# Memory Systems of the Brain

# MEMORY SYSTEMS OF THE BRAIN

## ANIMAL AND HUMAN COGNITIVE PROCESSES

EDITED BY

**Norman M. Weinberger**
**James L. McGaugh**
**Gary Lynch**
University of California, Irvine

THE GUILFORD PRESS
*New York • London*

A Division of Guilford Publications, Inc.
200 Park Avenue South, New York, N.Y. 10003



Printed in the United States of America

This work relates to Department of Navy Grant N00014-84-G-0108 issued by the Office of Naval Research. The United States Government has a royalty-free license throughout the world in all copyrightable material contained herein.

**Library of Congress Cataloging in Publication Data**

Main entry under title:

Memory systems of the brain.

Papers from the Second Conference on the Neurobiology of Learning and Memory, held Oct. 6–9, 1984, at Irvine, Calif. and organized by the Center for the Neurobiology of Learning and Memory.
Includes bibliographies and indexes.
1. Memory—Physiological aspects—Congresses.
2. Learning—Physiological aspects—Congresses.
3. Cognition—Physiological aspects—Congresses.
I. Weinberger, Norman M. II. McGaugh, James L.
III. Lynch, Gary. IV. University of California, Irvine.
Center for the Neurobiology of Learning and Memory.
V. Conference on the Neurobiology of Learning and Memory (2nd : 1984 : Irvine, Calif.)
QP406.M46 1985 153.1′2 85-24756
ISBN 0-89862-666-8

# CONTRIBUTORS

Wickliffe C. Abraham, Department of Psychology, University of Otago, Dunedin, New Zealand; present affiliation: Department of Physiology, University of Göteborg, S-400 33 Göteborg, Sweden

Daniel L. Alkon, Section on Neural Systems, Laboratory of Biophysics, IRP, National Institute of Neurological and Communicative Disorders and Stroke, National Institutes of Health at the Marine Biological Laboratory, Woods Hole, Massachusetts

John H. Ashe, Department of Psychology, University of California, Riverside, California; Center for the Neurobiology of Learning and Memory, University of California, Irvine, California

C. A. Barnes, Department of Psychology, University of Colorado, Boulder, Colorado

Theodore W. Berger, Departments of Psychology and Psychiatry, University of Pittsburgh, Pittsburgh, Pennsylvania

David H. Cohen, Department of Neurobiology and Behavior, State University of New York, Stony Brook, New York

Neal J. Cohen, Department of Psychology, The Johns Hopkins University, Baltimore, Maryland

I. Cooke, Department of Biology, Princeton University, Princeton, New Jersey

Richard G. Coss, Department of Psychology, University of California, Davis, California

Robert G. Crowder, Department of Psychology, Yale University, New Haven, Connecticut

Sam A. Deadwyler, Department of Physiology and Pharmacology, Bowman Gray School of Medicine, Wake Forest University, Winston-Salem, North Carolina

K. Delaney, Department of Biology, Princeton University, Princeton, New Jersey

Michela Gallagher, Department of Psychology, University of North Carolina, Chapel Hill, North Carolina

A. Gelperin, Department of Molecular Biophysics, AT&T Bell Laboratories, Murray Hill, New Jersey; Department of Biology, Princeton University, Princeton, New Jersey

Stephen E. Glickman, Department of Psychology, University of California, Berkeley, California

Graham V. Goddard, Department of Psychology, University of Otago, Dunedin, New Zealand

James L. Gould, Department of Biology, Princeton University, Princeton, New Jersey

William T. Greenough, Departments of Psychology and of Anatomical Sciences, and Neural and Behavioral Biology Program, University of Illinois, Urbana–Champaign, Illinois

Mary-Louise Kean, Cognitive Science Group and Department of Psychobiology, and Center for the Neurobiology of Learning and Memory, University of California, Irvine, California

N. J. Mackintosh, Department of Experimental Psychology, University of Cambridge, Cambridge, England, UK

Euan M. Macphail, Department of Psychology, University of York, Heslington, York, England, UK

H. Matthies, Institute of Pharmacology and Toxicology, Medical Academy, 3010 Magdeburg, GDR

B. L. McNaughton, Department of Psychology, University of Colorado, Boulder, Colorado

Richard G. M. Morris, MRC Cognitive Neuroscience Research Group, University of St. Andrews, St. Andrews, Fife, Scotland

Robert A. Rescorla, Department of Psychology, University of Pennsylvania, Philadelphia, Pennsylvania

Mark R. Rosenzweig, Department of Psychology, University of California, Berkeley, California
Daniel L. Schacter, Unit for Memory Disorders, Department of Psychology, University of Toronto, Toronto, Ontario, Canada
Robert J. Sclabassi, Department of Neurological Surgery, Center for Neuroscience, University of Pittsburgh, Pittsburgh, Pennsylvania
Sara J. Shettleworth, Department of Psychology, University of Toronto, Toronto, Ontario, Canada
Larry R. Squire, Veterans Administration Medical Center, San Diego, California; Department of Psychiatry, University of California, San Diego, La Jolla, California
J. E. R. Staddon, Department of Psychology, Duke University, Durham, North Carolina
L. Weiskrantz, Department of Experimental Psychology, University of Oxford, Oxford, England, UK
J. Wenzel, Institute of Anatomy, Humboldt University, 1040 Berlin, GDR
Stuart Zola-Morgan, Veterans Administration Medical Center, San Diego, California; Department of Psychiatry, University of California, San Diego, La Jolla, California

# ACKNOWLEDGMENTS

The conference on which this book is based was supported by a number of organizations including the University of California, Irvine; the Office of Naval Research; the Air Force Office of Scientific Research; Monsanto Company; Allergan Pharmaceuticals, Inc.; Health Resources Corporation of America; and The Irvine Company. We would also like to acknowledge and thank Lynn Brown, Nan Collett, Rita Stephens, and Jacqueline Weinberger for their meticulous and dedicated help in planning and coordinating the conference and for their efforts to assure the timely completion of this book. We are pleased to acknowledge the indexing labors of David Lane for the subject index, Lisa Weinberger for the author index, and Robert Finn for invaluable advice and assistance.

# PREFACE

Brains reasonably may be considered to be information processing systems, which acquire, store, and manipulate information in the service of adaptive behavior. Accordingly, learning and memory (i.e., acquisition and storage, respectively) are critical and central topics in neurobiology. A greatly increasing volume of research on learning and memory is a significant characteristic of current biological and behavioral approaches. There is ample reason to believe that this trend will continue because of the many advances that have emerged from recent studies relating learning and memory to their neural substrates, on the one hand, and placing them within their evolutionary and ecological contexts, on the other hand.

This volume is a product of the Second Conference on the Neurobiology of Learning and Memory, which was held at Irvine, California, October 6–9, 1984, and organized by the Center for the Neurobiology of Learning and Memory. Its focus differs from the previous volume that grew out of the first Irvine conference, marking the inauguration of the Center. That book (Lynch, McGaugh, & Weinberger, 1984) was more concerned with recent advances in cellular and brain system mechanisms and modulators and less concerned with relating findings from animal studies to human memory. Both volumes are concerned with presenting concepts and findings that characterize current research, organized on the basis of enduring problems and themes. As in the case of the previous monograph, this book is divided into major sections, each of which contains main chapters followed by directed comments and critiques. Its broad scope is intended to reflect some of the varied lines of inquiry into learning and memory, each of which has a rich primary source literature. The bibliographies provide a sense of this literature as well as focal points of entry for the reader who wants to embark on a more detailed journey into an area of interest.

Following an introductory chapter, the book begins with consideration of cellular- and systems-level mechanisms in diverse organisms and neural substrates. Not surprisingly, the mammalian hippocampus receives much attention, reflecting a current major focus of research. The second section concerns learning and memory from a comparative point of view. This section reflects increasing concern with delineating learning and memory characteristics and capacities in settings appropriate to the subject's ecological niche as well as other issues concerning beliefs about what is learned and the prospects for developing general process theories of learning. The final section juxtaposes human and animal studies of learning and memory, bringing similarities and differences into the same arena for direct comparison. This final section also places some emphasis upon a thread that runs thoughout the fabric of the book as it did in animated discussions during the Conference: Is there more than one form of memory, and just how is this issue to be settled?

An important point that emerged from the Conference, and which we hope is adequately reflected in the book, is that understanding how the brain acquires and stores experience constitutes a very central and complex task of very large proportions. It requires inquiry at several levels, from the molecular to that of behavioral ecology, as well as ways of bridging these levels. Of equal importance, and perhaps of greater difficulty, are the conceptual problems. In this regard, implicit assumptions should be made explicit so that they can be addressed directly. Furthermore, it is essential to realize that the need for conceptual advances is not relaxed by the gathering of new data, but on the contrary, becomes more urgent.

## REFERENCE

Lynch, G., McGaugh, J. L., & Weinberger, N. M. (Eds.). *Neurobiology of learning and memory.* New York: Guilford Press, 1984.

# CONTENTS

Introduction 1
*Norman M. Weinberger, James L. McGaugh, and Gary Lynch*

## I. BRAIN SYSTEMS AND LEARNING

1. Conditioning-Induced Changes of *Hermissenda* Channels: Relevance to Mammalian Brain Function 9
*Daniel L. Alkon*

2. Some Organizational Principles of a Vertebrate Conditioning Pathway: Is Memory a Distributed Property? 27
*David H. Cohen*

3. Spatial Information: How and Where Is It Stored? 49
*C. A. Barnes and B. L. McNaughton*

4. Multiple Traces of Neural Activity in the Hippocampus 62
*Wickliffe C. Abraham and Graham V. Goddard*

5. The Possible Role of Experience-Dependent Synaptogenesis,or Synapses on Demand, in the Memory Process 77
*William T. Greenough*

### Critical Commentaries

6. A Possible Enabling and Enhancing Function for Catecholamines in Neuronal Plasticity 107
*John H. Ashe*

7. Nonlinear Systems Analysis and Its Application to Study of the Functional Properties of Neural Systems 120
*Theodore W. Berger and Robert J. Sclabassi*

8. Involvement of Hippocampal Systems in Learning and Memory 134
*Sam A. Deadwyler*

9. Morphological Changes in the Hippocampal Formation Accompanying Memory Formation and Long-Term Potentiation 150
*J. Wenzel and H. Matthies*

## II. COMPARATIVE ASPECTS OF LEARNING AND MEMORY

10. Complex Computation in a Small Neural Network 173
*I. Cooke, K. Delaney, and A. Gelperin*

11. Learning and Memory in Honey Bees 193
*James L. Gould*

12. Associative Learning: Some Consequences of Contiguity 211
*Robert A. Rescorla*

13. Food Storing by Birds: Implications for Comparative Studies of Memory 231
*Sara J. Shettleworth*

### Critical Commentaries

14. Evolutionary Restraints on Learning: Phylogenetic and Synaptic Interpretations 253
*Richard G. Coss*

15. Ecology and Intelligence 279
*Euan M. Macphail*

16. Inference, Memory, and Representation 287
*J. E. R. Staddon*

17. Comparison of Learning Abilities among Species 296
*Mark R. Rosenzweig and Stephen E. Glickman*

## III. LEARNING, MEMORY, AND COGNITIVE PROCESSES

18. Re-Viewing Modulation of Learning and Memory 311
*Michela Gallagher*

19. Varieties of Conditioning 335
*N. J. Mackintosh*

20. Multiple Forms of Memory in Humans and Animals 351
*Daniel L. Schacter*

21. On Issues and Theories of the Human Amnesic Syndrome 380
*L. Weiskrantz*

**Critical Commentaries**

22. Levels of Analysis in Memory Research: The Neuropsychological Approach 419
*Neal J. Cohen*

23. On Access and the Forms of Memory 433
*Robert G. Crowder*

24. Disconnected Memories 442
*Mary-Louise Kean*

25. Moving On from Modeling Amnesia 452
*Richard G. M. Morris*

26. Complementary Approaches to the Study of Memory: Human Amnesia and Animal Models 463
*Stuart Zola-Morgan and Larry R. Squire*

Author Index 479

Subject Index 496

# Introduction

**Norman M. Weinberger**
**James L. McGaugh**
**Gary Lynch**
University of California, Irvine

This volume is divided into three sections: Brain Systems and Learning; Comparative Aspects of Learning and Memory; and Learning, Memory, and Cognitive Processes. Each section begins with chapters on selected topics and ends with critical commentaries. The inclusion of these commentaries reflects the need to examine the assumptions and approaches of all lines of inquiry, not merely those that are included in this volume.

Despite the breadth of topics and the variety of approaches, certain themes are common to the entire volume. These include whether memory is unitary or has multiple forms, the degree to which learning mechanisms have been conserved in evolution, the sense in which human memory is qualitatively different from that of other animals, and the nature of what is actually learned and how it is represented in brains.

## BRAIN SYSTEMS AND LEARNING

The first section concerning neural systems deals with substrates of learning and memory. It addresses several important issues, including the nature of relevant cellular mechanisms, loci of learning-induced plasticity within the nervous system, and the role of the hippocampus, and long-term plasticity within the hippocampus, in memory.

Dominant theories have assumed that learning requires synaptic change. However, the impressive analysis of classical conditioning in *Hermissenda* by Alkon and his associates reveals changes in calcium-dependent potassium channels rather than direct changes in synaptic function. The locus of change is at the extreme periphery, in the photoreceptor itself, which receives convergent input from the conditioned visual and unconditioned vestibular stimuli. This biophysical change is reported to occur also in the hippocampus of the rabbit during classical conditioning, a finding suggesting an evolutionary conservation of mechanism despite vast differences between gastropod and mammalian brains.

Plasticity in the sensory system of the conditioned stimulus also develops in the pigeon, as delineated in the extensive studies of David Cohen. Here the plasticity is seen not in the photoreceptors but in the avian "equivalent" of the lateral geniculate nucleus. This might suggest phylogenetic encephalization of plastic loci within the sensory system of the conditioned stimulus. Cohen also points out that multiple sites of plasticity may develop somewhat independently even within the same general circuitry for a particular conditioned response, a finding that argues against strict localization of a memory trace.

Neural plasticity that accompanies learning is, in any event, not restricted to sensory systems. Barnes and McNaughton argue that place learning involves the selective distribution of changes in synaptic strength in the hippocampus of the rat; furthermore, the storage of information is said to correspond to this distribution. This conclusion is based upon the use of high-frequency stimulation of selected hippocampal paths to produce "long-term enhancement" of transmission in a wide variety of circumstances. However, they conclude that the hippocampus need not be viewed as a site of permanent storage of spatial information, but rather may be a shorter term store upon which the neocortex draws information.

Although long-term enhancement/potentiation within the hippocampus is proving to be an important tool in the study of mechanisms of memory, it may not be a simpler model process than is experience-induced learning. Abraham and Goddard point out that electrical stimulation within the hippocampal formation, which causes "long-term potentiation," actually produces at least four long-term effects or traces. Although it would be premature to conclude that each of these physiological effects is isomorphic with a separate memory of the type associated with an environmental event, these findings do demonstrate that a neural substrate is capable of establishing multiple, independent traces. This is consistent with the view that multiple memories are formed during a behavioral learning episode. Direct behavioral evidence supporting this view is provided by Rescorla and also by Mackintosh in Sections II and III, respectively.

Given Alkon's findings, it might be thought that hippocampal long-term potentiation might involve changes in membrane channels. However, Greenough's findings indicate that morphological synaptic changes are involved. He also presents several pieces of evidence to support the idea that synapses are formed in the neocortex of rats during learning experiences. At the same time, Greenough indicates the additional criteria that need to be met to conclude that learning does cause the formation of new synapses. Even though it might appear that "synapses on demand" are in conflict with the role of channels in plasticity, Greenough notes that different mechanisms for plasticity may be related to the very different durations of various memories. Here again, the issue of multiple memory mechanisms is evident.

In commentary, Ashe points out that mechanisms of cellular plasticity also involve an enabling and enhancing role for catecholamines. It is particularly noteworthy that some of the synaptically mediated effects demonstrated have a time course orders of magnitude longer than the textbook descriptions of synaptic potentials. Moreover, Ashe has extended these findings from the superior cervical ganglion to the hippocampus, thus suggesting an evolutionarily conserved process. Wenzel and Matthies present additional strong evidence that long-term potentiation critically involves the formation, or perhaps uncovering, of synapses in the hippocampus. Deadwyler provides a comprehensive study of how potentials evoked by hippocampal stimulation are altered during a behavioral learning situation. His findings suggest that the hippocampus acts like a limited capacity buffer that can hold the results of recent experiences. Berger and Sclabassi argue that the analysis of hippocampal or other circuits requires nonlinear systems analysis because of the involved complexity. Applying this analysis to long-term potentiation, they find that high-frequency stimulation actually makes this nonlinear system operate in a more linear fashion. Although these findings are difficult to incorporate into other data, the power of the technique strongly indicates that such approaches must take an important place in the study of brain changes related to learning and memory.

## COMPARATIVE ASPECTS OF LEARNING AND MEMORY

Reviews and discussions of the comparative approach to memory occupy the middle third of the book. Gould describes the remarkable memory of bees for flowers and shows that, among other items, they retain information about odors, colors, shapes, and locations. The question of how relatively simple nervous systems can accomplish all of this leads to the idea that learning consists of changes in the strength of genetically dictated circuitries, suggesting in turn that learning and memory organization need to be analyzed in terms of the innate behavior patterns formed over evolutionary history.

Shettleworth takes up the question of memory for food location in birds. She reviews recent work that convincingly demonstrates an immense capacity and extreme duration of spatial memory and then considers in detail the question of what it is that the birds remember. The all-important comparative issue of how spatial memory in birds relates to that in other animals, and in particular the much studied radial maze learning of rats, is also discussed. Laboratory studies of conditioning in the slug *Limax* are reviewed and discussed by Cooke, Delaney, and Gelperin. The vast body of literature describing conditioning in birds and mammals allows for a quite detailed comparison of this form of learning between different groups, and most notably between vertebrates and invertebrates. One can only be impressed with the many features of Pavlovian conditioning possessed by the slugs, including the apparent necessity for predictability between stimulus events for conditioning to occur. These points of contact do suggest that the same phenomenon is present across much of the animal kingdom and therefore that deductions about mechanisms arrived at from studies in the invertebrates will have broad applicability. The simple nervous systems of the invertebrates should also be amenable to computer modeling of learning effects and the chapter by Cooke and colleagues describes some recent efforts in this direction. The chapter by Rescorla provides another view of conditioning. For birds and rats, at least, conditioning involves formations of numerous associations other than those that have been concentrated upon in the past. It now seems clear that the animal forms links between stimulus elements, between those elements and the consequents, and between the context and events occurring within it, all during a typical Pavlovian conditioning experiment. Rescorla raises the very significant point that these varieties of learning may follow different rules and therefore that psychological and neurobiological models of associative conditioning are quite possibly greatly oversimplified.

Coss emphasizes evolutionary restraints on learning. He argues that learning may best be viewed as an adjustment of instinct related to variations in ecological niche. Analysis of the antisnake behavior of ground squirrels indicates the retention of information about a specific habitat for thousands of generations. Macphail emphasizes the similarities in learning capacity across phyla, arguing that no species differences have been demonstrated. However, Rosenzweig and Glickman offer a sharply contrasting view. Staddon emphasizes the interplay of selection and variation as determinants of learning. He sees learning as inferences based on two sets of rules: one specific to ecological niche, the other more general.

Overall, these chapters reflect a vital area of rapidly growing interest and attention, the implications of which are critical for neurobiological attempts to understand learning and memory.

## LEARNING, MEMORY, AND COGNITIVE PROCESSES

One of the central issues in research on the neurobiology of learning and memory is the question of whether all learning, in humans as well as animals, is based on a single set of principles. This issue is the focus of the chapters in the third section of this book. As the discussions in these chapters indicate, there is currently a growing consensus that there are different forms of learning and memory and that the different forms may be based on different neuronal systems.

At one level, however, the various forms of learning, as seen in various learning tasks, appear to share a common basis. Gallagher presents evidence that treatments affecting endogenous opioid systems have comparable effects in several types of learning tasks in rats. Further, the modulating effects of opioid hormones on memory seem to work, at least in part, through influences on brain regions—amygdala and hippocampus—and on transmitter systems—adrenergic and cholinergic—that appear, on the basis of evidence from numerous studies, to be involved in information storage in several species.

At another level, however, there appear to be various forms of learning. Mackintosh summarizes evidence showing that animals learn about the relationships among stimuli and that *what* an animal learns when it is trained depends upon the specific way in which information is presented. His view that conditioning consists of acquiring declarative knowledge rather than procedural knowledge contrasts sharply with older as well as some current views that suggest that conditioned response learning consists of learning responses. He also proposes that different forms of learning may involve different neural systems. For example, systems underlying preparatory learning (e.g., affective responses) may differ from those involved in representing the specific information provided by the training stimuli.

This general theme of multiple forms of learning is continued in Schacter's chapter. He argues that, at a descriptive level, some learning and memory is based on explicit recognition and recollection whereas other forms, including skill learning and priming effects, are implicit; that is, they do not depend upon explicit conscious recollection. Further, both memory capacities appear to be intact in amnesic patients. Even though Schacter attempts to remain at a descriptive level, his suggestions and findings immediately raise the question of mechanisms. Do these findings argue that different neuronal systems are involved in these different forms of learning? Further, are forms of memory spared in amnesic patients, based on the same processes? Are there additional forms that have not as yet been identified? Schacter's chapter suggests that there are—or might be.

Schacter's findings and conclusions agree with earlier evidence from studies by Weiskrantz that some form of memory is spared in amnesic patients. As Weiskrantz points out, this evidence argues against the view that amnesics are generally defective in the ability to store new information. Although there is now broad agreement that there is sparing as well as loss of memory in amnesia, there remains disagreement as to whether there is more than one form of amnesia. Weiskrantz argues that there is one core form of the amnesia syndrome and that the memory impairment involves a common neural system.

In contrast, Zola-Morgan and Squire suggest that there is more than one form of amnesia and that different forms are due to damage of different neural structures. Thus, although there is general agreement that memory is spared in amnesic patients, there is, as yet, no consensus concerning the brain regions involved in the memory loss. Further, as Neal Cohen points out, it is not at all clear which structures are responsible for the memory spared in amnesics. This is, of course, an equally important issue. As Crowder emphasizes, the issues of the brain systems involved in declarative and procedural learning will be difficult to address in view of the evidence summarized by Mackintosh indicating that conditioning procedures seem to engage a declarative system. Finally, Kean argues that there are other grounds for suspecting that it will be difficult to identify the neural structures responsible for different forms of memory loss in amnesics. Any given behavior, she notes, no doubt engages the interaction of many different systems and, thus, any lesion might simply impair memory through disruption of the interactions among the systems. According to this view, it may be premature to identify specific neuronal systems as having specific functions in memories spared and lost in amnesics.

These, then, are the issues addressed in the chapters in the final section of the book. Obviously, attempts to understand the neural basis of learning and memory are enormously complicated by the accumulating evidence that memory may come in many forms. If the many forms are based on different brain systems, the problem is complicated still further. But, the weight of the evidence as well as the thrust of current thinking suggests that it may be unwise to make any simpler assumptions.

SECTION I

# BRAIN SYSTEMS AND LEARNING

CHAPTER 1

# Conditioning-Induced Changes of *Hermissenda* Channels: Relevance to Mammalian Brain Function

**Daniel L. Alkon**
National Institutes of Health at the
Marine Biological Laboratory

Humans are capable of associating almost any bit of information that they can sense with any other bit. A number or sequence of numbers can be associated with a place—a letter or sequence of letters with a face. Even a sequence of nonmeaningful numbers or letters can at will be associated with each other. Consideration of the extremely brief time (e.g., 1–2 seconds) required to form such associations suggests that the relevant neural pathways already exist in the human brain—they do not grow or develop at least within the *initial* learning period.

With progressively less evolved species, the potential for learning associations is progressively reduced, as is the complexity of the neural pathways. The complexity of neural systems that may mediate the learning of associations is most likely not only reflected by the *number* of potential associations that can be made. The simplicity of neural systems should also be manifest by a diminished capacity to discriminate which stimuli are associated and a concomitantly diminished capacity to generalize from one stimulus to another. Finally, we also might expect less fine tuning in the system's resolution of the temporal relationship between the associated stimuli.

Given these intuitively reasonable interspecies differences between neural systems and the learning they control as well as many other known differences in neuronal and synaptic properties (such as impulse duration, synaptic delay, transduction, and generator potentials), is it reasonable to expect that biophysical and biochemical mechanisms defined for animals with several thousand neurons can teach us anything about such mechanisms for animals with several billion or more neurons? Although an answer to this question must await some definitive demonstration of such mechanisms for a higher vertebrate, there are some intuitively reasonable possibilities that might motivate a research strategy.

It is *possible* that parts of neural systems, such as convergence points between pathways that are crucial for achieving certain aspects of associative learning, occur with very high frequency in the mammalian brain. The same or similar components might also occur, albeit with much lower frequency within neural systems of invertebrate species such as the mollusks. Although there might be obvious differences in such components between species, their basic physiology might be quite similar. For example, convergence between sensory modalities of the nudibranch mollusk *Hermissenda* occurs on the sensory receptor cells themselves (Figure 1.1) (Alkon, 1973, 1974b, 1975, 1983), whereas in mammalian species it occurs on neurons that are well along the sensory chain, that is, after four or five synaptic connections between successive neurons have been made (Alkon, 1983). Yet the way the converging sensory signals, when they are associated, affect those neuronal sites where the information is actually stored may be quite similar for the mammal and the mollusk.

It is now known, for example, that a sequence of biophysical steps (Figures 1.2 and 1.3) precedes the storage of a learned association for *Hermissenda* (Alkon, 1979, 1982, 1982–1983, 1984a, 1984b). This sequence begins with pairing-and stimulus-specific depolarization of neuronal membranes (Alkon, 1980; Crow & Alkon, 1980). This depolarization is accompanied by prolonged elevation of intracellular calcium (Connor & Alkon, 1984), which in turn causes inactivation of specific $K^+$ channels (Figures 1.2 and 1.3; Alkon & Sakakibara, 1984; Alkon, Shoukimas, & Heldman, 1982). Potassium channel inactivation lasting at least for several days (Alkon, Lederhendler, & Shoukimas, 1982; Farley, Sakakibara, & Alkon, 1984; Forman *et al.*, 1984) effects increased excitability of specific cells (West, Barnes, & Alkon, 1982), the increased impulse activity of which (Farley & Alkon, 1982) in response to the conditioned stimulus is responsible for a new, conditioned behavioral response (Alkon, 1974a; Crow & Alkon, 1978; Lederhendler, Gart, & Alkon, 1983). This then is a biophysical memory trace: semipermanent calcium-mediated inactivation of $K^+$ channels (Alkon, 1984a; Alkon, Shoukimas, & Heldman, 1982) that stores a memory at least for several days.

Ionic channels, known to occur in mammalian central neurons, are remarkably similar to those found within the membranes of those *Hermissenda* neurons—the type B photoreceptors—that encode the learned association between the conditioned stimulus (light) and the unconditioned response (rotation-elicited "clinging" or foot contraction). Again, components of neural systems only now at the level of ionic channels are shared by the *Hermissenda* nervous system and the central mammalian nervous system. Hippocampal CA1 neuron somata have across their membranes an early outward rapidly activating and inactivating $K^+$ current known as $I_A$; a slowly activating outward $K^+$ current that is dependent on the level of intracellular calcium,

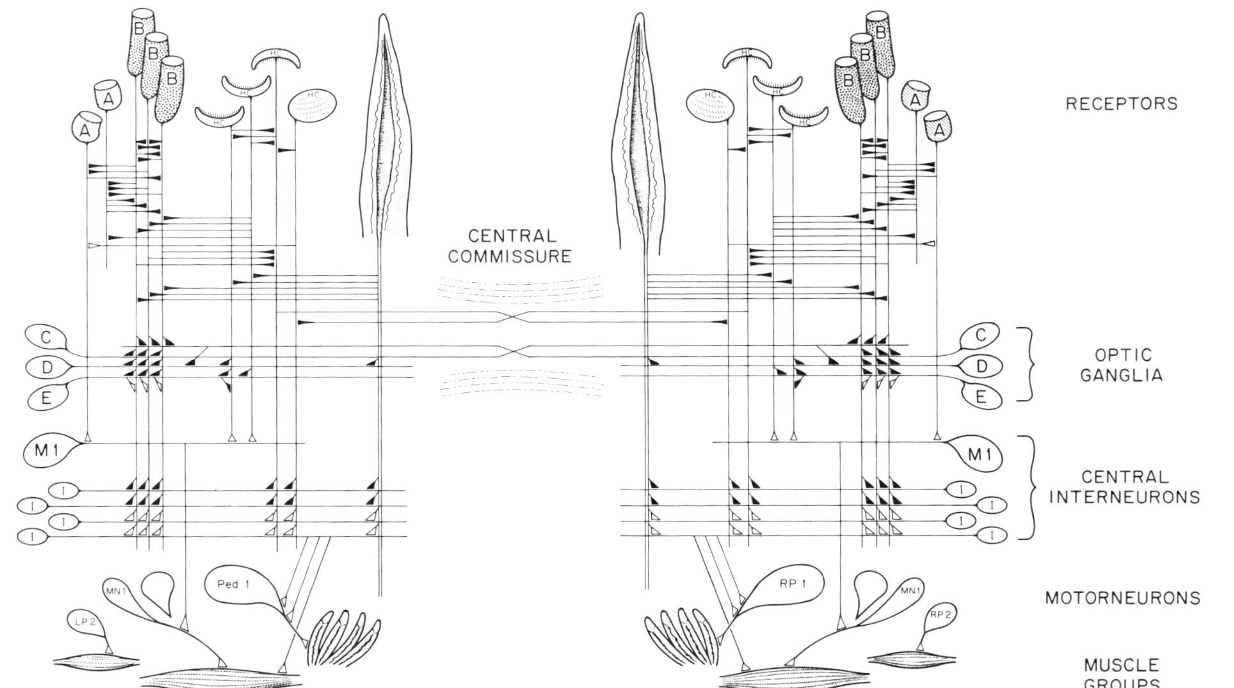


**FIGURE 1.1.** Schematic summary of synaptic interactions in the neural systems of *Hermissenda*. Interactions within and between three sensory pathways are included. The visual pathway begins with the five photoreceptors (two type A and three type B) of each eye. The afferent cells of the vestibular pathway, the 13 hair cells in each statocyst, are labeled HC. The tentacle, represented as an intact structure in the diagram, has chemosensory receptors distributed on its surface. Inhibitory synaptic interactions are indicated by filled endings; excitatory interactions are indicated by open endings. Muscle groups innervated by the motor neurons are pictured at the bottom of the figure. Each interaction represented was established to be reliably present in the adult nervous system by simultaneous pre- and postsynaptic intracellular recording. Not all known interactions are included (Alkon, 1982–1983).

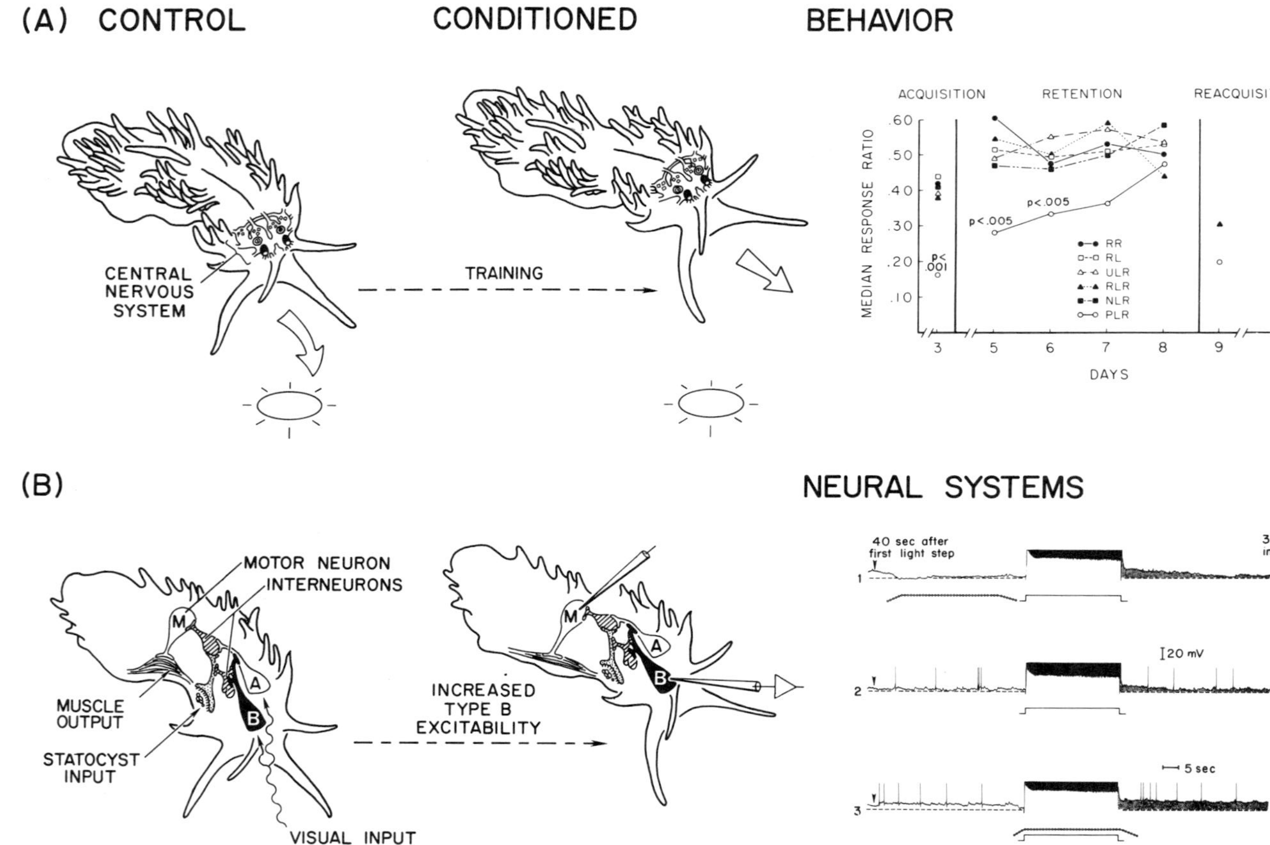

(A) CONTROL
CONDITIONED
BEHAVIOR
CENTRAL
NERVOUS
SYSTEM
TRAINING
ACQUISITION
RETENTION
REACQUISITION
MEDIAN RESPONSE RATIO
.60
.50
.40
.30
.20
.10
p<
.001
p<.005
p<.005
RR
RL
ULR
RLR
NLR
PLR
3
5
6
7
8
9
11
DAYS
(B)
NEURAL SYSTEMS
MOTOR NEURON
INTERNEURONS
M
A
B
MUSCLE
OUTPUT
STATOCYST
INPUT
VISUAL INPUT
INCREASED
TYPE B
EXCITABILITY
40 sec after
first light step
30 sec
interval
1
2
3
20 mV
5 sec

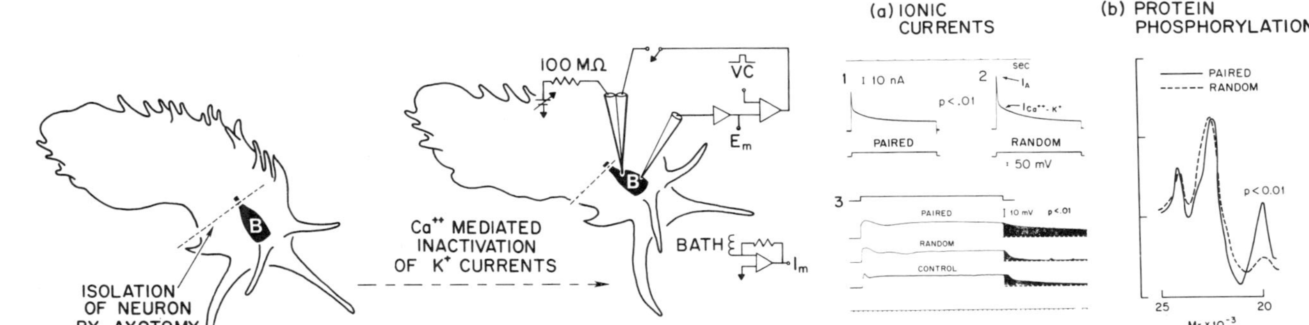


**FIGURE 1.2.** Cellular analysis of *Hermissenda* associative learning. (A) *Behavior*. Reduction of positive phototaxic response in *Hermissenda* as a result of conditioning procedure. The plot on the right represents data on the median response ratios for acquisition, retention, and reacquisition of a long-term behavioral change after a light stimulus [random rotation (●), random light (□), unpaired light and rotation (△), random light and rotation (▲), nothing (■), and paired light and rotation (○)]. (B) *Neural systems*. Critical input and output neurons, a few of many, that mediate learning the association of light and rotation. Type B and type A photoreceptors are indicated by B and A; M indicates the pedal ganglion motor neuron the activity of which regulates turning movements. Intracellular recordings from intact type B cells during and after light and rotation stimuli. *Trace 1*: Responses to the second of two succeeding 30-second light steps (with a 90-second interval intervening), each preceded by rotation. *Trace 2*: Responses to the second of two light steps without rotation. *Trace 3*: As in traces 1 and 2, with the onset of each light step followed by onset after 1 second of maximal rotation. (C) *Membrane channels*. Type B cells are isolated by axotomy subsequent to behavioral measurements made before and after training. The circuit for the voltage clamp experiment with two microelectrodes is shown in the center. The ionic currents were measured from a holding potential of $-60$ mV. *Trace 1*: Paired $I_A$ (early peak outward $K^+$ current) and $I_{Ca^{2+}-K^+}$ (late current, maximum at 300 msec after onset of command) are smaller than random (*Trace 2*) or control values (not shown). *Trace 3*: Paired steady-state depolarization during and after (shaded areas) a light step (monitored by top trace) are larger than random and control. The data on protein phosphorylation are represented by densitometric scans of autoradiograms of samples of eye proteins in the molecular weight range of 20,000 to 25,000 obtained 1 to 2 hours after animals received the third training session of paired or random light and rotation (Alkon, 1984a).

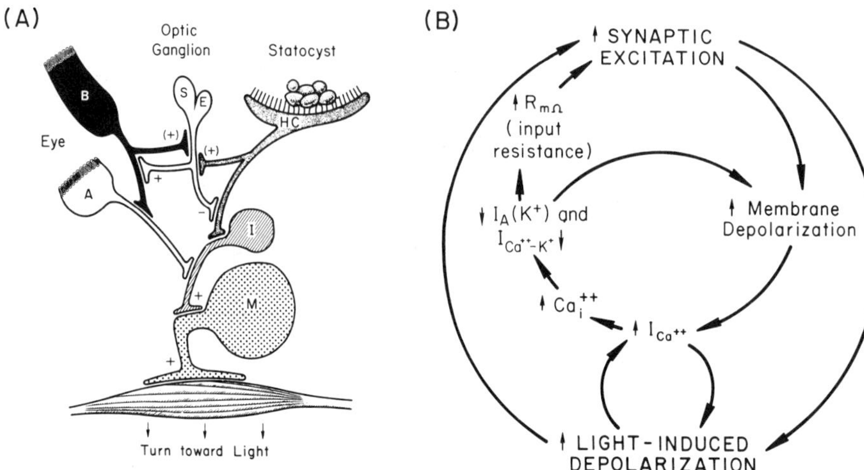


**FIGURE 1.3.** (A) Schematic diagram of visual pathway and its convergence with the statocyst pathway. The type B photoreceptor (B) causes monosynaptic inhibition of the medial type A photoreceptor (A). The medial type A photoreceptor causes monosynaptic excitation of ipsilateral interneurons (I), which are also excited by ipsilateral hair cells (HC). The ipsilateral interneuron in turn excites the motorneuron (M). Ipsilateral hair cell impulses and type B impulses cause a transient inhibition (not shown here) and are followed by long-lasting effective excitation (+) of the S-E optic ganglion cell and thereby the type B cell (Goh & Alkon, 1984). (B) Regenerative synaptic and light-induced excitation of the type B photoreceptor. Light-induced depolarization facilitates synaptic excitation and vice versa in response to temporally associated light and rotation. Analyzed in biophysical terms, synaptic depolarization causes transient activation and then prolonged inactivation of $I_A$ and $I_{Ca^{2+}-K^+}$ and enhancement of a voltage-dependent $Ca^{2+}$ current. Increased intracellular $Ca^{2+}$ causes further inactivation of $I_A$ and $I_{Ca^{2+}-K^+}$ and thus a further increase of effective input resistance. These in turn cause more membrane depolarization (Alkon, 1984a).

$I_{Ca^{2+}-K^+}$; an early inward rapidly activating and inward $Na^+$ current, $I_{Na^+}$; and a sustained voltage-dependent calcium current, $I_{Ca^{2+}}$ (Clark & Wong, 1983; Segal & Barker, 1984). Virtually the same currents have been measured across isolated type B somata. It is the sustained calcium current that is activated by paired presentations of the conditioned and unconditioned stimuli to *Hermissenda* (Alkon, Farley, Sakakibara, & Hay, 1984). It is the two outward $K^+$ currents, $I_A$ and $I_{Ca^{2+}-K^+}$, that are inactivated by the prolonged elevation of mean intracellular calcium that results from activation of the sustained calcium current (Alkon *et al.*, 1984). It is reasonable to expect then that repeated depolarization of CA1 somata (and/or the dendrites) due to activation of the Schaffer collaterals paired with additional stimulus-induced depolarization will result in calcium-mediated $K^+$ current reduction similar if not identical to those demonstrated to cause *Hermissenda* conditioning. These changes have been shown to occur on the somata of the *Hermissenda* type B cells. They might more commonly occur on dendrites of mammalian central neurons. This is more likely, given that the most common site for convergence of inputs to a neuron are on the dendritic tree where the proximity of distinct inputs resembles the proximity (within 80 μm) of the light-receptive membrane and the membrane postsynaptic to rotation-induced presynaptic signals. In fact, John Disterhoft, Douglas Coulter, and I have obtained evidence that such membrane changes intrinsic to CA1 neurons occur in hippocampal slices from classically conditioned rabbits but not from control animals (Disterhoft, Coulter, & Alkon, 1984).

Neural system components may be conserved during evolution at the molecular as well as the membrane and pathway levels. Phosphorylase kinase, isolated from vertebrate tissues, for example, when iontophoresed into isolated type B somata caused a prolongation and enhancement of calcium-mediated decrease of $I_A$ and $I_{Ca^{2+}-K^+}$ and a resulting increase of input resistance (Acosta-Urquidi, Alkon, & Neary, 1984; Figures 1.4 and 1.5). A similar change of input resistance followed iontophoresis of the

**FIGURE 1.4.** Effects of phosphorylase kinase (A) and 4-aminopyridine (B) on input resistance ($R_{in}$) in axotomized type B photoreceptors in normal (10 m*M*) $Ca^{2+}$-ASW. Each point is a mean of five cells; standard errors are smaller than symbols. (A) Steady-state voltage–current plots before (control, ●) and after phosphorylase kinase injections. A single injection (□, 36 nC) followed by three light steps increased $R_{in}$ over the entire range. A second injection (△, 54 nC) followed by two additional light steps further increased $R_{in}$. $R_{in}$ (− 0.2 nA, 800-msec pulses) did not increase after an injection given in the dark (inset). (B) 4-Aminopyridine (△) (5 m*M*), which preferentially blocks $I_A$, mimicked the increase in $R_{in}$ induced by phosphorylase kinase (Acosta-Urquidi, Alkon, & Neary, 1984).

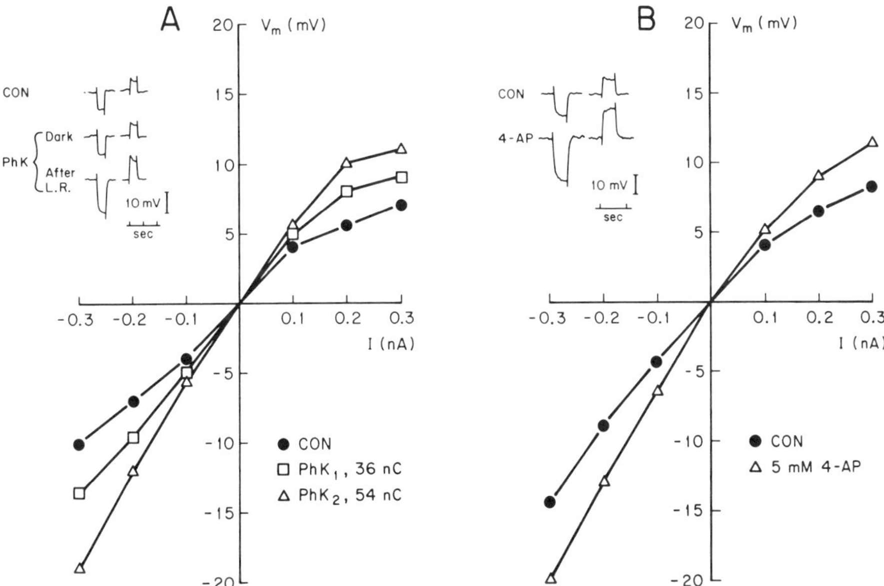

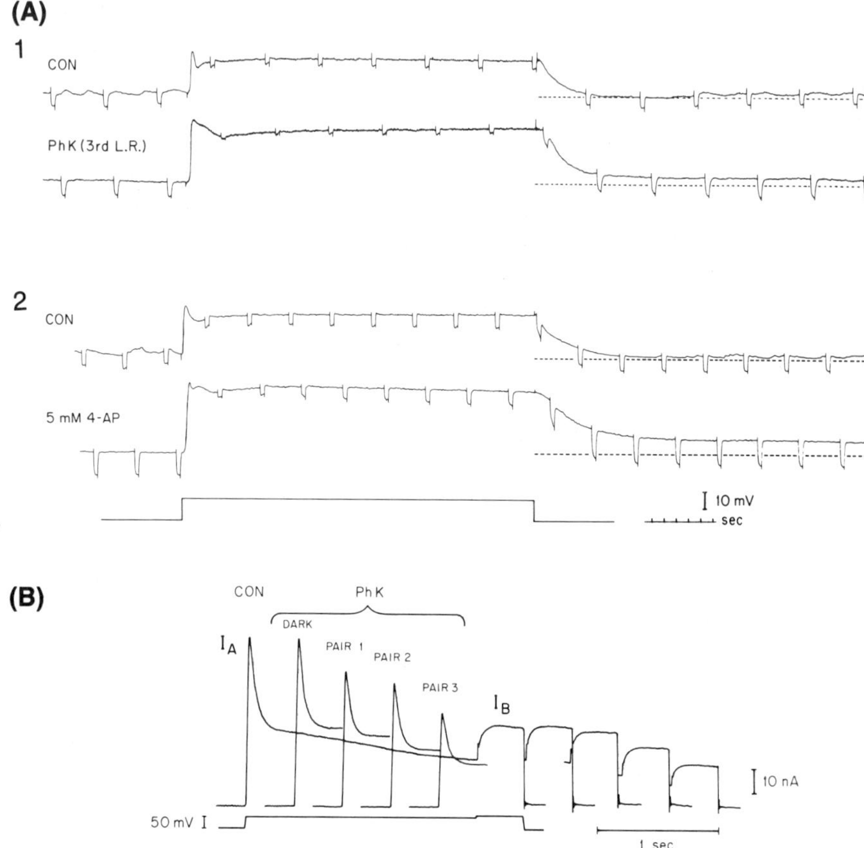


**FIGURE 1.5.** (A) Effects of phosphorylase kinase (1) and 4-aminopyridine (2) on the light response in axotomized type B photoreceptors in normal $Ca^{2+}$–ASW. (1) Before (control) and 10 minutes after single injections (36 nC, third light response). (2) 4-Aminopyridine (5 m*M*) mimicked the enhancement of all components of the light response by phosphorylase kinase. Constant current pulses (−0.2 nA, 400 msec) monitored $R_{in}$ before, during, and after the light response. The dotted baseline shows the magnitude of LLD after each treatment. (B) Effects of a single injection of phosphorylase kinase (60 nC) on axotomized type B photoreceptor $K^+$ currents in normal $Ca^{2+}$–ASW. From a $V_H$ of − 60 mV, $I_A$ (left) was elicited by the first command step to −10 mV and decayed within approximately 1 second to the steady state. A second superimposed step to 0 mV, applied 1.9 seconds after the first step, elicited $I_B$. The family of $K^+$ currents ($I_A$ and corresponding $I_B$) show that phosphorylase kinase had no effect on $I_A$ or $I_B$ in darkness but reduced $I_A$ after a 20-second pairing of light with depolarization to give a $Ca^{2+}$ −load (pair 1, to −10 mV). Further reduction of $I_A$ and also $I_B$ was evident after two additional pairings associated with increasing command steps (pair 2, to 0 mV; pair 3, to 15 mV). A full record is shown only for the control condition before the phosphorylase kinase injection (Acosta-Urquidi, Alkon, & Neary, 1984).

same enzyme and presumed depolarization-induced influx of calcium into neurons of cat motor cortex (Woody, Alkon, & Hay, 1984). Two-dimensional gel electrophoresis revealed that specific low-molecular-weight proteins from the eyes undergo decreased phosphorylation for conditioned but not control animals (Neary, Crow, & Alkon, 1981). Phosphorylation of these proteins is calcium-dependent and has now been related to the activation states of the same $K^+$ channels (for $I_A$ and $I_{Ca^{2+}-K^+}$) that change with *Hermissenda* conditioning (Alkon *et al.*, 1984; Neary & Alkon, 1983). Perfusion with inhibitors of calmodulin (calmidozolium or trifluoroperazine) block $Ca^{2+}$-dependent phosphorylation as well as the $Ca^{2+}$-mediated reduction of $I_{Ca^{2+}-K^+}$ (Alkon *et al.*, 1984). Intracellular iontophoresis of a $Ca^{2+}$-calmodulin-dependent protein kinase enhances and prolongs the $Ca^{2+}$-mediated reduction of $I_{Ca^{2+}-K^+}$ (Figure 1.5; Acosta-Urquidi *et al.*, 1984). Other manipulations that produce similar reduction of $I_A$ and $I_{Ca^{2+}-K^+}$ include iontophoresis of inosital triphosphate ($IP_3$) (but not $IP_1$) into type B somata (Sakakibara *et al.*, in press) and activation of endogenous C-kinase (Neary, Naito, & Alkon, in press). These results suggest that activation of the $Ca^{2+}$-calmodulin-dependent and C-kinase-dependent processes can act synergistically to effect long-term conditioning-induced modification of membrane channels.

The degree to which these features of neural systems are shared by the mammalian brain and molluscan ganglia should also be reflected in the number of common features that characterize the learning behavior. Divergence of the learning behaviors between species will indicate the necessity of seeking properties unique to mammalian neural systems, properties that could arise at any one or all of the aforementioned levels, namely, pathway, membrane, or molecular.

Classical conditioning of *Hermissenda* (Figure 1.2) (Alkon, 1974a; Crow & Alkon, 1978) in fact resembles in many respects that of mammalian species. It shows temporal or pairing specificity (Crow & Alkon, 1978), stimulus specificity (Farley & Alkon, 1982), acquisition (Crow & Alkon, 1978), retention for periods as long as a few weeks, extinction (Richards, Farley, & Alkon, 1983), savings, and a requirement for contingency (Farley, in press). As a result of conditioning, the conditioned stimulus—light—was shown to elicit a new muscular response—foot contraction (Figure 1.6)—which is elicited without training by the unconditioned stimulus—rotation (Lederhendler *et al.*, 1983). There is also no long-term (more than 1–2 hours) retention of habituation or sensitization effects due to repeated presentation of the conditioned stimulus (CS) or unconditioned stimulus (US) or both (Crow, 1983). Analysis of how *Hermissenda* neural systems accomplish these features of conditioning, therefore, might suggest how they are accomplished by vertebrate neural systems. The pairing and stimulus specificity arise out of the beautifully ordered details of synaptic interaction between the visual and statocyst pathways (Figures 1.1 and 1.2). This synaptic organization is ge-

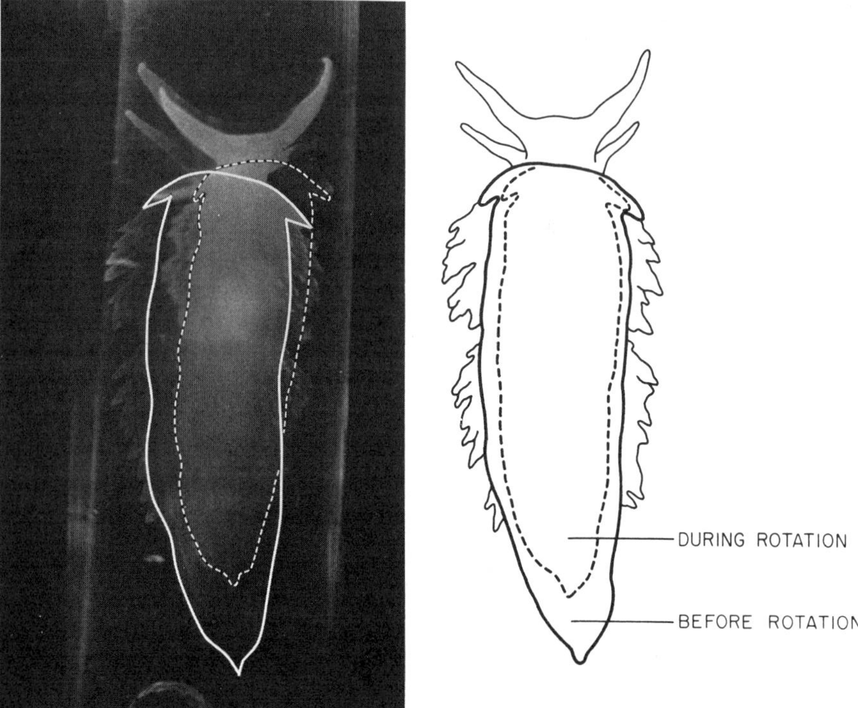


**FIGURE 1.6.** Time-lapse measurement of *Hermissenda* foot contraction. On the left are actual photographs (from below) of *Hermissenda* foot immediately before and 3 seconds after the onset of rotation. On the right are traces of the photographs on the left to highlight the contraction of the caudal half of the foot within 3 seconds of rotation onset. This contraction, part of a "clinging response" is reliably elicited by the US (rotation) before and after training. Light, the CS, only elicits this response after associative training in which light and rotation are repetitively paired (Lederhendler & Alkon, in preparation).

netically specified—it exists and is determined *prior to* acquisition of the learned behavior. Does this mean that the learning is "prewired"—that it is already genetically determined? By no means. It does mean that *the potential* for learning particular stimulus associations is predetermined. If those stimuli are encountered repetitively with a certain relationship in time, the potential is realized. Although such potential may exist for an incredibly greater number of stimuli in the mammalian nervous system, the principle could very well be the same: the organization of preexisting synaptic interactions will determine which stimuli can be associated and where in the mammalian nervous system the associations will be encoded and stored (Figure 1.7).

Pairing and stimulus specificity of *Hermissenda* conditioning depend on membrane channel physiology and neuronal biochemistry as well as on synaptic organization. If the CS precedes the US by too long a time interval or if the US precedes the CS, maximal activation of the critically involved voltage-dependent calcium current will not occur (Figure 1.8). Because those potassium currents that undergo calcium-mediated inactivation are on that neuronal membrane receptive to the CS, on retention days the B cell (which inhibits phototaxis) will be more excitable in response to the CS but not in response to the US. This depends on the fact that the US effect on the type B cell never brings the potential of the membrane that stores the association into a voltage range sufficient to activate and thus express the learning-induced difference of $K^+$ currents. Programmed within the neural system of *Hermissenda* are sites where membrane channels have the *potential* to change when the CS and US are appropriately timed; when the change occurs, the sites are programmed so that the learning-induced difference in membrane channels will only be expressed with subsequent presentations of the CS (but not the US). Again, a myriad of preexisting loci for changes of channels on dendritic membrane of the mammalian nervous system would not be unreasonable. The fine-tuning resolution of the temporal specificity and stimulus specificity might be of a much different order of magnitude than that observed for *Hermissenda*, but the principle could be the same. The separation of CS and US inputs on distinct dendritic spines, which were not electrically remote from each other, would serve in a manner analogous to the separation of light and rotation sites (i.e., at the soma, and approximately 80 $\mu$m away on postsynaptic terminal branches) on the *Hermissenda* type B cell.

As already alluded to, a major difference between *Hermissenda* loci for encoding a learned association and mammalian loci is undoubtedly the *number* of cells involved. The conditioned association of light and rotation is encoded within type B and probably type A photoreceptors. Although other cellular loci cannot be ruled out, the changes within the type B and type A cells are sufficient to account for much if not all of the learned behavior. Involvement of a relatively small number of cells has implications for choice of investigative strategies. With *Hermissenda* it has been possible to impale the implicated cells, produce the membrane changes that were found to occur with learning, and then on subsequent days to actually measure behavioral changes similar to those produced by conditioning (Farley, Richards, Ling, Liman, & Alkon, 1983). Accumulated clinical evidence suggests that human learning is represented diffusely throughout the brain. Pathological lesion of one brain area where the learning is stored does not necessarily abolish other areas where it is stored. Lesions that eliminate an area necessary for acquisition or expression of learned behavior do not necessarily affect storage sites. The learning of a stimulus association by a mammal most likely involves membrane changes in entire *sets* of neurons, and it is the collective effect of these sets of changes that ultimately encode a memory with its full meaning (Figure 1.7). In a mammal, lesions are undoubtedly useful for working out relevant neural pathways, but they

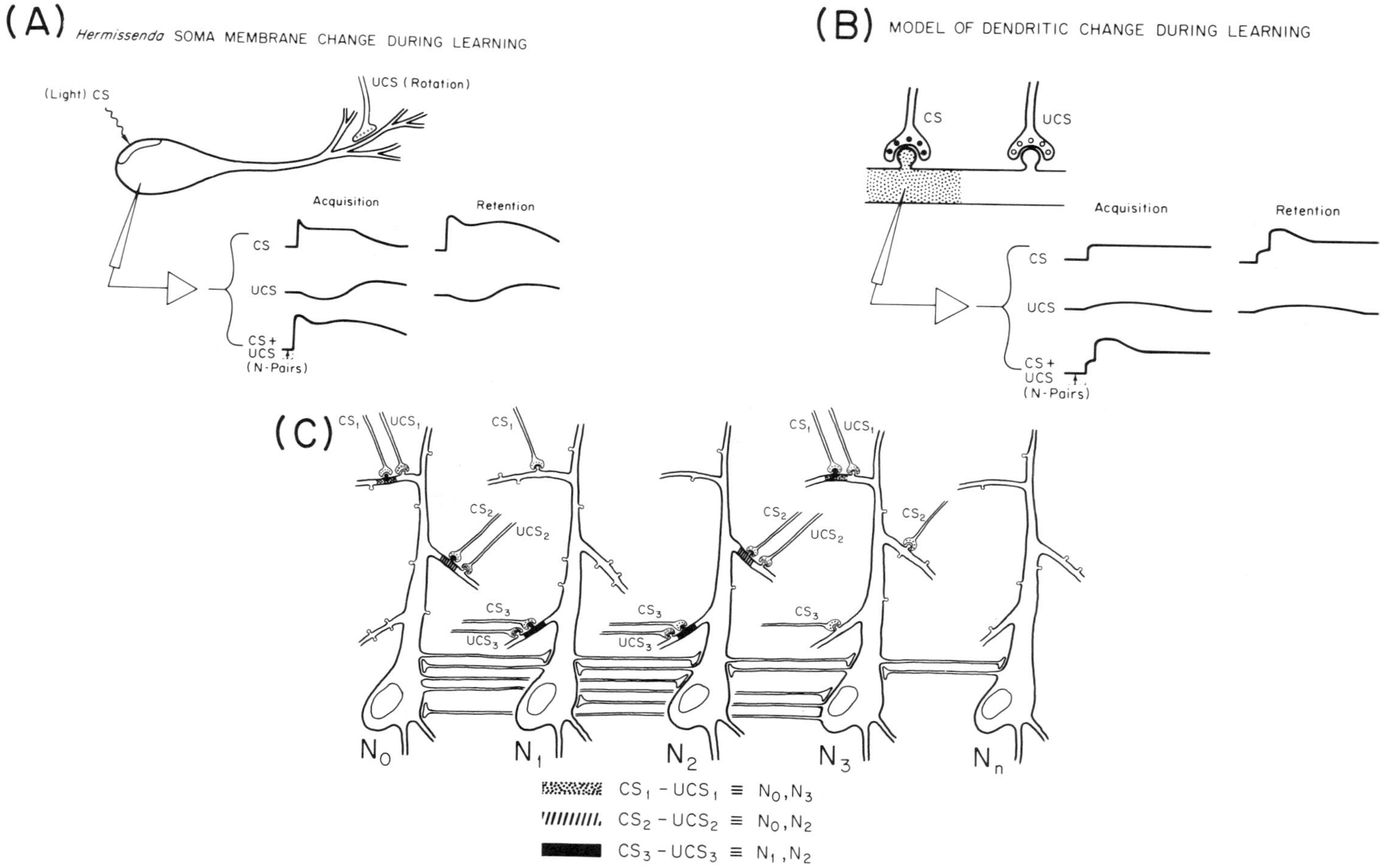

(A) *Hermissenda* SOMA MEMBRANE CHANGE DURING LEARNING
(Light) CS
UCS (Rotation)
Acquisition
Retention
CS
UCS
CS + UCS (N-Pairs)
(B) MODEL OF DENDRITIC CHANGE DURING LEARNING
CS
UCS
Acquisition
Retention
CS
UCS
CS + UCS (N-Pairs)
(C)
$CS_1$ $UCS_1$
$CS_2$ $UCS_2$
$CS_3$ $UCS_3$
$N_0$ $N_1$ $N_2$ $N_3$ $N_n$
$CS_1 - UCS_1 \equiv N_0, N_3$
$CS_2 - UCS_2 \equiv N_0, N_2$
$CS_3 - UCS_3 \equiv N_1, N_2$

**FIGURE 1.7.** (A) Schematic summary of conditioning-induced membrane changes in *Hermissenda*. Paired light and rotation are followed in the type B cell by an enhanced long-lasting depolarizing response (LLD) to light. Repeated pairings (lower left records) lead to cumulative membrane depolarization, enhanced response during and after the light, decreased voltage-dependent $K^+$ currents, increased input resistance, and thus increased excitability. On the days after training, that is, during retention of the learning, the cumulative depolarization is no longer present, whereas the other changes remain. (B) Model of conditioning-induced membrane changes in a dendritic branch. The genesis of these membrane changes could arise in a manner analogous to that observed for *Hermissenda* type B cells. (C) Hypothetical neural system changes during associative learning. Potential CS pathways synapse on postsynaptic dendritic membrane in proximity to postsynaptic sites for US pathways. Repetition of temporally associated stimulation of preexisting CS and US inputs that share a common postsynaptic dendritic branch cause persistent increases of postsynaptic excitability at the CS site (shaded areas). For a given set of neurons ($N_0 \ldots N_n$) different combinations of neurons will show increased excitability in response to a CS, depending on which stimuli were paired during training and depending on the genetically constrained features of the already formed neural systems. Horizontal processes ending on cell bodies represent inhibitory presynaptic endings (Alkon, 1984b).

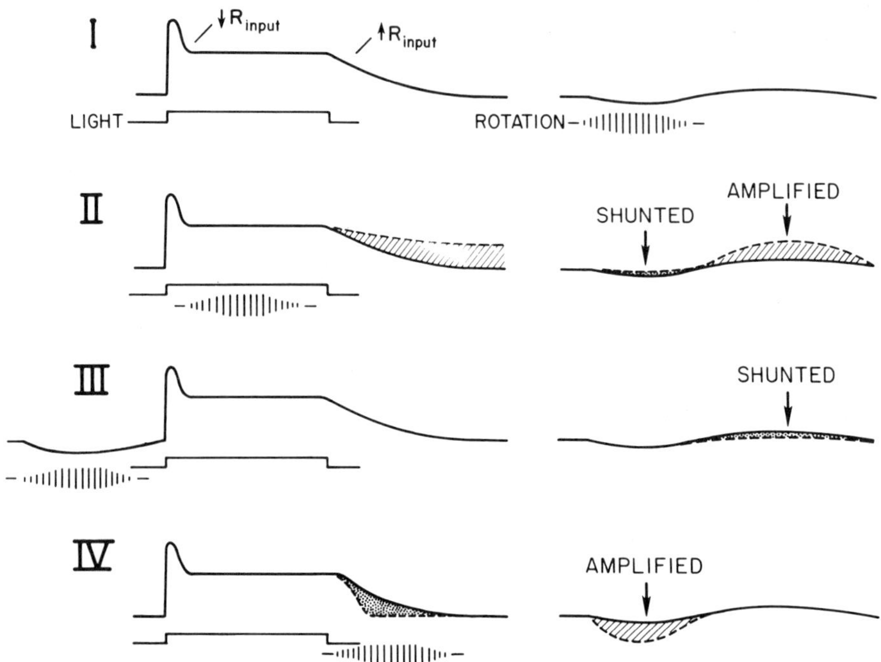


**FIGURE 1.8.** Effects of temporal relationship of light and rotation stimuli on type B photoreceptor responses. Schematic responses to light stimuli (bars) are on left; responses to rotation stimuli (sequence of vertical lines) are on right. During light input, resistance ($R_{\text{input}}$) of type B cell is low, thus shunting synaptic current due to activation of statocyst synaptic effects by rotation. Immediately after light, input resistance is two to three times higher than that prior to light, thereby amplifying rotation-induced synaptic input (Alkon, in press).

may be quite limited in achieving a conclusive demonstration of a site of memory storage. Similarly, neural correlates of learning are useful and certainly necessary as a first step in defining a storage site—but not conclusive. For *Hermissenda*, neural correlates of retention of conditioned behavior (Alkon, Lederhendler, & Shoukimas, 1982; Crow & Alkon, 1980; Farley & Alkon, 1982; West *et al.*, 1982) focused subsequent experimental approaches that would be helpful in the mammalian brain. The *Hermissenda* neurons, the type B cells, the activity changes of which were correlated with learning were first analyzed as to their position within neural pathways (Alkon, 1974b; Goh & Alkon, 1984; Tabata & Alkon, 1982). These learning-induced activity changes at the input stage of the visual pathway were shown to account for and cause learning-induced activity change of motor neurons (at the output stage) that control turning movements of the animal toward light (Goh & Alkon, 1984; Goh, Lederhendler, & Alkon, 1985; Lederhendler, Goh, & Alkon, 1982). Type B cells were then isolated from the *Hermissenda* nervous systems after conditioning (as well as control paradigms) and shown to contain intrinsic membrane changes—which could not simply be a reflection of presynaptic changes elsewhere in the nervous system (Alkon, Lederhendler, & Shoukimas, 1982; Farley *et al.*, 1984; Forman *et al.*, 1984; West *et al.*, 1982). Furthermore, cellular models of *Hermissenda* conditioning could be constructed by electrically stimulating key elements of the conditioned (visual) and unconditioned (statocyst) pathways that produced the same membrane changes in the type B cell (Farley & Alkon, in press). Other models could be constructed by the appropriate current injections into the isolated type B soma itself. Thus, repeated pairing of depolarizing current injections into the caudal hair cell with light steps caused prolonged depolarization and increased input resistance of the type B cell. Repeated pairing of light steps with the appropriate depolarizing current injection into the type B cell also produced these and related changes (Alkon, Shoukimas, & Heldman, 1982; Farley *et al.*, 1983).

Mammalian conditioning might be better understood at the cellular level by means of experiments analogous to *some* of those just described for *Hermissenda*. Brain regions in which short latency neural correlates of acquisition and retention of the learning were obtained could be sampled with the brain slice technique. If electrical changes (or other types of change such as structural and/or biochemical) could be measured within these slices, they could not be explained as simply reflecting learning-induced presynaptic modification located elsewhere in the brain. The learning-induced changes would then of necessity reside within the slice itself (as has recently been demonstrated—see Disterhoft *et al.*, 1984). Those cells and membranes on which intrinsic conditioning-induced changes occurred (i.e., where the association was being stored) could then be determined. Once intrinsic learning-induced changes of identified cell types were found, cellular models could be tested. Paired stimulation of pathways impinging on the critical storage sites could be evaluated for their effectiveness in producing the previously determined neuronal changes. An approach that was used successfully in *Hermissenda* but could not easily be attempted with vertebrates involves artificial production of conditioning-induced membrane changes in single neurons. Electrical stimulation of aggregates of neurons rather than of individual neurons would undoubtedly be necessary to simulate the effects of training and bring about the behavioral changes.

Taken together these different experimental approaches might provide insight as to how repeated stimulus patterns within the environment ultimately result in transformation of mammalian brain. It probably cannot be overemphasized that taken separately these approaches yield results that must be interpreted with great caution. Learning is a behavioral phenomenon that ultimately must be explainable by cell physiology. Cell models without correlation with learning behavior, however, are myriad and they do not *necessarily* account for learning or behavior at all, for that matter. Electrical stimulation of a neuronal aggregate to effect high-frequency impulse activity is not *necessarily* what happens during behavior or learning unless such activity is demonstrated to occur within a well-defined behavioral context in response to well-defined stimulus patterns. Similarly, injection of current into identified neurons within a neural system to produce changes of those neurons, be they short- or long-term changes, be they in *Hermissenda* or a hippocampal slice, is not learning or a learning mechanism unless those changes are given meaning by establishing their relationship to the function of intact animals. Finally, once these different approaches together have yielded a storage site and a sequence of physiological events that precede storage, as have now been revealed in *Hermissenda*, the question of generality (among neural systems within the same animal and of diverse species) *must* be painstakingly addressed. The reasonable relevance of the *Hermissenda* mechanisms to mammalian learning mechanisms has been suggested in the preceding discussion and lent considerable credence by the intrinsic neuronal changes recently demonstrated by Disterhoft *et al.* (1984) in hippocampal brain slices of conditioned rabbits. It, of course, remains to be seen whether what is reasonable within a limited conceptual framework agrees with what of neural systems' functions was conserved within the framework of species' evolution.

## REFERENCES

Acosta-Urquidi, J., Alkon, D. L., & Neary, J. T. $Ca^{2+}$-dependent protein kinase injection in a photoreceptor mimics biophysical effects of associative learning. *Science*, 1984, *224*, 1254–1257.

Alkon, D. L. Intersensory interactions in *Hermissenda*. *Journal of General Physiology*, 1973, *62*, 185–202.

Alkon, D. L. Associative training of *Hermissenda*. *Journal of General Physiology*, 1974, *64*, 70–84. (a)

Alkon, D. L. Sensory interactions in the nudibranch mollusc *Hermissenda crassicornis*. *Federation Proceedings, Federation of American Societies for Experimental Biology*, 1974, *33*, 1083–1090. (b)

Alkon, D. L. A dual synaptic effect on hair cells in *Hermissenda*. *Journal of General Physiology*, 1975, *65*, 385–397.

Alkon, D. L. Voltage-dependent calcium and potassium ion conductances: A contingency mechanism for an associative learning model. *Science*, 1979, *205*, 810–816.

Alkon, D. L. Membrane depolarization accumulates during acquisition of an associative behavioral change. *Science*, 1980, *210*, 1375–1376.

Alkon, D. L. A biophysical basis for molluscan associative learning. In C. D. Woody (Ed.), *Conditioning: Representation of involved neural functions*. New York: Plenum Press, 1982.

Alkon, D. L. Regenerative changes of voltage-dependent $Ca^{2+}$ and $K^{+}$ currents encode a learned stimulus association. *Journal of Physiology* (*Paris*), 1982–1983, *78*, 700–706.

Alkon, D. L. Intersensory convergence: A prerequisite for primary membrane changes of molluscan associative learning. In G. Horn (Ed.), *Multimodal convergences in sensory systems*. Stuttgart–New York: Gustav Fischer Verlag, 1983.

Alkon, D. L. Calcium-inactivated potassium currents: A biophysical memory trace. *Science*, 1984, *226*, 1037–1045. (a)

Alkon, D. L. Persistent changes of identified membrane currents as a cause of associative learning. In D. L. Alkon & J. Farley (Eds.), *Primary neural substrates of learning and behavioral change*. New York & London: Cambridge University Press, 1984. (b)

Alkon, D. L. Changes of membrane currents and calcium-calmodulin-dependent phosphorylation of specific proteins during associative learning. In D. L. Alkon & C. D. Woody (Eds.), *Neural mechanisms of conditioning*. New York: Plenum Press, in press.

Alkon, D. L., Farley, J., Sakakibara, M., & Hay, B. Voltage-dependent calcium and calcium-activated potassium currents of a molluscan photoreceptor. *Biophysical Journal*, 1984, *46*, 605–614.

Alkon, D. L., Lederhendler, I., & Shoukimas, J. J. Primary changes of membrane currents during retention of associative learning. *Science*, 1982, *215*, 693–695.

Alkon, D. L., & Sakakibara, M. Prolonged inactivation of a $Ca^{2+}$-dependent $K^+$ current but not $Ca^{2+}$-current by light induced elevation of intracellular calcium. *Society for Neuroscience Abstracts*, 1984, *10*, 10.

Alkon, D. L., Shoukimas, J., & Heldman, E. Calcium-mediated decrease of a voltage-dependent potassium current. *Biophysical Journal*, 1982, *40*, 245–250.

Clark, R. B., & Wong, R. K. S. Three components of outward current in isolated mammalian cortical neurons. *Society for Neuroscience Abstracts*, 1983, *9*, 601.

Connor, J., & Alkon, D. L. 1984. Light- and voltage-dependent increases of calcium ion concentration in molluscan photoreceptors. *Journal of Neurophysiology*, 1984, *51*, 745–752.

Crow, T. J. Conditioned modification of locomotion in *Hermissenda crassicornis*: Analysis of time-dependent associative and non-associative components. *Journal of Neuroscience*, 1983, *3*, 2621–2628.

Crow, T. J., & Alkon, D. L. Retention of an associative behavioral change in *Hermissenda crassicornis*. *Science*, 1978, *201*, 1239–1241.

Crow, T. J., & Alkon, D. L. Associative behavioral modification in *Hermissenda*: Cellular correlates. *Science*, 1980, *209*, 412–414.

Disterhoft, J. F., Coulter, D. A., & Alkon, D. L. Conditioning causes intrinsic membrane changes of rabbit hippocampal neurons *in vitro*. *Biological Bulletin (Woods Hole, Massachusetts)*, 1984, *167*, 526. (Abstract)

Farley, J. Contingency-learning and causal detection in *Hermissenda*: Behavioral and cellular mechanisms. *Behavioral Neuroscience*, in press.

Farley, J., & Alkon, D. L. Associative neural and behavioral change in *Hermissenda*: Consequences of nervous system orientation for light- and pairing-specificity. *Journal of Neurophysiology*, 1982, *48*, 785–807.

Farley, J., & Alkon, D. L. Associative training results in persistent reductions in a calcium-activated potassium current in *Hermissenda* type B photoreceptors. *Journal of Neurophysiology*, in press.

Farley, J., Richards, W. G., Ling, L. J., Liman, E., & Alkon, D. L. Membrane changes in a single photoreceptor cause associative learning in *Hermissenda*. *Science*, 1983, *221*, 1201–1203.

Farley, J., Sakakibara, M., & Alkon, D. L. Associative training correlated changes in $I_{Ca\text{-}K}$ in *Hermissenda* Type B photoreceptors. *Society for Neuroscience Abstracts*, 1984, *10*, 270.

Forman, R., Alkon, D. L., Sakakibara, M., Harrigan, J., Lederhendler, I., & Farley, J. Changes in $I_A$ and $I_C$ but not $I_{Na}$ accompany retention of conditioned behavior in *Hermissenda*. *Society for Neuroscience Abstracts*, 1984, *10*, 121.

Goh, Y., & Alkon, D. L. Sensory, interneuronal and motor interactions within the *Hermissenda* visual pathway. *Journal of Neurophysiology*, 1984, *52*, 156–169.

Goh, Y., Lederhendler, I., & Alkon, D. L. Input and output changes of an identified neural pathway are correlated with associative learning in *Hermissenda*. *Journal of Neuroscience*, 1985, *5*, 536–543.

Lederhendler, I., & Alkon, D. L. In preparation.

Lederhendler, I., Gart, S., & Alkon, D. L. Associative learning in *Hermissenda crassicornis* (Gastropoda): Evidence that light (the CS) takes on characteristics of rotation (the UCS). *Biological Bulletin (Woods Hole, Massachusetts)*, 1983, *165*, 528. (Abstract)

Lederhendler, I., Goh, Y., & Alkon, D. L. Type B photoreceptor changes predict modification of motorneuron responses to light during retention of *Hermissenda* associative conditioning.

*Society for Neuroscience Abstracts*, 1982, *8*, 824.

Neary, J. T., & Alkon, D. L. Protein phosphorylation/dephosphorylation and the transient, voltage-dependent potassium conductance in *Hermissenda crassicornis*. *Journal of Biological Chemistry*, 1983, *258*, 8979–8983.

Neary, J. T., Crow, T. J., & Alkon, D. L. Change in a specific phosphoprotein band following associative learning in *Hermissenda*. *Nature (London)*, 1981, *293*, 658–660.

Neary, J. T., Naito, S., & Alkon, D. L. $Ca^{2+}$-activated, phospholipid-dependent protein kinase (C-kinase) activity in the *Hermissenda* nervous system. *Society for Neuroscience Abstracts*, in press.

Richards, W., Farley J., & Alkon, D. L. Extinction of associative learning in *Hermissenda*: Behavior and neural correlates. *Society for Neuroscience Abstracts*, 1983, *9*, 916.

Sakakibara, M., Alkon, D. L., Neary, J. T., DeLorenzo, R., Gould, R., & Heldman, E. $Ca^{2+}$-mediated reduction of $K^+$ currents is enhanced by injection of $IP_3$ or neuronal $Ca^{2+}$/calmodulin kinase type II. *Society for Neuroscience Abstracts*, in press.

Segal, M., & Barker, J. L. Rat hippocampal neurons in culture: Potassium conductances. *Journal of Neurophysiology*, 1984, *51*, 1409-1433.

Tabata, M., & Alkon, D. L. Positive synaptic feedback in the visual system of the nudibranch mollusc *Hermissenda crassicornis*. *Journal of Neurophysiology*, 1982, *48*, 174-191.

West, A., Barnes, E. S., & Alkon, D. L. Primary changes of voltage responses during retention of associative learning. *Journal of Neurophysiology*, 1982, *48*, 1243–1255.

Woody, C. D., Alkon, D. L., & Hay, B. Depolarization-induced effects of $Ca^{2+}$-calmodulin-dependent protein kinase injection, in vivo, in single neurons of cat motor cortex. *Brain Research*, 1984, *321*, 192–197.

CHAPTER 2

# Some Organizational Principles of a Vertebrate Conditioning Pathway: Is Memory a Distributed Property?

**David H. Cohen**
State University of New York, Stony Brook

## INTRODUCTION

For many years symposia on the neural mechanisms of learning and memory were characterized by intense speculation with few factual constraints, a situation of frustration to some and of delight to others. However, the development of effective experimental model systems over the past decade and a half has generated an impressive body of knowledge and has initiated the era of a true cellular–molecular biology of learning (e.g., Kandel & Schwartz, 1982). Much of this progress has derived from simpler invertebrate models, principally *Aplysia* (Kandel, 1976) and *Hermissenda* (Alkon, 1982). However, more recently, a few vertebrate model systems have begun to yield cellular data as well (e.g., Cohen, 1982; Thompson *et al.*, 1982; Tsukahara, 1982).

Each model system tends to have its unique strengths and weaknesses. Indeed, it is probably inappropriate to think in terms of a single best system. Only with the development of many models can we hope to achieve a reasonable perspective on issues such as how neural networks are organized to store and retrieve information in different contexts, the possibility of different forms of memory, and the range and generality of various mechanisms. Although the number of effective systems at this time is admittedly rather small, the field has perhaps attained a stage of development where interim conclusions regarding selected issues can be productively considered. This is approached by starting with an overview of the model system we have been investigating for some years and then using it as a foundation for discussing selected issues.

## VISUALLY CONDITIONED HEART RATE CHANGE IN THE PIGEON: AN OVERVIEW OF A VERTEBRATE MODEL SYSTEM

### Analytic Strategy

To develop this particular model system, we applied a rather straightforward analytic strategy (Cohen, 1969, 1974). The initial task was to develop a standardized behavioral paradigm that would assure long-term associative learning and be as compatible as possible with the technical demands of cellular neurophysiological analysis. Given an effective behavioral model, the subsequent task was to delineate the neuronal circuitry mediating the acquisition of the learned change in heart rate. This, in turn, established a basis for utilizing cellular neurophysiological methods to determine the temporal properties of the information flow along the identified pathways. Such an analysis is important for evaluating the amenability of the system to cellular analysis. The subsequent phase of the program then involved searching for sites where training-induced modification actually occurs. Identifying such modifiable sites is, of course, the prerequisite for analyzing the cellular–molecular mechanisms of information storage.

### Behavioral Model

A robust and effective behavioral model is now well developed and extensively characterized (see Cohen & Goff, 1978). It involves the classical conditioning of heart rate change to a visual stimulus. The standardized paradigm involves the repeated presentation of a 6-sec pulse of whole-field illumination—the conditioned stimulus (CS)—immediately followed by a 500-msec foot shock—the unconditioned stimulus (US). The US elicits cardioacceleration; and after a sufficient number of CS–US pairings, the CS alone reliably evokes cardioacceleration of predictable dynamics—the conditioned response (CR). Stable conditioning develops within 10 CS–US presentations and asymptotic performance is achieved by 30 pairings (Figure 2.1). This CR is highly resistant to extinction, and orienting and sensitization responses contribute minimally to the response.

Through various investigations, summarized by Cohen and Goff (1978), we have characterized a number of the principal variables controlling response acquisition and have shown that the heart rate CR interacts minimally, if at all, with concomitantly developing conditioned responses. Moreover, in a pharmacologically immobilized preparation, the CR can be established in a single training session, where stable responses occur within 30 min and asymptotic performance in less than 2 hr (Gold & Cohen, 1981a).

### Neuronal Circuitry

Given an effective behavioral model, identifying the neuronal circuitry mediating acquisition of the CR is the most essential criterion the model system

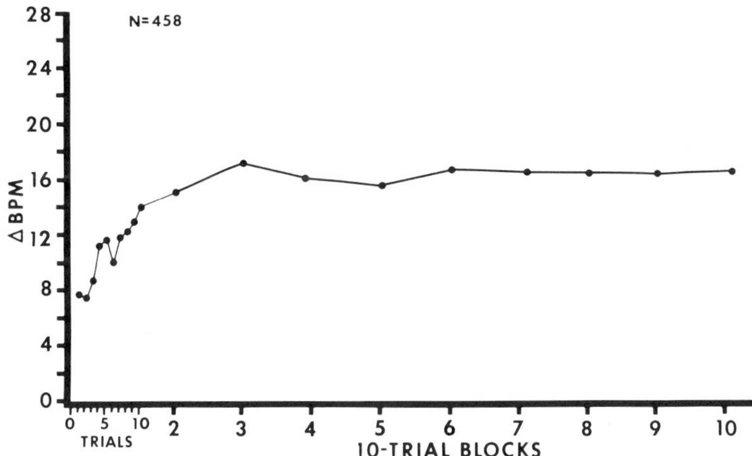


**FIGURE 2.1.** Acquisition of conditioned heart rate change. The curve represents mean heart rate changes in beats per minute (BPM) between the 6-sec CS and the immediately preceding 6-sec control periods. Each point represents a group mean for a block of 10 training trials, with the exception of the first block for which individual trial means are shown. (Adapted from Cohen & Goff, 1978.)

must satisfy (Cohen, 1969; Kandel & Spencer, 1968). We approached this by defining four segments of the system: (1) the visual pathways transmitting the CS information; (2) the somatosensory pathways transmitting the US information; (3) the descending pathways mediating expression of the CR; and (4) the efferent pathways mediating the unconditioned response (UR). We then began our analysis at the periphery of each segment and mapped the pathways systematically centrally. It was assumed that such an analysis of the input and output segments of the relevant neuronal circuitry would lead to the identification of sites of convergence of the CS and US pathways, as well as to their sites of coupling to the CR pathways.

This approach has proved rather successful, and we have now established a first approximation to a necessary pathway from the eye to the heart (Cohen, 1980). The following summary of the CS and CR pathways illustrates this.

## Visual Pathways Transmitting the CS Information

It was first established that bilateral enucleation precludes development of the CR, excluding participation of any nonretinal photoreceptors and nonvisual stimuli (Cohen, 1974; Cohen & Broyles, in preparation) (see Figure 2.2). We next evaluated the various retinorecipient cell groups and found that no deficits in conditioning followed destruction of any single optic tract target (Cohen, 1974; Cohen & Broyles, in preparation). This is not surprising because all such cell groups respond to whole-field illumination and thus provide considerable opportunity for parallel transmission of CS information.

Given the mammalian literature on structures involved in visual learning, we evaluated the possible involvement of the visual pathways ascending to the telencephalon—the thalamofugal and tectofugal pathways (see Figure 2.3). These are homologous respectively to the mammalian geniculo-striate and tecto-thalamo-extrastriate visual pathways (Cohen & Karten, 1974). We initially asked whether interruption of either of these pathways would affect CR acquisition. Even though the results were negative, we did find that the combined interruption of both by a lesion of their telencephalic targets (the visual Wulst and the ectostriatum) prevented CR development (Cohen, 1974, 1980; Cohen & Broyles, in preparation) (Figure 2.2). An attempt to validate this finding by combined interruption of the two pathways at the thalamic level produced only a transient deficit, a finding leading us to hypothesize the involvement of a third ascending pathway. Extending the subtelencephalic lesion to include the pretectal terminal field of the optic tract produced deficits comparable to those following the combined telencephalic lesion (Figure 2.2), and we thus hypothesized that the third pathway is of pretectal origin (Cohen, 1974, 1980). However, recent anatomical and physiological studies (Gamlin & Cohen, 1982, in preparation-a, in preparation-b), indicate that the third pathway is a second ascending tectofugal system and that the pretectal lesion interrupted the efferent tectal fibers of this pathway.

It thus appears that the thalamofugal and the two tectofugal pathways each transmit effective CS information, and it is only with their combined interruption that CR acquisition is precluded.

### Descending Pathways Mediating CR Expression

Our initial efforts to describe the CR pathway began at the motor periphery—the cardiac motoneurons. A behavioral study involving various combinations of cardiac denervation and pharmacological blockade indicated that the CR is entirely mediated by the extrinsic cardiac nerves (Cohen & Pitts, 1968). Although both the vagi and the cardiac sympathetics contribute to the CR, the sympathetic innervation provides the major contribution. Subsequent anatomical and electrophysiological studies characterized these motoneuronal pools in considerable detail and established electrophysiological criteria for identifying the cardiac motoneurons in the unanesthetized bird (see Cohen, 1982).

Given a comprehensive description of the final common path for the CR, we turned our attention to delineating the central pathways that converge upon these neurons and are involved in mediating the expression of the CR. Through this effort (see Cohen, 1980), we have identified a pathway that, upon electrical stimulation, produces striking pressor–accelerator responses and that, upon interruption, prevents the CR. This pathway courses from the posteromedial hypothalamus through the ventromedial brain stem

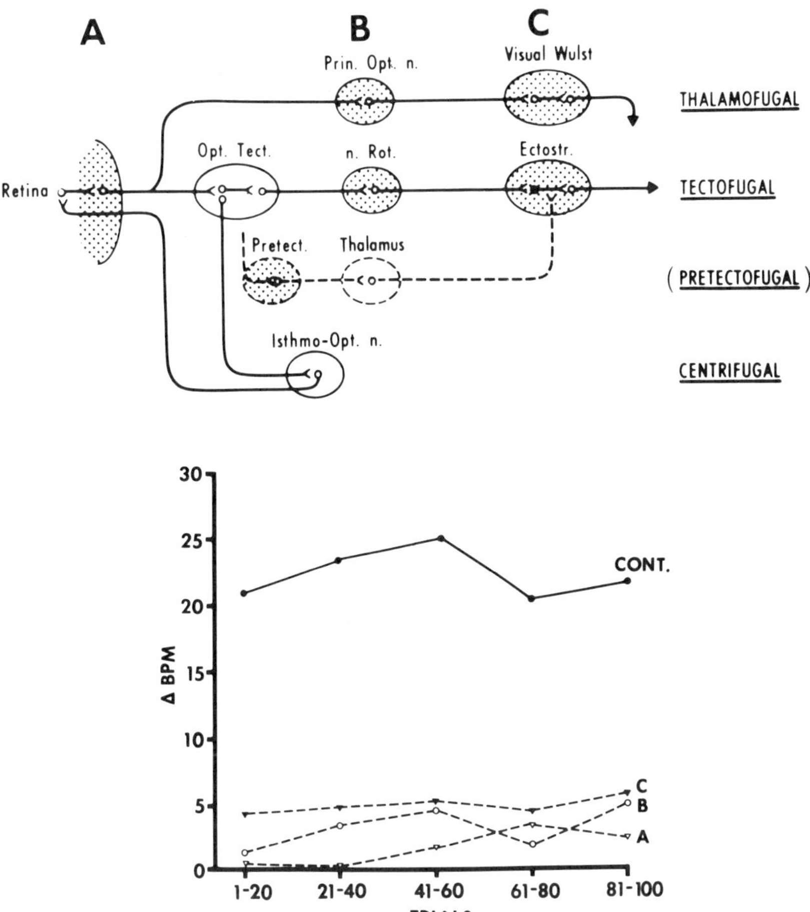


**FIGURE 2.2.** Visual system lesions that prevent CR acquisition. Each broken line represents an experimental group; the solid line shows the performance of control birds (CONT). Curve A illustrates the performance of animals with bilateral enucleation (A in upper panel). Curve B illustrates the performance of animals with a combined lesion of the principal optic nucleus, nucleus rotundus, and the pretectal terminal field of the optic tract (B in upper panel). (Note that the pretectal lesion interrupts efferent tectal fibers of a second tectofugal pathway; a pretectofugal pathway is no longer considered to be involved; see text.) Curve C illustrates the performance of animals with a combined lesion of the visual Wulst and ectostriatum (C in upper panel). For all curves, each point represents the mean heart rate changes in BPM between the 6-sec CS period and an immediately preceding 6-sec control period. Ectostr., ectostriatum; Isthmo-Opt. n., isthmo-optic nucleus; n. Rot., nucleus rotundus; Opt. Tect., optic tectum; Pretect., pretectal region; Prin. Opt. n., principal optic nucleus of the thalamus (dorsal lateral geniculate equivalent, or LGNe). (From Cohen, 1980.)

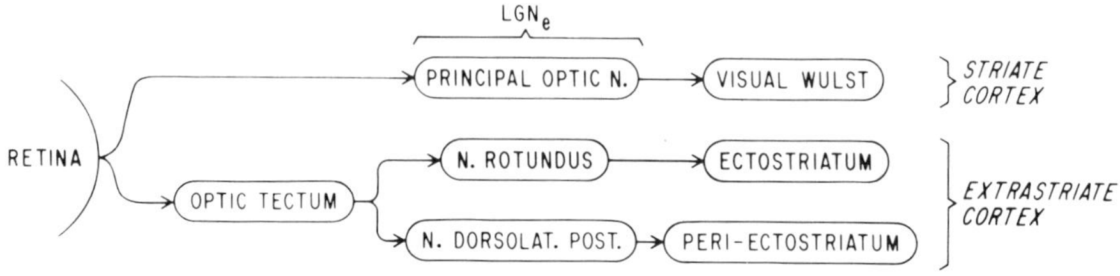


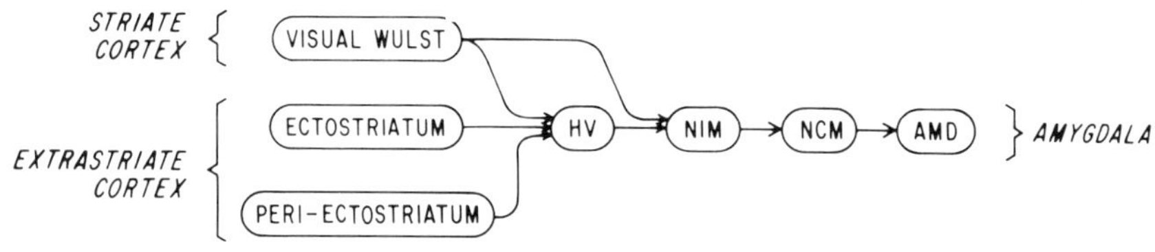


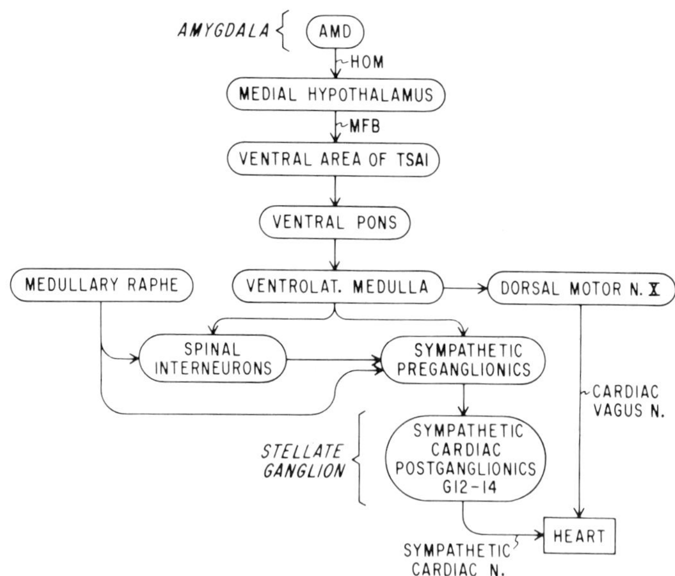


**FIGURE 2.3.** Schematic illustration of the CS–CR pathways and their coupling. *CS path*. Three ascending visual pathways each transmit effective CS information. The thalamofugal pathway involves a retinal projection to the principal optic nucleus of the thalamus, which is equivalent to the mammalian dorsal lateral geniculate nucleus and is designated LGNe. LGNe then

at mesencephalic and rostral pontine levels, where it then shifts to a ventrolateral position that is maintained through the medulla. Fibers then project dorsomedially to access the dorsal motor nucleus of the vagus, while the spinal continuation of the pathway occupies a position in the lateral funiculus. Another important feature of this pathway is that its most rostral component—the posteromedial hypothalamus—receives a projection via a well-defined pathway from the most "cardioactive" structure of the telencephalon—the avian amygdalar homologue.

Lesions at various sites along this pathway, including the amygdala, totally prevent expression of the CR. In contrast, large lesions nearby have virtually no effect, and destruction of other "cardioactive" areas is also without effect. A schematic diagram of the CS and CR pathways, including their coupling through intratelencephalic connections, is shown in Figure 2.3.

### Temporal Properties of Information Flow along the Identified Pathways

The heart rate CR has a latency of approximately 1 sec and persists for approximately 6 sec (see Cohen & Goff, 1978). To evaluate the CR in a neurophysiological, rather than a behavioral, time domain, we studied the discharge characteristics of the cardiac motoneurons during conditioned responding (see Cohen, 1982).

With respect to the sympathetic component of the final common path, we found that the cardiac postganglionic neurons respond weakly to the visual stimulus prior to any training. The latency of this orienting response

---

projects to the visual Wulst, the analogue of striate cortex. The other two pathways are tectofugal pathways. One relays through the nucleus rotundus of the thalamus and then to the ectostriatum. The other relays through the nucleus dorsolateralis posterior of the thalamus (N. DORSOLAT. POST.) and then to a periectostriatal region. The ectostriatal and periectostriatal terminal regions are considered analogous to mammalian extrastriate cortex. *Intratelencephalic path.* The most rostral component of the descending (CR) path is the avian amygdalar homologue, and the relevant telencephalic visual areas access the amygdala through intratelencephalic (equivalent to intracortical) circuitry. HV, hyperstriatum ventrale; NIM, neostriatum intermedium, pars mediale; NCM, neostriatum caudale, pars mediale. NCM then projects upon archistriatum mediale, pars dorsalis (AMD), which is the nucleus of the avian amygdala that is involved in the conditioning pathway. *CR path.* This segment of the system begins at the amygdala (AMD) and projects upon the medial hypothalamus via the tractus occipitomesencephalicus, pars hypothalami (HOM). The pathway exits the hypothalamus via the medial forebrain bundle (MFB) and maintains a ventromedial course through rostral pons. It then shifts laterally to occupy a ventrolateral position in the medulla (VENTROLAT. MEDULLA), where a contingent of fibers courses dorsomedially to access the vagal cardiac neurons in the dorsal motor nucleus. The caudal continuation of the pathway is through the lateral funiculus to influence, directly and/or through interneurons, the cardiac sympathetic preganglionic and subsequently the cardiac postganglionic neurons.

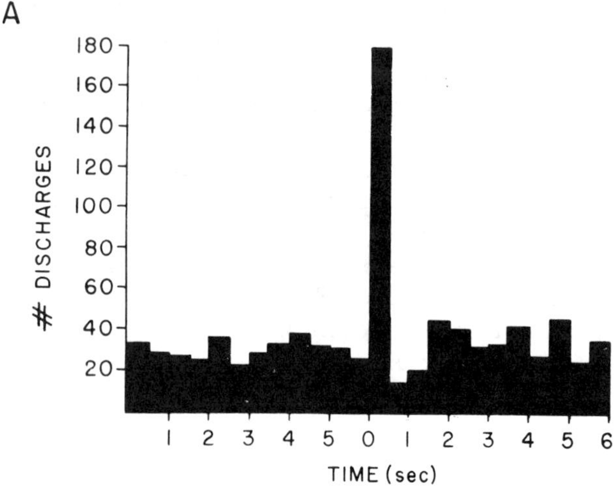


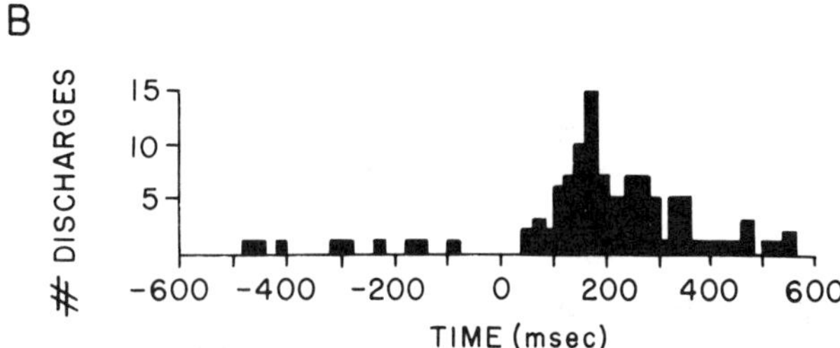


**FIGURE 2.4.** Discharge of cardiac sympathetic postganglionic neurons during conditioned responding. (A) Summary peristimulus time histogram of the responses of nine cardiac postganglionic neurons to 10 CS presentations. The onset of the 6-sec CS is at time 0; bin width is 500 msec. Note that the phasic response is confined to the first 500-msec bin. (B) Peristimulus time histogram of the discharges of three neurons for the 600 msec immediately before and after CS onset. Note that the phasic component of the response has a latency of approximately 100 msec (first significant deviation from maintained activity) and a duration of 300–400 msec. (Adapted from Cohen, 1980.)

is approximately 100 msec, and it consists of a short burst of action potentials, followed by a brief depression of discharge and a return to maintained activity levels. This response habituates rapidly; but with CS–US pairing, its probability of occurrence and its magnitude rapidly increase. An important feature of this response is that it consists almost exclusively of a transient discharge at CS onset with a latency of approximately 100 msec and a duration of 300–400 msec (Figure 2.4). This suggests that the central processing time for the 6-sec behavioral CR does not exceed 400 msec and that there is a highly nonlinear input–output relation between the sympathetic innervation and the heart.

The vagal cardiac neurons also respond to the CS prior to training, but with decreased discharge (Gold & Cohen, 1981b, 1984). Like the cardiac sympathetics, the vagal response has a prominent phasic component (Figure 2.5), although in contrast to the sympathetics there is a tonic component as well. Associative training enhances the magnitude of this decrease in discharge, as well as shortening its latency to 60–80 msec at asymptotic performance (Figure 2.5).

Our findings for the final common path generate the following conclusions:

1. The sympathetic and vagal cardiac innervations contribute synergistically to the CR.
2. The sympathetic outflow provides the principal contribution to the CR and occurs at a latency of 100 msec.
3. The sympathetic discharge evoked by the CS persists for only 300–400 msec.
4. Associative training increases the probability of occurrence and magnitude of the initial light-evoked responses of the cardiac motoneurons.

Together, these results suggest that the conditioned heart rate change is mediated by enhancement of a short-latency, short-duration motoneuronal response that initially occurs at light onset. This response attenuates (habituates) during nonassociative training.

These motoneuronal data can be utilized to estimate the central processing time for the CR, and the precision of this estimate can be increased if the delay at the CS periphery is known (Cohen, 1982). In that regard, it has been shown that the retinal ganglion cells respond to whole-field illu-

**FIGURE 2.5.** Poststimulus histogram showing the latency of the discharge change of vagal cardiac neurons in response to the CS during asymptotic performance. The ordinate indicates the standardized score for each 20-msec bin relative to the baseline distribution, and the arrow indicates the standardized score ($z = -1.65$) below which values differ significantly from baseline at the .05 level. (From Cohen, 1982.)

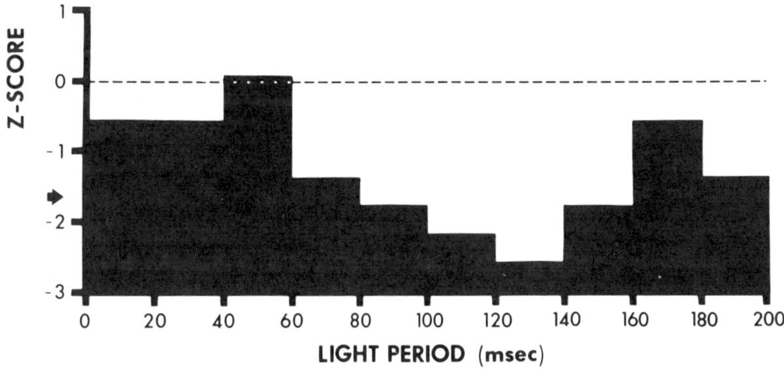

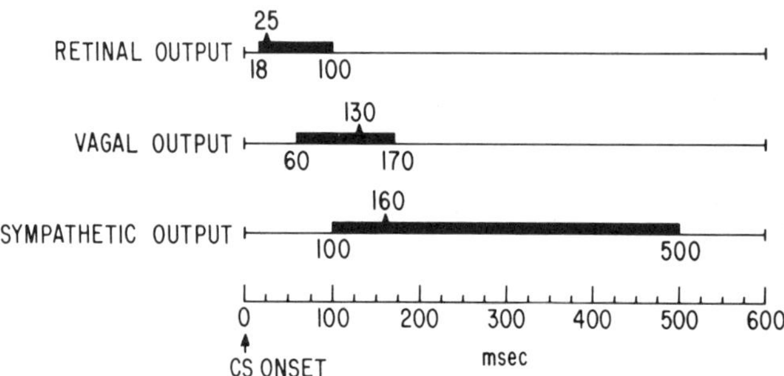


**FIGURE 2.6.** Summary illustration for estimating the central processing time for the CR. The bars are extrapolated from poststimulus histograms at CS onset. The numbers below each bar indicate the temporal range of the phasic response to the CS. The number above each bar indicates the interval (in milliseconds) between CS onset and the mode of the poststimulus histogram. (From Cohen, 1984.)

mination as a rather homogeneous population, bursting briefly at CS onset and largely ceasing activity during the remainder of the sustained illumination (Duff & Cohen, 1975a, 1975b). This "on" burst has a minimum latency of 16 msec and a maximum duration of 80 msec and is unaffected by either associative or nonassociative training (Wild & Cohen, 1985). Calculating the differences between the modes of the response histograms of the retinal ganglion cells and cardiac motoneurons gives an estimate of 105 msec for the central processing time for the vagal component of the CR and 135 msec for the sympathetic component (Figure 2.6). Calculating the differences for the shortest latency responses gives estimates of 40 msec for the most rapid vagal response and 80 msec for the earliest sympathetic response (Figure 2.6). The important point is that the central processing for the CR is in the domain of milliseconds rather than seconds, as originally suggested by the temporal properties of the behavioral response. Thus, although not a "simple system," perhaps the model could be viewed as a "relatively simple system."

## Sites of Neuronal Modification

### Analysis of CS Pathways

Given a first approximation to the relevant neuronal circuitry and an estimate of the central processing time, we turned our attention to identifying sites along the identified pathways where training-induced modification of CS-evoked discharge might occur (Cohen, 1984). Training-related discharge changes clearly occur at the level of the motoneurons. However, it is difficult to determine whether such changes merely reflect modification of more rostral structures. Consequently, we adopted an approach of undertaking cellular neurophysiological analysis of the CS pathways, beginning at the sensory periphery. Our strategy has been to examine successively more central cell groups until the most peripheral site(s) of associative change in discharge is identified. Such a strategy also addresses the issue of whether the involved sensory pathways behave merely as input lines or are plastic.

Investigation of the retinal output established that the retinal ganglion cells show no change in either maintained or CS-evoked activity over conditioning (Wild & Cohen, 1985). Given an invariant input from the periphery, we selected the tectofugal pathway for our initial analysis of the central CS pathways. Because it seemed possible, if not likely, that these pathways behave only as input lines, we first explored the telencephalic target of that pathway, the ectostriatum (see Figure 2.3). The rationale was that if ectostriatal neurons were invariant with training one could infer that the subtelencephalic components of the pathway would also be invariant. However, the data clearly indicated that certain classes of ectostriatal neurons show modification of their CS-evoked discharge during conditioning (Wall, Gibbs, Broyles, & Cohen, in press; Wall, Wild, Broyles, Gibbs, & Cohen, 1980). An examination of the thalamic relay of the tectofugal pathway, the nucleus rotundus (see Figure 2.3), similarly demonstrated classes of neurons the discharge of which changed as a function of associative training (Wall *et al.*, 1980, in press).

At that point we turned our attention to the thalamic relay of the thalamofugal pathway, the avian homologue of the geniculo-striate system; we refer to this as the lateral geniculate equivalent or LGNe. This permitted us (1) to assess the generality of the plasticity of the tectofugal pathway, and (2) by studying retinorecipient cells, to determine whether modification occurs that peripherally along an involved visual pathway (Cohen, 1984). The results clearly showed robust training-induced modification in the LGNe (Gibbs & Cohen, 1980; Gibbs, Cohen, & Broyles, in press) (Figure 2.7). Consequently, at least two of the three involved CS pathways undergo associative modification, and this can occur as peripherally as retinorecipient neurons.

## Some Properties of Training-Induced Modification of Visual Neurons

The plasticity of LGNe neurons during associative learning suggested various properties of training-induced modification. The modifiable neurons initially respond to both the CS and the US, a finding suggesting the necessity for convergence of CS and US inputs (Gibbs *et al.*, in press). The effect of associative training on such neurons is to enhance their initial CS-evoked response; with nonassociative training it generally attenuates or, less frequently, remains unchanged. Moreover, this associative enhancement is largely restricted to the short-latency, transient response to the visual stim-

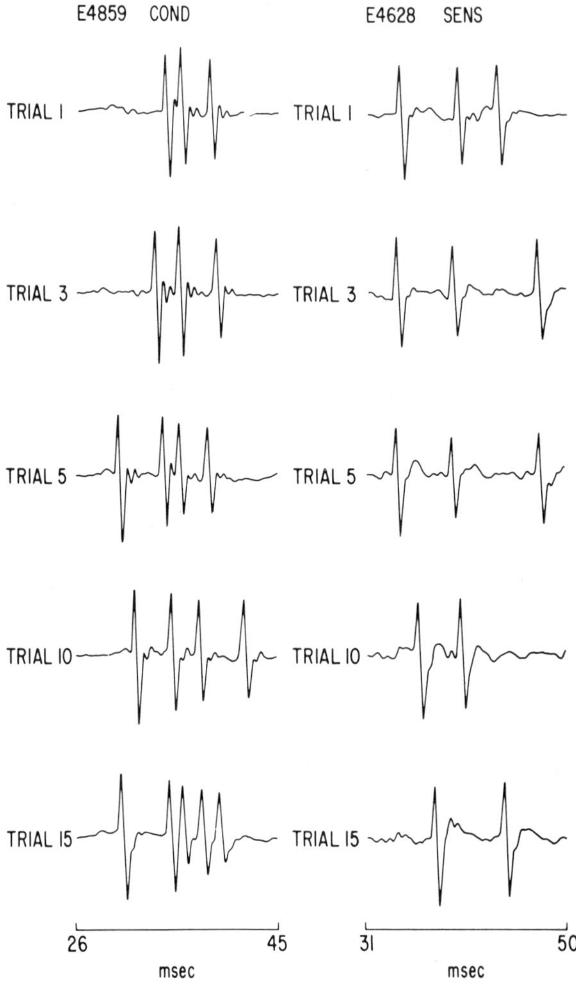


**FIGURE 2.7.** Examples of the behavior of single LGNe neurons during conditioning (COND; left column) and during unpaired lights and shocks (SENS; right column). The training trial from which each record was sampled is indicated to the left of that record. The bar below each column indicates the time period after CS onset for the records shown. (From Cohen, 1984.)

ulus, a phenomenon also observed in other structures along the identified pathways (Cohen, 1982). Tonic responses during sustained illumination either remain unchanged or attenuate, irrespective of the behavioral treatment. The response enhancement also seems to be independent of the nature of the light-evoked response; the modifiable cells simply do more of what they initially did upon light presentation. (We are presently conducting a study of the receptive fields to evaluate this conclusion more stringently.) Yet another important feature is that discharge modification of the CS pathways (Figure 2.8) either precedes or parallels the acquisition of the behavioral CR (Figure 2.1), such that these neuronal changes could well contribute to CR development.

It was concluded earlier that CS–US convergence is necessary for associative modification. However, our results also indicate that it is not sufficient because modifiability depends upon particular response properties to the US (Cohen, 1984; Gibbs *et al.*, in press; Gibbs, Cohen, Broyles, & Solina, 1981). In the specific case of the LGNe, only cells in which discharge is decreased by the US show associative modification (Figure 2.8). Thus, the properties of the US input are apparently more important than the properties of the CS input in determining a neuron's modifiability. Furthermore, because modifiable LGNe cells can show either increased or decreased discharge to the CS, the directions of the CS- and US-evoked responses need not be the same.

In recent experiments we have obtained evidence that the effective US input to the LGNe originates in the region of the locus ceruleus (Cohen, 1984; Cohen, Gibbs, Siegelman, Gamlin, & Broyles, 1982; Gibbs, Broyles, & Cohen, 1983), a finding possibly suggesting involvement of a biogenic amine as the neurotransmitter. The necessity of this input is suggested by preliminary experiments showing that interruption of the projection from the locus ceruleus eliminates the modifiability of LGNe neurons. Its sufficiency is suggested by experiments showing that electrical stimulation of the locus ceruleus serves as an effective US (Gibbs *et al.*, 1983).

## PROGNOSIS FOR VERTEBRATE MODEL SYSTEMS

The appreciation that emerged in the 1960s of the need to develop experimental model systems for the cellular analysis of learning (Cohen, 1969; Kandel & Spencer, 1968) stimulated a thrust toward "simple systems." These involved primarily invertebrate preparations in which the relevant neuronal circuitry included a limited number of frequently identifiable and large neurons. The challenging prospect of delineating the relevant circuitry in complex vertebrate brains understandably discouraged many serious efforts to develop vertebrate models. Although progress in developing vertebrate models has indeed been slow, as reviewed in the preceding sections, our experience with visually conditioned heart rate change suggests the task is by no means insurmountable. This view is reinforced by successes with other vertebrate models, such as conditioning of the nictitating membrane response in the rabbit (Thompson *et al.*, 1982) and an analogue conditioning model involving the red nucleus of the cat (Tsukahara, 1982). Moreover, advances in neuroanatomical methods for pathway tracing and

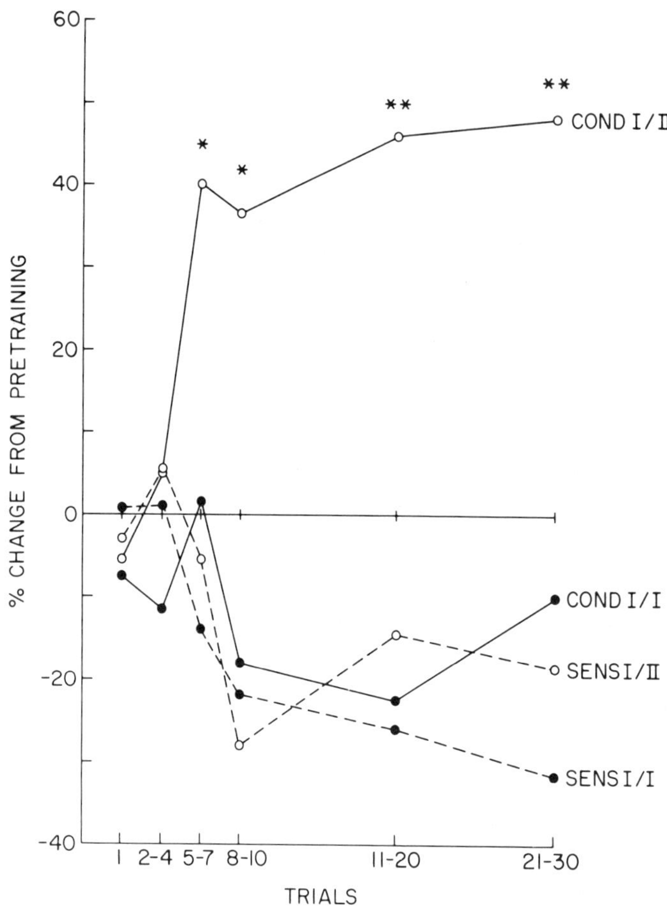


**FIGURE 2.8.** Demonstration that training-induced modification of LGNe neurons is a function of the response to the US. The data for the LGNe neurons showing excitatory responses to the CS (type I) are subdivided on the basis of the response to the US. Thus, I/II indicates cells that increase their discharge at CS onset and decrease their discharge at US onset. I/I refers to cells that increase their discharge at CS onset and US onset. COND refers to neurons studied during associative training, and SENS refers to units studied during nonassociative training. The curves show the mean percentage change from the response to the light prior to training, and the results shown are for the phasic responses at CS onset. Note that the only group showing response enhancement during associative training is that in which the neurons showed decreased discharge at US onset. The associative training group showing increased discharge at US onset does not differ from neurons given nonassociative training (SENS), and all three of these groups show habituation of the CS-evoked response over training. (From Cohen, 1984.)

for the morphological description of physiologically characterized neurons are significantly facilitating the specification of relevant circuitry in vertebrate systems.

Although vertebrate systems lack the very attractive feature of identifiable neurons, they do have identifiable neuronal populations; and although vertebrate models are unlikely to offer "simple systems," they may well provide "relatively simple systems." Moreover, technical advances in recent years, such as tissue slice methods, increase the feasibility of reducing segments of identified vertebrate circuitry to *in vitro* analogue models. This is extremely important because the need in the field is for a broad repertoire of model systems, invertebrate and vertebrate. Each system tends to have its unique advantages, and it is only with a broad repertoire of models that we can hope to gain an appropriate perspective on (1) the generality of mechanisms deriving from the study of any specific system and (2) the range of mechanisms utilized to store information under different behavioral demands.

## LOCALIZATION OF THE ENGRAM

Lashley's (1950) pursuit of the "engram" was instrumental in propagating the view that particular structures of the brain are specialized for storing information. The clinical neurology literature on human memory deficits consequent to brain damage (see Squire, 1982) significantly contributed to this view as well, a view that in fact remains prominent (e.g., Thompson *et al.*, 1976).

"Simple systems" cannot definitively address this issue. More appropriate in this regard are vertebrate models in which (1) the relevant circuitry is specified and (2) this circuitry is systemically probed to identify sites where active or primary training-induced change occurs. Unfortunately, no vertebrate model has yet been analyzed sufficiently to allow firm conclusions, but existing data do permit some preliminary suggestions.

### Modifiability of Sensory Pathways

A consequence of the concept of the "engram" is the tendency to assume that information storage during learning is localized to a limited number of central structures such as the hippocampus, amygdala, or cerebellum. A corollary of this position is that other segments of the participating circuitry, such as the sensory and motor pathways, are not sites of information storage. However, our findings clearly demonstrate that (1) the visual pathways transmitting the CS information for heart rate conditioning undergo plastic change specific to associative learning and (2) such training-induced modification can occur as peripherally as retinorecipient neurons. Furthermore, these changes precede or parallel the behavioral CR, a result suggesting that they contribute to its acquisition.

Plasticity of sensory pathways as a function of their inputs is well established for both developing (see Sherman & Spear, 1982) and adult (Killackey & Belford, 1980; Merzenich *et al.*, 1984) brain. In the context of learning, invertebrate model systems clearly establish that primary sensory neurons transmitting the CS information are modifiable (Alkon, 1982; Kandel & Schwartz, 1982), and our results extend the generality of changes along CS pathways to a vertebrate model. However, such changes may not be a necessary component of learning in all systems. For example, Thompson *et al.* (1982) reported that neurons along the CS (auditory) pathway show no modification during nictitating membrane conditioning in the rabbit. Similarly, it has been reported that the lemniscal ventral medial geniculate does not show plasticity during pupillary conditioning in the cat (Ryugo & Weinberger, 1978; Weinberger, 1982), avoidance conditioning in the rabbit (Gabriel, Miller, & Saltwick, 1976), or appetitive conditioning in the rat (Birt & Olds, 1981). In contrast, Oleson, Ashe, and Weinberger (1975) have reported changes in the cochlear nucleus, nonlemniscal medial geniculate, and auditory cortex during pupillary conditioning in the cat. The changes in auditory cortex and nonlemniscal medial geniculate paralleled the acquisition of the behavioral CR. However, they preceded changes in the cochlear nucleus that occurred after the appearance of the behavioral CR.

Thus, the conditions under which sensory pathways are plastic during learning remain to be clarified. Our findings for the LGNe suggest that this may be more related to the nature of the US than to the properties of the CS or to the particular training paradigm. As to the possible role of CS pathway modification in our specific model, we have hypothesized that it may function to increase the effectiveness of the CS input and thereby facilitate training-induced modification in more central structures (Gibbs *et al.*, in press). This is further elaborated in the following section.

### A Distributed Network for Learning

The modification of the CS pathways in our model, although in all likelihood contributing to CR acquisition, would not itself be capable of "driving" the behavioral response. This implies that information storage must occur in other structures along the pathway as well. Our working hypothesis is that convergent CS and US inputs are necessary, although not sufficient, for the associative modifiability of any given neuron along the relevant pathway. Because such convergence seems ubiquitous throughout the pathway, we suggest that information storage occurs at most sites along it (Cohen, 1984).

For heuristic purposes consider the relevant pathway as a "serial array" of neurons from the retina to the cardiac motoneurons (Figure 2.9). We have shown that the neurons of this array are responsive to the CS prior

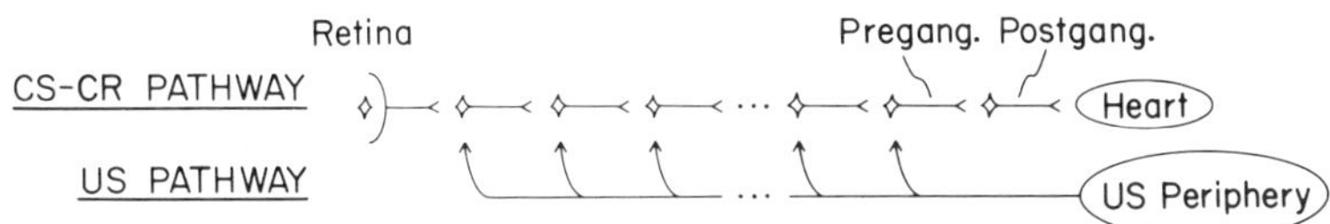


**FIGURE 2.9.** Hypothetical model of the organization of the neuronal circuitry mediating acquisition of the CR. The CS–CR pathway from the retina to the motoneurons is shown for heuristic purposes as a serial chain of neurons. The pathway transmitting the US information is shown as providing input to all central elements along the CS–CR pathway. (From Cohen, 1984.)

to training. Substantial US-responsiveness is also common throughout the array, with the exception of the retinal ganglion cells (Wild & Cohen, 1985). Our model thus proposes CS–US convergence at each central structure along the identified pathway (Figure 2.9). Such convergence establishes the substrate for some sort of long-term heterosynaptic facilitation at each of these structures, and such facilitation would be sufficient to account for the training-induced discharge changes we observe.

It is important to appreciate that this model allows for parallel changes at each relay because every neuron receiving convergent CS–US information is capable of modification irrespective of what occurs at other relays along the pathway. One implication of this property is that the order in which training-induced changes occur along the pathway need not be serial and that it is possible for more caudally located cells to show modified discharge first. However, as neuronal modification occurs, a "serial component" is introduced into the system. For example, the enhanced CS-evoked discharge of LGNe neurons would increase the magnitude of their input to their telencephalic target neurons, and this could well facilitate training-induced modification at that level.

A broader implication of this model is that information storage is "localized" in that it occurs only along the specific neural pathways that mediate the heart rate CR. However, within that neuronal circuitry, storage is "distributed" throughout. Thus, there may be an "engram" in the sense that information storage is restricted to a specified pathway. However, the distributed nature of the changes along that pathway is not entirely in the spirit of the classic view of the "engram."

## Compartments within a Distributed Network?

If information storage is indeed distributed as previously hypothesized, it is important to consider the possibility that the changes in different segments of the network serve different functions and possibly involve different cellular mechanisms. For example, the CS pathways might be viewed as constituting one "compartment" of the system. For our model we have suggested that the changes in this particular "compartment" function to increase the effectiveness of the CS and to thus facilitate modification in more central structures. It is possible that modification in this segment or "compartment" of the system is neither necessary nor sufficient for CR development but that it merely assists CR acquisition, perhaps primarily in early learning. Modification in other "compartments," such as that including the amygdala, might well be more powerfully involved in the actual shaping and driving of the behavioral CR.

Although we lack sufficient information for serious conclusions in this regard, it nonetheless seems worthwhile raising the issues because they may provide an impetus for developing additional model systems that can address such questions.

## POSSIBLE CONDITIONS FOR ASSOCIATIVE NEURONAL MODIFICATION

Neurophysiological investigation of the sensory and motor segments of our model system over the past few years have begun to generate some possible rules for associative neuronal modification; these are summarized below.

1. All modifiable neurons respond to the visual stimulus prior to training.
2. Conditioning then enhances this initial response, whereas nonassociative training either leads to its attenuation or has no effect.
3. This associative enhancement is largely restricted to the phasic, CS-evoked response.
4. Neurons showing associative modification are also US-responsive.
5. However, although US-responsiveness is apparently necessary, it is not sufficient because the specific nature of the US response seems critical.
6. The characteristics of the response to the US are more important for modifiability than are the characteristics of the response to the CS.
7. A neuron need not be excited by either the CS or the US because modification can occur with CS- and/or US-evoked decreases in discharge.
8. Additionally, the directions of the discharge changes evoked by the CS and the US need not be the same.
9. Finally, the training-induced neuronal modification precedes or parallels the acquisition of the behavioral CR.

The generality of these rules is certainly not established, even within our own model system. However, they have some implications worth consideration at this time. For our model, these findings suggest that at the visual periphery the CS evokes a short-latency burst of activity of limited duration. This traverses the identified pathways rather synchronously to be expressed as a burst of activity at the motoneurons of the system. The effect of associative training is to facilitate this CS-evoked response at multiple sites along the pathway. Such facilitation in all likelihood occurs only in neurons that receive convergent CS and US inputs. However, modification probably requires that the US input have particular properties that may relate more to the neurotransmitter, or other synaptically released substances, than to the sign of the postsynaptic response.

Initial responsiveness to the CS and US is characteristic of reduced invertebrate model systems, although their simplified circuitry does not provide a challenging test of the need for such responsiveness. More challenging in this regard is the nictitating membrane model, and in that case initial responsiveness seems to be the case (Berthier & Moore, 1983). Related to this is the necessity for CS–US convergence at a modifiable neuron, and, again, the literature supports this classic assumption. In more general terms, available data thus suggest that associative modification in classical conditioning involves the facilitation of CS-evoked responses along well-defined pathways that are "prewired" for responsiveness to the stimuli used as the CS and US. It should be reemphasized that this is a working model and that the generality of the findings on which it is based requires further validation.

## PHYLOGENETIC CONSIDERATIONS

Given the earlier plea in this chapter for the active development of many more invertebrate and vertebrate model systems, it is perhaps appropriate to consider briefly possible phylogenetic differences with respect to mechanisms of learning. One could hardly dispute an enormous variation among species with respect to learning capability. This is well documented by the application of standardized learning paradigms in a comparative context. However, rigorous neurobiological data regarding phylogenetic differences are not available.

Differences in learning capability, quantitative or qualitative, certainly suggest significant differences in neural organization. It seems difficult to escape the conclusion that at the integrative or systems level there must be striking species differences with respect to how arrays of neurons are organized to mediate the self-adaptive behavior reflected by learning. For example, the primate prefrontal cortex has been implicated in certain learning tasks. However, there is no apparent homologue to this cortical region in many vertebrate species capable of complex learning. A similar statement applies to the hippocampus. An ultimate understanding of learning at this more integrative level will undoubtedly require a concerted long-term effort at exploring a broad range of more complex model systems.

In contrast, the cellular–molecular mechanisms of information storage may well have considerable phylogenetic generality. This seems to be the case for synaptic mechanisms more generally, and it would be surprising if storage mechanisms discovered in invertebrates are not also found in vertebrates. If the growing suspicion of multiple storage mechanisms is correct, then it is quite possible that a greater range of mechanisms has evolved over phylogeny. Nevertheless, it seems likely that phylogenetically older mechanisms are conserved, and we can thus expect important information to derive from every rigorous exploration of cellular–molecular mechanisms of learning, irrespective of the species of the model system.

## CONCLUDING COMMENTS

In concluding, I would like to elaborate briefly on an extremely important feature of more complex model systems for learning. A comprehensive understanding of learning obviously requires a detailed specification of the various molecular mechanisms that are involved. However, equally important are descriptions of how arrays of neurons are organized to store and retrieve information for the guidance of goal-directed behavior.

The more complex vertebrate models have the feature of permitting the pursuit of both of these important directions in single systems. For example, despite the fact that we have analyzed only a few components of the conditioning pathway in our model system, some potentially interesting ideas as to its integrative properties have already begun to emerge. These include the necessity for CS–US convergence, the initial responsiveness of the relevant circuitry to the CS and the US, the particular importance of the properties of the US input, the modifiability of the CS pathways, and the possibly distributed nature of storage throughout the relevant neuronal circuitry.

At the same time, this system now has exciting potential for analyzing cellular mechanisms at one particular locus, the LGNe. The associative modifiability of the geniculate neurons and the possibility of producing such plasticity in an *in vitro* analogue model involving a thalamic slice raise the prospect of pursuing cellular mechanisms at this particular relay of the system at a level of resolution that could approach that of "simple systems."

## REFERENCES

Alkon, D. L. A biophysical basis for molluscan associative learning. In C. D. Woody (Ed.), *Conditioning*. New York: Plenum Press, 1982.

Berthier, N. E., & Moore, J. W. The nictitating membrane response: An electrophysiological study of the abducens nerve and nucleus and the accessory abducens nucleus in rabbit. *Brain Research*, 1983, *258*, 201–210.

Birt, D., & Olds, M. E. Associative response changes in lateral midbrain tegmentum and medial geniculate during differential appetitive conditioning. *Journal of Neurophysiology*, 1981, *46*, 1039–1055.

Cohen, D. H. Development of a vertebrate experimental model for cellular neurophysiologic studies of learning. *Conditional Reflex*, 1969, *4*, 61–80.

Cohen, D. H. The neural pathways and informational flow mediating a conditioned autonomic response. In L. V. DiCara (Ed.), *Limbic and autonomic nervous systems research*. New York: Plenum Press, 1974.

Cohen, D. H. The functional neuroanatomy of a conditioned response. In R. F. Thompson, L. H. Hicks, & V. B. Shvyrkov (Eds.), *Neural mechanisms of goal-directed behavior and learning*. New York: Academic Press, 1980.

Cohen, D. H. Central processing time for a conditioned response in a vertebrate model system. In C. D. Woody (Ed.), *Conditioning*. New York: Plenum Press, 1982.

Cohen, D. H. Identification of vertebrate neurons modified during learning: Analysis of sensory pathways. In D. L. Alkon & J. Farley (Eds.), *Primary neural substrates of learning and behavioral change*. London & New York: Cambridge University Press, 1984.

Cohen, D. H., & Broyles, J. The visual pathways transmitting conditioned stimulus information for visually conditioned heart rate change. In preparation.

Cohen, D. H., Gibbs, C. M., Siegelman, J., Gamlin, P., & Broyles, J. Is locus coeruleus involved in plasticity of lateral geniculate neurons during learning? *Neuroscience Abstracts*, 1982, *8*, 666.

Cohen, D. H., & Goff, D. M. Conditioned heart rate change in the pigeon: Analysis and prediction of acquisition patterns. *Physiological Psychology*, 1978, *6*, 127–141.

Cohen, D. H., & Karten, H. J. The structural organization of the avian brain: An overview. In I. J. Goodman & M. W. Schein (Eds.), *Birds: Brain and behavior*, New York: Academic Press, 1974.

Cohen, D. H., & Pitts, L. H. Vagal and sympathetic components of conditioned cardioacceleration in the pigeon. *Brain Research*. 1968, *9*, 15–31.

Duff, T. A., & Cohen, D. H. Retinal afferents to the pigeon optic tectum: Discharge characteristics in response to whole field illumination. *Brain Research*, 1975, *92*, 1–19. (a)

Duff, T. A., & Cohen, D. H. Optic chiasm fibers of the pigeon: Discharge characteristics in response to whole field illumination. *Brain Research*, 1975, *92*, 145–148. (b)

Gabriel, M., Miller, J. D., & Saltwick, S. E. Multiple unit activity of the rabbit medial geniculate nucleus in conditioning, extinction, and reversal. *Physiological Psychology*, 1976, *4*, 124–134.

Gamlin, P. D. R., & Cohen, D. H. A possible second ascending avian tectofugal pathway. *Neuroscience Abstracts*, 1982, *8*, 666.

Gamlin, P. D. R., & Cohen, D. H. Projections of retinorecipient pretectal nuclei in the pigeon. In preparation. (a)

Gamlin, P. D. R., & Cohen, D. H. Anatomical and electrophysiological evidence for a second ascending tectofugal visual pathway. In preparation. (b)

Gibbs, C. M., Broyles, J. L., & Cohen, D. H. Further studies of the involvement of locus coeruleus in plasticity of avian lateral geniculate neurons during learning. *Neuroscience Abstracts*, 1983, *9*, 641.

Gibbs, C. M., & Cohen, D. H. Plasticity of the thalamofugal pathway during visual conditioning. *Neuroscience Abstracts*, 1980, *6*, 424.

Gibbs, C. M., Cohen, D. H., & Broyles, J. L. Plasticity of lateral geniculate neurons during visual learning. *Journal of Neuroscience*, in press.

Gibbs, C. M., Cohen, D. H., Broyles, J. L., & Solina, A. Conditioned modification of avian dorsal geniculate neurons is a function of their response to the unconditioned stimulus. *Neuroscience Abstracts*, 1981, *7*, 752.

Gold, M. R., & Cohen, D. H. Heart rate conditioning in the pigeon immobilized with α-bungarotoxin. *Brain Research*, 1981, *216*, 163–172. (a)

Gold, M. R., & Cohen, D. H. Modification of the discharge of vagal cardiac neurons during learned heart rate change. *Science*, 1981, *214*, 345–347. (b)

Gold, M. R., & Cohen, D. H. The discharge characteristics of vagal cardiac neurons during classically conditioned heart rate change. *Journal of Neuroscience*, 1984, *4*, 2963–2971.

Kandel, E. R. *Cellular basis of behavior*. San Francisco: Freeman, 1976.

Kandel, E. R., & Schwartz, J. H. Molecular biology of learning: Modulation of transmitter release. *Science*, 1982, *218*, 433–443.

Kandel, E. R., & Spencer, W. A. Cellular neurophysiological approaches in the study of learning. *Physiological Reviews*, 1968, *48*, 65–134.

Killackey, H. P., & Belford, G. R. Central correlates of peripheral pattern alterations in the trigeminal system of the rat. *Brain Research*, 1980, *183*, 205–210.

Lashley, K. S. In search of the engram. In *Symposium of the society for experimental biology*. London & New York: Cambridge University Press, 1950.

Merzenich, M. M., Nelson, R. J., Stryker, M. P., Cynader, M. S., Schoppmann, A., & Zook, J. M. Somatosensory cortical map changes following digit amputation in adult monkeys. *Journal of Comparative Neurology*, 1984, *224*, 591–605.

Oleson, T. D., Ashe, J. H., & Weinberger, N. M. Modification of auditory and somatosensory system activity during pupillary conditioning in the paralyzed cat. *Journal of Neurophysiology*, 1975, *38*, 1114–1139.

Ryugo, D. K., & Weinberger, N. M. Differential plasticity of morphologically distinct neuron populations in the medial geniculate body of the cat during classical conditioning. *Behavioral Biology*, 1978, *22*, 275–301.

Sherman, S. M., & Spear, P. D. Organization of visual pathways in normal and visually deprived cats. *Physiological Reviews*, 1982, *62*, 738–855.

Squire, L. R. The neuropsychology of human memory. *Annual Review of Neuroscience*, 1982, *5*, 241–273.

Thompson, R. F., Berger, T. W., Berry, S. D., Clark, G. A., Ketter, R. N., Lavond, D. G., Mauk, M. D., McCormick, D. A., Solomon, P. R., & Weisz, D. J. Neuronal substrates of learning and memory: Hippocampus and other structures. In C. D. Woody (Ed.), *Conditioning*. New York: Plenum Press, 1982.

Thompson, R. F., Berger, T. W., Cegavske, C. F., Patterson, M. M., Roemer, R. A., Teyler, T. J., & Young, R. A. The search for the engram. *American Psychologist*, 1976, *31*, 209–227.

Tsukahara, N. Classical conditioning mediated by the red nucleus of the cat. In C. D. Woody (Ed.), *Conditioning*. New York: Plenum Press, 1982.

Wall, J. T., Gibbs, C. M., Broyles, J. L., & Cohen, D. H. Modification of neuronal discharge along the tectofugal pathway during visual learning. *Brain Research*, in press.

Wall, J. T., Wild, J. M., Broyles, J., Gibbs, C. M., & Cohen, D. H. Plasticity of the tectofugal pathway during visual conditioning. *Neuroscience Abstracts*, 1980, *6*, 424.

Weinberger, N. M. Sensory plasticity and learning: The magnocellular medial geniculate nucleus of the auditory system. In C. D. Woody (Ed.), *Conditioning*. New York: Plenum Press, 1982.

Wild, J. M., & Cohen, D. H. Invariance of retinal output during visual learning. *Brain Research*, 1985, *331*, 127–135.

CHAPTER 3

# Spatial Information: How and Where Is It Stored?

**C. A. Barnes**
**B. L. McNaughton**
University of Colorado, Boulder

Although the mnemonic capabilities of invertebrates have been shown in recent years to be astoundingly complex (cf. Hawkins & Kandel, 1984; Sahley, Rudy, & Gelperin, 1981), these complexities serve, in the minds of many investigators, to emphasize the additional and unique learning capability of the vertebrate species, especially mammals. Although there continues to be considerable controversy over how best to define this additional capability, one of its attributes appears to be a very large representational capacity. An important instance of such behavior is place learning, a salient attribute of which is the formation of a large number of associations among environmental features in a short period of time. The result is an internal representation of the environment that is highly resistant to disruption by removal of any specific part of the original feature set.

This chapter represents a summary of ongoing research that attempts to relate spatial learning and memory to changes in the efficacy of hippocampal synaptic transmission. The central hypothesis here is that place learning involves a selective change in the distribution of synaptic strengths in the hippocampus and that the stored information corresponds in a direct, one-to-one fashion with this distribution. This hypothesis is based on three principal lines of evidence. Lesion studies indicate the necessity of an intact hippocampus for (among other things) place learning (Jarrard, 1983; Morris, 1983; Morris, Garrud, Rawlins, & O'Keefe, 1982; O'Keefe, Nadel, Keightly, & Kill, 1975; Olton, Walker, & Gage, 1978; Sutherland, Kolb, & Whishaw, 1982). Analysis of single unit activity in unrestrained animals strongly suggests that spatial information processing is one of the principal preoccupations of the hippocampus (Hill, 1978; Kubie & Ranck, 1983; McNaughton, Barnes, & O'Keefe, 1983; O'Keefe, 1976; Olton, Branch, & Best, 1978). Finally, evoked field potential studies have shown that hippocampal synaptic strengths can be altered in interesting ways by electrical stimuli designed to mimic, to some extent, the effects of intense activity of the afferent fibers occurring from natural stimulation.

It has only been relatively recently that convincing evidence has been found for synaptic modification of sufficient duration to be taken seriously as a candidate mechanism for mammalian long-term memory. In 1973, Lømo, Bliss, and Gardner-Medwin were able to show long-lasting increases in hippocampal field responses. Following brief episodes of high-frequency stimulation, these increases persisted for hours in acute preparations (Bliss & Lømo, 1973) and for days in chronic preparations (Bliss & Gardner-Medwin, 1973). This enduring change in synaptic strength, initially called long-lasting potentiation, was later shown to require the association of activity of input fibers for its induction (McNaughton, Douglas, & Goddard, 1978). This cooperativity effect made the phenomenon a prime candidate mechanism of associative information storage in this system. Because it has been shown that this type of synaptic change is not merely a longer lasting form of posttetanic potentiation (McNaughton, 1982), a process that has been analyzed in detail at, for example, neuromuscular synapses (e.g., Liley & North, 1953; Magleby & Zengel, 1975, 1976a, 1976b), the term "long-term enhancement" (LTE) will be used here. The essence of the distinction is that "potentiation" is a *nonassociative* synaptic change that also occurs at the same hippocampal synapses exhibiting *associative* "LTE" (McNaughton, 1982).

The properties of LTE, as it has been observed following electrical stimulation of afferent fibers, are in agreement with many of the *a priori* assumptions that have been made in models of associative learning in neural networks. These properties have been reviewed elsewhere (e.g., McNaughton, 1983). This chapter deals with the question of the behavioral relevance of LTE: Is there any demonstrable relation between LTE and memory? In particular, we are interested in the relation between LTE and *spatial* memory because LTE is most conveniently studied in the hippocampus and because spatial memory is at least one of the major involvements of this system. While LTE-like phenomena have also been observed in a variety of other central nervous system responses both *in vivo* and *in vitro* (e.g., Lee, 1983; Racine, Milgram, & Hafner, 1983; Weinberger, 1982), it is only in the projection of the perforant path to the fascia dentata where one can discretely activate and modify a significant proportion of the excitatory afferent synapses from a single stimulus site. The following discussion is a summary of some of the evidence that has been gathered in examination of the hypothesis that LTE at hippocampal synapses (in fascia dentata) underlies spatial memory.

Before going on to consider the evidence, a brief review of the behavioral and electrophysiological methodology that will be discussed in the following experiments is in order. The spatial problem employed involved escape from a brightly illuminated circular platform into a darkened goal tunnel concealed below the maze surface (see Figure 3.1). Access to the tunnel was available through only 1 of 18 holes located at the platform periphery. A trial began by placing the animal into a false-bottomed, cylindrical, starting

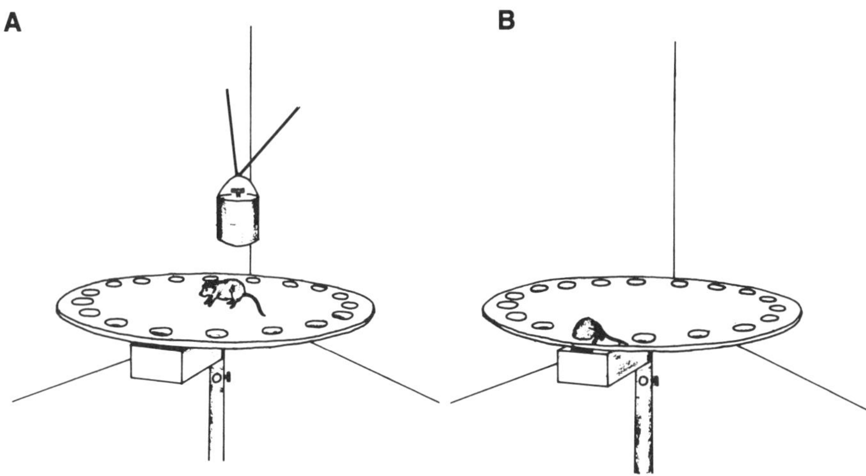


**FIGURE 3.1.** Circular platform apparatus. At the beginning of a trial (A), the start cylinder is raised and the animal is free to explore the platform surface. Underneath the maze is a dark escape tunnel, which is always in the same spatial location in the room. The animals learn to escape from the brightly illuminated maze surface into the tunnel. Through a series of controls, the use of motor sequences and local maze cues can be eliminated as possible strategies, forcing the animal to use extramaze spatial cues to solve the problem.

chamber in the center of the platform. Through a system of pulleys this chamber could be raised, leaving the animal to move freely on the surface of the maze. The animals' task was to learn in which direction from the central starting point the tunnel was located. Because the rat was placed in the central chamber in a random orientation and because the maze surface itself was rotated randomly from trial to trial, the learning of spatial information was required. Two different measures were taken on this task: number of incorrect holes investigated (errors) and initial heading (measured as deviation of the first hole investigated from the correct hole). For electrophysiological measurements, animals underwent surgical implantation of electrodes for extracellular stimulation of perforant path fibers and recording of synaptic field potentials in the fascia dentata of the hippocampus (see Figure 3.2). The implantations were bilateral, and the animals were given several weeks to recover from this surgery before testing began. Testing of synaptic efficacy was carried out using low-frequency stimulation (1/15 Hz), which induced no persistent change in the synaptic response. Long-term enhancement was induced by delivering bursts of high-frequency stimulation (400 Hz, 8 pulses per burst).

The first evidence in support of the notion that LTE and spatial memory were related came from a comparison of these phenomena in young and old rats (Barnes, 1979). When given one trial per day on the circular platform, animals reach asymptotic performance in approximately 10 trials. However, the average asymptotic performance of older animals on this task was poorer

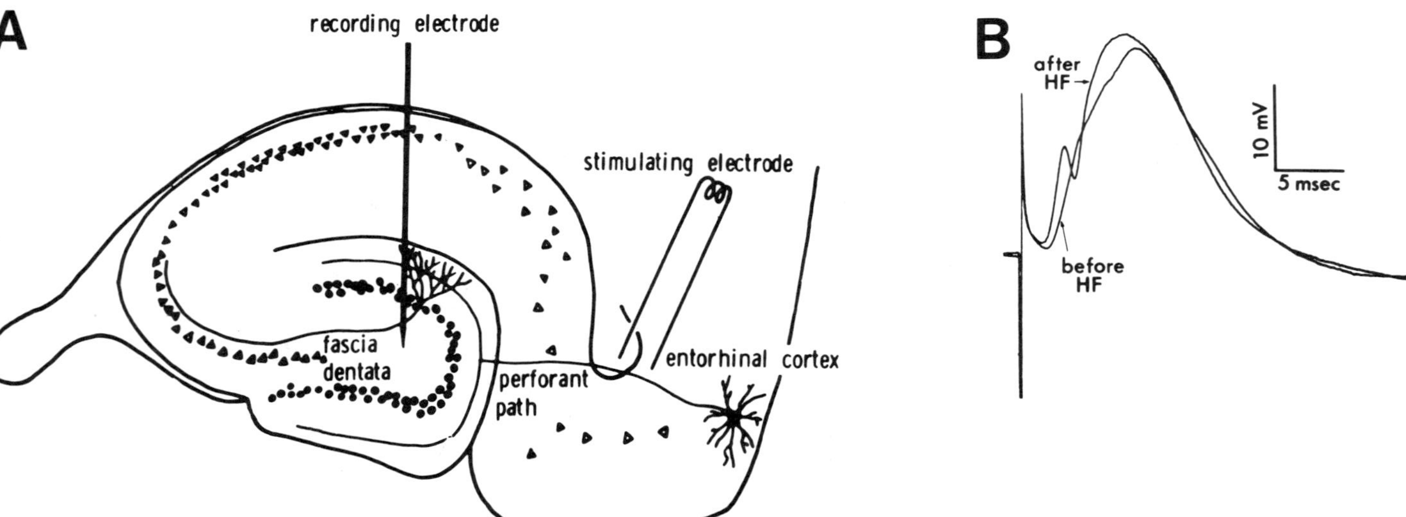


**FIGURE 3.2.** (A) For the electrophysiological studies, stimulation and recording electrodes were bilaterally implanted in the perforant pathway and fascia dentata, respectively. Large extracellular field potentials can be recorded from the fascia dentata of such a preparation following single stimuli to the perforant pathway. These responses generally remain stable for many months. Brief episodes of high-frequency stimulation (HF) result in a substantial long-lasting enhancement of both the synaptic potential and the postsynaptic population spike. (B) Representative examples of such responses, before and after the generation of LTE by HF stimulation.

than that of younger animals (Barnes, 1979). After the behavioral data were collected from these rats, they were prepared for chronic stimulation and recording of perforant path–dentate evoked responses. When baseline amplitudes of evoked synaptic responses were established in all animals, high-frequency stimulation was given to induce LTE. The mean decay of LTE was faster for the old animals (average decay time constant of 17 days) than it was for the young animals (average decay time constant of 37 days). These data showed a significant correlation, between groups, in the persistence of LTE and the performance of a spatial memory problem. More important, there was a small but statistically significant *within*-group correlation between the maintenance of LTE and the performance scores on the circular platform. That is, those animals in a given age group with the most persistent LTE also tended to show better performance on the circular platform than did animals with less persistent LTE. Although not definitive, this evidence is at least consistent with the notion that LTE and spatial memory are related.

Additional evidence along these lines has recently been provided in a comparison of the rates of forgetting of the goal location in the circular platform task and the rates of decay of LTE in young and old animals (Barnes & McNaughton, 1984). In this study rats were trained to asymptotic performance on the circular platform spatial memory task. The animals were subdivided into retention interval groups and were given a single retest of their ability to locate the tunnel at either 10, 20, 30, 45, or 60 days following the last training session. Retention was defined as the proportion of animals in each retention interval group making fewer than 10% more errors than their average errors at asymptotic performance during training. The retention function declined exponentially toward zero with time in a manner similar to the decline of LTE with time after stimulation. A direct comparison of the decay rates of LTE and spatial memory, however, is not possible because the choice of 10% as the cutoff point for errors is arbitrary and different cutoffs generate different rates. Furthermore, it would be naive to suppose that behavioral performance should be a linear function of the strength of the physical memory trace. Nonetheless, an indirect comparison of the decay rates is afforded by the existence of age differences in both measures. When the *relative* age differences in rate of decay of LTE and rate of forgetting of the goal tunnel location were compared, they were found to agree to within 1%. We interpret this to be rather compelling evidence that LTE has a fundamental involvement in the storage of spatial information. Of course, this does not necessarily imply that the spatial information is stored at *hippocampal* synapses because LTE at synapses in other structures may well show similar age differences in decay kinetics.

A brief note is warranted here concerning the "exponential" decay of LTE and/or spatial memory. Close examination of the LTE decay curves almost invariably reveals a faster decay in the early portion of the curves

(Barnes & McNaughton, 1980; McNaughton, 1983; Racine *et al.*, 1983). Racine *et al.* have argued that there must therefore be two separate processes, which they have labeled LTP1 and LTP2. We feel that the observation that more of the variance can be accounted for in the decay curve using two exponentials than by using one is not sufficient evidence for the definition of two processes. An equally viable hypothesis, for example, is that different synapses in the same population exhibit slightly different decay rates, depending either on local conditions or on past histories. Barnes (1979), for example, showed that the decay time constant of LTE changed dramatically as a function of the number of repetitions of the high-frequency stimulation given. Thus, it is highly probable that there are multiple decay rates present in the population at any given time. This would lead to an *apparently* multiexponential decay curve.

Most studies on LTE have employed electrical stimulation of afferent fibers for its induction. Although the frequency characteristics of this stimulation are within the physiological range of afferent fiber discharge (Douglas, 1977), the synchronous activation of a relatively large proportion of the afferent population required for LTE induction (McNaughton *et al.*, 1978) is not. This has led to the question whether LTE could occur under conditions of environmentally driven afferent activity. One argument in favor of this possibility is that the threshold number of afferent fibers that must be active to induce LTE is approximately the same as the number needed to generate measurable discharge in the receiving population. Although it has been shown that there is no physical coupling between postsynaptic discharge and the initiation of LTE (McNaughton *et al.*, 1978; Wigström, McNaughton, & Barnes, 1982), the observation that postsynaptic neurons fire frequently makes it likely that the amount of convergence necessary for the generation of LTE occurs reasonably frequently as well, under normal physiological conditions.

The preceding argument notwithstanding, it would still be encouraging if one could show a spontaneous change in synaptic strength during the course of acquisition of new spatial information. There is an *a priori* argument, however, that should make one somewhat pessimistic about the possibility of detecting such a change. An animal such as a rat is capable of storing a vast quantity of spatial information. It is expected, therefore, that a given learning experience will involve only a small proportion of the available modifiable synapses. Hence, one would suppose that detection of any synaptic change underlying the storage of one specific set of information would be extremely difficult. The apparently spontaneous decay of LTE, however, provides a possibility of circumventing this difficulty. If the information stored at the synapses under study is primarily of a spatial nature and if animals are maintained in a spatially restricted environment for a period corresponding to several decay time constants of LTE, then most of the synaptic weights should have returned to their lowest, ground state. Against this reduced background noise, it might then be possible to detect increases in the average synaptic strength of the population resulting from spatial information storage.

With this conceptual basis in mind, the following experiment was conducted (Sharp, McNaughton, & Barnes, 1983): Animals with chronically implanted electrodes were housed in individual cages in a quiet, dimly lit room for a period of 2 to 3 months. During this time they were removed once a day for 0.5-hour recording session to measure the size of the perforant path evoked population excitatory postsynaptic potential (EPSP) and postsynaptic population spike. They were then transferred to individual large rooms containing numerous ramps, boxes, tunnels, and so on to provide a spatially complex environment. They remained in these rooms for the duration of this experiment, with the exception of the daily recording sessions, which were continued in the same fashion as during the baseline period. Over the course of about 3 days, a significant increase developed in both the field EPSP and population spike. This increase persisted for at least 1 week and was not correlated with changes in the animals' overt behavioral state during the recording sessions themselves. Thus, it appears that during a period when an animal is engaged in learning about a new environment there is an increase in the synaptic responsiveness in the hippocampus that resembles electrically induced LTE. Although considerably more work will be required to determine whether the spontaneous change is indeed mechanistically the same as the electrically induced one, this observation is nevertheless consistent with the general hypothesis under consideration.

A large literature exists on the influence of internal state variables on learning ability. If a relationship exists between LTE and learning, then it is expected that at least some of these state variables would directly influence the LTE mechanism. One of the earliest demonstrations of such a correlation was provided by Laroche and Bloch (1982). Previous work from their laboratory had demonstrated that weak electrical stimulation of the mesencephalic reticular formation (MRF) during the posttrial period facilitated acquisition (Bloch, Denti, & Schmaltz, 1966; Deweer, 1976) of several simple learning tasks. The same form of stimulation delivered to the MRF for a period of 60 seconds following high-frequency activation of perforant path fibers resulted in a significant increase in the magnitude of the resulting LTE. Because one of the effects of MRF stimulation appears to be an increase in the arousal state of the animal, one might predict from these findings that the sleep–waking cycle would modulate LTE (as in fact it does the size of the evoked response itself; Winson & Abzug, 1978).

Recent work (Jones Leonard, McNaughton, & Barnes, 1984) has confirmed this prediction. Animals with chronically implanted electrodes were placed in the recording chamber in their home cages. Test stimuli were delivered at 15-second intervals while the animals fell asleep. When the animals exhibited EEG and behavioral indications of slow-wave sleep, ten high-frequency stimulus bursts were delivered to the perforant path. Some of the animals awakened during this stimulation. These animals exhibited normal LTE. The animals that remained asleep, however, showed no significant change from their prestimulation baseline response. After awakening *these* animals, a second series of high-frequency stimuli were delivered. These stimuli resulted in normal LTE. Thus, it is clear that some internal state variable that fluctuates with the sleep–waking cycle, has a profound influence on LTE. Furthermore, it appears as though this suppression of LTE during sleep must be mediated by an active process because animals anesthetized with either sodium pentobarbital or urethane exhibit robust and reliable LTE.

The evidence discussed up to this point is generally consistent with the hypothesis that LTE represents a fundamental mechanism of information storage in the mammalian central nervous system, and in particular that LTE of hippocampal synapses plays a role in the storage of spatial representations. In its simplest form, this hypothesis predicts that bilateral saturation of the LTE mechanism in a large proportion of perforant path terminals should both disrupt stored spatial memories and should prevent acquisition of new spatial information. If one supposes that the spatial information is stored as a specific distribution of synaptic strengths in the perforant path terminals, then artificially driving all synaptic strengths to their maximum value should destroy the information content of this distribution. Thus, the ability to recall previously stored spatial representations should be disrupted. Furthermore, the storage of new representations should be prevented because the capacity for further increasing synaptic strength would have been saturated.

To test this hypothesis, animals were trained to asymptotic performance on the circular platform task described earlier. They were then prepared with electrodes implanted bilaterally in fascia dentata and perforant path. Half of the animals were given six high-frequency stimulation sessions distributed over 2 days. This stimulation resulted in a near saturation of the LTE mechanism. The other half of the animals received the same number of stimulation pulses at a low frequency that induced no LTE. Twenty-four hours after the last stimulation session, the animals were tested on a modified problem on the circular platform. During this test, the goal tunnel was rotated 135° away from the original learned location. Two dependent measures were taken of the animals' performance: initial deviation from the previously correct goal location and number of errors. These measures permitted an assessment of both the retention of the *original* problem and the acquisition of the *new* problem. As predicted, saturation of LTE produced a large and statistically significant impairment in the acquisition of the new tunnel location. Indeed, there was no trend toward improvement in performance over the course of five daily sessions. Contrary to the prediction of the hypothesis, however, LTE saturation produced no change in the retention score for the original problem. Analysis of the initial deviation scores during repeated training sessions revealed no tendency to deviate from the accurate performance relative to the initial location acquired during prestimulation training (Barnes & McNaughton, 1983).

These results stand in marked contrast to the findings of Berger (1984), who recently reported that generation of LTE, using procedures very similar to those employed in the present experiments, resulted in a facilitation of the acquisition of a conditioned nictitating membrane response to air puffs. These contrasting effects of perforant path LTE on spatial memory and on simple conditioning suggest that the information content of the hippocampal synaptic distribution is important for the former, whereas in the latter, the hippocampal involvement may be one of supplying tonic excitation to other neural structures more directly involved in the storage of the information. This tonic excitation might well be expected to increase following the general increase in perforant path excitatory synaptic efficacy. Whatever the explanation, these divergent findings serve to emphasize the distinction between spatial learning, which requires a high information capacity, and the conditioned response, which has a comparatively small information content. These types of memory either involve different physiological mechanisms or are stored in different locations (Berger & Orr, 1983; Lincoln, McCormick, & Thompson, 1982).

A number of experiments will be required to clarify these results. In particular, control studies must be carried out to answer the question whether the behavioral effects result specifically from LTE or from other unspecified effects of stimulation. Nevertheless, taken at face value, these data support the general conclusions others have made on the basis of animal lesion experiments and human amnesic syndromes—that the hippocampus plays a role in acquisition of information, but that information is not actually stored there (e.g., Cohen & Squire, 1980; Jarrard, 1983; Squire, 1983). An alternative hypothesis that may account for more of the evidence follows a suggestion made by Marr (1971). He proposed that the structure and connectivity of the hippocampus made it (in theory) ideal for the storage of large numbers of "simple representations." These simple representations of the animal's immediate experience would be stored in the hippocampus regardless of their adaptive significance to the animal. If, in retrospect, a given item of information stored in the hippocampus turned out to be important, that information would be relocated to a more permanent neocortical store. Otherwise, it would simply fade from the system and be lost. In other words, according to this notion, the hippocampus serves as a high-capacity storage device from which the neocortex draws relevant information, which it stores in a more permanent fashion. Disruption of the ability to store information in the hippocampus would thus prevent acquisition but would leave well-learned information intact.

For a number of years a controversy has existed in the literature between the "cognitive mapping" (O'Keefe & Nadel, 1978) and "working memory" (Olton, Becker, & Handelmann, 1979; Walker & Olton, 1984) views of hippocampal function. The latter theory proposes that the role of the hippocampus is that of "short-term" storage of information that is relevant only to the immediate task at hand (but see Kesner, 1980). This type of memory is exemplified by the foraging type of paradigm in which an animal must learn not to return to locations from which it has already obtained reward in a given trial. This behavior has been well studied in rats in experiments using the elevated eight-arm radial maze. Whereas normal rats learn this task readily, animals with hippocampal lesions are severely impaired. It has been suggested that one possible mechanism for working memory might involve the active generation and subsequent erasure of LTE. For this and other reasons, it was of interest to assess the effects of LTE saturation on the performance of a *well-learned* radial maze problem (B. L. McNaughton, M. Rasmussen, & C. A. Barnes, unpublished data). Animals were trained to a high level of performance on the eight-arm radial maze and then underwent surgical implantation of electrodes. Following several weeks of recovery, radial maze training was resumed until the animals regained criterion levels of performance. During the retraining period, baseline levels of synaptic strength were measured daily following the behavioral sessions. When the behavioral criterion was reached, high-frequency stimulation was delivered over several days to maximize LTE. In contrast to its effects on circular platform performance, the resulting LTE produced no detectable alteration of performance on the radial maze problem. It thus appears that, if the hippocampus does play a role in working memory, this role does not involve the storage of new information through modification of synaptic efficacy in its major afferent system. Nor, indeed, is the specific distribution of synaptic strengths in this pathway important for working memory. One possible interpretation of these results is that the working memory system must be activated by environmental information that has passed through a reference or recognition memory filter. This would be consistent with the observation of Gallagher (Chapter 18, this volume) that animals require retraining on the radial maze if the maze is transferred to a different location. The prediction is then that induction of LTE should impair acquisition of the radial maze problem in a new environment but leave performance of the problem in a familiar environment unchanged.

In conclusion, the evidence presented, although incomplete, supports the general notion that LTE of hippocampal synapses is involved in the storage of spatial information. The precise nature of this involvement, however, remains elusive. It is likely that the hippocampus is not the only structure involved in "cognitive mapping" (e.g., Kolb, Sutherland, & Whishaw, 1983), and conversely that the storage and processing of spatial information is not the sole function carried out by the hippocampus (e.g., Berger & Orr, 1983; Hirsh, 1974; Squire, 1983). In considering the common thread to recent theories of hippocampal function, it appears that a useful conceptual framework might be the information capacity demands of the memory process under study. Classical conditioning and "procedural" learning events require relatively few bits of information to describe them. Spatial memory, which we would subsume under the category of declarative memory, requires relatively large amounts of information. For an animal such as a rat, it may be that spatial memory is the most important form of declarative memory that the animal uses. This would account for the relative predominance of spatial determinants of hippocampal unit discharge. It must also be emphasized that, although modification of existing synapses through LTE-like mechanisms may well play an important role in these processes, the evidence to date suggests that LTE, as measured in the rat (Barnes & McNaughton, 1980; Racine *et al.*, 1983), decays much too rapidly to account for all forms of long-lasting memory observed in humans. Either there exist large interspecies differences in decay kinetics or we have yet to identify the major basis of enduring memories.

## REFERENCES

Barnes, C. A. Memory deficits associated with senescence: A neurophysiological and behavioral study in the rat. *Journal of Comparative and Physiological Psychology*, 1979, *93*, 74–104.

Barnes, C. A., & McNaughton, B. L. Spatial memory and hippocampal synaptic plasticity. In D. Stein (Ed.), *The psychobiology of aging: Problems and perspectives*. New York: Elsevier/North-Holland, 1980.

Barnes, C. A., & McNaughton, B. L. Where is the cognitive map? *Society for Neuroscience Abstracts*, 1983, *9*, 649.

Barnes, C. A., & McNaughton, B. L. An age comparison of spatial forgetting and the decay of LTE. *Society for Neuroscience Abstracts*, 1984, *10*, 773.

Berger, T. W. Long-term potentiation of hippocampal synaptic transmission affects rate of behavioral learning. *Science*, 1984, *224*, 627–630.

Berger, T. W., & Orr, W. B. Hippocampectomy selectively disrupts discrimination reversal conditioning of the rabbit nictitating membrame response. *Behavioral Brain Research*, 1983, *8*, 49–68.

Bliss, T. V. P., & Gardner-Medwin, A. R. Long-lasting potentiation of synaptic transmission in the dentate area of unanesthetized rabbit following stimulation of the perforant path. *Journal of Physiology (London)*, 1973, *232*, 357–374.

Bliss, T. V. P., & Lømo, T. Long-lasting potentiation of synaptic transmission in the dentate area of the anaesthetized rabbit following stimulation of the perforant path. *Journal of Physiology (London)*, 1973, *232*, 331–356.

Bloch, V., Denti, A., & Schmaltz, G. Effets de la stimulation réticulaire sur la phase de consolidation de la trace mnésique. *Journal of Physiology (Paris)*, 1966, *58*, 469–470.

Cohen, N. J., & Squire, L. R. Preserved learning and retention of pattern analyzing skill in amnesia: Dissociation of knowing how and knowing that. *Science*, 1980, *210*, 207–209.

Deweer, B. Selective facilitative effect of post-trial reticular stimulation in discriminative learning in the rat. *Behavioral Proceedings*, 1976, *1*, 243–257.

Douglas, R. M. Long-lasting synaptic potentiation in the rat dentate gyrus following brief high-frequency stimulation. *Brain Research*, 1977, *126*, 361–365.

Hawkins, R. D., & Kandel, E. R. Is there a cell-biological alphabet for simple forms of learning? *Psychological Review*, 1984, *91*, 375–391.

Hill, A. J. First occurrence of hippocampal spatial firing in a new environment. *Experimental Neurology*, 1978, *62*, 282–297.

Hirsh, R. The hippocampus and contextual retrieval of information from memory: A theory. *Behavioral Biology*, 1974, *12*, 421–444.

Jarrard, L. E. Selective hippocampal lesions and behavior: Effects of kainic acid lesions on performance of place and cue tasks. *Behavioral Neuroscience*, 1983, *97*, 873–890.

Jones Leonard, B., McNaughton, B. L., & Barnes, C. A. Diminution of long-term synaptic enhancement during sleep. *Society for Neuroscience Abstracts*, 1984, *10*, 126.

Kesner, R. P. An attribute analysis of memory: The role of the hippocampus. *Physiological Psychology*, 1980, *8*, 189–197.

Kolb, B., Sutherland, R. J., & Whishaw, I. Q. A comparison of the contributions of frontal and parietal association cortex to spatial localization in rats. *Behavioral Neuroscience*, 1983, *97*, 13–27.

Kubie, J. L., & Ranck, J. B., Jr. Sensory–behavioral correlates in individual hippocampus neurons in three situations: Space and context. In W. Seifert (Ed.), *Neurobiology of the hippocampus*. New York: Academic Press, 1983.

Laroche, S., & Bloch, V. Conditioning of hippocampal cells and long-term potentiation: An approach to mechanisms of post-trial memory facilitation. In C. Ajmone Marsan & H. Matthies (Eds.), *Neuronal plasticity and memory formation* (IBRO Monograph Series). New York: Raven Press, 1982.

Lee, K. S. Sustained modification of neuronal activity in the hippocampus and neocortex. In W. Seifert (Ed.), *Neurobiology of the hippocampus*. New York: Academic Press, 1983.

Liley, A. W., & North, K. A. K. An electrical investigation of effects of repetitive stimulation on mammalian neuromuscular junction. *Journal of Neurophysiology*, 1953, *16*, 509–527.

Lincoln, J. S., McCormick, B. A., & Thompson, R. F. Ipsilateral cerebellar lesions prevent learning of the classically conditioned nictitating membrane/eyelid response. *Brain Research*, 1982, *242*, 190–193.

Magleby, K. L., & Zengel, J. E. A quantitative description of tetanic and post-tetanic potentiation of transmitter release at the frog neuromuscular junction. *Journal of Physiology (London)*, 1975, *245*, 183–208.

Magleby, K. L., & Zengel, J. E. Augmentation: A process that acts to increase transmitter release at the frog neuromuscular junction. *Journal of Physiology (London)*, 1976, *257*, 449–470. (a)

Magleby, K. L., & Zengel, J. E. Long-term changes in augmentation, potentiation and depression of transmitter release as a function of repeated synaptic activity at the frog neuromuscular junction. *Journal of Physiology (London)*, 1976, *257*, 471–494. (b)

Marr, D. Simple memory: A theory for archicortex. *Philosophical transactions of the Royal Society of London, Series B*, 1971, *262*, 23–81.

McNaughton, B. L. Long-term synaptic enhancement and short-term potentiation in rat fascia dentata act through different mechanisms. *Journal of Physiology (London)*, 1982, *324*, 249–262.

McNaughton, B. L. Activity dependent modulation of hippocampal synaptic efficacy: Some implications for memory processes. In W. Seifert (Ed.), *Neurobiology of the hippocampus*. New York: Academic Press, 1983.

McNaughton, B. L., Barnes, C. A., & O'Keefe, J. The contributions of position, direction and velocity to single unit activity in the hippocampus of freely-moving rats. *Experimental Brain Research*, 1983, *52*, 41–49.

McNaughton, B. L., Douglas, R. M., & Goddard, G. V. Synaptic enhancement in fascia dentata: Cooperativity among coactive afferents. *Brain Research*, 1978, *157*, 277–293.

Morris, R. G. M. An attempt to dissociate "spatial-mapping" and "working-memory" theories of hippocampal function. In W. Seifert (Ed.), *Neurobiology of the hippocampus*. New York: Academic Press, 1983.

Morris, R. G. M., Garrud, P., Rawlins, J. N. P., & O'Keefe, J. Place navigation impaired in rats with hippocampal lesions. *Nature (London)*, 1982, *297*, 681–683.

O'Keefe, J. Place units in the hippocampus of the freely moving rat. *Experimental Neurology*, 1976, *51*, 78–109.

O'Keefe, J., & Nadel, L. *The hippocampus as a cognitive map*. Oxford: Clarendon Press, 1978.

O'Keefe, J., Nadel, L., Keightly, S., & Kill, D. Fornix lesions selectively abolish place learning in the rat. *Experimental Neurology*, 1975, *48*, 152–166.

Olton, D. S., Becker, J. T., & Handelmann, G. E. Hippocampus, space, and memory. *Behavior and Brain Science*, 1979, *2*, 313–365.

Olton, D. S., Branch, M., & Best, P. J. Spatial correlates of hippocampal unit activity. *Experimental Neurology*, 1978, *58*, 387–409.

Olton, D. S., Walker, J. A., & Gage, F. H. Hippocampal connections and spatial discrimination. *Brain Research*, 1978, *139*, 295–308.

Racine, R. J., Milgram, N. W., & Hafner, S. Long-term potentiation phenomena in the rat limbic forebrain. *Brain Research*, 1983, *260*, 217–231.

Sahley, C. L., Rudy, J. W., & Gelperin, A. An analysis of associative learning in a terrestrial mollusc: I. Higher order conditioning, blocking, and a transient US preexposure effect. *Journal of Comparative Physiology*, 1981, *144*, 1–8.

Sharp, P. E., McNaughton, B. L., & Barnes, C. A. Spontaneous synaptic enhancement in hippocampi of rats exposed to a spatially complex environment. *Society for Neuroscience Abstracts*, 1983, *9*, 647.

Squire, L. R. The hippocampus and the neuropsychology of memory. In W. Seifert (Ed.), *Neurobiology of the hippocampus*. New York: Academic Press, 1983.

Sutherland, R. J., Kolb, B., & Whishaw, I. Q. Spatial mapping: Definitive disruption by hippocampal or medial frontal cortex damage in the rat. *Neuroscience Letters*, 1982, *31*, 271–276.

Walker, J. A., & Olton, D. S. Fimbria-fornix lesions impair spatial working memory but not cognitive mapping. *Behavioral Neuroscience*, 1984, *98*, 226–242.

Weinberger, N. M. Sensory plasticity and learning: The magnocellular medial geniculate nucleus of the auditory system. In C. D. Woody (Ed.), *Conditioning: Representation of involved neural functions*. New York: Plenum Press, 1982.

Wigström, H., McNaughton, B. L., & Barnes, C. A. Long-term synaptic enhancement in hippocampus is not regulated by postsynaptic membrane potential. *Brain Research*, 1982, *233*, 195–199.

Winson, J., & Abzug, C. Dependence upon behavior of neuronal transmission from perforant pathway through entorhinal cortex. *Brain Research*, 1978, *147*, 422–427.

CHAPTER 4

# Multiple Traces of Neural Activity in the Hippocampus

**Wickliffe C. Abraham**
**Graham V. Goddard**
University of Otago
Dunedin, New Zealand

Long-lasting alterations in transmission efficacy resulting from neural activity have been observed in several regions of the mammalian nervous system (Baranyi & Feher, 1981; Bliss & Lømo, 1973; Brons & Woody, 1980; Brown & McAfee, 1982; Ito, Sakurai, & Tongroach, 1982; Racine, Milgram, & Hafner, 1983). Many of these changes exhibit different properties and are governed by different rules, a finding suggesting that neural activity leaves a variety of lasting traces, each depending on the network involved. The focus of our recent work in the hippocampus has been to ask whether neural activity can leave multiple traces, all within the same brain region. More specifically, does high-frequency activity in the perforant path leave one or multiple long-lasting traces in its target zone, the dentate gyrus? There is considerable evidence that perforant path synapses, following high-frequency activity, can exhibit a lasting increase in synaptic strength known as long-term potentiation (LTP; Bliss & Lømo, 1973). Until recently, however, the possibility that other traces may have been left by the high-frequency activity has gone largely unexplored.

The granule cells of the dentate gyrus receive powerful excitatory monosynaptic inputs from the medial and lateral entorhinal cortex. These two sets of entorhinal fibers, which travel in the perforant path, terminate respectively on the middle and outer thirds of granule cell dendrites (Figure 4.1d). Circuitry that can modulate the granule cell responsiveness to this perforant path excitatory drive includes local recurrent and feed-forward inhibitory neurons and afferents from the contralateral dentate hilus, medial septal nuclei, hypothalamic nuclei, and brain stem monoaminergic nuclei.

Present affiliation for Wickliffe C. Abraham: University of Göteborg, Göteborg, Sweden.

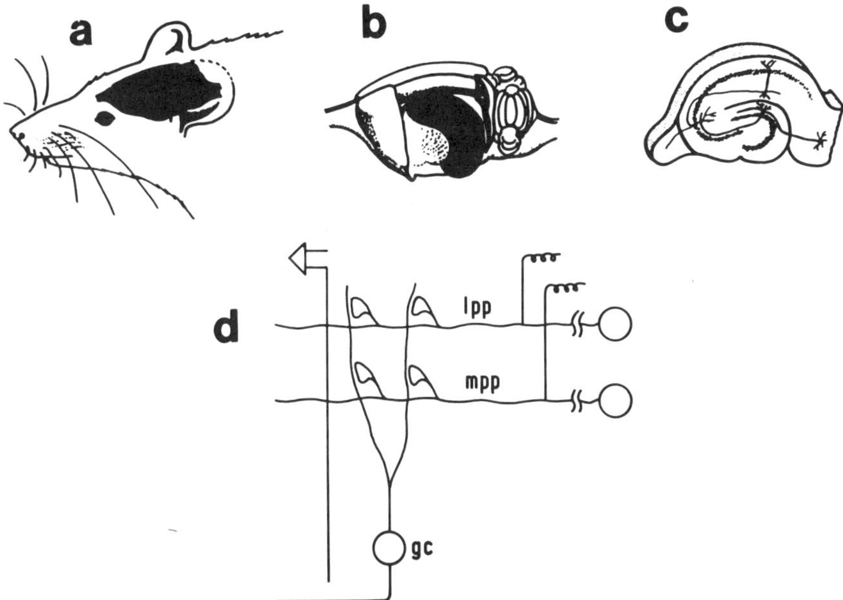


**FIGURE 4.1.** Schematic drawings of (a) the rat brain *in situ*, (b) a lateral view of the hippocampus (filled area) with the overlying cortex dissected away, and (c) a cross-sectional view of the hippocampal cell layers and intrinsic excitatory circuitry. (d) Simple dentate gyrus circuit diagram showing the monosynaptic connections made by the lateral perforant path (lpp) and the medial perforant path (mpp) onto granule cells (gc). Stimulating electrodes were placed in the angular bundle, and extracellular field recordings were made in the dentate hilus, deep to the granule cell layer.

The efficacy of perforant path transmission to the granule cells has been studied by measuring the field potentials recorded extracellularly in the hilus of the dentate gyrus following test shocks to the perforant path. At low stimulus strengths, one records a short-latency positive potential, which represents the sum of individual perforant path–granule cell excitatory postsynaptic potentials (EPSPs) passively conducted to the somata from the dendritic synaptic sites. This potential has been called the population EPSP (Lømo, 1971) but will be referred to here simply as the EPSP. At higher stimulus strengths, a negative-going potential becomes superimposed on the EPSP. It represents summed granule cell action potentials and has been termed the population spike (Andersen, Bliss, & Skrede, 1971).

To obtain a full assessment of the input-output characteristics of the pathway, we normally deliver 32 variable-strength test shocks to the perforant path, making sure to include stimuli that are above and below the population spike threshold. Synaptic strength is assessed by plotting the slope of the rising phase of the EPSP against the log of the stimulus strength. The responsiveness of the granule cells to this perforant path synaptic input is examined separately by plotting population spike height against EPSP slope, creating an "E-S" (EPSP–spike) curve. Both of the curves thus generated are linear over much of their extent, and linear regressions are used to describe them. Experimentally induced changes in the field potentials are thus analyzed in terms of the slopes and $x$-intercepts of these fitted regressions. The experiments described in this chapter were typically conducted in rats anesthetized with sodium pentobarbital.

Short periods of imposed neural activity result in changes that may be short lasting or long lasting. The short-lasting, graded alterations of perforant path synaptic efficacy may involve either synaptic strengthening or weakening (McNaughton, 1982; Teyler & Alger, 1976), depending on the frequency and duration of activation (Abraham, Rogers, & Hunter, 1984; Alger & Teyler, 1976). These short-lasting traces have been described and discussed in more detail elsewhere (Abraham & Bliss, 1985; Goddard, 1980; McNaughton, 1980, 1982). Here we shall focus on long-lasting traces, that is, traces persisting for at least 15 minutes following termination of perforant path stimulation.

## LONG-LASTING TRACES

An episode of high-frequency activity in the perforant path can result in an increase in the efficacy of this pathway (LTP) that lasts for days or even weeks (Bliss & Gardner-Medwin, 1973; Bliss & Lømo, 1973). Long-term potentiation is manifested as an increase in the size of both the population EPSP and the population spike responses to a constant intensity test stimulus delivered to the perforant path (Figure 4.2A) and results from an increase in synaptic efficacy that is confined to the activated synapses (Bliss & Dolphin, 1982). Of the two measures, the population EPSP most accurately reflects synaptic efficacy, and the term "long-term potentiation" will be used in this chapter to refer to changes in this measure only.

In the initial study of LTP, Bliss and Lømo (1973) reported that increases in population spike height, or reductions in population spike latency, sometimes followed high-frequency activity without alteration of the EPSP. Furthermore, even when LTP was observed, the population spike often showed disproportionately greater potentiation. This increase in the spike–EPSP relation (E-S curve) following conditioning has also been observed in CA1 *in vitro* (Andersen, Sundberg, Sveen, Swann, & Wigström, 1980). In CA1 it was observed as a decrease in $x$-intercept (shift to the left) of the E-S curve and was termed E-S potentiation by Andersen *et al.* (1980). Although E-S potentiation has now also been observed in other laboratories (Bliss, Goddard, & Riives, 1983; Wilson, Levy, & Steward, 1981), it is not at all clear whether, in the dentate gyrus, it reflects an independent trace or whether it is related in some way to a single mechanism also responsible for LTP.

In collaboration with Bliss, we decided to examine the characteristics of E-S potentiation in detail. A series of graded-intensity stimuli was delivered

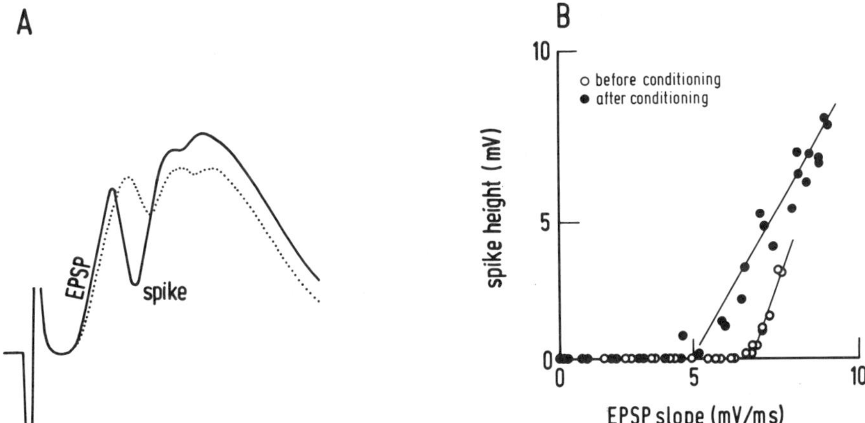


**FIGURE 4.2.** (A) Sample perforant path evoked responses before (dotted line) and after (solid line) 400-Hz stimulation of the perforant path. Each waveform is an average of two responses to constant intensity perforant path test pulses. (B) EPSP–spike (E-S) curves generated from a stimulus intensity series before (○) and after (●) perforant path conditioning. All data are taken from a single animal.

before, and at least 15 minutes after, high-frequency stimulation of the perforant path (16–20 400-Hz trains, each of 20 msec duration). Such conditioning stimulation parameters typically elicit both LTP and E-S potentiation. We found that the conditioning stimulation altered the E-S curve in two ways (Figure 4.2B): (1) a decrease in slope of the fitted regression line and (2) a reduction in $x$-intercept of the regression line (Abraham, Bliss, & Goddard, in press).

Functionally, the two changes in the E-S function represent opposing influences on granule cell input–output coupling: The smaller $x$-intercept reflects a lower spike threshold and a greater sensitivity of the granule cells to excitatory synaptic input, but the reduced slope indicates a decreased responsiveness that partially counteracts the increase in coupling, especially at the higher levels of synaptic input. The opposing nature of these E-S changes in terms of granule cell input–output coupling renders the term "E-S potentiation" ambiguous. Thus, for the moment, we shall refer to the two types of changes as the E-S left-shift and E-S slope depression. Because the high-intensity conditioning stimulation produced LTP and the two E-S changes concurrently and because all three appeared to be long lasting, it was unclear whether or not the three phenomena were interdependent.

The left-shift of the E-S curve has been interpreted as representing a generalized increase in granule cell excitability (Bliss *et al.*, 1983). If this is the case, these cells should then show greater firing to tests of other, unconditioned, excitatory inputs. Similarly, if the E-S slope depression reflects a decrease in granule cell excitability, then it should also be observable heterosynaptically. We tested these hypotheses by selective stimulation of the medial and lateral components of the perforant path. Because the lateral path does not elicit easily identifiable population spikes, we could only perform the heterosynaptic test in one direction, that is, by conditioning the lateral path and testing the unconditioned medial path. The parameters of conditioning stimulation were those that, when applied to the medial path, normally produce slope and $x$-intercept changes in the E-S relationship of that pathway.

Repeated high-frequency stimulation of the lateral path resulted in a significant shift to the left of the medial path E-S curve (Figure 4.3B; Abraham *et al.*, 1984). The left-shift was parallel, involving no significant change in slope. This production of a left-shift without a slope change implies that the slope and the $x$-intercept of the E-S function are manifestations of independent mechanisms. Because the left-shift was observed heterosynaptically, it probably involves some general postsynaptic mechanism. The slope change, on the other hand, being pathway specific, likely involves more localized alterations.

Another aspect of the heterosynaptic left-shift was that it was reliably obtained even though lateral path LTP was only occasionally observed, a result suggesting that LTP and the E-S left-shift may also be independent phenomena.

Finally, the lateral path conditioning resulted in smaller medial path EPSPs (Figure 4.3A). Such heterosynaptic EPSP depression has been observed by others, but typically it has lasted less than 5 minutes (Andersen *et al.*, 1980; McNaughton & Barnes, 1977; but see also Levy & Steward, 1979). In

**FIGURE 4.3.** Heterosynaptic consequences of conditioning the lateral perforant path. Synaptic stimulus–response (A), E-S–amplitude (B), and spike stimulus–response (C) curves are plotted for the medial perforant path from data obtained before and 15 minutes after conditioning of the lateral path. Arrows point toward the postconditioning curve in A and B. Filled circles define the postconditioning curve in C. Heterosynaptic depression of the EPSP is seen in A and E-S potentiation in B. The net result of these effects is that the spike stimulus–response curve is unchanged (C).

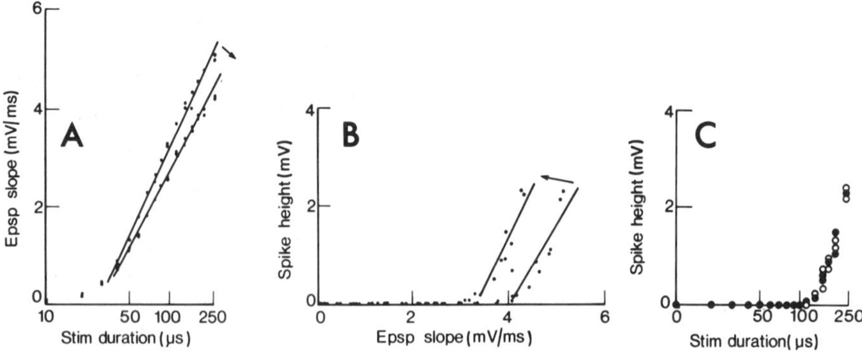

our experiments, the depression lasted at least 3 hours (Abraham & Goddard, 1983), a result indicating that heterosynaptic EPSP depression may be yet another long-term consequence of perforant path activity.

The combined consequence of the heterosynaptic E-S left-shift and the heterosynaptic EPSP depression was that there was no net change in the medial path spike height per afferent volley (Figure 4.3C). The importance of this result is twofold. First, it suggests that heterosynaptic EPSP depression and E-S potentiation may be produced by a common underlying process because one would not expect two independent processes to result in such a near-perfect cancellation of their effects on the amplitude of the population spike. Supporting this notion is the fact that the heterosynaptic effects were highly correlated in magnitude ($r = .81$). Second, it raises doubt about whether the E-S left-shift should be called an increase in granule cell excitability. Strictly speaking, the heterosynaptic E-S left-shift did occur as predicted by the hypothesis of altered excitability; however, it was not manifested as an increase in granule cell output to a given afferent volley, as one would also have expected.

In summary, the two experiments provide evidence that (1) the E-S left-shift is independent of LTP; (2) the E-S left-shift is postsynaptically mediated; (3) the E-S left-shift may be linked in some way to heterosynaptic depression; and (4) the E-S slope depression is pathway specific and independent of the E-S left-shift.

To carefully examine heterosynaptic EPSP depression, we gave consecutive conditioning trials to the medial and lateral pathways, with eight animals receiving medial conditioning trains first and eight animals receiving lateral conditioning trains first (Abraham & Goddard, 1983). Synaptic depression (15–20% decrease) in the unconditioned pathway was observed in each condition in naive animals and was independent of the amount of LTP observed in the conditioned pathway. The depression often lasted as long as 3 hours in acute experiments and has been seen to last for 2 days in a chronic experiment.

Once a pathway had been conditioned, however, and regardless of whether observable LTP had actually been induced, subsequent depression was never seen when the other pathway was stimulated. These data differ from the phenomenon of reversible potentiation and depotentiation as observed in the crossed perforant path (Levy & Steward, 1979). The reason for the protection from depression observed in our study is unclear. It is possible that the initial conditioning trials saturated the mechanism of depression throughout the cell, homosynaptically as well as heterosynaptically, with the homosynaptic depression being masked by the concurrent homosynaptic LTP. Depression, being saturated, would not then be increased by subsequent stimulation of any other pathway. This hypothesis may explain why stimulation of the lateral pathway does not often produce observable LTP in naive animals: The high-frequency stimulation, being only just above threshold for LTP due to low-stimulus strengths and low lateral path synaptic efficacy (McNaughton, 1980), induces LTP, but only just enough to cancel the effects on that pathway of the concurrent depression. In accord with this hypothesis, LTP in the lateral path is observed more reliably when the depression in that pathway has already been saturated by prior medial path conditioning (Abraham & Goddard, 1983).

## FURTHER TESTS OF TRACE INDEPENDENCE

Taken together, the preceding evidence indicates that high-frequency perforant path activity results in multiple changes in both perforant path synaptic input (homosynaptic long-term potentiation and heterosynaptic long-term depression) and the coupling between that input and granule cell output (E-S left-shift and E-S slope depression). Although some of the data presented earlier indicated that many of these traces are independent, a more direct approach to this question was required. The approach we chose was a comparison of the threshold and saturation levels of stimulation for each of the various traces.

A series of 250-Hz conditioning trains, which increased in duration from 10 to 290 msec, was delivered to the medial perforant path (one train every 5–10 minutes). A set of 400-Hz trains was given at the end of some experiments to produce maximal alterations in the evoked responses. Stimulus intensity series were run before each series of trains, after a few trains had been delivered, and from 10 to 60 minutes after the last and longest train. Long-term potentiation, E-S slope depression, and the E-S left-shift each developed with different thresholds (Abraham, 1984); LTP was observed under all conditions. In 3/7 experiments involving trains of short duration (<90 msec), LTP occurred in the absence of any E-S changes, a finding suggesting that this trace has the lowest threshold (Figure 4.4A). The E-S slope depression had the next lowest threshold. It was observed in the remaining experiments (4/7) involving short-duration trains and was nearly always seen following trains longer than 90 msec in duration (Figure 4.4B). Besides always being accompanied by LTP, the E-S slope depression was also occasionally accompanied by a small increase in the $x$-intercept of the E-S function. The E-S left-shift exhibited the highest threshold. It occurred in less than 50% of the experiments involving trains up to 190 msec long and became 100% reliable only after several 290-msec trains (Figure 4.4C). It was often accompanied by additional LTP and additional E-S slope depression, yet there were times when the E-S left-shift increased without further increments in any of the other measures.

The fact that LTP could be observed in the absence of any E-S changes suggests that LTP is independent of the other traces. Similarly, the E-S left-shift also appears to be an independent trace. It has been reported to occur occasionally in the absence of LTP (Bliss & Lømo, 1973); and in the present

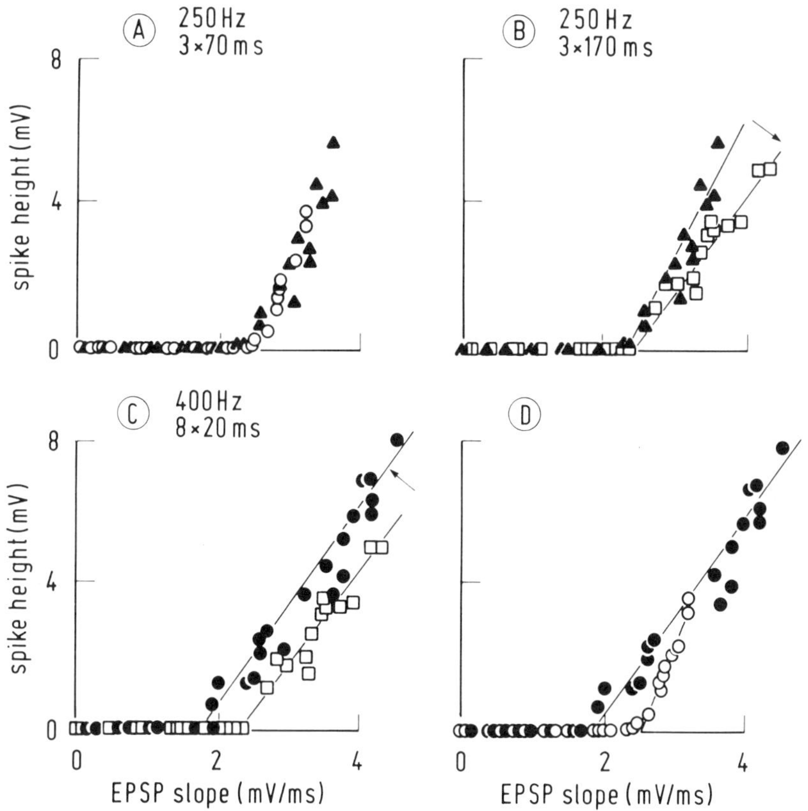


**FIGURE 4.4.** E-S curves from a single animal generated before and 10 minutes after each stage of E-S development. Linear regression lines are drawn for each curve, except in A, where a slight decrease in slope was observed without a change in threshold. Arrows point to the postconditioning curves. (A) Before (○), after (▲); (B) before (▲), after (□); (C) before (□), after (●); (D) comparison of the initial baseline curve (○) with the one generated after delivery of all trains (●).

experiment, once all three effects had been produced, additional E-S left-shifts could occur alone. On the other hand, E-S slope depression, when it occurred, was always accompanied by LTP and thus may not be independent of it.

The threshold of the fourth trace—heterosynaptic EPSP depression—is currently being examined by delivering test pulses to the lateral path before and after each train of an ascending series delivered to the medial path. The recent data from this experiment shows that the threshold of synaptic depression differs from both that of LTP and that of the E-S left-shift and appears to be similar to that of E-S slope depression. These data suggest a relationship different from that described earlier, where the magnitude of heterosynaptic depression was highly correlated with the E-S left-shift and their combined effects on the population spike per unit stimulus strength canceled to zero. Perhaps then, EPSP depression is unrelated to either the E-S left-shift or E-S slope depression. Such a hypothesis is consistent with finding that heterosynaptic EPSP depression was not accompanied by heterosynaptic E-S slope depression and, in the threshold experiment, did not always appear concurrently with the E-S left-shift.

Another method of trace separation would be to compare the time courses of decay. Racine and colleagues (1983), using chronic recording techniques, have followed the decay of LTP back to baseline. The decay was described by two exponentials, with time constants of about 2 hours (LTP1) and several days (LTP2). Their results suggest that even LTP is not a unitary phenomenon but may involve two separate mechanisms. Unfortunately, the authors did not report decay constants for measures of the E-S function. However, the population spike, measured in isolation, decayed with a double exponential in which the constants were somewhat longer than those observed for the EPSP, a result implying that the E-S function also has longer decay constants than LTP. Currently we are trying to repeat these decay experiments while extending them to include heterosynaptic and E-S measures. Although we have observed all four traces decaying over a period of 2–4 days in one chronic preparation (D. Pritchard & W. C. Abraham, unpublished observations), more observations will be required to detect the subtle differences that may exist between the decay constants of the several measures.

A third approach to the separation of the several traces of perforant path activity is the selective alteration of one trace, leaving others unchanged. Chronic norepinephrine depletion has been shown to impair LTP while leaving the E-S left-shift unaltered (Bliss *et al.*, 1983). Robinson and Racine (1983) repeated the monoamine depletion experiment and demonstrated that such treatment selectively affects the fast-decaying LTP1 component of LTP but not the longer lasting LTP2 component. Conversely, in animals tested 8–16 weeks after 5 months of chronic ethanol consumption, perforant path conditioning produced less than normal increases in the spike–EPSP relation, despite producing normal levels of LTP (Abraham *et al.*, 1984). In both this and the monoamine depletion studies, the short-term traces remained unaffected by the treatments. Finally, short periods of norepinephrine application iontophoretically to the dentate gyrus have been shown to produce increases in the spike–EPSP relation lasting several hours, but with little or no change in the amplitude of the EPSP (Neuman & Harley, 1983). Unfortunately, full input–output curves were not generated in either this or the alcohol study. In none of these studies has heterosynaptic EPSP depression or E-S slope depression been examined. Nonetheless, the above findings support the hypothesis that LTP and the E-S left-shift are independent traces that are formed by different underlying mechanisms.

## TRACE MECHANISMS

There is widespread agreement that LTP is an increase in synaptic efficacy that is confined to some proportion of synapses participating in the high-frequency activity (Bliss & Dolphin, 1982; Swanson, Teyler, & Thompson, 1982). Our data are consistent with this view. In the circuit diagram of Figure 4.5, granule cell LTP would occur at either the mpp–gc or the lpp–gc synapses, depending on which pathway was conditioned. Unfortunately, there is no direct evidence regarding the mechanisms of the remaining traces, so we can only speculate about their underlying mechanisms.

Depression of the E-S slope represents a subtle decrease in the responsiveness of granule cells to perforant path input, particularly at higher stimulus strengths. This effect is anomalous because its sign is opposite that of the other traces; that is, it represents a decrease in information flow through the dentate gyrus via the conditioned pathway. Our current hypothesis is that E-S slope depression results from an increase in efficacy of local inhibitory circuitry, perhaps via LTP of excitatory contacts made by the perforant path onto feed-forward inhibitory interneurons (e.g., mpp–ii synapse of Figure 4.5; see also Brassel, Levy, & Steward, 1982). Evidence supporting this hypothesis comes largely from a study by Buzsaki and Eidelberg (1982). Individual neurons were recorded in the dentate gyrus,

**FIGURE 4.5.** Simple circuit diagram of the dentate gyrus similar to that of Figure 4.1d but including an inhibitory interneuron (ii, filled neuron). The interneuron is depicted as mediating both recurrent and feed-forward inhibition, although two separate classes of neurons may actually subserve these two functions. lpp, lateral perforant path; mpp, medial perforant path; gc, granule cell.

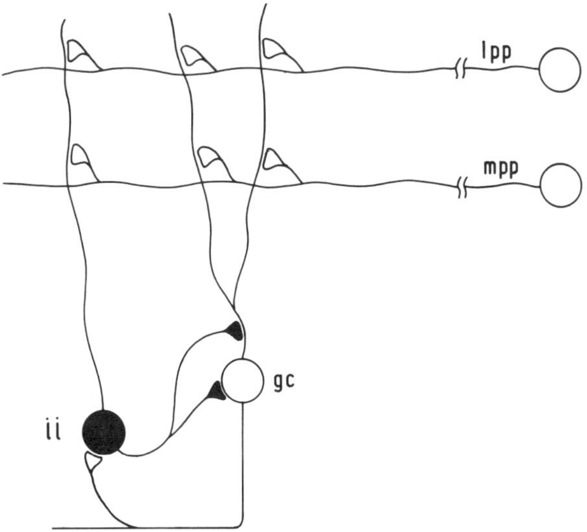

which responded repetitively to perforant path test pulses with latencies and thresholds below those for the granule cell population spike. Interestingly, these neurons showed a lasting enhancement of responding to perforant path stimuli following 40-Hz, 5-sec conditioning stimulation of the perforant path. These neurons were concluded to be feed-forward inhibitory interneurons receiving monosynaptic perforant path input capable of sustaining LTP.

Increased feed-forward inhibition would account for a number of our results. First, it would explain the decreased granule cell response to the more intense perforant path inputs (E-S slope depression). Assuming that the feed-forward inhibitory interneurons project laterally along the septotemporal axis of the hippocampus, the set of granule cells contributing to the population spike would receive increasing feed-forward inhibitory drive as more perforant path fibers are recruited by the larger stimulus intensities. Second, it explains why E-S slope depression was only observed homosynaptically. Long-term potentiation only occurs on the activated pathway, and thus LTP of the perforant path–inhibitory interneuron synapses can only be assessed by test pulses to the same pathway. Finally, the hypothesis would account for why E-S slope depression was always accompanied by granule cell LTP because it is based on LTP at other nearby synapses. To be consistent with the results of the threshold experiment, interneuron LTP is postulated to have a slightly higher threshold than granule cell LTP (possibly because the perforant path innervation of the interneurons is less dense than that of the granule cells). If interneuron spike threshold is likewise higher on average than granule cell spike threshold, it may contribute to the E-S curve being depressed more at higher stimulus strengths than at population spike threshold.

We have previously discussed the hypothesis that the E-S left-shift and heterosynaptic EPSP depression may both be a reflection of granule cell depolarization (Abraham *et al.*, 1984). In this hypothesis, the decreased EPSP is a result of a decreased driving force for the depolarizing synpatic potentials. The homo- and heterosynaptic E-S left-shifts are then explained by the granule cells being closer to firing threshold and thus more sensitive to a given synaptic input. The hypothesis predicts an increase in the spontaneous activity of granule cells, and although this effect has been observed up to 20 minutes postconditioning (Deadwyler, Gribkoff, Cotman, & Lynch, 1976), no longer term studies have been reported.

The depolarization hypothesis was attractive because it simply encompassed several phenomena and was in theory relatively easily to test. However, a number of findings argue against it. First, it predicts that more cells should fire to a given test stimulus applied to a converging unconditioned pathway; but our tests did not detect a net increase of the heterosynaptic population spike. Second, the antidromic granule cell spike elicited by mossy fiber stimulation should be reduced in amplitude, also as a result of a decrease in driving potential. However, in 5/5 cases we have been unable to detect alterations in the antidromic spike after perforant path conditioning trains (G. V. Goddard & W. C. Abraham, unpublished observations). Similar results have been obtained in CA1 (Alger, Megela, & Teyler, 1978). Third, our threshold experiments have shown EPSP depression to reach both threshold and saturation earlier than the E-S left-shift. Finally, intracellular recordings from CA1 pyramidal cells have failed to detect any changes in either membrane potential, resistance, or excitability under conditions of LTP and E-S left-shifts (Andersen *et al.*, 1980; Wigström, McNaughton, & Barnes, 1982). Such experiments must also be conducted in the dentate granule cells, though, because heterosynaptic EPSP and E-S effects were not observed in the CA1 studies.

Alternatively, it may be that EPSP depression and the E-S left-shift are independent traces. The EPSP depression observed heterosynaptically may represent a decrease in efficacy of the unconditioned synapses due to local synaptic or dendritic modifications, and the E-S left-shift may result from more general alterations in the excitability of the granule cell membrane. At present our data do not allow us to choose among the various hypotheses. Clearly intracellular recordings from granule cell somata and dendrites are required to resolve these issues.

## TRACE TERMINOLOGY

With the evidence of multiple traces arises the difficult problem of naming them. Operationally we have used "LTP" to denote long-lasting, pathway-specific increases in the field EPSP, chiefly because this is the term most commonly used to describe the primary effect of increased efficacy of the conditioned pathway. At one time this term was apt, as it succinctly described two prominent features of the phenomenon, that is, the slow decay function and the increase in response amplitude. The term "enhancement" has also been used to describe this phenomenon (McNaughton, 1982). The discovery that the decay of LTP (enhancement) is described by two exponentials with markedly differing constants questions whether these terms denote a single phenomenon. A further complication is that the properties of slow decay and increased response are shared by at least one other trace, the E-S left-shift (E-S potentiation), which can occur independently.

"Heterosynaptic EPSP depression" describes the reduced EPSP recorded in the unconditioned converging pathway, but the term would be misleading if the change should prove to occur at all synapses, including those of the conditioned pathway, perhaps as a result of a change in the membrane properties of the postsynaptic cell. The "E-S left-shift" and "E-S slope depression" have also been labeled solely on observed evoked potential changes; and, as might be expected at this early stage, the terms do not indicate what mechanisms are involved or over what time courses they decay.

Clearly we are in need of an updated terminology that uniquely identifies each of the long-lasting traces. Unfortunately, we have not yet progressed far enough in our understanding of their underlying mechanisms, or any relations between them, to safely suggest anything more than the descriptive labels used in this chapter. It is our hope that improved knowledge of the cellular mechanisms underlying these effects will suggest a clear and precise terminology, with a smaller number of actual "traces."

Network theories of learning, such as those of Hebb (1949) or Uttley (1979), have usually relied on a single mechanism to provide lasting changes in the efficacy of neural connections throughout the brain. Thus, they may be viewed as single trace theories of long-term information storage, although Hebb, for example, proposed a second, faster-decaying reverberatory trace to account for short-term information storage. We now have evidence in the perforant path–dentate gyrus circuit that as many as four (or five if LTP has two components) long-lasting traces may result from activity in this pathway. A detailed understanding of these traces and the involved local circuitry should allow us to build a multitrace model of dentate gyrus plasticity that has a solid empirical footing. Such a model will not only enhance our understanding of hippocampal function but will give us a base from which to generate more realistic network theories of learning.

## SUMMARY

Physiological studies in the hippocampus over the last 10 years have revealed that perforant path–granule cell synapses can exhibit a lasting increase in efficacy following high-frequency activity. This phenomenon has been called long-term potentiation. Recently we have shown that at least four separable lasting traces of perforant path activity can be observed: (1) LTP (which may itself have two components); (2) heterosynaptic EPSP depression; (3) a shift to the left of the EPSP–spike (E-S) function both homosynaptically and heterosynaptically; and (4) a decrease in slope of the E-S function homosynaptically. These four traces reach threshold and saturation separately and may be differentially affected by experimental manipulations. Depression of the E-S slope (trace 4) is hypothesized to result from an increase in inhibitory synaptic input to the granule cells, which is due to LTP of perforant path synapses onto feed-forward inhibitory interneurons and thus may be a special case of trace 1. Heterosynaptic EPSP depression (trace 2) and the E-S left-shift (trace 3) remain to be explained mechanistically in a way that accounts for all the data, but functionally they sharpen LTP by improving the flow of information in the conditioned pathway. Further studies are required to determine the cellular mechanisms of the various traces, to determine how many of them are independent, and to suggest an appropriate terminology to name them.

## REFERENCES

Abraham, W. C. Multiple long-term effects of perforant path tetanisation on input/output coupling in the dentate gyrus. *Proceedings of the University of Otago Medical School*, 1984, *62*, 67–68.

Abraham, W. C., & Bliss, T. V. P. An analysis of the increase in granule cell excitability accompanying habituation in the dentate gyrus of the anesthetized rat. *Brain Research*, 1985, *331*, 303–313.

Abraham, W. C., Bliss, T. V. P., & Goddard, G. V. Heterosynaptic effects accompany long-term but not short-term potentiation in the rat perforant path. *Journal of Physiology (London)*, in press.

Abraham, W. C., & Goddard, G. V. Asymmetric relations between homosynaptic long-term potentiation and heterosynaptic long-term depression. *Nature (London)*, 1983, *305*, 717–719.

Abraham, W. C., Rogers, C. J., & Hunter, B. E. Chronic ethanol-induced decreases in the response of dentate granule cells to perforant path input in the rat. *Experimental Brain Research*, 1984, *13*, 215–225.

Alger, B. E., Megela, A. L., & Teyler, T. J. Transient heterosynaptic depression in the hippocampal slice. *Brain Research Bulletin*, 1978, *3*, 181–184.

Alger, B. E., & Teyler, T. J. Long-term and short-term plasticity in the CA1, CA3, and dentate regions of the rat hippocampal slice. *Brain Research*, 1976, *110*, 463–480.

Andersen, P., Bliss, T. V. P., & Skrede, K. K. Unit analysis of hippocampal population spikes. *Experimental Brain Research*, 1971, *13*, 208–221.

Andersen, P., Sundberg, S. H., Sveen, O., Swann, J. W., & Wigström, H. Possible mechanisms for long-lasting potentiation of synaptic transmission in hippocampal slices from guinea-pigs. *Journal of Physiology (London)*, 1980, *302*, 463–482.

Baranyi, A., & Feher, O. Synaptic facilitation requires paired activation of convergent pathways in the neocortex. *Nature (London)*, 1981, *290*, 413–415.

Bliss, T. V. P., & Dolphin, A. C. What is the mechanism of long-term potentiation in the hippocampus? *Trends in NeuroSciences*, 1982, *5*, 289–290.

Bliss, T. V. P., & Gardner-Medwin, A. R. Long-lasting potentiation of synaptic transmission in the dentate area of the unanaesthetized rabbit following stimulation of the perforant path. *Journal of Physiology (London)*, 1973, *232*, 357–374.

Bliss, T. V. P., Goddard, G. V., & Riives, M. Reduction of long-term potentiation in the dentate gyrus of the rat following selective depletion of monoamines. *Journal of Physiology (London)*, 1983, *334*, 475–491.

Bliss, T. V. P., & Lømo, T. Long-lasting potentiation of synaptic transmission in the dentate of the anaesthetized rabbit following stimulation of the perforant path. *Journal of Physiology (London)*, 1973, *232*, 331–356.

Brassel, S., Levy, W. B., & Steward, O. Feed-forward inhibition and the regulation of cell discharge following long-term potentiation. *Society for Neuroscience Abstracts*, 1982, *8*, 740.

Brons, J. F., & Woody, C. D. Long-term changes in excitability of cortical neurons after Pavlovian conditioning and extinction. *Journal of Neurophysiology*, 1980, *44*, 605–615.

Brown, T. H., & McAfee, D. A. Long-term synaptic potentiation in the superior cervical ganglion. *Science*, 1982, *235*, 1411–1413.

Buzsaki, G. & Eidelberg, E. Direct afferent excitation and long-term potentiation of hippocampal interneurons. *Journal of Neurophysiology*, 1982, *48*, 597–607.

Deadwyler, S. A., Gribkoff, V., Cotman, C., & Lynch, G. Long lasting changes in the spontaneous activity of hippocampal neurons following stimulation of the entorhinal cortex. *Brain Research Bulletin*, 1976, *1*, 1–7.

Goddard, G. V. Component properties of the memory machine: Hebb revisited. In P. W. Jusczyk & R. M. Klein (Eds.), *The nature of thought: Essays in honor of D. O. Hebb*. Hillsdale, N.J.: Erlbaum, 1980.

Hebb, D. O. *The organization of behavior*. New York: Wiley, 1949.

Ito, M., Sakurai, M., & Tongroach, P. Climbing fibre induced depression of both mossy fibre responsiveness and glutamate sensitivity of cerebellar purkinje cells. *Journal of Physiology (London)*, 1982, *324*, 113–134.

Levy, W. B., & Steward, O. Synapses as associative memory elements in the hippocampal formation. *Brain Research*, 1979, *175*, 233–245.

Lømo, T. Potentiation of monosynaptic EPSPs in the perforant path–dentate granule cell synapse. *Experimental Brain Research*, 1971, *12*, 46–63.

McNaughton, B. L. Evidence for two physiologically distinct perforant pathways to the fascia dentata. *Brain Research*, 1980, *199*, 1–20.

McNaughton, B. L. Long-term synaptic enhancement and short-term potentiation in rat fascia dentata act through different mechanisms. *Journal of Physiology (London)*, 1982, *324*, 249–262.

McNaughton, B. L., & Barnes, C. A. Physiological identification and analysis of dentate granule cell responses to stimulation of the medial and lateral perforant pathways in the rat. *Journal of Comparative Neurology*, 1977, *175*, 439–454.

Neuman, R. S., & Harley, C. W. Long-lasting potentiation of the dentate gyrus population spike by norepinephrine. *Brain Research*, 1983, *273*, 162–165.

Racine, R. J., Milgram, N. W., & Hafner, S. Long-term potentiation phenomena in the rat limbic forebrain. *Brain Research*, 1983, *260*, 217–232.

Robinson, G. B., & Racine, R. J. Long-term potentiation of the perforant path–granule cell synapse in the chronic rat preparation: Effects of catecholamine depletion. *Society for Neuroscience Abstracts*, 1983, *30*, 8.

Swanson, L. W., Teyler, T. J., & Thompson, R. F. (Eds.). *Hippocampal long-term potentiation: Mechanisms and implications for memory*. Cambridge, Mass.: MIT Press, 1982.

Teyler, T. J., & Alger, B. E. Monosynaptic habituation in the vertebrate forebrain: The dentate gyrus examined in vitro. *Brain Research*, 1976, *115*, 413–426.

Uttley, A. *Information transmission in the nervous system*. London: Academic Press, 1979.

Wigström, H., McNaughton, B. L., & Barnes, C. A. Long-term synaptic enhancement in hippocampus is not regulated by postsynaptic membrane potential. *Brain Research*, 1982, *233*, 195–199.

Wilson, R. C., Levy, W. B., & Steward, O. Changes in translation of synaptic excitation to dentate granule cell discharge accompanying long-term potentiation: II. An evaluation of mechanisms utilizing dentate gyrus dually innervated by surviving ipsilateral and sprouted crossed temporodentate inputs. *Journal of Neurophysiology*, 1981, *46*, 339–355.

CHAPTER 5

# The Possible Role of Experience-Dependent Synaptogenesis, or Synapses on Demand, in the Memory Process

**William T. Greenough**
University of Illinois, Urbana–Champaign

## SOME PRELIMINARY CONSIDERATIONS

There are two basic research approaches to brain memory substrates: *intervention* experiments, which use agents that disrupt or enhance memory processes, and *correlative* experiments, which assess physiological, metabolic, or structural changes in the nervous system associated with learning or a model of it. Intervention experiments indicate that memory formation takes time, may be modulated, and may involve or require macromolecular synthesis. Correlative experiments, such as those discussed in adjacent chapters, have shown metabolic and electrophysiological alterations in the brain during or consequent upon training. Recently, as a follow-up to studies of effects of experience on the developing brain, structural correlates of training have begun to be described.

Studies of structural consequences of training or in model systems have a much shorter history than other correlative approaches, perhaps because the notion of structural plasticity in the adult nervous system was not widely accepted until a few years ago. Despite this recency, an increasingly strong case can be made for the involvement of synapse formation and maintenance in information storage, including traditionally conceived memory, in the developing and adult mammalian nervous system. I shall begin by considering some criteria by which the involvement of a correlate of training in the memory process might be evaluated and shall then consider, in historical context, the degree to which the structural substrates that we have been studying appear to fulfill them.

Perfect knowledge of the mechanisms of learning would allow us to state what is necessary and sufficient for its occurrence. In practice, work has been restricted to attempts to demonstrate the necessity of a brain change to learning or memory formation. Showing that some set of changes is *sufficient* for information storage will be vastly more difficult in a system as complex as the mammalian brain because more than a single, isolated engram is likely to be involved. [Even in the putatively best understood model of learning (Kandel & Schwartz, 1982), there has been no attempt to demonstrate sufficiency of the physiological changes described to the learning process.] Nonetheless, there are some criteria that we can apply as we determine whether continued pursuit of specific substrates of information storage in the mammalian brain is likely to be fruitful:

1. There should be a positive relationship between the amount of information stored and the magnitude of change in the proposed substrate. This relationship, in the case of memory, would probably not be linear even if we could somehow meaningfully quantify the amount of information stored because the storage of some information can enhance the ability to store more by providing more efficient ways to encode it.

2. The criterion of necessity noted above should survive experimental challenge by such techniques as lesions to areas in which correlates have been identified and administration of substances that prevent the occurrence of correlates (e.g., structural change) as they become available.

3. The (ultimate) changes should persist for as long as the memory persists. Changes involved in establishing memory, such as macromolecular synthesis, may be transient, however. Whether studies indicating increased stability of memories over years in humans and weeks in animals (Squire & Cohen, 1984) indicate continued changes in the form memories take in the brain, as opposed to changes in the strength or number of associations to other memories, is uncertain. If the form in the brain were to change, novel cellular mechanisms might be involved, but this seems unlikely.

4. The changes should not occur if learning (or information storage) does not occur. This criterion has been a problem in a large number of correlative studies because it is not sufficient merely to show that the subject did not learn what the experimenter intended.

5. Activity of nerve cells in which correlates are produced by a training experience should be correlated with the behavior and altered as the behavior is acquired.

6. Changes compatible with the proposed substrate should be initiated by events that lead to memory.

A still popular notion, perhaps arising from hopes engendered by recent invertebrate work, is that memories will be more or less localized in the higher vertebrate brain (e.g., Thompson, 1983). It seems unlikely, however, that the "engram" for most learned behaviors would reside exclusively in a single brain area or localized set of synapses. Indeed, use of the terms engram or memory trace may be misleading when applied to any very complicated behavior, and the notion that we may be able to track a mammalian memory to a single set of synapses in a manner similar to what has been presented in mollusks seems to overlook a considerable amount of electrophysiological and metabolic data indicating involvement of an array of regions in the acquisition and performance of learned tasks (e.g., Gabriel, Foster, Orona, Saltwick, & Stanton, 1980; Gallistel, Karreman, & Reivich, 1977; Schwartzman, Greenberg, Reivich, Klose, & Alexander, 1981; also see later). Conversely, it seems unlikely that the representation of a learned behavior in the brain would involve plastic change in all of the structures activated during acquisition and performance of the task. Structures associated with nonspecific activation, for example, might be involved in learning without themselves changing on a long-term basis. Certain structures may play general sensory or motor roles in behavioral performance that do not need to be modified for a specific behavior. Finally, it seems unlikely that structures not differentially activated by acquisition or performance of the learned task would show plastic change consequent on learning, if the changes are related to the acquisition of the task. Thus, the newly acquired behavior might involve fairly widespread brain representation of various components, but nothing of a "holographic" sort is expected. A "circuit," conceptually like that in simple systems, though vastly more complex, would remain an accurate description (see Bullock, 1984, for an interesting discussion of the units that might be involved). However, it is not required that one describe the entire circuit before studying processes leading to or involved in its formation.

The rest of this chapter focuses upon evidence that changes in the number and/or pattern of synaptic connections are involved in the memory process. This possibility has been relatively neglected by memory researchers despite more than 15 years of research indicating altered patterns of connections as a result of experience manipulations in development and more recent data indicating similar results in adulthood. The research to date makes a reasonably strong case for the involvement of altered patterns of synaptic connectivity in the memory process, although the data remain correlative. Other theories of neural memory mechanisms also focus upon the synapse as the most likely site of change, but, for the most part, models currently in vogue propose changes in ionic channel characteristics (Alkon, Chapter 1, this volume; Kandel & Schwartz, 1982), in neurotransmitter receptor availability (Lynch & Baudry, 1984), or in regulation of neurotransmitter release (Kandel & Schwartz, 1982; Skrede & Malthe-Sorenssen, 1981). There is no inherent incompatibility between these proposals and that of alterations in the pattern of synapses actually present for at least two reasons:

1. Higher mammals, which have evolved a lifestyle that depends heavily for survival upon the ability to acquire information through experience, seem quite likely to have evolved multiple mechanisms for storing that information. Even within LTP, there are multiple, temporally separate phases (Lynch & Baudry, 1984; Racine, Milgram, & Hafner, 1983) that suggest mediation by separate mechanisms. Thus, it is quite possible that several mechanisms exist and even that they may be used in combination in the

storage of information. Whether mechanisms would be shared with phyla that diverged from the line leading to modern mammals perhaps half a billion years ago has been an important question, and Alkon's report (Chapter 1, this volume) suggests that they might be. If so, it seems highly unlikely that the mechanisms evolved specifically to subserve learning.

2. Different mechanisms are, of course, likely to underlie memories with different time constants. The changes in ionic channel characteristics modulating membrane conductance and neurotransmitter release and the changes in receptor availability proposed to underlie various forms of synaptic plasticity in simpler systems seem more likely to be involved in shorter term forms of plasticity, as their proponents have noted (Kandel & Schwartz, 1982; Lynch & Baudry, 1984). [Increased neurotransmitter binding (Lynch & Baudry, 1984) could also indicate that additional synapses had formed.] Their involvement in long-term memory, however, other than as part of the process of initiation of long-term change, seems unlikely. Long-term memory may last for tens of years in a human and for up to several years in animals. The average life span of a brain protein, of which channels and receptors are composed, ranges from a few hours to a few weeks (Droz, Koenig, & Di Giamberardino, 1973; Korr, 1981), orders of magnitude shorter; and it is difficult to assume that changes involving phosphorylation or exposure of receptor proteins would either preserve them indefinitely against degradation or be passed to their newly synthesized successors. It is similarly improbable that a 90-year memory would involve a slight change in the width of an action potential. Thus, considering substrates likely to persist in the brain for as long as long-term memories are known to persist, altered patterns of synaptic connectivity seem more likely to have the requisite stability.

## EVIDENCE FOR SYNAPTIC NUMBER CHANGES ASSOCIATED WITH LEARNING

The pioneering research of Rosenzweig and colleagues (Bennett, Diamond, Krech, & Rosenzweig, 1964; Rosenzweig, Bennett, & Diamond, 1972) had indicated that rats reared in complex environments (large, toy-filled, group cages, with additional extracage experience) had a number of regions of the cortex, particularly in the posterior dorsal or occipital region, that were heavier and thicker than in rats reared in standard laboratory cages, and similar findings had also been reported in adults. Following a tentative early report (Holloway, 1966), we initially found (Greenough & Volkmar, 1973) that animals reared from weaning in environmental complexity (EC) had more extensive dendritic fields in occipital cortex than did littermates reared socially (SC) or individually (IC) in standard laboratory cages. These differences were large, averaging about 20% between EC and IC in three upper occipital cortex neuron types, with SC rats intermediate. The pattern of results bears upon the first criterion presented in the preceding section, in the sense that the three-way difference among the groups reflects differences in the amount of information available in the three rearing environments. The differences in dendritic fields suggested that occipital neurons in these groups differed in the number of synapses. However, it was possible that (1) the additional dendrite in the ECs was not innervated, (2) innervation density was lower on dendritic fields of ECs, (3) the Golgi methods used stained different neurons in the different groups, or (4) Golgi impregnation differed across groups in a way not visible in the light microscope.

To determine whether these quantitative dendritic field measures reflected differences in the number of synapses per neuron (S/N), we have (Turner & Greenough, 1985) used electron microscopy to assess synaptic density and light microscopy to assess neuronal density. It was not possible to infer S/N merely by counting synapses on electron micrographs or tissue sections because (1) counts must be corrected for any differences in size (larger synapses will appear more often in sections) and (2) reported differences among these groups in estimates of cortical tissue volume (Diamond, 1967) rendered synaptic density alone relatively meaningless. When both synaptic and neuronal density were estimated using appropriate stereological corrections, the S/N ratio in layers I to IV of visual cortex was about 20% higher in EC than in IC rats, with SC values again intermediate (Figure 5.1). This result indicates that inferences regarding synapse numbers may be based on quantitative dendritic field analysis.

The third criterion (see preceding section) requires that putative or alleged memory substrates persist for as long as the memory does. In the

**FIGURE 5.1.** Synaptic and neuronal density and synapses per neuron, corrected for group differences in size according to Coupland (1968) for synapses and Weibel (1979) for neuronal nuclei, in upper visual cortex of rats reared for 30 days after weaning in environmental complexity (EC), social cages (SC), or individual cages (IC). Lower density of neurons in EC and SC rats is assumed to reflect increases in neuropil and associated tissue elements. The greater number of synapses per neuron in the EC group confirms predictions from Golgi stain studies showing greater dendritic length per neuron. (After Turner & Greenough, 1985. Copyright 1984, Elsevier Science Publishers.)

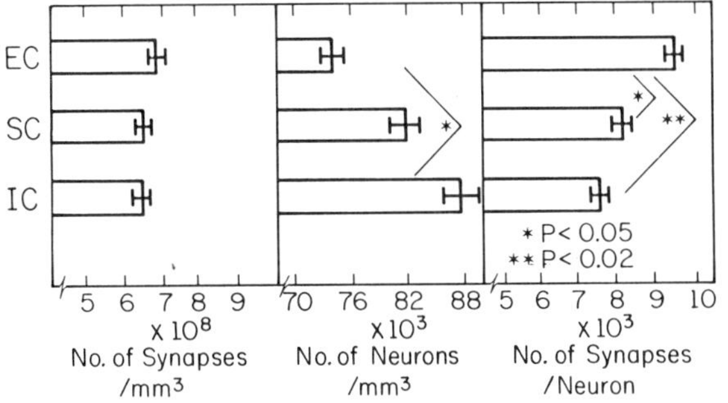

case of the effects of rearing in complex environments, the "memory"—in the sense of altered learning ability—appears to persist to some degree for at least much of the life of the animal (e.g., Forgays & Read, 1962). Studies of gross brain measures such as weight and thickness, in contrast, suggest relatively rapid declines in EC effects when the animals are returned to laboratory cages, although glia to neuron ratios and neuronal density values are more stable (Bennett, Rosenzweig, Diamond, Morimoto, & Hebert, 1974; Katz & Davies, 1984). In a study still in progress (J. E. Camel & W. T. Greenough, unpublished), our preliminary data for layer IV stellate neurons in occipital cortex indicate that most of the dendritic field size differences induced by 30 days of postweaning exposure to EC survive an additional 30 days of individual housing in standard laboratory cages. Although we have yet to examine longer durations of post-EC laboratory housing—and we would expect some declines paralleling behavioral losses—these data do make a good case for persistence of these plausible structural substrates of behavioral change, at least when induced during development.

Evidence that the complex-environment effects on dendritic fields were, like the differences in cortical weight and thickness (Rosenzweig *et al.*, 1972), not merely a developmental phenomenon, came from quantitative Golgi experiments in which young-adult (Juraska, Greenough, Elliott, Mack, & Berkowitz, 1980; Uylings, Kuypers, & Veltman, 1978) and middle-aged (Green, Greenough, & Schlumpf, 1983) rats housed under Ec and IC conditions for several weeks showed dendritic field differences qualitatively, if not quantitatively, similar to those of weanlings. These findings pointed to the possible involvement of synapse number and/or pattern changes in adult storage of information from experience.

To investigate whether similar changes might be involved in memory, we (Greenough, Juraska, & Volkmar, 1979) assessed effects of extensive maze training on occipital cortical dendritic fields. Rats given 3½ weeks of training on a changing series of maze patterns had more oblique branches on apical dendrites of layers IV and V pyramidal neurons than did controls that were handled and given a drink of water (the maze reward) when the others received maze trials (Figure 5.2, left bar). Data supporting this finding have been presented by others. For example, living in a maze with food at one end and water at the other has been reported to increase the weight of and ratio of RNA to DNA in occipital cortex in young animals (Bennett, Rosenzweig, Morimoto, & Hebert, 1979), and Hebb–Williams maze training was reported to increase the overall dimensions of the cerebral cortex in middle-aged rats (Cummins, Walsh, Budtz-Olsen, Konstantinos, & Horsfall, 1973).

To assess the specificity of this effect to the regions of the brain that were processing information from the training experience, we used unilateral eye occluders and a split-brain procedure to restrict visual input from the maze largely to one hemisphere (Chang & Greenough, 1982). After similar

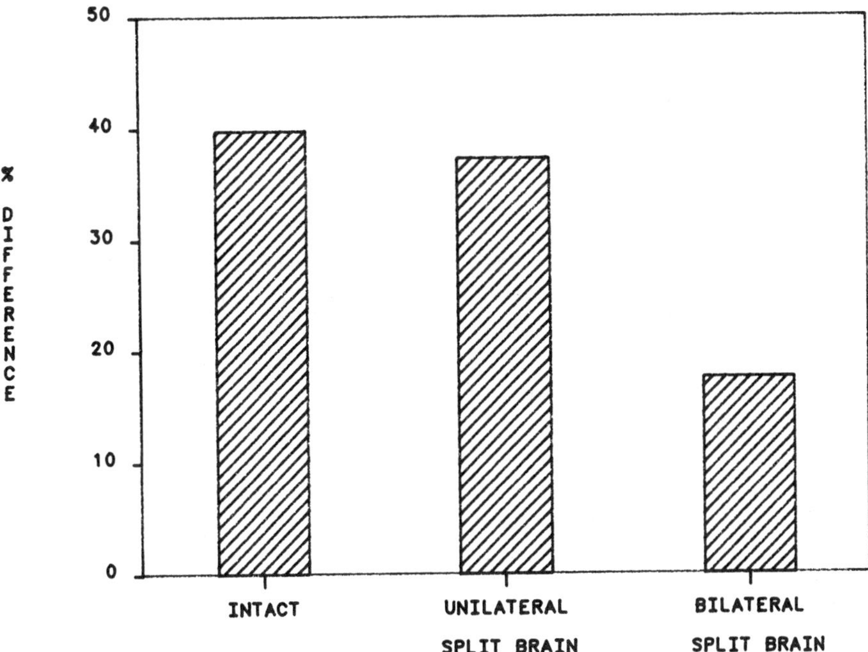


**FIGURE 5.2.** Effects of maze training on total length of oblique branches from the distal region of apical dendrites of layer V visual cortex pyramidal neurons. Percentage difference between trained and nontrained animals or hemispheres, $[(T - N)/N] \times 100$, is plotted. Intact animals are from Greenough, Juraska, and Volkmar (1979). Unilaterally trained, split-brain animals and bilaterally trained or nontrained, split-brain animals are from Chang and Greenough (1982). The smaller difference in the bilaterally trained, split-brain animals may reflect their having been trained with alternating daily eye occlusion, such that each hemisphere received only half as much training. Although these localized differences are quite large, they represent differences of only 2.5–5%, relative to the entire apical dendrite ($p < .01$ for all differences).

training, apical dendritic fields of occipital cortex layer V pyramidal neurons were more highly branched in the hemisphere opposite the nonoccluded eye (Figure 5.2, center bar). Two other conditions in this experiment, a group trained with alternating daily occluder insertion and a nontrained control group subdivided into alternating and fixed position of occluders, replicated the findings of the first maze training experiment (Greenough *et al.*, 1979), showing a between-animal effect of training (Figure 5.2, right bar), and also showed that there was no effect of occluder insertion alone. To some extent, this result (and those of the experiments described later) is compatible with the fourth criterion (see preceding section)—that changes should be related to memory rather than to performance of the learned behavior. More specifically, the unilateral effect of training in this experiment rules out mere generally acting hormonal or metabolic sources of the training-induced structural differences because visual input from the training governs the appearance of structural effects.

These experiments suggested that altered numbers or patterns of synaptic connections might be involved in long-term memory. To examine the generality of this effect across types of learning, we utilized a different learning paradigm—one that involves the forelimb area of somatosensory–somatomotor cortex. The behavior required of the rats is to reach into a chamber for bits of sweetened food, as shown in Figure 5.3A. An extensive series of studies (Peterson, 1934, 1951; Peterson & Devine, 1963; and our observations) indicates that individual rats can be trained to alter their preferred reaching forepaw, that training on the preferred forepaw strengthens original preference, and that induced preference shifts last for at least several months. Lesions of this area shift intrinsic or acquired forepaw preference (Peterson & Devine, 1963), which is compatible with the criterion of necessity of the area to performance of the learned task noted earlier. In addition, lesion studies indicate the importance of pyramidal tract axons, many of which arise from this area, in fine motor control in the rat (Castro, 1972b). We trained groups of seven rats using either the preferred or the nonpreferred reaching forepaw or both (on alternate days) for 16 days (approximately 1600 reaches) and preference-tested seven nontrained controls. In the initial study (Larson & Greenough, 1981), the cortical area associated with the forelimb was defined as the region of lowest threshold for epidural electrical stimulation-induced reaching responses (often with some grasp components). Layer V pyramidal neurons in both hemispheres of each subject within a 1-mm column centered on this point were sampled in six or seven subjects per group. In nontrained controls, there was a tendency for oblique branches from the apical dendrite to be more profuse in the hemisphere opposite the preferred forepaw. In animals trained with the preferred paw this tendency was strengthened, whereas in reversal trained animals it was reversed. Alternation-trained animals' results were inconsistent, despite a tendency for training to strengthen the original preference. Thus, reach training, which increases preference and deftness of reaching with the trained forepaw whether preferred or nonpreferred, altered the structure of motor cortex neurons involved in the behavior. This result suggests involvement of these structural changes in the learning or memory of the behavior.

This paradigm for studies of potential structural substrates of learning/memory has the following advantages: (1) The neocortical neurons studied appear to be critically involved in performance of the learned behavior based upon lesion (Peterson & Devine, 1963) and metabolic studies (see later) and upon the fact that the axons of these neurons appear to be especially important in flexor and digit movement (Castro, 1972a, 1972b). (2) The task appears quite "natural" to rats, which seem more "primate-like" than "cat-like" in the use of their forepaws in behaviors requiring dexterity.

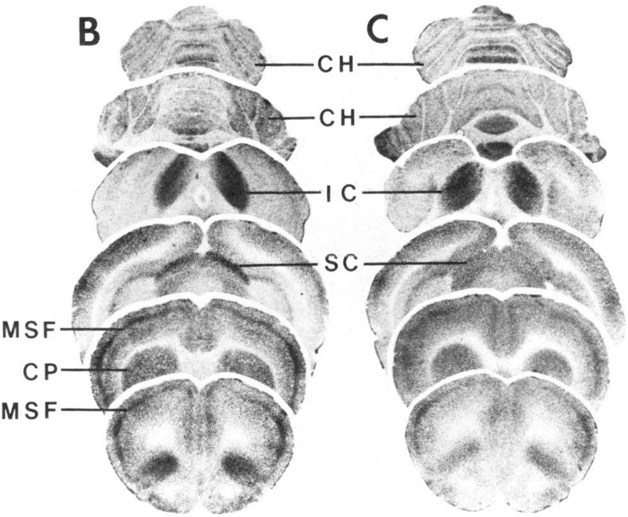


FIGURE 5.3. (A) Reach-training apparatus. Rats are required to reach into a tube or similar enclosure for pieces of sweetened food. Partition to rat's left prevents reaching with right forepaw. (B) 2-Deoxyglucose uptake in brain of rat reaching with left forepaw. Right hemisphere (on left in figure) shows greater uptake in motor–sensory forelimb (MSF) cortex and caudate–putamen (CP). Left superior colliculus (SC) shows greater uptake, probably as a result of use of the eye contralateral to the reaching forepaw, a function of the shape of the apparatus. Asymmetric uptake is also evident in the inferior colliculus (IC) and in regions of the ipsilateral cerebellar hemisphere (CH). (C) 2-Deoxyglucose uptake in nontrained rat eating from a dish shows little asymmetry. (Fuchs, Bajjalieh, Hoffman, & Greenough, 1983; B and C, copyright 1984, Elsevier Science Publishers.)

The region localized by electrical stimulation varied somewhat in its position across subjects, however; and it seemed advisable to try to locate the cortical region involved in reaching by other means. Using regional $[^{14}C]$2-deoxyglucose (2dg) uptake in animals performing the learned reaching task, we traced the region of increased labeling in the anterior neocortex from five rats on outlines of brain sections (Fuchs, Bajjalieh, Hoffman, & Greenough, 1983). There was a remarkable consistency in the position of the region of higher uptake opposite the trained forepaw across subjects (as well as consistent labeling of other regions; see Figure 5.3B and C). Ipsilateral hemisphere uptake was comparable to that of controls (placed in the apparatus with or without food). The term "motor–sensory forelimb cortex" (MSF cortex) is used in Figure 5.3 because (1) microstimulation mapping studies (e.g., Donoghue & Wise, 1982) have shown motor responses to be elicited from both the primary somatomotor area (MI; also termed lateral agranular cortex, Donoghue & Wise, 1982) and the medial portion of the primary somatosensory area (SI), (2) both regions project to cervical spinal cord (e.g., Wise, Murray, & Coulter, 1979), and (3) the anterior cortical region of heavy 2dg uptake also overlaps these two areas and is in reasonably good agreement with recent maps of cortical forelimb representation (e.g., Sanderson, Welker, & Shambes, 1984).

Because the regions of increased 2dg uptake in MSF cortex are remarkably consistent across subjects, this technique appears to define the area that is active during reaching with greater precision, relative to our original electrical stimulation technique. Hence, we sampled neurons from reach-trained subjects using this more well defined region of increased 2dg uptake, projected upon the Golgi-stained sections, as sample area boundaries. Results for apical dendrites of layer V pyramids are shown in Figure 5.4 for the combined trained versus nontrained hemispheres across all groups and the reverse-trained group. The data support the preceding study, indicating that the region which is active during training is altered structurally.

An important question is whether the structural effects of training are restricted to brain regions involved in the performance of the learned task. We selected a region posterior and medial to the forelimb motor and somatosensory cortex region shown to take up 2dg asymmetrically during performance of the reaching task. The area selected corresponds roughly to that designated hindlimb motor cortex in electrophysiological studies (Hall & Lindholm, 1974; Sanderson *et al.*, 1984) and, judging by metabolic criteria, is not (unilaterally) involved specifically in the task (although the rat must maintain hindlimb posture). Although there were some regional differences within the apical dendrite that we do not yet understand, there was no statistical overall bilateral asymmetry in the branching of apical dendrites of large layer V pyramidal neurons (the type that were asymmetric in branching in the MSF region) in the same animals from which the MSF

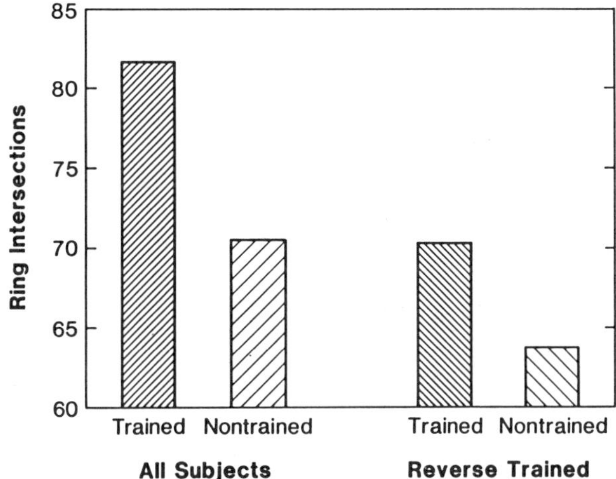


**FIGURE 5.4.** Mean total intersections with concentric rings (a measure of the amount of dendrite) at 10-micrometer intervals away from the cell body of apical dendrites of MSF cortex layer V pyramidal neurons in nontrained, bilaterally trained, preference trained, and reverse-trained rats. These data represent neurons selected from the region of asymmetric uptake of 2dg, which was microprojected on the sections. There is a high degree of consistency across animals in the location of the cortical region of high metabolic activity (see Figure 5.3B). Ten-micrometer ring intervals were used, for greater accuracy, rather than the 20-micrometer distance used in prior studies. Also, unlike the data in Figure 5.5, the apical shaft itself is included in the Figure 5.4 data. (G. S. Withers, J. R. Larson, & W. T. Greenough, unpublished data.)

data were obtained (Figure 5.5). This finding indicates a degree of specificity of the structural effects to the areas involved in performance of the learned task beyond that of bilateral asymmetry—areas apparently most differentially involved in the performance of the task are selectively structurally altered when animals learn it. The fact that the structural changes occur primarily in an area activated during performance of the task is compatible with the fifth criterion (see preceding section)—that activity of the area in which a proposed substrate occurs is systematically related to performance of the learned task. In addition, J. Disterhoft and I (unpublished observations) have recorded unit activity from the forelimb area that correlates with performance of the reaching behavior.

We have also followed up prior work by Hyden and co-workers (Hyden & Egyhazi, 1964) indicating regional protein synthesis changes during reversal training. In contrast to that report, we were not able to detect asymmetries within trained animals in MSF cortex [$^3$H]leucine uptake during training (Fuchs *et al.*, 1983). No differences were evident in other forebrain regions

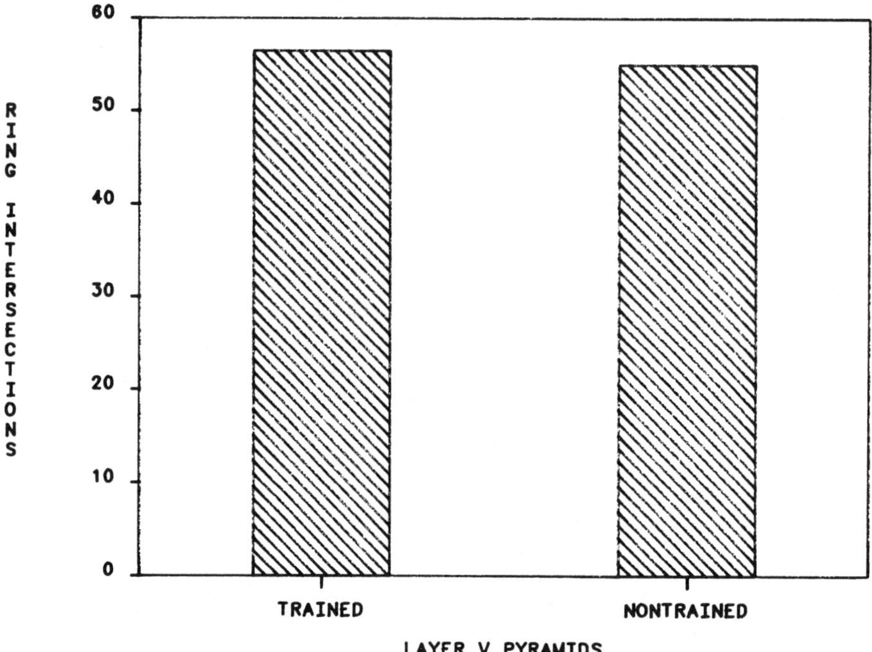


**FIGURE 5.5.** Mean ring intersections with apical dendrites of layer V pyramids in a *nonforelimb* region of motor cortex in the reverse-trained rats depicted in Figure 5.4. The effect of training appears largely restricted to the MSF region. (L. Simonson, J. R. Larson, & W. T. Greenough, unpublished data.)

as well, although we have not yet quantitatively compared whole-brain photodensitometry scans. In addition, following reports of acetylcholine receptor changes after imprinting and training (e.g., Horn, 1981; Rose, Gibbs, & Hambley, 1980), we have examined binding of $^{125}$I-labeled α-bungarotoxin (probable nicotinic ligand) and [$^3$H]quinuclidinyl benzilate (QNB) (muscarinic ligand) in trained animals. Again, eyeball analyses indicate no regional changes, but we have not yet scanned the sections with a photodensitometer, which might reveal small differences. Certainly, neither of these analyses has revealed anything even vaguely comparable to the dramatic differences in the 2dg analyses. The absence of detectable leucine incorporation is somewhat troubling in light of our findings regarding polyribosomal aggregations discussed later. It may be that the synthesis of protein associated with synaptogenesis is at too low a level to be detected with this rather crude light microscopic approach. In a reinnervation paradigm in which massive, synchronous synaptogenesis occurs, Fass and Steward (1983) have reported dramatically increased leucine incorporation.

## HOW MIGHT STRUCTURAL EFFECTS OF TRAINING ORIGINATE? CONSTITUTIVE SYNAPSE TURNOVER VERSUS "SYNAPSES ON DEMAND"

Assuming, for the purposes of this section, that the dendritic field differences arising after training are involved in its memory and that these differences reflect altered synaptic connectivity as we have shown in the complex-environment rearing study (Turner & Greenough, 1985), the issue of *how* training-related neural activity could meaningfully alter synaptic patterns is of significant interest. One current proposal as to where these new synapses come from involves an extension of the synapse overproduction model of development sometimes termed "synapse turnover" (e.g., Changeaux & Danchin, 1976; Cotman & Nieto-Sampedro, 1984; Dyson & Jones, 1984). In both the peripheral and central nervous system, developmental overproduction, first of neuroblasts, then of synapses, often occurs, followed by a selection or stabilization process that leaves behind a subset of the original neurons or connections (Changeaux & Dauchin, 1976; LeVay, Wiesel, & Hubel, 1980; Purves & Lichtman, 1980). It has been proposed that such a mechanism can be used to specify connections in cases in which certain features of the environment, such as binocular patterned light stimulation, can be relied upon to occur, based on the evolutionary history of the species (see later).

An extension of this model to the adult brain (Greenough, 1978), depicted schematically in Figure 5.6A, proposed that *transient or potential connections are formed* between proximate neural elements on a constitutive (nonmodulated) basis and that their *long-term survival as synapses requires confirmation* by the same (or a similar) mechanism to that operative in the developmental overproduction–loss process. Thus, the neural activity associated with a to-be-encoded event would selectively stabilize available transient synapses most appropriate to the encoding of the information. There is little support for the view that synapses constantly form without direction or some type of activating mechanism in the brain (indeed, this would be difficult to demonstrate), although there is some evidence for instability or turnover of synaptic connections in some regions of the intact adult brain (e.g., Sotelo & Palay, 1971) and considerable evidence for sprouting or reactive synaptogenesis in deafferented brain regions (Cotman & Nieto-Sampedro, 1984).

An *alternative* to this view, depicted in Figure 5.6B, is that *synapses can form "on demand"* either as a direct result of the neural activity involved with the processing of information from experience or as a result of some neuromodulatory event arising as a consequence of experience. Historically, the idea that specific connections can form in response to neural activity

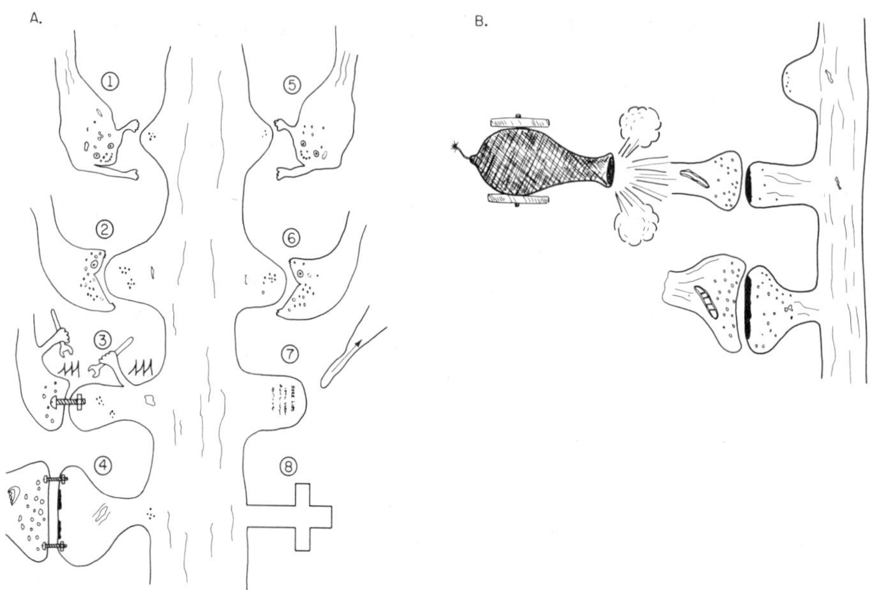


**FIGURE 5.6.** Schematic depiction of two hypothetical mechanisms whereby neural activity arising from experience could bring about synaptic number increases. (A) Constitutive turnover-selective preservation mechanism: Synapses are generated independently of neuronal impulse activity (1, 2, 5, 6); connections between processes that are activated are stabilized, presumably as a consequence of neural activity (3), and become mature (4). In the absence of activity, synapses regress (7), leaving little trace of their prior existence (8). (B) Activity-dependent "synapses on demand" mechanism: Synapses are generated as a consequence of neural activity. Later selective stabilization may determine ultimate survival of a subset of those generated.

has received little support since the initial proposal of electrically directed "neurobiotaxis" (Kappers, 1917), largely because plausible mechanisms for the expression of neural activity in specific growth patterns have not been presented. It should be noted, however, that connections thus formed would not need, initially, to form a change in circuitry that specifically encoded the information. Rather, connections could be generated nonsystematically among activated neurons (and, perhaps, their inactive close neighbors) such that a selective stabilization process could operate upon them, promoting survival of the connections appropriate to that encoding.

We have argued elsewhere (Black & Greenough, in press; Greenough, 1984b) that both modulation of turnover, or selective stabilization within an overproduced population of synapses, and active formation of synapses in response to the need for information storage may be used by the nervous system, depending upon the type of information to be stored. Developmental overproduction of synapses appears often to occur in situations in which specific events can be "expected" by the nervous system, based upon its evolutionary history. For example, mammalian visual systems have evolved in environments in which patterned binocular stimulation is available during development, and at least some mammals appear to have evolved an overproduction-selective stabilization mechanism that allows this information to fine tune the developing systems by weeding out (or in) connections activated by the stimulation (LeVay *et al.*, 1980). In contrast, certain experiential information, including that usually termed "learning," is unique to the individual. Mechanisms have evolved to store such information, but, unlike binocular patterned stimulation available to all members of a species, the character of what is to be learned will vary across individuals. Because the nature of the information cannot be anticipated, the nature of the circuitry necessary to store it cannot be known in advance, and synapse overproduction or continuing nervous system-wide synapse turnover would seem to be a rather inefficient way in which to prepare for it. Thus, experience-dependent synaptogenesis (or synaptogenesis on demand) seems an evolutionarily logical and metabolically more sensible mechanism for the storage of memories unique to the individual.

Recent evidence that synapses can form rapidly in adult brain tissue in response to neural activity is compatible with the proposal of synaptogenesis on demand. Lee, Schottler, Oliver, and Lynch (1980) and Lee, Oliver, Schottler, and Lynch (1981) reported that new synapses form in the hippocampus *in vitro* and *in vivo* following electrical stimulation that induces long-term potentiation (LTP). We (Chang & Greenough, 1984) have noted that these synapses form in relatively large numbers within 10–15 minutes of the eliciting stimulation and persist for at least 8 hours thereafter in the hippocampal slice *in vitro* (see Figure 5.7). We do not, of course, know whether these newly formed synapses mediate or are involved in LTP, although it is tempting to speculate that they play some role, perhaps in the longest lasting aspects of the phenomenon (Racine *et al.*, 1983). In any case, this rate of formation seems far too rapid to be mediated via modulation of synapse turnover. The relevance of LTP to the natural situation remains a question because it is unlikely that the hippocampus in general ever has a proportion of its afferents comparable to those activated in experimental LTP studies firing synchronously at high frequencies. Teyler and Discenna (1984) note that near-synchronous coincidental firing of hippocampal units could produce local active foci where individual neurons receive sufficient high-frequency activation to yield LTP. Behaviorally, increased responsiveness of hippocampal units to perforant path stimulation in an associative conditioning paradigm (Weisz, Clark, Yang, Thompson, & Solomon, 1982) has been interpreted as an example of "behavioral LTP" (Teyler & Discenna, 1984). In addition, recent demonstrations of LTP-like changes in hippocampal formation neurons as a consequence of exposure to complex spatial environments (see Figure 5.8) provide some evidence that a related process

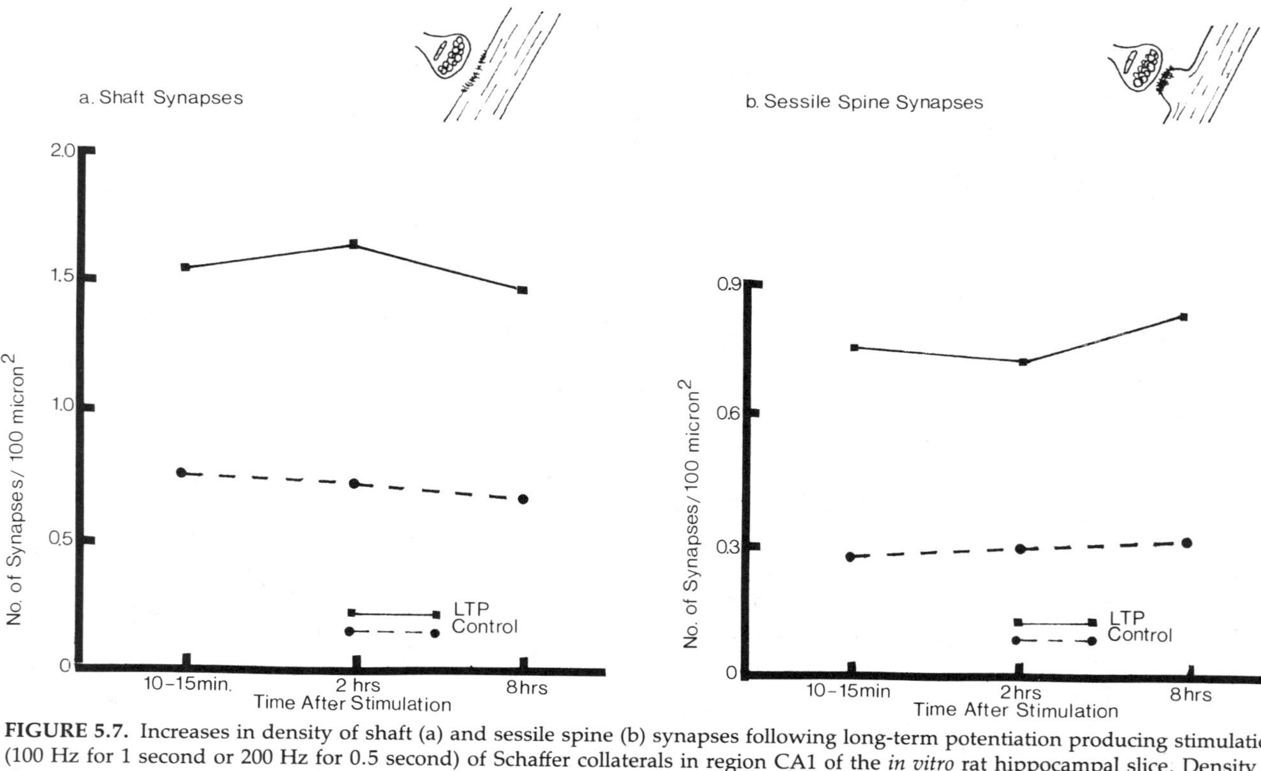


**FIGURE 5.7.** Increases in density of shaft (a) and sessile spine (b) synapses following long-term potentiation producing stimulation (100 Hz for 1 second or 200 Hz for 0.5 second) of Schaffer collaterals in region CA1 of the *in vitro* rat hippocampal slice. Density of the more common headed spine synapses was not affected. Equivalent stimulation at lower frequency or more prolonged stimulation at equivalent frequencies, which did not produce long-term potentiation, did not affect synapse density. (Chang & Greenough, 1984. Copyright 1984, Elsevier Science Publishers.)

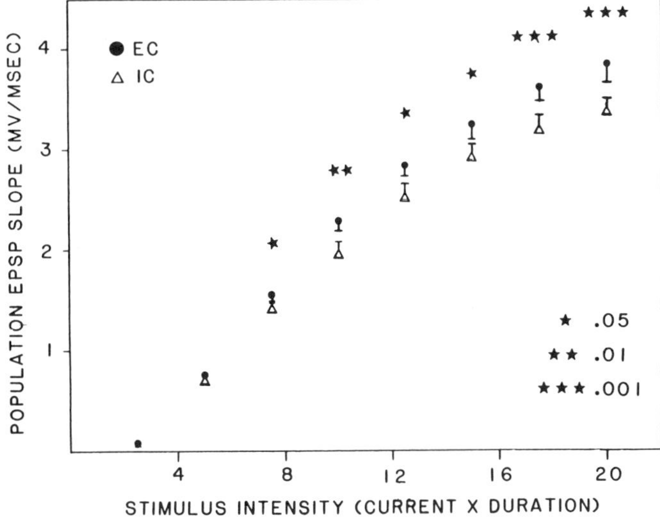


**FIGURE 5.8.** Dentate gyrus population EPSP in response to stimulation of afferents in middle molecular layer in *in vitro* slices from rats reared in EC or IC environments. Responses, at higher stimulus intensities, are larger in EC rats, a finding indicating an enhanced functional connectivity between perforant path axons and dentate granule cells. There were no differences in the granule cell population response to antidromic activation, a finding indicating that the differences in EPSP size were not due to differences in tissue impedance. (Green & Greenough, 1984.)

occurs under more normal circumstances (Green & Greenough, 1984; Sharp, McNaughton, & Barnes, 1983).

Given that synapses *can* form in response to neural activity, it seems reasonable to consider this process a possible mechanism underlying the appearance of increased numbers of connections (or, at least, increased postsynaptic surface) following postweaning and adult exposure to complex environments and learning tasks. Conceptually it seems reasonable that, if the nervous system encodes some types of extrinsically originating information in its pattern of connections, it would have a mechanism for generating connections in positions most appropriate to the incorporation of that information, and those positions might well be some of the ones activated by the processing of the information.

These two models—selective preservation within synapse turnover and synaptogenesis on demand—make one obvious differential prediction: There should be more new synapses forming when animals are learning or forming memories than when they are not, if active formation is involved. To test this hypothesis requires a way of identifying newly forming synapses. Studies of postnatal synaptogenesis in mammalian neocortex suggest that, for spine synapses, a sequence of morphologically distinguishable phases is involved (Adinolfi, 1972; DeGroot & Vrensen, 1978; Dyson & Jones, 1980, 1984; Freire, 1978; Hwang & Greenough, 1984; Juraska & Fifkova, 1979; Miller & Peters, 1981). As indicated in Figure 5.9, the first spines seen are typically of the sessile (Jones & Powell, 1969) or "nubbin"-shaped type, lacking clearly discernible heads and necks. These spines may contain cisternal material or have it at the base in the dendritic shaft, but well-developed spine apparatuses are rarely seen. With increasing age, heads and necks become discernible and cisternal material more reminiscent of the spine apparatus is present. Still later, large, mushroom-shaped spines with mature spine apparatuses appear and become increasingly frequent. This sequence is compatible with our observation (Chang & Greenough, 1984) of an increase in the numbers of sessile spines in hippocampal CA1 following long-term potentiation inducing electical stimulation. The shape changes are paralleled by an increasing thickness of the postsynaptic density (PSD) (Adinolfi, 1972; DeGroot & Vrensen, 1978), possible decreases in cleft width (Armstrong-James & Johnson, 1970), changes in the curvature of the contact zone (Dyson & Jones, 1980), and the increasingly frequent appearance of perforations in the postsynaptic density (DeGroot & Vrensen, 1978; Dyson & Jones, 1984; Greenough, West, & DeVoogd, 1978). Of particular interest is the fact that the location of "polyribosomal aggregates" (PRA) may provide a relatively specific marker of newly forming synapses. Gray and Guillery (1963) first noted organelles resembling the spine apparatus in the somata of neurons and pointed out a tendency for them to be associated with rough endoplasmic reticulum and free polyribosomal aggregates, but they reported that ribosomes were never found in the spine cytoplasm (in dog sensory–motor cortex). More recently, Steward (1983) has reported a dramatic increase in the frequency of occurrence of PRA at the base of spines as well as their occurrence within the spine itself (otherwise rare) during postdeafferentation reinnervation in the rat dentate gyrus and during postnatal synaptogenesis in this region. Similarly, we (Hwang & Greenough, 1984) have found, in a serial thin-section study, an increase of about 400% in the number of PRA in the spine head or neck in rat visual cortex during periods of peak synaptogenesis (postnatal days 13, 15, and 20) compared to adult values.

There is no guarantee, of course, that synaptogenesis in late development or adulthood will share morphological characteristics with that of early development or in response to damage. However, a recent finding is compatible with PRA location as an indicator of synaptogenesis in later development. We (Greenough, Hwang, & Gorman, in press) examined over 2000 spine synapses, using random single sections, in layer IV of occipital cortex of EC, SC, and IC rats after 30 postweaning days of exposure. The number of spines with PRA present was about 20% higher in the EC rats than in the other two groups (see Figure 5.10). In addition, the tendency for PRA to be in the spine head or stem, rather than at the base, was much

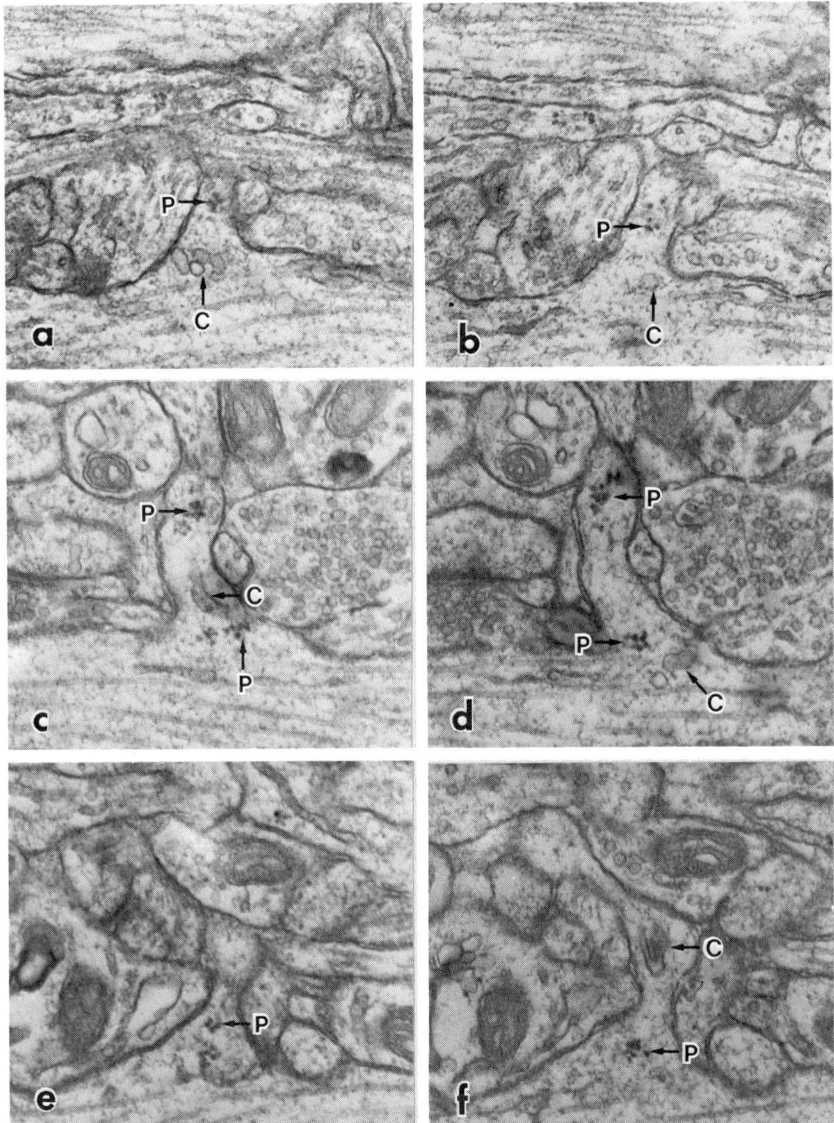


**FIGURE 5.9.** Proposed sequence of morphological development of spines in visual cortex. Pairs of micrographs are adjacent sections in a series. a–b, Sessile spine, polyribosomal aggregation (P) in stem/head, cisternae (C) at base; c–d, spine with just discernable head and stem, polyribosomal aggregation in head and base, cisternae at base; e–f, mushroom-shaped spine with mature-appearing spine apparatus, polyribosomal aggregation at base. (Hwang & Greenough, 1984.)

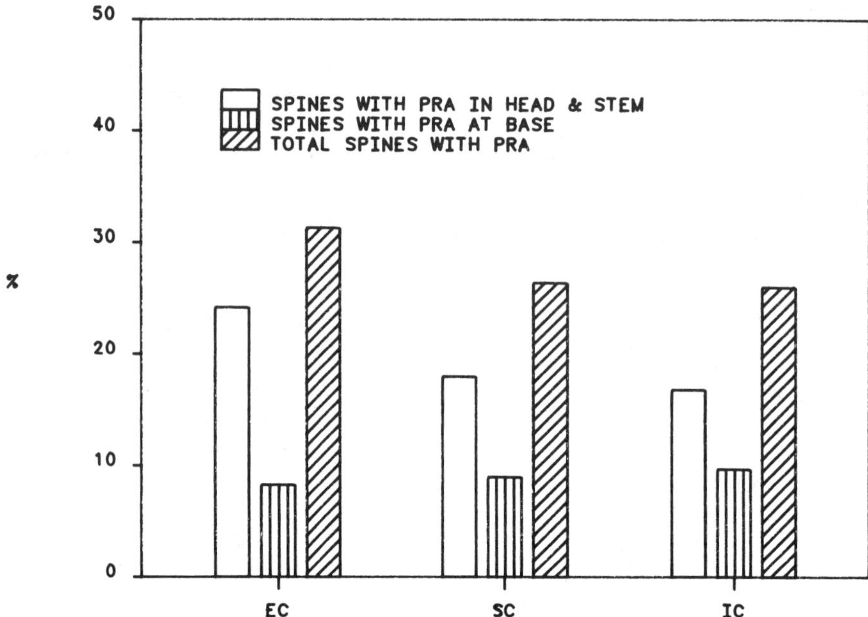


**FIGURE 5.10.** Location of polyribosomal aggregates (PRA) in spines in layer IV of occipital cortex of rats from environmental complexity (EC), social cage (SC), or individual cage (IC) rearing environments. The first two bars do not sum to the third bar in each condition because some spines have PRA in both head or stem and base. Statistics ($\chi^2$): For both proportion of spines associated with PRA (in head, stem, and/or base) and proportion with PRA in head and stem: EC versus IC, $p < .001$; EC versus SC, $p < .01$. (Greenough, Hwang, & Gorman, in press.)

higher in the ECs: The ratio of PRA in spine to in base was 70% higher in the EC than in the IC rats, and the percentage of spines with PRA in heads and stems was 40% higher.

Taken with the finding of higher numbers of synapses per neuron in EC rats, this finding strongly suggests that the location of PRA provides a marker for newly formed synapses and also suggests that experience-triggered (or "on demand") synaptogenesis occurs in the developmental environmental complexity paradigm. (We must, however, also consider that PRA may aggregate in and near spines to perform functions associated with increased activity or other types of synapse modification or maintenance). An obvious next step is to determine whether a similar increase in spine-located PRA occurs in adult animals during learning. This provides a test of the sixth criterion (see Some Preliminary Considerations) that changes compatible with the proposed memory substrate should be initiated by events that lead to memory formation.

## EVIDENCE FOR CHANGES IN PREEXISTING SYNAPSES

Although it is not a focus of this chapter, it should be noted in passing that structural changes in the characteristics of synapses have been identified as a consequence of experience manipulations and that these phenomena also remain viable candidate memory mechanisms. As noted earlier higher vertebrates depend heavily upon use of stored experiential information for their survival, and it certainly seems possible that multiple mechanisms may have evolved to enhance the quality of the storage process. There have been several reports of synapse size changes following differential experience (e.g., Cragg, 1967; Diamond, Lindner, Johnson, Bennett, & Rosenzweig, 1975; Sirevaag & Greenough, 1985; West & Greenough, 1972), and various structural changes have been described following long-term potentiating stimulation of various regions of the hippocampal formation (Chang & Greenough, 1984; Desmond & Levy, 1983; Fifkova & Anderson, 1981; Fifkova & Van Harreveld, 1977; Lee *et al.*, 1980, 1981; Moshkov & Petrovskaya, 1983). In addition, the frequency of perforations in synaptic densities, a potential correlate of use or plastic change (Greenough *et al.*, 1978; Hatton & Ellisman, 1982), has been reported to increase following extensive visual discrimination training in adult rabbits (Vrensen & Cardozo, 1981). (There was also a noticeable difference in synaptic density in the Vrensen and Cardozo study; but because the number of synapses per neuron was not reported, it cannot be clearly interpreted.) More recently, the excellent set of biochemical studies of Rose and his co-workers has been followed up at a structural level. Changes in the structural characteristics of synapses have been reported following both imprinting and passive avoidance learning (Horn, 1981; Stewart, Rose, King, Gabbott, & Bourne, 1984), and unilateral shifts in synapse density, also difficult to interpret in the absence of neuronal density data, have been described in the imprinting paradigm and may reflect increases in the formation or selective preservation of synapses. I shall not detail the argument here because it appears in a prior contribution in this series (Greenough, 1984a), but it remains difficult to discern whether changes in synapse characteristics result from the addition of new synapses with different characteristics or from changes in existing synapses in many of the foregoing studies. In either case, we must realize that changes other than formation of more of the same kind of synapses may be involved in memory.

## CONCLUSIONS

At this point, the correlative evidence for the involvement of altered patterns of synaptic connections in the memory process is intriguing but far from compelling. There is strong evidence that when animals are placed in situations in which learning (or related, perhaps physiologically identical, processes involving the storage of extrinsically originating information) takes place, the structure of cerebral neurons is altered in ways that, in other paradigms, indicate the formation or selective retention of synapses. In at least two cases (Chang & Greenough, 1982; Larson & Greenough, 1981), possible involvement of hormonal or other general nonspecific consequences of the training process in the generation of structural effects of training has been largely ruled out through use of within-subject designs. The possibility that the structural changes are merely a consequence of neural activity, occurring whether or not that activity results in the storage of information, has not been ruled out, although in the study of LTP-associated synaptogenesis mentioned earlier (Chang & Greenough, 1984) we did note that patterns of stimulation that did not produce LTP did not increase synapse density, even when a higher total number of stimuli was delivered than in the LTP treatment. Moreover, experience-dependent changes in dendritic field dimensions have been described in neurons when there were no detectable changes in other neurons that were the only excitatory afferents to the regions that changed, which is certainly not compatible with general effects of neural activity on neuronal structure (Floeter & Greenough, 1979).

With regard to the criteria outlined in the section Some Preliminary Considerations, existing evidence is compatible on all points, but we still fall well short of making a concrete case for synaptogenesis on demand as a memory mechanism. Specifically,

1. *The relationship between the amount of information stored and the magnitude of change in the proposed substrate should be positive*: In the complex-environment paradigm, there is a positive relationship across groups between the relative complexity of, or information available in, the rearing environments and the extent of the difference, above the IC level, in the amount of dendrite or number of synapses per neuron in the occipital cortex.

2. *The substrate, and the region in which the change occurs, should be necessary for memory*: In the reaching paradigm, the brain region in which the structural changes occur has been shown to be essential to performance by the lesion technique. This does not, however, mean that any part of the memory for the behavior resides there. Spinal motoneurons and muscles are also essential to performance of the task. Numerous studies have similarly shown visual cortex to be important to maze learning, and at least some effects of environmental complexity on maze learning survive blinding (Hymovitch, 1952), a finding indicating that the visual cortex role may extend beyond merely seeing the maze.

3. *Changes in the substrate should persist for as long as the memory*: Dendritic field differences between rats reared in EC and IC housing outlast the treatment period by at least an equivalent duration, paralleling the behavioral differences. There is no way of knowing whether the *same connections* persist, however, and the effects of environmental complexity could be self-maintaining if, for example, they caused the animals to attend more to the world

outside their cages (as the report of Will, Pallaud, Ungerer, & Ropartz, 1979, suggests). The same argument could be applied to reach training because induced preference shifts generalize to other tasks to some extent (J. R. Larson & W. T. Greenough, unpublished observations).

4. *Substrate changes should not occur unless memory occurs*: The two experiments indicating lateralized effects of training, as well as the relative absence of effects of reach training on nonforelimb cortex, indicate quite convincingly that these structural effects are specific to areas that appear (see following point) to be involved in the task. In this sense, the changes do not occur when (where?) learning does not. In addition, in the artificial LTP situation only stimulation patterns yielding LTP alter synapse numbers, and the lack of structural changes in excitatory afferents to experientially altered dendrites mentioned earlier argues against one nonlearning effect—neural activity—routinely affecting neuronal structure.

5. *Activity of nerve cells exhibiting substrate changes should correlate with performance of the learned task*: Metabolic and preliminary electrophysiological studies of reach-trained animals indicate involvement of the MSF region of cortex in the reaching task, as would be expected from a history of work on these cortical areas, some of which is cited earlier.

6. *Changes compatible with the substrate should be initiated by events leading to memory*: Structural indicants of synaptogenesis are seen in the occipital region in which other work has indicated higher numbers of synapses per neuron following exposure to environmental complexity. Similar studies have yet to be carried out in adults following EC housing or training.

## ACKNOWLEDGMENTS

Work described in this chapter and not otherwise yet reported was supported by NSF BNS 82-16916, NIMH 35321, NIH RR 07030, PHS 5 T-32EY07005, PHS 5 T-32GM7143, The Retirement Research Foundation, The System Development Foundation, and the University of Illinois Research Board. I thank E. J. Green and H.-M. Hwang for helpful comments.

## REFERENCES

Adinolfi, A. M. The organization of paramembranous densities during postnatal maturation of synaptic junctions in the cerebral cortex. *Experimental Neurology*, 1972, *34*, 383–393.

Armstrong-James, M., & Johnson, R. Quantitative studies of postnatal changes in synapses in rat superficial motor cerebral cortex. *Zeitschrift für Zellforschung und Mikroskopische Anatomie*, 1970, *110*, 559–568.

Bennett, E. L., Diamond, M. C., Krech, D., & Rosenzweig, M. R. Chemical and anatomical plasticity of brain. *Science*, 1964, *146*, 610–619.

Bennett, E. L., Rosenzweig, M. R., Diamond, M. C., Morimoto, H., & Hebert, M. Effects of successive environments on brain measures. *Physiology and Behavior*, 1974, *12*, 621–631.

Bennett, E. L., Rosenzweig, M. R., Morimoto, H., & Hebert, M. Maze training alters brain weights and cortical RNA/DNA ratios. *Behavioral and Neural Biology*, 1979, *26*, 1–22.

Black, J., & Greenough, W. T. Developmental approaches to the memory process. In J. L. Martinez, Jr. & R. P. Kesner (Eds.), *Learning and memory: A biological view*. New York: Academic Press, in press.

Bullock, T. H. Comparative neuroscience holds promise for quiet revolutions. *Science*, 1984, *225*, 473–478.

Castro, A. J. The effects of cortical ablations on digital usage in the rat. *Brain Research*, 1972, *37*, 173–185. (a)

Castro, A. J. Motor performance in rats: The effects of pyramidal tract section. *Brain Research*, 1972, *44*, 313–323. (b)

Chang, F.-L. F., & Greenough, W. T. Lateralized effects of monocular training on dendritic branching in adult split-brain rats. *Brain Research*, 1982, *232*, 283–292.

Chang, F.-L. F., & Greenough, W. T. Transient and enduring morphological correlates of synaptic activity and efficacy change in the rat hippocampal slice. *Brain Research*, 1984, *309*, 35–46.

Changeaux, J.-P., & Dauchin, A. Selective stabilization of developing synapses as a mechanism for the specification of neuronal networks. *Nature (London)*, 1976, *264*, 705–712.

Cotman, C. W., & Nieto-Sampedro, M. Cell biology of synaptic plasticity. *Science*, 1984, *225*, 1287–1294.

Coupland, R. E. Determining sizes and distribution of sizes of spherical bodies such as chromaffin granules in tissue sections. *Nature (London)*, 1968, *217*, 384–388.

Cragg, B. G. Changes in visual cortex on first exposure of rats to light. Effect on synaptic dimensions. *Nature (London)*, 1967, *215*, 251–253.

Cummins, R. A., Walsh, R. N., Budtz-Olsen, O. E., Konstantinos, T., & Horsfall, C. R. Environmentally-induced changes in the brains of elderly rats. *Nature (London)*, 1973, *243*, 516–518.

DeGroot, D., & Vrensen, G. Postnatal development of synaptic contact zones in the visual cortex of rabbits. *Brain Research*, 1978, *147*, 362–369.

Desmond, N. L., & Levy, W. B. Synaptic correlates of associative potentiation/depression: An ultrastructural study in the hippocampus. *Brain Research*, 1983, *265*, 21–30.

Diamond, M. C. Extensive cortical depth measurements and neuron size increases in the cortex of environmentally enriched rats. *Journal of Comparative Neurology*, 1967, *131*, 357–364.

Diamond, M. C., Lindner, B., Johnson, R., Bennett, E. L., & Rosenzweig, M. R. Differences in occipital cortical synapses from environmentally enriched, impoverished, and standard colony rats. *Journal of Neuroscience Research*, 1975, *1*, 109–119.

Donoghue, J. P., & Wise, S. P. The motor cortex of the rat: Cytoarchitecture and microstimulation mapping. *Journal of Comparative Neurology*, 1982, *212*, 76–88.

Droz, B., Koenig, H. L., & Di Giamberardino, L. Axonal migration of protein and glycoprotein to nerve endings. I. Radioautographic analysis of the renewal of protein in nerve endings of chicken ciliary ganglion after intracerebral injection of [$^3$H]lysine. *Brain Research*, 1973, *60*, 93–127.

Dyson, S. E., & Jones, D. G. Quantitation of terminal parameters and their interrelationships in maturing central synapses: A perspective for experimental studies. *Brain Research*, 1980, *183*, 43–59.

Dyson, S. E., & Jones, D. G. Synaptic remodelling during development and maturation: Junction differentiation and splitting as a mechanism for modifying connectivity. *Developmental Brain Research*, 1984, *13*, 125–137.

Fass, B., & Steward, O. Increases in protein precursor incorporation in the denervated neuropil of the dentate gyrus during reinnervation. *Neuroscience*, 1983, *9*, 633–664.

Fifkova, E., & Anderson, C. L. Stimulation-induced changes in dimensions of stalks of dendritic spines in the dentate molecular layer. *Experimental Neurology*, 1981, *74*, 621–627.

Fifkova, E., & Van Harreveld, A. Long-lasting morphological changes in dendritic spines of dentate granular cells following stimulation of the entorhinal area. *Journal of Neurocytolology*, 1977, *6*, 211–230.

Floeter, M. K., & Greenough, W. T. Cerebellar plasticity: Modification of Purkinje cell structure by differential rearing in monkeys. *Science*, 1979, *206*, 227–229.

Forgays, D. G., & Read, J. M. Crucial periods for free-environmental experience in the rat. *Journal of Comparative and Physiological Psychology*, 1962, *45*, 322–328.

Freire, M. Effects of dark rearing on dendritic spines in layer IV of the mouse visual cortex. A quantitative electron microscopical study. *Journal of Anatomy*, 1978, *126*, 193–201.

Fuchs, J. L., Bajjalieh, S. M., Hoffman, C. A., & Greenough, W. T. Regional brain 2-deoxyglucose uptake during performance of a learned reaching task. *Society for Neuroscience Abstracts*, 1983, *9*, 54.

Gabriel, M., Foster, K., Orona, E., Saltwick, S. E., & Stanton, M. Neuronal activity of cingulate cortex, anteroventral thalamus, and hippocampal formation in discriminative conditioning: Encoding and extraction of the significance of conditional stimuli. *Progress in Psychobiology and Physiological Psychology*, 1980, *9*, 125–131.

Gallistel, C. R., Karreman, G. A., & Reivich, M. [$^{14}$C]-2-Deoxyglucose uptake marks systems activated by rewarding brain stimulation. *Brain Research Bulletin*, 1977, *2*, 149–152.

Gray, E. G., & Guillery, R. W. A note on the dendritic spine apparatus. *Journal of Anatomy*, 1963, *97*, 389–391.

Green, E. J., & Greenough, W. T. Functional correlates of differential rearing in rat dentate gyrus. *Society for Neuroscience Abstracts*, 1984, *10*, 579.

Green, E. J., Greenough, W. T., & Schlumpf, B. E. Effects of complex or isolated environments on cortical dendrites of middle-aged rats. *Brain Research*, 1983, *264*, 233–240.

Greenough, W. T. Development and memory: The synaptic connection. In T. Teyler (Ed.), *Brain and learning*. Stanford, Conn.: Greylock Publishers, 1978.

Greenough, W. T. Possible structural substrates of plastic neural phenomena. In G. Lynch, J. L. McGaugh, & N. M. Weinberger (Eds.), *Neurobiology of learning and memory*. New York: Guilford Press, 1984. (a)

Greenough, W. T. Structural correlates of information storage in the mammalian brain: A review and hypothesis. *Trends in NeuroSciences*, 1984, *7*, 229–233. (b)

Greenough, W. T., Hwang, H.-M., & Gorman, C. Evidence for active synapse formation, or altered postsynaptic metabolism, in visual cortex of rats reared in complex environments. *Proceedings of the National Academy of Sciences, U.S.A.*, in press.

Greenough, W. T., Juraska, J. M., & Volkmar, F. R. Maze training effects on dendritic branching in occipital cortex of adult rats. *Behavioral and Neural Biology*, 1979, *26*, 287–297.

Greenough, W. T., & Volkmar, F. R. Pattern of dendritic branching in occipital cortex of rats reared in complex environments. *Experimental Neurology*, 1973, *40*, 491–504.

Greenough, W. T., West, R. W., & DeVoogd, T. J. Subsynaptic plate perforations: Changes with age and experience in the rat. *Science*, 1978, *202*, 1096–1098.

Hall, R. D., & Lindholm, E. P. Organization of motor and somatosensory neocortex in the albino rat. *Brain Research*, 1974, *66*, 23–38.

Hatton, J. D., & Ellisman, M. H. A restructuring of hypothalamic synapses is associated with motherhood. *Journal of Neuroscience*, 1982, *2*, 704–707.

Holloway, R. L. Dendritic branching: Some preliminary results of training and complexity in rat visual cortex. *Brain Research*, 1966, *2*, 393–396.

Horn, G. Neural mechanisms of learning: An analysis of imprinting in the domestic chick. *Proceedings of the Royal Society of London, Series B*, 1981, *213*, 107–137.

Hwang, H.-M., & Greenough, W. T. Spine formation and synaptogenesis in rat visual cortex: A serial section developmental study. *Society for Neuroscience Abstracts*, 1984, *10*, 579.

Hyden, H., & Egyhazi, E. Changes in RNA content and base composition in cortical neurons of rats in a learning experiment involving transfer of handedness. *Proceedings of the National Academy of Sciences, U.S.A.*, 1964, *52*, 1030–1035.

Hymovitch, B. The effects of experimental variations on problem solving in the rat. *Journal of Comparative and Physiological Psychology*, 1952, *45*, 313–321.

Jones, E. G., & Powell, T. P. S. Morphological variations in the dendritic spines of the neocortex, *Journal of Cell Science*, 1969, *5*, 509–529.

Juraska, J. M., & Fifkova, E. An electron microscope study of the early postnatal development of the visual cortex of the hooded rat. *Journal of Comparative Neurology*, 1979, *183*, 257–268.

Juraska, J. M., Greenough, W. T., Elliott, C., Mack, K., & Berkowitz, R. Plasticity in adult rat visual cortex: An examination of several cell populations after differential rearing. *Behavioral and Neural Biology*, 1980, *29*, 157–167.

Kandel, E. R., & Schwartz, J. H. Molecular biology of learning: Modulation of transmitter release. *Science*, 1982, *218*, 433–443.

Kappers, C. U. A. Further contributions on neurobiotaxis. IX. An attempt to compare the phenomena of neurobiotaxis with other phenomena of taxis and tropism. The dynamic polarization of the neurone. *Journal of Comparative Neurology*, 1917, *27*, 261–298.

Katz, H. B., & Davies, C. A. Effects of differential environments on the cerebral anatomy of rats as a function of previous and subsequent housing conditions. *Experimental Neurology*, 1984, *83*, 274–287.

Korr, H. Light microscopical autoradiography of CNS tissue. In C. Heym & W.-G. Forssman (Eds.), *Techniques in neuroanatomical research*. Berlin & New York: Springer-Verlag, 1981.

Larson, J. R., & Greenough, W. T. Effects of handedness training on dendritic branching of neurons in forelimb area of rat motor cortex. *Society for Neuroscience Abstracts*, 1981, *7*, 65.

Lee, K. S., Oliver, M., Schottler, F., & Lynch, G. Electron microscopic studies of brain slices: The effects of high-frequency stimulation on dendritic ultrastructure. In G. A. Kerkut & H. V. Wheal (Eds.), *Electrophysiology of isolated mammalian CNS preparations*. New York: Academic Press, 1981.

Lee, K. S., Schottler, F., Oliver, M., & Lynch, G. Brief bursts of high-frequency stimulation produce two types of structural change in rat hippocampus. *Journal of Neurophysiology*, 1980, *44*, 247–258.

LeVay, S., Wiesel, T. N., & Hubel, D. H. The development of ocular dominance columns in normal and visually deprived monkeys. *Journal of Comparative Neurology*, 1980, *191*, 1–51.

Lynch, G., & Baudry, M. The biochemistry of memory: A new and specific hypothesis. *Science*, 1984, *224*, 1057–1063.

Miller, M., & Peters, A. Maturation of rat visual cortex. II. A combined Golgi-electron microscope study of pyramidal neurons. *Journal of Comparative Neurology*, 1981, *203*, 555–573.

Moshkov, D. A., & Petrovskaya, L. L. Time-dependent ultrastructural changes in the hippocampal synapses after potentiation. *Tsitologiya*, 1983, *25*, 500–507.

Peterson, G. M. Mechanisms of handedness in the rat. *Comparative Psychology Monographs*, 1934, *9*, 1–67.

Peterson, G. M. Transfers of handedness in the rat from forced practice. *Journal of Comparative and Physiological Psychology*, 1951, *44*, 184–190.

Peterson, G. M., & Devine, J. V. Transfer of handedness in the rat resulting from small cortical lesions after limited forced practice. *Journal of Comparative and Physiological Psychology*, 1963, *56*, 752–756.

Purves, D., & Lichtman, J. W. Elimination of synapses in the developing nervous system. *Science*, 1980, *210*, 153–157.

Racine, R. J., Milgram, N. W., & Hafner, S. Long-term potentiation phenomena in the rat limbic forebrain. *Brain Research*, 1983, *260*, 217–231.

Rose, S. P. R., Gibbs, M. E., & Hambley, J. Transient increase in forebrain muscarinic cholinergic receptor binding following passive avoidance learning in the young chick. *Neuroscience*, 1980, *5*, 169–172.

Rosenzweig, M. R., Bennett, E. L., & Diamond, M. C. Chemical and anatomical plasticity of brain: Replications and extensions. In J. Gaito (Ed.), *Macromolecules and behavior* (2nd ed.). New York: Appleton-Century-Crofts, 1972.

Sanderson, K. J., Welker, W., & Shambes, G. M. Reevaluation of motor cortex and of sensorimotor overlap in cerebral cortex of albino rats. *Brain Research*, 1984, *292*, 251–260.

Schwartzman, R. J., Greenberg, J., Reivich, M., Klose, K. J., & Alexander, G. M. Functional metabolic mapping of a conditioned motor task in primates using 2-[$^{14}$C]deoxyglucose. *Experimental Neurology*, 1981, *72*, 153–163.

Sharp, P. E., McNaughton, B. L., & Barnes, C. A. Spontaneous synaptic enhancement in hippocampi of rats exposed to a spatially complex environment. *Society for Neuroscience Abstracts*, 1983, *9*, 647.

Sirevaag, A. M., & Greenough, W. T. Differential rearing effects on rat visual cortex synapses. II. Synaptic morphometry. *Developmental Brain Research*, 1985, *19*, 215–226.

Skrede, K. K., & Malthe-Sorenssen, D. Increased resting and evoked release of transmitter following repetitive electrical tetanization in hippocampus: a biochemical correlate to long-lasting synaptic potentiation. *Brain Research*, 1981, *208*, 436–441.

Sotelo, C., & Palay, S. L. Altered axons and axon terminals in the lateral vestibular nucleus of the rat. *Laboratory Investigation*, 1971, *25*, 653–671.

Squire, L. R., & Cohen, N. J. Human memory and amnesia. In G. Lynch, J. L. McGaugh, & N. M. Weinberger (Eds.), *Neurobiology of learning and memory*. New York: Guilford Press, 1984.

Steward, O. Polyribosomes at the base of dendritic spines of CNS neurons: Their possible role in synapse construction and modification. *Cold Spring Harbor Symposia on Quantitative Biology*, 1983, *48*, 745–759.

Stewart, M. G., Rose, S. P. R., King, T. S., Gabbott, P. L. A., & Bourne, R. Hemispheric asymmetry of synapses in chick medial hyperstriatum ventrale following passive avoidance training: A stereological investigation. *Developmental Brain Research*, 1984, *12*, 261–269.

Teyler, T. J., & Discenna, P. Long-term potentiation as a candidate mnemonic device. *Brain Research Reviews*, 1984, *7*, 15–28.

Thompson, R. F. The engram found? Initial localization of the memory trace for a basic form of associative learning. *Progress in Psychobiology and Physiological Psychology*, 1983, *10*, 167–196.

Turner, A. M., & Greenough, W. T. Differential rearing effects on rat visual cortex synapses. I. Synaptic and neuronal density and synapses per neuron. *Brain Research*, 1985, *329*, 195–203.

Uylings, H. B. M., Kuypers, K., & Veltman, W. A. M. Environmental influences on neocortex in later life. *Progress in Brain Research*, 1978, *48*, 261–274.

Vrensen, G., & Cardozo, J. N. Changes in size and shape of synaptic connections after visual training: An ultrastructural approach of synaptic plasticity. *Brain Research*, 1981, *218*, 79–97.

Weibel, E. R. *Stereological methods* (Vol. 1: *Practical methods for biological morphometry*). New York: Academic Press, 1979.

Weisz, D. J., Clark, G. A., Yang, B., Thompson, R. F., & Solomon, P. R. Activity of dentate gyrus during NM conditioning in rabbit. In C. D. Woody (Ed.), *Conditioning: Representation of involved neural functions*. New York: Plenum Press, 1982.

West, R. W., & Greenough, W. T. Effect of environmental complexity on cortical synapses of rats: Preliminary results. *Behavioral Biology*, 1972, *7*, 279–284.

Will, B., Pallaud, B., Ungerer, A., & Ropartz, P. Effects of rearing in different environments on subsequent environmental preference in rats. *Developmental Psychobiology*, 1979, *12*, 151–160.

Wise, S. P., Murray, E. A., & Coulter, J. D. Somatotopic organization of corticospinal and corticotrigeminal neurons in the rat. *Neuroscience*, 1979, *4*, 65–78.

# CRITICAL COMMENTARIES

CHAPTER 6

# A Possible Enabling and Enhancing Function for Catecholamines in Neuronal Plasticity

**John H. Ashe**
University of California, Riverside
and University of California, Irvine

## INTRODUCTION

One important aspect of changes in behavior that can be attributed to learning is a systematic, and relatively stable, variation between the input stimulus and the output response. The most obvious implication of this observation is that at least certain aspects of nervous system function must be equally flexible and capable of systematic long-term modification. Consequently, considerable research has been directed to the identification and study of cellular integrative properties that can be characterized by their capability for enduring and systematic modification.

The study of mechanisms of long-term cellular modification from the morphological, biophysical/biochemical, and physiological point of view has been of undoubted importance to the behavioral sciences. There has been a considerable quantity of new data generated that has led to productive debate and refinement of concepts (Abraham & Goddard, Chapter 4, this volume; Alkon, Chapter 1, this volume; D. H. Cohen, Chapter 2, this volume; Greenough, Chapter 5, this volume). However, it is also clear that the nature of the dynamic relationship between cellular plasticity and learning has not been established in any firm manner supported by a substantial data base. Thus, the developing theme of multiple memory mechanisms and traces (Abraham & Goddard, Chapter 4, this volume; Barnes & McNaughton, Chapter 3, this volume; D. H. Cohen, Chapter 2, this volume) should be of particular interest to those concerned with cellular mechanisms because the cardinal task is not merely to identify isolated instances of enduring differences in cellular activity and determine their relationship to behavior but also to understand how various distinctive aspects of cellular plasticity are organized in some manner that may account for vertebrate associative learning and memory. If there are multiple distinct mechanisms of cellular plasticity, is there an obligatory interaction such that each is involved, in perhaps some variable way, in every associative learning task? Are particular modifiable cellular processes specific to certain types of associative learning? At another level, is the question whether enduring changes are retained at the synapse or whether synaptic activity might be of crucial importance for learning by leading to long-term modification of the extrasynaptic membrane (Alkon, Chapter 1, this volume).

The problem extends not only to those mechanisms that may be specifically related to learning but also to nonspecific mechanisms that may nevertheless be critical for cellular plasticity and learning. Catecholamine systems have been implicated as having an important function in cellular networks that undergo systematic long-lasting modification (e.g., Abraham & Goddard, Chapter 4, this volume; Barnes & McNaughton, Chapter 3, this volume; D. H. Cohen, Chapter 2, this volume; Kasamatsu, 1983; Kety, 1970; Libet, 1984; Sakakibara, Alkon, Lederhendler, & Heldman, 1984). Although there is no evidence that catecholamines have a specific function in neuronal plasticity, it does appear that these substances function as neuromodulators to promote and perhaps maintain plasticity between neurons (for review, see Kasamatsu, 1983). It is also of interest that the autonomic nervous system, the major modulatory and integrative division of the nervous system, functions via a strong dependence upon the action of catecholamines. For the most part, the autonomic system acts prior to somatic behavior (Brooks, 1979) and acquires conditioned responses more rapidly than somatic responses (Weinberger, Diamond, & McKenna, 1984); and the autonomic system is perhaps more retentive of information than is the somatic system (Brooks, 1979).

## DOPAMINE MODULATION OF SYNAPTIC AND CELLULAR EXCITABILITY

Dopamine (DA) and norepinephrine (NE) have now been shown to have pronounced effects on neuronal sensitivity. Altered neuronal sensitivity is long-lasting, extending well beyond the actual presence of these agents and any direct effects that they may have at the membrane (Ashe & Libet, 1981a; Freedman, Hoffer, Woodward, & Puro, 1977; Koketsu, Akasu, Miyagawa, & Hirai, 1981; Libet, Kobayashi & Tanaka, 1975; Reader, Ferron, Descarries, & Jasper, 1979; Rowgaski & Aghajanian, 1980). For example, initial studies using the *in vitro* mammalian superior cervical ganglion as a model for the study of synaptic action and plasticity demonstrated the ability of DA to initiate cellular events that result in long-lasting potentiation of slow postsynaptic potentials. The slow postsynaptic responses of sympathetic ganglion are particularly interesting in that they differ in very important ways from other well-known synaptic potentials (Libet, 1984). Perhaps the most important is that they have durations in seconds and minutes rather than in milliseconds (Ashe & Libet, 1981b; Libet, 1984). This prominent feature is of obvious significance in that the slow postsynaptic potentials are ideally suited for extended temporal summation, even at very low input frequencies, and thus provide a relatively long period of altered synaptic excitability. A brief exposure to DA produces a long-lasting enhancement of the amplitude of the ganglionic slow, inhibitory postsynaptic potential and slow excitatory postsynaptic potential (Ashe & Libet, 1981a), potentials mediated by acetylcholine acting at pharmacologically distinct muscarinic receptor subtypes (Ashe & Yarosh, 1984; Ashe, Yarosh, & Crawford, 1983). The available evidence implicates a function for intracellular cyclic nucleotides in development of this type of long-lasting synaptic potentiation in sympathetic ganglia (Ashe & Libet, 1981a; Kobayashi, Hashiguchi, & Ushiyama, 1978; Libet *et al.*, 1975), as is the case for similar potentiating actions of biogenic amines at other synaptic loci (Brunelli, Castellucci, & Kandel, 1976; Koketsu *et al.*, 1981; Kuba, Kato, Kumamoto, Koketsu, & Hirai, 1981).

Modifications of receptor number and/or receptor sensitivity have been suggested to be important for establishing changes in synaptic efficacy (Daly, Hoffer, & Dismukes, 1980; Fuxe *et al.*, 1983). Thus, an important question for consideration is whether synaptic potentials generated via neurotransmitter interaction with different subtypes of receptors are equally susceptible to modification. The observation that both the muscarinic slow, inhibitory postsynaptic potential and slow, excitatory postsynaptic potential are potentiated by DA exposure (Ashe & Libet, 1981a), even though mediated via different subtypes of muscarinic receptors (Ashe & Yarosh, 1984), suggests that if DA-induced enhancement of the slow postsynaptic potentials requires modification of the properties of muscarinic receptors, the locus of the effect is likely to be at some portion of the receptor complex other than the binding site. Furthermore, these findings suggest that the cellular modifications initiated by exposure to DA affect muscarinic synaptic transmission through intracellular pathways governed by both receptor types.

Analogous studies of the enhancing action of DA have been initiated in the central nervous system to furher elucidate its ability to produce long-term changes in cellular excitability (Gribkoff & Ashe, 1984a, 1984b). The *in vitro* hippocampal slice preparation was used for this investigation as this cortical structure has been used extensively to study cellular mechanisms that may underlie changes in synaptic efficacy, and perhaps learning and memory (Levy & Steward, 1979; Swanson, Teyler, & Thompson, 1982). Following repetitive stimulation of afferent pathways, hippocampal principal neurons demonstrate pronounced and long-term potentiation (LTP) of the amplitude of responses elicited by single afferent volleys (for review, see Swanson *et al.*, 1982). This striking change in neuronal excitability has resulted in LTP being strongly promoted as a possible model for long-term memory (for review, see Swanson *et al.*, 1982). These observations have led to the investigation of the modulatory actions of DA on hippocampal pyramidal neurons of area CA1. The results of recent studies by others now provide evidence for an influence of catecholamines on LTP (Bliss, Goddard, & Riives, 1984; Gold, Delanoy, & Merrin, 1984; Hopkins & Johnston, 1984).

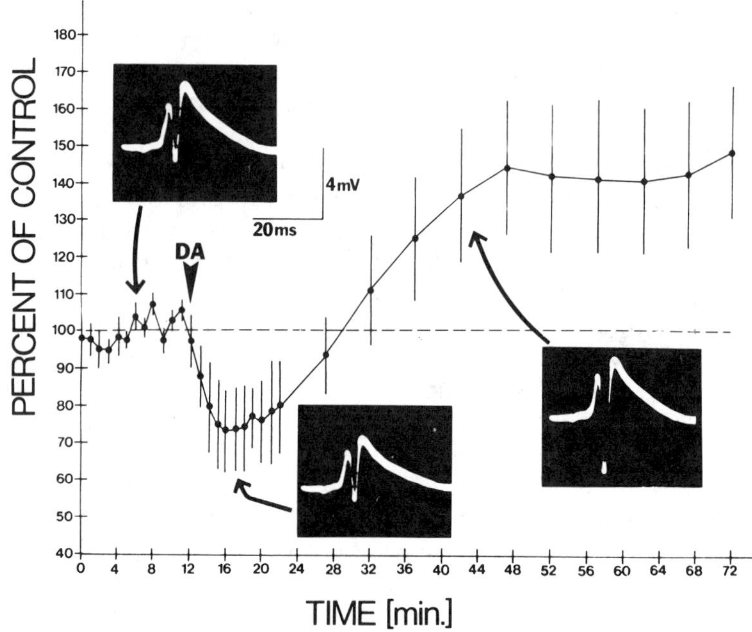


**FIGURE 6.1.** Effect of microtopical application of dopamine (1 m*M*, 0.2 μl) on the amplitude of population spikes recorded from rat hippocampal area CA1. Responses where elicited by single stimulus volleys to the Schäffer collateral fiber tract at a rate of one per minute. Mean and standard error of eight *in vitro* slice preparations. Individual means are plotted as the percentage of the mean of the 12 control responses elicited prior to exposure to dopamine (DA). Insets: Oscilloscope records of individual population responses that are representative of the mean response elicited at the times designated by the arrows.

Studies using anatomical and biochemical techniques have provided evidence for a physiological function of DA in the hippocampus (Bischoff, Bittiger, & Krauss, 1980; Bischoff, Scatton, & Korf, 1979; Ishikawa, Ott, & McGaugh, 1982; Scatton, Simon, LeMoal, & Bischoff, 1980; Schröder, Kammerer, & Matthies, 1982; Schwab, Javay-Agrid, & Agrid, 1978; Simon, LeMoal, & Calas, 1979; Wyss, Swanson, & Cowan, 1979). This evidence recently has been supplemented with physiological evidence that demonstrates the ability of DA to produce short- and long-term changes in the excitability of CA1 pyramidal cells (Benardo & Prince, 1982; Gribkoff & Ashe, 1984a, 1984b; Marciani, Calabresi, Stanzione, & Bernardi, 1984).

When recorded with extracellular electrodes, the typical effects of addition of DA to the bathing medium (.1–1.0m*M*) or of microtopical application (Figure 6.1) is an initial suppression of the area CA1 population spike. This initial suppression is followed by a progressive and long-lasting increase in population spike amplitude (Figure 6.1) (Gribkoff & Ashe, 1984a, 1984b). Addition of spiroperidol (5–10 μ*M*), an antagonist of DA at its receptors

(Seeman, 1982), disrupts late-developing DA-induced potentiation but appears to be without effect on DA-induced suppression of population response amplitude (Gribkoff & Ashe, 1984a). Dopamine-induced potentiation of the slow muscarinic synaptic potentials of superior cervical ganglia is also depressed by spiroperidol or butaclamol, DA antagonists that depress DA stimulation of adenylate cyclase in ganglia (Libet, 1984); in contrast, metoclopramide and sulpiride, DA antagonists that do not depress DA stimulation of adenylate cyclase, are ineffective for blockade of DA-induced potentiation (Ashe & Libet, 1981a). Specific binding sites in hippocampus for [$^3$H]spiroperidol have been reported (Bischoff *et al.*, 1979), as has the presence of a DA-sensitive adenylate cyclase (Dolphin, Hamont, & Bockaert, 1980). Although the precise nature of the spiroperidol binding site and of spiroperidol's effectiveness in antagonizing DA-induced elevations of cyclic AMP in hippocampus remain to be determined, the data suggest that the long-lasting action of DA is receptor-mediated and may involve modification of adenylate cyclase activity.

Results obtained with intracellular electrodes indicate that a brief exposure of area CA1 neurons to exogenous DA produces a biphasic modification of cellular excitability. The initial effect of microtopical application of DA is the production of membrane hyperpolarization usually accompanied by a decrease in membrane input resistance ($R_i$), and suppression of the rate of spontaneously occurring membrane fluctuations and spike potentials. Those initial effects are commonly followed by a long-lasting membrane depolarization, decreased membrane conductance, and an increase in the rate of spontaneous membrane fluctuations and spike potentials (Figures 6.2 and 6.3).

**FIGURE 6.2.** Intracellular records of the effect of microtopical application of dopamine (DA) (1 m$M$, 0.2 μl) on membrane potential. Chart recording of DA-induced changes in membrane potential from a resting potential of −65 mV. The initial effect of DA on membrane is hyperpolarization accompanied by a decrease in the number of rapid spontaneous membrane depolarizations. These initial effects are followed by a sustained membrane depolarization that is accompanied by an increase in the number of rapid depolarizing deflections of the membrane potential (Gribkoff & Ashe, 1984a).

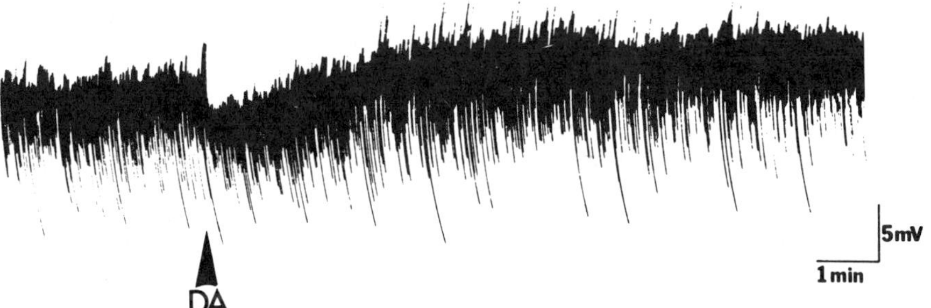

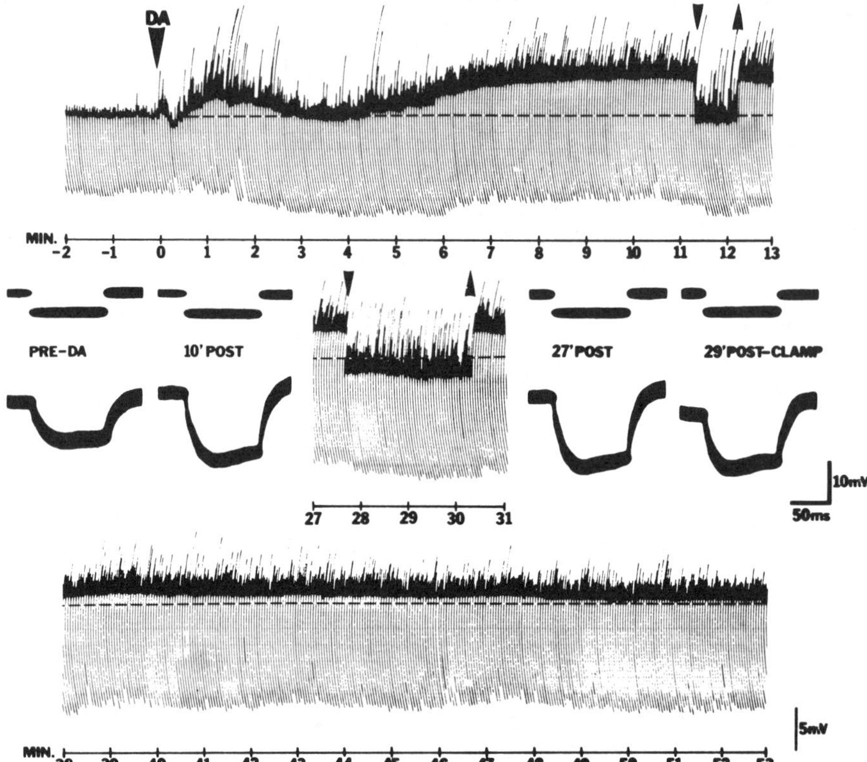


**FIGURE 6.3.** Strip chart and oscilloscope records of the effect of microtopical application of dopamine (DA) (1 m*M*, 0.2 μl) on membrane potential and responses to hyperpolarizing current pulses (0.6 mA, 100 msec, 0.3 per second) passed through a balanced bridge circuit. Initial $V_m = -72$ mV. Illustrated is the continuous strip-chart record of membrane potential with the exception of minutes 13–27 and 31–38, which are not shown in order to condense the illustration. Application of DA produced an initial membrane depolarization of about 4 mV peak amplitude and 3 minutes in duration. This was followed by a depolarization that attained a peak amplitude of about 9 mV and was of much longer duration, exceeding 45 minutes. Both components are accompanied by an increase in $R_i$, as indicated by the increase in the amplitude of membrane responses to hyperpolarizing constant-current pulses (cf. the amplitude of the downward deflections of membrane potential before and after DA application). These effects occur in parallel with a pronounced increase in the frequency of spontaneous membrane depolarizations.

Oscilloscope traces at the left and right center of the figure illustrate the effect of DA on $R_i$ with greater temporal resolution (note 50-msec calibration bar). The top trace displays the current monitor; the lower traces display membrane responses elicited, at the indicated times, by the hyperpolarizing current pulses. The increase in the amplitude of membrane responses to constant current pulses reflects an increase in $R_i$.

Manual clamping of the membrane potential, during the slow-developing long-lasting depolarization, to its initial potential level reduced DA-induced increase in $R_i$ from approximately 37% to 23% for the first period (top; arrowheads) and from approximately 43% to 23% for the second clamp period (center; arrowheads). Manual clamping of the membrane potential to its pre-DA level was totally ineffective in reducing DA-induced increase in spontaneous depolarizing and action potentials.

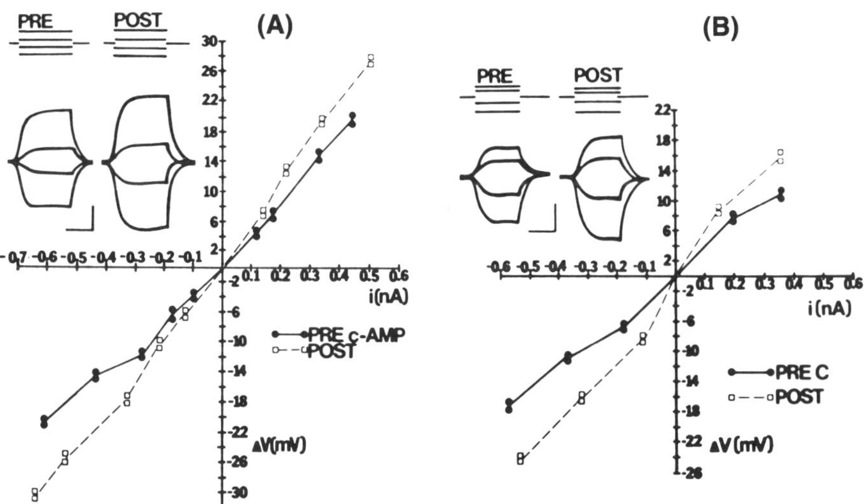


**FIGURE 6.4.** Current–voltage plots that illustrate the increase in membrane $R_i$ before (circles) and after (squares) intracellular injection of either cAMP (A) or the catalytic subunit of cAMP-dependent protein kinase (B). (A) Postinjection records were obtained 10 minutes after injection of cAMP (1 m*M* in 3 *M* $K^+$-acetate) by passage of hyperpolarizing current pulses. Injection of cAMP produced no significant change in resting membrane potential (−69 mV) of this particular neuron. Calibration: X-axis, 0.1-nA steps from an origin of zero; Y-axis, 2-mV steps from an origin of zero. Inset: Membrane responses (lower traces) to hyperpolarizing and depolarizing current pulses (upper traces). Calibration: 1 nA, 50 msec (upper); 10 mV, 50 msec (lower). (B) Postinjection records were obtained about 7 minutes after injection of the catalytic subunit (C) of cAMP-dependent protein kinase (6.25 μg/ml in 0.1 *M* Tris and 1.9 *M* $K^+$-acetate). There was no change in resting membrane potential (−64 mV). Calibration: X-axis, 0.1-nA steps from an origin of zero; Y-axis, 2-mV steps from an origin of zero. Inset: Membrane responses (lower traces) to hyperpolarizing and depolarizing current pulses (upper traces). Calibration: 1 nA, 50 msec (upper); 10 mV, 50 msec (lower).

The latter changes usually follow the initial membrane hyperpolarization and decreased input resistance but can also be initiated in neurons that have no detectable early change in excitability. In spite of the similarity in time course of the change in membrane potential and resistance, it is clear that the increase in $R_i$ is not totally attributable to membrane depolarization. Manual clamping of the membrane potential effectively uncouples the apparent relationship between depolarization and increased $R_i$ (Figure 6.3). This procedure reduces only a portion of the increased $R_i$, perhaps a component due to anomalous rectification (Hotson, Prince, & Schwartzkroin, 1979), but a substantial portion of the total increase in $R_i$ is uneffected. Nor does clamping the membrane potential effect in any appreciable manner DA-induced increase in spontaneous fluctuations of the membrane potential. Also, the duration of the late increase in $R_i$ often exceeds that of the late

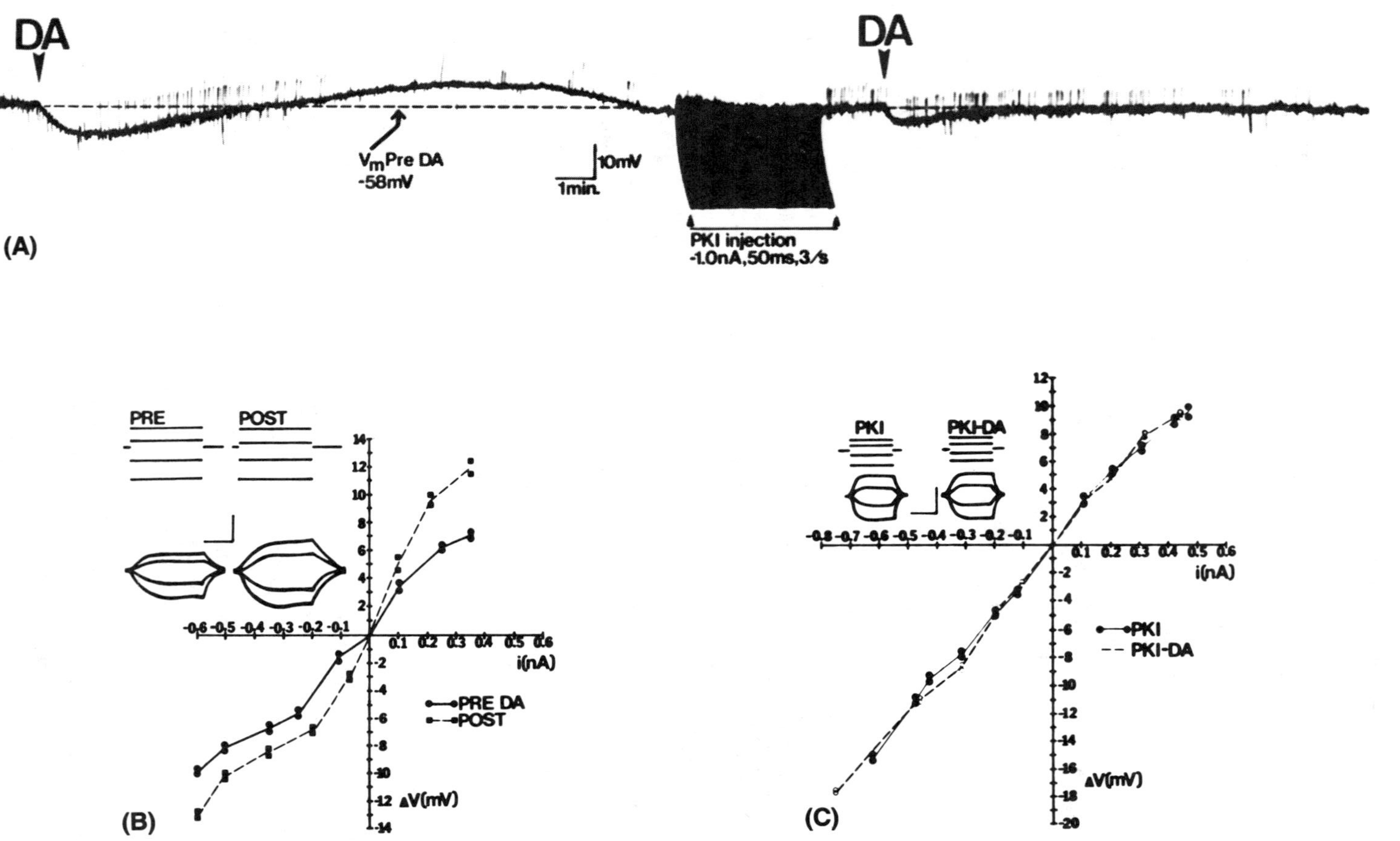
DA
DA
Vm Pre DA
-58mV
10mV
1min.
PKI injection
-1.0nA,50ms,3/s
(A)
PRE
POST
i(nA)
PRE DA
POST
ΔV(mV)
(B)
PKI
PKI-DA
i(nA)
PKI
PKI-DA
ΔV(mV)
(C)

**FIGURE 6.5.** Effect of intracellular injection of cAMP-dependent protein kinase inhibitor protein (PKI) (Fletcher & Byus, 1982) on dopamine (DA)-induced hyperpolarization, depolarization, and late increase in membrane input resistance. (A) Microtopical application of DA (1 m*M*, 0.2 μl) produces an initial membrane hyperpolarization that is followed by a long-lasting membrane depolarization. The resting membrane potential (−58 mV) is indicated by the dashed line. Following intracellular injection of PKI (12.5 μg/ml in 3 *M* $K^+$-acetate) by hyperpolarizing current pulses, DA application produces only a small hyperpolarizing change, but no depolarizing change, in membrane potential. (B) Current–voltage plot that illustrates the input–output function before (circles, solid line) and 10 minutes after (squares, dashed line) application of DA. In this neuron DA, produced no deviation of the membrane potential (−68 mV). The large increase in membrane input resistance is independent of membrane depolarization and therefore independent of anomalous rectifying properties of the membrane (Hotson, Prince, & Schwartzkroin, 1979). Calibration: X-axis, 0.1-nA steps from an origin of zero; Y-axis, 2-mV steps from an origin of zero. Inset: Membrane responses (lower traces) to hyperpolarizing and depolarizing current pulses (upper traces). Calibration: 0.5 nA, 50 msec (upper); 10 mV, 20 msec (lower). (C) Action of PKI on DA-induced increase in membrane input resistance. Current–voltage plots of input–output function before (closed circles, solid line) and 10 minutes after DA injection (open circles, dashed line). Five minutes subsequent to injection of PKI, DA (1 m*M*, 0.2 μl, two drops separated by 3 minutes) was applied and produced brief hyperpolization but no depolarization. The post-DA current–voltage plot was obtained 10 minutes following DA exposure. Calibration: X-axis, 0.1-nA steps from an origin of zero; Y-axis, 2-mV steps from an origin of zero. Inset: Membrane responses (lower traces) to hyperpolarizing and depolarizing current pulses (upper traces). Calibration: 0.5 nA, 50 msec (upper); 10 mV, 50 msec (lower).

depolarization and can occur in neurons in which DA did not induce a depolarization.

The cellular mechanism by which DA, or for that matter any other putative neuromodulatory substance, acts to modify neuronal excitability has not yet been fully elucidated. However, protein phosphorylation reactions have been implicated in synaptic transmission and plasticity (Browning, Dunwiddie, Bennett, Gispen, & Lynch, 1979; Castellucci *et al.*, 1980; Nestler & Greengard, 1982), and evidence indicates that phosphorylation can be regulated by DA, most likely via a receptor-mediated mechanism (Jork *et al.*, 1984; Nestler & Greengard, 1980). We now have evidence that suggests an important role for cyclic AMP-dependent phosphorylation reactions in DA-induced enhancement of CA1 neuronal excitability (Gribkoff, Ashe, Fletcher, & Lekawa, 1984). Extracellular application of 8-bromoadenosine 3′,5′-cyclic monophosphate (8-bromo-cAMP), or intracellular microinjection of cAMP or catalytic subunit of cAMP-dependent protein kinase all result in the production of a long-lasting increase in $R_i$ (Figure 6.4). Moreover, the enduring increase in $R_i$ that is initiated by microtopical application of DA is reduced or eliminated by prior microinjection of cAMP-dependent protein kinase inhibitor protein (Figure 6.5). These data provide important evidence that the long-lasting effect of DA in the hippocampus involves modification of the phosphorylative state of one or more proteins associated with CA1 pyramidal neurons.

## SUMMARY

Studies using model systems from both peripheral and central sites clearly have demonstrated a function for catecholamines in synaptic and neuronal plasticity. The foregoing, as well as other lines of evidence, support the view that catecholamines may have a general modulatory or enabling action on cellular processes likely involved in formation of specific learned associations (Abraham & Goddard, Chapter 4, this volume; Bliss *et al.*, 1983; Hopkins & Johnson, 1984). The important empirical finding is that catecholamines are predominately involved in the production of a relatively long-lasting modification of the reactivity state of neurons. Thus, it is likely that these agents are of fundamental importance for integrative functions of the nervous system and for the maintenance of synaptic activity, for example, providing for an extended period for temporal summation. The data trend toward a view that these agents produce alterations in neuronal reactivity by involvement of intracellular mediators and metabolic pathways that may result in long-term changes in membrane input resistance. Increased membrane input resistance, apparently mediated by protein phosphorylation reactions, has been related to acquisition and retention of learned behaviors in both vertebrate (Woody, 1984) and invertebrate (Alkon, Chapter 1, this volume) nervous systems. The similarities of the long-term effects on neuronal reactivity produced by both catecholamines and conditioning procedures may reflect activation of common intracellular mechanisms.

## ACKNOWLEDGMENTS

Unpublished data discussed in this chapter are from experiments done in collaboration with Dr. V. K. Gribkoff and C. A. Yarosh. This work was supported by NSF Research Grants PRM-8200575 and RII-8200575-01, and NIH BRSG-RR070101-17.

## REFERENCES

Ashe, J. H., & Libet, B. Modulation of slow postsynaptic potentials by dopamine, in rabbit sympathetic ganglion. *Brain Research*, 1981, *217*, 93–106. (a)

Ashe, J. H., & Libet, B. Orthodromic production of non-cholinergic slow depolarizing response in the superior cervical ganglion of the rabbit. *Journal of Physiology (London)*, 1981, *320*, 333–346. (b)

Ashe, J. H., & Yarosh, C. A. Differential and selective antagonism of the slow-inhibitory postsynaptic potential and slow-excitatory postsynaptic potential by gallamine and pirenzepine in the superior cervical ganglion of the rabbit. *Neuropharmacology*, 1984, *23*, 1321–1329.

Ashe, J. H., Yarosh, C. A., & Crawford, M. R. Ganglionic slow postsynaptic potentials and muscarinic asynchronous discharge in postganglionic nerve elicited by orthodromic stimulation. *Experimental Neurology*, 1983, *82*, 635–649.

Benardo, L. S., & Prince, D. A. Dopamine action on hippocampal pyramidal cells. *Journal of Neuroscience*, 1982, *2*, 415–423.

Bischoff, S., Bittiger, H., & Krauss, J. *In vivo* [$^3$H]spiperone binding to the rat hippocampal formation: Involvement of dopamine receptors. *European Journal of Pharmacology*, 1980, *68*, 305–315.

Bischoff, S., Scatton, B., & Korf, J. Biochemical evidence for a transmitter role of dopamine in the rat hippocampus. *Brain Research*, 1979, *165*, 161–165.

Bliss, T. V. P., Goddard, G. V., & Riives, H. Reduction of long-term potentiation in the dentate gyrus of the rat following selective depletion of monoamines. *Journal of Physiology (London)*, 1983, *334*, 475–491.

Brooks, C. McC. The development of our knowledge of the autonomic nervous system. In C. McC. Brooks, K. Koezumi, & A. Sato (Eds.), *Integrative functions of the autonomic nervous system*. Tokyo: University of Tokyo Press, 1979.

Browning, M., Dunwiddie, T., Bennett, W., Gispen, W., & Lynch, G. Synaptic phosphoproteins: Specific changes after repetitive stimulation of the hippocampal slice. *Science*, 1979, *103*, 60–62.

Brunelli, M., Castellucci, V., & Kandel, E. R. Synaptic facilitation and behavioral sensitization in Aplysia: Possible role of serotonin and cyclic AMP. *Science*, 1976, *194*, 1178–1181.

Castellucci, V. F., Kandel, E. R., Schwartz, J. H., Wilson, F. D., Nairn, A. C., & Greengard, P. Intracellular injection of the catalytic subunit of cyclic AMP-dependent protein kinase stimulates facilitation of transmitter release underlying behavioral sensitization in *Aplysia*. *Proceedings of the National Academy of Sciences, U.S.A.*, 1980, *77*, 7492–7496.

Daly, J. W., Hoffer, B. J., & Dismukes, R. K. Mechanisms of regulation of neuronal sensitivity. *Neuroscience Research Program Bulletin*, 1980, *18*, 325–456.

Dolphin, A., Hamont, M., & Bockaert, J. The resolution of dopamine and $B_1$ and $B_2$ – adrenergic sensitive adenylate cyclic activities in homogenates of cat cerebellum, hippocampus and cerebral cortex. *Brain Research*, 1979, *179*, 305–317.

Fletcher, W. H., & Byus, C. V. Direct cytochemical localization of catalytic subunits dissociated from cAMP-dependent protein kinase in reuber H-35 Lepatoma cells. I. Development and validation of fluorescinated inhibitor. *Journal of Cell Biology*, 1982, *93*, 719–726.

Freedman, R., Hoffer, B. J., Woodward, D. J., & Puro, D. Interaction of norepinephrine with cerebellar activity evoked by mossy and climbing fibers. *Experimental Neurology*, 1977, *55*, 269–288.

Fuxe, K., Agnati, L. F., Benfenati, F., Celeni, M., Zini, I., Zoli, M., & Mutt, V. Evidence for the existence of receptor–receptor interactions in the central nervous system: Studies on the regulation of monoamine receptors by neuropeptides. *Journal of Neural Transmission, Supplement*, 1983, *18*, 165–179.

Gold, P. E., Delanoy, R. L., & Merrin, J. Modulation of long-term potentiation by peripherally administered amphetamine and epinephrine. *Brain Research*, 1984, *305*, 103–107.

Gribkoff, V. K., & Ashe, J. H. Modulation by dopamine of population responses and cell membrane properties of hippocampal CA1 neurons *in vitro*. *Brain Research*, 1984, *292*, 327–338. (a)

Gribkoff, V. K., & Ashe, J. H. Modulation by dopamine of population spikes in area CA1 hippocampal neurons elicited by paired stimulus pulses. *Cellular and Molecular Neurobiology*, 1984, *4*, 177–183. (b)

Gribkoff, V. K., Ashe, J. H., Fletcher, W. H., & Lekawa, M. L. Dopamine, cyclic AMP, and protein kinase produce a similar long-lasting increase in input resistance in hippocampal CA1 neurons. *Society for Neuroscience Abstracts*, 1984, *10*, 898.

Hopkins, W. F., & Johnston, D. Frequency-dependent noradrenergic modulation of long-term potentiation in the hippocampus. *Science*, 1984, *226*, 350–352.

Hotson, J. R., Prince, D. A., & Schwartzkroin, P. A. Anomalous inward rectification in hippocampal neurons. *Journal of Neurophysiology*, 1979, *42*, 889–895.

Ishikawa, K., Ott, T., & McGaugh, J. L. Evidence for dopamine as a transmitter in dorsal hippocampus. *Brain Research*, 1982, *282*, 222–226.

Jork, R., deGraan, P. N. E., Van Dongen, C. J., Zwiers, H., Matthiews, H., & Gispen, W. H. Dopamine-induced changes in protein phosphorylation and polyphosphoinositide metabolism in rat hippocampus. *Brain Research*, 1984, *291*, 73–81.

Kasamatsu, T. Neuronal plasticity maintained by the central norepinephrine system in the cat visual cortex. In J. M. Sprague & A. N. Epstein (Eds.), *Progress in psychobiology and physiological psychology*. New York: Academic Press, 1983.

Kety, S. S. The biogenic amines in the central nervous system: Their possible role in arousal, emotion, and learning. In F. O. Schmitt (ed.), *The neurosciences: Second study program*. New York: Rockefeller University Press, 1970.

Kobayashi, H., Hashiguchi, T., & Ushiyama, N. S. Postsynaptic modulation of excitatory processes in sympathetic ganglia by cycle AMP. *Nature (London)*, 1978, *271*, 268–270.

Koketsu, K., Akasu, T., Miyagawa, M., & Hirai, K. Modulation of nicotinic transmission by biogenic amines in bullfrog sympathetic ganglia. *Journal of the Autonomic Nervous System*, 1981, *6*, 47–53.

Kuba, K., Kato, E., Kumamoto, E., Koketsu, K., & Hirai, K. Sustained potentiation of transmitter release by adrenaline and dibutyryl cyclic AMP in sympathetic ganglia. *Nature (London)*, 1981, *291*, 654–656.

Levy, W. B., & Steward, O. Synapses as associative memory elements in the hippocampal formation. *Brain Research*, 1979, *175*, 233–245.

Libet, B. Heterosynaptic interaction at a sympathetic neuron as a model for induction and storage of a postsynaptic memory trace. In G. Lynch, J. L. McGaugh, & N. M. Weinberger (Eds.), *Neurobiology of learning and memory*. New York: Guilford Press, 1984.

Libet, B., Kobayashi, H., & Tanaka, T. Synaptic coupling into the production and storage of a neuronal memory trace. *Nature (London)*, 1975, *258*, 155–157.

Marciani, M. G., Calabresi, P., Stanzione, P., & Bernardi, G. Dopaminergic and noradrenergic responses in the hippocampal slice preparation: Evidence for different receptors. *Neuropharmacology*, 1984, *23*, 303–307.

Nestler, E. J., & Greengard, P. Dopamine and depolarizing agents regulate the state of phosphorylation of protein I in the mammalian superior cervical sympathetic ganglion. *Proceedings of the National Academy of Sciences, U.S.A.*, 1980, *77*, 7479–7483.

Nestler, E. J., & Greengard, P. Nerve impulses increase the phosphorylation state of protein I in rabbit superior cervical ganglion. *Nature (London)*, 1982, *296*, 452–454.

Reader, T. A., Ferron, A., Descarries, L., & Jasper, H. H. Modulatory role for biogenic amines in the cerebral cortex: Microiontophoretic studies. *Brain Research*, 1979, *160*, 217–229.

Rowgaski, M. A., & Aghajanian, G. K. Modulation of lateral geniculate neurone excitability by noradrenaline microiontophoresis or locus coeruleus stimulation. *Nature (London)*, 1980, *289*, 731–734.

Sakakibara, M., Alkon, D. L., Lederhendler, I., & Heldman, E. $\alpha_2$-Receptor control of $Ca^{++}$ mediated reduction of voltage-dependent $K^+$ currents. *Society for Neuroscience Abstracts*, 1984, *10*, 950.

Scatton, B., Simon, H., LeMoal, M., & Bischoff, S. Origin of dopaminergic innervation of the rat hippocampal formation. *Neuroscience Letters*, 1980, *18*, 125–131.

Schröder, H., Kammerer, E., & Matthies, H. Biochemical evidence for dopaminergic transmission in the rat hippocampus. In C. Ajmone Marsan & H. Matthies (Eds.), *Neuronal plasticity and memory formation*. New York: Raven Press, 1982.

Schwab, M. E., Javay-Agrid, F., & Agrid, Y. Labeled wheat germ agglutinin as a newly, highly sensitive retrograde tracer in the rat brain hippocampal system. *Brain Research*, 1978, *152*, 145–150.

Seeman, P. Brain dopamine receptors. *Pharmacological Review*, 1982, *32*, 229–313.

Simon, H., LeMoal, M., & Calas, A. Efferents and afferents of the ventral tegmental AIO region studied after local injection of [$^3$H]leucine and horseradish peroxidase. *Brain Research*, 1979, *178*, 17–40.

Swanson, L. W., Teyler, T. J., & Thompson, R. F. Hippocampal long-term potentiation: Mechanisms and implications for memory. *Neuroscience Research Program Bulletin*, 1982, *20*(5), 617–769.

Weinberger, N. M., Diamond, D. M., & McKenna, T. M. Initial events in conditioning: Plasticity in the pupillomotor and auditory systems. In G. Lynch, J. L. McGaugh, & N. M. Weinberger (Eds.), *Neurobiology of Learning and Memory*. New York: Guilford Press, 1984.

Woody, C. D. Studies of Pavlovian eye-blink conditioning in awake cats. In G. Lynch, J. L. McGaugh, & N. M. Weinberger (Eds.), *Neurobiology of learning and memory*. New York: Guilford Press, 1984.

Wyss, J. M., Swanson, L. W., & Cowan, W. M. A study of subcortical afferents to the hippocampal formation in rat. *Neuroscience*, 1979, *4*, 463–476.

CHAPTER 7

# Nonlinear Systems Analysis and Its Application to Study of the Functional Properties of Neural Systems

**Theodore W. Berger**
**Robert J. Sclabassi**
University of Pittsburgh

The previous chapters have emphasized either the localization of specific sites within the nervous system that are altered as a result of behavioral conditioning (Alkon, Chapter 1, this volume; D. H. Cohen, Chapter 2, this volume; Greenough, Chapter 5, this volume) or the electrophysiological and behavioral impact of changes in synaptic efficacy that occur within a localized region of a brain structure (Barnes & McNaughton, Chapter 3, this volume; Abraham & Goddard, Chapter 4, this volume). In either case, the discussions have focused on changes in the functional properties of the elemental unit of brain systems, that is, the individual neuron. In contrast, we would like to concentrate on the functional properties of the brain system itself and address the specific issue of how the functional properties of the larger neural network are altered as a result of changes that occur in a subpopulation of its elements.

A second, common theme in the preceding chapters underscores the difficulty in assessing the impact of behavioral conditioning or high-frequency stimulation on the functional properties of neural networks. Specifically, what emerges as a principle from their findings is that experimental manipulations that result in synaptic plasticity produce, not a single form of plasticity at a single site within the brain, but instead, multiple forms at multiple sites. For example, D. H. Cohen (Chapter 2, this volume) presented evidence for changes in the CS-evoked responsiveness of neurons at several sites in the visual system of the pigeon. His data suggest that changes at each node in that system may be independent of each other, rather than simply reflecting the altered output of the neural element that is most peripheral. In addition, the data of Abraham and Goddard (Chapter 4, this volume) reveal that long-term potentiation (LTP) consists of changes in several characteristics of perforant path–dentate synaptic transmission that are relatively independent of one another. Furthermore, their results show that different components of LTP can have opposing functional consequences; that is, one effect of high-frequency stimulation increases the excitability of dentate granule cells, whereas a separate effect of the same stimulation appears to decrease their excitability. Thus, the general problem may be summarized as follows: If experimental manipulations result in changes in synaptic efficacy at several loci within a neural system and if these changes are qualitatively and quantitatively different, then predicting the resultant summary effect on total system output becomes a considerably more difficult task, demanding a more theoretically based experimental strategy.

We have been developing such an experimental strategy utilizing nonlinear systems analysis, which was originally developed within the disciplines of engineering and mathematics (Lee & Schetzen, 1965; Volterra, 1959; Wiener, 1958) and has been adopted for measuring the functional properties of neural systems (Krausz & Friesen, 1977; Marmarelis & McCann, 1973; Marmarelis & Naka, 1972; Sclabassi, Hinman, Kroin, & Risch, 1977; Sclabassi & Noreen, 1981; Sclabassi, Vries, & Bursick, 1982). We have extended the application of these methods to the study of the functional consequences of stimulation-induced neural plasticity within the mammalian hippocampus; in particular, the network of mono- and polysynaptic pathways that determine granule cell excitability (Berger, Balzer, Eriksson, & Sclabassi, 1984; Berger, Eriksson, Ciarolla, & Sclabassi, 1983; Sclabassi, Eriksson, & Berger, 1984). This chapter reviews selected aspects of this work to illustrate how the functional properties of a neural system or network can be characterized and how the parameters of that characterization are altered by the induction of LTP, a potent form of synaptic plasticity.

## EXPERIMENTAL AND THEORETICAL CONSIDERATIONS

All experiments were performed on male, New Zealand white rabbits that either were acutely prepared and maintained on halothane anesthesia or were chronically implanted with stimulation and recording electrodes. Experiments in chronically implanted animals were conducted while the animals were awake and mildly restrained. Axons of entorhinal cortical neurons (i.e., the perforant path) were stimulated with electrical impulses of 100-μsec duration while extracellular field potentials were recorded from the granule cell body layer of the dentate gyrus. Previous work of Andersen (Andersen, Bliss, & Skrede, 1971), Lømo (1971a), and others has established that short-duration, low-intensity stimulation of the perforant path (Figure 7.1A) results in a positive wave (Figure 7.1B) within the granule cell layer of the dentate gyrus, reflecting synaptic currents within dendritic processes. Higher intensity stimulation results in the development of a prominent

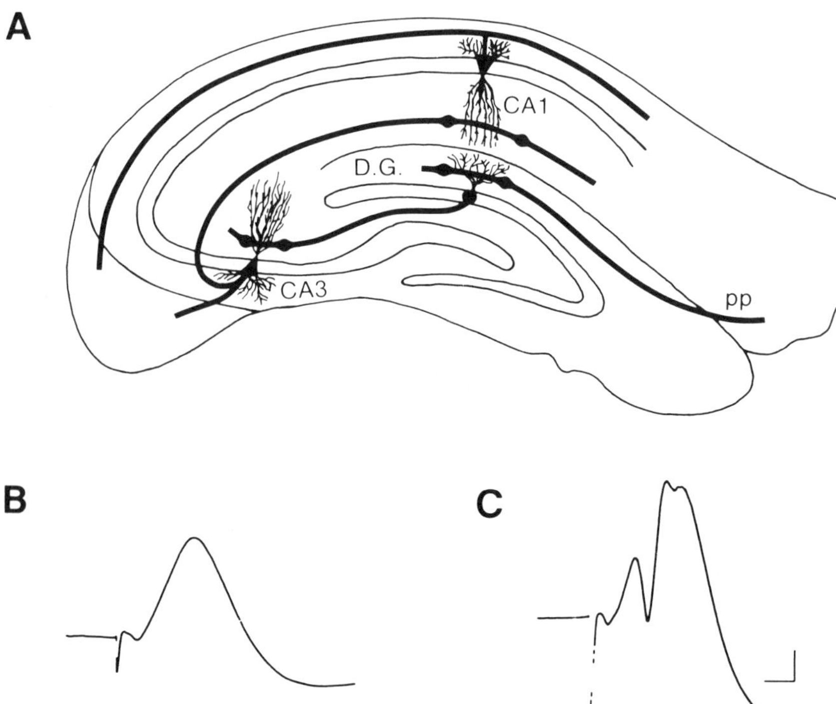


**FIGURE 7.1.** (A) Schematic of a cross-section through the hippocampus. For the experiments reported here, stimulating electrodes were implanted in the perforant path (pp) and a recording electrode was implanted in the cell body layer of the dentate gyrus (D.G.). (B) Positivity recorded in the dentate granule cell body layer reflecting synaptic events in the dendritic region evoked by low-intensity perforant path stimulation. (C) Negativity recorded in the dentate granule cell body layer reflecting action potential currents in response to suprathreshold perforant path stimulation. Calibrations: 200 μV and 2 msec.

negative wave (Figure 7.1C), called the population spike, that reflects the summed action potential currents of many granule cells. It is the amplitude of this population spike in response to impulse stimulation of the perforant path that we measured and analyzed.

The perforant path-dentate projection is known to be monosynaptic (Andersen, Holmqvist, & Voorhoeve, 1966; Lømo, 1971a). It is also known that a single stimulation impulse affects the excitability of dentate granule cells polysynaptically via several short- and long-loop feedback and feed-forward pathways (Andersen, Eccles, & Loyning, 1964; Andersen *et al.*, 1966; Beckstead, 1978; Fricke & Cowan, 1978; Sørensen & Shipley, 1979; Swanson & Cowan, 1977). Some of the more well established polysynaptic pathways are illustrated diagrammatically in Figure 7.2. The functional impact of these feedforward and feedback pathways can be assessed by testing the change in excitability of granule cells as a function of the interstimulus interval between a first stimulation impulse and a second, following impulse. This, of course, is the logic for the twin-impulse or paired-impulse paradigm that has been used extensively in the study of perforant path–dentate synaptic transmission (Andersen *et al.*, 1964; Lømo, 1971b). If we extend that logic to its limit, however, the functional impact of all possible feedforward and feedback pathways, known or unknown, can be measured with the use of a random stimulus train containing all possible pairs of stimulation impulses (as well as all possible triplets and so on). It was our thesis that the functional impact of all feedback and feedforward pathways could be assessed by applying a properly designed random stimulus train to the perforant path and analyzing the data in the appropriate fashion. Throughout the remainder of this text we shall use "perforant path–dentate system" to refer to the set of mono- and polysynaptic pathways that influence granule cell excitability. We shall use "perforant path–dentate synapse" to refer to the monosynaptic connection only.

It has been shown that when input to a system is allowed to vary randomly, the functional properties of the system can be represented by a functional power series. In this approach the transformational properties of the system are idealized as a stochastic transformation between the stimulus input, the random stimulus train, and the observed evoked neuroelectric

**FIGURE 7.2.** (A) Schematic of some of the major feedback pathways that are known to affect granule cell excitability in response to perforant path (pp) activation. comm., commissural connections. (B) In the experiments reported here we treated the network of mono- and polysynaptic pathways shown in A as a neural network or system and characterized that system output, $y(t)$, in response to random impulse stimulation, $x(t)$, of the perforant path (pp).

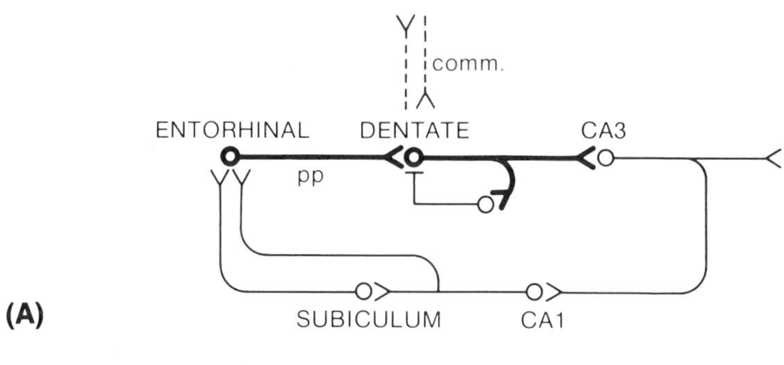


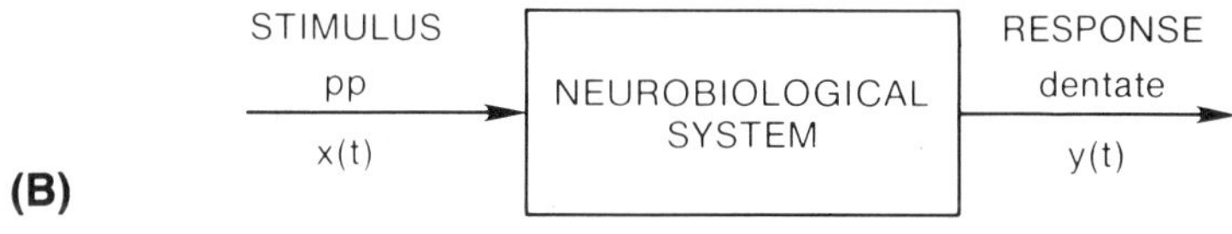

activity. In our case, the output, $y(t)$, of the perforant path–dentate system was approximated by a series of functionals, $G_i[h,x(t)]$, related to the random stimulus train input $x(t)$:

$$y(t) = G_0 + G_1[h_1,x(t)] + G_2[h_2,x(t)] + G_3[h_3,x(t)] + \ldots \quad (1)$$

where

$$G_0 = h_0 \quad (2)$$

$$G_1 = \int_0^\infty h(\tau)\, x(t - \tau)d\tau \quad (3)$$

$$G_2 = \iint_0^\infty h_2(\tau_1,\tau_2)\, x(t - \tau_1)\, x(t - \tau_2)d\tau_1,d\tau_2 \quad (4)$$

$$G = \iiint_0^\infty h_3(\tau_1,\tau_2,\tau_3)\, x(t - \tau_1)\, x(t - \tau_2)\, x(t - \tau_3)d\tau_1,d\tau_2,d\tau_3 + E \quad (5)$$

and $(G_i)$ is a set of mutually orthogonal functionals, $(h_i)$ is a set of symmetrical kernels that characterize the relationship between the input and output, and $E$ is an error term due to truncation. The kernels are obtained by the process of orthogonalization (Wiener, 1958) using the cross-correlation technique of Lee and Schetzen (1965) applied to a point process input (Krausz, 1975; Ogura, 1972) under the assumptions of stationarity and ergodicity.

The train of discrete stimulus impulses represented by $x(t)$ is a delta-function, the interevent intervals of which are drawn from an exponential distribution. The distribution of intervals in these experiments had a mean interval of 500 msec (2.0 Hz), with intervals ranging from 5 sec to 1msec (0.2 to 1000 Hz). A total of 4064 impulses were utilized in a stimulus train, and the stimulus intensity was held constant at a level that produced a population spike approximately 10–20% of maximum.

## LINEAR AND NONLINEAR CHARACTERISTICS OF SYNAPTIC TRANSMISSION IN THE PERFORANT PATH–DENTATE SYSTEM

Three characteristics of the perforant path–dentate system were examined in the present experiments (see Figure 7.3): (1) the linear responsiveness of the system represented by the first-order kernel, $h_1(\tau)$, which is obtained by averaging the field potentials over an observation period after each stimulation whether or not another impulse occurs during the observation period;

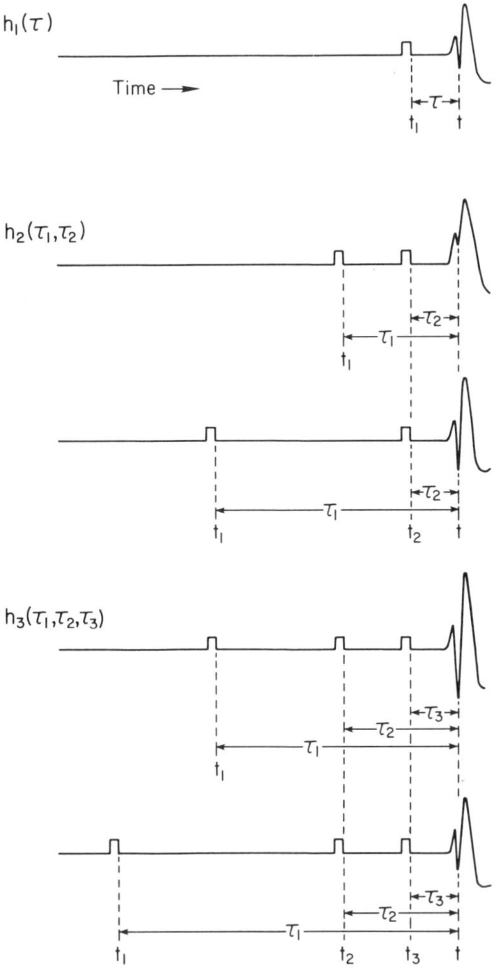


**FIGURE 7.3.** Diagrammatic representation of the measurement of first-order, $h_1$ ($\tau$), second-order, $h_2(\tau_1,\tau_2)$, and third-order, $h_3$ ($\tau_1,\tau_2,\tau_3$) interactions between stimulation impulses on granule cell population spike amplitude. $h_1$ reflects the average population spike amplitude sampled at time $t$ after all 4064 impulses in the random train. $h_2$ measures variation in population spike amplitude to an impulse occurring at $t_2$ as a result of a preceding impulse at $t_1$. $h_3$ measures variation in population spike amplitude to an impulse occurring at $t_3$ as a result of preceding impulses at $t_1$ and $t_2$. Thus, even when $\tau_2$ is equal for two different triplets of stimulation impulses, differences in the interval represented by $\tau_1$ may influence spike amplitude.

(2) the modulatory influence of a previous impulse on the activity evoked by the current stimulus whether or not other impulses occur between the two, represented by the second-order kernel, $h_2(\tau_1,\tau_2)$; and (3) the modulatory influence of any pair of preceding intervals on the activity evoked by the most current stimulus, represented by the third-order kernel $h_3(\tau_1,\tau_2,\tau_3)$,

independent of whether or not other impulses occur during the preceding intervals.

Because in these experiments we limited our analysis to amplitude of the population spike, $h_1$ is quite similar to the averaged population spike amplitude of all 4064 impulses in the train. If the perforant path–dentate system were linear with respect to stimulation interval such that population spike amplitude was dependent only on stimulus intensity, then spike amplitude to each impulse in the train would be equivalent except for variation due to uncontrolled variables (i.e., changes in the excitability of other afferents to dentate granule cells). An example of $h_1$ computed on data collected from a chronically implanted animal is seen in the top panel of Figure 7.4A. Note that, as expected, the value of $h_1$ is significantly non zero only at postimpulse latencies consistent with monosynaptic activation of dentate granule cells.

From past work by others using paired-impulse techniques, we know that perforant path–dentate synaptic transmission is influenced by the preceding stimulus as a function of the interstimulus interval (Andersen *et al.*, 1964; Lømo, 1971b). This modulatory influence is by definition nonlinear; that is, the resultant response to the paired stimuli cannot be predicted by the superposition of the response to the same two stimuli administered in isolation of one another. These nonlinearities are evident in the second-order kernel, $h_2$, an example of which is given in Figure 7.4B for the same data set utilized to calculate $h_1$. These values have been normalized relative to the peak value for $h_1$, so that percentage variation in population spike amplitude is plotted as a function of the interval from the population spike to the first impulse of the pair. Note that at short interstimulus intervals, the population spike is completely inhibited for intervals as long as 50 msec. At interstimulus intervals of 50 to approximately 325 msec, there is a dramatic facilitation of population spike amplitude that reached 75% in this preparation. Beyond 325 msec, the perforant path–dentate system demonstrates no modulatory activity to preceding impulses in the second-order kernel; that is, the system responds in a linear fashion.

The second-order kernel may be conceived of as a recovery function (Sclabassi, Hinman, Kroin, & Risch, in press); that is, the first impulse of a pair of impulses perturbates the perforant path-dentate system and the second impulse tests the time course, direction, and magnitude of the effects of the numerous short-loop and long-loop pathways activated by the first impulse. The response of granule cells to the second impulse thus provides a measure of the system recovery to the preperturbation state. It is possible, however, that the particular recovery function derived from a pair of impulses is dependent on the stimulation interval that precedes that impulse pair; that is, the functional properties of the perforant path–dentate system may be described accurately not by one recovery function but instead by a family of conditional recovery functions. Each recovery function would be conditional on the stimulation interval preceding the pair of impulses that measures second-order interactions. The third-order kernel, $h_3$, is calculated

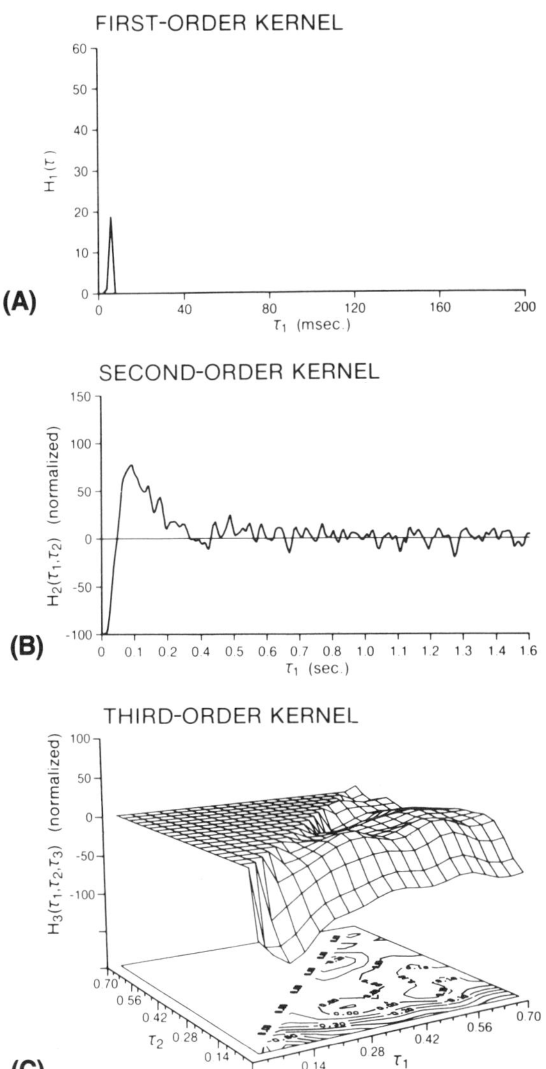


**FIGURE 7.4.** First-, second-, and third-order kernels computed from granule cell population field potentials recorded in response to random train stimulation of the perforant path. All data were recorded before long-term potentiation (LTP) was induced. Only population spike amplitudes were used in these computations.

to test the latter hypothesis. In calculating $h_3$, the data sets of $h_1$ and $h_2$ are used to predict dentate granule cell response to three impulses. As shown in Figure 7.3, amplitude of the population spike to the most recent impulse may be predicted using $h_1$, and alterations in that $h_1$ predicted by the intervals $\tau_1$ and $\tau_2$ using $h_2$. If amplitude of the population spike deviates significantly from that prediction, then the system in question exhibits third-order nonlinearities; that is, computation of a family of conditional recovery functions is necessary to accurately describe the system response, and the second-order kernel calculated from all 4064 impulses in the train represents an average of that family of conditional recovery functions.

We have found that the perforant path–dentate system exhibits significant third-order nonlinearities. An example of a third-order kernel computed from the same data used to compute $h_1$ and $h_2$ described earlier is shown in Figure 7.4C. Figure 4 shows a two-dimensional plot of $h_3$ values normalized relative to the peak $h_1$ value as a function of both $\tau_1$ and $\tau_2$. (Because we restrict $\tau_2$ always to be less than $\tau_1$, only half of the graphic space is utilized). First note that most of the third-order interactions result in smaller population spike amplitudes than would be predicted from the first- and second-order kernels; that is, most of the $h_3$ values are negative. Second, note that significant third order interactions occur in relation to three ranges of intervals. The most obvious set involves intervals of $\tau_2$ = 35–105 msec. When $\tau_2$ = 35–105 msec, amplitude of the population spike is significantly reduced regardless of the value of $\tau_1$. For these intervals of $\tau_1$ and $\tau_2$, amplitude of the population spike can be reduced as much as 60%. The second set of intervals involves cases when $\tau_1$ and $\tau_2$ are nearly equivalent. Thus, for many of the points along the diagonal of the three-dimensional graph, $h_3$ values are again negative. For these cases, population spike amplitude can be up to 40% below the peak $h_1$ value. The third set of intervals involves deviations from $\tau_1$ and $\tau_2$ predictions that are smaller in magnitude but, nevertheless, consistently seen across preparations. For this particular preparation, $\tau_1$ intervals ranging from 350 to 735 msec in combination with $\tau_2$ intervals ranging from 105 to 385 msec produce facilitative third-order interactions equivalent to 5–20% of the peak $h_1$ value. Data we are currently collecting strongly suggest that the nature of second- and third-order interactions in this system varies as a function of the mean frequency and intensity of stimulation. Although the latter must await further corroboration, it suggests that the description of second- and third-order kernels given here must eventually be parameterized by those two variables. A summary of the current stage of our analysis is that (1) the perforant path–dentate system is highly nonlinear at certain stimulation intervals; (2) those nonlinearities exist both with respect to the preceding interval of stimulation and with respect to the two preceding intervals of stimulation; and (3) third-order interactions occur in response to remarkably long stimulation intervals, for example, 700 msec.

## THE EFFECT OF LTP ON PEFORANT PATH–DENTATE SYSTEM RESPONSE

With this as a description of system characteristics, we next asked how these system properties might be altered by an experimental manipulation that induces synaptic plasticity in one or more of the system elements.

Although our ultimate interest is in behavioral conditioning as that experimental manipulation, we first used high-frequency stimulation that is known to produce LTP. These experiments were conducted on the same animals used to obtain data about the normal characteristics of perforant path–dentate synaptic transmission described earlier, so each animal served as

**FIGURE 7.5.** First-, second-, and third-order kernels computed from granule cell population field potentials recorded in response to random train stimulation of the perforant path. All data were recorded from the same animal shown in Figure 7.4, but after LTP was induced.

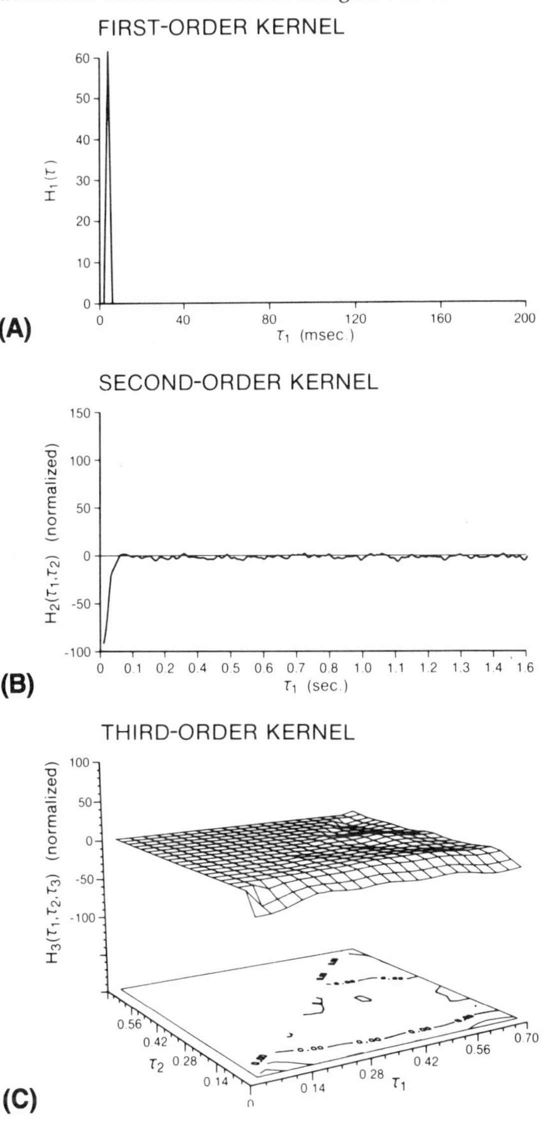

its own control. High-frequency stimulation (at least 10 trains of 400 Hz, 20-msec duration) was given over the course of 2–3 days following the last random impulse train delivery used to obtain baseline data. The perforant path then was stimulated using random impulse trains at the same intensity used before LTP was induced. Results for the first-, second-, and third-order kernels are shown in Figure 7.5.

It was predicted that LTP would increase the peak amplitude of $h_1$ because LTP is evidenced by an increase in amplitude of the population spike to the same stimulation intensity used prior to high-frequency stimulation. This was found to be the case and can be seen in Figure 7.5A as a 200% increase in the peak value of $h_1$. The latency at which the peak $h_1$ value occurs is also decreased after LTP. The second- and third-order kernels, however, were also significantly altered. In $h_2$, whereas inhibition of the population spike still occurs at short intervals of stimulation, virtually no facilitation is seen at longer intervals. Before LTP, the perforant path–dentate system in this preparation does not respond linearly until intervals of stimulation reach approximately 325 msec. After LTP, however, the system responds linearly at intervals greater than approximately 70 msec. Thus, LTP significantly reduces the range of stimulation intervals to which the system responds in a nonlinear fashion. Likewise, LTP virtually abolishes third-order interactions. As shown in the bottom panel of Figure 7.5, facilitative third-order interactions do not exceed 5% of the peak $h_1$ value for any combination of $\tau_1$ and $\tau_2$ intervals. Inhibitory third-order interactions do not exceed 10% except for a restricted range of intervals that includes $\tau_1$ = 35–140 msec and $\tau_2$ = 35–105 msec. Thus, before LTP, at least the two preceding intervals must be used to accurately predict granule cell output. After LTP, however, only magnitude of the preceding interval is needed to predict the system response.

## THE FUNCTIONAL IMPACT OF A REDUCTION IN PERFORANT PATH–DENTATE SYSTEM NONLINEARITIES

High-frequency stimulation of perforant path fibers produces a dramatic change in the response characteristics of the network of neurons influenced by perforant path–dentate synaptic connections. That change can be summarized as an increase in the linearity and a decrease in the nonlinearity of the system response to interstimulus interval. As a result, post-LTP granule cell excitability is much less dependent on stimulation interval and thus relatively more dependent on stimulus intensity. From this perspective, high-frequency stimulation of perforant path fibers results in a neural network that varies in output only in response to changes in one dimension of the input—stimulus intensity—whereas prior to high-frequency stimulation, system output varies in response to changes in two dimensions of the input—stimulus intensity and interstimulus interval. Restated, the post-

LTP neural system still transmits information with respect to stimulus intensity, but transmits much less, if any, information with respect to interstimulus interval. This characterization of the effects of high-frequency stimulation is not meant to minimize the functional significance of the enhancement of perforant path–granule cell synaptic efficacy that originally characterized LTP. Instead, we wish to emphasize that, at least for the perforant path–dentate system, the enhancement of one dimension of system output—amplification or gain—occurs at the expense of another dimension of system output—frequency responsiveness.

Whether this combination of changes in system properties enhances or degrades the mnemonic function normally performed by the hippocampus, and thus positively or negatively affects learned behavior, is an empirical question. We have recently shown that inducing LTP in the perforant path–dentate synapse enhances the rate at which naive animals subsequently learn a classical conditioning task (Berger, 1984). However, Barnes and McNaughton (see Chapter 3, this volume) have found that when LTP is induced in animals previously trained on a maze task, subsequent reversal learning is disrupted. Thus, hippocampal LTP apparently can have either beneficial or deleterious effects on learned behavior depending on the task requirements. While the hippocampus may play a mnemonic role during both types of learning, these differences in LTP's behavioral effects may reflect the fact that during classical conditioning tasks the perforant path–dentate system normally functions with high gain and increased linearity but that during operant maze learning tasks a different set of system characteristics predominates. As a result, inducing one set of system characteristics would be facilitative for one class of learned behaviors (e.g., classical conditioning) and yet disruptive for another class (e.g., maze learning).

Although admittedly speculative, this line of reasoning suggests a dynamic characterization of brain system function. Stable environmental variables are likely to have a significant influence on the properties of a neural system through the profile of extrinsic activity to that system (e.g., Winson, 1980). As a result, the same set of neural elements may have different transformational capabilities in different environmental settings. Not only will the stimuli impinging on an organism be different across learning tasks, but the manner in which the neural representations of those stimuli are transformed may also be different. If this speculation is supported, both single cell activity and the system properties that form the "context" for single cell responses must be considered in characterizing the role of brain systems in learning.

## ACKNOWLEDGMENTS

This research was supported by grants from The Whitaker Foundation and NIMH (MH00343).

## REFERENCES

Andersen, P., Bliss, T. V. P., & Skrede, K. K. Unit analysis of hippocampal population spikes. *Experimental Brain Research*, 1971, *13*, 208–221.

Andersen, P., Eccles, J. C., & Loyning, Y. Location of postsynaptic inhibitory synapses on hippocampal pyramids. *Journal of Neurophysiology*, 1964, *27*, 592–607.

Andersen, P., Holmqvist, B., & Voorhoeve, P. E. Entorhinal activation of dentate granule cells. *Acta Physiologica Scandinavica*, 1966, *66*, 448–460.

Beckstead, R. M. Afferent connections of the entorhinal area in the rat as demonstrated by retrograde cell-labeling with horseradish peroxidase. *Brain Research*, 1978, *152*, 249–264.

Berger, T. W. Long-term potentiation of hippocampal synaptic transmission affects rate of behavioral learning. *Science*, 1984, *224*, 627–630.

Berger, T. W., Balzer, J. R., Eriksson, J. L., & Sclabassi, R. J. Long-term potentiation alters nonlinear characteristics of hippocampal perforant path–dentate synaptic transmission. *Society for Neuroscience Abstracts*, 1984, *10*, 1047.

Berger, T. W., Eriksson, J. L., Ciarolla, D. A., & Sclabassi, R. J. Non-linear systems analysis of perforant path–dentate synaptic transmission in the hippocampus. *Society for Neuroscience Abstracts*, 1983, *9*, 220.

Fricke, R., & Cowan, W. M. An autoradiographic study of the commissural and ipsilateral hippocampo-dentate projections in the adult rat. *Journal of Comparative Neurology*, 1978, *181*, 253–270.

Krausz, H. I. Identification of nonlinear systems using random impulse train inputs. *Biological Cybernetics*, 1975, *19*, 217–230.

Krausz, H. I., & Friesen, W. O. The analysis of nonlinear synaptic transmission. *Journal of General Physiology*, 1977, *70*, 243–265.

Lee, Y. W., & Schetzen, M. Measurement of the kernels of a non-linear system by cross-correlation. *International Journal of Control*, 1965, *2*, 237–254.

Lømo, T. Patterns of activation in a monosynaptic cortical pathway: The perforant path input to the dentate area of the hippocampal formation. *Experimental Brain Research*, 1971, *12*, 18–45. (a)

Lømo, T. Potentiation of monosynaptic EPSPs in the perforant path–dentate granule cell synapse. *Experimental Brain Research*, 1971, *12*, 46–63. (b)

Marmarelis, P. Z., & McCann, G. D. Development and application of white-noise modeling techniques for studies of insect visual nervous systems. *Kybernetik*, 1973, *12*, 74–89.

Marmarelis, P. Z., & Naka, K.-I. White noise analysis of a neuron chain: An application of the Wiener theory. *Science*, 1972, *175*, 1276–1278.

Ogura, H. Orthogonal functionals of the poisson process. *IEEE Transactions on Information Theory*, 1972, *IT-18*, 473–481.

Sclabassi, R. J., Eriksson, J. L., & Berger, T. W. Nonlinear characteristics of hippocampal perforant path–dentate synaptic transmission are different for synaptic and action potential currents. *Society for Neuroscience Abstracts*, 1984, *10*, 1047.

Sclabassi, R. J., Hinman, C. L., Kroin, J. S., & Risch, H. The modulatory effect of prior input upon afferent signals in the somatosensory system. *Proceedings of the Joint Automatic Control Conference, IEEE*, 1977, *12*, 787–795.

Sclabassi, R. J., Hinman, C. L., Kroin, J. S., & Risch, H. A. A nonlinear analysis of afferent modulatory activity in the cat somatosensory system. *Electroencephalography and Clinical Neurophysiology*, in press.

Sclabassi, R. J., & Noreen, G. K. The characterization of dual-input evoked potentials as nonlinear systems using random impulse trains. *Proceedings of the Pittsburgh Modeling and Simulation Conference*, 1981, *12*, 1123–1130.

Sclabassi, R. J., Vries, J. K., & Bursick, D. M. Somatosensory evoked potentials to random stimulus trains. *Annals of the New York Academy of Sciences*, 1982, *388*, 695–701.

Sørensen, K. E., & Shipley, M. T. Projections from the subiculum to the deep layers of the ipsilateral presubicular and entorhinal cortices in the guinea pig. *Journal of Comparative Neurology*, 1979, *188*, 313–334.

Swanson, L. W., & Cowan, W. M. An autoradiographic study of the organization of the efferent connections of the hippocampal formation in the rat. *Journal of Comparative Neurology*, 1977, *172*, 49–84.

Volterra, V. *Theory of functionals and of integral and integro-differential equations*. New York: Dover Publications, 1959.

Wiener, N. *Nonlinear problems in random theory*. New York: Wiley, 1958.

Winson, J. Influence of raphe nuclei on neuronal transmission from perforant path through dentate gyrus. *Journal of Neurophysiology*, 1980, *44*, 937–950.

CHAPTER 8

# Involvement of Hippocampal Systems in Learning and Memory

**Sam A. Deadwyler**
Bowman Gray School of Medicine
Wake Forest University

## CELLULAR BASIS OF LEARNING AND THE MAMMALIAN BRAIN

The issue of learning and memory at the cellular level in the mammalian brain has been investigated now for over 20 years and there have been significant advances in this area (Kandel & Spencer, 1968; Thompson, Berger, & Madden, 1983). It now appears as though mammalian nerve cells can, in fact, learn. However, whether or not the manner in which the brain analyzes and stores information is the same as occurs in cellular models of learning distinguishes to some extent the theoretical biases of researchers in the field. Some investigators (Alkon, Chapter 1, this volume) suggest that the cellular mechanisms shown to be operative in "simpler" invertebrate systems could subserve the same functions in the mammalian brain although, admittedly, the interactions would be much more iterative and complex. The more recent *in vitro* brain slice techniques have yielded a different set of candidate processes that could lead to the same changes in cellular physiology (Barrionuevo & Brown, 1983; Lynch & Baudry, 1984; Skrede & Malthe-Sorenssen, 1981). Whether or not similar or different mechanisms are the basis of learning at the cellular level in the mammalian brain and in simpler nervous systems appears to be an open question.

The issue of cellular learning in the mammalian brain has also been attacked at a morphological level. The evidence seems clear that plastic changes in synaptic structure can be obtained by a number of manipulations that also produce functional changes (Desmond & Levy, 1983; Fifkova & Anderson, 1981; Fifkova & Van Harreveld, 1977; Greenough, 1984; Lee, Schottler, Oliver, & Lynch, 1981). Evidence that is rapidly accumulating indicates that synaptic changes of the type discussed by Greenough (1984, and Chapter 5, this volume) represent the basis for behavioral changes observed following these manipulations.

There are, however, discrepancies in the current literature regarding the pre- and/or postsynaptic nature of altered cellular physiology produced during behavioral conditioning. Changes in ion channel permeability represent the critical events for cellular learning in simpler systems (Alkon, Lederhendler, & Shoukimas, 1982; Klein, Shapiro, & Kandel, 1980; Siegelbaum, Camardo, & Kandel, 1982), whereas the findings in vertebrate models seem to emphasize a change in synapse formation or alteration in existing synaptic structure as the basis for neurophysiological change accompanying mammalian behavioral plasticity and learning (Lynch & Baudry, 1984). To resolve these differences, perhaps one could assume that the structural changes observed in the mammalian brain during various environmental and behavioral manipulations are coupled to the same membrane processes that produce alterations in membrane conductances during associative learning in simpler systems. Alternatively, as Greenough (1984) suggested, it may be the case that structural changes of the type exhibited by mammalian brain systems do not occur in the simpler models of associative learning because they are not required.

A third possibility suggests that modification of cellular events could occur at many places along the appropriate neural circuits in the brain and eventually lead to a convergence of conditioned stimulus (CS) and unconditioned stimulus (US) modified impulse flow at different locations in a central processing network. D. H. Cohen (Chapter 2, this volume) asserts that it is unlikely that a single locus or set of neural processes that is totally responsible for training-induced changes at the cellular level will be identified in vertebrate brains. Cardiac conditioning in the pigeon produces multiiple changes along the CS and US pathways (D. H. Cohen, 1982). In this system, the CS and US appear to activate specialized target neurons within the learning circuit of the pigeon, but the process seems to be biased toward activation by the US. The system, therefore, has specialized node points of modifiability although other linkages in the circuit may be less plastic. The question is, How can these regions be identified? And what are their critical features? As Cohen suggests, the number of possible combinations of cellular interactions rapidly grows into the unmanageable range for vertebrate models of learning. Thus, although attempts to directly apply invertebrate models of cellular learning to the vertebrate brain are attractive, the levels of analysis necessary to locate and identify similar mechanisms *in vivo* are not currently available.

## CELLULAR PLASTICITY AND INFORMATION STORAGE IN THE HIPPOCAMPUS

A widely held opinion of most researchers in the learning and memory field is that the hippocampus is critically involved in the storage and/or retrieval of information in the mammalian brain. More specifically, it has been suggested that the hippocampus and related limbic structures participate in the formation of associative connections necessary for some types of learning and memory. Two lines of experimental evidence have been instrumental in providing the basis for these assumptions. The first is the human literature, which suggests that the hippocampus is required for the retention of information relevant to the occurrence of events in the immediate past (N. J. Cohen & Squire, 1980; Squire, 1981; Squire, Cohen, & Nadel, 1984). The current status of this position is discussed by N. Cohen (Chapter 22, this volume) and Weiskrantz (Chapter 21, this volume). The second type of evidence implicating hippocampus in memory is the emergence of studies in animals in which associative learning and cognitive-like processes appear to be coded by hippocampal unit discharges that have been shown to reflect both the spatial and temporal aspects of learning and performance (cf. O'Keefe & Nadel, 1978; Thompson, 1982).

Although cellular plasticity may be necessary for information storage in the mammalian brain, it is unlikely that this would be sufficient in the case of hippocampal involvement in human memory formation. In simpler systems, appropriate pairing of the CS and US seems to be adequate to produce sustained changes in neuronal mechanisms subserving behavioral conditioning. However, in more complex vertebrate brain models, additional criteria appear to be necessary. Abraham and Goddard (1983, and Chapter 4, this volume) have shown that in the hippocampus different types of information might be stored in different ways by the same cell populations, depending upon the patterning and intensity of activity within the input pathways.

## ROLE OF HIPPOCAMPAL LTP IN LEARNING AND MEMORY

If long-term potentiation (LTP) can be demonstrated in other neural structures (Brown & McAfee, 1982; Gerren & Weinberger, 1983; Lee, 1983) and in other species (Lewis, Teyler, & Shashoua, 1981), what is its *specific* role in relation to hippocampal influences in learning and memory? Long-term potentiation *per se,* therefore, may not be critical for learning and memory, but certain structures with intrinsic cell populations in which LTP can be generated would be critical. Thus, hippocampal LTP may be unique because of the functional nature of the synaptic circuitry for producing it and not simply because hippocampal synapses can be artificially (electrically) induced to exhibit LTP. The question reduces to a distinction between LTP as a process that is utilized naturally by certain key structures with the appropriate circuitry (i.e., hippocampus) and LTP as a phenomenon that many disparate brain cells display when subjected to LTP-like stimulation.

A second consideration is whether the cellular plasticity illustrated by LTP, even though long lasting, is the "substrate" for memories formed by associative conditioning processes. In examining this question in detail, two factors must be considered. First, what is the process mimicked by the LTP experimental manipulation with regard to the functional change at the synapse or membrane structure of the cell. That is, can a neural process be identified that, when activated by naturally occurring stimuli, produces changes that are quantitatively as well as qualitatively similar to those effected by LTP? The current status of knowledge regarding this issue suggests that certain neurophysiological features of LTP correlate with learning (Berger, 1984), but there is little evidence indicating that LTP has actually been induced by or is the basis for the behavioral changes produced during associative conditioning.

Barnes and McNaughton (Chapter 3, this volume) report that LTP "saturation" did not affect place responding that was already learned but rather disrupted acquisition of new place learning. The reason for the difference in effects of LTP stimulation was attributed to the differential nature of the two tasks—the one that required acquisition of new place responding, according to Barnes and McNaughton, also required more information storage "capacity," hence LTP saturation disrupted acquisition of the new response more than performance of the old response.

An alternative explanation could account for this result by assuming that the one type of memory may be more susceptible to disruption by saturable LTP stimulation than the other. Because it has been known for some time that hippocampal pathways show variation in synaptic efficacy during different behavioral states (Winson & Abzug, 1978), the effectiveness of LTP stimulation in the aforementioned task should be assessed in terms of background variability produced by the behavioral change. Under these conditions, it cannot be assumed that behavior has no influence on LTP, even though the opposite is being tested. As with any other brain–behavior correlate, the role of LTP must be analyzed within well-controlled testing situations in which the chance of the behavior acting back to influence LTP is minimized.

## SIMILARITIES AND DIFFERENCES BETWEEN LTP AND CONDITIONED CELLULAR CHANGES

How is LTP, if it is the basis of learning at the cellular level, generated in successful (Berger & Orr, 1982; Thompson, 1982; Woody, 1984) mammalian associative conditioning paradigms? How is the critical pattern of afferent neural activity required to produce LTP generated within each system? These questions point out several contrasts relative to the observed effects of conditioning and LTP generation on single hippocampal cells (Berger, 1982).

According to Alkon (Chapter 1, this volume) classical conditioning of the nictitating membrane produces a change in calcium conductance in hippocampal cells when measured *in vitro*, a change that results in potassium channel inactivation and an increase in both excitatory postsynaptic potential

(EPSP) amplitude and membrane resistance measured with somal electrodes. Associative LTP produced in the *in vitro* hippocampal slice does not produce detectable postsynaptic changes of this type (Barrionuevo & Brown, 1983). The increased EPSP amplitude produced by associative LTP was most likely due to increased synaptic efficacy (pre- or postsynaptic) at distant dendritic sites that was undetectable by a somal electrode (Brown & Johnston, 1983). It is puzzling, therefore, why *in vivo* conditioning would promote changes that cannot be mimicked by *in vitro* LTP-stimulation techniques—unless possibly the two processes (LTP and conditioning) are not the same.

Associative conditioning paradigms require presentation of stimuli in pairs, with critical intervals between the CS and US to induce cellular changes *in vivo*. Long-term potentiation, is the result of high-frequency activity in a critical number of input fibers (McNaughton, 1983). Unless one assumes that the "cooperativity" among input fiber populations is analogous to some degree with "associative activation" of pre- or postsynaptic elements produced by CS–US pairings, the relationship between LTP and the successful conditioning paradigm is not isomorphic. If we are to assume that LTP does underlie learning at the cellular level in the hippocampus or any other structure, it will be necessary to examine in much more detail the synaptic activity within convergent afferent pathways that are critical for producing conditioned postsynaptic changes to establish whether they satisfy criteria for producing LTP.

## HETEROSYNAPTIC INTERACTION DURING LEARNING AND MEMORY

It seems logical that the plasticity underlying learning and memory reflect both decreased and increased synaptic and cellular excitability. Synapses within the hippocampus have been shown to increase and decrease in efficacy as well as remain unaltered following several types of physiological manipulations (Abraham & Goddard, 1983; Andersen, Sundberg, Sveen, Swann, & Wigström, 1980; Levy & Steward, 1979; Lynch, Dunwiddie, & Gribkoff, 1977). An important requirement, therefore, would appear to be the *precision* with which such synaptic and cellular changes are produced if they are to serve as the biological substrates of associative learning and memory.

It is frequently implicit in most discussions of LTP that the biochemical or biophysical events that underlie the neurophysiological correlates of LTP are themselves the representations of sensory events made significant during learning. In this regard, it may be more productive when considering hippocampal involvement in such processes to determine how other synaptic mechanisms in addition to LTP (i.e., depression, posttetantic potentiation, facilitation, inhibition) participate in memory storage and retrieval. There are a number of different ways in which such elemental synaptic and cellular processes could be integrated to provide stable ongoing representations of mammalian experiences without assuming a long-term unalterable change in efficacy of one set of synapses.

Abraham and Goddard's (1983, see also Chapter 4, this volume) analyses of extracellular events accompanying different patterns and intensities of stimulation suggest that the input characteristics of the signal will produce differing types of cellular and synaptic "traces" that could account for many more of the neural phenomena associated with behavioral aspects of learning and memory than LTP alone (i.e., "forgetting," short-term or intermediate memory). Similarly, the work of Levy and Steward (1983) suggests that fluctuations in neural transmission within specific hippocampal cell populations will be dynamically regulated by changing patterns of afferent input activity (see also Levy, Brassel, & Moore, 1983). It therefore seems reasonable to assume that all identified hippocampal synaptic processes are at one time or another involved in processing of sensory information during learning.

## INFORMATION PROCESSING WITHIN A HIPPOCAMPAL PATHWAY

A necessary step in the analysis of the relevance of LTP for learning and memory would be to determine whether or not hippocampal circuitry exhibits long-term synaptic changes during the establishment and performance of sensory discrimination learning. This approach provides the means of investigating hippocampal activity with relevance to the issues of (1) the nature of the sensory information transmitted to the hippocampus, (2) determination of the rule(s) tht govern how this information is selected, and, perhaps more important, (3) how such information is processed. In this section, some recent findings pertaining to these issues will be discussed.

Animals were trained to make an auditory discrimination as evidenced by selective responding in the presence of a tone stimulus. Individual tone-evoked potentials (EPs) were recorded from the outer molecular layer of the dentate gyrus in the region of perforant path terminals and averaged over 50–100 trials (Deadwyler, West, & Robinson, 1981a). The averaged tone-evoked potential from the outer molecular layer (OM AEP) exhibited a characteristic waveform, which included two prominent negative components labeled $N_1$ and $N_2$ (Figure 8.1). Past investigations have shown that the $N_1$ component reflects activity conveyed via connections between the entorhinal cortex and hippocampus and that the $N_2$ component is modulated by afferent input from the medial septal nucleus (Deadwyler, West, & Robinson, 1981a, 1981b). Behavioral control of the OM AEP has been documented by the fact that both components are differentially altered during acquisition and extinction of a single-tone discrimination task (Deadwyler *et al.*, 1981a, 1981b).

In contrast, during differential (successive) two-tone discrimination learning and performance, the OM AEP exhibits more complex changes

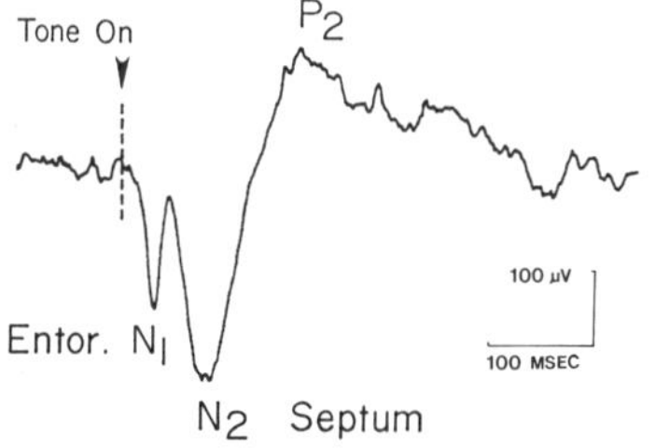


**FIGURE 8.1.** Representative 50-trial average tone-evoked potential recorded from the outer molecular layer of the dentate gyrus (OM AEP) during tone discrimination learning. $N_1$ and $N_2$ are the two negative components that have been previously shown to be mediated via projections from entorhinal cortex (Entor.) or the medial septal nucleus (Septum).

(West, Christian, Robinson & Deadwyler, 1982). Averages across all 50 negative (nonreinforced) tone trials within a 100-trial session revealed OM AEPs that do not differ in amplitude or waveform from averages of the remaining 50 positive (reinforced) tone trials, even though behavioral performance with respect to both tones is highly differentiated (Deadwyler, 1982). These findings suggest that more subtle factors than merely the associated reward values of the individual tone stimuli controlled the amplitudes of the $N_1$ and $N_2$ components of the OM AEP. This was confirmed following sequential analyses of the trial-to-trial fluctuations in the OM AEP, which showed that during criterion behavioral performance the $N_1$ component of the potential displayed a high degree of within-session amplitude variability (Deadwyler, 1982; West *et al.*, 1982). Systematic computer sorts of OM AEPs based upon the preceding pattern or sequence of positive and negative trials revealed that the amplitude fluctuation of the $N_1$ component was tightly regulated and followed a definable principle (Deadwyler, West, & Christian, 1982; West *et al.*, 1982). The preceding sequence of trials controlled more than 90% of the variance in the amplitude of $N_1$, while $N_2$ remained relatively stable across the same trial sequences (Figure 8.2).

From such analyses, four important features of the data provided insight into the nature of processes regulating the magnitude of the sensory-evoked potentials recorded in the dentate gyrus. First, the adequate stimulus for increasing $N_1$ amplitude was the negative (nonreinforced) stimulus whereas the positive (reinforced) stimulus produced a reduction in $N_1$. Second, the

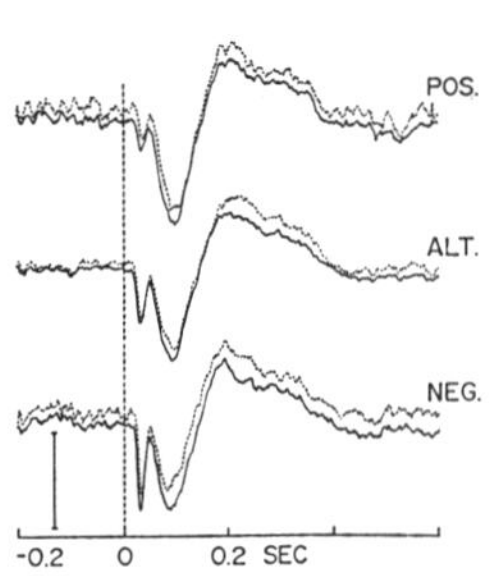


**FIGURE 8.2.** Sequence-dependent fluctuations in $N_1$ component of the OM AEP during criterion performance of two-tone differential discrimination learning. OM AEPs are averaged according to sequences of runs of positive and negative trials preceding the trial on which individual evoked potentials occurred. During positive (POS) trial sequences, $N_1$ was small; $N_1$ was intermediate during alternating sequences (ALT) and largest during negative (NEG) trial sequences. The three OM AEPs were constructed by averaging and normalizing unique trials sorted on the basis of prior runs of two to five similar trials or trials that were preceded by only alternating sequences. Dotted curves represent standard errors. Calibration: 300 µV.

$N_1$ amplitude changes associated with or conditioned to the tone stimuli did not occur on the same trial in which the potential was evoked by the tone stimulus; the effect was delayed until the occurrence of the tone on the next trial (West *et al.*, 1982). Third, there was a monotonic increase or decrease in the amplitude of $N_1$ as a function of the number of trials following a run of similar trials. Finally, single alternating positive and negative trials produced $N_1$ amplitudes that were midway between the extremes effected by runs of positive or negative trials (Figure 8.2).

The preceding analyses revealed a strong tendency for the $N_1$ component amplitude to vary in accordance with the preceding trial sequence. However, the rule by which the $N_1$ amplitude changes were regulated could not be determined unless the pattern of transition between the run series and alternating series could also be described. It was therefore necessary to sort and average individual EPs on the basis of all possible combinations of five trial sequences preceding the trial on which the potential was evoked by the tone stimulus. The computer program employed sorted, averaged, and normalized individual tone-evoked potentials into 32 different categories representing each possible preceding five-trial combination of positive and negative tones. Because each five-trial combination could also be associated with (i.e., elicited by) a positive or negative tone on the current trial, a total of 64 possible unique OM AEPs representing each preceding five-trial combination was required to reconstruct the trial-by-trial sequential dependency.

Figure 8.3 shows the entire data set of traces for one animal as an array of sequence-coded, normalized OM AEPs displayed as a three-dimensional

**FIGURE 8.3.** The entire set of 64 OM AEPs obtained from sorting each trial on the basis of its unique preceding five-trial sequence. The OM AEPs were amplitude ranked and plotted relative to the combined cumulative probability of a negative trial within the preceding sequence of five trials. The 64 combinations result from $2^5$ possible combinations of positive and negative trials within the preceding sequence increased by a factor of 2 to account for whether a positive or negative tone occurred on the current trial (see text).

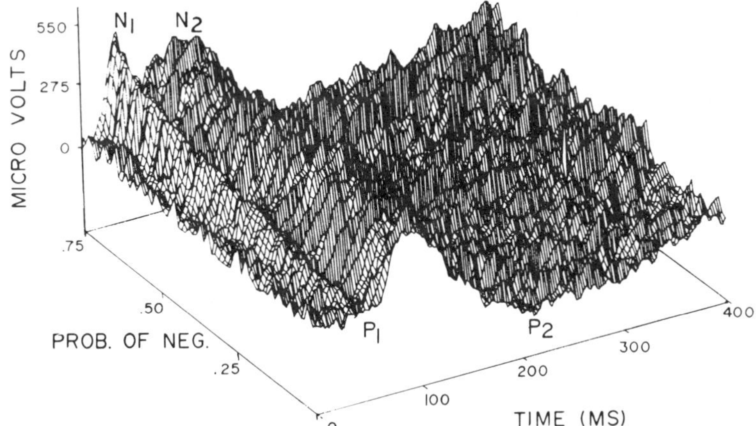

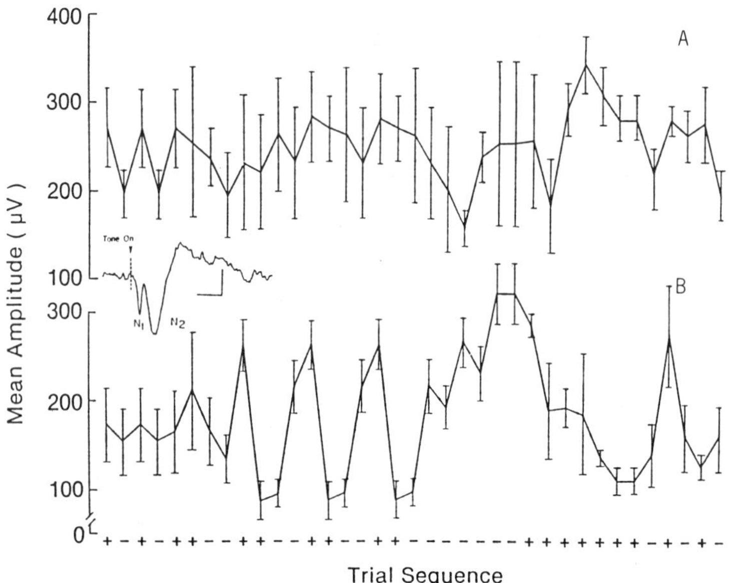


**FIGURE 8.4.** Variation in amplitude of $N_1$ and $N_2$ components of the OM AEP as a function of trial sequence. (A) $N_2$ amplitude fluctuation shows no significant relationship to the trial sequence plotted on the abscissa. (B) $N_1$ amplitude fluctuations during the same sequence. Note large oscillations in $N_1$ during double alternation series. Bars represent *SEM*.

surface in which the amplitude of $N_1$ and $N_2$ are shown as peaks and the positive $P_1$ and $P_2$ waves as valleys. The potentials are ranked according to $N_1$ amplitude (low-to-high), and the Z-axis is labeled with the corresponding maximal range of cumulative probability of a negative trial within the five-trial sequence that preceded each potential. It is clear that $N_1$ amplitude was closely related to the likelihood of a negative trial predicted by the prior sequence. Figure 8.3 also indicates that $N_2$ amplitude did not change systematically as a function of either sequence or variation in $N_1$ amplitude (Z-axis).

Data from four different animals were sorted and categorized in the preceding manner. It was then possible to serially reconstruct sequential changes in the OM AEP component amplitudes for any series of trials utilizing these 64 unique five-trial combinations for each animal. Figure 8.4 depicts one such reconstruction. Mean $N_2$ (A) and $N_1$ (B) amplitudes are plotted serially as a function of a specified 37-trial sequence (bottom axis). Whereas $N_2$ amplitude variation was not significantly correlated with any specific feature of the sequence of trials.[1] $N_1$ amplitude varied dramatically

1. The large standard errors in this plot result from the fact that $N_2$ amplitudes were not normalized across animals as percentage changes. Peak amplitudes were plotted in this manner to illustrate the uniformity relative to $N_2$ (A) of $N_1$ (B) amplitude changes across different animals.

in conjunction with certain aspects of the same trial sequence. Runs of three or more like trials produced $N_1$ components that were at the extreme maximum or minimum amplitude ranges depending upon whether the run included positive or negative trials. Single alternation trial sequences produced $N_1$ amplitudes intermediate between these two extremes (Deadwyler *et al.*, 1982; West *et al.*, 1982).

An unexpected finding resulting from such reconstructions was the potency of double alternating trial sequences. When a repeating series of double alternating trials was reconstructed, the repetition set up near-maximal oscillations in $N_1$ amplitude (Figure 8.4). The changes in $N_1$ amplitude during both double alternating sequences and runs of three or more like trials were highly significant by two-way ANOVA ($F_{3,9} = 10.01$, $p < 01$; and $F_{4,12} = 14.96$, $p < .001$, respectively).

These investigations showed that the preceding pattern or sequence of trials significantly affected the amplitude of auditory-evoked potentials recorded in the dentate gyrus. On the basis of previous studies in which destruction of the entorhinal cortex eliminated the $N_1$ component in the OM AEP (Deadwyler, 1982; Deadwyler *et al.*, 1981a), it is very likely that the sequential dependency of the $N_1$ amplitude is determined in part by changes in perforant path synaptic input. This assumption was confirmed by obtaining direct measures of perforant path excitability on the same trials in which tone-evoked potentials were recorded. In these experiments, the perforant path was stimulated 200 msec prior to the onset of the tone stimulus, and extracellular monosynaptic perforant path field potentials were recorded from the same electrode as the OM AEP. The field potentials were sorted, averaged, and normalized in the same manner as the OM AEPs (Foster, Hampson, & Deadwyler, 1984). Perforant path field potentials showed relatively small but significant fluctuations in peak amplitude during the same trial sequences as the $N_1$ component. Figure 8.5 indicates that perforant path field potentials exhibited near-maximum peak amplitude changes associated with single and double alternating trial sequences simultaneously with similar changes in the $N_1$ component of the OM AEP recorded on the same trials.

Although the fluctuations in the field potential amplitudes were not large (10–20% of the 2 mV total amplitude), the range of amplitude changes (100–400 $\mu$V) were within the mean maximum and minimums exhibited by the $N_1$ component of the OM AEP (Figure 8.4). This indicates that if a change in synaptic efficacy was the basis of the $N_1$ amplitude fluctuation then only a small percentage of the electrically activated perforant path synapses were affected. These results suggest two possibilities: (1) that not all perforant path fibers carry auditory information, or (2) that only a small proportion of the possible number of perforant path synapses are affected by sequential influences on any given trial.

The relative contribution of each trial position in the preceding sequence to the total amplitude of $N_1$ was determined by systematically averaging

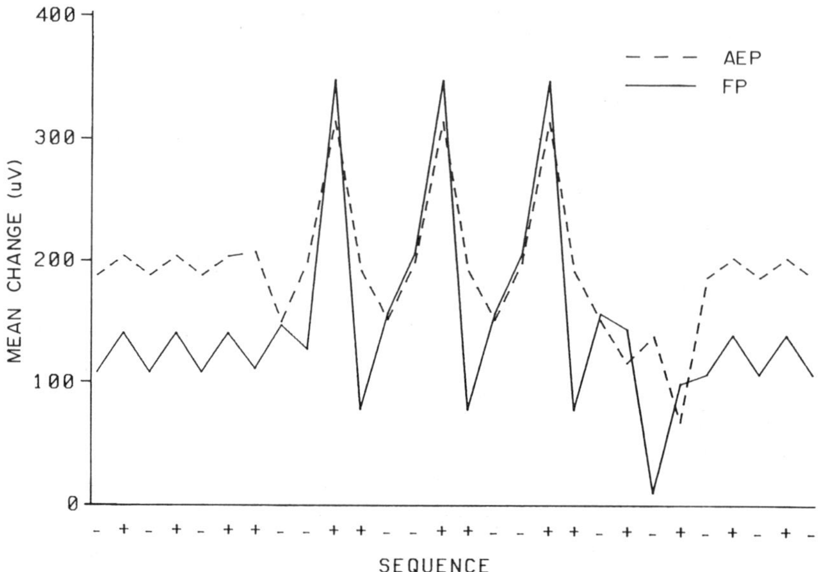


**FIGURE 8.5.** Simultaneous variation in mean OM AEP (AEP) and perforant path field potential (FP) amplitudes as a function of single and double alternating trial sequences. Perforant path field potentials were elicited 200 msec prior to tone onset.

OM AEPs with similar sequences following elimination of positions two through five in the sequence. The results are shown in Figure 8.6. Reducing the number of trials in the preceding trial sequence from five to one produced a 20–40% reduction in $N_1$ amplitude during a run of all negative trials. Clearly, the first or most recent trial in the sequence had the largest influence on $N_1$ amplitude. The second through fifth trials in the sequence contributed proportionately less to $N_1$ amplitude. However, the fact that the fifth trial showed an increase in two of the four animals indicates that time elapsed since the current trial was not the only determinant of the sequential dependency. Analyses with other types of trial sequences suggests different magnitudes of recency influence for each trial position (Hampson, West, Christian, Foster, & Deadwyler, 1984).

## WHAT IS HIPPOCAMPAL MEMORY?

These findings indicate that sensory information is transmitted to the hippocampus via the perforant path under strict regulation by an endogenous synaptic "filter-like" process that is heavily biased by the context of successively experienced events. This process can best be described in the rat as an updateable "buffer" with a moderately limited capacity (five to six trials). The relative influence of each successive position in the buffer in relation to sensory input on the current trial may differ under different behavioral circumstances, but preliminary evidence suggests recency as the major determinant. Because these changes in hippocampal electrophysiology are dissociated from ongoing behavioral processes, they cannot be viewed as consequences of behavioral state changes (Winson & Abzug, 1978) nor alterations in the manner in which the tone stimuli are presented to the animal.

Several features of this model incorporate contemporary hypothesized characteristics of hippocampal function. These characteristics include contextual representation and retrieval of sensory stimuli (Hirsh, 1980), de-

**FIGURE 8.6.** Relative contribution of each trial in the preceding sequence to $N_1$ amplitude during runs of five negative trials. Each line indicates a separate animal ($n$ = 4). Trial 1 represents the most recent relative to the current trial on which the potential was recorded, trial 2 the next successively removed in time, and trial 5 the most remote in time.

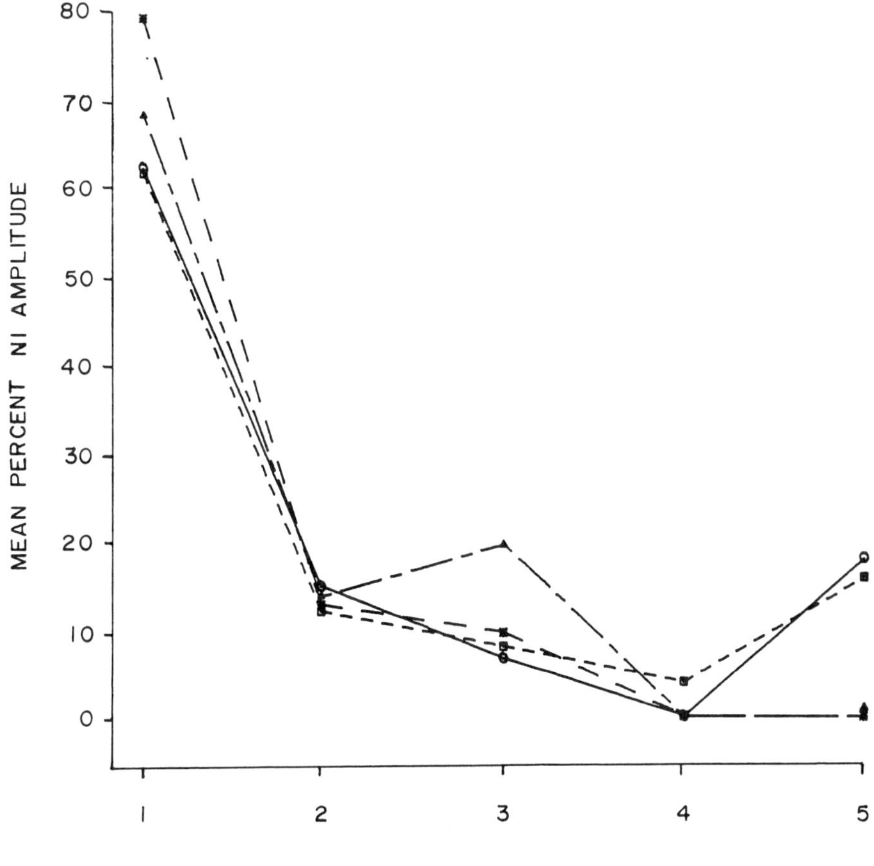

clarative or episodic memory (Kinsborne & Wood, 1975; Squire & Cohen, 1984), working memory (Olton & Feustle, 1981), serial learning dependency (Kesner, 1982), "attentional tuning" (Solomon, 1980), and "experience expectant" information storage (Greenough, 1984).

Within the behavioral paradigm used here, there was little chance for spatial information to be of any significance in determining the fluctuations in the $N_1$ component and perforant path field potential amplitudes. This suggests that the hippocampus processes nonspatially significant sensory information differently from the spatial contexts hypothesized by O'Keefe and Nadel (1978). There are, however, common aspects of hippocampal involvement in spatial and nonspatial memory that are subserved by the model. The first is that representations of sensory events in the hippocampus will be heavily biased by short-lasting temporal as well as the perceptual contexts in which behaviorally relevant stimuli are encountered (Marr, 1971). This view agrees with those presented by Rescorla (Chapter 12, this volume) and MacKintosh (Chapter 19, this volume) with respect to what animals learn and remember within laboratory experimental conditioning paradigms. The second way in which the model accounts for hippocampal function in memory is through the trial-to-trial flexibility of the perforant path synapses. Rather than preserving information for long-term storage, the synapses seem primed to accurately change efficacy to conform to the stimulus context experienced in the present and immediate past (Hirsh, 1980). From a cognitive viewpoint, the latter function would be in keeping with the capacity of the mammalian brain to deal with moment-to-moment fluctuations in the stimulus environment while at the same time extracting critical contiguities (associations) among sensory events to determine future actions.

## ACKNOWLEDGMENTS

The contributions of Robert Hampson and Tom Foster to many facets of the research reported in this chapter are greatly appreciated. The efforts of Sonia Stitcher in helping to prepare the manuscript are also appreciated. Supported by NIH Grants NS18288, DA02048, and DA03502.

## REFERENCES

Abraham, W. C., & Goddard, G. V. Asymmetric relations between homosynaptic long-term potentiation and heterosynaptic long-term depression. *Nature (London)*, 1983, *305*, 717–719.

Alkon, D. L., Lederhendler, I., & Shoukimas, J. J. Primary changes of membrane currents during retention of associative learning. *Science*, 1982, *215*, 693–695.

Andersen, P., Sundberg, S. H., Sveen, O., Swann, J. W., Wigström, H. Possible mechanisms for long-lasting potentiation of synaptic transmission in hippocampal slices from guinea-pigs. *Journal of Physiology (London)*, 1980, *302*, 463–482.

Barrionuevo, G., & Brown, T. H. Associative long-term potentiation in hippocampal slices. *Proceedings of the National Academy of Sciences, U.S.A.*, 1983, *80*, 7347–7357.

Berger, T. W. Hippocampal cellular plasticity induced by classical conditioning. In L. W. Swanson, T. Teyler, & R. F. Thompson (Eds.), *Neuroscience research program bulletin*. Cambridge, Mass.: MIT Press, 1982.

Berger, T. W. Long-term potentiation of hippocampal synaptic transmission affects rate of behavioral learning. *Science*, 1984, *224*, 627–630.

Berger, T. W., & Orr, W. B. Hippocampectomy selectively disrupts discrimination reversal conditioning of the rabbit nictitating membrane response. *Behavioral Brain Research*, 1982, *8*, 49–68.

Brown, T. H., & Johnston, D. Interpretation of voltage-clamp measurements in hippocampal neurons. *Journal of Neurophysiology*, 1983, *50*, 464–486.

Brown, T. H., & McAfee, D. A. Long-term synaptic potentiation in the superior cervical ganglion. *Science*, 1982, *215*, 1411–1413.

Cohen, D. H. Central processing time for a conditioned response in a vertebrate model system. In C. R. Woody (Ed.), *Conditioning: Representation of involved neural functions*. New York: Plenum Press, 1982.

Cohen, N. J., & Squire, L. R. Preserved learning and retention of patterned analyzing skill in amnesia: Dissociation of knowing how and knowing that. *Science*, 1980, *210*, 207–209.

Deadwyler, S. A. The functional basis of LTP in the behaving animal. Sensory evoked potentials in the dentate gyrus. In L. Swanson, T. Teyler, & R. Thompson (Eds.), *Neurosciences research program bulletin*. Cambridge, Mass.: MIT Press, 1982.

Deadwyler, S. A., West, M. O., & Christian, E. P. Neural activity in the dentate gyrus of the rat during the acquisition and performance of simple and complex sensory discrimination learning. In C. Woody (Ed.), *Conditioning: Representation of involved neural functions*. New York: Plenum Press, 1982.

Deadwyler, S. A., West, M. O., & Robinson, J. H. Entorhinal and septal inputs differentially control sensory-evoked responses in the rat dentate gyrus. *Science*, 1981, *211*, 1181–1183. (a)

Deadwyler, S. A., West, M. O., & Robinson, J. H. Evoked potentials from the dentate gyrus during auditory stimulus generalization in the rat. *Experimental Neurology*, 1981, *71*, 615–624. (b)

Desmond, N. L., & Levy, W. B. Synaptic correlates of associative potentiation/depression: An ultrastructural study in the hippocampus. *Brain Research*, 1983, *265*, 21–30.

Fifkova, E., & Anderson, C. L. Stimulation-induced changes in dimensions of stalks of dendritic spines in the dentate molecular layer. *Experimental Neurology*, 1981, *74*, 621–627.

Fifkova, E., & Van Harreveld, A. Long-lasting morphological changes in dendritic spines of dentate granular cells following stimulation of the entorhinal area. *Journal of Neurocytology*, 1977, *6*, 211–230.

Foster, T. C., Hampson, R. E., & Deadwyler, S. A. Sequential dependencies regulate sensory evoked potentials and perforant path field potentials in the dentate gyrus. *Society for Neuroscience Abstracts*, 1984, *10*, 124.

Gerren, R. A., & Weinberger, N. M. Long-term potentiation in the magnocellular medial geniculate nucleus of the anesthetized cat. *Brain Research*, 1983, *265*, 138–142.

Greenough, W. T. Structural correlates of information storage in the mammalian brain: A review and hypothesis. *Trends in NeuroScience*, 1984, *7*, 229–233.

Hampson, R. E., West, M. O., Christian, E. P., Foster, T. C., & Deadwyler, S. A. Principal component analyses of sensory evoked potentials in the dentate gyrus of the rat. *Society for Neuroscience Abstracts*, 1984, *10*, 1141.

Hirsh, R. The hippocampus, conditional operations and cognition. *Physiological Psychology*, 1980, *8*, 175–182.

Kandel, E. R., & Spencer, W. A. Cellular neurophysiological approaches in the study of learning. *Physiological Review*, 1968, *48*, 68–134.

Kesner, R. Serial position curve in rats: Role of dorsal hippocampus. *Science*, 1982, *218*, 173–174.

Kinsbourne, M., & Wood, F. Short-term memory processes and the amnesic syndrome. In D. Deutsch, & J. A. Deutsch (Eds.), *Short-term memory*. New York: Academic Press, 1975.

Klein, M., Shapiro, E., & Kandel, E. R. Synaptic plasticity and the modulation of the $Ca^{2+}$ current. *Journal of Experimental Biology*, 1980, *89*, 117–157.

Lee, K. S. Sustained modification of neuronal activity in the hippocampus and neocortex. In W. Seifert (Ed.), *Neurobiology of the hippocampus*. New York: Academic Press, 1983.

Lee, K. S., Schottler, F., Oliver, M., & Lynch, G. Brief bursts of high-frequency stimulation produce two types of structural change in rat hippocampus. *Journal of Neurophysiology*, 1981, *44*, 247–258.

Levy, W. B., Brassel, S. E., & Moore, S. D. Partial quantification of the associative synaptic learning rate of the dentate gyrus. *Neuroscience*, 1983, *8*, 799–808.

Levy, W. B., & Steward, O. Synapses and associative memory elements in the hippocampal formation. *Brain Research*, 1979, *175*, 233–245.

Levy, W. B., & Steward, O. Temporal contiguity requirements for long-term associative potentiation/depression in the hippocampus. *Neuroscience*, 1983, *8*, 791–797.

Lewis, D., Teyler, T., & Shashoua, V. Development of long-term potentiation in the *in vitro* goldfish optic tectum. *Society for Neuroscience Abstracts*, 1981, *7*, 66.

Lynch, G. L., & Baudry, M. The biochemistry of memory: A new and specific hypothesis. *Science*, 1984, *224*, 1057–1063.

Lynch, G. L., Dunwiddie, T., & Gribkoff, V. Heterosynaptic depression: A post-synaptic correlate of long-term potentiation. *Nature (London)*, 1977, *266*, 737–739.

Marr, D. Simple memory: A theory of archicortex. *Philosophical Transactions of the Royal Society of London*, 1971, *262*, 23–85.

McNaughton, B. L. Activity dependent modulation of hippocampal synaptic efficacy: Some implications for memory processes. In W. Seifert (Ed.), *Neurobiology of the hippocampus*. New York: Academic Press, 1983.

O'Keefe, J., & Nadel, L. *The hippocampus as a cognitive map*. Oxford: Oxford University Press, 1978.

Olton, D. S., & Feustle, W. A. Hippocampal function required for nonspatial working memory. *Experimental Brain Research*, 1981, *41*, 380–389.

Siegelbaum, S. A., Camardo, J. S., & Kandel, E. P. Serotonin and cyclic AMP close single $K^+$ channels in *Aplysia* sensory neurones. *Nature (London)*, 1982, *299*, 413–417.

Skrede, K. K., & Malthe-Sorenssen, D. Increased resting and evoked release of transmitter following repetitive electrical tetanization in hippocampus: A biochemical correlate of longer lasting synaptic potentiation. *Brain Research*, 1981, *208*, 436–441.

Solomon, P. R. A time and place for everything? Temporal processing views of hippocampal function with special reference to attention. *Physiological Psychology*, 1980, *8*, 254–261.

Squire, L. R. Two forms of amnesia: An analysis of forgetting. *Journal of Neuroscience*, 1981, *1*, 635–640.

Squire, L. R., & Cohen, N. J. Human memory and amnesia. In G. Lynch, J. L. McGaugh, & N. M. Weinberger (Eds.), *Neurobiology of learning and memory*. New York: Guilford Press, 1984.

Squire, L. R., Cohen, N. J., & Nadel, L. The medial temporal region and memory consolidation. In H. Weingartner & E. Parker (Eds.), *Memory consolidation*. Hillsdale, N.J.: Erlbaum, 1984.

Thompson, R. F. Training-induced increase in hippocampal unit activity. In L. W. Swanson, T. Teyler, & R. F. Thompson (Eds.), *Neuroscience research program bulletin*. Cambridge, Mass.: MIT Press, 1982.

Thompson, R. F., Berger, T. W., & Madden, J., IV Cellular processes of learning and memory in the mammalian CNS. *Annual Review of Neuroscience*, 1983, *6*, 447–491.

West, M. O., Christian, E. P., Robinson, J. H., & Deadwyler, S. A. Evoked potentials in the dentate gyrus reflect the retention of past sensory events. *Neuroscience Letters*, 1982, *28*, 319–324.

Winson, J., & Abzug, C. Neuronal transmission through hippocampal pathways dependent on behavior. *Journal of Neurophysiology*, 1978, *41*, 716–732.

Woody, C. R. Studies of Pavlovian eye-blink conditioning in awake cats. In G. Lynch, J. L. McGaugh, & N. M. Weinberger (Eds.), *Neurobiology of learning and memory*. New York: Guilford Press, 1984.

CHAPTER 9

# Morphological Changes in the Hippocampal Formation Accompanying Memory Formation and Long-Term Potentiation

**J. Wenzel**
Humboldt University
Berlin, GDR

**H. Matthies**
Medical Academy
Magdeburg, GDR

The investigation of processes connected with learning and memory formation is one of the most fascinating and difficult fields of neurobiology. Among various theories of learning and memory processes today, we favor the storage of information by changes in the interneuronal connectivity within the neuronal network (D. H. Cohen, Chapter 2, this volume; Eccles, 1972; Hebb, 1949; Matthies, 1974, 1981; Wenzel, Kammerer, Frotscher *et al.*, 1977; Wenzel, Kammerer, Kirsche *et al.*, 1977; Wenzel *et al.*, 1980).

In studying memory formation, we are confronted with the problem of information storage brain circuitries and thus of morphofunctional structure, which we choose to define by number and properties of its elements as well as of their mutual relations. The acquisition and consolidation of a new behavior resulting in a more or less permanent memory trace necessitate the activity and functional change of a large number of cells in many structures of the brain, particularly in the hippocampus and the neocortex. It can be assumed that a series of events takes place before the permanent trace has been formed, each of which is characterized by a particular molecular or cellular mechanism, by its time course, and by its reaction to various chemical and physiological influences. In this connection the plastic properties of the nervous tissue have to be taken into consideration.

It is widely assumed that short- and long-term plastic processes are based on changes in synaptic efficiency or synaptic connectivity and can be related to either presynaptic or postsynaptic mechanisms. Long-term memory storage, however, most probably depends on macromolecular synthesis and transport, necessary for the production of material to be newly incorporated into synaptic structures in order to permanently change their functional properties (and efficiency) and leading in the end to a modified pattern of connectivity in neuronal circuitries (Matthies, 1974, 1981; Rosenzweig, Bennett, & Flood, 1982; Thompson, Berger, & Madden, 1983; Wenzel, David, Pohle, Marx, & Matthies, 1975).

As discussed in several earlier chapters (Barnes & McNaughton, Chapter 3, this volume; Abraham & Goddard, Chapter 4, this volume; Greenough, Chapter 5, this volume), the mechanisms underlying memory formation and long-term potentiation (LTP) are quite possibly closely related. Long-term potentiation can be elicited by brief trains of high-frequency stimulation, delivered to monosynaptic pathways in the hippocampus; and it consists of an increase in the amplitude of evoked potentials, lasting for several hours or even days. It provides an interesting and suitable model for analyzing permanent changes in the synaptic efficiency of the type that might well form the neuronal substrate for learning and memory (Bliss & Dolphin, 1982). At present, a complete understanding of the underlying mechanisms for the LTP is still lacking, although some progress has been made in identifying physiological and biochemical events that in sum generate the LTP effect (Alger & Teyler, 1976; Andersen, Sundberg, Sveen, Swann, & Wigström, 1980; Baudry & Lynch, 1980, 1981, 1982; Dolphin, Errington, & Bliss, 1982; Duffy, Teyler, & Shashoua, 1981; Krug, Lössner, & Ott, 1984; Lynch & Baudry, 1984; Lynch, Halpain, & Baudry, 1982; Lynch, Kessler, & Baudry, 1984; McNaughton, Douglas, & Goddard, 1978; Shashoua & Teyler, 1982). There also exists a considerable body of evidence that LTP involves structural changes in synapses (Chang & Greenough, 1984; Desmond & Levy, 1983; Fifkova, Anderson, Young, & Van Harreveld, 1982; Fifkova & Van Harreveld, 1977; Lee, Oliver, Schottler, & Lynch, 1981; Lee, Schottler, Oliver, & Lynch, 1980; Moshkow, Petrovskaia, & Bragin, 1980; Van Harreveld & Fifkova, 1975, as discussed by Greenough, Chapter 5, this volume).

In this chapter we shall briefly review some recent work from our laboratory that directly bears on the models discussed in the preceding paragraph. It was the aim of our studies to test for possible structural changes in synapses and neurons as morphological correlates of the memory formation and LTP in rat brains. We particularly concentrated on the following questions:

1. Is there any relationship between the acquisition of a new behavior and changes in the synaptic connectivity, for example, by a *de novo* formation of synapses?
2. Is the memory formation process accompanied by changes in protein synthesis?
3. Does long-term potentiation result in permanent morphologically detectable changes in the ultrastructure of synapses?

4. Is the phenomenon of LTP accompanied by changes in protein synthesis systems as well?

To solve these problems we used three different methodological approaches: First, to study the effects of learning and memory formation on neuronal ultrastructure, we trained rats on a foot shock-motivated, brightness-discrimination task in a Y-shaped maze and examined the hippocampus. Second, to generate the long-term potentiation effect, we used high-frequency stimulation of the perforant path fibers, recorded from an electrode in the molecular layer of the fascia dentata, and examined the tissue up to 48 hours later. Third, in hippocampal slices, the LTP phenomenon was generated by high-frequency stimulation of the Schaffer–commissural fibers and recorded from CA1 neurons. The tissue was investigated at 15 and 75 minutes following the stimulation.

## RIBOSOMAL SYSTEMS AND SYNAPSES IN THE HIPPOCAMPUS DURING LEARNING BEHAVIOR

A brightness discrimination in a semiautomatic Y-maze served as the training paradigm. This required the rats to learn—against their instinctive behavior—to run into the illuminated alley of the maze to avoid a foot shock. The training was considered successful when the rats responded correctly after each of five successive changes of the position of the illuminated alley during a mean period of training of 45 minutes. As active controls we used rats that performed the same number of trials and received the same number of punishments as trained animals. Naive (untrained) rats of the same age and weight from the same strain served as passive controls.

Autoradiographic and radiochemical studies on the incorporation of RNA and protein precursors during learning showed that trained animals had a significantly increased incorporation of tritium-labeled material and an enchanced incorporation of labeled fucose into hippocampal glycoproteins (Pohle & Matthies, 1974; Popov, Pohle, Rüthrich, Schulzeck, & Matthies, 1976; Popov, Rüthrich, Pohle, Schulzeck, & Matthies, 1976; Matthies 1981).

The electron microscopic investigations of the brains comprised quantitative anlyses of the distribution of ribosomes in the cytoplasm of CA1 and CA3 neurons of hippocampus 70 minutes following training and morphometrical investigations on the number and various parameters of the synapses in CA1 and CA3 (at 70 minutes, 24 hours, and 14 days following training). The quantitative evaluation of the ribosomes gave the following results (Figure 9.1): The total number of ribosomes in both CA1 and CA3 increased significantly over the passive and active controls—by 18% in CA1 and 17% in CA3 cells. From these results we can conclude that the quantitative increase in ribosomal units, especially of the polysomes and membrane-bound ribosomes, reflects a true enhancement of the protein synthesis. Our

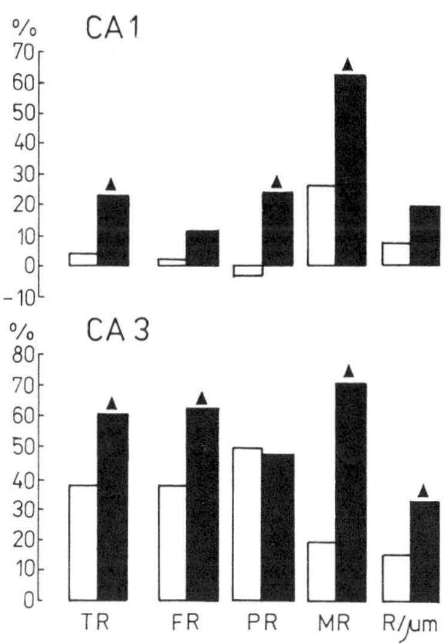


**FIGURE 9.1.** Increase of ribosomes in CA1 and CA3 pyramidal neurons of rats after training (shock-motivated brightness discrimination). TR, total ribosomes: FR, free ribosomes: PR, ribosomes in polysomes: MR, membrane-bound ribosomes: R/µm, ribosomes per micrometer of endoplasmic membrane. White columns, active controls; black columns, trained animals; ▲, significant increase ( $p < .01$) in trained animals over active controls; ordinate, percentage increase over passive controls. (Modified from Wenzel, David, Pohle, Marx, & Matthies, 1975.)

morphological findings are considered to be the expression of an enhanced macromolecular synthesis during the acquisition of a new behavior.

Because synaptic structures are likely to be candidates for transient alterations during short-term as well as intermediate memory storage, we investigated the synaptic structures in the stratum radiatum of CA1 of the hippocampus after the brightness discrimination task by electron microscopical and morphometrical methods. At 1 hour after training, we observed an increase in the number of electron microscopically detectable synapses. These changes disappeared slowly during the following days. Figure 9.2 shows the mean number of synapses per unit area of the neuropil at different periods after training. In the trained animals the synaptic density was substantially (39%) and significantly higher than in the active and passive controls. Fourteen days after training, the mean synaptic density in the trained animals was markedly reduced. Combining the biochemical results by Matthies (1982) with these findings leads us to propose that the observed increase of structures reflect the transformation of performed synapses into an activated state as a result of the enhanced neuronal function during the acquisition phase.

In principle, however, *de novo* formation of synapses during training might also occur because the number of very small axon–spine–dendritic synapses (diameter $< .25$ µm) increased by 10% in the trained animals in comparison to the active control (Wenzel *et al.*, 1980). This finding is comparable with the observation of Chang and Greenough (1984; see Greenough, Chapter 5, this volume) that in the rat the number of small "sessile" spines on hippocampal CA1 neurons increases following the induction of LTP.

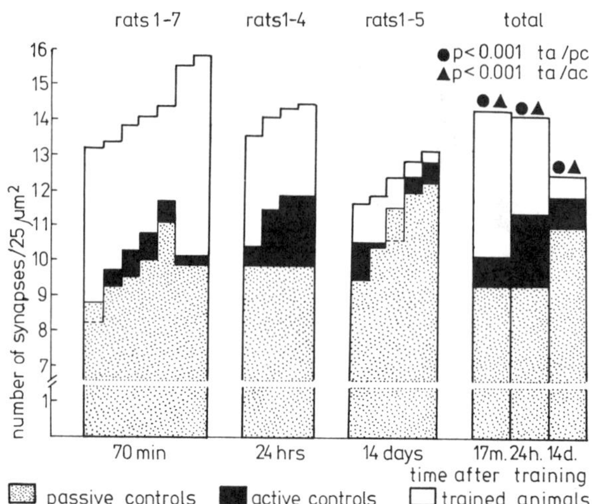


**FIGURE 9.2.** Graphic representation of changes in the number of synapses per area neuropil (stratum radiatum of CA1) in passive controls (dotted), active controls (black), and trained animals (white) 70 minutes, 24 hours, and 14 days after training. ●, significant increase ($p <$ .001) in trained animals over passive controls; ▲, significant increase ($p <$ .001) in trained animals over active controls. (Modified from Wenzel *et al.*, 1980.)

## RIBOSOMAL SYSTEMS AND SYNAPSES IN THE HIPPOCAMPUS DURING LONG-TERM POTENTIATION OF THE PERFORANT PATH IN INTACT ANIMALS

In a second series of experiments, we searched for changes in the ultrastructure of synapses in the neuropil of the fascia dentate as well as for ribosomal shifts in the granular cell cytoplasm following high-frequency stimulation of the perforant path. The data were collected 48 hours after tetanization. Figure 9.3 shows the experimental arrangement of the electrodes used for the *in vivo* and *in vitro* investigations of the hippocampal formation. The first experimental paradigm called for stimulation of the perforant path (the stimulating electrode was implanted in the medial entorhinal cortex) and recording of the extracellular field potential in the middle stratum moleculare of the gyrus dentatus.

Test stimuli were applied using single pulses with .1-msec duration (.2 Hz stimulus frequency). For tetanization, a train consisting of 300 pulses divided into groups of 15 was applied; the group interval was 5.0 sec and the stimulus frequency within the groups was 200 Hz. To obtain the long-term potentiation effect, it proved necessary to employ four such pulse series with 300 single pulses in each series and a stimulus frequency of 200 Hz. The trains were separated by 30 minutes. For controls, we used three different groups: "short term-potentiated" rats received 1 train with 300 pulses (200 Hz); "active controls" were stimulated with 1200 single pulses

(.2 Hz); "passive controls" had the electrodes implanted but received no pulses.

Several experiments were carried out to follow the time course of the potentiation by recording test-evoked responses up to 7 days after the potentiation (Figure 9.4). The time course of the LTP showed a long-lasting effect over several days, visible in the high amplitudes of the extracellular excitatory postsynaptic potential and of the population spike.

For the evaluation of electron micrographs of the stratum moleculare of the hippocampal dentate gyrus from stimulated animals, we estimated quantitatively the following morphological synaptic parameters: distribution

**FIGURE 9.3.** (A) Scheme of the interneuronal connections and position of the electrodes in the hippocampus dentate gyrus and entorhinal cortex. MF, mossy fiber; PP, perforant path; SC, Schaffer collaterals; Subic., Subiculum; TA, tractus angularis. (B) Scheme of the stimulation and recording sites used in both long-term potentiation experiments: medial entorhinal cortex to middle third of the dentate molecular layer via perforant path; CA3 neurons to the CA1 neurons via the Schaffer collaterals.

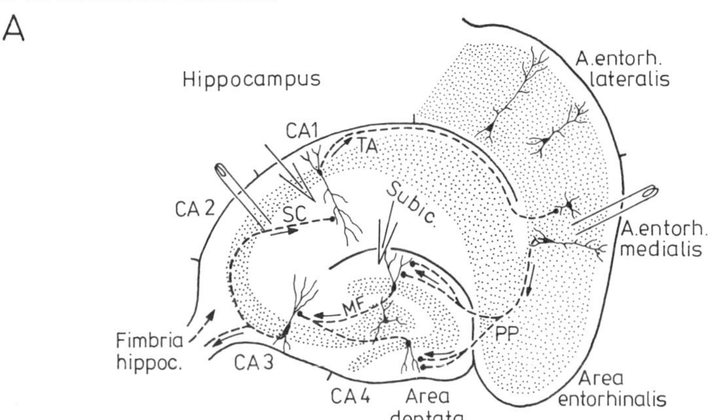


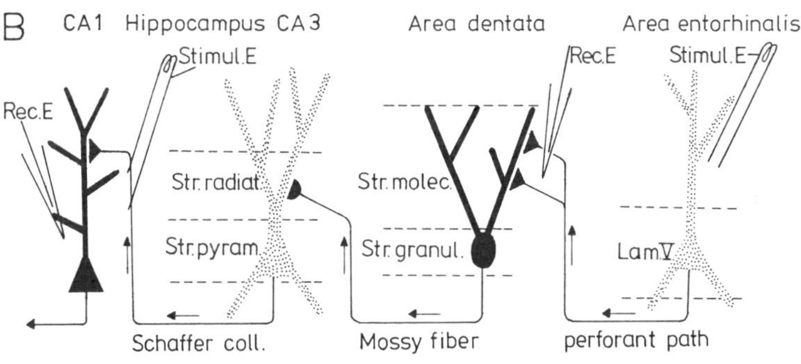

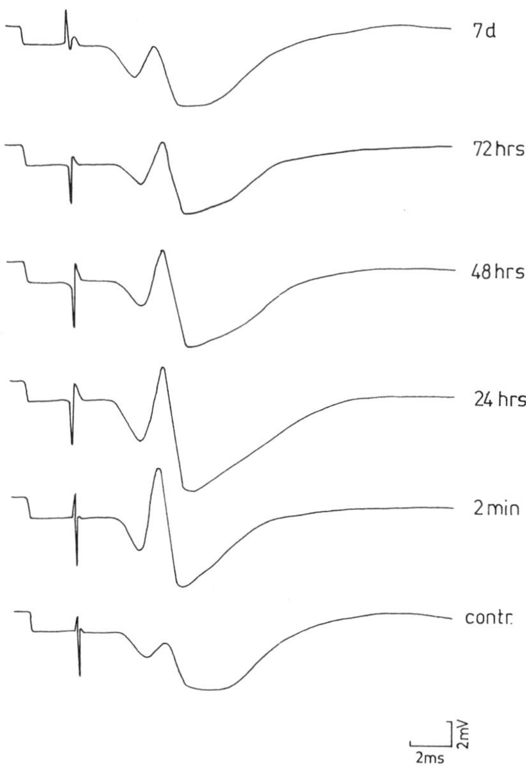


**FIGURE 9.4.** Traces of evoked potentials recorded from the stratum moleculare of fascia dentata in response to stimulation of the area entorhinalis medialis. Time course of LTP after a repetitive high-frequency stimulation and recording of the extracellular EPSP and the population spike. (From M. Krug, personal communication.)

of synaptic vesicles, size of the presynaptic terminal and postsynaptic spine, and length of the postsynaptic density 48 hours after the experiment.

After counting the number of vesicles in the various zones of the presynaptic terminal in potentiated animals, we found the number of vesicles reduced in the zone near the synaptic membrane. The postsynaptic spine area and the presynaptic terminal area showed no significant differences between potentiated rats and the control groups (Figure 9.5).

In these experiments we found the total number of synapses in potentiated animals not significantly changed when compared to the controls (passive, active, or short-term potentiation); however, the number of axodendritic contacts (nonspiny or shaft synapses) was enhanced by 40% (Figure 9.6). This result is in good agreement with the changes in the synapse population 15 minutes after LTP reported by Lynch and co-workers and might indicate a specific shift in the synaptic efficiency and/or synaptic connectivity (Chang & Greenough, 1984; Desmond & Levy, 1983; Greenough, Chapter 5, this volume; Lee *et al.*, 1980, 1981). At present we are not able to present an adequate explanation for these shifts in the synapse population. The existence of different pools of synapses that are specifically affected by the LTP as well as a *de novo* formation of synapses belonging to granule or basket cells has been discussed (Abraham & Goddard, Chapter 4, this volume; Barnes & McNaughton, Chapter 3, this volume; Matthies, 1982; Teyler & Discenna, 1984). Teyler and Discenna (1984) have suggested that "one pos-

**FIGURE 9.5.** Electron micrographs showing synapses in the dentate molecular layer of active controls (A), after short-term potentiation (B), and after long-term potentiation (C, D).

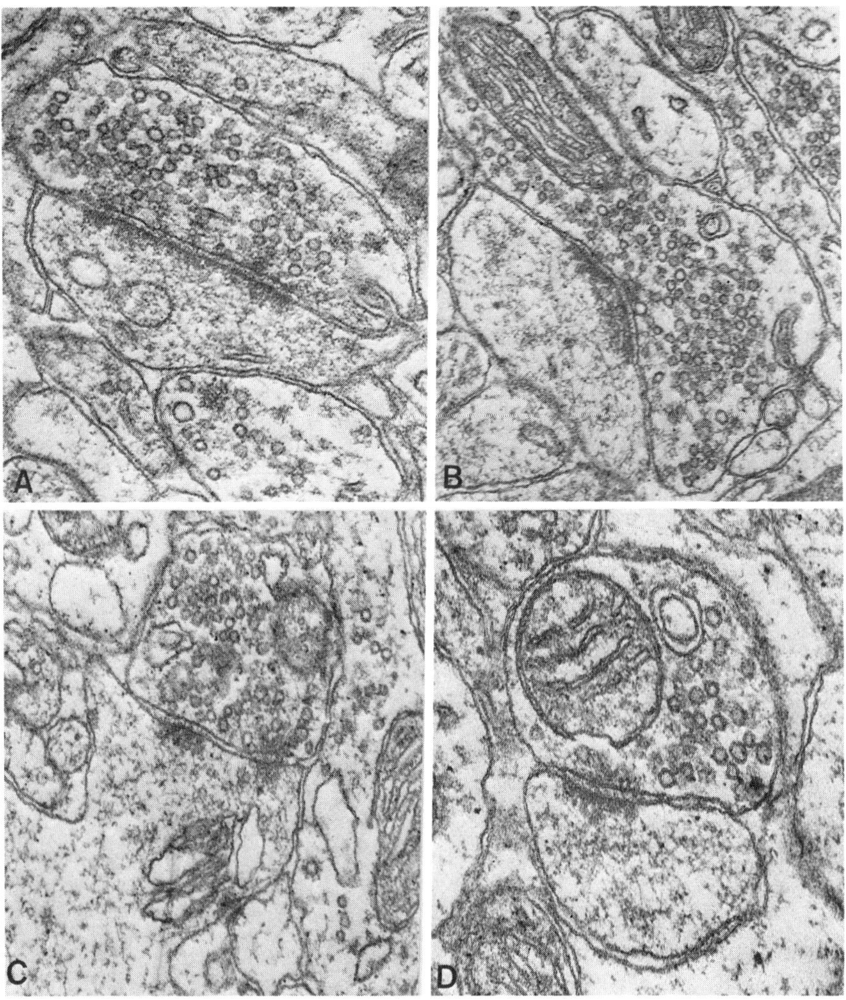

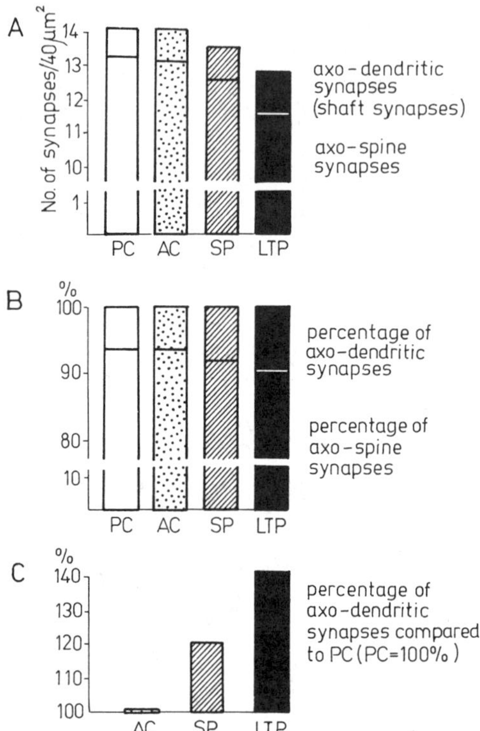


**FIGURE 9.6.** Numerical density of synapses in the dentate molecular layer of control and potentiated animals. (A) Numerical density of axo-dendritic contacts (shaft synapses) and axo-spine synapses. (B) Percentage relation of both types of synapses. (C) Relative increase of shaft synapses in potentiated animals; passive control = 100%. PC, passive control; AC, active control; SP, short-term potentiated animals; LTP, long-term potentiated rats.

sibility is that as the synapses become consolidated via LTP, more plastic synapses are formed by the cell and/or additional neurons, thus preserving a pool of plastic synapses for future use."

Fifkova *et al.* (1982) demonstrated in their investigations that the stimulation-induced spine enlargement in the dentate fascia can be suppressed by protein synthesis-blocking drugs (e.g., anisomycin), an observation suggesting that a link may exist between LTP and the metabolic processes that lead to protein synthesis in the hippocampus. Therefore, it can be concluded that biochemical and physiological processes during LTP should be reflected by morphological changes of the ribosomes. In fact, the evaluation of the ribosomal systems in the granular cell somata 48 hours following LTP revealed significant increases in the number of polysomes and especially of the membrane-bound ribosomes in potentiated animals (Figures 9.7–9.9).

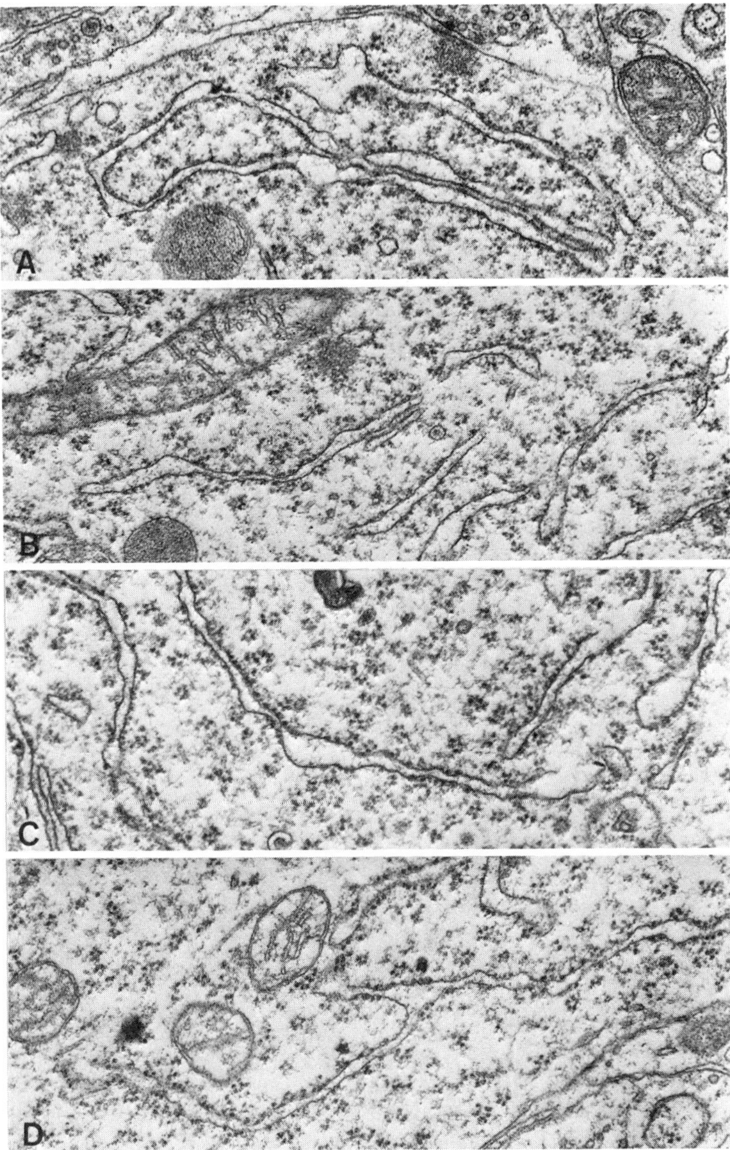


**FIGURE 9.7.** Electron micrographs showing the granular endoplasmic reticulum in passive controls (A), active controls (B), and short-term (C) and long-term potentiated animals (D). There is a marked increase in polysomes and membrane-bound ribosomes in potentiated animals (C and D).

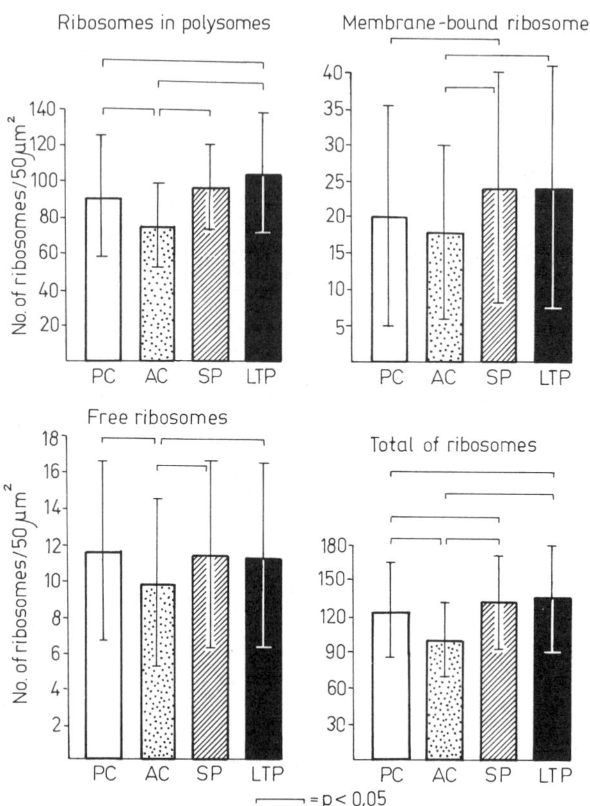


**FIGURE 9.8.** Numerical density of the ribosomes within the cytoplasm of dentate granule cells from control and potentiated animals. PC, passive control; AC, active control; SP, short-term potentiation; LTP, long-term potentiation.

## RIBOSOMAL SYSTEMS IN THE HIPPOCAMPUS USING BRAIN SLICES FOR THE LTP EXPERIMENT

Electrophysiological and electron microscopic methods were used to investigate (in collaboration with F. Schottler, M. Kessler, and G. Lynch) possible structural modifications associated with synaptic LTP in hippocampal slices on the level of the ribosomal systems. The hippocampal slices were processed for the electron microscopy 15 and 75 minutes after the stimulation for LTP. The perikarya of CA1 pyramids and the neuropil of the stratum radiatum were investigated. In these slices brief bursts of high-frequency stimulation of the Schaffer collaterals produced long-lasting changes of the synaptic response of CA1 pyramids (Figure 9.3).

In one group of slices, four trains of stimulation were administered at a frequency of 100 Hz (potentiated slices), and a second group was stimulated at .2 Hz for 3 minutes (active control; Figure 9.10). The electron microscopic investigation was carried out in the pyramidal neurons of the CA1 region in potentiated and control slices. The following parameters were evaluated:

1. total number of ribosomes per 50 μm² cytoplasm
2. membrane-bound ribosomes
3. ribosomes in polysomes
4. free ribosomes

The pictures taken from the hippocampal slices demonstrate that the tissue was maintained in good morphological condition (Figures 9.11–9.13). The perikarya of the CA1 pyramids and the structure of the synapses appeared quite normal and not unlike those observed *in vivo*.

Fifteen minutes after LTP, no significant changes could be detected in the ribosomes as compared to unspecifically stimulated controls. But all slices underwent a slight shrinkage during longer incubation time, a change resulting in an increasing density of the ribosomes in the cytoplasm (Figure 9.14). From these results we might conclude that the first period after high-frequency stimulation (LTP) does not lead to morphologically detectable changes in the protein synthesis.

Seventy-five minutes after high-frequency stimulation of the Schaffer collaterals, the number of polysomes and membrane-bound ribosomes was markedly increased in the cytoplasm of the CA1 pyramids of the potentiated slices (Figure 9.15). This effect was evaluated quantitatively by an increase of 25% against the active control, maninly of polysomes and membrane-bound ribosomes (Figure 9.16).

Several authors (e.g., Duffy *et al.*, 1981; Shashoua & Teyler, 1982) have reported that LTP results in an increase in the incorporation of labeled amino acids into slides. This was found for potentiation of the Schaffer collaterals as well as for perforant path. These results seem to support the hypothesis of a multiphasic development of the LTP phenomenon (Barnes & McNaughton, Chapter 3, this volume; Racine, Milgram, & Hafner, 1983;

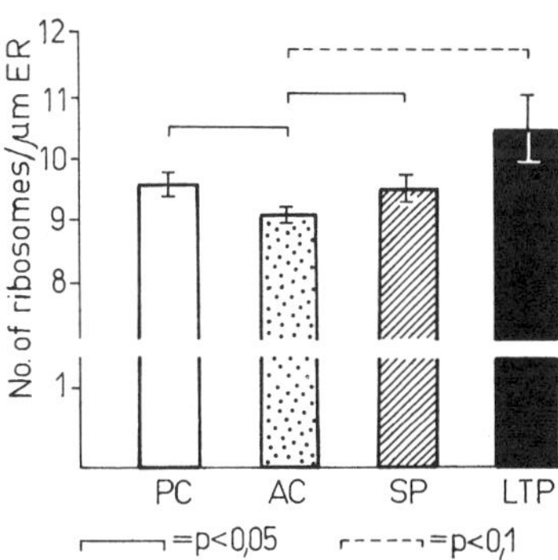


**FIGURE 9.9.** Number of membrane-bound ribosomes per micrometer of membrane length within the cytoplasm of dentate granule cells from passive controls (PC), active controls (AC), and short-term (SP) and long-term potentiated rats (LTP).

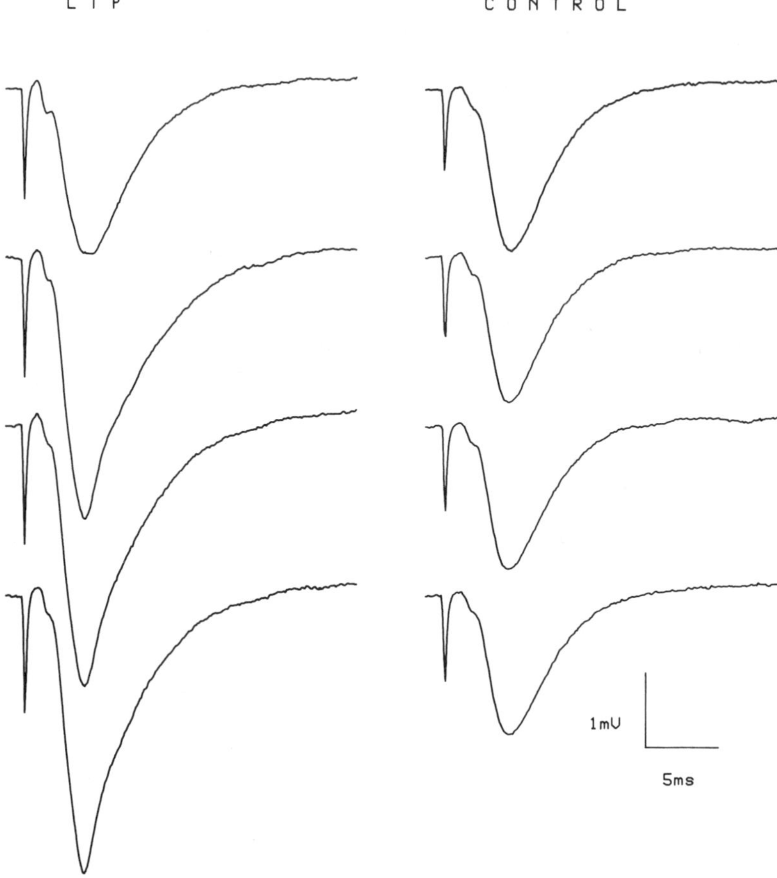


**FIGURE 9.10.** Traces of evoked potentials recorded from stratum pyramidale/stratum radiatum of CA1 of a hippocampal slice in response to stimulation of the Schaffer collaterals. Control: traces obtained following a train of low-frequency stimulation (.2 Hz for 3 minutes). LTP: long-lasting potentiation of CA1 responses to repetitive high-frequency stimulation of the Schaffer collaterals (latest recording after 75 minutes).

Teyler & Discenna, 1984). The enhancement in the number of ribosomes observed only during later stages of the LTP development may indicate that the protein synthesis is involved in the stablization of the morphological and biochemical processes at the one hand, or as proposed by Shashoua, increases in a compensatory manner for the resynthesis of proteins exhausted during the initial phases of the LTP.

Results of Krug *et al.* (1984) also support the hypothesis of protein synthesis being involved in the late phase of the LTP development. They found a permanent suppression of the stimulation-induced enlargement of

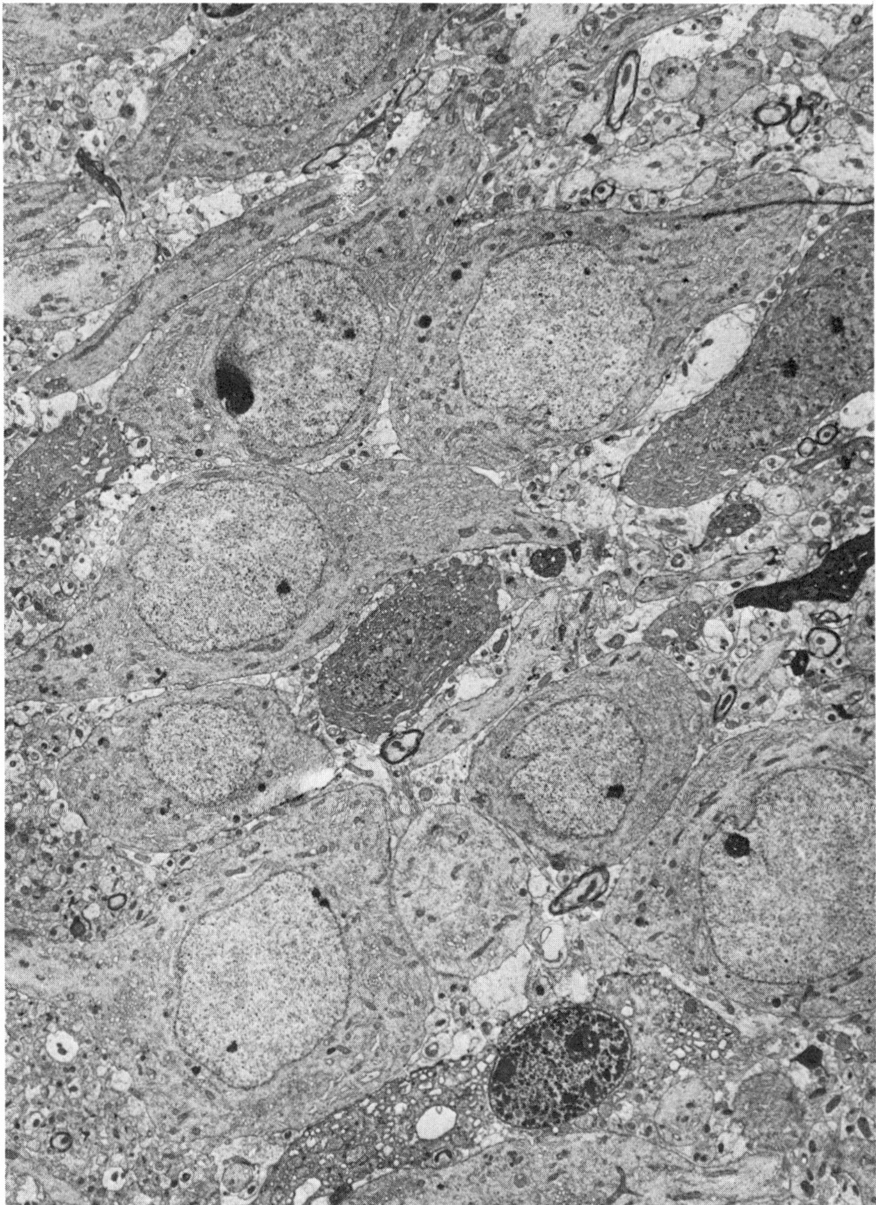

**FIGURE 9.11.** Electron micrograph of the CA1 pyramidal layer in a hippocampal slice. Most of the pyramidal cells showed a well-preserved structure even after 3 hours *in vitro*. Only single neurons exhibit signs of degeneration (shrinkage, vacuolization of cytoplasm and nuclear pyknosis as a result of the preparation of the slices).

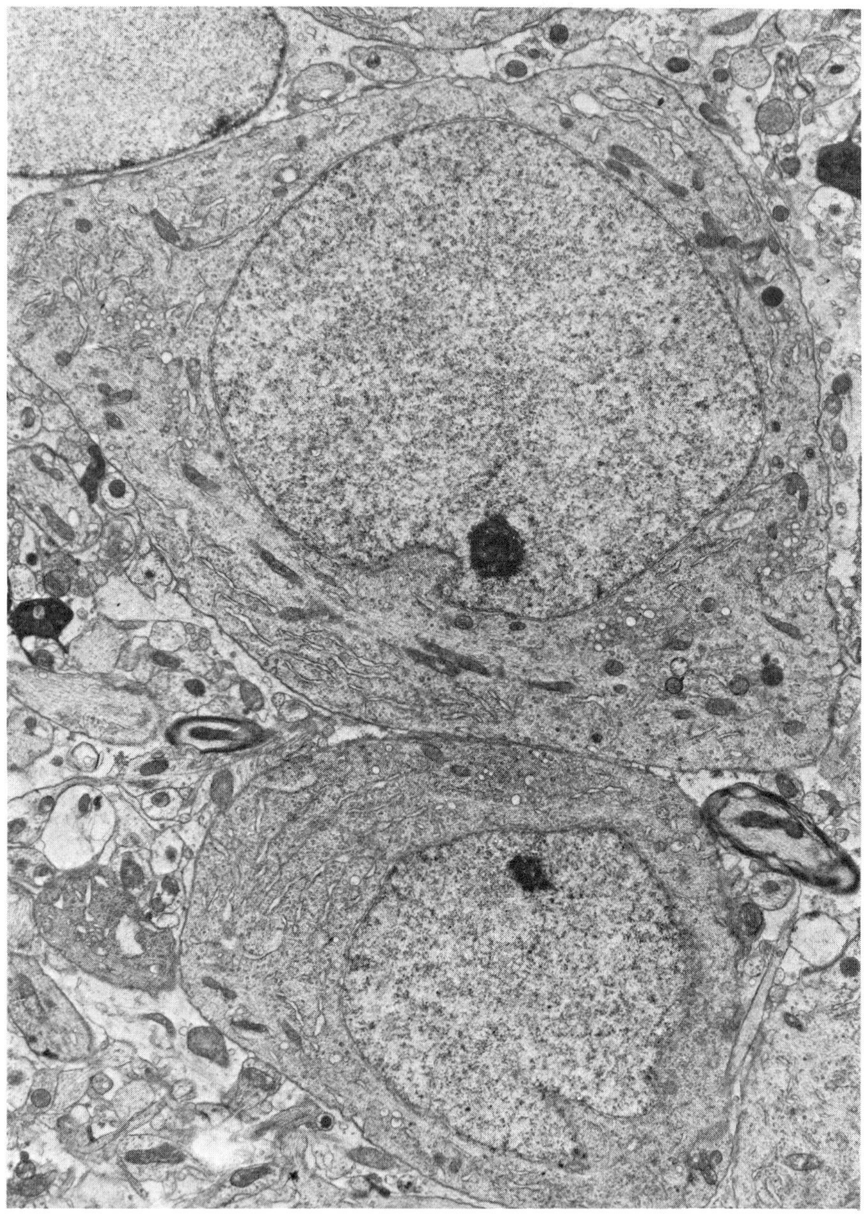

**FIGURE 9.12.** Electron micrograph showing two pyramidal neurons in CA1 of a hippocampal slice, maintained *in vitro*. Cytoplasm and nuclei show no pathological changes.

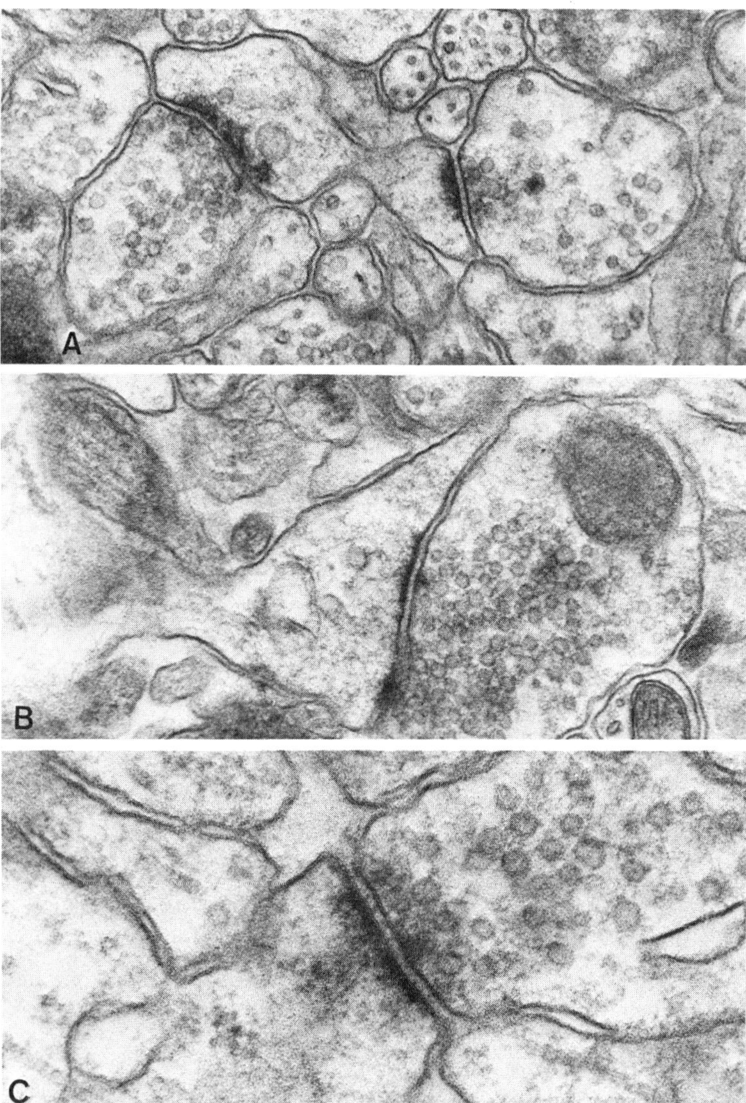


**FIGURE 9.13.** Electron micrographs of axo-spine-dendritic synapses from the radiate layer of CA1 in a hippocampal slice. After 3 hours *in vitro*, synaptic membranes, vesicles, and mitochondria are morphologically well preserved.

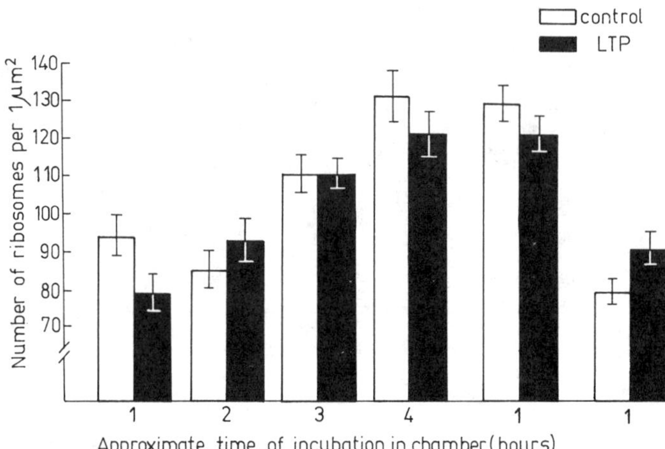


**FIGURE 9.14.** Numerical density of ribosomes within the cytoplasm of CA1 pyramidal neurons. White columns, control slices, after low-frequency stimulation; black columns, potentiated slices, 15 minutes after repeated high-frequency stimulation (LTP). No significant differences were found in potentiated and control slices, but increasing values in dependence of the incubation time *in vitro*.

the EPSP amplitude or of the population spike when they administered the inhibitor of the protein synthesis anisomycin.

We propose that two types of results are of particular importance in elucidating the mechanisms underlying the phenomenon of LTP: (1) demonstration of changes in the spine morphology and of the increase of the number of axo-dendritic synapses (shaft or nonspiny synapses) (Chang & Greenough, 1984; Desmond & Levy, 1983; Fifkova *et al.*, 1982; Fifkova & Van Harreveld, 1977; Lee *et al.*, 1980, 1981); and (2) demonstration of biochemical changes in postsynaptic structures (Baudry & Lynch, 1980, 1981; Lynch & Baudry, 1984; Lynch *et al.*, 1982, 1984) and changes of the protein synthesis due to LTP (Duffy *et al.*, 1981; Shashoua & Teyler, 1982; Teyler & Discenna, 1984).

These results together with our findings provide the following answer to our initial model: The biochemical and other physiological processes underlying the phenomena of learning and LTP are reflected by morphological changes in the synaptic level as well as by changes in the ribosomal systems. The observed changes can be summarized as three points:

1. The memory process resulted in an increase of the number of neuropil synapses in the hippocampus; however, the LTP effect was a shift to a relatively more dendritic shaft synapse with no higher density of all synapses. These facts reflect the relatively long-lasting changes in the neuronal connectivity as a result of both experimental conditions.

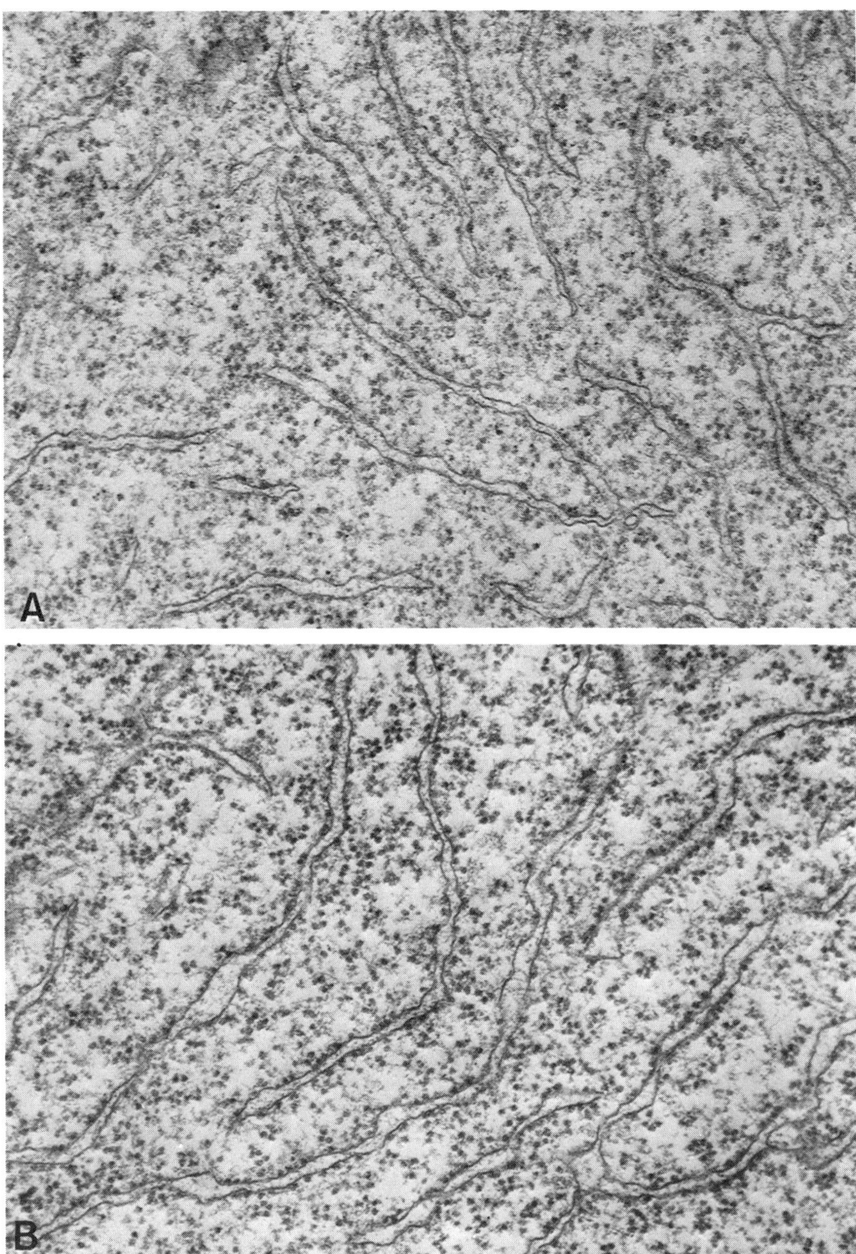


**FIGURE 9.15.** Electron micrographs showing parts of the cytoplasm of CA1 pyramids in a hippocampal slice (A, control slice; B, potentiated slice). A marked increase in polysomes and membrane-bound ribosomes was found 75 minutes after the high-frequency stimulation (LTP) (B).

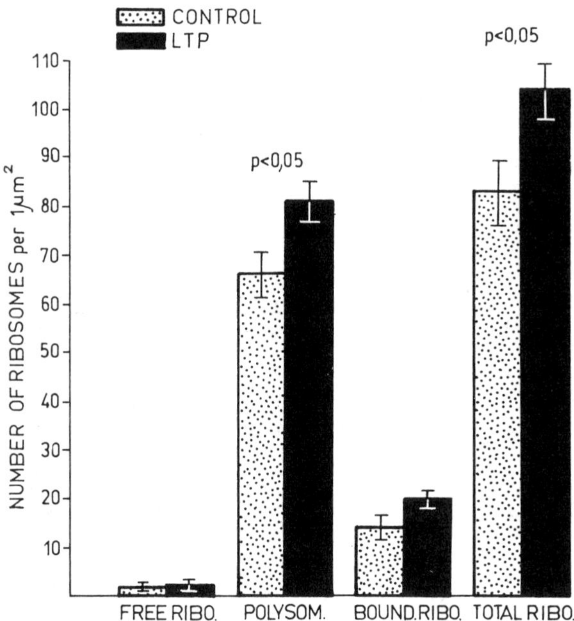


**FIGURE 9.16.** Numerical density of ribosomes in the CA1 pyramidal cytoplasm in hippocampal slices after high-frequency stimulation (black columns, LTP; white columns, control). There is a significant increase in total ribosomes (25%, $p < .05$) and polysomes (23%, $p < .05$) 75 minutes after high-frequency stimulation (LTP).

2. The changes in the synaptic connectivity observed during the memory formation process are accompanied by an enhanced protein synthesis activity.

3. LTP is characterized by various morphological changes pointing to an early phase with transient effects on the ultrastructure of the synapses and to a late phase with activated protein synthesis systems to stabilize a long-lasting shift in the neuronal connectivity.

## REFERENCES

Alger, B. E., & Teyler, T. J. Long-term and short-term plasticity in the CA1, CA3 and dentate region of the rat hippocampal slice. *Brain Research*, 1976, *110*, 463–480.

Andersen, P., Sundberg, S. H., Sveen, O., Swann, J. W., & Wigström, H., Possible mechanisms for long-lasting potentiation of synaptic transmission in hippocampal slices from guinea-pigs. *Journal of Physiology (London)*, 1980, *302*, 463–482.

Baudry, M., & Lynch, G. Hypothesis regarding the cellular mechanisms responsible for long-term synaptic potentiation in the hippocampus. *Experimental Neurology*, 1980, *68*, 202–204.

Baudry, M., & Lynch, G. Hippocampal glutamate receptors. *Molecular and Cellular Biochemistry*, 1981, *38*, 5–18.

Baudry, M., & Lynch, G. Properties and mechanisms of LTP: Possible mechanisms of LTP: Role of glutamate receptors. *Neurosciences Research Program Bulletin*, 1982, *20*, 663–670.

Bliss, T. V. P., & Dolphin, A. C. What is the mechanism of long-term potentiation in the hippocampus? *Trends in NeuroScience*, 1982, *5*, 289–290.

Chang, F.-L., & Greenough, W. T. Transient and enduring morphological correlates of synaptic activity and efficacy change in the rat hippocampal slice. *Brain Research*, 1984, *309*, 35–46.

Desmond, N. L., & Levy, W. B. Synaptic correlates of associative potentiation/depression: An ultrastructural study in the hippocampus. *Brain Research*, 1983, *265*, 21–30.

Dolphin, A. C., Errington, M. L., & Bliss, T. V. P. Long-term potentiation of the perforant path in vivo is associated with increased glutamate release. *Nature (London)*, 1982, *297*, 496–497.

Duffy, C., Teyler, T. J., & Shashoua, V. E. Long-term potentiation in the hippocampal slice: Evidence for stimulated secretion of newly synthesized proteins. *Science*, 1981, *212*, 1148–1151.

Eccles, J. C. Possible synaptic mechanism subserving learning. In A. G. Karczmar & J. C. Eccles (Eds.), *Brain and human behavior*. Berlin & New York: Springer-Verlag, 1972.

Fifkova, E., Anderson, C., Young, S. J., & Van Harreveld, A. Effect of anisomycin on stimulation-induced changes in dendritic spines of the dentate granule cells. *Journal of Neurocytology*, 1982, *11*, 183–210.

Fifkova, E., & Van Harreveld, A. Long-lasting morphological changes in dendritic spines of dentate granular cells following stimulation of the entorhinal area. *Journal of Neurocytology*, 1977, *6*, 211–230.

Hebb, D. O. *The organization of behavior*. New York: Wiley, 1949.

Krug, M., Lössner, B., & Ott, T. Anisomycin blocks the late phase of long-term potentiation in the dentate gyrus of freely moving rat. *Brain Research Bulletin*, 1984, *13*, 39–42.

Lee, K. S., Oliver, M., Schottler, F., & Lynch, G. Electron microscopic studies of brain slices: The effects of high-frequency stimulation on dendritic ultrastructure. In G. Kerkut & H. V. Wheal (Eds.), *Electrical activity in isolated mammalian C.N.S. preparations*. New York: Academic Press, 1981.

Lee, K. S., Schottler, F., Oliver, M., & Lynch, G. Brief bursts of high-frequency stimulation produce two types of structural change in rat hippocampus. *Journal of Neurophysiology*, 1980, *44*, 247–258.

Lynch, G., & Baudry, M. The biochemistry of memory: A new and specific hypothesis. *Science*, 1984, *224*, 1057–1063.

Lynch, G., Halpain, S., & Baudry, M. Effects of high-frequency synaptic stimulation on glutamate receptor binding studied with a modified in vitro hippocampal slice preparation. *Brain Research*, 1982, *244*, 101–111.

Lynch, G., Kessler, M., & Baudry, M. Correlated electrophysiological and biochemical studies of hippocampal slices. In R. Dingledine (Ed.), *Brain slices*. New York: Plenum Press, 1984.

Matthies, H. The biochemical basis of learning and memory. *Life Sciences*, 1974, *15*, 2017–2031.

Matthies, H. Biochemical, electrophysiological and morphological correlates of brightness discrimination in rats. In M. A. B. Brazier (Ed.), *Brain mechanisms in memory and learning*. New York: Raven Press, 1981.

Matthies, H. Memory formation: A model of corresponding neuronal processes. In R. Sinz & M. R. Rosenzweig (Eds.), *Psychophysiology 1980*. Amsterdam: Elsevier Biomedical Press, 1982.

McNaughton, B. L., Douglas, R. M., & Goddard, G. V. Synaptic enhancement in fascia dentata: Cooperativity among coactive afferents. *Brain Research*, 1978, *157*, 277–293.

Moshkow, D. A., Petrovskaia, L. L., & Bragin, A. G. Ultrastructural study of the bases of postsynaptic potentiation in hippocampal sections by the freeze-substitution method. *Tsitologia*, 1980, *22*, 20–26.

Pohle, W., & Matthies, H. Incorporation of RNA-precursors into neuronal and glial cells of rat brain during a learning experiment. *Brain Research*, 1974, *65*, 231–237.

Popov, N., Phole, W., Rüthrich, H.-L., Schulzeck, S., & Matthies, H. Time course and disposition of fucose radioactivity in rat hippocampus. A biochemical and microautoradiographic study. *Brain Research*, 1976, *101*, 283–293.

Popov, N., Rüthrich, H.-L., Pohle, W., Schulzeck, S., & Matthies, H. Increased fucose incorporation into rat hippocampus during learning. A biochemical and microautoradiographic study. *Brain Research*, 1976, *101*, 295–304.

Racine, R. J., Milgram, N. W., & Hafner, S. Long-term potentiation phenomena in the rat limbic forebrain. *Brain Research*, 1983, *260*, 217–231.

Rosenzweig, M. R., Bennett, E. I., & Flood, J. F. Tests of the protein-synthesis-hypothesis of formation of long-term memory. In R. Sinz & M. R. Rosenzweig (Eds.), *Psychophysiology 1980*. Amsterdam: Elsevier Biomedical Press, 1982.

Shashoua, V. E., & Teyler, T. J. Properties and mechanisms of LTP: Possible mechanisms of LTP: Role of secreted proteins. *Neurosciences Research Program Bulletin*, 1982, *20*, 671–680.

Teyler, T. J., & Discenna, P. Long-term potentiation as a candidate mnemonic device. *Brain Research Reviews*, 1984, *7*, 15–28.

Thompson, R. F., Berger, T. W., & Madden, J., IV. Cellular processes of learning and memory in the mammalian CNS. *Annual Reviews of Neuroscience*, 1983, *6*, 447–491.

Van Harreveld, A., & Fifkova, E. Swelling of dendritic spines in the fascia dentate after stimulation of the perforant fibers as a mechanism of posttetanic potentiation. *Experimental Neurology*, 1975, *49*, 736–749.

Wenzel, J., David, H., Pohle, W., Marx, I., & Matthies, H. Free and membrane-bound ribosomes and polysomes in hippocampal neurons during a learning experiment. *Brain Research*, 1975, *84*, 99–109.

Wenzel, J., Kammerer, E., Frotscher, M., Joschko, R., Joschko, M., & Kaufmann, W. Elektronenmikroskopische und morphometrische Untersuchungen an Synapsen des Hippocampus nach Lernexperimenten bei der Ratte. *Zeitschrift für Mikroskopisch-Anatomische Forschung*, 1977, *91*, 74–93.

Wenzel, J., Kammerer, E., Frotscher, M., Kirsche, W., Matthies, H., & Wenzel, M. Electronmicroscopical and morphometrical investigations on the plasticity of the synapses in the hippocampus of the rat following conditioning. *Journal für Hirnforschung*, 1980, *21*, 647–654.

Wenzel, J., Kammerer, E., Kirsche, W., Matthies, H., Joschko, R., Joschko, M., & Kaufmann, W. Der Einfluss eines Lernexperimentes auf die Synapsenanzahl im Hippocampus der Ratte. Elektronenmikroskopische und morphometrische Untersuchungen. *Zeitschrift für Mikroskopisch-Anatomische Forschung*, 1977, *91*, 57–73.

SECTION II

# COMPARATIVE ASPECTS OF LEARNING AND MEMORY

CHAPTER 10

# Complex Computation in a Small Neural Network

**I. Cooke**
**K. Delaney**
Princeton University
**A. Gelperin**
AT&T Bell Laboratories
and Princeton University

> The head of the slug was broader than the rest, and was topped by twin antennae, each of which bore a knob. These it waved here and there, testing the air. And this slug was nude, having neither plate nor shell. I understood at once. Such beauty disdains any covering save the perfect stocking of its own integument. The enchantment it evokes is quite enough protection. (R. Selzer, *Letters To A Young Doctor*)

The slug encountered by Selzer was *Limax maximus*, described as "brown as Morocco. The forepart of the back was golden with tiny leopard spots which coalesced into stripes that ran the length of the tail. Thick as a finger it was, and full of wet stuff." Although rarely serving to evoke the Muse, *Limax* and its gastropod kin are increasingly seen as representing an optimal compromise between simplicity of neural organization and complexity of behavior. Students of associative learning have been particularly drawn to marine and terrestrial slugs (Alkon, 1984; Davis, 1984; Hawkins & Kandel, 1984). The difficulties of devising optimal learning experiments for such nonmammalian forms are more than offset by the accessibility of their neurons. Slug ganglia, comprising several hundred to a few thousand neurons (Boyle, Cohen, Macagno, & Orbach, 1983), can mediate associative learning, including such higher order learning phenomena as second-order conditioning and blocking. The demonstration that such a limited number of neurons can mediate such sophisticated mental calculations has stimulated new thinking about the synaptic processing underlying these functions (Gelperin, Hopfield, & Tank, 1985).

Using the terrestrial gastropod *Limax maximus*, we have demonstrated new levels of complexity and sophistication in the mental operations ac-

| | |
|---|---|
| 1st ORDER CONDITIONING: | $A^+ + Q^- \rightarrow A^-, B^+$ |
| 2nd ORDER CONDITIONING: | $A^+ + Q^-; B^+ + A^- \rightarrow A^-, B^-, C^+$ |
| | $A^+ + Q^-; (A^- B^+) \rightarrow A^-, B^-, C^+$ |
| COMPOUND CONDITIONING: | $(A^+ B^+) + Q^- \rightarrow A^-, B^-, C^+$ |
| BLOCK OF CONDITIONING: | $A^+ + Q^-; (A^- B^+) + Q^- \rightarrow A^-, B^+$ |
| EXTINCTION AFTER CONDITIONING: | $A^+ + Q^-; (A^- B^+); A^-, A^- \ldots \rightarrow A^+, B^+$ |
| | $A^+ + Q^-; B^+ + A^-; A^-, A^- \ldots \rightarrow A^+, B^-$ |
| APPETITIVE CONDITIONING: | $X^- + F^+ \rightarrow X^+, Y^-$ |

**FIGURE 10.1.** A summary of the associative learning functions of the *Limax* central nervous system as demonstrated with behavioral conditioning experiments. Stimuli in parentheses are presented simultaneously.

complished by molluscan ganglia. A testable model for the synaptic processing mediating the associative learning, including the higher order conditioning phenomena, has been developed and embodied in a computer simulation called LIMAX. First we shall outline the learning phenomena demonstrated with intact *Limax* and then describe the learning ability of its isolated cerebral ganglia. Second, several approaches to determining the synaptic processing used by *Limax* to accomplish the learning tasks will be outlined. Finally, we shall describe experiments designed to explore the extent of the congruence between synaptic mechanisms used by *Limax* and LIMAX.

## *LIMAX* LEARNING PHENOMENA

Our catalog of the associative learning abilities of *Limax* is derived from Pavlovian conditioning experiments using attractive food odors and tastes as the conditioned stimuli (CS) and repellent and/or toxic agents as the unconditioned stimuli (US). Pairing a CS and US causes a clear and dramatic change in the response to the CS. Before training, the CS causes approach and ingestion. After training, the CS causes aversion and rejection. Specifically, an odor CS will promote directed locomotion toward the source of the CS before training but directed locomotion away from the CS source after training. A taste CS will promote lip extension and ingestion before training but head withdrawal and writhing after training. A precise behavioral characterization of the responses to the CS before and after training is crucial to a complete description of the changes in motoneuronal activation that are used to monitor the learning of isolated preparations and may provide information about strategic sites of synaptic modulation (see later).

The results of an extensive series of behavioral experiments based on standard Pavlovian conditioning paradigms are summarized in Figure 10.1. The associative nature of these phenomena is indicated by the results obtained from a variety of control procedures fully summarized elsewhere (Sahley, Barry, & Gelperin, in press; Sahley, Gelperin, & Rudy, 1981; Sahley, Rudy, & Gelperin, 1981). These associative abilities are comparable to mammalian results, not only qualitatively (Rudy, 1984), but also in the reliability and robustness of the phenomena within individuals of the species. The existence of the Kamin blocking effect suggests that *Limax* possesses a type of internal representation of the stimulus contingencies that leads to an expectation of future contingencies. Both appetitive and aversive conditioning have been observed.

## POSTINGESTIVE CONDITIONING

We have found aversive conditioning to artificial diets lacking a single essential amino acid that depends on postingestive sequelae caused by the deficient diet (Delaney & Gelperin, submitted for publication). The results of an experiment demonstrating the rapidity and specificity of the postingestive conditioning are shown in Figure 10.2. Groups of five or six slugs were individually offered preweighed pellets of either the complete diet containing

**FIGURE 10.2.** Consumption of artificial diet during one meal. Bars indicate means for groups of six slugs given either a complete diet containing 20 amino acids or a diet that was devoid of either alanine or methionine. Slugs were allowed to consume one meal during a 3-hour period each day for 3 days. One standard error of the mean is indicated above each bar.

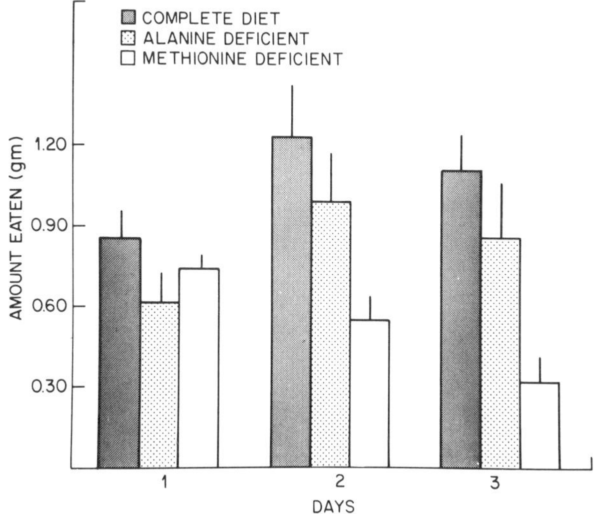

all 20 amino acids, a diet missing a nonessential amino acid (alanine), or a diet missing an essential amino acid (methionine). Each slug was given one feeding opportunity per day, with consumption measured at the end of the first feeding bout (usually 20–30 minutes) or 180 minutes after offering the food pellet, whichever came first. Slugs in the three groups were offered only one diet, *not* a choice between them. All slugs were starved for 13 days before the start of the experiment to ensure a high level of responsiveness to food. As shown in Figure 10.2, consumption of all three diets during the first meal on day 1 was the same. On days 2 and 3, whereas intake of the complete diet and the alanine-deficient diet increased somewhat, intake of the methionine-deficient diet decreased significantly. Removal of tryptophan or phenylalanine and to a lesser degree tyrosine also caused a diet to become aversive after ingestion (data not shown).

Evidence obtained to date indicates that the animals cannot discriminate between these different diets on the basis of smell or taste. This is most clearly seen in results from experiments in which, after a period of feeding on either the complete *or* methionine-deficient diets, the diets are switched so that animals previously given the complete diet are now given the methionine-deficient diet and animals previously given the methionine-deficient diet are now given the complete diet (Figure 10.3). The slugs treat the new diet as though it were the old diet until after their first meal of the new diet. Then the slugs previously fed the complete diet and switched to the methionine-deficient diet dramatically *decrease* their intake and the slugs previously fed the methionine-deficient diet and switched to the complete diet *increase* their intake. Further evidence that the methionine-deficient

**FIGURE 10.3.** Effect of switching diets on consumption. Dark bars represent mean consumption of diet during one meal per day for eight slugs fed the complete diet on days 1–3. Open bars show mean consumption of nine slugs fed one meal per day of the methionine-deficient diet on days 1–3. On days 4–10, the slugs previously fed the complete diet were fed the methionine-deficient diet and slugs fed the methionine-deficient diet were switched to the complete diet. Both groups were starved on day 11 and then fed rat chow in agar on day 12.

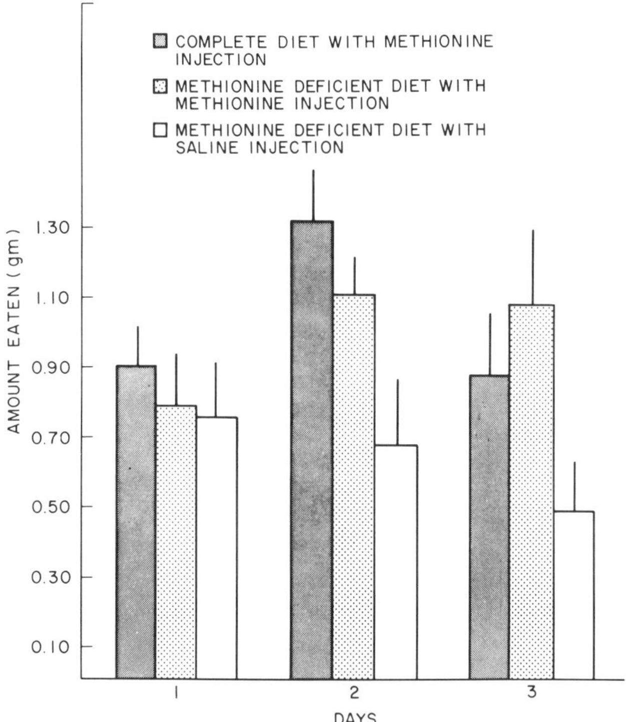


**FIGURE 10.4.** Consumption of artificial diets by slugs given injections of either saline or saline containing methionine after the completion of a meal. One group of six slugs was given the complete diet and then given an injection of *Limax* saline containing methionine directly into the hemocoel 1 hour after the completion of a meal. Another group of six slugs was given a methionine-deficient diet and injected with saline containing methionine in a similar manner. A third group of five slugs was fed the deficient diet and injected with saline without methionine. Methionine was added to saline so that .25 milliliters contained as much methionine as 1 gram of the complete diet, .0024 grams. Slugs were then injected with .25 milliliters of saline or saline with methionine for each gram of food they ate. The solutions and diets were coded so that the experimenter had no knowledge of what was being fed to a particular slug nor what was being injected. Means and one standard error of the mean are presented.

diet is not intrinsically less attractive than the complete diet was derived from replacement-therapy experiments in which the appearance of the aversion to the methionine-deficient diet was blocked by postprandial injections of methionine directly into the blood (Figure 10.4).

We have used the postingestive learning paradigm to demonstrate memory retention of 127 days. Young slugs were given either the complete diet containing all 20 amino acids plus carbohydrates and lipids or a diet missing one essential amino acid (methionine) with all other components held constant. Daily consumption of preweighed agar pellets of diet was measured for three groups of five slugs offered each diet for 10 days. During

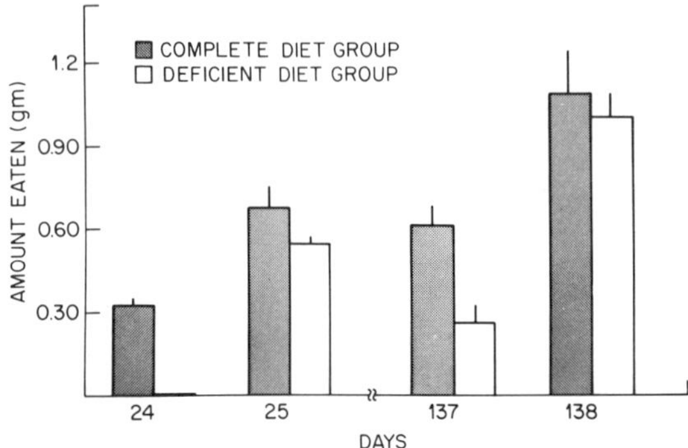


**FIGURE 10.5.** Consumption of artificial diets by young slugs demonstrating retention of a learned aversion to a methionine-deficient diet. Bars on day 24 show the mean amount of complete diet eaten by three groups of five slugs or the amount of methionine-deficient diet eaten by another three groups of five slugs during 24 hours access to the food. Day 25 shows the amount of rat chow in agar eaten by these same slugs. Not shown are data from day 23 when the same slugs were given the artificial diets and the groups given the complete diet ate an average of .46 grams whereas the groups offered the deficient diet ate nothing. From day 25 to day 126, all the slugs were fed rat chow pellets and then starved from day 127 to 136. On day 137, the 10 largest slugs originally fed the complete diet and the 10 largest slugs originally fed the deficient diet were individually given the artificial diets and allowed to eat one meal during a 4-hour period. On day 137, the mean weights of the group of slugs fed the complete diet was 8.43 grams and that of the group fed the deficient diet was 8.41 grams. The amount of rat chow in agar eaten by these slugs is shown on day 138. Standard errors of the means are indicated above each bar. See the text for more details of the feeding protocol.

this period a marked aversion to the methionine-deficient diet developed. On days 11–21 of the experiment, the slugs were fed rat chow. They were starved for 1 day (22) and then reoffered for 2 days (23, 24) the same artificial diet experienced on days 1–10. None of the animals offered the methionine-deficient diet on days 1–10 ate it, and therefore they received no postingestive negative reinforcement. All slugs were then maintained on rat chow for 101 days (25–126), starved for 10 days (127–136), and then tested with their original artificial diets for 1 day (137) and with rat chow the following day (138). The results of the tests on days 24, 25, 137, and 138 are shown in Figure 10.5. The retention of the aversion to the methionine-deficient diet over the 127-day interval (day 10 to day 137) is very clear, as is the demonstration that the animals in the two groups ate the same amount of rat chow on the day following their demonstrated aversion to the methionine-deficient diet (day 25 and day 138).

## STIMULUS TIMING

The summary of Figure 10.1 does not adequately represent the critical importance of the temporal relations between stimuli during conditioning trials. Although all of the possible timing relations between CS and US have not yet been systematically explored, we have found no conditioning when the US precedes the CS (backward conditioning). Some timing requirements for learning are measured in minutes, whereas others are measured in seconds. A novel taste or odor CS given alone remains in memory for tens of minutes in a form that can be associated with a subsequent US (Chang & Gelperin, 1980; Gelperin, 1975). The postingestive learning paradigm also contains delays of many minutes between CS and US (Delaney & Gelperin, submitted for publication). Conversely, the outcome of a three-phase training procedure used to test the stimulus–stimulus versus stimulus–response nature of second-order conditioning (Rescorla, 1984) can be completely different depending on a few seconds difference in stimulus timing during the second phase of conditioning, as diagrammed in Figure 10.1 (Sahley, Rudy, & Gelperin, 1984).

Our catalog of learning phenomena is probably not complete. Operant conditioning phenomena are yet to be investigated. Recent work on the water regulatory behaviors of *Limax* and their effects on feeding behavior (Phifer & Prior, in press; Prior, 1983, 1984) suggest that rehydration after dessication may be a powerful positive reinforcement for learning.

## LEARNING BY ISOLATED BRAINS

Our experimental attack on the synaptic mechanisms of learning in *Limax* makes use of an isolated preparation of the lips and the central nervous system (CNS). This preparation reliably produces the motor program for ingestion (feeding motor program, FMP) when palatable food extracts are applied to the lips (Gelperin, Chang, & Reingold, 1978). Responsiveness to food is retained for several days when the preparation is maintained in culture conditions. Chang and Gelperin (1980) showed that it is possible to produce one-trial, first-order, discriminative conditioning of this response by pairing the application of an aversive taste stimulus to the lips (quinidine sulfate) with the application of a particular palatable taste (the CS). Following pairing, the response of the preparation to the CS is suppressed, yet responses to other palatable tastes not paired with quinidine sulfate remain normal. The possibility that this associative change results merely from sensory adaptation or damage to peripheral sensory receptors has been disproved (Culligan & Gelperin, 1983). It is also possible to train the intact slug and then, using cold anesthesia, prepare a CNS preparation from it and show that the memory implanted *in vivo* can be expressed *in vitro* (Gelperin & Culligan, 1984). Finally, the isolated lip–brain preparation can be trained using shock of the lip as the US (Delaney & Gelperin, 1984).

Our behavioral analysis of the response to the CS before and after training indicates that other neuronal systems besides that for generation of the ingestive FMP are affected by the pairing of an attractive odor or taste with a noxious stimulus. After training, application of the formerly attractive taste produces head withdrawal, accompanied by withdrawal of the anterior portion of the foot. This finding led us to examine a bilateral pair of nerves that innervate the anterior portion of the foot from the pedal ganglion. Stimulation of one or both of these pedal nerves, either *en passant* or via the cut peripheral stumps, in both semiintact and highly dissected preparations evokes a strong, short-latency withdrawal response of the anterior portion of the foot. Similarly, brief stimulation of a central stump of an anterior pedal nerve elicits a short-latency foot withdrawal when the contralateral anterior pedal nerve still connects the pedal ganglion and anterior portion of the foot. The same stimulus regime applied to the cut central stump of an anterior pedal nerve as it exits the pedal ganglion is sufficient to terminate food-elicited FMP in the lip–brain preparation and suppress activity of buccal motor neurons for several minutes following the offset of the stimulus. Application of a food extract to the lips evokes a small and transient increase in efferent pedal nerve activity. Activity in anterior pedal nerves is greatly increased by noxious stimuli such as quinidine sulfate or strong electric shock applied to the lips, and this increased activity persists for several minutes following the offset of the noxious stimulus. Pairing the application of a food extract to the lips with strong electric shock of a lip results in a strong and prolonged increase in efferent pedal nerve activity to subsequent applications of the food paired with shock but not to other foods not paired with shock. This finding suggests another neural locus that is appropriate for examination of learning-related changes and emphasizes that a multiplicity of neural effects underlies the behavioral changes we interpret as learning in the whole animal (Delaney & Gelperin, 1984).

These results encourage us to believe that we will be able to use this preparation to study causative changes in cells involved in food-related learning processes. However, the frequency with which we presently can condition isolated brains successfully is less than our success rate with the whole animal. This is not surprising, for several reasons. First, the isolated preparation lacks much of the sensory feedback that would normally modulate and shape the complex feeding behavior of the intact animal. One result of this is that bouts of FMP elicited by stimulation of the lips in the isolated preparation usually far outlast the duration of stimulus appplication, in contrast to the behavior of the intact slug, which always ceases biting movements soon after the lips lose contact with food. Second, the paradigm that we have used to perform taste CS–taste US conditioning of the isolated lip–brain preparation with FMP as the physiological assay is not exactly analogous to the paradigm that has best demonstrated the impressive learning capabilities of intact slugs. The behavioral paradigm involves odor–taste association and an odor–choice assay, in which the relative preference of the slug for orientation toward test odors is assessed. The *in vitro* paradigm involves taste–taste association, and the assay is an absolute one, assessing whether or not FMP is expressed in response to a standard taste stimulus. Both differences are likely to affect the measured learning performance. The odor–taste association paradigm more closely approximates the normal foraging strategy of the whole animal, which will have been subject to selection pressure to maximize its efficiency. The odor-choice assay permits subtle changes in food preference to be detected, whereas the FMP assay used for the *in vitro* preparation can only detect major changes in taste palatability and may not resolve other associative changes occurring in the preparation.

Part of our current research effort is directed at improving the training procedure used with the isolated lip–brain preparation. We are studying in more detail elements of the foraging and feeding behavior of *Limax* that might permit the development of a better paradigm or preparation with which to study food aversion learning in the isolated *Limax* CNS (e.g., Delaney & Gelperin, 1984). We are looking for agents or conditions that will permit better control over the excitability of the isolated lip–brain preparation and allow us to detect more subtle changes in its output as a result of conditioning procedures.

## ENGRAM PURSUIT STRATEGY

One goal of this work is to understand the synaptic mechanisms by which memories of food odors and tastes are stored in the *Limax* CNS and the synaptic mechanisms by which the behavioral outcome of invoking such memories is altered by associative conditioning. Given an ensemble of neurons that can be associatively conditioned *in vitro*, one strategy is to determine the complete connectivity pattern between the chemosensory input and FMP output and then pinpoint the loci of synaptic and membrane changes that represent the information storage events (D. H. Cohen, Chapter 2, this volume). This is an ambitious undertaking, given the complexity and hierarchical nature of the neural circuitry that is likely to be involved in behaviors as complex as food aversion learning, even in the restricted population of neurons in the *Limax* cerebral ganglia.

Our strategy is to localize directly interneurons that seem likely to play a critical, perhaps even causative role in food-related learning. Feeding interneurons are deemed likely candidates for the study of learning-related changes if on anatomical or physiological grounds they represent convergence points for sensory integration and motor control. The localization is being done with a variety of techniques, including ablation experiments, mapping of neurons with axons in nerves for which stimulation dramatically affects FMP (internal lip nerve and subcerebral nerve), immunocytochemical mapping of neurons containing neurotransmitters affecting FMP, and/or learning and examination of the homologues of feeding interneurons documented in other molluscan systems (Benjamin, 1983; Croll, Kovac, Davis, & Matera, 1985; Rosen, Weiss, Cohen, & Kupfermann, 1982). The collected set of learned logic operations performed by the neural hardware of *Limax* indicates a sophistication of information processing far beyond our previous expectations for molluscan ganglia. The optimum engram pursuit strategy thus entails using several different lines of experimental attack so as to optimize the probability of localizing and characterizing causative cellular events underlying the learning and memory storage functions.

## ANATOMICAL LOCALIZATION

Having shown that the cerebral and buccal ganglia can accomplish first-order conditioning, we focused our attention on the cerebral ganglia, assuming that the buccal ganglia are not crucially involved in decision making. The cerebral ganglia are organized into three major lobes, each containing several cell clusters, some of which have anatomically complex areas of synaptic interaction adjacent to them (Veratti, 1900; Zs-Nagy & Sakharov, 1970). The cerebral ganglia receive direct input from the lips and noses. The most striking anatomical feature of the *Limax* cerebral ganglia is the pair of procerebral lobes (Van Mol, 1967). These ear-like projections from the edges of the cerebral ganglia arise just lateral to the entry of the large olfactory nerves, from which the procerebral lobes receive significant input (Chetail, 1963). The geometry of the intrinsic procerebral interneurons is complex, as is the extent and layering of neuropil adjacent to the distal layer of cell bodies (see Bullock & Horridge, 1965, p. 1308). The intrinsic procerebral neurons are numerous and small (5 to 7 μm), so we wished to know whether they were necessary for the taste–taste learning ability of the isolated lip–brain preparation.

First we determined that the reflex pathway from lip chemoreceptors to feeding motoneurons was functional in the absence of the procerebral lobes. Attractive food extracts placed on the lips of a naive lip–brain preparation triggered normal FMP in the absence of both procerebral lobes. Preliminary evidence suggests that a conditioned lip–brain preparation retains its selective response suppression after removal of the procerebral lobes. However, additional controls need to be done. These experiments also need to be extended before we will know whether procerebral lobe circuits have effects on the time course of learning or forgetting. If the procerebral lobes prove to be unnecessary for taste–taste learning, this would greatly simplify the possible anatomical substrates of first-order conditioning within the cerebral ganglia, particularly given the number of cerebral cells devoted to neuroendocrine regulation of sexual maturation (Van Minnen & Sokolove, 1981).

Two further points about the procerebral lobe ablation experiments should be made. First, the procerebral lobe on anatomical grounds is very likely to be necessary for the processing of olfactory input. Second, as yet the higher order conditioning phenomena have only been documented with olfactory CSs. Behavioral training experiments with anosmic slugs or further neurophysiological training experiments with the lip–cerebral ganglia preparation can determine if the higher order conditioning phenomena are obtained with taste CS–taste US training. A nose–brain preparation (Egan & Gelperin, 1981) can be used to clarify the role of the procerebral lobes in processing olfactory afference by recording from many neurons simultaneously using voltage-sensitive dyes (Kauer, Senseman, & Cohen, 1984) while applying food odor puffs to the olfactory epithelium.

## IMMUNOCYTOCHEMICAL LOCALIZATION

We are using a combination of pharmacological and immunocytochemical techniques to locate areas in the nervous system of *Limax* worthy of careful examination in our attempts to find the anatomical loci of synaptic changes involved in learning. The approach involves screening for pharmacological agents that affect the feeding or food-related learning behavior of *Limax* and then using immunocytochemistry to map the location and organization of cells containing these transmitters. Thus far we have identified a number of pharmacological agents that affect the expression of FMP by the isolated lip–brain preparation. These include dopamine, serotonin, γ-aminobutyric acid (GABA) and the tetrapeptide FMRFamide (Greenberg *et al.*, 1983). Dopamine has been shown to play a fundamental role in triggering FMP when the lips receive chemosensory input (Wieland & Gelperin, 1983). Serotonin appears to play a modulatory role in the control of feeding, enhancing the intensity of bouts of FMP elicited by lip stimulation (Gelperin, 1981). More recent experiments indicate that both FMRFamide and GABA exert an inhibitory influence on specific elements of the feeding system and on the overall output of the system.

Application of FMRFamide to the isolated lip–brain preparation at $10^{-7}$ *M* (Figure 10.6) abolishes the spontaneous bursting activity of the fast salivary burster neuron (Prior & Gelperin, 1977) without affecting the activity of the slow salivary burster (Copeland & Gelperin, 1983). FMRFamide, $10^{-7}$ *M*, also shortens the bout of FMP elicited by stimulation of the lips with a standard amount of food extract whereas a $10^{-5}$ *M* dose all but abolishes

**FIGURE 10.6.** Recording of activity in the salivary nerve in a lip–brain preparation showing the suppression of spontaneous bursting in the fast salivary burster (SB) neuron by $10^{-7}$ *M* FMRFamide.

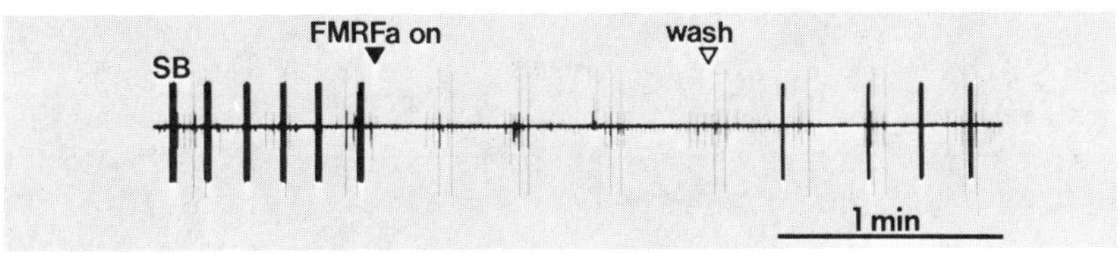

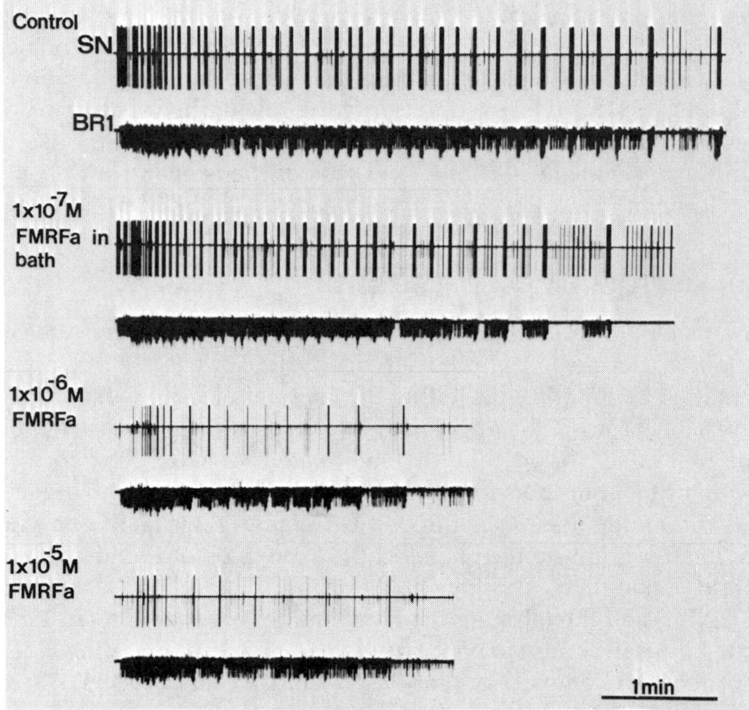


**FIGURE 10.7.** Series of recordings from a salivary nerve (SN) and a buccal root 1 (BR1) showing the effects of different concentrations of FMRFamide on FMP responses evoked by stimulation of the lips with potato extract.

the response (Figure 10.7). The inhibitory effect of FMRFamide on FMP can be seen both in the diminished intensity of the response components (lower bite rate and fewer motoneuron spikes per bite) and in the shortened duration of the FMP response. GABA, $10^{-6}$ *M*, suppresses the spontaneous bursting of the salivary fast burster, increases the firing of the slow burster, and slightly suppresses the intensity and duration of the FMP response to lip stimulation (Figure 10.8). GABA, $10^{-4}$ *M*, causes much stronger suppression of FMP (Figure 10.8).

FMRFamide-like immunoreactivity is extremely widespread in the nervous system of *Limax*. Large numbers of FMRFamide-like immunoreactive (FLI) cells are present in the buccal and cerebral ganglia, and there are numerous FLI fibers in the interganglionic connectives and peripheral nerves (Figure 10.9). These results are consistent with FMRFamide having both central and peripheral neurotransmitter functions in *Limax*. In addition, there are numerous fine, varicose FLI fibers in the connective tissue of the ganglionic and peripheral nerve sheaths and covering various organs including the salivary ducts and glands (Figure 10.9). The appearance of these fibers at the light microscopic level is strikingly similar to that of known neurosecretory fibers in the lobster (Beltz & Kravitz, 1983; Livingstone, Schaeffer, & Kravitz, 1981), an observation suggesting that FMRFamide might also play a hormonal role in *Limax*. Marchand, Sokolove, and Dubois (1984) have shown the colocalization of FMRFamide and somatostatin immunoreactivity in cerebral neurons of *Limax*.

GABA-like immunoreactive (GLI) neurons are found in the cerebral, buccal, and pedal ganglia. Two distinct classes of GLI cells are found: small (15–20 μm) unipolar cells that are aggregated in clusters and larger, solitary multipolar cells (Figure 10.10). GLI fibers are found in the interganglionic connectives but not in any of the peripheral nerves, a finding suggesting that GABA acts strictly as a central transmitter in *Limax*. We plan to use antisera to map the distribution of other classes of neurons that affect the feeding behavior of *Limax* as these reagents become available.

## NEUROCHEMICAL MANIPULATIONS

Another vital tool for dissecting circuit function that is readily implemented with the isolated lip–brain preparation involves direct chemical measurement of neurotransmitters present in the tissue, followed by pharmacological assessment of their effects on the lip input–FMP output reflex and learning ability (Sahley *et al.*, in press; Wieland & Gelperin, 1983).

**FIGURE 10.8.** Response of the isolated lip–brain preparation to GABA. SN, salivary nerve; BR1, buccal root 1. (A) GABA ($10^{-6}$ *M*) added to the bath interrupts the spontaneous bursting of the salivary burster neuron and excites several other salivary neurons. Stimulation of the lips still elicits vigorous FMP. (B) GABA ($10^{-4}$ *M*) interrupts spontaneous salivary burster activity and also suppresses the intensity of FMP.

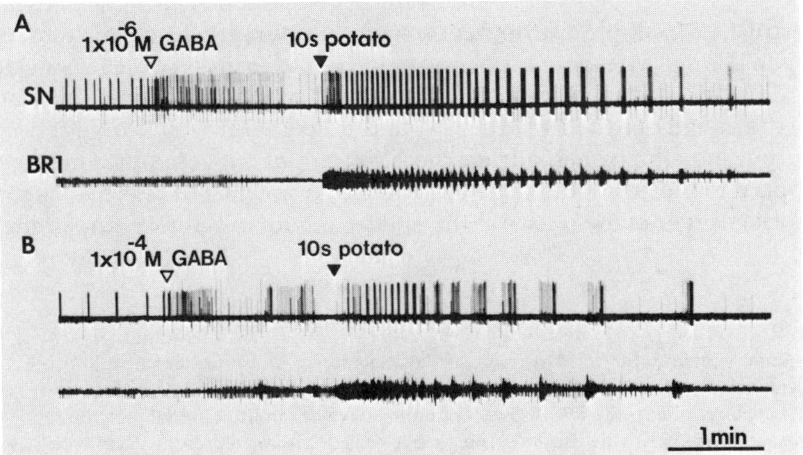

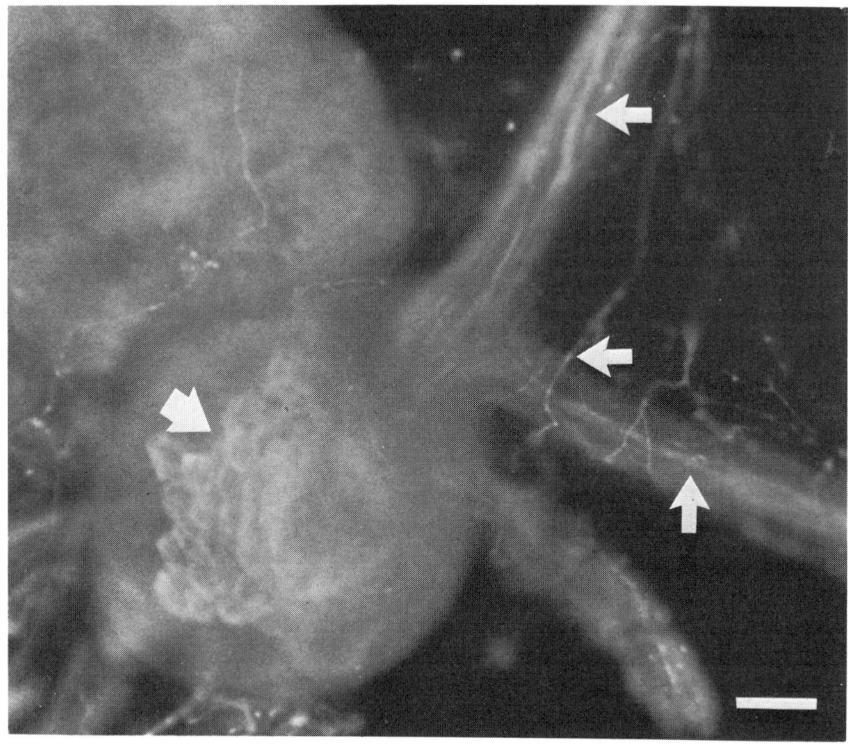

**FIGURE 10.9.** Fluorescence micrograph showing FMRFamide-like immunoreactivity in the buccal ganglion and peripheral nerve roots. A large number of neurons in the lateral lobe of the ganglion stain strongly (large arrow), as do fibers in the roots and in the connective tissue sheaths of the roots and ganglion (small arrows). Scale bar represents 25 micrometers

The involvement of dopamine in the generation of FMP is a particularly instructive example of the neurochemical approach to circuit dissection. Upon finding large amounts of dopamine in acid extracts of the *Limax* cerebral and buccal ganglia, it was discovered that low doses of dopamine applied to the ganglia of the isolated lip–brain preparation would trigger a motor output indistinguishable from the FMP output triggered by food extracts applied to the lips of the same preparation. A potent and selective dopamine blocker, ergonovine, blocked the ability of both exogenous dopamine and

---

**FIGURE 10.10.** (A) Fluorescence micrograph showing GABA-like immunoreactivity in the cerebral ganglion. Several clusters of small cells (arrows) are present in the vicinity of the metacerebral giant cell (MGC). Scale bar represents 100 micrometers. (B) Fluorescence micrograph of a solitary, multipolar GABA-like immunoreactive cell in the cerebral ganglion and several smaller, unipolar GABA-like immunoreactive cells. Scale bar represents 50 micrometers.

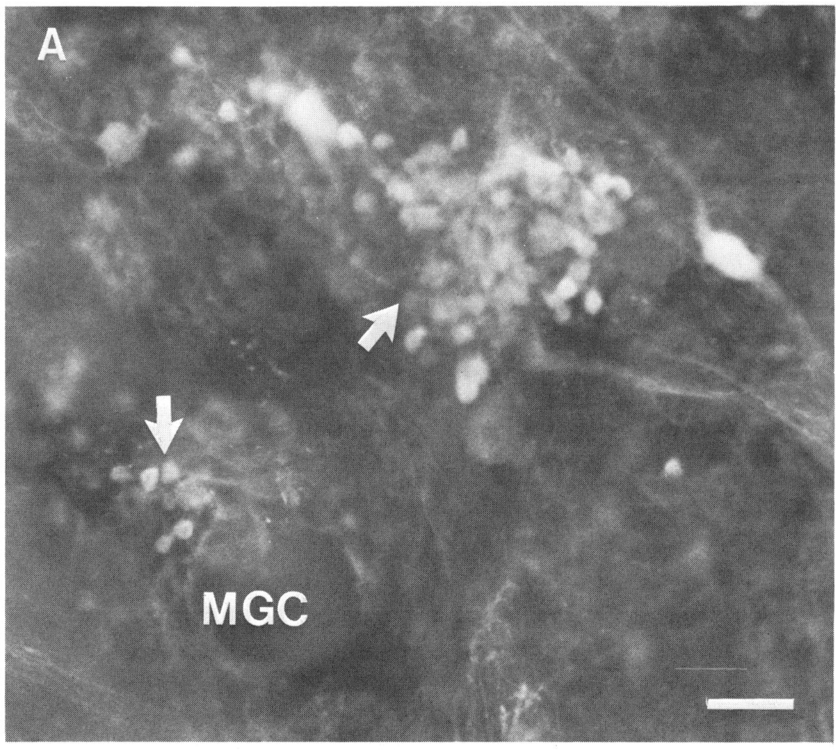
A
MGC

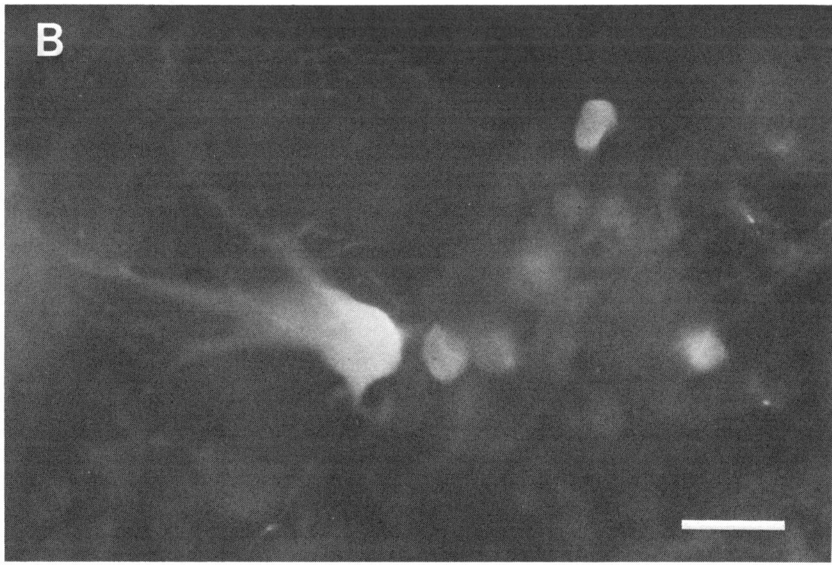
B

lip chemostimulation to trigger FMP (Wieland & Gelperin, 1983). Given that the operation of a set of dopaminergic synapses is obligatory for the operation of the taste input–FMP output reflex, we are approaching the involvement of dopaminergic synapses in learning by preparing brains with altered synaptic stores of dopamine for learning studies. The inhibitor α-methyl-*p*-tyrosine (AMPT) blocks dopamine synthesis in *Limax* neurons as in mammalian neurons (Wieland, Jahn, & Gelperin, submitted for publication). Determination of the differential effects of AMPT on storage pool versus readily releasable dopamine (Wieland, Jahn, & Gelperin, 1984) sets the stage for learning studies on brains with altered central stores of dopamine to determine if there is a differential effect of dopamine depletion on learning in addition to the expected effect on the FMP reflex. The modulation of molluscan dopaminergic synapses by opiate agonists such as met-enkephalin (Stefano, 1982) and morphine (Kavaliers, Hirst, & Teskey, 1984) suggests an intrinsic peptidergic control of dopaminergic neurotransmission.

## MODELING STUDIES

A model that has been developed containing an explicit mechanism of network interaction and synaptic alteration simulates many of the learning abilities of *Limax* (Gelperin *et al.*, 1985). This model (called LIMAX) has been implemented as a computer program that allows one to perform taste–taste associative conditioning experiments on-line. An essential element of the model is a highly interconnected network of neurons that can display several different stable states, that is, stable patterns of action potential activity within the network (Hopfield, 1984). The stable states of the network are determined by the strength of the synaptic connections between the neurons (Hopfield, 1982). An emergent feature of the network's operation is that if it is driven into an activity pattern similar to one of the stable activity patterns, it will converge to the most similar stable activity pattern and remain in the stable state unless perturbed again. Each stable state can be thought of as a memory stored in the network. The memory storage network is connected to an array of taste receptors through which distinct activity patterns arising from taste inputs can be imposed on the memory storage network and become stable states. Neurons in the memory storage network make connections with two motor command cells, called the "feed" and "flee" neurons. These synaptic connections between the memory network neurons and the command neurons are modified in strength by presynaptic facilitation or antifacilitation, triggered by activation of a labeled-line for aversive inputs such as quinidine. The synapse change algorithm initiated by quinidine stimulation contains timing relationships that enable forward conditioning but not backward conditioning. The network can simulate first-order conditioning, second-order conditioning, and both possible outcomes of the three-phase training procedure wherein the conditioned aversion to a stimulus is extinguished after using that stimulus to achieve second-order conditioning of a second stimulus (Sahley *et al.*, 1984; see Figure 10.1). The model has been extended more recently to simulate extinction and blocking.

The model is striking in its simplicity, its use of neurophysiologically realistic synaptic mechanisms, and the range of complex associative conditioning it can accomplish (see also Hawkins & Kandel, 1984). The model also is powerful because it makes specific predictions, behavioral and neurophysiological, that can be experimentally tested. For example, if aversive inputs operate as in our model, the quinidine stimulus should not decrease in aversiveness no matter how many times it is paired with attractive taste stimuli because aversive stimuli are not processed by the taste memory network in our model. An obvious cellular prediction is the existence of a group of highly interconnected interneurons, receiving direct sensory input, which is driven into a stable, reproducible pattern of membrane electrical activity by repeated application of a chemostimulus to the receptors activating the input. The olfactory input–procerebral lobe network will be used to test this prediction using multineuron optical recording techniques adequate to the task of recording network activity patterns.

The model is not yet complete. It does not account for different forms of memory storage that undoubtedly obtain at different times after conditioning. Some of its details are surely wrong. The importance of the model derives from its demonstration of how sophisticated logic operations can be performed by a small number of neural elements and by its predictive power and testability. Given that the phenomena of *Limax* conditioning are representative of a large array of vertebrate conditioning data (Rudy, 1984), the model may be of general utility at the behavioral level independent of its generality at the mechanistic level.

The work on *Limax* learning is part of a broad effort analyzing neural networks in a variety of vertebrate and invertebrate preparations. Although the neural networks being dissected are diverse in their phyletic origins, the goal of explaining learned behavioral changes in terms of the biochemistry of membrane receptors, ion channels, and synapse shape changes is broadly shared among the community of neuroscientists involved in this work. The learning results with *Limax* and LIMAX show that small neural networks can mediate complex neural calculations. When experiments with *Limax* identify critical interneurons and synapses as candidate loci for learning-related cellular changes, analysis can progress to the level of ionic conductances (Hockberger & Connor, 1984), cyclic nucleotide levels (Yamane & Gelperin, in preparation), and neuronal phosphoproteins (Oestereicher, Yamane, & Gelperin, 1984). The molecular mechanisms underlying the neuronal computations performed by the *Limax* CNS will then be open to analysis.

## ACKNOWLEDGMENTS

Work done at Princeton University was supported by NIMH Grant MH39160 (to A. G.) and a Natural Sciences and Engineering Research Council of Canada Postgraduate Scholarship (to K. D.). We thank B. Beltz for advice on immunocytochemical techniques.

## REFERENCES

Alkon, D. L. Calcium-mediated reduction of ionic currents: A biophysical memory trace. *Science*, 1984, *226*, 1037–1045.

Beltz, B., & Kravitz, E. A. Mapping of serotonin-like immunoreactivity in the lobster nervous system. *Journal of Neuroscience*, 1983, *3*, 585–602.

Benjamin, P. R. Gastropod feeding: behavioral and neural analysis of a complex multicomponent system. In A. Roberts & B. L. Roberts (Eds.), *Neural control of rhythmic movements*. London & New York: Cambridge University Press, 1983.

Boyle, M. B., Cohen, L. B. Macagno, E. R., & Orbach, H. The number and size of neurons in the CNS of gastropod molluscs and their suitability for optical recording of activity. *Brain Research*, 1983, *266*, 305–317.

Bullock, T. H., & Horridge, G. A. *Structure and function in the nervous systems of invertebrates* (Vol. 2). San Francisco: Freeman, 1965.

Chang, J. J., & Gelperin, A. Rapid taste aversion learning by an isolated molluscan central nervous system. *Proceedings of the National Academy of Sciences, U. S. A.*, 1980, *77*, 6204–6206.

Chetail, M. Etude de la régéneration du tentacule oculaire chez un arionidae (*Arion rufus*) et un Limacidae (*Agriolimax agrestis*). *Archives d'Anatomie Microscopique et de Morphologie Expérimentale*, 1963, *52*, 129–203.

Copeland, J., & Gelperin, A. Feeding and a serotonergic interneuron activate an identified autoactive salivary neuron in *Limax maximus*. *Comparative Biochemistry and Physiology*, 1983, *76*, 21–30.

Croll, R. P., Kovac, M. P., Davis, W. J., & Matera, C. M. Neural mechanisms of motor program switching in the mollusk Pleurobranchaea. III. Role of the paracerebral neurons and other identified brain neurons. *Journal of Neuroscience*, 1985, *5*, 64–71.

Culligan, N., & Gelperin, A. One-trial associative learning by an isolated molluscan CNS: Use of different chemoreceptors for training and testing. *Brain Research*, 1983, *266*, 319–327.

Davis, W. J. Neural mechanisms of behavioral plasticity in an invertebrate model system. In A. I. Selverston (Ed.), *Model neural networks and behavior*. New York: Plenum Press, 1985.

Delaney, K., & Gelperin, A. Rapid food-aversion learning with shock as UCS in *Limax maximus*. *Society for Neuroscience Abstracts*, 1984, *10*, 509.

Delaney, K., & Gelperin, A. Postingestive food-aversion learning to amino acid deficient diets by the terrestrial slug *Limax maximus*. Submitted for publication.

Egan M., & Gelperin, A. Olfactory inputs to a bursting serotonergic interneuron in a terrestrial mollusc. *Journal of Molluscan Studies*, 1981, *47*, 80–88.

Gelperin, A. Rapid food-aversion learning by a terrestrial mollusk. *Science*, 1975, *189*, 567–570.

Gelperin, A. Synaptic modulation by identified serotonin neurons. In B. Jacobs & A. Gelperin (Eds.), *Serotonin neurotransmission and behavior*. Cambridge, Mass.: MIT Press, 1981.

Gelperin, A., Chang, J. J., & Reingold, S. C. Feeding motor program in *Limax*. I. Neuromuscular correlates and control by chemosensory input. *Journal of Neurobiology*, 1978, *9*, 285–300.

Gelperin, A., & Culligan, N. In vitro expression of in vivo learning by an isolated molluscan CNS. *Brain Research*, 1984, *304*, 207–213.

Gelperin, A., Hopfield, J. J., & Tank, D. W. The logic of *Limax* learning. In A. I. Selverston

(Ed.), *Model neural networks and behavior*. New York: Plenum Press, 1985.

Greenberg, M. J., Painter, S. D., Doble, K. E., Nagle, G. T., Price, D. A., & Lehman, H. K. The molluscan neurosecretory peptide FMRFamide: Comparative pharmacology and relationship to the enkephalins. *Federation Proceedings, Federation of American Societies for Experimental Biology*, 1983, *42*, 82–86.

Hawkins, R. D., & Kandel, E. R. Is there a cell-biological alphabet for simple forms of learning? *Psychological Review*, 1984, *91*, 375–391.

Hockberger, P., & Connor, J. A. Alteration of calcium conductances and outward current by cAMP in neurons of *Limax maximus*. *Cellular and Molecular Neurobiology*, 1984, *4*, 319–338.

Hopfield, J. J. Neural networks and physical systems with emergent collective computational abilities. *Proceedings of the National Academy of Sciences, U. S. A.*, 1982, *79*, 2554–2558.

Hopfield, J. J. Neurons with graded response have collective computational properties like those of two-state neurons. *Proceedings of the National Academy of Sciences, U. S. A.*, 1984, *81*, 3088–3092.

Kauer, J. S., Senseman, D., & Cohen, L. B. Voltange-sensitive dye recording from the olfactory system of the tiger salamander. *Society for Neuroscience Abstracts*, 1984, *10*, 846.

Kavaliers, M., Hirst, M., & Teskey, G. C. Opioid-induced feeding in the slug *Limax maximus*. *Physiology and Behavior*, 1984, *33*, 765–767.

Livingstone, M. S., Schaeffer, S. F., & Kravitz, E. A. Biochemistry and ultrastructure of serotonergic nerve endings in the lobster: Serotonin and octopamine are contained in different nerve endings. *Journal of Neurobiology*, 1981, *12*, 27–54.

Marchand, C.-R., Sokolove, P. G., & Dubois, M. P. Immunocytological localization of a somatostatin-like substance in the brain of the giant garden slug, *Limax maximus*. *Cell Tissue Research*, 1984, *238*, 349–353.

Oestereicher, B., Yamane, T., & Gelperin, A. Dopamine alters the phosphorylation of specific proteins from cerebral neurons of *Limax maximus*. Unpublished manuscript, 1984.

Phifer, C. B., & Prior, D. J. Body hydration and haemolymph osmolality affect feeding and its neural correlate in the terrestrial gastropod, *Limax maximus*. *Journal of Experimental Biology*, in press.

Prior, D. J. Hydration-induced modulation of feeding responsiveness in terrestrial slugs. *Journal of Experimental Zoology*, 1983, *227*, 15–22.

Prior, D. J. Analysis of contact-rehydration in terrestrial gastropods: Osmotic control of drinking behavior. *Journal of Experimental Biology*, 1984, *111*, 63–73.

Prior, D., & Gelperin, A. Autoactive molluscan neuron: Reflex function and synaptic modulation during feeding in the terrestrial slug *Limax maximus*. *Journal of Comparative Physiology*, 1977, *114*, 217–232.

Rescorla, R. A. Comments on three Pavlovian paradigms. In D. Alkon & J. Farley (Eds.), *Primary neural substrates of learning and behavioral change*. London & New York: Cambridge University Press, 1984.

Rosen, S. C., Weiss, K. R., Cohen, J. L. & Kupfermann, I. Interganglionic cerebral-buccal mechanoafferents of *Aplysia*: Receptive fields and synaptic connections to different classes of neurons involved in feeding behavior. *Journal of Neurophysiology*, 1982, *48*, 271–288.

Rudy, J. W. An appreciation of higher-order conditioning and blocking. In M. Commons, R. Herrnstein, & A. R. Wagner (Eds.), *Quantitative analyses of behavior* (Vol. 3: *Acquisition*). Cambridge, Mass.: Ballinger, 1984.

Sahley, C. L., Barry, S. R., & Gelperin, A. Dietary choline augments associative memory function in *Limax maximus*. *Journal of Neurobiology*, in press.

Sahley, C., Gelperin, A., & Rudy, J. W. One-trial associative learning modifies food odor preferences of a terrestrial mollusc. *Proceedings of the National Academy of Sciences, U. S. A.*, 1981, *78*, 640–642.

Sahley, C. L., Rudy, J. W. & Gelperin, A. An analysis of associative learning in a terrestrial mollusc: higher-order conditioning, blocking and a transient US pre-exposure effect. *Journal of Comparative Physiology*, 1981, *144*, 1–8.

Sahley, C. L., Rudy, J. W., & Gelperin, A. Associative learning in a mollusc: A comparative analysis. In D. L. Alkon & J. Farley (Eds.), *Primary neural substrates of learning and behavioral change*. London & New York: Cambridge University Press, 1984.

Stefano, G. B. Comparative aspects of opioid-dopamine interaction. *Cellular and Molecular Neurobiology*, 1982, *2*, 167–178.

Van Minnen, J., & Sokolove, P. G. Neurosecretory cells in the central nervous system of the giant garden slug, *Limax maximus*. *Journal of Neurobiology*, 1981, *12*, 297–301.

Van Mol, J. Etude morphologique et phylogénétique du ganglion cérébroide des Gasteropodes Pulmones. *Memories de l'Académie Royale de Médecine de Belgique*, 1967, *37*(5), 1–168.

Veratti, E. Ricerche sul sisterna nervoso dei *Limax*. *Memorie dell'Istituto Lombardo di Scienzee Lettere*, 1900, *18*, Fasc. 9.

Wieland, S. J., & Gelperin, A. Dopamine elicits feeding motor program in *Limax maximus*. *Journal of Neuroscience*, 1983, *3*, 1735–1745.

Wieland, S. J., Jahn, E. G., & Gelperin, A. Measurement and control of dopamine and serotonin release from *Limax* ganglia in vitro. *Society for Neuroscience Abstracts*, 1984, *10*, 690.

Wieland, S. J., Jahn, E., & Gelperin, A. Localization and synthesis of monoamines in regions of *Limax* CNS controlling feeding behavior. Submitted for publication.

Yamane, T., & Gelperin, A. Effects of dopamine and serotonin on cyclic AMP levels in procerebral neurons of *Limax maximus*. In preparation.

Zs-Nagy, I., & Sakharov, D. A. The fine structure of the procerebrum of pulmonate molluscs, *Helix* and *Limax*. *Tissue and Cell*, 1970, *2*, 399–411.

CHAPTER 11

# Learning and Memory in Honey Bees

**James L. Gould**
Princeton University

## INTRODUCTION

This chapter serves two purposes: first, to attempt to relate laboratory work on learning to naturalistic observations and experiments, thereby deriving testable models for learning in animals under naturalistic conditions; and second, to describe and analyze honey bee learning from this perspective. Earlier papers by Gould and Marler (1984) and Gould (1984) have explored these two general topics in a more detailed, though preliminary way; a forthcoming paper by Gould (in press-a) will deal with some of these ideas in greater detail.

## THE ETHOLOGY OF LEARNING

Ethologists are concerned with the mechanisms and evolution of behavior. They are interested, then, in what an animal is born knowing—instinct—and what it learns; they are interested in how innate knowledge is stored and used and in how learned knowledge is acquired and employed; and finally, they are interested in understanding the evolutionary pressures that have led to differences in the innate behavior and learning of different species. As reductionists, they assume there are common mechanisms underlying instinct and learning, despite the striking species-specific differences in behavior. I shall review very briefly the mechanistic explanations for innate behavior accepted by most ethologists and then shall turn to ethological and psychological studies of learning.

### Mechanisms of Innate Behavior

The mechanisms of innate behavior are relevant to learning because, as I shall argue, they are intimately involved in learning programs. The most important in the present context are releasers or sign stimuli. These are relatively simple, abstract cues, apparently analogous (and perhaps identical) to the disembodied features to which "feature detectors" in the nervous system selectively respond (Gould, 1982); they serve to direct and trigger innate behavior. Sign stimuli will be important to my discussion of associative learning in the next section.

Motor programs consist of endogenously generated and coordinated, relatively automatic and stereotyped muscle movements. They are relevant to learning because many learned behavioral performances are learned motor programs; they will be especially important in my later discussion of trial-and-error learning.

Drive is the endogenously controlled alteration of behavioral responsiveness and behavioral priorities. Drive is relevant to learning because the capacity for some sorts of learning in many animals is internally modulated.

Bird song learning (Gould, 1982; Gould & Marler, 1984; Marler, 1984) provides a cogent example of how the interaction of these three innate mechanisms can create a learning program. To take a specific and relatively typical case, white-crowned sparrows reared in isolation will sing a very simple song—in some sense an outline of a normal song (Figure 11.1). A deafened bird will sing an unpatterned, nonmelodic song (Figure 11.1), an observation suggesting that feedback matching—hearing one's sound output, comparing it against an innate model of some sort, and modifying the output accordingly—must be necessary to sing even the innate song. (This is in sharp contrast to the two dozen or so innate calls—the mating call, for instance—found in most species, which require no initial feedback; moreover, some species like the mourning dove have songs that are also completely innate and require no feedback.) This process of feedback matching in white-crowned sparrows occurs when the drive to start vocal experimentation begins at about 150 days of age. Birds subsequently store the instructions for singing even the innate song as a motor program, and so deafening after full song appears has little or no effect on fully developed innate song.

Normally, however, young birds learn to sing elaborate versions of their species' songs—versions that closely resemble those they heard when young. Experiments on laboratory-reared birds demonstrate that the learning is almost exclusively restricted to songs of the learner's own species and to a particular period in the bird's life—the "sensitive period." The learning, then, occurs in two steps: First, an endogenous system makes the bird receptive over a relatively brief period to songs containing acoustic sign stimuli diagnostic of its species' songs. The song meeting these criteria is committed to memory, perhaps being "written over" the innate song model in the brain. Second, an endogenous system later causes the bird to begin vocal experimentation, to match the stored song, and to commit the appropriate series of instructions to memory as a motor program. Except for the involvement of a learned motor program, bird song learning is virtually identical to classical imprinting: There is a sensitive period; learning is trig-

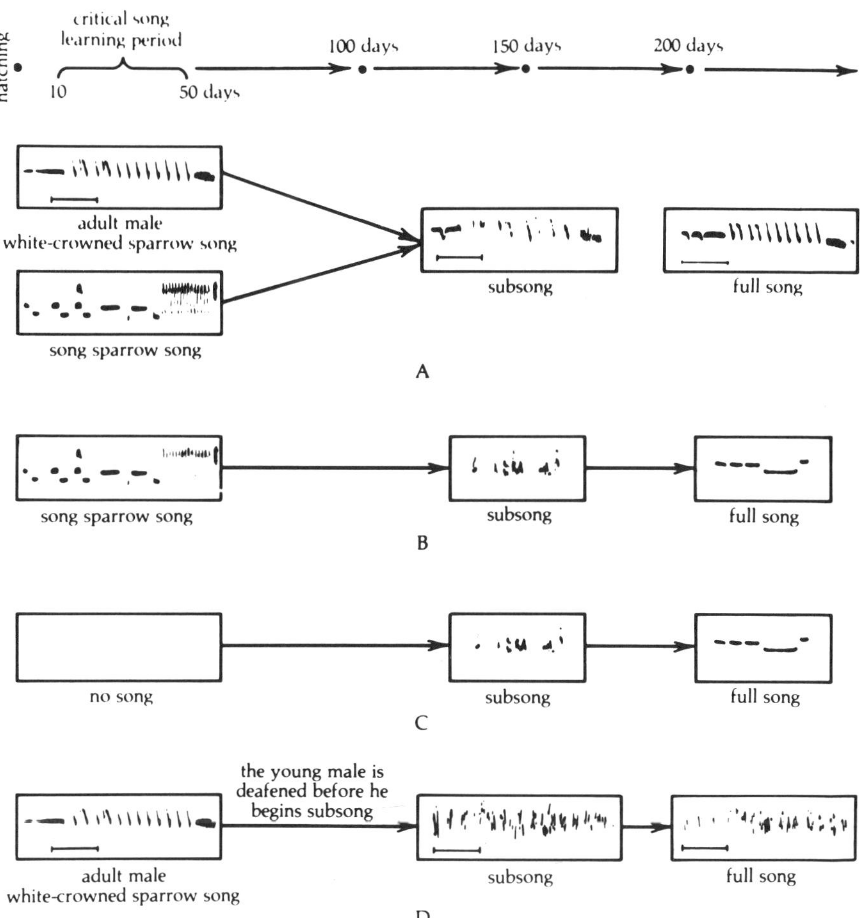


**FIGURE 11.1.** Song learning. White-crowned sparrows learn their species song during a sensitive period from 10 to 50 days of age. At about 150 days they begin to vocalize and practice making syllable sounds. By 200 days they have developed a stable song that closely matches the song heard during the sensitive period. Song learning is selective, so that if offered a choice, birds will learn only their own species' song (A); if offered the wrong song (B) or no song at all (C), the birds will learn nothing and sing only a simple innate song. If deafened before he begins to practice (D), the bird will never sing anything melodic, whereas deafening after song "crystallizes" at about 200 days leaves singing almost unaffected. (From Gould, 1982.)

gered by innately recognized cues; there is no overt reward; and the learning can be relatively irreversible. The claim still heard from some writers (e.g., Macphail, Chapter 15, this volume) that all vertebrate learning is identical ignores the fact that only some species imprint on their young, only some memorize their eggs, only some imprint on their parents, only some learn their courtship songs, and so on (Gould & Marler, 1984). These differences, the evolutionary significance of which is obvious in light of the natural history of the species, imply adaptive differences in the neural wiring associated with learning, though the basic mechanisms may be (and we hope are) identical.

### Associative Learning: Classical Conditioning

Classical conditioning (Schwartz, 1984) involves learning a positive correlation between a novel stimulus or stimulus set—the conditioned stimulus (CS)—and an innately recognized stimulus—the unconditioned stimulus (US). Initially, the US triggers an innate behavior—the unconditioned response (UR)—but if the CS is sufficiently predictive of the US, the CS will come to trigger the behavior itself. In the language of ethology, the US is a sign stimulus, the UR a motor program, and the CS (loosely) a search image. To ethologists, the selective value—the "purpose"—of associative learning seems clear: A relatively crude sign stimulus (or more often, set of sign stimuli) is replaced by a more precise set of stimuli, as when a herring gull chick, who initially responds to its parent on the basis merely of its vertical beak and red spot moving horizontally, replaces this very crude but diagnostic pair of releasers with a "picture" of the parent sufficient to distinguish it even from other herring gulls [Hailman, 1967; habituation and conditioned inhibition are also important (Dollinger, Gordon, & Gould, in review; Margolis, Mariscal, & Gould, in review)].

It is worth emphasizing that most innate behavior is triggered by a small constellation of sign stimuli, each of which can be effective by itself. Herring gull chicks, for example, will peck at and learn to prefer a model with a vertical bill but no spot, or a spot without a bill (Dollinger *et al.*, in review). The same is true of laughing gulls, where the vertical red beak of the normal adult can be divided into a vertically oriented shape and the color red (Margolis *et al.*, in review). In both cases, the two stimuli are more effective when presented together, a frequently observed phenomenon known to ethologists as "heterogeneous summation." Some psychological analyses of imprinting (Shettleworth, 1983), attempting to reason out whether imprinting is or is not a case of associative learning, make the mistake of assuming there is a unitary US (usually said to be movement), whereas the species-specific exodus call and speculum color are also effective (Hess, 1972) and sum heterogeneously (Horner, Acuña, & Gould, in preparation). In fact, the speculum response of mallards is itself probably a result of heterogeneous summation of two separate color releasers (Durkis & Gould, in preparation). Moreover, Gould and Marler (1984) point out the frequent distinction between Innate Learning Triggers—cues that specify the context for a specific kind of learning and bring about an alteration in the nervous system that makes specific USs effective—and both the USs themselves and the potential CSs an animal can learn in the particular context. [The phenomenon of heterogeneous summation, where several cues can be independently effective simultaneously, should not be confused with cases—particularly common in courtship displays—in which several cues are involved but are each essential and must be encountered in a particular sequence (Gould, 1982).] Beyond the problem of considering the US as a single entity, some writers have made the analogous mistake of assuming there is a unitary CS. In fact, there is usually a hierarchy (e.g., Horner *et al.*, in preparation), a fact that will become clear in the contest of flower learning by bees described later.

It is striking how much of associative learning is innate: the US, the UR, and the wiring for extracting correlations. In many—perhaps most—cases, even the range and relative salience of potential CS cues are also innately specified. This latter conclusion is suggested by the observation that many species are subject to learning biases; pigeons, for example, learn an auditory CS predicting danger faster than a visual one, but they learn a visual CS predicting food faster than an auditory one.

For ethologists, it is tempting to think of associative learning as a sort of covert alpha conditioning—normal or "overt" alpha conditioning is learning in which there is some slight initial response to the CS that is quickly amplified during conditioning. Suppose that the cells responsible for learning the US–CS correlation initially "listen" primarily to inputs from the US feature detectors but are also weakly wired to various potential CSs. Suppose further that collaterals from the US input interact with the CS inputs such that correlated firing leads to strengthening of the active CS connections, whereas uncorrelated or negatively correlated firing leads to weakening or inhibition. The number, nature, and initial strength of the CS connections would then be the likely source of learning biases, with unusually strong connections giving rise to the overt phenomenon of alpha conditioning. This kind of model parallels the results obtained by N. J. Cohen (Chapter 22, this volume) on pigeons.

This kind of model, variants of which have been proposed by Changeaux and Dauchin (1976), Edelman and Mountcastle (1978), Hawkins and Kandel (1984), Gould (1982), and Gould and Marler (1984), places associative learning in a clear evolutionary context: Through natural selection, a particular range of plausible, species-specific preassociations can be prewired for each of several behavioral situations to facilitate rapid learning of the cues most likely to be salient. Extraneous stimuli unlikely to provide useful information would thus be largely ignored, at least initially. Over a wide range of lifestyles, animals with such wiring would tend to be more fit than those with no preexisting biases. In the discussion of honey bee learning presented later, another possible role of these biases will become evident. A model that has

## Associative Learning: Trial-and-Error Learning

Operant (instrumental) conditioning allows animals to learn novel motor behaviors to gain rewards or avoid punishments (Schwartz, 1984). Ethologists have little trouble seeing a chickadee experimenting with and "solving" a sunflower seed, for example, as an example of trial-and-error learning in the wild. In fact, observations of animals under natural conditions suggest that trial-and-error learning may be more adaptive and species-specific than is often thought. One point is that novel behaviors frequently become as automatic as innate motor programs, as in the case of bird song, where deafening after "crystallization" has little effect. Reducing a frequent behavior to an automatic motor program has the advantage of freeing an animal's attention for other tasks—watching for predators or conspecifics, for example.

Another ethological observation is that the motor experimentation used in the initial stages of learning to perform a behavior is often composed of a group of individual, species-specific gestures appropriate to the behavioral context. Marler (1984) has gone so far as to interpret the babbling phase of bird song learning in this framework, with each syllable constituting a single innate vocal gesture. Some uses of trial-and-error learning, then, might involve selecting and ordering prewired gestures (Gould & Marler, 1984). Moreover, as already mentioned, the gestures actually used in experimentation appear to be context specific—singing versus seed opening, for example—thus suggesting that the "design logic" in at least some cases of trial-and-error learning may be similar to the more tightly programmed cases of associative learning discussed earlier. Indeed, some of the "biases" in operant conditioning this perspective would predict are well known: Pigeons, for example, learn more readily to peck than to bar-press for food, but can be more easily taught to bar-press than to peck to avoid danger. A pigeon that has wiring predisposing it to experiment initially on potential food items by pecking and to try using its legs or wings rather than its neck to find ways of avoiding potential danger is probably more fit than a bird with no motor biases. A degree of internal guidance in trial-and-error situations must often be adaptive.

Some ethologists have found the distinction between classical and operant conditioning to be relatively artificial because the two—learning to recognize and learning how to behave—are usually linked in the real world. Indeed, if classical conditioning is often context specific—and trial-and-error learning can be as well—then it would be surprising if the wiring for the two kinds of learning in the same context were not at least tentatively linked for efficiency. It may be that the phenomenon of autoconditioning (in which animals spontaneously perform unnecessary but "sensible" behavior in a classical conditioning paradigm) reflects this linkage.

Ethologists, among others, would also be tempted to interpret some of the more unusual response patterns on various ratio schedules in terms of a mismatch between the often-deterministic situation presented to the animal and the probabilistic "expectations" incorporated through natural selection into the animal's nervous system (Staddon & Gould, in preparation).

## FLOWER LEARNING BY HONEY BEES

The lifestyle of honey bees offers many opportunities for the kinds of preadapted learning emphasized in the preceding discussion. In essence, this is because they live in a world of the *predictably unpredictable*: They must learn many things to survive, but the proper context for this learning and the range of likely possible answers to the questions that must be answered can be specified in advance with fair precision. Hence, selection can and has worked to make them learning specialists. The larger range of learning tasks bees face—particularly those related to navigation—are discussed elsewhere (Gould, 1984); here I wish to focus entirely on what and how bees learn about flowers, and why.

### Odor Learning

As von Frisch (1967) showed more than 70 years ago, honey bees learn to recognize the odor of flowers rapidly and with considerable precision. In one case, bees successfully located a species of flower on the basis of its odor from some 700 alternatives. Menzel and his colleagues (Menzel & Erber, 1978) have shown that for most odors, only a single trial is necessary to reach a 90% criterion in a two-choice test (Figure 11.2). Lindauer (1969) has shown that different odors are learned at different rates and that different geographical races of bees learn certain odors at very different rates—rates that he concludes reflect the occurrence of flowers with that kind of odor

**FIGURE 11.2.** Learning rates in bees. The percentage of correct choices in a two-choice test is plotted for bees rewarded one to nine times in the presence of a color or odor cue. The color curve is for blue. (From Gould, 1982.)

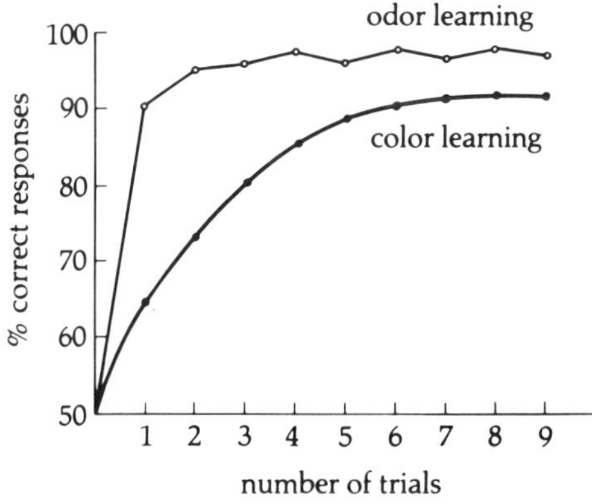

in their habitat. The possibility that these biases reflect the sort of covert alpha conditioning preassociations discussed earlier is reinforced by Erber's (1981) finding that only nerve cells in the brain of bees that initially show some slight response to both sucrose solution (the US) and the particular odor to be tested (the CS, which by itself does not initially trigger a behavioral response) show a dramatic change in activity after the two are paired.

## Color Learning

Von Frisch (1967) demonstrated early in the century that bees could learn the color of a food source. Later, Opfinger (1931) demonstrated that this learning took place only on the approach to the flower, and Menzel (Menzel & Erber, 1978) found that only the color seen in the last 2 or 3 seconds was remembered; this is typical of the temporal relationship expected between CS and US in associative learning situations.

Not all colors are learned equally fast; as Menzel has shown (Figure 11.3), violet is learned very quickly (better than 90% after one trial in a two-

**FIGURE 11.3.** Color learning by honey bees. Average learning curves in a two-color choice test for 11 colors visible to bees. The alternative was always the complement. The line connecting these results after one trial is highlighted. (From Menzel, Erber, & Masuhr, 1974.)

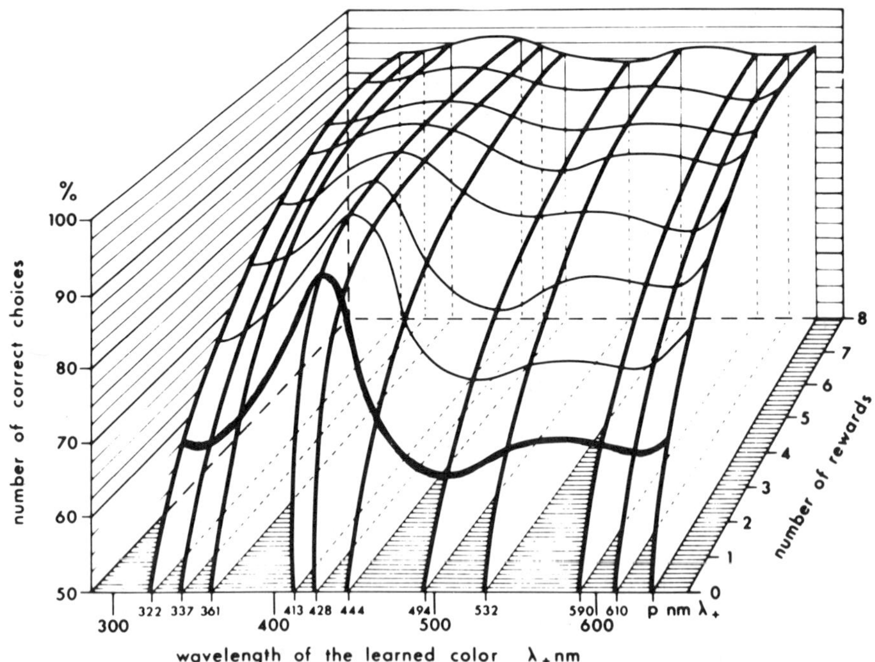

choice test), whereas blue-green is learned more slowly (about 65% in one trial). The three color receptors of honey bees have maximum sensitivities for the ultraviolet (UV), blue, and green wavelengths, so that the enhanced learning of violet involves some sort of processing between receptor and brain. It is perhaps also interesting that, given a choice of targets of different colors, naive bees will spontaneously land on violet targets and search there for food more often than on other hues. Now bees scouting for new food sources must experiment by exploring some very small but plausible subset of the many possibilities they encounter in the field. Clearly, an undiscriminating exploration of every stone and blade of grass would be maladaptive. Instead, bees have certain "preconceptions" that guide them to experiment on likely targets. Those spontaneous preferences include not only the color violet, but odors containing geraniol (a frequent component of floral scents), targets that are UV-dark in the center and UV-bright around the center, and highly dissected shapes (that is, targets with many petals). None of these biases is absolute, however; bees will try all sorts of targets but will most often try ones that have one or more of these heterogeneously summing stimuli and that appear to offer the best chance of success.

A possible lesson is suggested by the spontaneous biases of bees: They may reflect the strength of the preexisting CS wiring in the network responsible for learning about flowers. Indeed, we could imagine this network as corresponding to the IRM (innate releasing mechanism) of classic ethology, responsible for summing the relevant, context-specific sensory inputs (heterogeneous summation again), but capable of altering its selectivity through associative learning. Associative learning might then be thought of in such cases as a mechanism for replacing the innate, spontaneous preferences—the "default" parameters in computer jargon—with a set of cues more precisely "tuned" to the contingencies of the real world.

## Shape and Pattern Learning

Hertz (1929, 1930, 1931) originally concluded that the spontaneous preference of honey bees for highly dissected targets was so great that only the crudest sort of pattern discrimination is possible. Later workers (Anderson, 1972, 1977b, 1977c; Cruse, 1972; Ronacher, 1979a, 1979b; Schnetter, 1972; Wehner, 1972) demonstrated that bees have a good ability to learn shapes and patterns but that the dissectedness—or, more precisely, spatial frequency—of a target was perhaps its most salient characteristic for bees. With the initial exception of Wehner, the consensus of opinion was that bees do not store pictorial representations—eidetic images—of flowers but rather remember a series of abstract parameters like spatial frequency. Wehner (1972), on the other hand, at first concluded from his experiments, which showed that bees could learn the orientation of a set of parallel lines presented on a vertical surface, that bees could remember pictures. Later, Wehner (1981) pointed out that because the visual systems of many animals have feature detector circuits specific to all possible line angles, his bees could have remembered line angle as a parameter. Various authors suggest different numbers of stored parameters, four being a typical figure.

The parameter hypothesis is attractive because it would probably require many fewer neurons than the picture hypothesis, and could be wired along the preassociational, alpha conditioning lines discussed earlier through the strategy of "reciprocal coding" (Gould, 1984). But as I have pointed out (Gould, 1984), the evidence for the parameter hypothesis is equivocal on several counts. Only tests in which the parameters are preserved but the spatial relationships between the elements are varied can distinguish clearly between the two.

I have performed a series of such experiments, a few of which are illustrated in Figure 11.4. In each case, the pattern marked "+" offered sugar solution and the one marked "−" did not. [The $S^-$ pattern was used to avoid the possibility of bees learning "part figures" in the manner of rats (Lashley, 1938) rather than the pattern as a whole.] The bees were able to distinguish most patterns with great reliability. Only when the number of elements was increased to 24 did the choices become nearly random. From this result and the distance from the targets at which bees hovered while making their choices, I estimate that each element in the most difficult pattern tested was seen by 25 ommatidia. This suggests that the resolution of the stored picture rather than visual resolution *per se* is the limiting factor. I was also able to demonstrate that bees learn to avoid the unrewarded target through conditioned inhibition. These experiments are reported in detail elsewhere (Gould, 1985, in press-b).

### Landmark Learning

Bees can learn and use three-dimensional landmarks near a food source to aid them in their final approach to a target (Wehner, 1981). Anderson (1977a) concluded that bees do not store images of landmarks but rather remember relatively crude parameters. Cartwright and Collett (1982, 1983), on the other hand, concluded that bees remember the landmarks pictorially. The two sets of experiments were quite different, and, in my opinion, the definitive test has yet to be done (Gould, 1984). Recent experiments (Gould, in preparation) explore this question in more detail and indicate that bees can learn the color of landmarks, the spatial relationship between landmarks of two colors—between, for example, a set of four evenly spaced vertical cylinders painted (running from left to right) blue, violet, violet, blue from a set painted violet, blue, blue, violet—and the shapes of landmarks with a resolution of 8–10° (Figure 11.5). These results strongly favor the picture hypothesis.

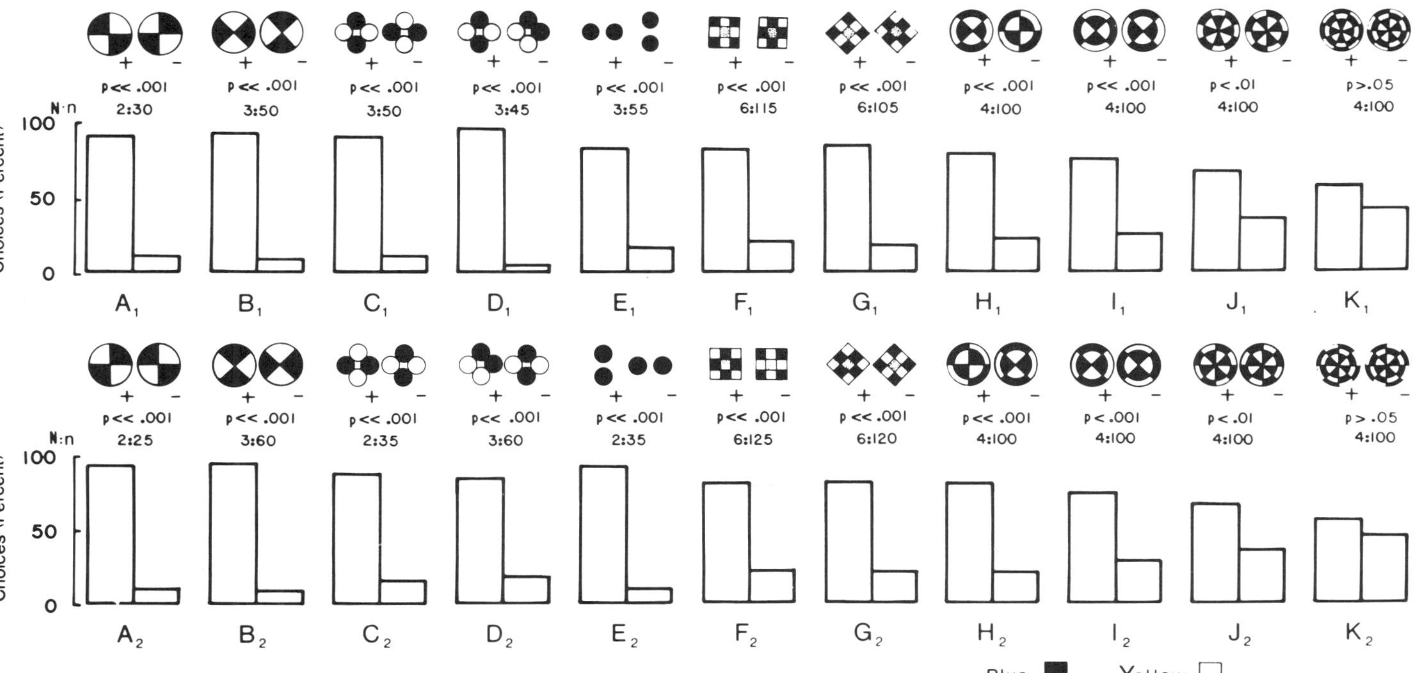


**FIGURE 11.4.** Pattern learning. Bees were offered two targets, but only rewarded when they chose the one marked "+". After each of the ten training visits, the left–right relationship of the targets was reversed (because otherwise some bees learned location rather than the pattern). Testing consisted of scoring landings on identical targets without food. Most patterns had identical spatial frequency, color areas, line angles, and so on; most differed in the spatial relationship between the elements. Bees learned to distinguish between all pattern pairs except the ones with 24 elements (far right). (Number of bees tested, $N$, and number of choices recorded, $n$, are shown above the bar graphs as $N{:}n$.)

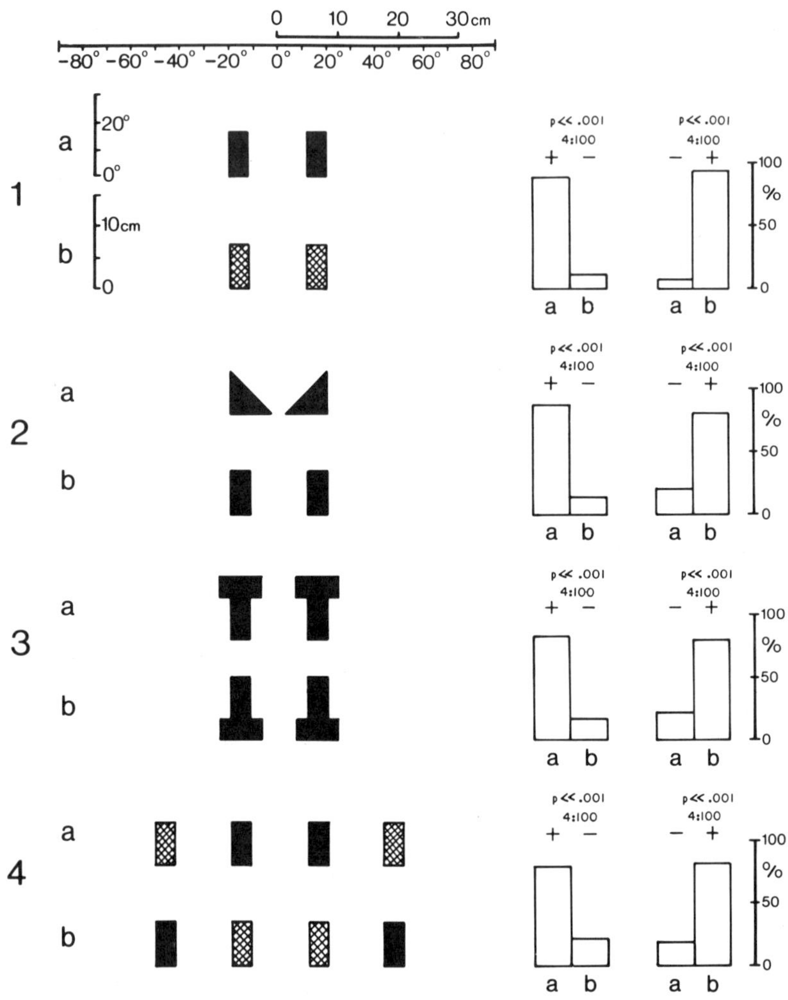


## Location Learning

Bees also learn the location of food sources. Initially, as recruits attending a recruitment dance in the hive, bees learn the distance and direction of the food (Gould, 1975; von Frisch, 1967). Scouts, who search for new food sources and so have not attended a dance, remember enough about the location of their discoveries to navigate back to the hive and perform dances encoding distance and direction. Whether the location memory of a scout or forager familiar with a good source is identical to that of a recruit is not known. A variety of experiments (Gould, 1984; Wehner, 1981) suggests that scouts and foragers, at least, use a learned, landmark-based, map-like rep-

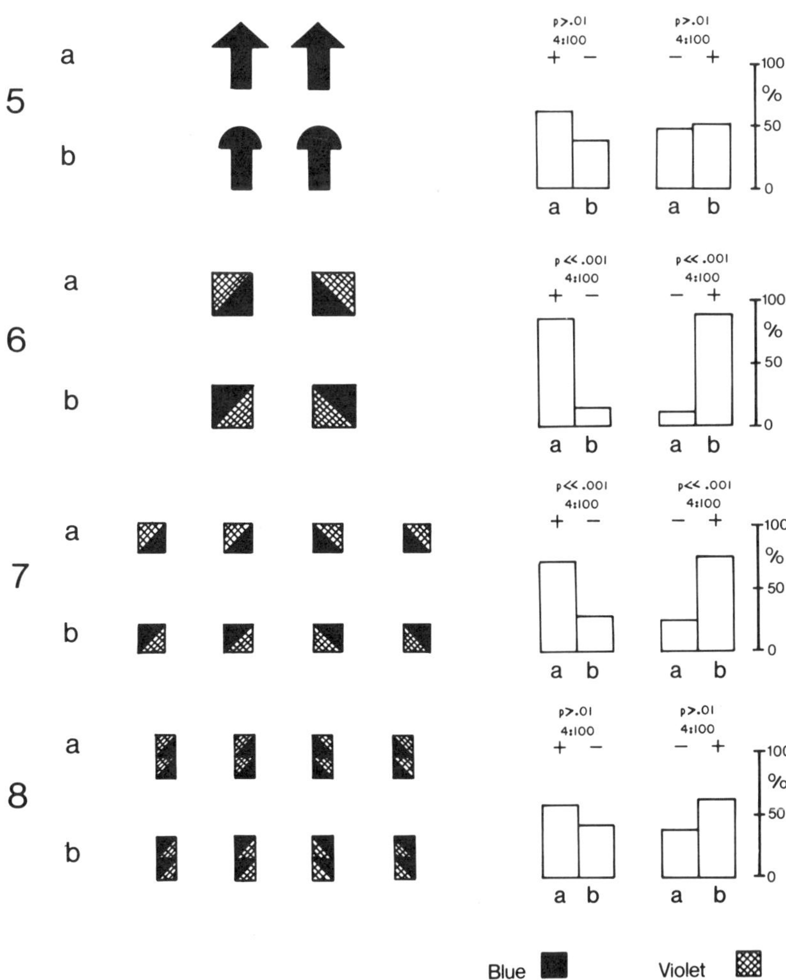


**FIGURE 11.5.** Landmark learning. Bees were offered two landmark arrays—(a) and (b)—of which one ($S^+$) provided food and one ($S^-$) did not. Landmarks are shown as seen from the location of the food. An absolute scale of centimeters and a relative scale of angular size are provided. The center of the array was defined as the direction away from the hive. Results are shown on the right, with the data for the $S^+$ pattern marked "+." Note that the two sets of data for each experiment came from reciprocal experiments—that is, the $S^+$ in one is the $S^-$ in the other. The number of bees tested ($N$) and the number of choices recorded ($n$) are shown above the data as $N$:$n$. The $p$ value for the summed data is also shown.

resentation of their surroundings for navigation and can extract distance and direction from this map. It may be that an experienced recruit can perform the opposite transformation (Gould, 1984). The nature, organization, and resolution of the honey bee locale map is one of the most interesting unsolved problems in invertebrate learning.

### Time Learning

Von Frisch (1967) discovered that bees remember the time of day particular flowers produce nectar and visit them only during those times. Individual bees specialize on different flowers at different times of day and maintain a learned periodicity indefinitely. Koltermann (1974) was able to train the same bees to visit nine different food sources during nine periods of the day, with a temporal resolution of 20 minutes. It could be that Koltermann's bees would have learned more than nine sources had he tried to teach them more. I will return to time learning later.

### Flower Handling

In addition to all of the US–CS pairing tasks by which a bee memorizes the information necessary to find and distinguish a particular species of flower, bees also face an operant task: How best to land on the flower and extract the nectar and/or pollen. There are many different flower morphologies, and most require very different strategies for harvesting the reward. Recruits to most artificial food sources are rather incompetent at getting the sucrose solution, but soon perfect a technique. At feeders for which a variety of strategies will work, different bees learn and remain faithful to very different approaches. The same thing happens at flowers, although the range of efficient strategies is usually more restricted: Bees experiment, perfect a technique through trial and error, and so greatly increase their harvesting efficiency (Heinrich, 1979). This efficiency is doubtless one of the reasons foragers specialize.

### Cue Hierarchies

Although an animal may learn or be capable of learning many things about a target, it may not use all the information or it may not weigh different cues equally in making a choice. Peking ducklings, for instance, learn, among other things, the color of their mother's speculum (the brightly colored patch on the wing), its location, and the mother's shape; and yet, given a choice between a model with, say, a speculum of a color different from the one seen during imprinting but in the correct location and on a model of the correct shape, as opposed to a model of the wrong shape with a misplaced speculum of the correct color, ducklings strongly prefer the latter model (Horner *et al.*, in preparation). (The hierarchy of learned preferences is color–shape–location.) So, too, it is with flower learning by bees; the rank order is odor–color–shape–landmarks for the Italian race, *Apis mellifera ligustica*, and odor–color–landmarks–shape for the German race, *A. m. carnica* (Hoefer & Lindauer, 1975; Koltermann, 1973; Lauer & Lindauer, 1971; Lindauer, 1969, 1976). These rankings appear to correspond both to the reliability of each cue in distinguishing between species of flowers as well as to the rate at which each cue is learned.

## Organization of Floral Memory

In the process of investigating how time is linked to other cues, Bogdany (1978) has uncovered a fascinating pattern of organization in flower learning. Consider the following experiment: We train a group of foragers to a blue, peppermint-scented, triangular target from 9:00 to 10:00 and then to a yellow, orange-scented, star-shaped target from 10:00 to 11:00. We repeat this sequence for a few days. On the next day, we set out both targets together, each supplied with sugar solution. The foragers appear at about 8:45 and land almost exclusively on the triangle. At about 9:45, they begin to switch from the triangular target, which still has food, to the star-shaped feeder. By 10:00, all the trained bees have abandoned the perfectly good triangle for the star. It is as though the bees have organized their daily activities by means of a mental appointment book listing all of the relevant cues for each time of day.

Bogdany also showed that if one component of an expected combination were changed, all of the components had to be relearned. For example, if at 9:30 we were to substitute rose for peppermint in the blue triangular target to which bees had been trained from 9:00 to 10:00 for several days, we would find that after landing, feeding, and returning to the hive, the forager on her next visit would be able to choose rose odor over a new odor at the 90% level but would be very poor at selecting the color blue or the triangle shape in a similar choice test even though they were nearly perfect at this task before the odor was switched. The bee also loses and must relearn the precise beginning and ending times for the food source. Apparently, the bee must start over and relearn each cue if any one is changed, each cue at its own specific rate.

The picture of storage in terms of sets of independently acquired cues is reinforced by the observation that if a cue—color or odor, for instance—is omitted initially but then added later, the set does *not* have to be relearned. Apparently the blank space for, say, odor can be filled in after the time-linked slots for color and shape have been filled.

It is tempting to think of flower memory organized as a kind of matrix. It is probably significant that although bees can learn that two different flowers have the same odor or color or other associated cue, they can only remember unique flower–time associations—that is, if they have learned flower A for the 10:00 to 11:00 "slot" and then are reinforced on a subsequent day to flower B from 10:00 to 11:00, they forget flower A; if, on the other hand, they are reinforced to flower B from 9:30 to 10:30, they remember flower A and fly to it from 10:30 to 11:00. Hence, a flower-learning matrix could consist of time-specific networks triggered by the US of sugar solution input for the various CSs. The different possibilities within each class of cue could be reciprocally coded to account for the exclusiveness of the learning within each cue domain (Gould, 1984). Such networks would have to have provision for storing or linking to flower-pattern and landmark pictures as well as the appropriate learned flower-handling motor program. Whether or not flower memory is organized in this way is not known, but this appears a plausible and testable way of accounting for one well-studied example of the widespread phenomenon of learning programs.

## CONCLUSION

From a comparison of laboratory and field work on learning in a variety of species, I conclude that in nature much—perhaps most—learning is integrated into highly evolved, context-specific learning programs based on a small number of general learning strategies that have been customized as necessary through natural selection. It may be that habituation, sensitization, classical conditioning, and trial-and-error learning are the building blocks of learning in general (and of learning programs in particular), rather than the consequences. A balanced consideration of these general mechanisms and their species-specific elaborations and coordination yields predictions consistent with field observations and suggests testable hypotheses at both the behavioral and neural levels.

## REFERENCES


Anderson, A. M. The ability of honey bees to generalize visual stimuli. In R. Wehner (Ed.), *Information processing in the visual system of arthropods*. Berlin & New York: Springer-Verlag, 1972.

Anderson, A. M. A model for landmark learning in the honey bee. *Journal of Comparative Physiology*, 1977, *114*, 335–355. (a)

Anderson, A. M. Shape perception in the honey bee. *Animal Behaviour*, 1977, *25*, 67–69. (b)

Anderson, A. M. Parameters determining the attractiveness of stripe patterns in the honey bee. *Animal Behaviour*, 1977, *25*, 80–87. (c)

Bogdany, F. J. Linking of learning signals in honey bee orientation. *Behavioral Ecology and Sociobiology*, 1978, *3*, 323–336.

Cartwright, B. A., & Collett, T. S. How honey bees use landmarks to guide their return to a food source. *Nature (London)*, 1982, *295*, 560–564.

Cartwright, B. A., & Collett, T. S. Landmark learning in bees. *Journal of Comparative Physiology*, 1983, *151*, 521–543.

Changeaux, J. P., & Dauchin, A. Selective stabilization of developing synapses as a mechanism for the specification of neuronal networks. *Nature (London)*, 1976, *264*, 705–712.

Cruse, H. A qualitative model for pattern discrimination in the honey bee. In R. Wehner (Ed.), *Information processing in the visual system of arthropods*. Berlin & New York: Springer-Verlag, 1972.

Dollinger, J., Gordon, J., & Gould, J. L. Ontogeny of species recognition in herring gull chicks. In review.

Durkis, D. A., & Gould, J. L. In preparation.

Edelman, G., & Mountcastle, V. *The mindful brain: cortical organization and the group-selection theory of higher brain function*. Cambridge, Mass.: MIT Press, 1978.
Erber, J. Neural correlates of learning in the honey bee. *Trends in NeuroScience*, 1981, *4*, 270–273.
Gould, J. L. Honey bee communication: The dance–language controversy. *Science*, 1975, *189*, 685–692.
Gould, J. L. *Ethology: The mechanisms and evolution of behavior*. New York: Norton, 1982.
Gould, J. L. The natural history of honey bee learning. In P. Marler & H. Terrace (Eds.), *The biology of learning*. Berlin & New York: Springer-Verlag, 1984.
Gould, J. L. Pattern learning by honey bees. *Science*, 1985, *227*, 1492–1494.
Gould, J. L. The natural history of learning. *Annual Review of Psychology*, in press. (a)
Gould, J. L. Shape learning by honey bees. *Animal Behavior*, in press. (b)
Gould, J. L. Landmark learning by honey bees. In preparation.
Gould, J. L., & Marler, P. Ethology and the natural history of learning. In P. Marler & H. Terrace (Eds.), *The biology of learning*. Berlin & New York: Springer-Verlag, 1984.
Hailman, J. P. The ontogeny of an instinct. *Behaviour, Supplement*, 1967, *17*, 1–159.
Hawkins, R. D., & Kandel, E. R. Is there a cell-biological alphabet for simple forms of learning? *Psychological Review*, 1984, *91*, 375–391.
Heinrich, B. *Bumble bee economics*. Cambridge, Mass.: Harvard University Press, 1979.
Hertz, M. Die Organisation des optischen Feldes bei der Biene. I. *Zeitschrift für Vergleichende Physiologie*, 1929, *8*, 693–748.
Hertz, M. Die Organisation des optischen Feldes bei der Beine. II. *Zeitschrift für Vergleichende Physiologie*, 1930, *11*, 107–145.
Hertz, M. Die Organisation des optischen Feldes bei der Biene. III. *Zeitschrift für Vergleichende Physiologie*, 1931, *14*, 629–674.
Hess, E. *Imprinting*. Princeton, N.J.: Van Nostrand Reinhold, 1972.
Hoefer, I., & Lindauer, M. Das Lernerhalten zweiger Bienenrassen unter veranderten Orientierungsbedingungen. *Journal of Comparative Physiology*, 1975, *99*, 119–138.
Horner, E., Acuña, K., & Gould, J. L. Learning hierarchies in imprinting. In preparation.
Koltermann, R. Rassen-bzw. artspezifische Duyftbewertung bei der Honigbiene und okologische Adaptation. *Journal of Comparative Physiology*, 1973, *85*, 327–360.
Kolterman, R. Periodicity in the activity and learning performance of the honey bee. In L. B. Brown (Ed.), *Experimental analysis of insect behavior*. Berlin & New York: Springer-Verlag, 1974.
Lashley, K. Conditioned reactions in the rat. *Journal of Psychology*, 1938, *6*, 311–324.
Lauer, J., & Lindauer, M. Genetische fixierte Lerndisposition bie der Honig bienen. In *Informationsaugnahme und Informationsverarbeitung im lebenden Organismus* (Vol. 1). Weisbaden: Franz Steiner Verlag, 1971.
Lindauer, M. Lernen und Vergessen bei der Honigbiene. *Proceedings of the Congress of IUSSI*, 1969, *6*, 153–158.
Lindauer, M. Recent advances in the orientation and learning of honey bees. *Proceedings of the International Congress of Entomology*, 1976, *15*, 450–460.
Margolis, R., Mariscal, S., & Gould, J. L. Ontogeny of species recognition in laughing gull chicks. In review.
Marler, P. The natural history of birdsong learning. In P. Marler & H. Terrace (Eds.), *The biology of learning*. Berlin & New York: Springer-Verlag, 1984.
Menzel, R., & Erber, J. Learning and memory in bees. *Scientific American*, 1978, *239*, 102–110.
Menzel, R., Erber, J., & Masuhr, J. Learning and memory in the honey bee. In L. B. Brown (Ed.), *Experimental analysis of insect behaviour*. Berlin: Springer-Verlag, 1974.
Opfinger, E. Uber die Orientierung der Biene an der Futterfuelle. *Zeitschrift für Vergleichende Physiologie*, 1931, *15*, 431–487.
Ronacher, B. Aquivalenz zwischen Gross und Helligkeitsunterschieden im Rahman der visuellen Wahrnehmung der Honigbiene. *Biological Cybernetics*, 1979, *32*, 63–75. (a)

Ronacher, B. Beitrag einzelner Parameter zum wahrnehmungsgema ss Unterschied von zusammengesetzten Reizen bei der Honigbiene. *Biological Cybernetics*, 1979, *32*, 77–83. (b)

Schnetter, B. Experiments on pattern discrimination in honey bee. In R. Wehner (Ed.), *Information processing in the visual system of arthropods*. Berlin & New York: Springer-Verlag, 1972.

Schwartz, B. *The psychology of learning and memory*. New York: Norton, 1984.

Shettleworth, S. J. Function and mechanism in learning. In M. D. Zeiler & P. Harzen (Eds.), *Advances in the analysis of behavior* (Vol. 3). New York: Wiley, 1983.

Staddon, J. R. R., & Gould, J. L. In preparation.

von Frisch, K. *The dance language and orientation of bees*. Cambridge, Mass.: Harvard University Press, 1967.

Wehner, R. Pattern modulation and pattern detection in the visual system of hymenoptera. In R. Wehner (Ed.), *Information processing in the visual system of anthropods*. Berlin & New York: Springer-Verlag, 1972.

Wehner, R. Spatial vision in arthropods. In H. Autrum (Ed.), *Handbook of sensory physiology*. Berlin & New York: Springer-Verlag, 1981.

CHAPTER 12

# Associative Learning: Some Consequences of Contiguity

**Robert A. Rescorla**
University of Pennsylvania

## INTRODUCTION

The intention of this chapter is to give a sampling of Pavlovian associative learning as studied in vertebrates. It is in the study of Pavlovian processes that students of animal learning have placed much of their energy in the last 15–20 years, and it is here that our understanding of learning processes is best worked out. It is no longer common to regard associative processes as providing a complete account of learning in rats and pigeons, let alone a full description of learning in all organisms. But it remains useful to consider our understanding of associative processes in vertebrates as a kind of model system. It is a system in which theoretical structures are well specified and in which various analytical and conceptual tools are well developed. Consequently, it often provides a kind of template against which to match other examples of learning in other species.

I find it useful to begin with a description of the study of learning that Rescorla and Holland (1976) articulated several years ago. According to this view, all modifications from experience can be characterized in terms of events that occur at two discrete times. At $t_1$ the organism undergoes some individual experience. As a result, its behavior at a later time, $t_2$, is different from that of an animal that was spared that $t_1$ experience. Learning situations can be characterized along two dimensions: the type of experience to which the organism is subjected at $t_1$ and the way in which the behavior differs at $t_2$.

One can consider various taxonomies of $t_1$ experiences, but the psychology of learning has commonly acknowledged two broad classes: experience with individual events and experience with relations among events. Experience with individual events includes treatments such as habituation and sensitization. Experience with relations among events includes relations among events located entirely in the world (as in Pavlovian conditioning) and relations between the animal's own behavior and a world event (as in instrumental learning). Many of the major advances have been made in the study of the first of these two relations, and the bulk of this chapter will concentrate on that case. However, I shall make occasional comments about non-Pavlovian relations and about individual-event learning.

One can consider various ways in which learning can exhibit itself at $t_2$. Most commonly we inspect the ability of some stimulus to evoke a response, expecting that ability to be enhanced or depressed by different $t_1$ experiences. But sometimes the assessment of learning requires procedures considerably more complex than the simple inspection of a response when a stimulus occurs. Several cases of that sort are described in following sections.

The key to understanding Pavlovian conditioning has always been the concept of contiguity. Consequently, the present discussion will be organized around the different kinds of learning that occur when a simple contiguity is arranged between two events at $t_1$. Consider a typical Pavlovian procedure in which a signal (such as a light, a tone, or a flavor) occurs in contiguity with some significant event (such as food delivery, pain, or the availablity of a sexual partner). It turns out that such an arrangement can result in a rich array of consequences. For present purposes I shall consider three kinds of consequences of such a contiguity: the formation of elementary associations among pairs of elements, the formation of more complex learning structures involving more than two elements, and what are here called "catalytic" functions. The discussion begins with the more familiar and better understood processes and moves progressively into more poorly explored territory.

## ASSOCIATIONS BETWEEN PAIRS

Modern studies of Pavlovian conditioning frequently arrange for the unconditioned stimulus (US) to be paired with a relatively complex conditioned stimulus (CS), consisting of two or more parts (e.g., A and B). In such an AB→US arrangement, one can identify three distinct classes of contiguous pairs. The most obvious, and the best studied, is the pairing of A and B each with the US. But, of course, A and B are paired not only with the US but also with each other. Moreover, this whole experience must take place in some context; the result is that both the CSs and the US are contiguous with the stimuli that define that context. It turns out that for many species and many types of events, this simple contiguity results in the learning of each of these different relations: between signal and consequent, within-signal, and context-event.

### Signal-Consequent Learning

A great deal is now known, of course, about the way in which associations occur between the US and its signals, A and B (e.g., Mackintosh, 1983).

This has been taken as a paradigm case, and most modern theories are directed toward its explanation. The major conceptual notion that dominates those theories is that of information. In recent years it has become clear that signals develop associations with consequences primarily under circumstances in which they provide information about those consequences. What that means is that not all contiguities between CS and US have the same implications for the formation of an association between them.

One way to see this is to consider various groups of animals, all of which receive conditioning trials of the form AB→US. However, suppose those groups differ in their history of experience with the A element; for some animals, A may have previously signaled the US on its own, for others A may have been exposed independently of the US, and for yet others A may have signaled that the US will not occur. For all animals, B is arranged to be contiguous with the US in the presence of A. However, the consequences of that contiguity will be quite different for the formation of a B–US association. The most well known comparison is that which Kamin (1968, 1969) made between a group for which A had previously been paired with the US and one for which that pairing was absent. When A had no history, the B–US association proceeded quite well. However, when A had an excitatory history, the B–US association was markedly attenuated (blocked). The intuition is simple: when A alone signals the US, the added B is redundant, whereas when A fails to signal the US, B is informative. The same contiguity has quite different consequences for associative learning, depending on the information value.

Kamin's result is one example of a general principle: the more excitatory A is, the less B is conditioned when AB is contiguous with the US. Another instance of this principle is the enhancement of conditioning that B undergoes if A has a history of inhibitory conditioning; under those circumstances B is especially informative and becomes well conditioned. Yet another instance occurs if A has a history of pairing with an especially strong US, stronger than that which occurs following AB. Under those conditions B may actually lose association with the US as a result of the AB→US pairings. The point is that the same contiguity between B and the US can result in excitation, no change, or inhibition, depending on the associative state of a concurrently present A (see Rescorla & Holland, 1982).

There are several modern theories of conditioning that capture this set of facts quite well and that attempt to give it a more detailed basis. For instance, one approach is to suggest that information affects the processing of the CS (e.g., Mackintosh, 1975). An informative A may be especially well processed, resulting in especially poor processing of B. As a result, the US is contiguous with a B that varies in its processing and so the association varies in its strength. Alternatively, one might argue that information affects the processing of the US. Some have suggested that USs vary in their effectiveness to the degree that they are poorly expected (e.g., Rescorla &

Wagner, 1972). When A is well associated with the US, then the US that follows AB is adequately anticipated and so is relatively less effective. Each of these approaches has been given rather precise mathematical formulation and each does rather well in describing quite detailed quantitative aspects of various Pavlovian conditioning experiments. Each has its virtues and its vices, but my point here is not to choose between them. Rather I want simply to call attention to the fact that even for standard Pavlovian CS–US learning the same contiguity can have a variety of consequences.

### Within-Stimulus Learning

The pairing of AB with a US results in A and B being contiguous, not only with the US, but also with each other. Recent evidence indicates that this contiguity is not lost on the animal. However, the detection of the learning that this contiguity produces is somewhat less straightforward for a number of reasons. First, A and B are normally relatively innocuous stimuli such that the formation of an association between them cannot itself be expected to endow either stimulus with a new response. Second, even if a response were observed to A or B, one could not uniquely attribute it to the A–B association rather than to the association of A or B each with the US.

Consequently, to detect the presence of an A–B association as a result of a $t_1$ presentation, one must use somewhat more complex $t_2$ assessment techniques. One technique that has proved especially useful in instances of this sort first arranges for A and B to be contiguous at $t_1$. Then at $t_2$, either A or B is endowed with some new ability, such as the power to evoke a new response. Then the response to the other stimulus is inspected. If one finds, as a result of the A–B contiguity and the establishment of a new response to B, that A also has developed the ability to evoke that response, he can infer the presence of an A–B association.

That logic is well illustrated by an experiment conducted some years ago by Rescorla and Cunningham (1978). We were interested in whether rats form associations between the component parts of a stimulus. Consequently, we exposed them to two stimulus events that had components known to be highly salient—flavors. Thirsty rats drank, for instance, a sweet–sour solution composed of sucrose and hydrochloric acid (SH), as well as a salty–bitter solution composed of salt and quinine (NQ). Other rats had the alternative pairings of SQ and NH. Then half the animals received H alone paired with a LiCl injection; half received Q alone paired with that injection. The injection rapidly resulted in rejection of the poisoned substance; our question was whether it would also lead to the specific rejection of the flavor that had been presented together with the poisoned substance. Consequently, the animals were given the choice of S and N to consume. Evidence of within-stimulus learning would take the form, for

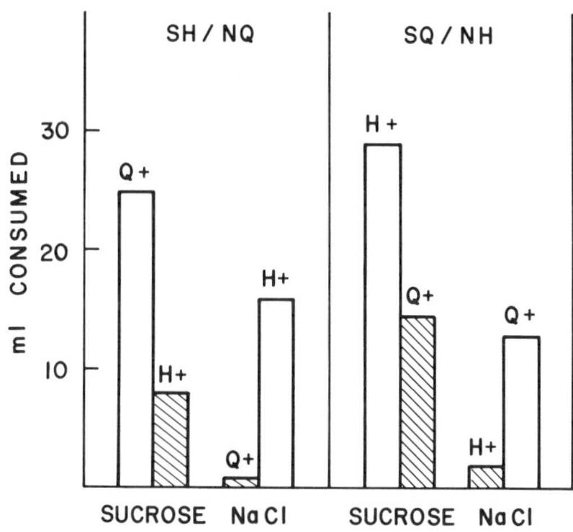


**FIGURE 12.1.** Within-event learning. Intakes of sucrose and salt solutions after exposure to either sucrose–hydrochloric acid (SH) and salt–quinine (NQ) or SQ and NH compounds. Either H or Q had been paired with a toxin prior to the test. Intakes of flavors the partners of which had been poisoned are cross-hatched. (From Rescorla & Cunningham, 1978. Copyright 1978 by the American Psychological Association. Reprinted by permission of the publisher.)

instance, of animals who had received SH and NQ exposure followed by H→LiCl pairings rejecting S in favor of N; animals with the same exposure and Q→LiCl pairings should reject N in favor of S. Similar reasoning applies to animals who had initially been exposed to SQ and NH.

Figure 12.1 shows the results of this experiment; the data are separated according to the various counterbalanced subgroups. The outcome was quite clear: Animals routinely rejected substances the partners of which had subsequently been poisoned. Figure 12.1 indicates those substances by cross-hatching and within each subgroup the intake was substantially less than the intake of the alternative fluid. With these particular parameters, this is an extremely powerful effect, normally observable in every subject.

This result turns out to have a fair degree of generality (see Rescorla & Durlach, 1981). It has been observed with various kinds of stimulus components: auditory and visual as well as gustatory. It has been observed in various species: pigeons, rats, monkeys, and bees. Moreover, we have detected its occurrence over a wide range of Pavlovian paradigms involving compound stimulus presentation. At present the best estimate is that whenever stimulus components occur jointly in a species known to show standard Pavlovian conditioning, one can anticipate the development of an association between those components. In fact, we have argued that some phenomena normally attributed to variation in the success of A–US or B–US associations are in fact attributable to variations in A–B associations.

### Associations with Context

Whenever we arrange for two events to be contiguous, the arrangement must take place in some general environment. It has been increasingly common to acknowledge that this context can have a profound effect on the learning that results. I will here just point to two elementary consequences of noting that contiguities occur in a context, both having to do with that context itself entering into associative connections.

Perhaps the most obvious possibility is that the context can become associated with the US. It would not be surprising if an organism that receives a significant event (such as food or shock) following a CS learned not only that the US follows a particular CS but also that it occurs in a particular setting. The detection of such learning is reasonably straightforward; animals that have repeatedly received a US in a context will commonly show behaviors in that context that differ from those they display in nonreinforced contexts. For instance, rats that receive tone–shock pairings will frequently display fear reactions, not only to the tone, but also to the experimental chamber (e.g., Bouton & Bolles, 1985). Similarly, pigeons that receive light–food pairings in a particular chamber will be considerably more active in that chamber than in another lacking food (e.g., Rescorla, Durlach, & Grau, 1985). This learning is often extremely rapid and powerful.

Moreover, modern theories of conditioning have accorded this context–US learning important roles in explaining a variety of phenomena. For instance, explanations of the US-preexposure effect, in which simple US presentation in a context retards the course of subsequent CS–US learning in that context, have leaned heavily on context–US learning (e.g., Randich & LoLordo, 1979; Tomie, 1980). Essentially they claim that the context plays the role of an alternative signal of the US that modulates the impact of the CS/US contiguity on the formation of the CS–US association, much in the way we described in the section Signal-Consequent Learning. Similarly, the importance of CS/US contingencies, demonstrated by the severe depressive effect on CS–US learning that results from presentation of USs at times other than during the CS, has been explained by context–US associations (e.g., Rescorla & Wagner, 1972). Consequently, there is little doubt that such learning occurs and has a profound impact both on the animal's performance and on modern theorizing.

But the context does not only become associated with significant events like the US; it also develops associations with innocuous events, such as the CS. There are a variety of results that have been interpreted as demonstrating such associations, but one of the most straightforward uses a technique like that of the Rescorla–Cunningham experiment described earlier. Recently, Rescorla (1984) conducted a study with pigeons in which each subject was exposed to two contexts differing in the pattern of wallpaper on the chambers. While in each chamber the pigeons received illuminations of one of two keylights, such that each keylight occurred uniquely in one chamber. Then, in a third (wallpaper-less) chamber, the birds had one of these keylights repeatedly paired with food; the other keylight was non-reinforced. With such exposures, of course, the birds rapidly formed the keylight–food associations and engaged in the standard autoshaped pecking at the reinforced keylight. But our interest centered on how the birds would react to the contexts that had previously contained these now differently valued keylights. The answer was quite straightforward: The birds were much more active when placed in the chamber the keylight of which had been paired with food than when placed in the chamber the keylight of which had not been reinforced. That differential outcome clearly indicates the presence of context–CS associations. Moreover, further analysis revealed that the excitation so induced to the context by these associations had many of the same effects on learning and performance as do context–US associations.

The point is that when two events are arranged to be contiguous in a context, one should anticipate that those events will not only become associated with each other; each will likely become associated with the context. Moreover, that learning will, under many circumstances, be more rapid and powerful than is the more specific CS–US learning we usually inspect. Consequently, the first and most easily observed learning may often involve associations with context.

## Response–Outcome Associations

Even in these simple Pavlovian paradigms, there is another event that we are yet to explicitly acknowledge: the animal's response. Typically the animal makes a discrete response to the US from the outset; what we have here termed associations with the US may in some instances actually be associations with the animal's response to the US. Moreover, as the signaling properties of A and B become learned, they will come to evoke responses. Those responses, too, can enter into associations with other events, such as the context.

But the case where such response learning has been most extensively discussed is, of course, that of instrumental learning, where the environment explicitly arranges a relation between the animal's response and some outcome. Pairwise associations between responding and some stimulus have long been the primary account of instrumental behavior. However, two quite different associative structures have been proposed, corresponding to associations between the response and various of the other events we have discussed. One possibility is that instrumental learning involves an association between the response (R) and some eliciting stimulus (S). The popular candidates have been the signaling stimulus, such as A or B (in the case of discrete trial procedures), and the contextual stimuli (in the case of free-operant behavior). This S–R possibility dominated much of the early theorizing about instrumental behavior, but I shall postpone its discussion until the section More Complex Structures.

Another possibility has recently had more intuitive appeal: instrumental learning may involve the formation of an association between the response and the reinforcing outcome that is arranged to be contingent upon it. According to this account the animal learns what the consequences of its actions are and generates responding based on that information. Essentially, the animal shows Pavlovian conditioning of a specialized sort in which the instrumental response plays the role of a signal of the outcome. It is then of interest to ask how one would collect evidence relevant ot that interpretation.

There are several strategies that have been followed, but perhaps the most straightforward is to demonstrate the existence of response–outcome associations. This can be done using an analogue to the Rescorla-Cunningham procedure; a recent experiment by Colwill and Rescorla (1985) illustrates the point. They trained rats to make two instrumental responses (lever pressing and chain pulling) by arranging for each to produce a unique outcome (sucrose pellets or Noyes pellets). Then they presented one of those outcomes freely in the absence of the response, and paired it with a toxin. Once the animals completely rejected the poisoned outcome, the manipulanda were returned and the animals were given a choice between

**FIGURE 12.2.** Response–outcome learning. Performance during an extinction test on two responses, one previously reinforced with sucrose and one with pellets. Either the sucrose or the pellets was paired with a toxin between training and test. (From Colwill & Rescorla, 1985.) Copyright 1985 by the American Psychological Association. Reprinted by permission of the publisher.)

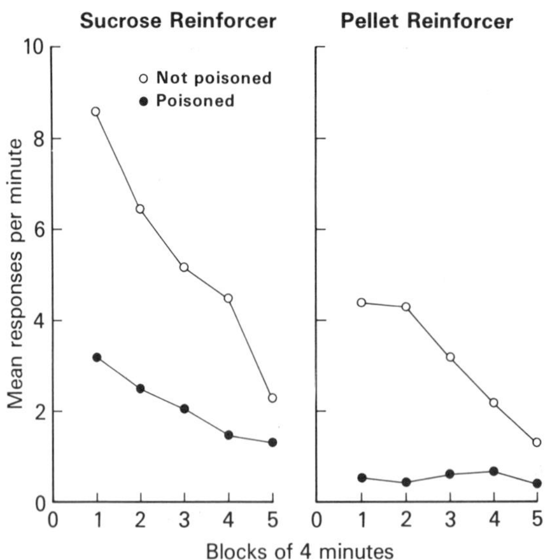

chain pulling and lever pressing; neither response now led to any outcome. The notion was that to the degree the animal had an association between a response and a particular outcome, it would now select the response the outcome of which had not been poisoned. Figure 12.2 shows that this expectation was confirmed. That figure shows the rate of executing the response that formerly led to each reinforcer, separated according to whether or not that reinforcer had been poisoned. Poisoning either outcome led to a specific reduction in the response that formerly produced it. These data show that animals can form response–outcome associations.

## Conclusion on Pairwise Associations

It seems clear from even this brief discussion that quite a range of pairwise associations can form as the result of an elementary CS–US pairing. We have seen evidence of signal–consequence, signal–signal, context–consequence, and context–signal associations. Moreover, there is some evidence that instrumental responding can play the role of a signal to become associated with its consequence. Some of these associations may form more rapidly than others, particularly for some kinds of stimuli in some kinds of species. Moreover, we do not know a great deal about the principles that these various kinds of associative learning show. It is convenient, as a first approximation, to assume that the rules that have been well explored in the case of signal–consequence learning can be applied to the other cases. In some instances, such as the case of context–US associations, that assumption has already yielded important theoretical power. However, it seems unlikely that all of these associations will follow exactly the same principles. For instance, the informational notion that is so central to signal–consequence learning seems less likely to be critical to the formation of associations within the signal itself (cf. Rescorla, 1981).

This multiplicity of associative learning has a number of implications of potential interest to neurobiologists. For instance, it greatly complicates the identification of a correspondence between a neural change and a particular instance of associative learning. Even in the simplest of Pavlovian situations, there may be many more associative changes taking place than our models normally acknowledge. Moreover, these changes are almost certainly occurring at different rates and interacting with each other. To make analysis even more complicated, some of those changes (such as the CS–US association or the response–reinforcer association) may readily be observable in behavior whereas others (such as context–CS associations or within-stimulus associations) may not have obvious behavioral consequences in the absence of special detection procedures. Clearly, the models we normally have in mind when we search for the (single or multiple) locus for Pavlovian CS–US learning are vastly oversimplified.

These results also suggest the possibility that many of the examples of learning that are commonly classified as nonassociative could in fact importantly involve associative mechanisms. For instance, the circumstances under which one observes context–stimulus and within-stimulus associations almost certainly include simple repeated presentation of a stimulus. Consequently, the changes that result from that procedure, which are normally identified as habituation or sensitization, may in fact have associative components. Indeed, there are currently available theories of these nonassociative situations that make appeals to just such associative mechanisms (e.g., Wagner, 1981).

Consequently, the observation of this richness of associative learning has important implications both for the complexity that we can anticipate at the neural level and for the nature of the neural mechanisms we may find.

## MORE COMPLEX STRUCTURES

The formation of associations between pairs of elements has been the staple of theories of learning. However, some authors have expressed increasing discomfort with the notion that all learning of relations can be understood in that way (e.g., Jenkins, 1977). Some phenomena seem to require learning structures that encode more than two elements. This section describes two types of such learning and gives an illustration of each. Both instances involve conditional discriminations, in which a consequence can be anticipated only by attention to its relation to two other events. However, they represent different kinds of solutions to that problem on the part of the learning organism.

### Formation of New Elements

Consider again the case in which an AB is followed by a US. In addition to the elemental A–US and B–US associations, sometimes the organism learns a more complex relation in which the US becomes associated with the joint occurrence of A and B. That outcome is especially encouraged if the environment arranges a discrimination of the form AB+, A−, B−, in which only the joint AB occurrence is reinforced. Such discriminations can often be learned, taking the form of the animal responding to the AB compound but not to either of its elements (e.g., Rescorla, 1973; Saavedra, 1975; Woodbury, 1943). One popular theoretical interpretation is that the organism forms a new element, AB, that is other than the simple combination of A and B (e.g., Spence, 1956). That interpretation can take several forms. For instance, the AB element may itself be a product of an associative process, as indicated in the previous discussion of within-stimulus learning. Alternatively, the AB element may involve a nonassociative process (see Rescorla & Durlach, 1981). But there is evidence that some form of constructing a new element occurs both for signals and for consequents.

Rescorla (1979) reported an experiment that illustrates that point. This experiment used an autoshaping preparation in which pigeon subjects receive presentations of a discretely localized disk (a keylight) followed, in a Pavlovian fashion, by food. As the birds learn that association, they come to peck at the key whenever it is illuminated by the signaling light. Moreover, a keylight that has been paired with food not only elicits pecking, it can also serve in place of food to establish pecking to another keylight that signals it. That is, second-order autoshaping can be readily produced (Rescorla, 1980). In this experiment we exploited that fact to study the formation of new units when a compound served both as a signal and as a consequent. Pigeons were intially given simple autoshaping in which a red (R) and a yellow (Y) half-keylight were each separately paired with food. Then R and Y were presented jointly, side by side, as the consequent to yet another keylight, a horizontally oriented black and white grid (H). The consequence was that the birds rapidly came to peck at H because it signaled RY. The question of interest is the structure of the learning that underlies that pecking. Has the organism formed a new unit (RY) from the components of H's consequent and associated H with that unit or has the organism simply formed elemental associations between H and each of the R and Y components? To answer that question, we explicitly subjected some animals to a conditional discrimination of the form RY+, R−, Y−; others received the reverse discrimination, RY−, R+, Y+. We then tested the animals for their pecking to H. We anticipated that responding to H would track the current value of its associate. If H is associated with an RY unit, then it should be pecked rapidly following the first discrimination but not the second. On the other hand, if H is associated with R and Y separately, responding should be high after the second, but not the first, discrimination.

Figure 12.3 shows the primary results. To the left is the keypecking to H at the end of second-order conditioning by RY. Responding is shown separately for those animals that would receive the different discriminations in the next phase of the experiment, but it is clear that substantial second-order conditioning of H had occurred. The middle panel shows responding to R, Y, and RY during the conditional discrimination training. It is clear that the animals learned whichever discrimination we taught them. Their successful differential responding is naturally interpreted in terms of their using a new signal element when a compound signal announces a consequent. But we were also interested in whether the animals had formed a new element when that compound had previously served as a consequent. To address that question, we tested the animals for their responding to H; those results are shown at the right in Figure 12.3. They too were positive: responding to H was more influenced by the state of the RY compound than by the state of its elements. Consequently, this experiment illustrates that when a compound is either a consequence or a signal, the organism sometimes learns a more complex relation involving more than two elements.

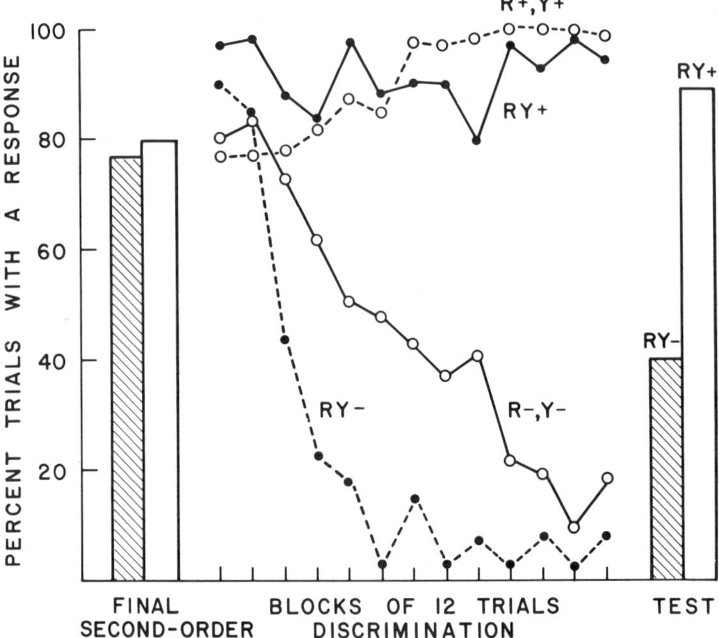


**FIGURE 12.3.** Hierarchical organization of between- and within-event learning. The left-hand panel shows performance in two groups of birds both given second-order conditioning of a grid pattern (H) by a compound color (RY) reinforcer. In the middle panel, one group received an RY+, R−, Y− discrimination; the other received the converse. The right-hand panel shows responding to H as a function of this discrimination. (From Rescorla, 1979. Copyright 1979 by the American Psychological Association. Reprinted by permission of the publisher.)

## Conditional Control

Another type of solution to such complex discriminations involves the organism's using one stimulus to tell it the relation between two others. Again three components are involved in the learning, but here one component provides the circumstances under which the relation between two others is in force. An experiment we recently did will illustrate this point for two different relations.

This experiment exploited an insufficiently appreciated fact about Pavlovian conditioning: the dependence of the conditioned response on the identity of the conditioned stimulus. In many conditioning situations, the same US results in quite different behavior patterns when it is paired with different CSs. In autoshaping with pigeons, this CS dependence is easily seen when auditory and visual stimuli are used. As noted earlier, when a discrete localized keylight becomes associated with food, the bird directs pecking at the keylight. However, when a diffuse auditory stimulus bears the same relation to food, the learning is exhibited not as directed pecking but instead as general activity. Moreover, when such a separately trained auditory stimulus is presented in conjunction with a previously trained keylight, there is little response interaction; in particular, keypecking is not enhanced. This means that one might arrange for the tone to signal the relation of the keylight to food and use different response topographies to determine the tone's function. For instance, one might arrange a discrimination of the form A−, AB+, where A is a keylight and B a tone. To the degree that B simply becomes a signal for food, we would expect responding to the AB compound to take the form of the response normally observed when B alone is conditioned—general activity. However, to the degree that B serves as a conditional signal, informing the animal that A signals food in B's presence but not in its absence, we would expect to see the response to the AB compound to be the same as that normally conditioned to A-directed pecking.

Figure 12.4 shows the result of one recent experiment in which both this A−, AB+ relation and its converse, A+, AB−, were arranged. Consider first the open symbols, from the A−, AB+ relation. There was initially pecking during both A alone and the AB compound; however, the former rapidly dropped out. Consequently, by the end of training the animal directed its response to A only in the presence of the auditory B. When B was presented alone, there was never any pecking to it. It seems clear that the role of the auditory B was to inform the animal about the A–US relation, not simple to become excitatory itself.

The converse relation, A+, AB− relation, was included not simply out of considerations of symmetry. That relation is a well-studied one in Pavlovian conditioning, the so-called conditioned inhibitory paradigm. A

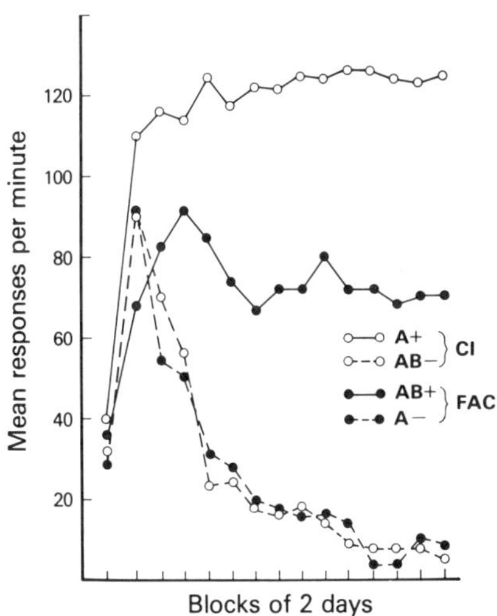


**FIGURE 12.4.** Conditional control. Autoshaped keypecking at a disk (A) the reinforcement of which was signaled by the presence or absence of a noise (B). For Group FAC (facilitation), A was reinforced only when B was present; for Group CI (conditioned inhibition) it was reinforced only when B was absent. (From Rescorla, 1985. Copyright 1985 by Lawrence Erlbaum Associates. Reprinted by permission.)

great many studies show results like those illustrated in Figure 12.4: responding to A when presented alone but not in the presence of B. Theories of that performance have normally appealed to the animal's learning an inhibitory relation between B and the reinforcer. The interpretation is that A is excitatory by virtue of its association with the US whereas B is inhibitory by virtue of an inhibitory relation with the US; the behavior to the compound is a consequence of the summation of these opposite tendencies. But in the present context another interpretation also seems possible—that B is a conditional stimulus that is informative about the circumstances under which A is reinforced that is, only in the absence of B. We have argued elsewhere that there may be a general class of functions in which one stimulus controls the relation among others (Rescorla, 1985).

This modulatory role that one stimulus can play with regard to others has only recently begun to receive investigation, but it may be rather widespread. For instance, we earlier saw evidence that contextual stimuli can enter into pairwise associations with single events. But is seems likely that contextual stimuli also play this conditional role: CS–US relations may obtain in one context but not in another. The most dramatic case of this is the classic switching experiment in which one explicitly arranges a discrimination in one context and its reversal in another (e.g., Asratyan, 1965). Similarly, one role that a discriminative stimulus might play in instrumental learning is as this sort of modulator. In many discrete trial procedures, the signal informs the animal that a response–reinforcer relation is in force. Although it has been popular to assume that this can result in a B (e.g., signal–response association [see later]), an alternative is suggested by the data presented in this section and in the section Response–Outcome Associations. The instrumental learning may take the form of a response–reinforcer association, and the signal may tell the animal when this relation obtains.

In any case, contiguities can result in learning structures that are more complex than simple pairwise associations. Clearly more experimental attention needs to be given to the analysis of such cases.

## CATALYTIC FUNCTIONS OF CONTIGUITY

The previous discussion has emphasized those consequences of contiguity that involve learning about the contiguous events. But another important result of contiguity is the modulation of learning about other stimuli. Sometimes an event will govern the learning about other events without itself entering into new learning. Both of the principal events in a standard Pavlovian procedure—the CS and the US—can serve this catalytic function.

### CSs as Catalysts

Those events that normally serve as signals can both help and hinder the associative learning of other signals, even if they themselves do not change associative strength. The primary case of interference has already been described earlier—the Kamin blocking effect. That is an instance in which the presence of one stimulus, A, interferes with the formation of an association between another stimulus, B, and the US, even when the latter two are contiguous. As we noted earlier, in this case the critical feature of A is its current associative strength: An excitatory A will interfere with learning about B, but an inhibitory A will promote the B–US association.

Another instance of an apparent catalytic function is the phenomenon of "potentiation" that has recently been described in several settings (e.g., Durlach & Rescorla, 1980; Kehoe, Gibbs, Garcia, & Gormezano, 1979; Rusiniak, Hankins, Garcia, & Brett, 1979). In some instances, a CS that is difficult for a US to condition can be made more conditionable by the presence of another CS. For instance, Rusiniak *et al.* (1979) reported that an odor that bore a trace relation to a toxin was poorly conditioned unless that odor was accompanied by a taste. Relatedly, studies of autoshaping, eyeblink conditioning, and conditioned suppression have all found that a trace CS receives improved conditioning by a US if another CS intervenes between the original two events (see Rescorla & Holland, 1982).

One instance of this sort of catalytic effect (Rescorla, 1982) is shown in Figure 12.5. That figure shows the development of pecking to two different keylights both paired with food in the same birds. Both keylights were separated from food by 5 seconds, an interval sufficient to markedly undermine the associative learning underlying autoshaping. However, for one keylight, a tone intervened between it and food; for the other stimulus, the interval was unfilled. Keypecking hardly developed to the keylight with the unfilled interval (open symbols) but proceeded moderately well to the keylight with the filled interval (closed symbols). The presence of the tone clearly potentiated conditioning of the keylight.

Potentiation results have been given various interpretations. In some instances, there is evidence that the greater conditioning that one stimulus

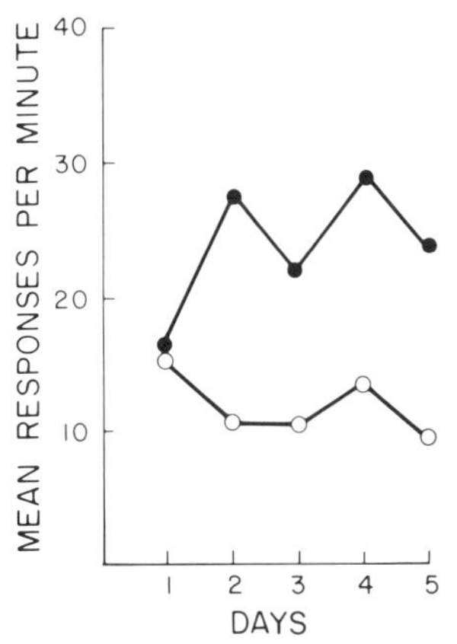


**FIGURE 12.5.** Catalytic effect of a tone on autoshaping. Autoshaped pecking at two keylights, both followed after 5 seconds by food. A tone intervened between one keylight and food (filled circle) but no stimulus occurred for the other keylight (open circle). (From Rescorla, 1982. Copyright 1982 by the American Psychological Association. Reprinted by permission of the publisher.)

A enjoys because of the presence of another stimulus B depends on B's playing a mediational role, becoming associated with both A and the US (e.g., Durlach & Rescorla, 1980). But other instances of potentiation seem to involve true improvement in the A–US association as a result of B's presence. Analysis of the autosphaping example shown in Figure 12.5 suggests that it is of this latter sort (Rescorla, 1982).

Some qualitative hypotheses have been advanced for explaining this potentiation result, but we have little detailed understanding of its underlying mechanism. Negative catalytic effects, such as blocking, seem more prevalent; but positive effects, such as potentiation, can be quite substantial in some instances. At present we cannot fully characterize the circumstances under which one or the other outcome will occur. But it seems clear that a contiguity can affect behavior not only by involving the stimulus in learning but also by allowing it to modulate the learning of other associations.

### USs as Catalysts

Historically, it has been more common to suggest that contiguous presentation of events that might otherwise serve as USs can have important impact on the learning of other relations. Both interfering and facilitating consequences have been proposed. For instance, there is a substantial literature on the effects of presentation of electroconvulsive shock (ECS) that suggests that it can interfere with the learning of another relation with which its presentation is contiguous. Although there are interpretations of such results that argue that the impact of an ECS involves its own participation in the learning, there is an important tradition that views its action as disruptive of the formation of other associations. More recently, there have been suggestions that somewhat more mild events, such as food presentations or other learning opportunities, can serve to interfere with other learning (e.g., Wagner, 1981). The point is that just because the action of these important US-like events depends on contiguity need not mean that the nature of that action is for them to participate in learning themselves. Instead they may act as a kind of catalyst.

There is also a strong tradition that suggests that US-like events that occur contiguously with the occurrence of a relation can promote learning of that relation. The clearest example arises in the case of instrumental learning. The classic S–R account of instrumental learning is that an association is formed between an antecedent stimulus and the response, with the reinforcer playing the role of a catalyst. In that account, the job of the reinforcer is not itself to enter into the learning, but rather to act as an agent that, because of its contiguity to the S–R pairing, makes the association take place. We saw in the section Response–Outcome Associations that this mode of action cannot fully account for all that is learned in instrumental training; there is also evidence that the organism learns about the reinforcer by associating it with the response. However, it is also possible that this sort of catalytic action occurs. Note, for instance, the incompleteness of the depressive effect on instrumental responding that Colwill and Rescorla (1985) sometimes observed when they poisoned a reinforcer. One possibility is that some of the instrumental learning in fact involves associations between antecedent stimuli and the response, associations that were strengthened by the contiguous presentation of the reinforcer but are no longer dependent on its having value.

It is important to realize that contiguity can also affect nonassociative learning in this catalytic fashion. Indeed, that affect may sometimes lead us to mistake the modulation of the success of nonassociative learning for an instance of associative learning. Consider, for instance, a case of habituation in which repeated presentation of a stimulus results in a reduced response to that stimulus. Suppose that we have a second stimulus that is a powerful disrupter of that learning, particularly when it occurs in close temporal contiguity. Then if the first stimulus were regularly followed by the second, we would anticipate that its habituation would proceed more slowly than if the two stimuli were separated in time. But that difference in outcome as a function of whether or not two stimuli are presented in contiguous fashion is routinely interpreted as evidence for associative learning. Yet it might as easily be an instance of the second event having a disruptive catalytic effect on the first. There is good evidence that such effects occur in habituation and the allied process of latent inhibition (e.g., Lubow, Schnur, & Rifkin, 1976; Wagner, 1976). Moreover, one should also anticipate that we will find instances of a positive catalytic effect on a fundamentally sensitization process. In that case, the result of a second stimulus would be to augment the sensitization effects of presenting the first. Indeed, in the absence of the catalytic effect of the second stimulus, the sensitization of the first might not otherwise be observable. That makes it very difficult to reject this sort of interpretation of many results usually taken to be assocative in nature.

These catalytic effects on what are basically nonassociative changes may well provide animals with one primitive way to encode contiguities in the world. They may even involve some of the same mechanisms as associative learning. But they are not associative consequences of contiguity as we normally use the term at the behavioral level. There is no encoding of two stimuli with some enhanced communication between their representations. Rather the contingity allows one stimulus to modulate the degree to which the other stimulus has its various effects.

It will not always be easy to separate the formation of associations from the catalytic effect on a nonassociative process. But two suggestions have been made. One approach is to carry out the sort of manipulation used in the section Associations between Pairs. If two stimuli, A and B, are associated and B is given a new response, then we might also see that response to A. On the other hand, if B has acted as a catalyst for A, that sort of transfer is not anticipated. Another approach is simply to look at the form of the response to A; to the degree that B has only modulated nonassociative change to A, there is no reason to expect the form of the response to A to depend on the B event. But if the two are associated, the response observed to A after A–B pairing should depend on the identity of the B event. This dependence of the conditioned response on the identity of the US may be the essential feature that many wished to capture in the historical emphasis upon similarity between the conditioned response and the unconditioned response.

But in any case, we must acknowledge that contiguity between two events has important consequences other than enabling them to become associated. Those other consequences may be both large and important. Certainly, if we want to conduct neurobiological investigation of the consequences of contiguity, we need to be sensitive to this array of possibilities.

## CONCLUSION

Contiguities among events in the environment can have varied consequences for learning. The present discussion has described three such consequences: the learning of pairwise associations, the formation of more complex learning structures, and the catalytic functions of an event. Theories and data from experimental psychology have emphasized associations among pairs. We have here noted the range of events that can enter into such pairwise associations. But we have also noted that pairwise associations seem unlikely to be the full story; more complex, conditional learning seems to occur. Finally, it is important to keep in mind that when several events are contiguous in time, they can affect learning in a "catalytic" fashion—by modifying what the animal learns without themselves being represented in that learning.

My aim here has been to lay out some of these possibilities and illustrate their occurrence. Obviously the degree to which these different forms of modification occur will vary with stimuli, situation, and species. Although we as yet have only a limited understanding of the mechanisms and circumstances of occurrence of some of these processes, we do have available some tools for their identification and analysis.

## ACKNOWLEDGMENTS

The research reported here was supported by grants from the National Science Foundation. This chapter was written while the author was a J. S. Guggenheim Fellow.

## REFERENCES


Asratyan, E. A. *Compensatory adaptations, reflex activity, and the brain*. Oxford: Pergamon Press, 1965.

Bouton, M. E., & Bolles, R. C. Contexts, event-memories, and extinction. In P. D. Balsam & A. Tomie (Eds.), *Context and learning*. Hillsdale, N.J.: Erlbaum, 1985.

Colwill, R. M., & Rescorla, R. A. Post-conditioning devaluation of a reinforcer affects instrumental responding. *Journal of Experimental Psychology: Animal Behavior Processes*, 1985, *11*, 120–132.

Durlach, P. J., & Rescorla, R. A. Potentiation rather than overshadowing in flavor-aversion learning: An analysis in terms of within-compound associations. *Journal of Experimental Psychology: Animal Behavior Processes*, 1980, *6*, 175–187.

Jenkins, H. M. Sensitivity of different response systems to stimulus-reinforcer and response-reinforcer relations. In H. Davis & H. M. B. Hurwitz (Eds.), *Operant–Pavlovian interactions*. Hillsdale, N.J.: Erlbaum, 1977.

Kamin, L. J. Attention-like processes in classical conditioning. In M. R. Jones (Ed.) *Miami symposium on the prediction of behavior: Aversive stimuli*. Coral Gables: Fla.: University of Miami Press, 1968.

Kamin, L. J. Predictability, surprise, attention, and conditioning. In B. Campbell & R. Church (Eds.), *Punishment and aversive behavior*. New York: Appleton-Century-Crofts, 1969.

Kehoe, E. J., Gibbs, C. M., Garcia, E., & Gormezano, I. Associative transfer and stimulus selection in classical conditioning of the rabbit's nictitating membrane response to serial compound CSs. *Journal of Experimental Psychology: Animal Behavior Processes*, 1979, *5*, 1–18.

Lubow, R. E., Schnur, P., & Rifkin, B. Latent inhibition and conditioned attention theory. *Journal of Experimental Psychology: Animal Behavior Processes*, 1976, *2*, 163–174.

Mackintosh, N. J. A theory of attention: Variations in the associability of stimuli with reinforcement. *Psychological Review*, 1975, *82*, 276–298.

Mackintosh, N. J. *Conditioning and associative learning*. Oxford: Oxford University Press, 1983.

Randich, A., & LoLordo, V. M. Associative and nonassociative theories of the UCS preexposure phenomenon: Implications for Pavlovian conditioning. *Psychological Bulletin*, 1979, *86*, 523–548.

Rescorla, R. A. Evidence for a unique-cue account of configural conditioning, *Journal of Comparative and Physiological Psychology*, 1973, *85*, 331–338.

Rescorla, R. A. Aspects of the reinforcer learned in second-order Pavlovian conditioning. *Journal of Experimental Psychology: Animal Behavior Processes*, 1979, *5*, 79–95.

Rescorla, R. A. *Pavlovian second-order conditioning: Studies in associative learning*. Hillsdale, N.J.: Erlbaum, 1980.

Rescorla, R. A. Simultaneous associations. In P. Harzem & M. Zeiler (Eds.), *Advances in analysis of behavior* (Vol. 2). New York: Wiley, 1981.

Rescorla, R. A. Effect of a stimulus intervening between CS and reinforcer in autoshaping. *Journal of Experimental Psychology: Animal Behavior Processes*, 1982, *8*, 131–141.

Rescorla, R. A. Associations between Pavlovian CSs and context. *Journal of Experimental Psychology: Animal Behavior Processes*, 1984, *10*, 195–205.

Rescorla, R. A. Conditioned inhibition and facilitation. In R. R. Miller & N. S. Spear (Eds.), *Information processing in animals: Conditioned inhibition*. Hillsdale, N.J.: Erlbaum, 1985.

Rescorla, R. A., & Cunningham, C. L. Within-compound flavor associations, *Journal of Experimental Psychology: Animal Behavior Processes*, 1978, *4*, 267–275.

Rescorla, R. A., & Durlach, P. J. Within-event learning in Pavlovian conditioning. In N. E. Spear & R. Miller (Eds.), *Information processing in animals: Memory mechanisms*. Hillsdale, N.J.: Erlbaum, 1981.

Rescorla, R. A., Durlach, P. J., & Grau, J. W. Contextual learning in Pavlovian conditioning. In P. D. Balsam & A. Tomie (Eds.), *Context and learning*. Hillsdale, N.J.: Erlbaum, 1985.

Rescorla, R. A., & Holland, P. C. Some behavioral approaches to the study of learning. In

M. R. Rosenzweig & E. L. Bennett (Eds.), *Neural mechanisms of learning and memory*. Cambridge, Mass.: MIT Press, 1976.

Rescorla, R. A., & Holland, P. C. Behavioral studies of associative learning in animals. *Annual Review of Psychology*, 1982, *33*, 265–308.

Rescorla, R. A., & Wagner, A. R. A theory of Pavlovian conditioning: Variations in the effectiveness of reinforcement and nonreinforcement. In A. H. Black & W. F. Prokasy (Eds.), *Classical conditioning II*. New York: Appleton-Century-Crofts, 1972.

Rusiniak, K., Hankins, W., Garcia, J., & Brett, L. Flavor-illness aversions: Potentiation of odor by taste in rats. *Behavioral Neural Biology*, 1979, *25*, 1–17.

Saavedra, M. A. Pavlovian compound conditioning in the rabbit. *Learning and Motivation*, 1975, *6*, 314–326.

Spence, K. W. *Behavior theory and conditioning*. New Haven, Conn.: Yale University Press, 1956.

Tomie, A. Effects of unpredictable food on the subsequent acquisition of autoshaping: Analysis of the context blocking hypothesis. In C. M. Locurto, H. S. Terrace, & J. Gibbon (Eds.), *Autoshaping and conditioning theory*. New York: Academic Press, 1980.

Wagner, A. R. Priming in STM: An information-processing mechanism for self-generated or retrieval-generated depression in performance. In T. J. Tighe & R. N. Leaton (Eds.), *Habituation: Perspectives from child development, animal behavior, and neurophysiology*. Hillsdale, N.J.: Erlbaum, 1976.

Wagner, A. R. SOP: A model of automatic memory processing in animal behavior. In N. E. Spear & R. Miller (Eds.), *Information processing in animals: Memory mechanisms*. Hillsdale, N.J.: Erlbaum, 1981.

Woodbury, C. B. The learning of stimulus patterns by dogs. *Journal of Comparative and Physiological Psychology*, 1943, *35*, 29–40.

CHAPTER 13

# Food Storing by Birds: Implications for Comparative Studies of Memory

**Sara J. Shettleworth**
University of Toronto
Toronto, Ontario, Canada

## INTRODUCTION

Animals store food in many different ways, but the scatter hoarding of some birds is particularly interesting to psychologists because of the feats of memory it involves. Tits and corvids, among others, store large numbers of items in scattered locations and recover them hours, days, even months, later. Although most early observers were skeptical that these birds use memory to recover their hoards, there is now good evidence that they do. Some food-storing birds appear to retain information about the locations of hundreds of stored items for intervals much longer than those over which other species have been demonstrated to retain spatial information in laboratory tasks. This raises the question whether, as an adaptation to their food-storing way of life, these birds have more persistent and larger-capacity spatial memory than nonstoring species. Strong behavioral evidence for superior spatial memory in food-storers might encourage a search for differences in their brains, along the lines of studies of differences in the vocal control system within and between species of songbirds (e.g., Nottebohm, 1981).

In a recent article on the prospects for comparative neuroscience, Bullock (1984, p. 477) drew attention to "the urgent need for better methods for assessing behavior in ways that will permit its variety to be better correlated with brain variables." This discussion of food storing is organized around the question whether the behavioral evidence is indeed such that we should expect to find any special features in the brains of food-storing species. I shall first briefly present the facts about food storing in field and laboratory. I shall then discuss what laboratory studies have revealed about the properties of memory for stored food and whether such studies are adequate to show how memory is used to recover stored food in the field. I shall also compare the properties of memory for stored food with the properties of memory in other species in laboratory situations. Finally, I shall outline an experimental approach to comparing memory for stored food with other forms of spatial memory in food storers and their relatives.

## NATURAL HISTORY OF FOOD STORING

Food storing is especially widespread among the chickadees and tits (*Paridae*) and among the corvids (crows, jays, and nutcrackers). Both groups are currently being studied by several independent teams of zoologists and psychologists. The tits are the subject of collaborative work by Krebs and his group in Oxford together with Sherry and me in Toronto. Clark's nutcracker (*Nycifraga columbiana*) and other corvids are being studied by Vander Wall (1982), Tomback (1980), Kamil and Balda (1985), and others. Sherry (1984b, in press) has reviewed much of this and earlier work.

Both tits and corvids vary considerably in the period for which food is stored and the extent to which a species relies on it for energy. Within the *Paridae*, for example, blue tits (*Parus caeruleus*) and great tits (*P. major*) hoard little or not at all. At the other extreme, the crested tits (*P cristatus L.*) and coal tits (*P. ater L.*) observed in Scandinavia by Haftorn (1956) appear to store up large numbers of pine seeds in the fall and consume them throughout the winter. And as an intermediate case, marsh tits (*P. palustris*) in Britain seem to use hoarding as a way to make the most of a temporary superabundance of food like a freshly opened seed pod or an experimentally introduced pile of sunflower seeds. Such a bonanza is too large for a 9-gram marsh tit to eat all at once or to defend from competitors for later consumption, but it evokes vigorous hoarding. Several hundred items may be stored in a day, each in a different place (Sherry, Avery, & Stevens, 1982). In Wytham Wood, Oxford, at least, such hoards are recovered or eaten by predators within 2 or 3 days (Cowie, Krebs, & Sherry, 1981). Nevertheless, as with storing up provisions for the winter, such opportunistic hoarding occurs most readily in fall and winter, even in constant conditions of food availability (Ludescher, 1980). Some hoarders also have a daily cycle of storage and recovery, storing early in the day when food is most abundant and recovering food near evening when they need to build up reserves to survive the night (Sherry, 1985).

Similar, but more extreme, variations occur in the corvids, where differences in reliance on stored food are correlated with numerous adaptations in morphology and behavior. These differences are most vividly illustrated by four species that cache conifer seeds in the American Southwest, Clark's nutcracker, the pinyon jay (*Gymnorhinus cyanocephalus*), Stellar's jay (*Cyanocitta stelleri*), and the scrub jay (*Aphelocoma coerulescens*; Vander Wall & Balda, 1981). When pine cones begin to ripen in August, Clark's nutcrackers pry out the seeds, load them into their sublingual pouches, and fly several kilometers to bury them. The seeds are deposited in caches of one to five on south-facing slopes where the snow will not be too deep later on. The seeds, amounting to several thousand caches, or a total of more than 30,000 individual items, are recovered and eaten throughout the winter. Clark's nutcracker is one of the earliest breeding birds in North America, and this aspect of its breeding biology is presumably related to its ability to feed its young on stored pine seeds.

The most extreme contrast in this group of species is the scrub jay. It has a short stubby bill that it cannot use to open pine cones, has no sublingual pouch, is not such a strong flier as the nutcracker, and does very little hoarding. Moreover, what little it does takes place in its territory, not in special sites kilometers away. Still another corvid, the Northwestern crow (*Corvus caurinus*), has a daily cycle of hoarding and recovery. At low tide, Northwestern crows take crabs and mussels from the shore and conceal them in nearby meadows. The prey are recovered during high tides over the next few days before they have time to rot (James & Verbeek, 1983).

Field evidence strongly suggests that some of the species mentioned earlier use memory to recover their stores. For example, Tomback (1980) concluded from the clusters of beak marks nutcrackers left in the snow that the birds could not have been searching randomly for caches. Cowie *et al.* (1981) allowed marsh tits to store radioactively labeled sunflower seeds, which the experimenters could then locate with a scintillation counter. The experimenters placed "near control" and "far control" seeds 10 and 100 cm, respectively, from the stored seeds, in sites as similar as possible to those chosen by the birds. Controls for seeds poked into broken nettle stems were poked into broken nettle stems; controls for seeds in cracks of bark were placed in cracks of bark, and so on. The seeds in locations chosen by the tits disappeared significantly sooner than the "far controls." On the assumption that predation was equally likely at all three types of sites, the seeds hoarded by the birds must have been recovered by the individuals that hoarded them, presumably using memory.A model that has

## LABORATORY STUDIES OF MEMORY: METHODS

Field studies are of limited usefulness for studying the details of a phenomenon that takes place over such a long time and is spread over such a wide area as food storing and recovery. Therefore, it is fortunate for those wanting to analyze the memory involved in food storing that several species hoard readily in captivity. Studies of captive birds have shown fairly conclusively that marsh tits, black-capped chickadees (*Parus atricapillus*), and Clark's nutcrackers, the three species tested most extensively, can use memory to recover stored items in the laboratory. Before reviewing the properties of this memory and comparing it to memory in other species, it is worth considering how these laboratory tests of memory for storage sites have been designed and how their demands compare to the demands of recovering stored food in the wild.

The first study of food storing in captive marsh tits was reported by Sherry, Krebs, and Cowie (1981). They offered birds in a 3 × 4 meter room trays of moss, each 1 meter square, where they could store sunflower seeds. The moss trays were rearranged on the floor of the aviary each day. On each trial a bird was allowed into the room for a 15-minute "prestorage phase" during which time spent on different parts of the moss was recorded. Opportunity to eat and/or store sunflower seeds for 15 minutes followed immediately; during this time the birds stored a mean of 8.8 seeds. All stored seeds were removed by the experimenters for the recovery test, which followed 3 or 24 hours later, with the birds deprived for 2 hours beforehand. Memory for the storage sites was assessed by comparing the times spent and numbers of visits to quandrants of moss used for storage in the recovery phase to those measures in the prestorage phase. The tits appeared to be searching for seeds by pulling and poking at the moss in the areas where they had been stored, and these measures provided significant evidence of memory at both retention intervals.

In an attempt to make recovery of stored food more like a conventional test of memory for identifiable items, John Krebs and I (Shettleworth & Krebs, 1982) allowed marsh tits to store hemp seeds in holes drilled in sections of tree branches set in tubs of cement or hung from the ceiling (Figure 13.1). There were 100 possible storage sites, each covered by a small flap of cloth that the bird had to lift when depositing or recovering seeds. Because, as a control experiment showed, the birds could not detect the seeds from a distance in this arrangement, seeds could be left in place for

**FIGURE 13.1.** Experimental aviary used by Shettleworth and Krebs (1982) for marsh tits. Small circles indicate locations of artificial storage sites. Emphasized and filled circles indicate sites used by one bird on 1 day in two bouts of hoarding separated by 2 hours.

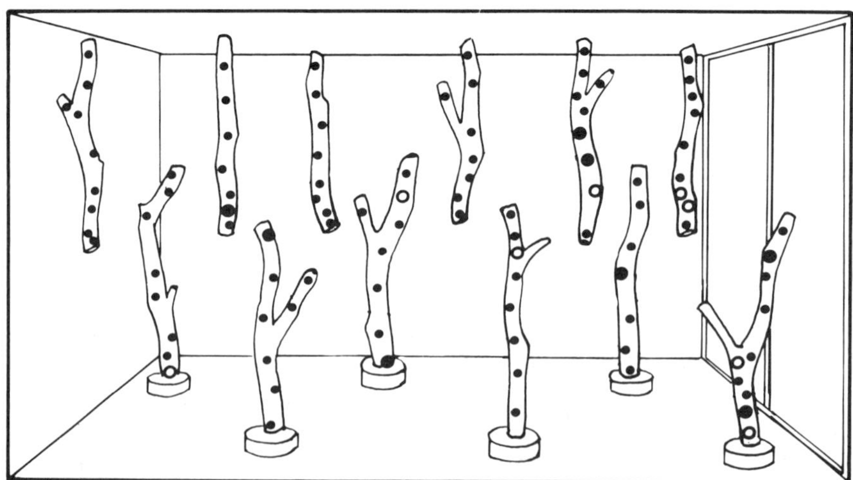

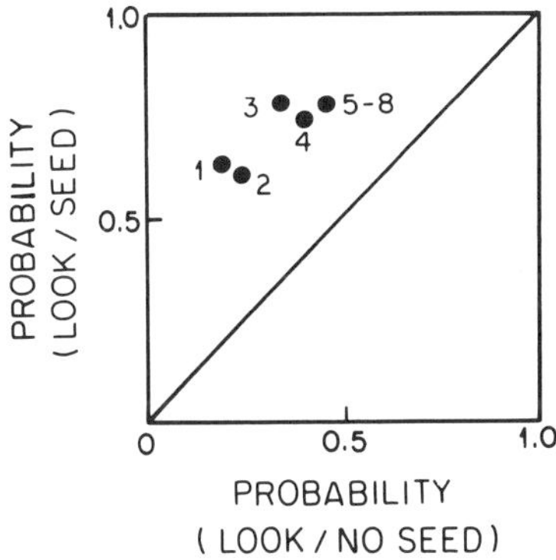


**FIGURE 13.2.** Signal detection analysis of one marsh tit's performance recovering 12 seeds on 12 trials in the aviary depicted in Figure 13.1. Data were grouped across holes used similar numbers of times for storage, indicated by numbers beside the data points. The probability of looking into given holes was greater on days when they had been used for storage than otherwise, indicating that memory is used. The existence of site preferences is indicated by the fact that frequently used holes are always visited more often. (Data from Shettleworth & Krebs, 1982. Reprinted by permission.)

the tests of memory. Recovery was tested 2 hours after storage of 8–16 seeds. Data analysis was based on the assumption that all looks into holes in recovery were attempts to recover seeds stored in that trial. Thus, looks into holes that had not been used that day were "errors." In our first experiment, the trees were always left in the same place so that data could be subjected to signal detection analysis (Figure 13.2). Probability of visiting a hole or set of holes on trials when they had been used for storage ("correct detections") could be compared to probability of visiting those same holes when they had not been stored in that day ("false reports"). This analysis showed that although the birds tended to develop preferences for certain storage sites, over and above this they used memory to locate stored items. In a second experiment the trees were rearranged each day, and there was less evidence for site preferences. Sherry (1984a) has used a very similar method with chickadees and also found good evidence for memory using measures of visits and times spent at given sites much like those used by Sherry *et al.* (1981).

Both continuous and discontinuous distributions of experimental storage sites have also been used for testing captive Clark's nutcrackers. Balda (1980; Balda & Turek, 1984) and Vander Wall (1982) allowed their subjects to bury pine seeds in a sand-covered aviary floor, whereas Kamil and Balda (1985) presented their subjects with an array of sand-filled holes in which to cache seeds. The latter experimenters introduced the further methodological refinement of forcing birds to store in an experimenter-selected subset of the holes by plugging some of them up. In this way a bird could be required to remember "items" "presented" by the experimenter rather than items it selected entirely on its own, and habitual storing in only a few sites could be eliminated. Retention intervals of 2 weeks or more have been used in some of these tests, as being more appropriate to a species that stores for months in the wild, and good evidence for memory has been obtained. Most studies have allowed the nutcrackers actually to find seeds in recovery because Balda (1980) reported that a captive Eurasian nutcracker (*Nucifraga caryocactes*) seemed to lose interest in storing in an aviary when it was never allowed to recover any of its caches. A control experiment reported by Vander Wall (1982) showed that Clark's nutcrackers are very poor at finding seeds buried by other nutcrackers, so the birds presumably do not use smell. In addition, before losing interest in storing, Balda's nutcracker continued to probe accurately in the absence of seeds.

Clearly, all these laboratory situations differ greatly from the situation confronted by a food storer in the field. The birds experience isolated episodes of storing and recovery in the testing environment while spending the rest of their time elsewhere, in a home cage. Recovery is observed while the hungry bird has no source of food other than its stores available. In effect, the recovery situation is modeled as one in which the bird must recall the locations of storage sites and set out to find them. However, it seems just as likely that marsh tits in the field would often recover stores by recognizing a storage site when passing near it during the course of normal foraging. Nutcrackers might have a hierarchical system, recalling whole slopes where caches are buried and recognizing individual sites within them (Balda & Turek, 1984). A factor limiting the extent to which recovering in either of these ways could be observed in the laboratory is the small areas that must be used. At any time the bird is within sight of most of the storage sites and could be recognizing each one in turn.

A further problem with testing in a small area is that items may be much closer together than they are in the field. Marsh tits store items an average of 7 meters apart in the Wytham Wood, Oxford (Cowie *et al.*, 1981); in the laboratory studies described above they were forced to store many items in a 4 × 3 meter room. This means that the storage sites are more similar spatially than they would be normally. Moreover, because sites are close together, there is little cost to searching them but considerable benefit, as they contain the only food available. These two factors might make accuracy of memory appear less than it would be in the field.

A further factor limiting what can be learned about accuracy of recovery is the type of experimental storage sites used. From this point of view, the ideal storage substrate is the sand floor used by Vander Wall (1982) and others for nutcrackers. In this arrangement the stored items can be present but concealed during recovery tests, and accuracy can be measured by how far from buried items the bird probes. Because nutcrackers probe and swipe from side to side with the bill, "successful" attempts can be counted as those near enough to a cache to uncover it within a single probe and swipe sequence. With a discontinous distribution of storage sites, like holes in trees or on the floor, the bird has only a limited number of places where it can look. The observed error rate is likely to be affected by the distance between sites, their number, and their similarity to one another.

Finally, all the studies mentioned consisted of a number of repetitions of the store–recover sequence, all in the same relatively small area with the same set of sites. Particularly in experiments with discrete storage sites, this means that the birds would be forced to reuse storage sites. Not only has reuse of sites not been observed in the wild (if sites were reused, predators would quickly learn this and empty them) but repeated trials in the same area would be expected to cause considerable proactive interference (cf. Roberts, 1984, for rats in the radial maze). Memory ought to be facilitated if novel sites are used each time (Mishkin & Delacour, 1975), as in the field. It could be argued, therefore, that rearranging the experimental aviary for each trial would improve memory, but if a bird needs to be able to localize a site within a familiar spatial array, rearranging sites each day confronts the bird with a situation where this is difficult.

It seems, then, that if we assume that factors such as interference and similarity of items affect memory for storage sites in the same way they affect memory for other kinds of items, the experimental situations in which memory for stored food has been studied would be expected to degrade that memory considerably. If their aim is to discover how tits and nutcrackers recover stored food in the wild, such studies cannot contribute much toward an answer. They can, however, contribute toward answering the more limited question, What are the properties of spatial memory for stored food in tits and nutcrackers? To apply knowledge gained from laboratory studies to analyzing what goes on in the field, we then must assume that the considerable differences between the field and laboratory situations do not affect the properties of memory in a qualitative way.

One key question in this regard is whether the properties of memory for storage sites are unique to memory for storage sites or whether they are general properties of spatial memory in food-storing species. That is, does the act of storing food in a location make the storage site remembered especially strongly or in a different way? John Krebs and I have begun some experiments aimed at answering this question. In one experiment marsh tits encountered seeds placed in storage sites by the experimenter while they were trying to store seeds themselves. The birds generally left the encountered seeds in place because they were already carrying a seed at the time and each storage site would only hold one seed. When allowed to search for seeds 2 hours later, they were as likely to recover the encountered seeds as the ones they had stored themselves. Although this experiment was done only with sets of 3–6 hoarded and 3–8 encountered seeds per trial and one retention interval, it does suggest that the act of storing confers no special memorial status on locations of food. Further work along these lines is described in a later section.

## PROPERTIES OF MEMORY FOR STORED FOOD

Memory for stored food in the wild appears to have remarkably large capacity and long persistence, especially in the corvids. It is clear that individuals may store many hundreds or thousands of items. For example, by providing a continuous supply of sunflower seeds, Sherry *et al.* (1982) were able to observe individual marsh tits hoarding more than 100 items in a day. Over a period of a few weeks a year, Clark's nutcrackers make many more caches than this. It is also clear that some items are recovered with great accuracy, as witness the observations of Tomback (1980) and Cowie *et al.* (1981) described earlier. What is more difficult to discover in the field is just what proportion of items stored is actually recovered. Stevens (1985) has reported one method for doing so. Marsh tits wore tiny magnets and detectors were placed near their hoarded seeds. Twenty to thirty percent of seeds marked in this way were visited within 3 days by the birds that hoarded them, whereas control sites were hardly visited at all.

Information of this kind is important because the relatively small size of areas used for laboratory studies of hoarding means that only relatively few items can be offered in one hoarding bout without hoarded items becoming so dense that the probability of recovering one by chance is unacceptably high. The reported laboratory studies of hoarding in marsh tits and chickadees have all involved less than 20 items per bout of hoarding and recovery. Upward of 150 caches have been used in studies with nutcrackers (Vander Wall, 1982). It seems unlikely that these numbers of items would tax the memory capacities of the subjects, although it must be recalled that individual items may be less memorable in the laboratory situation than they would be in the field. In any case, to compare memory for individual items when different numbers of items are hoarded, one would need a method of "probing" memory for a single storage site, something that might be difficult to devise in a situation where subjects are left to move freely among the storage sites.

Investigations of the persistence of memory lend themselves more readily to the laboratory, especially with marsh tits and chickadees, where the natural time intervals involved are not too long to make data collection practical over similar intervals in the laboratory. Sherry *et al.* (1981) found that marsh tits recovered as accurately after 24 hours as after 3. Preliminary evidence indicates that chickadees still recover seeds accurately 7 days after storing them, although performance seems a little worse after 14 days (Sherry, 1984b). Nutcrackers' recovery has been found to be quite accurate after intervals of 2 weeks or more in several experiments, but none have included comparisons of two or more retention intervals.

If marsh tits' and chickadees' memory for storage sites lasts for a week or more, as Sherry's results suggest, this would help to account for why the balance of the data indicates neither primacy nor recency effects in these birds (review in Sherry, 1984b). It has seemed of particular interest to some investigators (e.g., Shettleworth & Krebs, 1982) to look for a recency effect in recovery of stored items because it would be expected on functional grounds. If a stored item is more likely to have been lost to predators the longer it has been in place and if stored items are of equal initial value, then, on an item-by-item basis, a hoarder always has the most to gain from attempting to recover the item stored most recently (Stephens, 1982). John Krebs and I looked for the recency effect predicted by this hypothesis by allowing marsh tits to store two batches of seeds 2 hours apart and observing recovery of the whole hoard a further 2 hours later (Shettleworth & Krebs, 1982, Experiment 2). There was a significant tendency to recover more seeds from the later batch in two of three birds (i.e., a recency effect), but further tests with the double-hoarding design have not corroborated this effect (J. R. Krebs, personal communication). Several field studies with the radioactive seed technique have not corroborated it either (review in Sherry, 1984b). The possible intepretation of recency effects or the lack of them is discussed further in the next section.

Perhaps more informative than attempts to describe the quantitative properties of memory in absolute terms have been studies attempting to delineate the contents of memory, what the birds remember about a storage site. Marsh tits, at least, remember something equivalent to "there is an item there," a piece of information they can use in a fexible cognitive way. In the double-hoarding study designed to study recency, Krebs and I found that marsh tits were able to avoid visiting holes containing seeds from the first batch while hoarding the second batch (Figure 13.3). (In our arrangement, each hole would hold only one seed.) Yet they clearly knew the locations of items from the first batch because they recovered them accurately later on.

Not only do birds remember where stored items are, chickadees, at least, appear to remember something about their nature. When they have hoarded both sunflower seeds and less preferred safflower seeds, they spend more time at sunflower than at safflower seed sites in a recovery test

**FIGURE 13.3.** One marsh tit's rate of visiting holes holding stored seeds as a function of successive holes visited when eight seeds were stored among the 100 sites provided in the aviary shown in Figure 13.1. When the bird is recovering the stored seeds, full holes are visited at greater than the chance expectation, but if instead the bird is storing eight further seeds, it visits holes already holding seeds at the chance rate or slightly below. (Data from Shettleworth & Krebs, 1982. Reprinted by permission.)

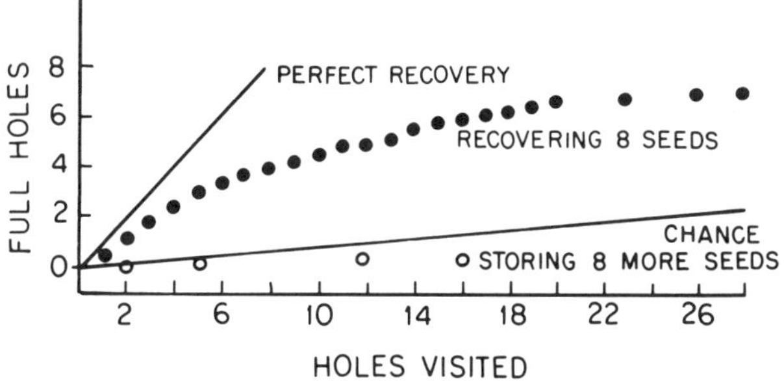

with all items removed (Sherry, 1984a). Contemporary theorizing about the cognitive basis of classically conditioned responding has inspired studies asking what aspects of food are learned about in conditioning (Rescorla, Chapter 12, this volume). Similar methods might be applied to food storing to analyze whether the birds simply associate greater value with sites holding preferred food at the time of storage or whether they recall the sensory properties of items stored in particular sites. This could be done by manipulating the value of a given item type after storage has taken place, for example, by satiating the bird on it or creating an aversion to it.

In addition to retaining considerable information about a storage episode, marsh tits and chickadees make use of information gained during recovery or attempted recovery. First of all, they tend not to revisit sites from which they have already recovered an item. This is true both within a relatively short bout of recovery (Shettleworth & Krebs, 1982) and from one bout of recovery to another one 24 hours later (Sherry, 1982). Chickadees seem to treat sites emptied by predators like those they have emptied themselves, spending little time at either in further bouts of recovery (Sherry, 1984a). However, marsh tits treat the sites of successful and unsuccessful recoveries differently when it comes to selecting storage sites in the future. If they are offered several types of storage site such as moss, bark, and nettle stems and one is "preyed on" consistently by the experimenter, they reallocate their storing effort to the types of sites where recovery is successful (Stevens, 1985).

Finally, some work has been done with nutcrackers on what cues birds use to locate storage sites. The two-dimensional sand-covered arena in which nutcrackers will store lends itself very well to this type of study because discrete objects can be introduced, moved around, or removed altogether and their effect on the location of recovery attempts measured in a continuous way. Vander Wall (1982) has shown through experiments of this sort that Clark's nutcrackers localize cache sites with respect to nearby prominent objects. This fits with field observations of nutcrackers digging down through snow straight to caches (e.g., Swanberg, 1951). However, the results of such studies will probably depend on the relative salience of the various cues that are offered. For example, with a sand-covered floor carefully smoothed over before each test, small local cues are not available, whereas they are in a bed of moss that might be offered to a marsh tit. Thus, it is questionable whether studies of what cues the birds use to locate their stores are likely to be very profitable.

## FOOD STORING AND RADIAL MAZES: A MODEL OF MEMORY

The problem confronting a marsh tit or a nutcracker recovering its stores is similar to that confronting a rat in a radial maze (Olton & Samuelson, 1976). A radial maze consists of a number of open, elevated arms radiating

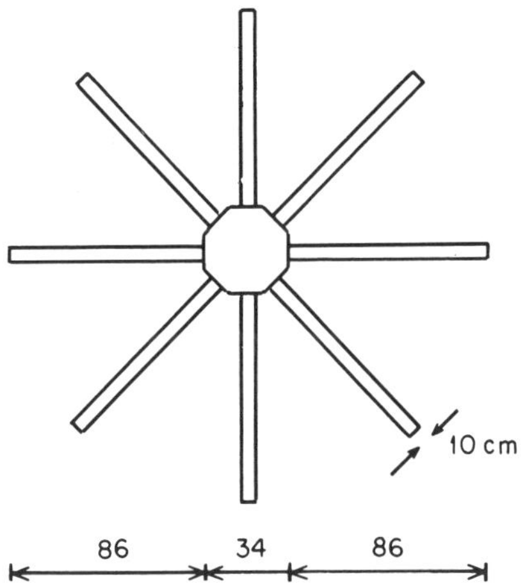


FIGURE 13.4. Schematic overhead view of a radial maze used for studying spatial memory in rats. Such a maze is typically elevated, with very low or no walls, so the rat is exposed to a rich variety of cues from the room surrounding the maze. (After Olton & Samuelson, 1976.)

out from a central platform (Figure 13.4). Rats are first accustomed to running around on the maze and finding food at the ends of the arms. The test of memory consists of daily trials in which each arm contains one item of food at the start and the rat is allowed to collect them all. Rats soon come to perform very efficiently, visiting each arm once and only once per trial. Numerous control experiments have shown that rats use memory for arms already visited, not such aids as odor trails or stereotyped ways of responding (review in Roberts, 1984).

In the typical radial maze task, there is a fixed rule about the locations of food: one item per arm per trial. In contrast, for a tit or nutcracker storing food, the locations of items change with each storage and recovery bout. In addition, although a tit in the field probably knows its territory very well, being permanently territorial, it has probably not identified any given storage site as such before using it for storage. Thus, learning what the sites are must take place very quickly, while the bird is depositing an item there. Having learned what the sites are, the food-storer, like the rat, is able to collect food from all of them with very few revisits to emptied sites.

Rats perform well in mazes with up to 32 different locations, and Roberts (1984) has argued that their spatial memory capacity is much larger than this, being limited only by the number of different locations they can discriminate. When allowed to visit four arms of an eight-arm maze and then held for up to 4 hours before being allowed to complete the trial, rats still perform well. Various interfering events such as trials on other mazes can be experienced during this retention interval without memory for the first four arms being much affected.

The radial maze is often described as a test of spatial "working memory," where working memory refers to memory for the aspects of a task that change from one trial to the next. Reference memory, in contrast, is memory for aspects of the task that remain the same, like the configuration of the maze or the general task requirements. Working memory in the radial maze does have a larger capacity and greater persistence than working memory in most other laboratory tasks, but this is not an inherent feature of spatial tasks. Rather, it is due to the radial maze task as it is usually run, having parameters particularly favorable to memory. This is shown most vividly by comparing results in a radial maze to results of a spatial delayed matching task with pigeons in a Skinner box (Wilkie & Summers, 1982).

Wilkie and Summers presented pigeons with an array of nine white pecking keys on one wall of an operant chamber. One key was lighted at the beginning of each trial. After the pigeon pecked it, a retention interval followed and then the original key (the "sample") and another key were lighted. When the pigeon pecked the sample, it was sometimes rewarded with food. With retention intervals of as little as 4–8 seconds, pigeons showed no evidence of memory for the location of the sample. These intervals are typical of delayed matching to sample with other types of visual cues and many trials a day. Their shortness is probably not indicative of a difference in spatial memory between rats and pigeons because pigeons can be induced to perform fairly well in a radial maze, although they need much more extensive training than do rats (Roberts & Van Veldhuizen, 1985). Pigeons can also perform delayed spatial alternation in a T-maze with retention intervals of 16 minutes or more (Olson & Maki, 1983).

Food storing and the radial maze task both differ from spatial delayed matching in a number of ways, all of which would be expected to improve memory. Locations to be remembered in a maze or food-storing situation are relatively far apart and differ in a number of visual aspects and perhaps on other dimensions. Food is located in the site to be remembered rather than offered elsewhere. The animal visits the places to be remembered rather than passively viewing them. Trials are usually given at the rate of one a day, in the case of mazes and laboratory studies of storage. In addition, in the wild, locations to be remembered are probably novel.

These sorts of parametric differences among different laboratory tests of memory can be encompassed in a single model (R. H. I. Dale & J. E. R. Staddon, unpublished; see Staddon, 1983, Chapter 12) that accounts for the differences in results between such tests as radial mazes, delayed alternation, and delayed matching. Locations to be remembered are identified in memory by a spatial code. This is what the rat is assumed to be acquiring in its initial explorations of the maze. (Memory tests like delayed matching presumably require some other sort of coding of the individual stimuli.) Locations are also tagged with information about when they were last visited. Memory for the last visit (the temporal tag) decays over a few hours so that eventually all arms are treated as visited equally recently. During a usual sort of radial maze trial, the rat must distinguish between arms tagged as visited that day and those not so tagged and go to the latter. Other response rules can be trained, but rats seem to use an "avoid the least recent" rule spontaneously.

The elements of this account of radial maze behavior, then, are a spatial code identifying places, a temporal tag identifying how recently a place has been visited, and a response rule indicating what kind of discrimination among temporal tags is required. This framework encompasses a wide range of species and task differences among laboratory tests of memory, but it is too simple to fit food storing without modification.

Consider first the situation confronting a chickadee or marsh tit recovering its stores. Once the bird has tagged a number of sites as holding food, it must visit them while avoiding sites already visited in recovery. It can do this even when storage takes place one day, some recovery on the next, and a final bout of recovery on the third day (Sherry, 1982). In Dale and Staddon's terms, by the third day it can still discriminate sites visited 24 hours earlier from those visited 48 hours earlier. It cannot just be using information about the time of last visit to a site, however. In the first bout of recovery, birds sometimes rehoarded a seed rather than eating it. That is, they removed it from its original storage site and stored it elsewhere. In the second recovery test, they visited sites with rehoarded seeds while at the same time not visiting sites of seeds recovered during the first recovery episode (Figure 13.5). If sites are merely tagged with the time of last visit, this discrimination would be impossible. The same conclusion that more

**FIGURE 13.5.** Mean percentage of time per site spent by black-capped chickadees at storage sites during a bout of searching for stored food. The test was conducted after an initial bout of recovery in which the birds were allowed to recover approximately half of their stores. They rehoarded some of the stored seeds at this time, moving them from one site to another. In the test, the sites holding seeds (HOARD-ONLY and RE-HOARD) were visited for significantly longer than in the prestorage phase, whereas those from which seeds had been removed were not. (Data from Sherry, 1984a. Reprinted by permission.)

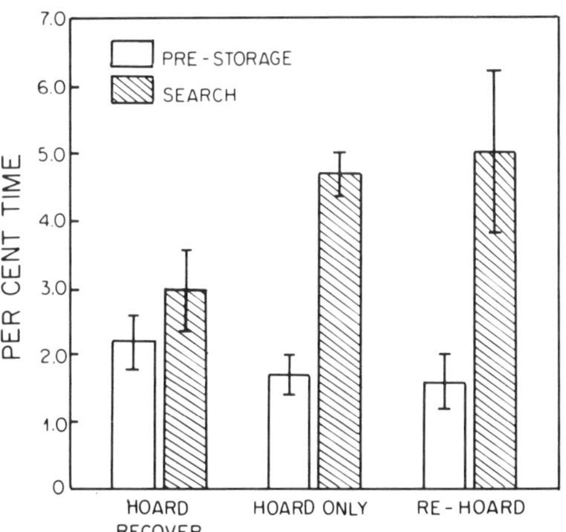

than just visiting sites is remembered follows from our observations (S. J. Shettleworth & J. R. Krebs, unpublished) that while storing seeds marsh tits visit some potential storage sites without using them, but in recovery they inspect these sites significantly less often than sites they actually used for storage.

Thus, although the behavior of rats in radial mazes may be accounted for in terms of simple temporal tags, a parallel account of the behavior of food-storing birds requires that possible storage sites be tagged as to the presence or absence of food. Whether they are tagged temporally as well is unclear because the best evidence for this would be the so far elusive recency effect. Consideration of Dale and Staddon's model for the decay, or change in discriminability, of temporal tags with time suggests that the best way to find a recency effect in food storing would be to have two bouts of storing quite far apart, say a day or more, with opportunity to recover both hoards very soon after the second storing bout. Such an experiment has not yet been done. If, however, what the bird remembers about a site is seen as a relatively enduring association of the site location with food or no food, primacy and recency effects might not be expected.

Some data suggest that for marsh tits and chickadees, at least, the act of storing or recovering food from a site does not have a special role in acquisition of information about the status of the site. Sites where seeds were encountered during storage are treated similarly to sites where seeds were stored by the bird itself. Similarly, birds seem equally to avoid revisiting sites they have taken seeds from, empty sites they have visited in error, and sites emptied by predators. Detailed comparisons of rates of revisiting all three types of sites need to be done, however, to test whether they indeed remain similar under a variety of conditions. For some purposes, marsh tits clearly do discriminate sites emptied by predators from sites they have emptied themselves. When they are offered several types of storage sites such as nettle stems, bark, and moss and one is consistently emptied of stored items by the experimenter, they reallocate their storage effort to safer sites (Stevens, 1985). At some level they must be storing information about more than just the presence or absence of food at the time of last visit to a site.

Thus, it appears that the memorial requirements of food storing and recovery can be described most simply as follows. In visiting a potential storage site, the bird encodes the site as such and tags it with information as to whether it contains food or not at the end of the visit. It also encodes the value and/or sensory qualities of the food. Information about the presence or absence of food seems to be stored regardless of whether the bird itself deposits or removes it or whether it simply observes the presence or absence of food. However, in recovery, the state of a site when the bird arrives there is compared with its remembered state at the end of the last visit, and this comparison influences future storage attempts. The information with which sites are tagged (or, equivalently, whether they are associated with food or not) is relatively enduring, unlike the temporal tags in rat spatial memory in the radial maze. Indeed, it is questionable whether information about the times of visits is stored at all. "Errors" in recovery, unlike errors in radial maze behavior as interpreted by Dale and Staddon, are probably due to similarities among spatial and other cues to site identity rather than to confusion of temporal tags. This implication of the present view, is supported by Kamil and Balda's (1985) data for Clark's nutcrackers. Finally, food-storing birds can switch readily between two response rules, either going to or avoiding locations with food depending on whether they are engaged in storage or recovery.

By this interpretation, radial maze behavior and recovering stored food involve memory for different types of events. Radial maze studies have not generally been designed to discriminate memory for time of last visit (temporal tags) from memory about the presence or absence of food. When depletion versus nondepletion of food at the ends of arms has been manipulated, this has been done between groups of animals experiencing different reinforcement contingencies (e.g., Gaffan, Hansel, & Smith, 1983; Haig, Rawlins, Olton, Mead, & Taylor, 1983).

Food-storing birds seem able to acquire and act on information about presence or absence of food on one brief visit to each of many sites. A laboratory situation for rats that has this requirement, although for only one site at a time is the Maier three-table task (cf. Haig *et al.*, 1983; Herrman, Bahr, Bremner, & Ellen, 1982). Here a rat is allowed to acquire spatial information about a complex room by freely exploring it. Among other things, the room contains three tables joined by rat walkways. The rat is then placed on one of the tables and fed, and the question is whether it will go back there when released on another one of the tables. If they are not allowed to deplete the food on the first table, rats perform well in this task (Herrman *et al.*, 1982). It might be seen as a very limited version of the task confronting a food hoarder, although it does differ in that the rat is passively transported to the food table the first time while the food hoarder actively inspects sites. In addition, the retention interval between placement on a table and opportunity to return has typically been only a few seconds.

## COMPARATIVE STUDIES OF MEMORY

In the foregoing account, an essential feature of the ability to recover stored food successfully is rapid association of food or absence of food with large numbers of storage sites or potential sites as they are inspected. The acts of storing and recovering do not seem to play an essential role in this. Storing food simply serves to bring the bird into contact with a large number of locations containing food. Suppose, then, we could arrange for a nonstoring species to come into contact in a similar way with locations containing food.

Would these animals show equally good memory or would their memory have less capacity and/or persistence than that of a food storer in a similar situation?

Functional arguments provide no guidance here. In favor of the food-storer performing better is the idea that by storing food items the tit or nutcracker is depositing them in places where they are not usually found, places only it knows. It is to the bird's advantage to remember them because it will be more likely to find them that way than by foraging at random in the same area (see Haftorn, 1956). In contrast, a single item encountered in random search would seem unlikely to remain where it is long enough for it to be worth any predator's remembering its location. (Note that this argument predicts a difference between memory for stored and encountered seeds, although we did not find one with the set of parameters we used.) Sherry (in press) has argued, however, that remembering where food has been encountered would be of advantage to any predator, and we should not expect food storers to have better-developed spatial memories than their nonstoring relatives.

Together with John Krebs, I have begun exploring a method for comparing the spatial memory of marsh tits and chickadees with that of nonstoring tits in a situation that does not require the birds to store food but has similar memory requirements to food storing. The situation resembles "window-shopping" by human consumers. While the shops are shut, the shopper, bird or human, observes where goods are to be found. If it remembers where the goods are, it can return when the shops open and collect them. Our "shops" are blocks of wood, each containing one hole big enough for half a shelled sunflower seed and a perch conveniently placed an inch or two below it. Each hole is concealed from a bird's distant view by a flap of black cloth, and it can also be covered by a small transparent Plexiglas "window." Black-capped chickadees stored and recovered seeds from these blocks in a procedure similar to that we had used with marsh tits (Shettleworth & Krebs, 1982). Recovery after 2 hours was reasonably good in this situation, especially considering that the sites were quite uniform and close together.

Having shown that these artificial sites supported normal storage and recovery behavior, we then forced our subjects to window-shop. The windows were closed and covered with the black cloths, and behind some of the closed windows were pieces of sunflower seed. Because they had been accustomed to looking under the cloths, the birds continued to do so, and when they saw a seed behind a window they stopped and pecked at it, sometimes quite persistently. On each of a number of trials the birds were allowed to discover four seeds in this way (the number used in the previous hoarding trials) and then let out of the aviary for 2 hours. When they returned, the seeds they had seen were accessible, and some birds showed evidence of remembering where they were.

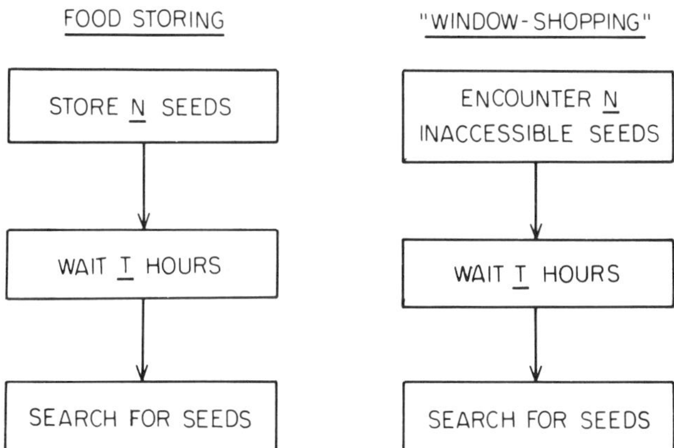


**FIGURE 13.6.** Schematic representation of how spatial memory for stored and "window-shopped" items can be compared for capacity ($N$) and persistence ($T$). The spatial arrangement and nature of to-be-remembered sites is the same in the two types of tests.

All we can say from this initial study is that chickadees can perform the window-shopping task. We cannot yet compare recovery of window-shopped seeds with recovery of hoarded seeds because all the window-shopping trials were performed late in the season, after all the storing trials. A further experiment balanced for experience and time of year is underway. Ideally, performance in the two tasks should be compared with various retention intervals and numbers of items (Figure 13.6). However, the similarity of memory for stored and merely encountered seeds in marsh tits suggests that window-shopping and storage will give similar results for at least some sets of parameters. If so, window-shopping performance in food-storing tits can be compared to window-shopping performance in tits that store little or not at all, such as blue and great tits, to determine whether the ability to remember the state of a large number of sites for a long time after brief exposure is better developed in birds that rely on this ability to recover their stores. Obviously there are many possible pitfalls in such a program, but it does offer the opportunity to compare food-storers with their nonstoring relatives on a task with the same spatial memory requirements as food storing.

If spatial memory turns out to be better in food storers than in nonstorers, the next question might be whether it is also exceptional in tasks not resembling food storing. For example, pigeons remember up to 160 pairs of slides for more than 2 years, although they need considerable training with them in the first place (Vaughan & Greene, 1984). The analysis of food storing presented here suggests that a nutcracker or a chickadee might acquire the initial discriminations much faster.

## SOME NEUROBIOLOGICAL SPECULATIONS

Rozin and Kalat (1971) introduced psychologists to the idea that there might be adaptive specializations of learning and memory. Food-storing birds are good candidates for possessors of adaptive specializations of spatial memory, at least in a quantitative way. However, as has been implicit in most of the preceding discussion, such adaptive specializations are notoriously hard to pin down. One approach to doing so has been sketched in the last section. The best subjects for this sort of approach might be corvids because some of these food-storing species possess such extreme specializations of morphology and behavior that it is easy to believe they might have concomitantly specialized memories (see Kamil & Balda, 1985).

If one were to identify an adaptive specialization of memory among food-storing birds, where might one look for its physiological basis? Presumably the considerable work on bases of spatial memory in mammals would lead one to look at homologous structures in birds. There are also a few clues in the literature on food storers. Sherry *et al.* (1981) found that if marsh tits stored seeds with one eye covered, they could only relocate the storage sites when that eye was in use. In effect this means that when storage takes place with binocular vision, memory for each site is stored in both hemispheres. Although this implication needs to be tested directly, it does suggest some constraints on the structures that are involved. It also suggests that in experiments to explore the effects of lesions on suspected structures, unilateral lesions could be employed and each subject used as its own control.

One set of lesion experiments on food-storing species has actually been reported. Krushinskaya (1966) lesioned the "hippocampus" of nutcrackers and found that while they still would store seeds in an aviary they could not relocate them more than 15 minutes later. Birds with control lesions still stored and recovered normally. The structure the absence of which causes such amnesia might be expected to be developed to different degrees in different species of corvids, depending on their specialization for food storing. These larger and more robust animals might be better subjects for physiological work than the tiny tits.

Like song learning, food storing differs widely across closely related species of birds. Both also occur on a seasonal basis. The spectacular success of neurobiological studies of song learning (e.g., Nottebohm, 1981) might encourage parallel investigations of the bases of memory for stored food. It is tempting to speculate, for example, that each summer in a nutcracker's brain, some cells die and others are born in preparation for remembering the next fall's storage sites. These may be exciting possibilities for the neurobiologist. However, a sobering thought is that although the ability to learn song seems to be confined to certain groups of birds, most vertebrates, and even some invertebrates (see Gould, Chapter 11, this volume), have the ability to remember at least some places where food is. Thus, on the basis of the behavioral evidence, food storing seems less likely than song learning to be subserved by specialized structures. And the behavioral evidence is as yet too limited to say whether the structures that subserve spatial memory should be any different in food-storers than in nonstoring species.

## ACKNOWLEDGMENTS

Preparation of this chapter was supported by a grant to the author from the Natural Sciences and Engineering Research Council of Canada (NSERC). Collaborative work with John Krebs was made possible by a NATO Grant for International Collaboration in Research to the author, John Krebs, and David Sherry and an International Scientific Exchange Award from NSERC. I thank Al Kamil, John Krebs, and David Sherry for comments and Cynthia Thomas for help with both the chickadees and the preparation of the manuscript.

## REFERENCES

Balda, R. P. Recovery of cached seeds by a captive *Nucifraga caryocatactes. Zeitschrift für Tierpsychologie*, 1980, *52*, 331–346.

Balda, R. P., & Turek, R. J. The cache-recovery system as an example of memory capabilities in Clark's nutcracker. In H. L. Roitblat, T. G. Bever, & H. S. Terrace (Eds.), *Animal cognition*. Hillsdale, N.J.: Erlbaum, 1984.

Bullock, T. H. Comparative neuroscience holds promise for quiet revolutions. *Science*, 1984, *225*, 473–478.

Cowie, R. J., Krebs, J. R., & Sherry, D. F. Food storing by marsh tits. *Animal Behaviour*, 1981, *29*, 1252–1259.

Gaffan, E. A., Hansel, H. C., & Smith, M. C. Does reward depletion influence spatial memory performance? *Learning and Motivation*, 1983, *14*, 58–74.

Haftorn, S. Contributions to the food biology of tits especially about storing of surplus food. A comparative analysis of *Parus atricapillus L., P. cristatus L.*, and *P. ater L. Skrifter, Kongelige Norske Videnskabers Selskab*, 1956, 4 (new series), 1–54.

Haig, K. A., Rawlins, J. N. P., Olton, D. S., Mead, A., & Taylor, B. Food searching strategies of rats: Variables affecting the relative strength of stay and shift strategies. *Journal of Experimental Psychology: Animal Behavior Processes*, 1983, *9*, 337–348.

Herrmann, T., Bahr, E., Bremner, B., & Ellen, P. Problem solving in the rat: Stay vs shift solutions on the three-table task. *Animal Learning & Behavior*, 1982, *10*, 39–45.

James, P. C., & Verbeek, N. A. M. The food storage behaviour of the Northwestern crow. *Behaviour*, 1983, *85*, 276–291.

Kamil, A. C., & Balda, R. C. Cache recovery and spatial memory in Clark's nutcrackers (*Nucifraga columbiana*). *Journal of Experimental Psychology: Animal Behavior Processes*, 1985, *11*, 95–111.

Krushinskaya, N. L. Some complex forms of feeding behavior of nutcrackers after removal of their old cortex. *Journal of Evolutionary Biochemistry and Physiology*, 1966, *11*, 564–568. (Translation by M. M. Clark)

Ludescher, F. B. Feeding and caching of seeds in willow-tits *Parus montanus* in the course of the year under constant feeding conditions. *Oekologie der Vogel*, 1980, *2*, 135–144.

Mishkin, M., & Delacour, J. An analysis of short-term visual memory in the monkey. *Journal of Experimental Psychology: Animal Behavior Processes*, 1975, *1*, 326–334.

Nottebohm, F. A brain for all seasons: Cyclical anatomical changes in song control nuclei of the canary brain. *Science*, 1981, *214*, 1368–1370.

Olson, D., & Maki, W. S. Characteristics of spatial memory in pigeons. *Journal of Experimental Psychology: Animal Behavior Processes*, 1983, *9*, 266–280.

Olton, D. S., & Samuelson, R. J. Remembrance of places passed: Spatial memory in rats. *Journal of Experimental Psychology: Animal Behavior Processes*, 1976, *2*, 97–116.

Roberts, W. A. Some issues in animal spatial memory. In H. L. Roitblat, T. G. Bever, & H. S. Terrace (Eds.), *Animal cognition*. Hillsdale, N.J.: Erlbaum, 1984.

Roberts, W. A., & Van Veldhuizen, N. Spatial memory in pigeons on the radial maze. *Journal of Experimental Psychology: Animal Behavior Processes*, 1985, *11*, 241–260.

Rozin, P., & Kalat, J. W. Specific hungers and poison avoidance as adaptive specializations of learning. *Psychological Review*, 1971, *78*, 459–486.

Sherry, D. F. Food storage, memory, and marsh tits. *Animal Behaviour*, 1982, *30*, 631–633.

Sherry, D. F. Food storage by black-capped chickadees: Memory for the location and contents of caches. *Animal Behaviour*, 1984, *32*, 451–464. (a)

Sherry, D. F. What food-storing birds remember. *Canadian Journal of Psychology*, 1984, *38*, 304–321. (b)

Sherry, D. F. Food storage by birds and mammals. *Advances in the Study of Behavior*, 1985, *15*, 153–188.

Sherry, D. F. Foraging for stored food. In M. L. Commons, A. Kacelnik, & S. J. Shettleworth (Eds.), *Quantitative analyses of behavior: Foraging*. Hillsdale, N.J.: Erlbaum, in press.

Sherry, D., Avery, M., & Stevens, A. The spacing of stored food by marsh tits. *Zeitschrift für Tierpsychologie*, 1982, *58*, 153–162.

Sherry, D. F., Krebs, J. R., & Cowie, R. J. Memory for the location of stored food in marsh tits. *Animal Behaviour*, 1981, *29*, 1260–1266.

Shettleworth, S. J., & Krebs, J. R. How marsh tits find their hoards: The roles of site preference and spatial memory. *Journal of Experimental Psychology: Animal Behavior Processes*, 1982, *8*, 354–375.

Staddon, J. E. R. *Adaptive behavior and learning*. London & New York: Cambridge University Press, 1983.

Stephens, D. W. *Stochasticity in foraging theory: risk and information*. Unpublished doctoral thesis, University of Oxford, 1982.

Stevens, T. A. *Food storing by marsh tits*. Doctoral thesis, Oxford University, 1985.

Swanberg, P. O. Food storage, territory, and song in the thick-billed Nutcracker. *Proceedings of the International Ornithological Congress*, 1951, *10*, 545–554.

Tomback, D. F. How nutcrackers find their seed stores. *Condor*, 1980, *82*, 10–19.

Vander Wall, S. B. An experimental analysis of cache recovery in Clark's nutcracker. *Animal Behaviour*, 1982, *30*, 84–94.

Vander Wall, S. B., & Balda, R. P. Ecology and evolution of food storage behavior in conifer-seed-caching corvids. *Zeitschrift für Tierpsychologie*, 1981, *56*, 217–242.

Vaughan, W., & Greene, S. L. Pigeon visual memory capacity. *Journal of Experimental Psychology: Animal Behavior Processes*, 1984, *10*, 256–271.

Wilkie, D. M., & Summers, R. J. Pigeon's spatial memory: Factors affecting delayed matching of key location. *Journal of the Experimental Analysis of Behavior*, 1982, *37*, 45–56.

# CRITICAL COMMENTARIES

CHAPTER 14

# Evolutionary Restraints on Learning: Phylogenetic and Synaptic Interpretations

**Richard G. Coss**
University of California, Davis

## INTRODUCTION

The notion that some organisms may have different propensities to learn specific relationships between themselves and their environments—relationships that have been important on the evolutionary time scale—has been emphasized by several of the contributors to this volume, notably Gould (Chapter 11) and Shettleworth (Chapter 13). In keeping with this theme, I shall examine several aspects of evolutionary restraints on learning, emphasizing two types of analysis: (1) correlations of behavioral and situational changes among animals in natural settings and (2) correlations of experiential and neuroanatomical changes generated by varying behavioral activities. Correlations of these disparate types of analyses are likely to reflect the influences of both phylogenetic and ontogenetic processes of adjustment, some of which have been restrained by phylogenetically old and important contexts.

### Levels of Analysis in the Laboratory and Field

Some aspects of the notion of evolutionary restraints have been incorporated into the development of general process learning theory, particularly the hypothesis of "preparedness" (Seligman, 1970), and have led to a large number of studies of taste aversion in a variety of taxa (Garcia, McGowan, & Green, 1972; but also see Cooke, Delaney, & Gelperin, Chapter 10, this volume, and Rescorla, Chapter 12, this volume). Theoretical arguments for more research on learning under natural conditions, as opposed to restricted laboratory conditions (see Johnston, 1981; Johnston & Turvey, 1980), have prompted new studies seeking to broaden the generality of experimental findings to both laboratory and field settings. However, problems of interpretation are encountered when laboratory conditions differ markedly from field conditions. As an example of the problems emerging in the study of food hoarding and recovery by marsh tits, Shettleworth and Krebs (1982) describe the limitations of confined aviaries that restrict the spacing and complexity of storage sites as compared with the high variability of natural habitats. From this perspective, it appears that the gain in experimental precision in laboratory settings may be offset by physical limitations imposed by those settings. Thus, Shettleworth (Chapter 13, this volume) concedes that laboratory studies may reveal little information about how birds store and recover food in the wild. On the other hand, experimental questions about learning and memory can be tailored specifically to the limitations imposed by laboratory setups. These limitations are most apparent in instrumental learning situations in which the availability of changing environmental features is severely restricted. For example, Rescorla (Chapter 12, this volume) discusses the experimental situations in which animals learn a wide range of signal–signal and signal–consequence associations.

In laboratory setups with little environmental variation, it is not surprising that animals learn to organize their behaviors in ways that maximize the processing of any *invariances* in environmental features (e.g., Gibson, 1966, 1979) that emerge from experimental manipulations. Because experience is restricted to these settings, the animal focuses its attention on subtle changes in organism–environment relationships that might be quite apart from those encountered in the wild (Menzel, 1975). The fact that animals born and reared under laboratory conditions almost never experience the ecologically important tasks of finding food in diverse microhabitats, of searching for mates and defending nest sites, and of engaging or avoiding predators, means that detection of minor variation of independent variables could become very important during associative learning in impoverished settings. In many ways, the rich complexity of pairwise associative learning described by Rescorla might represent a fraction of the true learning capabilities that animals exhibit in the wild.

In contrast with the desirability of extending laboratory studies to field conditions, laboratory studies are paramount for examining the neurobiology of learning and memory, particularly those involving invertebrate taxa that show Pavlovian conditioning (e.g., Alkon, Chapter 1, this volume; Cooke, Delaney, & Gelperin, Chapter 10, this volume). As compared with vertebrates and invertebrates that range over large areas while foraging or searching for mates away from nest sites, terrestrial and aquatic mollusks have limited behavioral repertoires that are quite amenable to laboratory study. The choice for laboratory study of the terrestrial slug (*Limax maximus*) has proved to be exceptionally fruitful, especially the documentation that these mollusks exhibit higher order conditioning (see Gelperin, Hopfield, & Tank, 1985). Furthermore, lip–brain preparations of *Limax* can retain for several hours higher order associations learned initially in intact animals.

As in the studies of *Aplysia* (Hawkins, Abrams, Carew, & Kandel, 1983; Walters & Byrne, 1983), however, the continued focus of attention on biophysical changes at the synaptic level restricts the range of inferences about how information emerges at the higher levels of functioning neuronal networks. Moreover, there is the ever present risk of treating any one level of analysis, such as synaptic modification (e.g., Kandel & Schwartz, 1982, p. 441), as if it had ontological primacy; that is, there is a tendency to collapse the hierarchy of higher levels of relationships, such as neuronal circuits and behaving organisms, into that one level of causal description (Marr, 1982; Overton, 1976; Rose, 1980). Computer models of neuronal networks with highly deterministic circuits, in which output behavior is modified by adjusting a single variable such as "synaptic strengths," also give primacy to a single level of analysis (e.g., Gelperin *et al.*, 1985). On the other hand, computer models that incorporate more than one level of analysis with probabilistic features, such as growth of new circuits (Pellionisz, Llinás, & Perkel, 1977), provide for more realistic simulations that could prompt further experimentation. Although molluscan neural circuits are often depicted as deterministic, recent findings by Bailey and Chen (1983) suggest that growth of new connections might be involved in modulating habituation and sensitization in *Aplysia*.

To summarize the preceding points, much of my critique has focused on the reductionistic error of giving primacy to any one level of analysis, molar or molecular. My concern here also extends to problems of generating inferences about how learning works from findings obtained under highly restricted circumstances. As I extend this argument further, dropping from one extreme level to the other, I shall concentrate on the integration of learning and instinct as a continuum of the same general phenomena, that is, multilevel adjustments of organisms to varying environmental conditions occurring over phylogenetic, ontogenetic, and proximate time scales (see Coss & Owings, 1985).

## LEARNING AS ADJUSTMENT OF INSTINCT

Based on his acute observations of the first behaviors of deprivation-reared chicks, Spalding (1873) was one of the earliest proponents of a hierarchical view that learning capabilities are restrained by instinctive mechanisms shaped over successive generations by natural selection. With birth or hatching, according to Spalding, "animals may be awaking up in a world with which they are, in greater or less degree, already acquainted." In essence, Spalding considered instinct to be a *product* of the process of natural selection, a view that was later elaborated by Lorenz (1950, 1951) and further exemplified by Riedl (1983) with his hierarchical structure of Aristotelian causes.

Gould (Chapter 11, this volume) continues this tradition, extending the ideas of how Pavlovian conditioning shares features in common with the ethological construct of the innate releasing mechanism (IRM). Although Lorenz (1950, 1951) also observed some of these similarities, noting that the

Pavlovian unconditioned response (UR) could be elicited by an IRM, he differs considerably from Gould's notion that the sign stimulus is just a tuned up conditioned stimulus (CS). The IRM, according to both Lorenz (1950, 1951) and Tinbergen (1951) is a receptory apparatus that inhibits the expression of innate activities. Such an apparatus, with peripheral or central filtering properties (Marler, 1961), releases its inhibition with perception of a simple, key stimulus element—the sign stimulus. The IRM was not thought to function at all in a cognitive manner in which a learned Gestalt was built up through successive experiences. In the case of foraging honey bees, an IRM "tuned" to radially symmetric flower forms could direct the circumstances for learning which flowers yielded pollen or nector; that is, the IRM was an adjunct system that complemented the learning process.

My own views of the IRM (Coss, 1965, 1968) have changed considerably as a result of more recent experiments on antipredator behavior showing that instinctive processes, such as predator recognition and concomitant orchestration of motor patterns, operate on Gestalt principles with cognitive properties not unlike those observed in associative learning (Coss, 1978a, 1979a). For example, taxa as diverse as newborn humans and newly hatched or isolation-reared African jewel fish (*Hemichromis bimaculatus*) innately recognize the lineamental Gestalt of two facing eyes as facial features (see Coss, 1979a, 1979b; Goren, Sarty, & Wu, 1975). Experience with faces subsequently results in the development of individual recognition that is guided by the salient aspects of two facing eyes. Learning specific facial features is a process of perceptual refinement embedded in the overall innate substrate, which affords the recognition of the Gestalt. This process of individual recognition can be disrupted by cerebral deficits leading to prosopagnosia in autistic children and by prolonged social deprivation in jewel fish (for review, see Coss, 1979a, 1979b; Coss & Globus, 1979). Unlike the higher order cognitive processes underlying individual recognition, which appear labile to developmental anomalies, recognition of two facing eyes persists as a deeply canalized perceptual process (Bateson, 1979; Coss, 1979a; Sæther, 1983; Waddington, 1957) engendering abnormal levels of gaze aversion and flight behavior in autistic children (Richer & Coss, 1976) and deprivation-reared jewel fish.

Because of the highly interactive nature of changing organism–environment relationships during ontogeny, it seems much more appropriate not to treat instinctive behaviors as mediated by isolated mechanistic variables (Pepper, 1942) like IRMs. I must note here that instinctive processes mediating the execution of relatively stereotyped behaviors to changes in highly specific environmental features appear mechanistic because they engage in very brief periods of decision making. Giant Mauthner cells in fish (Diamond, 1971; Eaton, 1983), for example, process sensory input extremely rapidly during the initation of escape behaviors. Similarly, but involving the operation of much more complex neural circuitry, prey-catching behavior by toads and frogs is thought to be mediated by a classic example of an IRM. Recent studies by Ewert, Burghagen, and Schürg-Pfeiffer (1983) have focused on the ability of this system to extract the Gestalt properties of prey-like visual patterns and engage in goal-oriented decision making. The cognitive, dynamic aspects of this innate system do not fit well with the original model of the IRM with its inhibition releasing properties proposed by Lorenz and Tinbergen. Contemporary use of this term by ethologists and neuroethologists best reflects the inertia of early ethological terminology rather than empirically derived functional interpretations.

Under circumstances in which urgency of correct performance has not received strong natural selection, innate behaviors are much more variable (Schleidt, 1974) and performances can be adjusted by repeated experiences. The learning of song dialect by some birds characterizes a less urgent context in which ontogenetic adjustments refine innate predispositions (Gould, Chapter 11, this volume; Marler, 1976), but even some of these assumptions are being challenged (see Baptista & Petrinovich, 1984). A similar case for ontogenetic adjustments can be made for learning cognitive maps (Menzel, 1978) of patchy food sources, refuge sites, and locations where predatory attacks might occur.

In our own work on the California ground squirrel (*Spermophilus beecheyi*), Leger, Owings, and Coss (1983) found that, under field conditions, the utility of some behaviors varied spatially with respect to the probability of encountering biologically important factors in different microhabitats. Extending this line of argument further, we have noted the numerous occasions in which ground squirrels appear to make cognitive inferences about both present and future contextual properties of these microhabitats (for review, see Coss & Owings, 1985). My use of the term "context" here differs considerably from that described by Rescorla (Chapter 12, this volume) in which context is treated as just another signal to be associated with a CS. I also use the term differently from that appearing in some of the communication literature (e.g., W. J. Smith, 1977), which is more in keeping with the above definition; that is, multiple sources of information outside the organism can be "contextual" to specific communicative events.

From an alternative point of view, context is the *entire set of circumstances*, comprising both the endogenous aspects of the organism, including its expectancies about future events and consequences, and the exogenous features of the locality. Because organisms are dynamic, contextual relationships are constantly in flux. Research by Shalter (1978) provides a clear example of how context is not just a set of adjunct environmental features associated with an important source of information. A stuffed pigmy owl (*Glaucidium passerinum*) was mounted on a pole facing each of the nest holes of seven resident pairs of pied flycatchers (*Ficedula hypoleuca*). These birds were quite disturbed by the presence of the model predator and exhibited mobbing calls that waned over a few minutes. The owl was then removed and replaced at 15-minute intervals and mobbing calls were again elevated in number. With successive trials, however, the tendency to mob began to habituate. Shalter then moved the owl about 90° relative to their nest holes. The birds were quite disturbed by the owl in its new location, which indicates that habituation had occurred to the nonrealistic, static owl–pied flycatcher relationship and not to the owl model *per se*.

## Ground Squirrel Antisnake Behavior

California ground squirrels during interaction with the predators that eat them, adjust their behaviors in ways that reflect the potential risks associated with each type of predator. Fast-moving predators, like eagles and hawks, engender conditions of great urgency after these predators are spotted at a distance. Ground squirrels typically emit single-note alarm calls when startled by the bird's appearance, and they dart toward their home burrows if the bird's trajectory places them at risk (Coss & Owings, 1985; Leger & Owings, 1978). Under less urgent conditions, in which a dog is seen at a distance, ground squirrels emit much more variable alarm calls and may not run to home burrows immediately but may choose to climb rocks to get a better view (Owings & Virginia, 1978).

Rattlesnakes (*Crotalus viridis oreganus*) and gopher snakes (*Pituophis melanoleucus catenifer*) are also important predators of ground squirrels and have been so for several million years. At the San Joaquin Experimental Range in the Sierra Nevada foothills near Fresno, ground squirrels may constitute up to 69% of the diet of rattlesnakes (Fitch, 1948). Unlike their mammalian and avian predators, these slow-moving predators can be approached safely. Ground squirrels will often harass and even attack them, employing behaviors similar to those seen during agonistic encounters among themselves.

Upon detection of rattlesnakes and gopher snakes, ground squirrels exhibit tail hair erection and flag their tails vigorously (see Hennessy, Owings, Rowe, Coss, & Leger, 1981). This activity may attract the attention of other squirrels (Figure 14.1). When snakes are approached cautiously, ground squirrels alternate between elongate investigative postures and crouching, which positions the hind legs for evasive leaping (Coss & Owings, 1985; Owings & Coss, 1981). Jumping back may occur without any apparent provocation by the snake, such as subtle turning of the snake's head or its more salient activities of hissing, rattling, and striking. Ground squirrels readily probe nonmoving snakes into action by their engaging in repeated bouts of substrate throwing (Rowe & Owings, 1978), a variant of the defensive burying behavior seen in rats (e.g., Pinel, Treit, Ladak, & MacLennan, 1980). Because snakes often strike after being hit by detritus, leaves, and twigs, ground squirrels are prepared to leap back and often do so without the snake striking out defensively.

**FIGURE 14.1.** Reconstruction (from video recordings) of five California ground squirrels harassing a tethered rattlesnake at the San Joaquin Experimental Range in the Sierra Nevada foothills, an area abundant in rattlesnakes. Ground squirrels on the far left and right are tail flagging vigorously and exhibiting cautious, elongate postures. The top middle squirrel is throwing loose substrate at the snake repeatedly. The bottom middle squirrel was first to detect the snake and has now retired from harassing the snake after her activity attracted the other squirrels.

In some circumstances, the squirrel may approach the snake closely and then freeze for several seconds, staring at the snake. This activity seems to intimidate gopher snakes (Coss, 1978b), but with rattlesnakes, this activity invariably leads to the snake striking and the squirrel jumping back dramatically. Analyses of slow-motion video playbacks of encounters between ground squirrels and rattlesnakes in the field have revealed unequivocal bites by striking snakes, but without evidence of serious envenomization. These observations prompted us to study whether ground squirrels had evolved innate immunity to rattlesnake venom. Research in progress using radioimmunoassays, which indicate the amount of binding between rattlesnake venom and ground squirrel serum, has shown that some ground squirrel populations have evolved serum components that are quite effective in neutralizing rattlesnake venom. But further, it must be noted that venom resistance works in concert with the squirrel's ability to regulate venom delivery. Ground squirrels can be killed if they fail to detect rattlesnakes, prepare themselves to leap, and execute jumps that disengage them quickly from embedded fangs.

## Extinction of Cognitive Information on the Phylogenetic Time Scale

Douglas ground squirrels (*S. b. douglasii*) living in the Coast Range foothills near Winters and Fisher ground squirrels (*S. b. fisheri*) at the San Joaquin Experimental Range in the Sierra Nevada foothills receive strong predation from both rattlesnakes and gopher snakes. Douglas ground squirrels living on the floor of the Great Valley on and near the University of California (U.C.) campus at Davis encounter only gopher snakes. The antisnake behaviors of these populations were compared during encounters with rattlesnakes, gopher snakes, and garter snakes in seminatural laboratory rooms with sand substrata. Douglas ground squirrels from the rattlesnake-free Davis area were much more likely to approach and harass snakes than were the Douglas and Fisher ground squirrels from habitats with both high rattlesnake and gopher snake densities (Owings & Coss, 1977). Subsequent comparative research has shown a consistent pattern of reduced caution toward rattlesnakes among ground squirrels from the Great Valley, which experience relaxed selection from rattlesnakes (Hennessy, 1982).

It was important to consider the possibility that these differences in antisnake behaviors reflected the different experiences with snakes in the wild. However, lab-reared, snake-inexperienced Fisher and Douglas pups, the mothers of which were trapped at the San Joaquin Experimental Range and U.C. Davis campus, respectively, exhibited marked differences in the way they treated a garter snake, which is a nonpredatory threat. First of all, the Douglas and Fisher pups recognized the snake on first encounter and applied the same general classes of antisnake behavior seen in their wild-caught adult counterparts, such as cautious, investigative approaches and substrate throwing, which agitated the snake (Owings & Coss, 1977).

Second, like the less cautious behavior of adults from the rattlesnake-free Davis area, Douglas pups treated the garter snake with much less caution than did the Fisher pups, the parents of which came from a rattlesnake habitat. Such adaptive variation in antisnake behavior, roughly correlated with relative rattlesnake and gopher snake abundance, afforded a paradigm for generating a phylogenetic time scale for extinction of the cognitive aspects of antisnake behavior.

A time scale for population divergence throughout California was developed by examining the genetic variation of Douglas and Beechey (*S. b. beecheyi*) ground squirrel subspecies distributed just north and south of the San Francisco Bay and Sacramento–San Joaquin Delta region (D. G. Smith & Coss, 1984). Nei's model for estimating the genetic distance ($D_v$) of two populations, in units that are linear in time (Nei, 1972, 1978), was calibrated on a .725-million-years-ago event in which the Sacramento and San Joaquin rivers began to drain through the San Francisco Bay. This sudden event, effectively blocking gene flow, initiated Douglas and Beechey subspeciation. The accuracy of this model has been corroborated using recent and ancient geological and fossil time markers (see Coss & Owings, 1985; D. G. Smith & Coss, 1984). Along with the use of this calibrated molecular clock and paleoclimatological evidence, we examined the differential venom resistance of 18 ground squirrel populations in California, selecting for behavioral study three populations with different histories of selection from rattlesnakes and gopher snakes (Coss, Poran, & Smith, in preparation).

Fisher ground squirrels were trapped at the snake-free campgrounds of the Folsom State Park in the Sierra Nevada foothills. Rattlesnakes are abundant within 3 kilometers of the trapping site, but gopher snakes are relatively rare. These Fisher squirrels have the highest venom resistance among the populations surveyed. Sierra ground squirrels (*S. b. sierrae*) were trapped in the Lake Tahoe Basin, an area totally free of rattlesnakes and gopher snakes. According to the molecular clock, these Fisher and Sierra populations diverged about 35 thousand years ago, but geological and paleoclimatological evidence, combined with evidence of moderate rattlesnake venom resistance in squirrels from the Lake Tahoe Basin and an adjacent population at Boca Reservoir, indicates that selection from rattlesnakes has been absent for only a few thousand years. Ground squirrels with very low venom resistance were trapped in the Sacramento Delta on Ryer Island and Little Holland Tract. These populations have been isolated for about 80–90 thousand years from their closest relative, the Fisher ground squirrel in the Sierra Nevada foothills. Although rattlesnakes are not found in the Delta, gopher snakes are found occasionally. Because the Delta was once a tidal marsh prior to land reclamation, a habitat relatively unsuitable to gopher snakes, the presence of these snakes may be a recent phenomenon.

Prior to testing, the animals were maintained under laboratory conditions for 9 months to equilibrate recent experiences among the groups. Unlike previous procedures in which ground squirrels and snakes interacted freely in 2.5 by 2.4 meter laboratory rooms with sand substrata, the procedure was changed so that a rattlesnake or gopher snake was confined by a 28 by 28 by 28 centimeter compartment with transparent top and 8-millimeter flexible wire mesh on the sides and bottom to prevent injury to either animal. View of the snake was not obstructed by the wire mesh, which is analogous in appearance to that of a grassy barrier. With the compartment centered in the rooms, video recordings were made in plan view from adjacent rooms via overhead and one-way mirrors. After the squirrels spent several weeks in the laboratory rooms in burrow-like nest boxes, the experiment was started by temporarily removing all animals and equipment except the subject squirrel ($n = 8$ per group) and its nest box. Snake presentation was made by raising this remaining nest box remotely. Ground squirrels denied this refuge typically approached the compartment where they discovered the snake. Both a rattlesnake and gopher snake were presented to squirrels in a balanced, repeated, measures design with a 5-day interval between 10-minute trials.

The initial results of this multivariate study provided evidence for the first time that information about former habitats can persist for many thousands of ground squirrel generations. For example, Sierra ground squirrels quickly recognized the snakes, especially the rattlesnake, and treated them as dangerous adversaries. On initial approach or bout of substrate throwing, some squirrels leaped back or sideways from the motionless rattlesnake. Such inference that this motionless form posed a distinct sort of threat suggested that the innate cognitive processes underlying snake recognition in ground squirrels included the expectations of what these snakes can do. Similar inferences of the relative risks of approaching snakes or throwing substrate at them had been noted previously among lab-reared, snake-inexperienced Fisher pups during encounters with a gopher snake in the aforementioned laboratory rooms and in an artificial burrow (Coss & Owings, 1978).

Among the three ground squirrel populations, the Sierra ground squirrels were the most excited during close-range interactions with the snakes as revealed by their tail pilomotor erection, an index of sympathetic nervous system arousal (Fulton, 1955), and persistence in harassing the snakes. In contrast, the rattlesnake-adapted Fisher squirrels tended to engage the snakes more intermittently and several of the squirrels retired after harassing the rattlesnake briefly.

The most important population differences appeared among the Delta ground squirrels, which exhibited the highest interanimal variability. As examples of this variability, some squirrels were slow to initiate their antisnake behaviors, appearing sluggish in their application of substrate throwing. Surprisingly, these particular animals began to habituate to the snakes, jumping back only during the first few snake strikes. Subsequent snake strikes appeared to be ignored. Fewer than one-half of the squirrels behaved as if the snakes constituted a serious threat; these particular ground squirrels, however, were vigorous in harassing the snakes.

On the whole, the Delta population comprised both highly excitable animals, like those characterizing the Sierra population, and animals that showed much less snake-directed activity in keeping with the Delta population's low venom resistance and rattlesnake-free habitat. Furthermore, the reduction of concern about the gopher snake by the latter group suggests that selection from both types of snake predators has been relaxed for some time, perhaps since the squirrels migrated into the Delta at the beginning of the last ice age.

Follow-up research on lab-reared Arctic ground squirrels (*S. parryii ablusus*), a species that has lived in a snake-free habitat for a least 3 million years (Coss & Owings, 1985) and has minimal resistance to rattlesnake venom, provided and important control for the novel aspects of snakes. Using the same snake-presentation protocol, the results of this study revealed that Arctic ground squirrels will treat a rattlesnake and gopher snake as an animate novel object, despite repeated snake strikes accompanied by hissing and rattling. When given the opportunity to interact freely with a gopher snake, however, they may treat the snake defensively as a threatening, novel animate object that bites by throwing substrate weakly at the snake. This behavior is not surprising because defensive burying behavior is seen in other rodents (e.g., Pinel *et al.*, 1980).

The finding that cognitive information about snakes under conditions of relaxed selection can persist for perhaps 100,000 years, but not 3 million years, prompted the examination of whether relatively recent relaxed selection from one type of snake predator would differentially affect the antisnake behaviors during encounters with both types of snake predators (Coss & Poran, in preparation). Lab-reared pups, the mothers of which were trapped on the U.C. Davis campus, were compared with lab-reared pups, the mothers of which were trapped at Sunol Regional Park in the Coast Range mountains southwest of Livermore. Genetic distance analysis calibrated to time suggests that Douglas ground squirrels from Davis experienced relaxed selection from rattlesnakes beginning about 3000 years ago when they migrated onto the floor of the Great Valley, an area abundant with gopher snakes. Beechey ground squirrels live in a habitat that has been a relatively stable refugium for both species of snakes. Snake-inexperienced Douglas and Beechey pups ($n$ = 8 per group) were tested at 60–70 days of age using the same protocol described earlier, with the exception that 5-minute rather than 10-minute trials were used.

The results of this study of the effects of relaxed selection from one type of snake predator, the rattlesnake, but not both types as in the previous study, indicates that ground squirrels can evolve relatively discrete patterns of information unique to each type of predator. Beechey pups, for example, appeared to differentiate the rattlesnake and gopher snake on a gradient of risk; they spent significantly more time-sampled bouts within striking range of the rattlesnake (Figure 14.2A), maintaining more time-sampled bouts of positive orientation that afforded better surveillance of the rattlesnake's activities (Figure 14.2B). In contrast, Douglas pups were equally vigilant toward both snakes, but they were less aroused by the rattlesnake, as compared with arousal by the gopher snake, exhibiting significantly fewer cycles of tail flagging (Figure 14.2C) and significantly fewer substrate throwing acts (Figure 14.2D).

**FIGURE 14.2.** Antisnake behavior of eight young snake-inexperienced Douglas and Beechey ground squirrel pups during 5-minute encounters alternately with a rattlesnake and gopher snake in seminatural laboratory settings with sand substrata. Each snake is confined by a wire-screened compartment resembling a grassy barrier. The Beechey pups, the parents of which came from a rattlesnake and gopher snake habitat, investigated the rattlesnake more intensely than they did the gopher snake, exhibiting significantly more time-sampled bouts within the rattlesnake's striking range (A, $p < .01$) and, within this range, a positive orientation (B, $p < .005$). Douglas pups harassed their natural enemy, the gopher snake, with significantly more tail-flagging cycles (C, $p < .005$) and substrate-throwing acts (D, $p < .05$) than they did the rattlesnake, a predator that has not provided the circumstances for selection for about 3000 years.

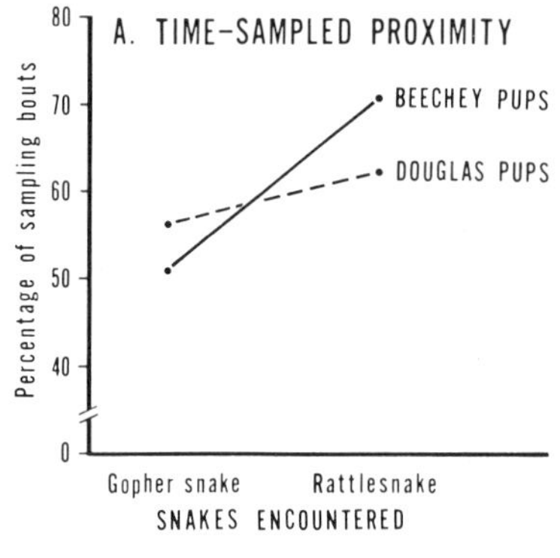


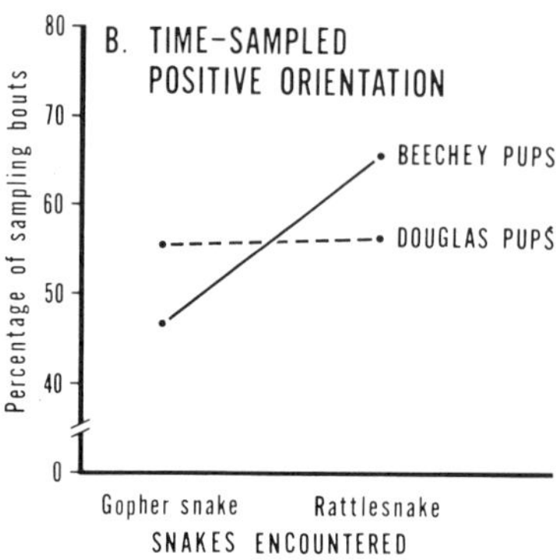


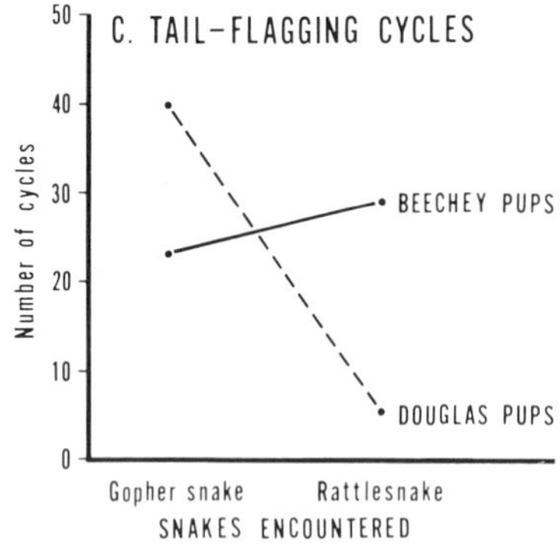


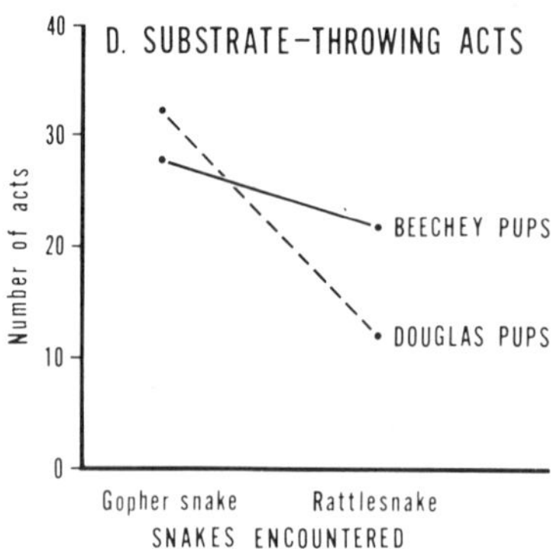

In short, Beechey and Douglas pups engaged in differential behaviors toward each predator for entirely different reasons. For Beechey pups, the intense selection from rattlesnakes engendered greater concern for keeping track of what the rattlesnake was doing throughout the trial even though they harassed both snakes with about equal intensity. Douglas pups, on the other hand, differentiated the snakes as a result of about 3000 years of relaxed selection from rattlesnakes, exhibiting a markedly reduced tendency to harass the rattlesnake as compared with the gopher snake.

Although these studies of adaptive variation in ground squirrel antisnake behaviors did not focus on the examination of learning *per se*, a number of field and laboratory observations provided ideas about how learning enhanced the effectiveness of these behaviors. Clearly, rapid learning goes on about specific features of *that* particular predator in *that* particular microhabitat, such as change in the predator's movement, orientation, size, and distance relative to the perceiver in its own microhabitat (see Coss & Owings, 1978; Leger *et al.*, 1983; Owings & Owings, 1979). Learning is thus congruent with the innate processes of predator recognition and concomitant inferences about the predator's capabilities vis-à-vis the perceiver; that is, the context for organizing and executing appropriate antipredator behavior emerges immediately upon perception of these variables.

In confined laboratory settings, wild-caught adult ground squirrels, presumably with snake experience (Owings & Coss, 1977), are less likely to exhibit the intense snake-directed behavior observed in snake-inexperienced pups. Changes in the adult's propensity to engage snakes in laboratory settings may well reflect differences in the context engendered by laboratory and field conditions as well as any previous snake experience. From this theoretical perspective, learning cannot be extricated as a separate entity from instinct, but could be considered as proximate and ontogenetic adjustments of a genetically orchestrated substrate, itself adjustable on the phylogenetic time scale (see Coss & Owings, 1985).

## NEUROBIOLOGICAL IMPLICATIONS

What are the neurobiological implications of the viewpoint that learning is part of a continuum of adjustment over phylogenetic, ontogenetic, and proximate time scales? First, rapid and cumulative experiences resulting from changing organism–environment relationships add supplemental information during ontogeny to a network of processes already roughly organized through phylogeny. In this view, these processes are restrained, not only by their adaptation to the environment, but also by their adaptation to each other (see Lewontin & Levins, 1978; Webster & Goodwin, 1982). Second, with intense persistent selection over phylogenetic time, genetic and epigenetic processes construct nervous systems with organizational properties and expectancies about specific types of habitat variation, but only approximately so. Learning thus provides the details about the organism–environment circumstances that are too variable to act as reliable sources of selection.

Gould (Chapter 11, this volume) describes the various properties of honey bee foraging in which certain "preconceptions" about the habitat, including its temporal properties, guide honey bees to appropriate sources of pollen and nectar. Similarly, food-storing birds appear to have expectations about the most suitable microhabitats for storing and recovering seeds as well as dealing with probabilistic factors like seed predation (Shettleworth, Chapter 13, this volume). California ground squirrels also seek suitable microhabitats for foraging and for maintaining vigilance after they have learned that a specific type of predator is in the area (Coss & Owings, 1985). Because such expectancies bias decision making, they are "seen" by selection when organisms fail to organize and execute behaviors with sufficient skill to survive and produce progeny. With prolonged relaxed selection, this innate information undergoes extinction, but as it does, it continues to bias decision making for many thousands of generations.

In the case of Sierra and Delta ground squirrels, gene substitutions, probably at regulatory loci, have undergone sufficient drift (random changes in genetic structure) to alter the functional integration of many genetic loci (Mayr, 1963; McDonald, 1983). Such subtle changes could markedly affect the pattern of neuronal organization, thus altering the *invariances* in the information emergent in interneuronal communication. A surprising aspect of this study, as manifested by the Sierra population, was evidence that during the early phase of relaxed selection from snakes, ground squirrel antisnake behavior becomes more excitable and consistent within members of the population. With more prolonged relaxed selection, however, antisnake behavior begins to dissipate in some of the animals. The sluggish, somewhat erratic application of antisnake behaviors by the least active Delta ground squirrels gives the figurative impression that the underlying cognitive organization has been disrupted, almost as if cloaked by mist.

### Adjustments in the Neuronal Substrate

Several types of neurobiological studies have shed some light on the evolutionary restraints discussed earlier. Studies of phenotype, behaviors, and neurotransmitter levels in *Drosophila melanogaster* have documented that single gene mutations can alter learning capabilities (see Byers, Davis, & Kiger, 1981; Quinn & Greenspan, 1984). Studies of homozygous weaver mice (Sotelo, 1975) and chromosome anomalies in humans (Marin-Padilla, 1974; Purpura, 1975; Takashima, Becker, Armstrong, & Chan, 1981) have shown aberrant changes in dendritic structure, especially the presence of unusually long dendritic spines.

The initial outgrowth of dendritic branches seems to be restrained more by endogenous cell processes than by the extrinsic influences of nearby afferent projections (e.g., Whitehead, 1979). Growth of multiple branch orders, however, can be sculpted by extrinsic factors (see review in Greenough, Chapter 5, this volume; Tieman & Hirsch, 1982; Vaughn, Henrikson, & Grieshaber, 1974). Dendritic growth, even late in life (Connor, Diamond, & Johnson, 1980; Connor, Melone, Yuen, & Diamond, 1981), associated with the organism's differential experience could be considered as an ontogenetic adjustment of a substrate previously organized by more intrinsic regulatory processes (Clark, 1976). It therefore seems reasonable to consider that the previous history of dendritic growth in some cells could restrain subsequent patterns of growth and connectivity.

An important question emerges when one considers the implications of dendritic growth, retraction, and other processes of dendritic remodeling (i.e., Mates & Lund, 1983). When neuronal networks undergo remodeling, how are previous invariances that constitute information preserved? In jewel fish, for example, innate recognition of two facing eyes begins promptly in fry on the 13th postspawning day of age and continues throughout life without disruption (Coss, 1978a, 1979a; Coss & Globus, 1979) even though the apical dendrites of tectal interneurons have elongated dramatically (see Figure 14.3). Preservation of such ecologically relevant information, despite massive neuronal growth, suggests that the information emerges in the proportional relationships among growing neurons rather than in the formation of absolute relationships that could be labile to growth. Because the brains of newly hatched fry are tiny relative to those of adults, fish have not adopted the strategy of synaptic overproduction and competition that is typically found in mammals (see Purves & Lichtman, 1980).

The sources of selection on young fish, such as predation, are probably too intense to permit the adoption of a less reliable process of connectivity during development; although it must be noted that competitive exclusion can be surgically induced in adult fish (Meyer, 1979). In contrast, the overproduction and subsequent stabilization of synapses in mammals (Greenough, Chapter 5, this volume) and in birds (Rausch & Scheich, 1982), probably reflects their overall growth trajectories. The notion that synapses can form "on demand," as proposed by Greenough, is a reasonable candidate for describing the changes in the neural circuitry that provide the potential for new neuronal relationships.

Formation of new synapses, however, is not a necessary component of learning. In short-lived holometabolis insects that emerge from pupation as adults, selection is especially intense for stable and reliable neural circuitry. Newly emerged and forager honey bees show no appreciable differences in spine density on Kenyon cells (see Figure 14.4) in the calyces of the mushroom bodies (Coss, Brandon, & Globus, 1980). At the other end of the developmental spectrum, adult jewel fish readily learn to recognize new mates long after the late juvenile developmental period in which the optic tectum shows little signs of further growth. Most dendritic growth occurs early in jewel fish development (Burgess & Coss, 1980), especially

**FIGURE 14.3.** Camera lucida tracings (1 μm = 6 mm) of spiny pyriform interneurons in the jewel fish optic tectum showing growth-related changes in the lower half of the dendritic trees. For scale, the hatch bars, depicting the stratum album centrale (SAC) plexiform layer are, from left, 7.3, 66.2, and 74.0 μm. At 13 postspawning days of age, all types of tectal neurons observed acquire the general appearance of their adult counterparts. Spines on 13-day-old interneurons are short, averaging 1.17 μm in length (range: .59–2.54 μm). At 30 days of age, spines average 1.85 μm in length (range: .59–3.38 μm), which falls within the adult average of 1.52–1.95 μm in length). Dendritic branches within the SAC of adults are labile to early deprivation rearing. Tectal thickness (basilar edge of SAC-pia) is, from left, 54, 217, and 370 μm.

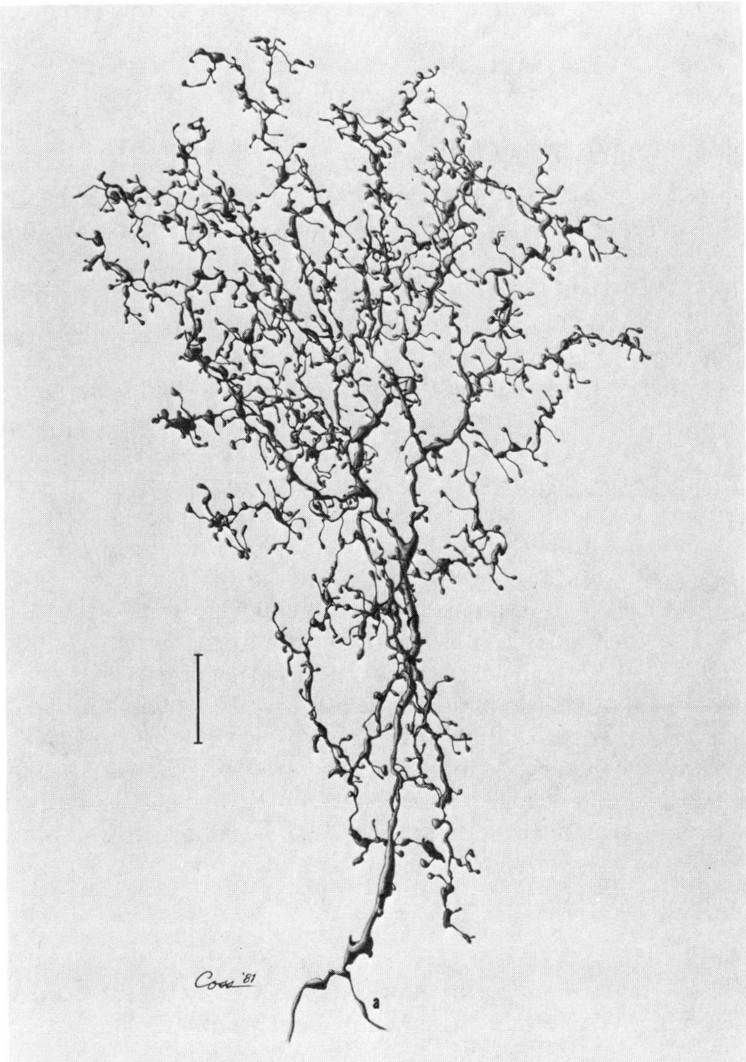


**FIGURE 14.4.** Spiny Kenyon cell (type II) in the calyces of the honey bee corpora pedunculata. Illustration was made from a camera lucida tracing (1 μm = 6 mm); scale bar represents 10 μm. On this type of interneuron, spine density per unit length of dendrite is stable in newly emerged, nurse, and forager honey bees. After honey bees take their first orientation flights lasting a few minutes, spine stems are found to be shorter on only the longest spines as a result of a process of elongated dilation of spine heads.

among newly formed cells in the germinal zones. Spine density is remarkably stable after 160 days of age at dendritic loci formerly sensitive to environmental variation (Burgess & Coss, 1982).

### Dendritic Spines as Adjustable Regulators

The probabilistic aspects of synaptic activity, as characterized by the stochastic process of neurotransmitter release, saturation of ionic channel binding sites, and variable channel opening time constants (Gage & McBurney, 1975; Kuno, 1964; Matthews-Bellinger & Salpeter, 1978; Redman & Walmsley, 1983), are likely to contribute to the already considerable noise in interneuronal communication. One function of dendritic spines may be to reduce this potential variance by restricting the amount of ion influx. Computer simulations of spine electrical properties (Kawato, Hamaguchi, Murikami, & Tsukahara, 1984; Koch & Poggio, 1983; Perkel, 1982–1983; Perkel & Perkel, 1985; Wilson, 1984) have converged on one important functional interpretation. Spines with long, narrow stems increase the input resistance at the synapse, and this property regulates synaptic conductance by creating a much larger depolarization in the spine head than in the parent dendrite. A rapid rise in spine head membrane voltage quickly approaches reversal potential, thus delimiting ion influx and current generation (see Stevens, 1984). With successive bouts of synaptic conductance, this putative regulatory property of spines could dampen variation in the rise time and peak depolarization at the same dendritic locus, the net effect being a more consistent pattern of voltage integration in the dendritic tree. Based on this argument, one might expect to find spines throughout a broad range of phylogenetically old and distant taxa; in addition to those taxa described earlier, spines are found in marine flatworms (Keenan, Coss, & Koopowitz, 1981) and molluscans, such as gastropods and cephalopods (Bailey & Thompson, 1979; Young, 1971).

A second characteristic of spines is evinced by their dynamic ability to change shape rapidly as a function of synaptic activity (Desmond & Levy, 1981; Greenough, Chapter 5, this volume; Lee, Schottler, Oliver, & Lynch, 1980; Van Harreveld & Fifkova, 1975) and under conditions of biologically important behavioral activity (Brandon & Coss, 1982; Burgess & Coss, 1983). Quantification of large numbers of spines in young and old honey bees and jewel fish has shown a consistent change in spine morphology. Spine stems are shortened successively by elongated dilation of spine heads without appreciable change in overall spine lengths (Brandon & Coss, 1982; Burgess & Coss, 1983; Coss *et al.*, 1980). Rapid and long-lasting unidirectional shortening of the spine stem is thought to lower the input resistance, and this factor changes two spine properties: (1) Lowering the input resistance also lowers peak spine head voltage, and this could affect synaptic conductance mediated by any appreciable number of voltage-dependent ion channels (see Miller, Rall, & Rinzel, 1985; Perkel & Perkel, 1985); (2) If synaptic conductance still matches the lowered input resistance, that is, if spine head voltage still approaches the reversal potential (Kawato *et al.*, 1984; Koch & Poggio, 1983), this lowered input resistance will enhance the transfer of electrical charge from the spine head to the parent dendrite. In short, spines seem capable of adjusting their regulatory properties in keeping with differential patterns of synaptic activity (for review, see Coss & Perkel, 1985).

A final important implication of spine-stem shortening takes us back into the theoretical realm of learning as adjustment of instinct. Clearly, long spines exhibit a greater potential range of stem shortening than do shorter spines (see Figure 14.5).

During jewel fish development, short spines appear earliest in fry and are followed by more variable spine lengths as fry disperse from parents, a developmental period in which learning is important (compare the 13- and 30-day-old interneurons depicted in Figure 14.3). Spine density becomes labile after this period, and developmentally deprived jewel fish have fewer,

**FIGURE 14.5.** Range of variation in spine morphology on Kenyon cells in 3- to 5-week-old forager honey bees. Black and hatched spine profiles are adapted from standard deviations of mean values. Note the overlap of stem shortening in spines 2 and 3 μm long. Between the newly emerged and forager stages of honey bee behavioral development, spines 2–3 μm long show progressive stem shortening, a process that culminates in foragers having a residual plasticity of about 16% narrow-headed spines (black profiles).

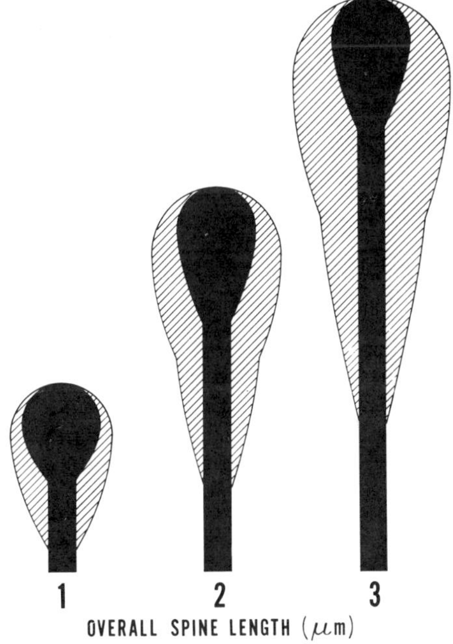

but longer spines (see Berard, Burgess, & Coss, 1981; Burgess & Coss, 1982; Coss & Globus, 1978). Similar findings of fewer, but longer spines appear in mammalian studies with experimental intervention (Berry & Bradley, 1976; Chen & Hillman, 1982; Tavares, Paula-Barbosa, & Gray, 1983) and genetic anomalies (Sotelo, 1975, 1978; Takashima *et al.*, 1981). Such observations have led to the "search and capture" hypothesis in which overall spine length is regulated by endogenous growth processes and extrinsic stabilization processes with synaptogenesis (see Llinás, Hillman, & Precht, 1973; Marin-Padilla, 1974), albeit, some long spines can be "naked" (Hirano & Dembitzer, 1975). In effect, the distribution of long and short spines in fish and mammals could reflect one genetic–epigenetic restraint on the overall adjustability of the neuron (Coss & Brandon, 1982), a restraint that combines both deterministic (genetic) and probabilistic (labile) attributes (Berard *et al.*, 1981).

As discussed earlier, honey bees exhibit stable spine densities on Kenyon cells after emergence from pupation, but overall spine length appears to be stable as well (Coss *et al.*, 1980). During the newly emerged to nurse stages of development, in which honey bees adjust many of their innate hive maintenance and brood care activities to match variable hive conditions, the shorter spines show acceleration in stem shortening. Conversely, during their first orientation flight when honey bees learn terrain landmarks and under the complex conditions of foraging (see Gould, Chapter 11, this volume), the longer spines undergo marked stem shortening (Brandon & Coss, 1982; Coss *et al.*, 1980). But also across an enormous phyletic gulf, jewel fish hatch with short spines when instinct predominates and the shorter spines show the most reliable stem shortening (Coss & Perkel, 1985) in older juveniles exhibiting prolonged escape behaviors requiring reliable behavioral expression (Burgess & Coss, 1983). Like that of honey bees engaging in complex behavioral activities requiring adjustments to varying environmental conditions, jewel fish which explore and control their physical and social environment (Coss & Globus, 1979) also show the most reliable stem shortening among their longest spines (see Coss & Globus, 1978).

Although spine stem adjustability, as a function of overall spine length, and the ecological requirements for behavioral adjustability are only roughly correlated in these taxa, any correlation at all provides ideas of how instinct and learning might reflect a continuum of the same cellular process. Furthermore, once spine-stem shortening has reached a stable asymptote in the long spines through elongated dilation of the spine head, a process that might occur rapidly (Lynch & Baudry, 1984; Robinson & Koch, 1984) and relatively early in development (Curcio & Hinds, 1983), the input resistance and regulatory properties of these long spines could approximate those of much shorter spines which have yet to undergo as much stem shortening (see Figure 14.5). If the stability of overall spine length seen in honey bees and jewel fish is similar to that of other taxa, a point that is still equivocal (see Lund, Boothe, & Lund, 1977), spines with short and shortened stems could be less plastic in their regulatory properties. The reciprocal of this reduction in plasticity at specific neural loci would likely manifest itself in the ability of an organism to now deal with environmental aspects only partly specified by selection on the phylogenetic time scale.

## CONCLUSION

I have presented a view of evolutionary restraints on learning, selecting two types of analysis for discussion—phylogenetic and synaptic. These two types of analyses could be considered part of a three-dimensional matrix characterizing processes of adjustment. Two of the axes represent phylogenetic and ontogenetic time scales, and the third axis could be viewed as a structural scale representing hierarchical levels of description. I treated organism–environment relationships as the highest level in the hierarchy and relationships of synaptic processes as the lowest level, both of which are interpretations embedded in the matrix of phylogenetic and ontogenetic time scales of adjustment. When viewed from the perspective of this three-dimensional matrix, learning could be considered as an adjustment of instinct at the level of organism–environment relationships. As evinced by behavior, instinct itself is restrained by all the processes constituting lower levels. My discussion of the synaptic level focused on the idea that invariances in interneuronal communication constitute information; and for information to be preserved, stable regulatory processes must emerge from initially adjustable processes. The dendritic spine was emphasized as a structural component of the synapse with putative voltage regulating properties. Dendritic spines of different overall lengths provide the potential for gradations of low and high adjustability by shortening their spine stems. Such changes are roughly correlated with the ecological demands for behavioral adjustability in members of two phyla. In light of the discussion of the probabilistic aspects of growth and connectivity in neural circuits and preservation of information, it seems remarkable that the mammalian nervous system can retain information about former habitats for thousands of generations. From the neurobiological perspective, slow extinction of information on the phylogenetic time scale means that neurons and neuronal circuits have histories that should not be ignored. Perhaps the most important implication is that learning and instinct might be mediated by the differential adjustability of the same neuronal processes. The variation of plasticity detected at one level may simply be the reciprocal of restraint engendered at the level by previous adjustments of plasticity over phylogeny.

## ACKNOWLEDGMENTS

The research described in this chapter was supported by Faculty Research Grant D-922 and National Science Foundation Grants No. BNS 79-0683 and BNS 84-06172. My appreciation goes to Ronald Goldthwaite, Naomie Poran, and Carol Tyler for helpful suggestions in the preparation of this chapter and to Drs. Donald H. Owings and David G. Smith for their important contributions in discussions about evolutionary issues. Theoretical exploration of spine function was supported by System Development Foundation Grant SDF-G00283 to Donald H. Perkel.

## REFERENCES

Bailey, C. H., & Chen, M. Morphological basis of long-term habituation and sensitization in *Aplysia*. *Science*, 1983, *220*, 91–93.

Bailey, C. H., & Thompson, E. B. Indented synapses in Aplysia. *Brain Research*, 1979, *173*, 13–20.

Baptista, L. F., & Petrinovich, L. Social interaction, sensitive phases and the song template hypothesis in the white-crowned sparrow. *Animal Behaviour*, 1984, *32*, 172–181.

Bateson, G. *Mind and nature: A necessary unity*. New York: Dutton, 1979.

Berard, D. R., Burgess, J. W., & Coss, R. G. Plasticity of dendritic spine formation: A state-dependent stochastic process. *International Journal of Neuroscience*, 1981, *13*, 93–98.

Berry, M., & Bradley, P. The growth of the dendritic trees of Purkinje cells in irradiated agranular cerebellar cortex. *Brain Research*, 1976, *116*, 361–387.

Brandon, J. G., & Coss, R. G. Rapid dendritic spine stem shortening during one-trial learning: The honeybee's first orientation flight. *Brain Research*, 1982, *252*, 51–61.

Burgess, J. W., & Coss, R. G. Crowded jewel fish show changes in dendritic spine density and spine morphology. *Neuroscience Letters*, 1980, *17*, 277–281.

Burgess, J. W., & Coss, R. G. Effects of chronic crowding stress on midbrain development: Changes in dendritic spine density and morphology in jewel fish optic tectum. *Developmental Psychobiology*, 1982, *15*, 461–470.

Burgess, J. W., & Coss, R. G. Rapid effect of biologically relevant stimulation on tectal neurons: Changes in dendritic spine morphology after nine minutes are retained for twenty-four hours. *Brain Research*, 1983, *266*, 217–223.

Byers, D., Davis, D. L., & Kiger, J. A. Defect in cyclic AMP phosphodiesterase due to the dunce mutation of learning in *Drosophila melanogaster*. *Nature (London)*, 1981, *289*, 79–81.

Chen, S., & Hillman, D. E. Plasticity of the parallel fiber–Purkinje cell synapse by spine takeover and new synapse formation in the adult rat. *Brain Research*, 1982, *240*, 205–220.

Clark, R. D. Structural and functional changes in an identified cricket neuron after separation from the soma. I. Structural changes. *Journal of Comparative Neurology*, 1976, *170*, 253–265.

Connor, J. R., Diamond, M. C., & Johnson, R. E. Occipital cortical morphology of the rat: Alterations with age and environment. *Experimental Neurology*, 1980, *68*, 158–170.

Connor, J. R., Melone, J. H., Yuen, A. R., & Diamond, M. C. Dendritic length in aged rat's occipital cortex: An environmentally induced response. *Experimental Neurology*, 1981, *73*, 827–830.

Coss, R. G. *Mood provoking visual stimuli: Their origins and applications* (Monograph). Los Angeles: University of California Press, 1965.

Coss, R. G. The ethological command in art. *Leonardo*, 1968, *1*, 273–287.

Coss, R. G. Development of face aversion by the jewel fish (*Hemichromis bimaculatus*, Gill 1862). *Zeitschrift für Tierpsychologie*, 1978, *48*, 29–46. (a)

Coss, R. G. Perceptual determinants of gaze aversion by the lesser mouse lemur (*Microcebus murinus*), the role of two facing eyes. *Behaviour*, 1978, *64*, 248–270. (b)

Coss, R. G. Delayed plasticity of an instinct: Recognition and avoidance of 2 facing eyes by the jewel fish. *Developmental Psychobiology*, 1979, *12*, 335–345. (a)

Coss, R. G. Perceptual determinants of gaze aversion by normal and psychotic children: The role of two facing eyes. *Behaviour*, 1979, *69*, 228–254. (b)

Coss, R. G., & Brandon, J. G. Rapid changes in dendritic spine morphology during the honeybee's first orientation flight. In M. D. Breed, C. D. Michener, & H. E. Evans (Eds.), *The biology of social insects*. Boulder, Colo.: Westview Press, 1982.

Coss, R. G., Brandon, J. G., & Globus, A. Changes in morphology of dendritic spines on honeybee calycal interneurons associated with cumulative nursing and foraging experiences. *Brain Research*, 1980, *192*, 49–59.
Coss, R. G., & Globus, A. Spine stems on tectal interneurons in jewel fish are shortened by social stimulation. *Science*, 1978, *200*, 787–790.
Coss, R. G., & Globus, A. Social experience affects the development of dendritic spines and branches on tectal interneurons in the jewel fish. *Developmental Psychobiology*, 1979, *12*, 347–358.
Coss, R. G., & Owings, D. H. Snake-directed behavior by snake-naive and experienced California ground squirrels in a simulated burrow. *Zeitschrift für Tierpsychologie*, 1978, *48*, 421–435.
Coss, R. G., & Owings, D. H. Restraints on ground squirrel antipredator behavior: Adjustments over multiple time scales. In T. D. Johnston & A. T. Pietrewicz (Eds.), *Issues in the ecological study of learning*. Hillsdale, N. J.: Erlbaum, 1985.
Coss, R. G., & Perkel, D. H. The function of dendritic spines: A review of theoretical issues. *Behavioral & Neural Biology*, 1985, *44*.
Coss, R. G., & Poran, N. Snake species discrimination by California ground squirrels: The effects of recent relaxed selection. In preparation.
Coss, R. G., Poran, N., & Smith, D. G. Pleistocene memories: The effects of differential relaxed selection on the behavioral and physiological antisnake defenses of California ground squirrels. In preparation.
Curcio, C. A., & Hinds J. W. Stability of synaptic density and spine volume in dentate gyrus of aged rats. *Neurobiology of Aging*, 1983, *4*, 77–87.
Desmond, N. L., & Levy, W. B. Ultrastructural and numerical alteration in dendritic spines as a consequence of long-term potentiation. *Anatomical Record*, 1981, *199*, 68A–69A.
Diamond, J. The Mauthner cell. In W. S. Hoar & D. J. Randall (Eds.), *Fish physiology* (Vol. 5). New York: Academic Press, 1971.
Eaton, R. C. Is the Mauthner cell a vertebrate command neuron? A neuroethological perspective on an evolving concept. In J.-P. Ewert, R. R. Capranica, & D. J. Ingle (Eds.), *Advances in vertebrate neuroethology*. New York: Plenum Press, 1983.
Ewert, J.-P., Burghagen, H., & Schürg-Pfeiffer, E. Neuroethological analysis of the innate releasing mechanism for prey-catching behavior in toads. In J.-P. Ewert, R. R. Capranica, & D. J. Ingle (Eds.), *Advances in vertebrate neuroethology*. New York: Plenum Press, 1983.
Fitch, H. S. Ecology of the California ground squirrel on grazing lands. *American Midland Naturalist*, 1948, *39*, 513–596.
Fulton, J. F. *A textbook of physiology*. London: Saunders, 1955.
Gage, P. W., & McBurney, R. N. Effects of membrane potential, temperature and neostigmine on the conductance change caused by a quantum of acetylcholine at the toad neuromuscular junction. *Journal of Physiology (London)*, 1975, *244*, 385–407.
Garcia, J., McGowan, B. K., & Green, K. F. Biological constraints on conditioning. In A. H. Black & W. F. Prokasy (Eds.), *Classical conditioning II*. New York: Appleton-Century-Crofts, 1972.
Gelperin, A., Hopfield, J. J., & Tank, D. W. The logic of *Limax* learning. In A. I. Selverston (Ed.), *Model neural networks and behavior*. New York: Plenum Press, 1985.
Gibson, J. J. *The senses considered as perceptual systems*. Boston: Houghton Mifflin, 1966.
Gibson, J. J. *The ecological approach to visual perception*. Boston: Houghton Mifflin, 1979.
Goren, C. C., Sarty, M., & Wu, P. Y. K. Visual following and pattern discrimination of face-like stimuli by newborn infants. *Pediatrics*, 1975, *56*, 544–549.
Hawkins, R. D., Abrams, T. W., Carew, T. J., & Kandel, E. R. A cellular mechanism of classical conditioning in *Aplysia*: Activity-dependent amplification of presynaptic facilitation. *Science*, 1983, *219*, 400–405.
Hennessy, D. F. *Functional significance of variation in predator harassment*. Doctoral dissertation, University of California, Davis, 1982.
Hennessy, D. F., Owings, D. H., Rowe, M. P., Coss, R. G., & Leger, D. W. The information

afforded by a variable signal: Constraints on snake-elicited tail flagging by California ground squirrels. *Behaviour*, 1981, *78*, 188–226.

Hirano, A., & Dembitzer, H. M. Aberrant development of the Purkinje cell dendritic spine. *Advances in Neurology*, 1975, *12*, 353–360.

Johnston, T. D. Contrasting approaches to a theory of learning. *Behavioral and Brain Sciences*, 1981, *4*, 125–173.

Johnston, T. D., & Turvey, M. T. A sketch of an ecological metatheory for theories of learning. In G. H. Bower (Ed.), *The psychology of learning and motivation* (Vol. 14). New York: Academic Press, 1980.

Kandel, E. R., & Schwartz, J. H. Molecular biology of learning: Modulation of transmitter release. *Science*, 1982, *218*, 433–443.

Kawato, M., Hamaguchi, T., Murakami, F., & Tsukahara, N. Quantitative analysis of electrical properties of dendritic spines. *Biological Cybernetics*, 1984, *50*, 447–454.

Keenan, C. L., Coss, R., & Koopowitz, H. Cytoarchitecture of primitive brains: Golgi studies of flatworms. *Journal of Comparative Neurology*, 1981, *195*, 697–716.

Koch, C., & Poggio, T. A theoretical analysis of electrical properties of spines. *Proceedings of the Royal Society of London, Series B*, 1983, *218*, 455–477.

Kuno, M. Quantal components of excitatory synaptic potentials in spinal motoneurones. *Journal of Physiology (London)*, 1964, *175*, 81–99.

Lee, K. S., Schottler, F., Oliver, M., & Lynch, G. Brief bursts of high-frequency stimulation produce two types of structural change in rat hippocampus. *Journal of Neurophysiology*, 1980, *44*, 247–258.

Leger, D. W., & Owings, D. H. Responses to alarm calls by California ground squirrels: Effects of call structure and maternal status. *Behavioral Ecology and Sociobiology*, 1978, *3*, 177–186.

Leger, D. W., Owings, D. H., & Coss, R. G. The behavioral ecology of time allocation in California ground squirrels (*Spermophilus beecheyi*): Microhabitat effects. *Journal of Comparative Psychology*, 1983, *97*, 283–291.

Lewontin, R. C., & Levins, R. Evoluzione. In *Enciclopedia. V: Divino-Fame*. Torino: Einaudi, 1978.

Llinás, R., Hillman, D. E., & Precht, W. Neuronal circuit reorganization in mammalian agranular cerebellar cortex. *Journal of Neurobiology*, 1973, *4*, 69–94.

Lorenz, K. Z. The comparative method in studying innate behavior patterns. *Symposia of the Society for Experimental Biology*, 1950, *4*, 221–268.

Lorenz, K. Z. The role of gestalt perception in animal and human behaviour. In L. L. Whyte (Ed.), *Aspects of form*. Bloomington, Ill.: Indiana University Press, 1951.

Lund, J. S., Boothe, R. G., & Lund, R. D. Development of neurons in the visual cortex (area 17) of the monkey (*Macaca nemestrina*): A Golgi study from fetal day 127 to postnatal maturity. *Journal of Comparative Neurology*, 1977, *176*, 149–188.

Lynch, G., & Baudry, M. The biochemistry of memory: A new and specific hypothesis. *Science*, 1984, *224*, 1057–1063.

Marin-Padilla, M. Structural organization of the cerebral cortex (motor area) in human chromosomal aberrations: A Golgi study. I. $D_1$ (13–15) Trisomy, Patau syndrome. *Brain Research*, 1974, *66*, 375–391.

Marler, P. The filtering of external stimuli during instinctive behavior. In W. H. Thorpe & O. L. Zangwill (Eds.), *Current problems in animal behaviour*. London: Cambridge University Press, 1961.

Marler, P. R. Sensory templates in species-specific behavior. In J. C. Fentress (Ed.), *Simple networks and behavior*. Mass.: Sinauer Associates, 1976.

Marr, D. *Vision, a computational investigation into the human representation and processing of visual information*. San Francisco: Freeman, 1982.

Mates, S. L. & Lund, J. S. Neuronal composition and development in lamina 4C of monkey striate cortex. *Journal of Comparative Neurology*, 1983, *221*, 60–90.

Matthews-Bellinger, J., & Salpeter, M. M. Distribution of acetylcholine receptors at frog neuromuscular junctions with a discussion of some physiological implications. *Journal of Physiology (London)*, 1978, *279*, 197–213.

Mayr, E. *The unity of the genotype*. Cambridge, Mass.: Harvard University Press, 1963.

McDonald, J. F. The molecular basis of adaptation: A critical review of relevant ideas and observations. *Annual Review of Ecology and Systematics*, 1983, *14*, 77–102.

Menzel, E. Natural language of young chimpanzees. *New Scientist*, 1975, *65*, 127–130.

Menzel, E. W. Cognitive mapping in chimpanzees. In S. H. Hulse & W. K. Honig (Eds.), *Cognitive processes in animal behavior*. Hillsdale, N. J.: Erlbaum, 1978.

Meyer, R. L. "Extra" optic fibers exclude normal fibers from tectal regions in goldfish. *Journal of Comparative Neurology*, 1979, *183*, 883–902.

Miller, J. P., Rall, W., & Rinzel, J. Synaptic amplification by active membrane in dendritic spines. *Brain Research*, 1985, *325*, 325–330.

Nei, M. Genetic distance between populations. *American Naturalist*, 1972, *106*, 283–292.

Nei, M. The theory of genetic distance and evolution of human races. *Japanese Journal of Human Genetics*, 1978, *23*, 341–369.

Overton, W. F. The active organism in structuralism. *Human Development*, 1976, *19*, 71–86.

Owings, D. H., & Coss, R. G. Snake mobbing by California ground squirrels: Adaptive variation and ontogeny. *Behaviour*, 1977, *62*, 50–69.

Owings, D. H., & Coss, R. G. How ground squirrels deal with snakes. *Anima*, 1981, *99*, 37–43.

Owings, D. H., & Owings, S. C. Snake-directed behavior by Black-tailed prairie dogs (*Cynomys ludovicianus*). *Zeitschrift für Tierpsychologie*, 1979, *49*, 35–54.

Owings, D. H., & Virginia, R. A. Alarm calls of California ground squirrels (*Spermophilus beecheyi*). *Zeitschrift für Tierpsychologie*, 1978, *46*, 58–70.

Pellionisz, A., Llinás, R., & Perkel, D. H. A computer model of the cerebellar cortex of the frog. *Neuroscience*, 1977, *2*, 19–35.

Pepper, S. C. *World Hypotheses: A study in evidence*. Berkeley: University of California Press, 1942.

Perkel, D. H. Functional role of dendritic spines. *Journal de Physiologie (Paris)*, 1982–1983, *78*, 695–699.

Perkel, D. H., & Perkel, D. J. Dendritic spines: Role of active membrane in modulating synaptic efficacy. *Brain Research*, *325*, 331–335.

Pinel, J. P., Treit, D., Ladak, F., & MacLennan, A. J. Conditioned defensive burying in rats free to escape. *Animal Learning and Behavior*, 1980, *8*, 447–451.

Purpura, D. P. Dendritic differentiation in human cerebral cortext: Normal and aberrant developmental patterns. *Advances in Neurology*, 1975, *12*, 91–116.

Purves, D., & Lichtman, J. W. Elimination of synapses in the developing nervous system. *Science*, 1980, *210*, 153–157.

Quinn, W. G., & Greenspan, R. J. Learning and courtship in *Drosophila*: Two stories with mutants. *Annual Review of Neuroscience*, 1984, *7*, 67–93.

Rausch, G., & Scheich, H. Dendritic spine loss and enlargement during maturation of the speech control system in the mynah bird (*Gracula religiosa*). *Neuroscience Letters*, 1982, *29*, 129–133.

Redman, S., & Walmsley, B. Amplitude fluctuations in synaptic potentials evoked in cat spinal motoneurones at identified group Ia synapses. *Journal of Physiology (London)*, 1983, *343*, 135–145.

Richer, J. M., & Coss, R. G. Gaze aversion in autistic and normal children. *Acta Psychiatrica Scandinavia*, 1976, *53*, 193–210.

Riedl, R. The role of morphology in the theory of evolution. In M. Grene (Ed.), *Dimensions of Darwinism*. Cambridge: Cambridge University Press, 1983.

Robinson, H., & Koch, C. *An information storage mechanism: Calcium and spines* (A.I. Memo 779, C.B.I.P Paper 004). Cambridge, Mass.: M.I.T., Artificial Intelligence Laboratory, 1984.

Rose, S. P. R. Can the neuroscience explain the mind? *Trends in Neuroscience*, 1980, *3*, 2–4.

Rowe, M. P., & Owings, D. H. The meaning of the sound of rattling by rattlesnakes to California ground squirrels. *Behaviour*, 1978, *66*, 252–267.

Sæther, O. A. The canalized evolutionary potential: Inconsistencies in phylogenetic reasoning. *Systematic Zoology*, 1983, *32*, 343–359.

Schleidt, W. M. How "fixed" is the fixed action pattern? *Zeitschrift für Tierpsychologie*, 1974, *36*, 184–211.

Seligman, M. E. P. On the generality of the laws of learning. *Psychological Review*, 1970, *77*, 406–418.

Shalter, M. D. Effect of spatial context on the mobbing reaction of pied flycatchers to a predator model. *Animal Behaviour*, 1978, *26*, 1219–1221.

Shettleworth, S. J., & Krebs, J. R. How marsh tits find their hoards: The roles of site preference and spatial memory. *Journal of Experimental Psychology: Animal Behavior Processes*, 1982, *8*, 354–375.

Smith, D. G., & Coss, R. G. Calibrating the molecular clock: Estimates of ground squirrel divergence made using fossil and geological time markers. *Molecular Biology and Evolution*, 1984, *1*, 249–259.

Smith, W. J. *The behavior of communicating an ethological approach*. Cambridge, Mass.: Harvard University Press, 1977.

Sotelo, C. Anatomical, physiological and biochemical studies of the cerebellum from mutant mice. II. Morphological study of cerebellar cortical neurons and circuits in the weaver mouse. *Brain Research*, 1975, *94*, 19–44.

Sotelo, C. Purkinje cell ontogeny: Formation and maintenance of spines. *Progress in Brain Research*, 1978, *48*, 149–170.

Spalding, D. A. Instinct. With original observations on young animals. *MacMillan's Magazine*, 1873, *27*, 282–293.

Stevens, C. F. Biophysical studies of ion channels. *Science*, 1984, *225*, 1346–1350.

Takashima, S., Becker, L. E., Armstrong, D. L., & Chan, F. Abnormal neuronal development in the visual cortex of the human fetus and infant with Down's syndrome. A quantitative and qualitative Golgi study. *Brain Research*, 1981, *225*, 1–21.

Tavares, M. R., Paula-Barbosa, M. M., & Gray, E. G. Dendritic spine plasticity and chronic alcoholism in rats. *Neuroscience Letters*, 1983, *42*, 235–238.

Tieman, S. B., & Hirsch, H. V. B. Exposure to lines of only one orientation modifies dendritic morphology of cells in the visual cortex of the cat. *Journal of Comparative Neurology*, 1982, *211*, 353–362.

Tinbergen, N. *The study of instinct*. Oxford: Clarendon Press, 1951.

Van Harreveld, A., & Fifkova, E. Swelling of dendritic spines in the fascia dentata after stimulation of the perforant fibers as a mechanism of post-tetanic potentiation. *Experimental Neurology*, 1975, *49*, 736–749.

Vaughn, J. E., Henrikson, C. K., & Grieshaber, J. A. A quantitative study of synapses on motor neuron dendritic growth cones in developing mouse spinal cord. *Journal of Cell Biology*, 1974, *60*, 664–672.

Waddington, C. H. *The strategy of the genes*. London: Allen & Unwin, 1957.

Walters, E. T., & Byrne, J. H. Associative conditioning of single sensory neurons suggests a cellular mechanism for learning. *Science*, 1983, *219*, 405–408.

Webster, G., & Goodwin, B. G. The origin of species: A structuralist approach. *Journal of Social and Biological Structures*, 1982, *5*, 15–47.

Whitehead, M. C. Growth of dendrites in the optic tectum of the chick embryo following destruction of the eye primordium. *Neuroscience*, 1979, *4*, 379–390.

Wilson, C. J. Passive cable properties of dendritic spines and spiny neurons. *Journal of Neuroscience*, 1984, *4*, 281–297.

Young, J. Z. *The anatomy of the nervous system of Octopus vulgaris*. Oxford: Clarendon Press, 1971.

CHAPTER 15

# Ecology and Intelligence

**Euan M. Macphail**
University of York
Heslington, York, England, UK

A bewildering variety of animal species, vertebrate and invertebrate, inhabit the earth. Each of these species has evolved through modification from its ancestors in response to environmental pressures associated with the ecological niches occupied through the evolutionary history of the species. Successive modifications of the anatomical structure of at least some species can be detected in the fossil record, and although behavioral patterns cannot be observed in—or even, except very indirectly, deduced from—the fossil record, there is equally no reason to doubt that genetically controlled components of those patterns also evolved through modification in response to environmental pressures and that the behavior patterns of ancestors of living species differed from those of their extant descendants in important ways. In other words, there is no dispute over the proposition that variations in genetically controlled components of behavior patterns are to be expected in animals occupying different ecological niches.

Intelligence, while not, perhaps, to be regarded as a pattern of behavior, may be seen as the behavioral capacity, or, more likely, set of capacities, that underlies the relatively predictable patterns of behavioral adjustment shown by individuals of a species in response to what are, to the individual, initially novel and unexpected events. (It is presumably because of the unpredictability on a large time scale of certain events—the availability of food in a particular place, for example—that intelligence evolved as a capacity to adjust behavior in response to events that are predictable only on a much smaller time scale.) It might be expected, then, that like other behavior patterns, the intellectual capacity (or capacities) of different species should vary in accordance with the demands made by the ecological niches occupied by the species and that a full understanding of the intelligence of a species could not be obtained without detailed consideration of its ecology.

Until relatively recently, however, comparative psychologists have pursued their analyses of intelligence by studying learning in laboratory tasks using species selected on grounds of contrasting phylogeny rather than contrasting ecology, and their investigations have paid little overt heed to the natural ecology of those species. Ethologists, on the other hand, have analyzed the behavior of animals in their natural environments but have shown little interest in the problem of intelligence and, in particular, of how animals might solve problems outside their natural environments. It is, then, a welcome development that bridges between ethological and comparative psychological modes of analysis are now being built. Attempts are being made to explain capacities observed in the laboratory in terms of adaptation to demands posed by the natural environment of a species, and, similarly, attempts are made to predict laboratory performance from observations made in the field. Olton and his colleagues, for example, who reported remarkably efficient performance by rats in the radial maze (e.g., Olton & Samuelson, 1976) went on to suggest (Olton & Schlosberg, 1978) that one reason for the rats' efficiency was their (innate) tendency when motivated by food reward to adopt a win–shift strategy, a strategy that was taken to reflect the fact that food resources in the natural environment of the rat were unreliable and easily depleted. A similar course was pursued in reverse by Kamil and his colleagues, who began (Kamil, 1978) by observing the foraging behavior of a species of nectar-feeding bird (the amakihi, *Loxop virens*, a Hawaiian honeycreeper species). These birds, having obtained nectar from one flower, go on to other flowers, systematically avoiding flowers already visited. Kamil generalized these findings to other nectar-feeding species and predicted that nectar-feeding birds would, when tested in a laboratory setting, tend to adopt win–shift strategies in food-rewarded tests; that prediction was confirmed in an experiment using individuals of three species of (nectar-feeding) hummingbirds (Cole, Hainsworth, Kamil, Mercier, & Wolf, 1982).

A further example of such bridge building is provided by workers investigating birds known to cache food in their natural environments. Field observations have suggested that these birds recover the caches by using memory, and attempts are now being made to gain close experimental control over their performance by testing the birds in what might be termed "seminatural" conditions in the laboratory (see Shettleworth, Chapter 13, this volume). Performance in these tasks has validated the claim that the birds rely on memory and suggests that the spatial memory of (at least some) of these birds may be more impressive than might previously have been expected on the basis of results using other avian species (and other techniques).

The correspondence between laboratory and field performances is reassuring, if only because it provides direct evidence that performance in artificial situations does not necessarily yield a distorted view of an animal's "true" capacities. It is, on the other hand, important to notice that congruence between a behavior pattern and an environmental demand does not force the conclusion that the pattern evolved to meet that demand. Although the results obtained from the cross-fertilization of ethology and comparative psychology have been of compelling interest, it is not clear that the theoretical accounts advanced for them are convincing at present, because there is a lack of evidence in support of the view that different ecologies would support different capacities. Such evidence could come from two soures: either from within-species contrasts observed when different environmental demands are relevant or from between-species contrasts, where a pressure supposedly relevant to the evolution of a capacity in one species differs significantly in some other species.

To return to the first of the examples cited earlier—namely, the suggestion that win–shift strategies have evolved in response to particular environmental resource distributions—this proposal has encountered difficulties (Macphail, 1985) because such strategies are seen in rats working for a reward (water) that is assumed to have a different (more dependable) distribution than food and because other species that have a more dependable distribution of food resources nevertheless show win–shift strategies when working for food reward. The second example cited, that of memory in food-storing birds, as yet awaits any direct evidence that the memory of these animals differs from that of birds that do not store food. It is a question of central importance to comparative psychologists (who will await with interest the results of the experiments outlined by Shettleworth); but in case it may be thought wholly implausible that the memory of, say, a pigeon, could match that of a Clark's nutcracker (which may remember the locations of thousands of caches), it may be valuable to point to two recent reports that could give encouragement to pigeon fanciers. First, Olson and Maki (1983) found successful performance by pigeons in a delayed-alternation task using a T-maze, when delays as long as 16 minutes were imposed; this contrasts markedly with the report of Wilkie and Summers (1982), who found that memory for location of a recently illuminated sample key (taken from an array of nine keys) decayed over a few seconds. Second, Vaughan and Greene (1984) have reported that pigeons showed no detectable loss of memory for the correct stimulus from 160 pairs of slides depicting natural objects and scenes, even after a 2-year delay. It should be noted that this particular test involved more than recognition memory because the birds were discriminating from 320 familiar stimuli the 160 that were associated with reward. In other words, both short- and long-term memory in the pigeon may be more resistant to decay and interference than might previously have been imagined. Finally, Vaughan and Greene emphasize that there is no reason to suppose that their experiments have reached a limit in number of items that pigeons may retain; in this context it will be recalled that, at a time when estimates of human recent memory capacity suggested a limitation (of approximately seven) in the number of items that could be stored, it came as something of a surprise when it was shown that human memory for pictorial items seen briefly and once only had a capacity, when tested using recognition techiques, of hundreds (Nickerson, 1965) or even of thousands (Standing, 1973) of items (and one might well ask what environmental demand led to the evolution of such a capacity in man?). To recapitulate—there is no unique measure of either the duration or the capacity of the memory of a species and no reason to suppose that the limits of a pigeon's memory capacity have yet been explored. Whether the memory capacity of food-storing birds exceeds that of pigeons (not to say those of close relatives of food-storing species) remains an open—and critical—question.

There have been, of course, numerous previous attempts by comparative psychologists to demonstrate species differences in learning or memory, and although the species for comparison were not selected on grounds of contrasting ecologies, there can be no doubt that the animals most commonly used (goldfish, turtles, pigeons, rats, rhesus monkeys) occupy very different environments and so should have been expected to have evolved different capacities. It is therefore relevant, in the present context of interest in the potential contribution of species-specific environmental pressures on the evolution of intellect, to record that when I surveyed the literature available on the comparative analysis of vertebrate intelligence (Macphail, 1982), I was unable to find compelling evidence for any species-differences in intellect among nonhuman vertebrates.

My reaction (Macphail, 1985) to the negative findings of that survey is that the null hypothesis cannot be rejected—that hypothesis being that there are, in fact, no differences within vertebrates (excluding humans) in intelligence. Not only that, but that the null hypothesis—the only tested and not disproved hypothesis available—should in fact be accepted, as is the normal scientific procedure. Now, of course, to accept the null hypothesis may appear to involve rejection of the notion that ecological factors are relevant to the evolution of intelligence. Before considering this implication further, I shall broaden the discussion somewhat to include a brief foray into invertebrate intelligence.

There are many more invertebrate species than vertebrate species, more than a million invertebrate species in all; and, of course, learning has been investigated in only a minute fraction of all invertebrate species. In most cases, moreover, little systematic analysis of learning capacity is available, investigators being concerned essentially to show that a given species can learn at least something. In only two groups of invertebrates have there been systematic investigations, those groups being, on the one hand, species from the phylum Mollusca, and, on the other, honey bees. Earlier molluscan studies concentrated on the octopus (e.g. Sutherland & Mackintosh, 1971), whereas the current emphasis is on somewhat less exotic species, such as the slug *Limax* (e.g., Cooke, Delaney, & Gelperin, Chapter 10, this volume), the sea hare *Aplysia* (e.g., Hawkins & Kandel, 1984), and the nudibranch mollusk *Hermissenda* (e.g., Alkon, Chapter 1, this volume). The attraction of these latter species lies to a large extent in their neuroanatomy because their nervous systems consist of a relatively small number of neurons in total, many of which are large and individually recognizable in different subjects. There is, in other words, promise that the way in which they learn may be accessible to detailed neurobiological analysis. Honey bee behavior has been investigated intensively over several decades; and there has, in particular, been a recent series of reports on their learning abilities using paradigms closely modeled on paradigms widely used in vertebrates. At present it is fair to say that the neurophysiological analysis of learning in bees is not far advanced, just as behavioral analyses of molluscan learning lag behind those available for bees. This latter fact will force an emphasis here on honey bees, as opposed to mollusks, when the question whether specific ecological factors contribute to the learning capacities of these invertebrates is considered.

Gould (Chapter 11, this volume) has suggested that an important contributory factor to association formation in bees might be "hard-wired" preassociations between cues and reinforcers, so that learning would be most rapid for cues likely (in the natural environment) to be relevant. Association formation in bees would, that is, largely be an instance of alpha conditioning. Apart from the fact that, for bees, some stimuli are more salient than others (a fact that is accommodated by all theories of learning), there is no direct behavioral evidence in support of the "alpha conditioning hypothesis." Indeed, if taken to its logical conclusion, there is direct evidence against the hypothesis. For if hard-wired stimulus-reinforcer preassociations are responsible for rapid association formation in bees, it should be difficult, if not impossible, for such stimuli to support conditioned inhibition (Hawkins and Kandel, 1984, acknowledge that a similar difficulty faces their current model of association formation in *Aplysia*). But there is evidence for honey bees (as there is not for *Aplysia*) of the generation of conditioned inhibition, using as cues odor stimuli that also allow substantial one-trial association formation (Bitterman, Menzel, Fietz, & Schafer, 1983). There is currently no evidence from experiments using honey bees that some cues are relatively more effective as conditioned excitors as opposed to conditioned inhibitors, nor that some cues are more readily associated with one reinforcer than with another; in the absence of such evidence, it is premature, to say the least, to adopt the alpha conditioning hypothesis. It may be added here that it is not clear that there is yet conclusive evidence for any such innate stimulus-reinforcer predispositions in vertebrates either. Many examples of selective association formation, initially taken to be demonstrations of the existence of "biological constraints" on learning are in fact amenable to interpretation in terms of "general process" theories, theories that apply equally to all types of stimuli and reinforcers (e.g., Macphail, 1985).

Gould also emphasizes the ability of honey bees to learn to visit different food sources according to the time of day; such an ability might, of course, be a species-specific adaptation, reflecting the fact that in the bees' natural environment most flowers yield nectar only at certain predictable and limited times of day. But it would seem more economical to regard this finding as reflecting simply the ability of bees to use cues derived from their internal clocks as discriminative stimuli in a simple conditional discrimination. Other animals having very different ecologies are capable of forming time-based discriminations (e.g, fish and birds, Fraisse, 1963; bullfrogs, Van Bergeijk, 1967; humans, Glaser, 1966); and as Bitterman and his colleagues have shown in an impressive series of experiments, there are striking parallels between the phenomena of learning obtained in bees and those known to occur in vertebrates. Bees show, for example, both response–stimulus and stimulus–stimulus association formation (Bitterman *et al.*, 1983; Couvillon & Bitterman, 1982; Sigurdson, 1981), generalization decrement, second-order conditioning, successive negative contrast, the overlearning extinction effect, and the partial reinforcement extinction effect (Bitterman *et al.*, 1983; Couvillon & Bitterman, 1980, 1984; Sigurdson, 1981).Phenomena of discrimination learning shown by bees and vertebrates include overshadowing, potentiation, summation, improvement across a series of spatial discrimination reversals, and superiority of intradimensional over extradimensional shift learning (Couvillon & Bitterman, 1980, 1982; Klosterhafen, Fischer, & Bitterman, 1978; Sigurdson, 1981). Moreover, as Menzel and Bitterman (1983) have emphasized, the behavioral findings from bees appear identical whether the experiments employ free-flying bees or bees that are individually captured and tested in "artificial" surroundings comparable in many ways to the various boxes in which vertebrate laboratory experiments are conducted.

The conclusion of this discussion is, then, that no between-species difference in learning or memory, attributable to a difference in ecological niche, has yet been demonstrated in either invertebrates or vertebrates. Such a conclusion naturally lends support to those general process theorists whose work concentrates on data obtained from two species, pigeons and rats. For although, of course, species differences in learning may ultimately be demonstrated, there can be little doubt that—at the least—there is much in common among the groups, both vertebrate and invertebrate, so far investigated. As general process theorists propose new principles—Rescorla's (Chapter 12, this volume) notion of the potential "catalytic" action of contiguous stimuli upon association formation between other stimuli provides a good example—the validity of those principles should be investigated in other groups, both closely and distantly related.

Even though the possibility that there exist species differences in intellect cannot (ever) be ruled out conclusively, we should perhaps finally consider the implications of a continuing failure to detect instances of them. Would it, for example, mean that intelligence has somehow evolved independently of ecology—and if not, how are the parallels between learning in invertebrate and vertebrate, in fish and bird, in rat and monkey, to be explained? There is one candidate for a relatively simple answer to such questions, and this is, that similar mechanisms of intelligence are encountered in these diverse groups because intelligence evolved in response to an environmental factor common to all ecological niches—namely, causality. Events are predictable to the extent that causal links between events are detected, and a number of learning theorists (e.g., Dickinson, 1980) have emphasized that mechanisms of association formation appear to possess precisely the properties required for the detection of causes. The broader in application such cause-detecting devices are, the more useful they should prove to their possessors in predicting future events. Perhaps, then, association formation evolved very early and proved so powerful as a predictive mechanism that subsequent improvements in problem solving have arisen largely from the undoubted improvements in the quality of sensory processing and in the variability and skill of motor response available.

## REFERENCES

Bitterman, M. E., Menzel, R., Fietz, A., & Schafer, S. Classical conditioning of proboscis extension in honeybees (*Apis mellifera*). *Journal of Comparative Psychology*, 1983, *97*, 107–119.

Cole, S., Hainsworth, F. R., Kamil, A. C., Mercier, T., & Wolf, L. L. Spatial learning as an adaptation in hummingbirds. *Science*, 1982, *217*, 655–657.

Couvillon, P. A., & Bitterman, M. E. Some phenomena of associative learning in honeybees. *Journal of Comparative and Physiological Psychology*, 1980, *94*, 878–885.

Couvillon, P. A., & Bitterman, M. E. Compound conditioning in honeybees. *Journal of Comparative and Physiological Psychology*, 1982, *96*, 192–199.

Couvillon, P. A., & Bitterman, M. E. The overlearning–extinction effect and successive negative contrast in honeybees (*Apis mellifera*). *Journal of Comparative Psychology*, 1984, *98*, 100–109.

Dickinson, A. *Contemporary animal learning theory*. Cambridge: Cambridge University Press, 1980.

Fraisse, P. *The psychology of time*. Westport, Conn.: Greenwood Press, 1963.

Glaser, E. M. *The physiological basis of habituation*. London: Oxford University Press, 1966.

Hawkins, R. D., & Kandel, E. R. Is there a cell-biological alphabet for simple forms of learning? *Psychological Review*, 1984, *91*, 375–391.

Kamil, A. C. Systematic foraging by a nectar-feeding bird, the Amakihi (*Loxops virens*). *Journal of Comparative and Physiological Psychology*, 1978, *92*, 388–396.

Klosterhafen, S., Fischer, W., & Bitterman, M. E. Modification of attention in honeybees. *Science*, 1978, *201*, 1241–1243.

Macphail, E. M. *Brain and intelligence in vertebrates*. Oxford: Clarendon Press, 1982.

Macphail, E. M. Vertebrate intelligence: The null hypothesis. *Philosophical Transactions of the Royal Society of London, Series B*, 1985, *308*, 37–51.

Menzel, R., & Bitterman, M. E. Learning by honeybees in a unnatural situation. In F. Huber & H. Markl (Eds.), *Neuroethology and behavioral physiology*. Berlin: Springer-Verlag, 1983.

Nickerson, R. S. Short-term memory for complex meaningful visual configurations, a demonstration of capacity. *Canadian Journal of Psychology*, 1965, *19*, 155–160.

Olson, D. J., & Maki, W. S. Characteristics of spatial memory in pigeons. *Journal of Experimental Psychology: Animal Behavior Processes*, 1983, *9*, 266–280.

Olton, D. S., & Samuelson, R. J. Remembrance of places past: Spatial memory in rats. *Journal of Experimental Psychology: Animal Behavior Processes*, 1976, *2*, 97–116.

Olton, D. S., & Schlosberg, P. Food searching strategies in young rats: Win–shift predominates over win-stay. *Journal of Comparative and Physiological Psychology*, 1978, *92*, 609–618.

Sigurdson, J. E. Automated discrete-trials techniques of appetitive conditioning in honey bees. *Behavior Research Methods and Instrumentation*, 1981, *13*, 1–10.

Standing, L. Learning 10,000 pictures. *Quarterly Journal of Experimental Psychology*, 1973, *25*, 207–222.

Sutherland, N. S., & Mackintosh, N. J. *Mechanisms of animal discrimination learning*. London: Academic Press, 1971.

Van Bergeijk, W. A. Anticipatory feeding behaviour in the bullfrog (*Rana catesbeiana*). *Animal Behaviour*, 1967, *15*, 231–238.

Vaughan, W., & Greene, S. L. Pigeon visual memory capacity. *Journal of Experimental Psychology: Animal Behavior Processes*, 1984, *10*, 256–271.

Wilkie, D. M., & Summers, R. J. Pigeons' spatial memory: Factors affecting delayed matching of key location. *Journal of the Experimental Analysis of Behavior*, 1982, *37*, 45–56.

CHAPTER 16

# Inference, Memory, and Representation

**J. E. R. Staddon**
Duke University

I shall begin with a general comment on the selectionist view of learning, then turn to three related themes: learning as an inference process and the roles of representation and memory in learning.

## SELECTION, VARIATION, AND INFERENCE

There is an emerging consensus that learning is best thought of as a joint process of *selection* and *variation* (Campbell, 1960; Staddon & Simmelhag, 1971). In recent years neurobiologists have tended to assume that selection means *neuro*selection, but of course we have little idea as yet of the units of selection, of what is selected. In simple creatures that show no associative learning, selection may just be of place (as in bacterial orientation) or of a particular motor pattern (as in the avoidance pattern of *Stentor* described by Jennings, 1906/1976). In more complex animals, capable of associative learning, reward or punishment act to produce a particular pattern of behavior, a *program* rather than a particular response, which is tied to a particular environmental context. Selection here is for the elements out of which this program is constructed (Staddon, 1981). We have no idea of the "language" in which behavioral programs are written or of the details of their physical embodiment. We can safely assume that the nervous system is involved, but, for vertebrate learning, at least, we know little at the level of organization—how the nervous system is altered by experience and how these alterations affect future behavior potential.

The experimental and theoretical work of Gelperin, Hopfield, and their associates with the invertebrate *Limax* points to some fascinating organizational possibilities. The invertebrate preparations are exciting just because they promise to reveal the "alphabet" (in the phrase of Hawkins & Kandel, 1984) of associative learning, the elements rearrangement of which, by the contingencies of operant and classical conditioning, yields up the programs—words and sentences—that are the outcome of learning. But much remains to be done: The Gelperin–Hopfield approach has the great virtue of dealing with a real working model, even if its links with the anatomical, biochemical, and neurophysiological details are still incomplete. Many other models are less convincing because we cannot be as sure that they really behave as described, quite apart from their connection with known neurophysiology. In all, the gulf between the growing mountain of sophisticated neurochemical and neurophysiological data and the behavior for which these processes are responsible—and for which they have evolved—is still wide.

If something is to be selected, it must first occur—at least in rudimentary form. It is, therefore, of great interest to see in the work of several of the contributors to this volume evidence that the "conditionability" of a stimulus depends upon the preexistence of appropriate "spontaneous" activity (data that lend support to Gould's "alpha conditioning" model; see Chapter 11, this volume). David Cohen (Chapter 2, this volume), for example, reports that there must be some initial neural response to the conditioned stimulus (CS) if the response is to be subsequently enhanced by pairing the CS with an unconditioned stimulus (US). In classical as in operant conditioning, the predictive relation (contingency) between a neutral event (stimulus or response) and a subsequent valued event (US) acts to select neural activity that allows the event to occur (if it is an activity) or be attended to (if it is a stimulus).

From a functional point of view, learning can be thought of as a process of *inference* (Staddon, 1983). Animals act as "inference engines," using built-in rules to anticipate, identify, and react appropriately to events of biological importance. For example, in classical conditioning, the stimulus followed most closely and reliably by an event of value is usually the one that becomes "conditioned," that is, evokes the appropriate anticipatory reactions.

Organisms use two kinds of rules to identify the CS: (1) General rules related to what might be called the "ecology of causation"—the principles of contiguity and invariable (or at least reliable) succession first described by David Hume and made exact by experimental psychologists in recent years. (2) Specific predictors related to the particular context and valued event that is to be predicted. Principles of the first kind reflect properties common to all ecological niches; priciples of the second kind reflect features specific to particular niches.

Specific predictors reflect properties of stimuli that have special significance in relation to particular to-be-predicted events: Taste may have a special significance as a predictor of sickness; sound, of danger; certain song elements as identifiers of species-specific bird song; and so on. In bee learning, odors are learned faster than colors and different colors are learned at different rates (see Gould, Chapter 11, this volume, for these and other examples).

Temporal contiguity is the chief general predictor: no matter what the situation, the time between potential cause and its effect is always useful, although the shortest time need not be the best predictor. When an effect is always delayed, for example, as sickness follows poisoning with a lag, intermediate times may carry the greatest weight. Even in standard laboratory classical conditioning, the optimal CS–US delay is not zero but half a second or so (Landauer, 1969; Staddon, 1973). Contingency, reliability of succession measured as a difference in conditional probability [$p(\text{US}|\text{CS}) > p(\text{US}|\overline{\text{CS}})$], is the other general predictor.

The general predictors are the selection rules the animal uses to weed out the predictive event from among a set of possibilities presented to it by processes of behavioral variation. The specific predictors are the set of "default" possibilities that are thus offered up. Learning constraints reflect both limitations on variation and rules of selection. For example, if in golden hamsters *grooming* is never a candidate as putative cause of food delivery, hamsters will be unable to learn to produce food by grooming (Shettleworth, 1975). (Notice that the limitation here is at the neural level: Grooming certainly *occurs* in a food context; but it cannot be connected to food. Perhaps recording studies will show that neural activity associated with grooming is not facilitated by food presentation or potential discriminative stimuli, whereas neural activity associated with lever pressing, say, is.) Rats cannot learn that a nontaste stimulus is a signal for poison, no matter how good the general predictors (contiguity and contingency). Even if a trace CS reliably predicts a US, animals may fail to detect the relation if the trace delay is too long—a limitation on the general laws. There are numerous other examples.

The two general predictors have a special status in that they reflect necessary properties of the world. Taste need not be the best predictor of sickness, and one can imagine worlds in which any specific predictor becomes invalid. But contingency almost defines what we mean by predictiveness. Temporal contiguity has no such necessary status, but it does reflect ineluctable limitations on information gathering, as well as a reliable feature of the real world: A cause remote in time from its effect will be hard to identify because intervening potential causes must first be eliminated (cf. Revusky, 1977), and most identifiable causes closely precede their effects. The only escape from the information-gathering limit is when potential causes for an effect differ in some consistent way from all intervening events—as in taste-aversion learning where a remote taste takes precedence over intervening nontaste stimuli.

Operant (instrumental) conditioning adds to the two general factors a third—*control* by the animal, who can produce a potential predictor (response) at will and thus test the degree of contingency between it and a valued consequence (reward or punishment).

Thinking of learning as an effect of different classes of predictors rather than as the automatic action of simple contiguity and contingency processes makes paradoxical effects less surprising—and also makes it harder to come up with realistic physiological mechanisms. For example, hungry pigeons easily learn to peck at brief stimuli that signal food—but still peck even if pecks turn off the stimulus and prevent food (Williams & Williams, 1969). Here a specific predictor—a good food signal, which induces pecking—overrides a general predictor, contiguity of the response with food. Given a single experience with electric shock, rats may later prefer to avoid a life-like novel object (rubber hedgehog) presented just after the shock than a relatively neutral object presented just before: The specific predictive property of the hedgehog overrides contiguity, the general predictor (Keith-Lucas & Guttman, 1975). Additional trials (denied the animal in this experiment) would presumably permit the contigency variable to override the high *a priori* danger probability of the novel hedgehog. It will be interesting to see under what conditions LIMAX—and *Limax*—will show backward conditioning.

## REPRESENTATION AND MEMORY

Roger Shepard (1984) has drawn a neat parallel between something most biologists take for granted—the ubiquity of circadian rhythms—and the problem of *representation* now much studied by psychologists (cf. Roitblat, 1982). Shepard points out that reliable properties of the environment are likely to be built into the organism. Biologists have long taken this view of morphological features: The form of the shark represents invariant properties of the fluid medium in which it lives; the morphology of wings, bones, and membranes all accommodates well-understood physical principles. I have argued that the general and specific learning predictors follow the same rule; for example, contiguity guides learning because it is a reliable feature of most causal relationships. Shepard points out that circadian rhythms can be thought of as a "mental representation" of another invariant, the 24-hour diurnal cycle. He goes on to argue that the invariant projective properties of rigid bodies as they move in three-dimensional space are similarly built into our perceptual systems and account for many of the illusions in which the Gestalt psychologists took such delight.

All this is by way of arguing that the notion of mental or neural representation, far from being a high-level "cognitive" construct, is, in fact, something fundamental to any adaptive system. Cooke, Delaney, and Gelperin (Chapter 10, this volume) point out how the "across-fiber" pattern of receptor responses represents taste in the LIMAX model and how stable configurations of the neural network represent particular remembered foods. A "neural representation" is just any stable state that can be identified with some invariant property of the world.[1]

1. Indeed, it may well be that the most significant changes in the nervous system associated with the evolution of learning ability have to do with the way that knowledge about the world is represented neurally. The switch-like properties of neural junctions, gating functions embodied

The simplest form of representation is a dyadic link, between stimulus and stimulus or between stimulus and response. There is little reason, other than history, for giving such representations a special status. Perhaps unfortunately, history has been decisive: The tradition of Locke and Hume led early learning theorists to assume that dyadic links between elements are the natural building blocks for all learning. In the ingenious hands of experimental psychologists such as Kamin, Rescorla, Wagner, and Mackintosh, the elementaristic approach led to the discovery and definition of what I have been terming general predictors. But, more recently, this same ingenuity has begun to turn up difficulties. For example, Rescorla (Chapter 12, this volume) describes experimental results that imply not only stimulus–stimulus links but also what he terms "catalytic" functions of stimuli; Rusiniak, Hankins, Garcia, and Brett (1979) have shown that an odor that precedes sickness will not become conditioned unless accompanied by a taste; hawks cannot learn to avoid mice of a particular color unless the color is associated with a special taste (Garcia, 1981). The traditional "stamping-in" role of reinforcement, now largely discredited, can be thought of in the same way: lever pressing will not become conditioned to a discriminative stimulus unless accompanied by reinforcement.

Similar effects have been known for some time in bee learning. For example, if bees learn to find a particular food source at a certain time of day, they will forget all and have to begin again if just one of its attributes—odor, color, time of day—is altered. Bogdany (1978) has shown that when bees learn to find a particular source at a particular time of day, they learn its other attributes better than when it is available at variable times—and, conversely, they learn the time poorly when the source has a variable color. These complex effects in rat, hawk, and bee learning do not fit easily into a dyadic form of data representation. They suggest a spatial or matrix type of data structure in which objects are represented as regions in a coordinate space. For example, the Bogdany data suggest that food sources are represented in an attribute space as regions for which "density" is related to food value. If an attribute is changed, then a new region is created, so that variability of an attribute must diminish the salience of its representation (see Staddon, 1983, p. 421). The data of Rusiniak *et al.* (1979) can perhaps be handled in a similar way, with the added constraint that an object must have a nonzero value on the taste dimension of a taste–odor–appearance space.

Gould's ingenious experiments on visual discrimination by bees led him to a different conclusion: Apparently bees encode appearance in a

---

in simple circuits, and principles of plasticity derived from basic learning processes, such as habituation, sensitization, and elementary classical conditioning, may well be universal, as several students of invertebrate learning have suggested. By the same token, information at this level can tell us little about behavioral differences between man and mollusk.

"picture" mode. The insects behave as if they were comparing a potential food source with a stored, low-resolution picture, rather than representing visual appearance by points in an attribute space. Although inefficient in terms of storage requirements, the "picture" mode has the advantage of flexibility: It does not prejudge the form of potential food sources and so enables the bee to learn to recognize anything that does not exceed its memory resolution. But there are other problems with an essentially unprocessed representation. For example, what of *constancy*? Before a flower can be identified, some way must be found to transform the retinal image to bring it into registry with the stored template. Here bee–flower coevolution may come to the aid of the bee: Most flowers are radially symmetrical (perhaps because this form is easiest for a template-recognition system to work with) and essentially two-dimensional in form. Consequently, *size* is the main thing the bee must adjust to bring image and representation into registry. Birds and mammals carry out this task neurally, by constancy processes that can compensate for distance and orientation and so identify an object at any distance or from any angle. Such mechanisms are complex and would surely tax the bee's limited processing capacity, but, happily, she may not need them: She can do the same job simply by adjusting her position in space. This hypothesis can easily be tested by testing the animals with artificial blossoms larger or smaller than the training blossoms; bees should hover further away from the large ones, but closer to the smaller ones, at distances predictable from hover distances in training.

Sara Shettleworth's account of the beautiful experiments with food-storing birds carried out at Oxford and Toronto suggests still another form of representation. Earlier work with rats in the now-familiar eight-arm radial maze had suggested to Robert Dale and me a simple encoding scheme in which each goal box is represented by a two-element vector, in which one element is the spatial location of the goal box and the other its *recency* (i.e., the time since it was last visited). The spatial-location element seems to correspond to the coordinates in a spatial map because animals are more confused when goal boxes are close together than when they are far apart (e.g., Horner, 1984): The spatial code is more than just ordinal. Most of the radial-maze data, and salient differences between animals' ability to solve delayed-alternation (DA) and delayed-matching-to-sample (DMTS) problems, on the one hand, and radial-maze problems, on the other, are consistent with this kind of representation, together with a rule to choose on the basis of recency: choosing the least recent option in the radial maze, the most recent in DMTS (see Staddon, 1983, Chapter 12; Staddon, 1984).

The radial-maze task requires the animal always to select unvisited locations, so there is no reason to invoke *value* as a goal box attribute; but, of course, rats must encode the value of locations—else they could not learn conventional mazes, in which the task is to find a single food source. If value is encoded, then in radial-maze tasks the animal could succeed either by choosing the least recently visited goal box or by *avoiding* empty goal boxes. Rats nevertheless seem to adopt the recency method, but it is not really clear why. The simplest possibility is that least-recent choice is the "default" rule the animals adopt for exploring a novel environment—*spontaneous alternation*. There are other data suggesting that events without a value connotation are sometimes hard to remember (cf. Staddon, 1974). We have just seen that an odor without a taste is not remembered; evidently an event without an associated positive or negative value may also sometimes be imperfectly stored. But these data may not apply to spatial learning, for which most animals require no reward.

Shettleworth's data from her food-hoarding *Paridae* imply a code in which the value of a food source, as well as its location, appearance, and recency, are represented. Because only full sites are of interest to the animal, it need not choose on the basis of recency but can go directly to the full sites. We do not know, apparently, whether the birds attend to site value when choosing hoarding sites: Do they selectively avoid filled sites or selectively choose sites with bigger, or newer, seeds? We know that they attend to at least some features of the sites in addition to location because they can learn to avoid sites that are frequently robbed.

The radial-maze task excited interest because it seemed to require a memory capacity much larger than that implied by rats' and pigeons' poor performance on DMTS and delayed-alternation tasks. Looking at these tasks as recency discriminations makes these differences more comprehensible: The DMTS task is difficult, not because rats cannot remember many things, but because they cannot discriminate recencies very well. Even radial-maze tasks do not require animals to store more than a dozen or so items (indeed, I have argued that radial-maze performance may be better than delayed-alternation performance partly because of a limit on the number of items—recencies—that can be stored in short-term memory). Shettleworth's birds so far show storage capacities on the same order. Yet in nature they may perhaps remember very many more food sites [recent experiments on long-term visual memory in pigeons show them able to remember 100 or more photographic-slide pairs for hundreds of days, for example (Vaughan & Greene, 1984) ].[2] It will be interesting to find the absolute limits on birds'

2. The apparent contrast between the large number of items birds seem to be able to retain in long-term memory and the much smaller capacity of short-term memory again points *recencies* as the critical factor. Short-term memory is the name we give to whatever faculty allows animals to learn under conditions of repeated exposure: DMTS, delayed-alternation, the radial-arm maze, and other similar tasks, where the animal sees the same physical events over and over again, each time with a different significance in terms of reward. The animal must learn not "which arm is baited (or unbaited)" but "which arm is baited *on this trial*." Long-term memory of the sort studied in the Vaughan and Greene experiment refers to retention of a discrimination whose features are constant in all the animal's experience: No matter how extensive the set of stimulus pairs, for any given pair the same one is always positive, the

ability to store information about food sites—and, as Shettleworth suggests, to see whether appropriate brain areas change seasonally in tune with the seasonal hoarding instinct or in response to memory demands placed on the animal. If marsh tits do have superior short-term memory and if they can be trained to perform on radial-maze tasks, then they may perhaps perform *less* well than rats, not because their short-term memory is inferior, but because it is superior, so that information from trial $N$ remains accessible and able to interfere with information from trial $N + 1$.

## REFERENCES

Bogdany, F. J. Linkage of learning signals in honey bee orientation. *Behavioral Ecology and Sociobiology*, 1978, *3*, 323–336.

Campbell, D. T. Blind variation and selective retention in creative thought as in other knowledge processes. *Psychological Review*, 1960, *67*, 380–400.

Garcia, J. Tilting at the paper mills of academe. *American Psychologist*, 1981, *36*, 149–158.

Hawkins, R. D., & Kandel, E. R. Is there a cell-biological alphabet for simple forms of learning? *Psychological Review*, 1984, *91*, 375–391.

Horner, J. The effect of maze structure upon the performance of a multiple-goal task. *Animal Learning and Behavior*, 1984, *12*, 55–61.

Jennings, H. S. *Behavior of the lower organisms*. Bloomington: Indiana University Press, 1976 (originally published, 1906).

Keith-Lucas, T., & Guttman, N. Robust-single-trial delayed backward conditioning. *Journal of Comparative and Physiological Psychology*, 1975, *88*, 468–476.

Landauer, T. K. Reinforcement as consolidation. *Psychological Review*, 1969, *76*, 82–96.

Revusky, S. H. Learning as a general process with emphasis on data from feeding experiments. In N. W. Milgram, L. Krames, & T. M. Alloway (Eds.), *Food aversion learning*. New York: Plenum Press, 1977.

Roitblat, H. L. The meaning of representation in animal memory. *Behavioral and Brain Sciences*, 1982, *5*, 353–406.

Rusiniak, K., Hankins, W., Garcia, J., & Brett, L. Flavor-illness aversions: Potentiation of odor by taste in rats. *Behavioral and Neural Biology*, 1979, *25*, 1–17.

Shepard, R. N. Ecological constraints on internal representation: Resonant kinematics of perceiving, imagining, thinking, and dreaming. *Psychological Review*, 1984, *91*, 417–447.

Shettleworth, S. J. Reinforcement and the organization of behavior in golden hamsters: Hunger, environment and food reinforcement. *Journal of Experimental Psychology*, 1975, *104*, 56–87.

Staddon, J. E. R. On the notion of cause, with applications to behaviorism. *Behaviorism*, 1973, *1*, 25–63.

---

other one always negative. Only short-term memory, therefore, requires the animal to discriminate between the most recent experience with the same physical event and earlier experiences—and this requirement is perhaps the main reason for the inferior capacity of short-term versus long-term memory.

Thus, the apparently extraordinary memory capacity of food-storing *Paridae* may perhaps reflect the rarity with which, in nature, they store food more than once in exactly the same site—or a time between repeat visits to the same sites that is long compared with the times typically used in animal-memory experiments. This issue could be easily settled in the elegant experimental situation Shettleworth and her colleagues have developed.

Staddon, J. E. R. Temporal control, attention and memory. *Psychological Review*, 1974, *81*, 375–391.

Staddon, J. E. R. Cognition in animals: Learning as program assembly. *Cognition*, 1981, *10*, 287–294.

Staddon, J. E. R. *Adaptive behavior and learning*. New York: Cambridge University Press, 1983.

Staddon, J. E. R. Time and memory. *Annals of the New York Academy of Sciences*, 1984, *423*, 322–334.

Staddon, J. E. R., & Simmelhag, V. The "superstition" experiment: A reexamination of its implications for the principles of adaptive behavior. *Psychological Review*, 1971, *78*, 3–43.

Vaughan, W., & Greene, S. L. Pigeon visual memory capacity. *Journal of Experimental Psychology: Animal Behavior Processes*, 1984, *10*, 256–271.

Williams, D. R., & Williams, H. Auto-maintenance in the pigeon: Sustained pecking despite contingent non-reinforcement. *Journal of the Experimental Analysis of Behavior*, 1969, *12*, 511–520.

CHAPTER 17

# Comparison of Learning Abilities among Species

**Mark R. Rosenzweig**
**Stephen E. Glickman**
University of California, Berkeley

## INTRODUCTION

Comparison of learning abilities among species is an important aspect, whether explicit or implicit, of several of the chapters in this volume. Some authors stress comparative aspects of learning and/or memory (Coss, Macphail, Shettleworth, Staddon), and others, while restricting themselves mainly to learning/memory in a single species, present interesting material that invites comparisons with other species (Alkon, Gelperin, Gould). We shall focus on Macphail's contribution because we believe that it represents an important challenge to the consensus of workers in this field about species differences in learning abilities and because it reflects on the problems of testing learning abilities.

## SOME HISTORICAL HIGHLIGHTS

The problems of comparing learning abilities among species and of evaluating the relative intelligence of different species have aroused speculation and stimulated research for over a century. As new methods have been introduced to attack these problems, as new evidence has been obtained, and as new criticisms have been leveled, the dominant opinion concerning species differences in learning ability and in intelligence has oscillated back and forth. As we shall see, differing views can still be held in the light of the available evidence. A few of the highlights in the history of the problem will be mentioned next, both to provide indications of how the field has progressed and because some earlier views resemble strongly some current views.

Darwin's follower Romanes (1883) tried to determine at what stages in evolution different abilities arose, using observational evidence. For certain faculties (e.g., imagination, abstraction) and for a number of abilities (e.g., formation of association by contiguity, reason, communication of ideas), Romanes indicated where in his scale of animals the ability first appeared (Table 17.1). Romanes' table suffers from acceptance of evidence that would certainly not meet modern standards and from his insistence on locating the emergence of human-like mental processes on a phyletic basis in an orderly arrangement of contemporary species. Furthermore, each phyletic group is treated as a unit with no consideration for the diversity that is at the heart of modern conceptions of evolution. However, the core idea of the gradual emergence of intellectual abilities as one moves "upward" on the "scale of nature" still hovers over this field in the present day.

At the end of the last century, Thorndike (1898) was the first to find a way to measure learning in animals. He proposed that basic mechanisms of learning and basic learning abilities are similar in different species. Then Hunter (1912), using his delayed response test, found evidence of differences in ability among species. Many researchers seized upon this method of scaling mental ability of species. By the middle 1930s, however, it had become apparent that the results obtained, in terms of the maximal possible delay, varied more as a function of the particular conditions of testing than as a function of the phyletic status of the species (Maier & Schnierla, 1935).

Pavlov's work on conditioning, especially when it was made the basis for Soviet psychology in 1950, appeared to provide a common mechanism

**TABLE 17.1.** Mental Evolution in Animals

| Faculties and abilities | Highest animals not showing the ability | Lowest animals showing the ability |
|---|---|---|
| Memory | Coelenterates | Echinoderms |
| Imagination | | |
| Association by contiguity | Annelids | Mollusks |
| Association by similarity | Insects | Fish and batrachia |
| Reason | Fish and batrachia | Higher crustacea |
| Communication of ideas | Reptiles and cephalopods | Hymenoptera |
| Abstraction | | |
| Understanding of mechanisms | Birds | Carnivora, rodents, and ruminants |
| Use of tools | Carnivora, rodents, and ruminants | Monkeys, cats, and elephant |
| Indefinite morality | Monkeys, cats, and elephant | Anthropoid apes and dog |

*Note.* Adapted and abridged from diagram in Romanes (1883).

for learning in a wide range of species. The only exception made from the start was for language, the second signal system, that human beings alone possess. As work on conditioning was pursued in a variety of vertebrate species, some qualitative species differences emerged, for example, in the rate of formation of multiple-component chain reflexes. Animals whose brains were taken as showing more complex evolution were found to acquire reversals and chain reactions more rapidly than simpler vertebrates, but "we can by no means state that there exists a specific qualitative difference between them. The point is that one and the same principle of individual adaptive reactions is of different significance on various levels of phylogenesis" (Voronin, 1962, p. 192). In modern birds and mammals, complex multistage temporary connections yield "concrete or image bearing thought," but only in man does the second signaling system "give rise to a new type of thought, namely, abstract thought" (p. 192).

The study of formation of learning sets (Harlow, 1949) appeared to offer a general-purpose intelligence test for animals. The improvement of children on a similar set of problems was found to be related to their intelligence as measured on an IQ test (Harter, 1965). A well-known compilation by Hodos (1970) of results of learning set studies with many species appeared to show large differences among species, and the ranking of species conformed in general to ideas about phylogenetic status. This compilation, rather than using absolute scores, measured the rate of improvement over large numbers of successive problems of the same general type. But closer attention to the studies showed that the different experimenters had used a variety of methods to train and test their subjects; for example, they gave different numbers of trials per problem, and this was found to affect the rapidity with which animals improve their performance in learning sets. Such criticisms threw into doubt again the possibility of comparing abilities of different species.

In an attempt to obtain as much as one could from the learning-set evidence, Passingham (1981) sought to find the largest set of results available for different species using the same method of training. Reports of experiments using six trials per problem were found for rhesus monkey, squirrel monkey, marmoset, cat, gerbil, rat, and squirrel. Among these species, the rhesus monkey was clearly the best; all three species of primates were better than the cat, and the cat's rate of improvement surpassed that of any of the three rodents. Thus, the results apparently support the existence of differences in "learning-to-learn" and intelligence among mammals. There does remain the concern that these experiments all used visual discrimination and may therefore have capitalized on the high visual acuity and color discrimination of primates. One study compared three species of platyrrhine monkeys using a common methodology and obtained significant species differences: Spider monkeys improved more rapidly than did cebus monkeys, and cebus monkeys more rapidly than squirrel monkeys (Shell & Riopelle, 1958).

Using a simpler sensory discrimination well within the sensory capacity of even nocturnal rodents, Riddell (1979) obtained a measure of flexibility in reversal learning for spatial and brightness cues. Successively better performance was shown by rats, shrews, squirrel monkeys, cebus monkeys, and people. When the behavioral index was plotted against a measure of encephalization (Nc, "extra" cortical neurons), a correlation of .94 was obtained. Passingham (1975) had reported a similar positive correlation between learning-set data in nine species of primates and a different index of encephalization (neocortical volume:medullary volume ratio). It should be noted that measures of encephalization such as Nc and the neorcortical:medullary volume ratio show more robust correlations with ability than does the encephalization quotient (EQ) on which Macphail focuses his discussion of brain measures and intelligence.

## MACPHAIL'S HYPOTHESIS

Differing sharply from the prevailing view, Macphail has proposed that, except for humans, species do not differ in intelligence and basic learning ability. Originally he proposed that this null hypothesis held for vertebrates (Macphail, 1982). In Chapter 15 (this volume) Macphail goes beyond his 1982 book in two ways: (1) He extends this hypothesis to invertebrates. (2) Accepting the lack of demonstration of differences in learning ability among species as proof that no such difference exists, Macphail asks how the essential similarity among species can be reconciled with differences among their ecologies. Differences in ecology have given rise to many other adaptive changes and might well have been expected to lead to species differences in learning abilities and intelligence. In answer to this question, he proposes that the mechanisms of formation of associations evolved early and proved so powerful in predicting events that these mechanisms were simply maintained without substantial change during evolution; subsequent improvements in problem-solving capacities, Macphail suggests, arose largely from improvements in sensory processing and in the variety and skill of motor responses.

In discussing Macphail's hypothesis and his examination of the data in this field, we shall restrict ourselves mainly to abilities to learn and remember, although we shall mention intelligence at some points.

## THE DISJUNCTION BETWEEN HUMAN BEINGS AND NONHUMAN VERTEBRATES

The same logic that Macphail has applied to possible differences among animals could be applied to the disjunction he sees between human beings and nonhuman vertebrates. Perhaps apes could be found to display the full range of human capacities if we were just better animal trainers? Certainly the history of language learning studies in apes gives considerable support to this argument. The chimpanzees trained by Gardner and Gardner (1984) have developed much larger vocabularies than the apes studied earlier by Kellogg and the Hayses. The chimpanzees of the Gardners' second set are only 5 years old at present, and, as they state, "It is clear that a 5-year-old chimpanzee is far from realizing the limits of chimpanzee intelligence and the full benefits of cross-fostering. The strongest conclusion that we can make about the results so far is that there is much more to be discovered about the continuity between human and non-human intelligence" (Gardner & Gardner, 1984, p. 403).

## ECOLOGICAL APPROACHES AND CONSTRAINTS ON LEARNING

During the early 1970s, information from such diverse areas as bird-song learning, bait-shyness learning, and imprinting coalesced to form a challenge to contemporary general-process views of learning. These particular cases were seen by many researchers as representing a more general proposition—that the learning capacities of species were tightly bound to their lifestyles in the habitats where they evolved. Some workers (e.g., Domjan & Galef, 1983; Johnston, 1981) have attempted to reconcile the specificity of the constraints literature with the search for generality. Others (e.g., Bitterman, 1975; Macphail, Chapter 15, this volume) have challenged the relevance of the constraints literature on a variety of grounds. For example, bird-song learning is often ignored as irrelevant to the issue of general intelligence, although there are theorists who believe it to be directly relevant (e.g., Rozin, 1976). The unique facets of bait-shyness learning are sometimes explained away as lacking proper controls, although again we judge the weight of evidence to favor the constraints position.

In Chapter 15 (this volume) Macphail focuses upon two issues in the constraints literature: (1) The remarkable memorial abilities of food-storing birds such as Clark's nutcrackers and marsh tits, and (2) the win-shift behavior of animals in various tests following food reward. We agree with Macphail's call for the appropriate comparative data, employing species in whom spatial memory for food stores or win–shift behavior would not be predicted by their ecology. Some work testing hypotheses that relate species differences in lifestyle to their individual learning abilities has begun to appear (e.g., Daly, Rauschenberger, & Behrends, 1982). However, there are some cautionary notes to be sounded with regard to interpretation of the available data.

First, a major part of the nutcracker case is built upon the spontaneity and speed of their learning of cache locations. Should non-food-storing species prove to be capable of broad memorial performance but only following a much larger number of experimenter-controlled trials, that would be very interesting but would clearly have different implications for survival in nature.

Second, we rarely have the detailed ecological information that would permit the further, more decisive studies that all of us would like to see. For example, consider the issue that Macphail raises in regard to the logically expected differences in responses to food rewards and water rewards. Macphail argues that win–shift behavior might be expected to follow food reward (assuming food to be a variable resource), whereas win–stay behavior should occur after water reward (presumably because water is a stable, replenishing resource). However, despite Macphail's apparently negative evidence concerning the occurrence of such differences, there are some reasons to pursue the question further. For example, there is evidence suggesting that alternation behavior in rats varies differentially as a result of food or water deprivation (Petrinovich & Bolles, 1954). The subsequent report (Bolles & Petrinovich, 1956) indicating that this was an artifact of weight loss need not be viewed as artifactual *if* the appropriate weight losses commonly cued searching for food or searching for water. What is generally lacking in much of the constraints literature to date is a thorough understanding of the patterns of behavior and their surrounding conditions in nature. For example, when we think of animals obtaining water, the most common image is a visit to the shore of a pond, lake, or stream. But some terrestrial and many aquatic animals obtain their water exclusively from food, and many other terrestrial animals obtain a large part of their water in this way. For a California vole, the evidence suggests that it obtains water in the summer by arising early to lick the dew from grasses (Pearson, 1960). The point here is that we need much more detailed natural habitat knowledge before we can set up the appropriate laboratory studies to really test ecological hypotheses. Again, this seems to be an area that calls for more and better comparative work, rather than acceptance of the null hypothesis.

## KINDS OF LEARNING TO BE CONSIDERED

In evaluating learning of different species, Macphail uses four categories of learning: habituation, classical conditioning, instumental conditioning, and a grab-bag residual category called "complex learning." He uses a number of specific kinds of complex learning that have been used to compare species, for example, serial reversal learning, formation of learning sets, and probability learning. While these are all worth considering, it should be pointed out that most investigators and theorists now believe that for complex (even verbal) material there are at least two and perhaps several major memory systems. Some of these have been mentioned by contributors to the volume reporting the previous Irvine Conference (Lynch, McGaugh, & Weinberger, 1984) and this volume. Tulving (1985) notes the consensus on plurality of memory systems as follows:

> Just about everyone agrees on the reality of a major division between procedural memory (stimulus–response memory, associative memory) on the one hand and the "other kind" on the other. The currently popular open question has to do with what this "other kind" is and whether it is one or two. Many investigators say "one." Different versions corresponding to the "one" position have been promulgated or approvingly mentioned. . . . Some others say "two." . . . A large majority of the students of learning and memory have yet to join the debate on either side.

In this and the previous volume (Lynch *et al.*, 1984), dichotomies of this sort have been presented:

| Associative memory | Cognitive memory | Reference |
|---|---|---|
| Procedural | Declarative | (N.J. Cohen, Chapter 22, this volume; Squire & Cohen, 1984) |
| Habit | Memory | (Mishkin, Malamut, & Bachevelier, 1984) |

Returning to the usage of the last century, such as that employed by William James, a habit is defined as a noncognitive stimulus–response bond, whereas a memory is cognitive information. Not only does this distinction relate to unconscious versus conscious aspects of learning and memory, but also to multitrial repetitive learning versus rapid (even single-trial) learning, to effortful versus effortless learning, and to long-term reliability versus short-term flexibility. There is also evidence that different brain regions subserve the two kinds of learning. Thus, people with damage to the medial temporal lobe who can no longer form memories of occurrences can nevertheless form habits, including some verbal habits. Furthermore, there is good evidence that the habit system matures earlier than the memory system, and Mishkin believes that it evolved earlier.

If this set of distinction holds, it would seem to have important implications for our topic. It suggests that it would be worthwhile to compare species for possible differences in the ability to form associations and also for possible differences in the ability to form cognitive representations; two species might be equal in ability to form habits but differ in the ability to form memories. There may well be species that can form habits but not memories; if so, this should be reflected in the lesser rapidity and power of their learning—or of their intelligence—as compared with species that do form memories.

Tulving (1985) suggests that the number of learning and memory systems is "at least three, and probably many more." Furthermore, it is possible, and even likely, that the more demanding types are more narrowly distributed among species. Thus, for example, Premack (1983) has reviewed evidence indicating that certain kinds of problems can be learned and solved in terms of representation in the form of images whereas other problems require abstract representation. In tasks solved by rats and pigeons and for which representation appears necessary (e.g., spatial location and temporal order), the representation could be of the imaginal kind. But certain tasks that primates can solve (e.g., same/different judgments about analogies) require the use of an abstract code. "The lack of . . . evidence [for abstract representation] in nonprimates, along with the improbability of obtaining it, is compatible with the view that these species have only imaginal representations" (Premack, 1983, pp. 360–361).

## QUANTITATIVE AND QUALITATIVE DIFFERENCES

Evidence has been presented for both quantitative and qualitative differences in learning ability and intelligence among species, but Macphail does not find either sort of evidence to be convincing. For example, in discussing research with learning sets, he concludes that the findings do not afford "evidence . . . for qualitative differences between species" (Macphail, 1982, p. 281). Furthermore, unlike such workers as Voronin, who found quantitative but not qualitative differences, Macphail discounts quantitative differences by showing that they can be influenced by the specific procedures employed in the experiments and maintains that it is most parsimonious to generalize this and reject the hypothesis of quantitative differences in intelligence between the various species (1982, p. 334). Because it is clear to other reviewers that when comparable procedures are used, there are large quantitative differences among species, both in the rate of improvement in learning problems of the same basic type and in the final level of performance obtained, it is worth considering this question: Are quantitative differences likely to be of significance for individual behavior and for evolution?

There is abundant evidence that quantitative differences in bodily structure and in behavior are important for survival. That greater abilities to learn and remember also confer selective benefits is widely believed. The small amount of evidence that Johnston (1982) was able to locate by which to test this hypothesis was consistent with it, but Johnston stressed "the paucity of ecologically motivated studies of learning" (p. 74). Certainly for many species under natural conditions, abilities to learn and remember have survival value. For example, birds that cache food (Shettleworth, Chapter 13, this volume; Kamil & Balda, in press) depend on memory for their caches to obtain sustenance during the winter. Experimenters who have tested numbers of birds or mammals of the same species testify to large and reliable individual differences in abilities to learn and remember, and presumably this affects individual survival and reproductive success. Selection programs based on quantitative differences in learning ability among laboratory rats have led, within a few generations, to large and significant differences. Occasional mutations among *Drosophila* have been found to affect learning and memory (Quinn & Greenspan, 1984). Originally some of these mutants were thought to be incapable of learning; more careful testing has now shown that they can learn but they forget much more rapidly than do wild-type flies. Thus, the difference that was thought to be qualitative has turned out to be quantitative, but this has not lessened the significance of the biochemical alterations in these mutant flies for understanding neurochemical processes in memory. We conclude that even if there turned out to be no qualitative differences among species in learning, memory, and intelligence—and we doubt that—nevertheless the quantitative differences that exist are important for both individual behavior and for evolution of behavior and its neural bases.

## COMMENTS ON GAPS IN THE DATA AND IN THE REVIEW

At various points in his book, and in Chapter 15 (this volume), Macphail notes that data are lacking that would permit a thorough test of the hypothesis. He reacts to such gaps in two ways, one of which we agree with and the other of which we do not. An example of the first sort occurs when Macphail points out that the importance of good memory in food-storing birds will be clear only when there is "direct evidence that the memory of these animals differs from that of birds that do not store food" (Chapter 15, this volume, p. 281). As discussed earlier, we agree that the design of such studies must be complete before any conclusion can be drawn with confidence, but we have also pointed out that better knowledge of behavior in natural habitats will be needed before crucial laboratory tests can be set up. An example of the second sort occurs when Macphail states that "although no efforts have been made to train amphibians on anything but relatively simple tasks, [there is] no direct comparative evidence that amphibians are either inferior or superior to any other group of vertebrates" (1982, p. 132). This lack of data may well not be accidental. Instead, it probably reflects the highly reasoned intuitions of experienced comparative psychologists. The burden of proof—that amphibia can not only demonstrate such feats as formation of learning sets but can do so at the level of a chimpanzee—would seem to fall on Macphail and those of similar opinion.

Some comments also seem in order concerning the completeness of Macphail's review and the way in which it attempts to integrate findings. Macphail's book is a scholarly review that cites about 1000 references. Nevertheless, in spite of its impressive scope, the book cannot cite all the pertinent studies, and we were often left wondering why some of our "favorite" studies (such as Passingham, 1981, and Riddell, 1979) were not taken into account. Furthermore, in areas in which there are either conflicting reports or suggestive but nonsignificant differences, Macphail discusses the findings in rather informal ways, usually concluding that no significant difference can be shown. Such incomplete and informal reviews are the norm, but there are now quantitative methods to summarize and analyze research literature, as reviewed by Green and Hall (1984). Such methods are variously called meta-analysis, research integration, and quantitative assessment of research domains. Features of such methods include attempts to locate and consider all of the relevant literature and also methods of combining statistics from different studies. These methods have been applied productively to such controversial topics as sex differences in personality and the effectiveness of psychotherapy, and they may well prove helpful in investigations of comparative behavior.

## CONCLUSIONS

On the basis of his analysis of the existent data, Macphail urges acceptance of the null hypothesis, that is, "that no between-species difference in learning or memory, attributable to a difference in ecological niche, has yet been demonstrated in either invertebrates or vertebrates" (Chapter 15, this volume, p. 284). We see many reasons to reject this course. Perhaps the primary reason is that "acceptance," in the broad sense, is not generative of the appropriate sort of research. In addition, as we have illustrated in this brief chapter, there are data that support such differences in some cases, and there are gaps in data sets that make conclusions premature in other cases. Virtually any behavioral literature in psychology, when scrutinized carefully, can be shown to demand further work. Given the methodological and conceptual complexities of comparative studies of learning abilities and intelligence, it is not surprising that Macphail has located such problems with the existent data set. But we find Macphail's admonition to be discordant with the general trends in the data set and also likely to dampen rather than encourage fruitful research.

Based on the evidence and conceptualizations reviewed in this and related papers at this conference, we offer the following tentative conclusions as consistent with the available evidence:

1. Certain kinds of nonassociative learning (habituation and sensitization) and of associative learning (classical and instrumental conditioning) occur throughout the vertebrates and also widely among arthropods and mollusks and perhaps some other phyla.

2. Cognitive learning (formation of declarative memories or "memories" in the Jamesian sense) occurs in primates and some other, but not all, mammals. It also occurs in some "large-brained" species of other phyla, for example, in some cephalopods.

3. Not only qualitative differences in abilities to learn and remember but also quantitative differences can be important for individual behavior and for evolution.

4. Further exploration seems in order with regard to the hypotheses offered by some investigators, such as Premack (1983), that particular complex cognitive abilites are found only within a few selected species.[1]

---

1. *Note added in proof*: Some theorists have claimed recently that the term "genetic constraints on learning" derives from the commitment of most psychologists to general process learning theory and that this concept is now outdated (Gould & Marler, in press; Jenkins, 1984). Rather than supposing that the genes of certain species constrain their general ability to learn and thereby make them selectively stupid, these workers hold it more likely that evolution creates specific learning abilities where these are needed. Several examples of bird species that do or do not learn to recognize their eggs or young are analyzed from the point of view of selective learning routines rather than constraints.

## REFERENCES


Bitterman, M. E. The comparative analysis of learning. *Science*, 1975, *188*, 699–709.

Bolles, R. C., & Petrinovich, L. Body weight changes and behavioral attributes. *Journal of Comparative and Physiological Psychology*, 1956, *49*, 177–180.

Daly, M., Rauschenberger, J., & Behrends, P. Food aversion learning in kangaroo rats: A specialist–generalist comparison. *Animal Learning and Behavior*, 1982, *10*, 314–320.

Domjan, M., & Galef, B. G. Biological constraints on instrumental and classical conditioning: Retrospect and prospect. *Animal Learning and Behavior*, 1983, *11*, 151–161.

Gardner, R. A., & Gardner, B. T. A vocabulary test for chimpanzees (*Pan troglodytes*). *Journal of Comparative Psychology*, 1984, *98*, 381–404.

Gould, J. L., & Marler, P. The biology of learning. *Annual Review of Psychology*, in press.

Green, B. F., & Hall, J. A. Quantitative methods for literature reviews. *Annual Review of Psychology*, 1984, *35*, 37–53.

Harlow, H. F. The formation of learning sets. *Psychological Review*, 1949, *56*, 51–65.

Harter, S. Discrimination learning set in children as a function of intelligence and mental age. *Journal of Experimental Child Psychology*, 1965, *2*, 31–43.

Hodos, W. Evolutionary interpretation of neural and behavioral studies of living vertebrates. In F. O. Schmitt (Ed.), *The neurosciences* (Vol. 2). New York: Rockefeller University Press, 1970.

Hunter, W. S. The delayed reaction in animals and children. *Behavior Monographs*, 1912, *2*, 1–85.

Jenkins, H. M. The study of animal learning in the tradition of Pavlov and Thorndike. In P. Marler & H. Terrace (Eds.), *The biology of learning*. Berlin: Springer-Verlag, 1984.

Johnston, T. D. Contrasting approaches to a theory of learning. *Behavioral and Brain Sciences*, 1981, *4*, 125–173.

Johnston, T. D. Selective costs and benefits in the evolution of learning. In J. S. Rosenblatt, R. A. Hinde, C. Beer, & M.-C. Busnel (Eds.), *Advances in the study of behavior* (Vol. 12). New York: Academic Press, 1982.

Kamil, A. C., & Balda, R. C. Cache recovery and spatial memory of Clark's nutcrackers (*Nucifraga columbiana*). *Journal of Experimental Psychology: Animal Behavior Processes*, in press.

Lynch, G., McGaugh, J. L., & Weinberger, N. M. (Eds.). *Neurobiology of learning and memory*. New York: Guilford Press, 1984.

Macphail, E. M. *Brain and intelligence in vertebrates*. London: Oxford University Press, 1982.

Maier, N. R. F., & Schnierla, T. C. *Principles of animal psychology*. New York: McGraw-Hill, 1935.

Mishkin, M., Malamut, B., & Bachevalier, J. Memories and habits: Two neural systems. In G. Lynch, J. L. McGaugh, & N. M. Weinberger (Eds.), *Neurobiology of learning and memory*. New York: Guilford Press, 1984.

Passingham, R. E. The brain and intelligence. *Brain, Behavior and Evolution*, 1975, *11*, 1–15.

Passingham, R. E. (1981). Primate specializations in brain and intelligence. *Symposia of the Zoological Society of London*, 1981, *46*, 361–388.

Pearson, O. P. Habits of *Microtus californicus* revealed by automatic photographic records. *Ecological Monographs*, 1960, *30*, 231–249.

Petrinovich, L., & Bolles, R. C. Deprivation states and behavioral attributes. *Journal of Comparative and Physiological Psychology*, 1954, *47*, 450–453.

Premack, D. Animal cognition. *Annual Review of Psychology*, 1983, *34*, 351–362.

Quinn, W. G., & Greenspan, R. J. Learning and courtship in *Drosophila*: Two stories with mutants. *Annual Review of Neuroscience*, 1984, *7*, 67–93.

Riddell, W. I. Cerebral indices and behavioral differences. In M. E. Hahn, C. Jensen, & B. C. Dudek (Eds.), *Development and evolution of brain size: Behavioral implications*. New York: Academic Press, 1979.

Romanes, G. J. *Animal intelligence*. New York: Appleton, 1883.

Rozin, P. The evolution of intelligence and access to the cognitive unconscious. In J. M. Sprague & A. N. Epstein (Eds.), *Progress in psychobiology and physiological psychology* (Vol. 6). New York: Academic Press, 1976.

Shell, W. F., & Riopelle, A. J. Progressive discrimination learning in platyrrhine monkeys. *Journal of Comparative and Physiological Psychology*, 1958, *51*, 467–470.

Squire, L. R., & Cohen, N. J. Human memory and amnesia. In G. Lynch, J. L. McGaugh, & N. M. Weinberger (Eds.), *Neurobiology of learning and memory*. New York: Guilford Press, 1984.

Thorndike, E. L. Animal intelligence: An experimental study of the associative processes in animals. *Psychological Review, Monograph Supplement*, 1898, *2*, 1–109.

Tulving, E. How many memory systems are there? *American Psychologist*, 1985, *40*.

Voronin, L. G. Some results of comparative physiological investigations of higher nervous activity. *Psychological Bulletin*, 1962, *59*, 161–195.

SECTION III

# LEARNING, MEMORY, AND COGNITIVE PROCESSES

CHAPTER 18

# Re-Viewing Modulation of Learning and Memory

**Michela Gallagher**
University of North Carolina, Chapel Hill

The term "modulation" is frequently encountered in recent research on the neurobiology of learning and memory. References to modulation are found in work on elementary forms of learning in simple invertebrate systems (Krasne, 1978; Walters & Byrne, 1983). Modulation is considered to serve a function in regulating several specific forms of neural plasticity in the mammalian brain (Bliss, Goddard, & Riives, 1983; Kasamatsu & Pettigrew, 1976). In research using considerably more complex behavioral tasks, the same term is called upon to account for the sensitivity of memory to a variety of pharmacological treatments (Gold & McGaugh, 1978; Kety, 1976; McGaugh & Gold, 1976). In surveying the breadth of neurobiological research on learning and memory, the concept of modulation might appear, at present, to provide one of the more unifying themes in the field. Although various approaches to the study of learning and memory are conducted at different levels of behavioral and/or neural analysis, the emergence of the concept of modulation appears to have signaled, in each case, a reorientation in thinking about the organization and function of biological mechanisms underlying learning and memory. An example from work on a simple invertebrate system will serve to illustrate some of the general properties ascribed to modulation.

The neural circuitry considered to underlie differential classical conditioning in a model invertebrate system is illustrated in Figure 18.1. The neural mechanisms involved in learning in this preparation represent an example of activity-dependent neuromodulation. When a conditioned stimulus (CS+) is delivered repeatedly to one input pathway in temporal contiguity with presentation of a strong unconditioned stimulus (US) to another pathway, a change occurs at synaptic connections in the CS+ pathway. In this system, the changes at synapses in the CS+ pathway are not governed solely by the pattern of activity at the synapses that become altered. Rather these changes are also regulated by another source of input that modulates

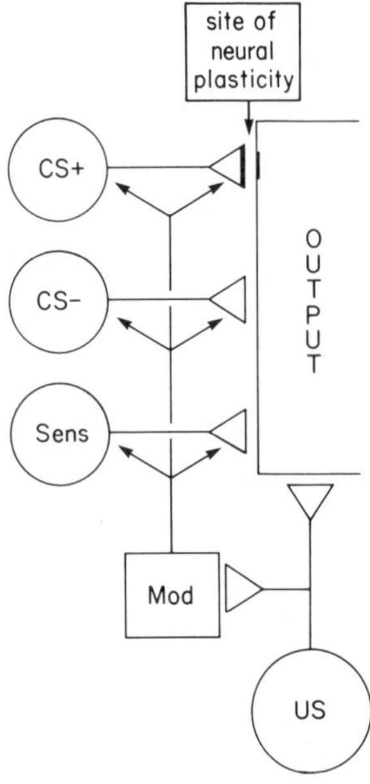


**FIGURE 18.1.** Schematic representation of activity-dependent neuromodulation during differential classical conditioning in a model invertebrate preparation. (Adapted from Walters & Byrne, 1983.)

change. Note that the modulating system is depicted as being sensitive to the US input but is not represented as part of the sensory system devoted to processing the US. The modulating system is, in addition, characterized as having widespread access to many different input pathways that could process other events presented during training. During conditioning the plasticity that occurs at selected sites is due to an optimal effect of the modulatory system on a recently activated set of connections.

From a neurobiological point of view, a primary function of modulators is to determine whether "synapses that are able to change their properties as a result of particular configurations of activity, will actually do so" (Krasne, 1978). The theoretical implications of modulation of neural plasticity are significant. Neurons that become functionally altered are not the sole source of candidate mechanisms for preserving information in the nervous system. A description of the biological process by which the nervous system is altered may include not only the sites and circuits where changes in synaptic function occur but also the action of other neural systems that impinge upon them.

The schematic depiction in Figure 18.1 could reflect an additional feature of modulatory systems that would be of considerable interest. In this model invertebrate preparation, the modulatory system is represented as being sensitive to an input that is capable of supporting conditioning, that is, a strong reinforcing US. If some modulatory systems were solely or especially sensitive to inputs that possess reinforcing properties, then the neural plasticity governed by such modulators could be regulated by the reinforcing dimensions of experiences. This view was indeed first proposed in some of the earliest discussions about modulation in neurobiological research on learning and memory. A brief presentation of the background from which this idea originally arose, followed by a consideration of some more current investigations, may broaden our understanding of the behavioral significance of modulation beyond the motivational/reinforcement framework that has predominated up to this point.

## MODULATION: THE EVOLUTION OF A CONCEPT

The earliest references to the concept of modulation in the field of learning and memory are found in research that was originally designed to investigate memory consolidation. In this research the phenomenon of retrograde amnesia had become well documented in laboratory animals by the early 1970s. Administration of a variety of treatments shortly after training produced subsequent alterations in retention. Initially this research was directed toward determining the specific sites and mechanisms that preserve information in the brain. In the earliest theoretical formulations, the posttraining period of susceptibility to amnestic treatments was proposed to reflect the time course for the formation of a long-term memory for the training experience (McGaugh, 1966). Posttraining treatments were viewed as acting on a biological storage process that would represent the content of memory independent of the many other functions that operate during training, that is, sensory processing, arousal, attention, and motivation. It became clear, however, that posttraining treatments may not necessarily reveal the identity of systems that contain information in memory. For example, it was found that the functional state of hormonal systems outside the brain could profoundly alter time-dependent memory processes (see McGaugh, 1983, for a recent review). By the mid-1970s the notion of modulation of memory emerged in this research to signal a significant reorientation in thinking about the organization and function of biological systems that influence memory. It was proposed that the neurobiological events underlying the preservation of information (i.e., the content of memory) could be influenced by other "nonspecific" systems (Kety, 1970; McGaugh & Gold, 1976). The activity in such nonspecific systems was envisioned to "affect synapses generally but with a greater effect on those recently activated, displaying some reverberating or 'hot-tube' quality" (Kety, 1976). In agreement with current descriptions in studies of neural plasticity, modulating systems were originally proposed to regulate changes in synaptic connections that could provide a basis for preserving recently acquired information.

The functional significance of memory modulation was also considered in early expositions of this concept. It was, in fact, proposed that the activity of modulators might be particularly attuned to the motivational/reinforcing aspects of training (Kety, 1976). According to this proposal, modulation could serve an adaptive role in selecting to preserve information derived from "significant experiences." The activation of modulating systems, particularly by rewarding or aversive events, would lead to an enhancement of neural plasticity that would ensure good memory. Conversely, those experiences that had negligible impact on an animal in failing to adequately activate modulators would be less likely to be preserved. It should be noted that this hypothesis was, at the time, consistent with some experimental findings. For example, pituitary–adrenal hormones that were implicated in the modulation of memory processes could be activated by the kinds of stimulus events typically used to support conditioning such as exposure to footshock. More recent work has provided further evidence that the responsiveness of some systems can vary with parametric manipulations of the aversive stimulus used during training. A case in point is illustrated by the work of Gold and his colleagues on epinephrine function (see Zornetzer & Gold, 1983, for a recent review of this work).

Originally it was found that posttraining epinephrine administration could alter subsequent retention of avoidance conditioning. More recently, Gold and his colleagues observed that following passive avoidance training, plasma levels of epinephrine (EPI) normally differ in animals that receive different intensities of footshock during conditioning. When a low intensity of footshock that normally supports rather weak retention is used, plasma levels of EPI measured after training are relatively low. Following training in which a more intense footshock that produces higher retention scores is used, plasma levels of EPI are also higher. If animals trained with the lower footshock receive posttraining injections of EPI, increased retention can be obtained with doses that elevate plasma EPI to the levels normally found following a high footshock training procedure. These results are consistent with the idea that epinephrine secretion constitutes a physiological response to the aversive stimulus used during training and that retention can vary depending upon the magnitude of the epinephrine response elicited during training. Another interesting finding in this research is that posttraining treatments that produce very high levels of plasma EPI, caused by either administering a high EPI dose or combining a lower dose with high footshock, can result in impaired retention. This type of dose–response function, which is observed with quite a number of other posttraining treatments, has been associated with the detrimental effects of high arousal levels on performance that are also characterized by U-shaped curves (Eysenck, 1982). Although these results are generally consistent with the view that memory modulation can occur through systems that are sensitive to the motivational/reinforcing aspects of training, they do not indicate whether such modulators are attuned to any specific reinforcement parameters of experience or are more generally sensitive to events that elicit arousal.

It is interesting that another approach to determining whether systems that modify retention are specifically attuned to reinforcement parameters has rarely been followed in this type of work. In particular, it would be of interest to investigate whether posttraining treatments are effective across tasks that entail the use of different reinforcement contingencies. In recent work conducted in several different laboratories, including our own, it appears that, in at least one instance, a system that is sensitive to posttraining manipulations can influence retention irrespective of whether reinforcement is either rewarding or aversive. Of even greater interest are the results of studies on this system in which the learning that is modulated can be characterized by the absence of reinforcement, that is, habituation and latent inhibition. The results of this research do not appear to fit within a motivational/reinforcement framework. It is perhaps surprising that this conclusion can be drawn from research on opioid peptides because traditionally many of the effects of opiates, and more recently opioid peptides, have been viewed within a motivational/reinforcement framework (Gallagher & Kapp, 1981; Mondadori & Waser, 1979; Stein & Belluzzi, 1979).

## FUNCTIONAL SIGNIFICANCE OF MODULATION: RE-VIEWING OPIOID PEPTIDES

In a number of studies using aversive tasks it was initially found that posttraining administration of morphine at very low doses impaired retention (Barrati, Introini, & Huygens, 1984; Castellano, 1975; Castellano & Pavone, 1984; Castellano, Pavone, & Puglisi-Allegra, 1984; Izquierdo, 1979; Jensen *et al.*, 1978; Messing, Rigter, & Nickolson, 1982). This effect of morphine was subsequently found to be shared by several opioid peptides (Izquierdo, 1980; Izquierdo & Dias, 1981; Izquierdo, Paiva, & Elisabetsky, 1980; Lucion, Rosito, Sapper, Palmini, & Izquierdo, 1982; Martinez & Rigter, 1980; Tazi, Dantzer, Mormede, & Le Moal, 1983). Evidence that endogenous opioid peptides normally influence retention was then provided by numerous reports that posttraining administration of naloxone, as well as other opiate antagonists, could increase retention when aversive training procedures were used (Barrati *et al.*, 1984; Carrasco, Dias, & Izquierdo, 1982; Castellano, 1981; Fulginiti & Cancella, 1983; Gallagher, 1982; Izquierdo, 1979; Messing *et al.*, 1979; Messing, Rijk, & Rigter, 1983; Tazi *et al.*, 1983). Figure 18.2 depicts the results of one experiment in which a number of different opiate antagonists were administered following passive avoidance conditioning (Gallagher, 1982).

In interpreting these findings, it was frequently emphasized that opiates are capable of attenuating affective responses to aversive stimuli (e.g., see Gallagher & Kapp, 1981). In addition, in light of evidence that opioid peptides can be activated by noxious or stressful events (Madden, Akil, Patrick, & Barchas, 1977), it was reasonable to regard opioid peptides as capable of providing an endogenous mechanism that could attenuate the impact of aversive experiences on an animal. In this context the effects of posttraining opiate antagonists, by interfering with opioid peptide function, could be

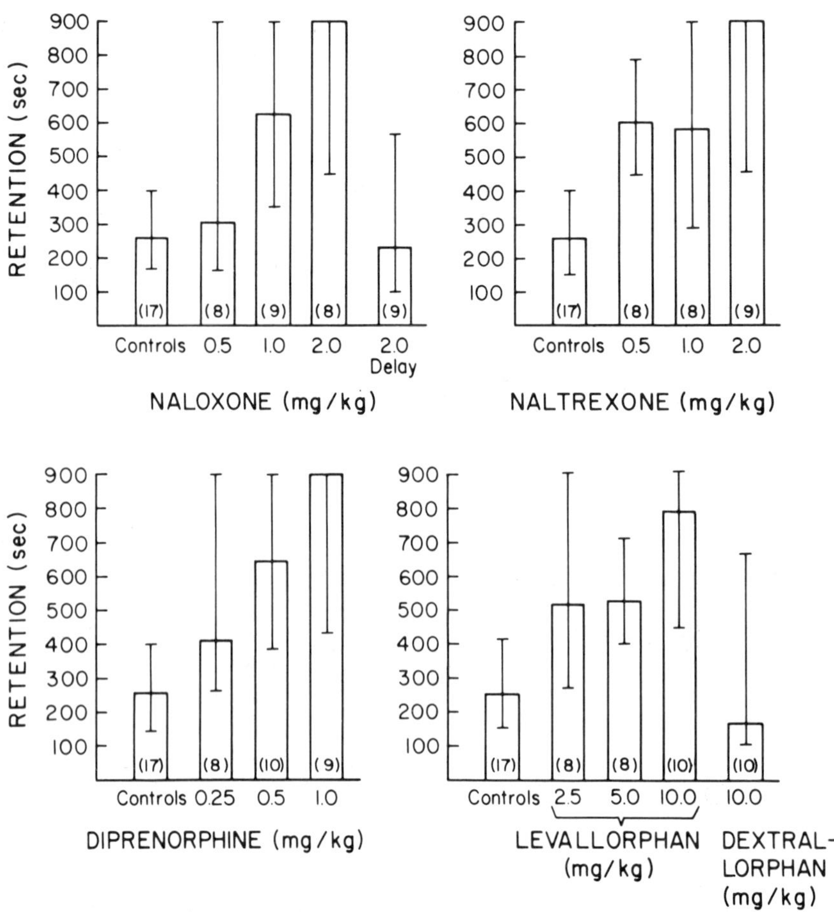


**FIGURE 18.2.** Effects of posttraining opiate antagonist administration on retention of one-trial step through passive avoidance conditioning. Median retention latencies and interquartile ranges are indicated for groups of rats. (From Gallagher, 1982. Reprinted by permission.)

viewed as augmenting the motivational/reinforcing effects of aversive conditioning. As appears to be the case with EPI, the increased retention latencies for passive avoidance produced by opiate antagonists might also reflect an augmentation of the posttraining physiological effects of footshock. Even within the context of experiments using aversive conditioning procedures, this interpretation has recently been questioned because, unlike EPI and a number of other posttraining treatments, opiate antagonists do not appear to interact with parametric manipulations of the aversive stimulus used during training. This point is illustrated in a recent study by Izquierdo and Dias (1983). In a passive avoidance experiment in which a low-intensity footshock was used, posttraining administration of EPI, adrenocorticotropic hormone (ACTH), or naloxone increased subsequent retention latencies. When a second passive avoidance experiment was conducted using a high footshock that elevated the retention latencies in the control group, retention deficits were observed in groups that received EPI and ACTH but not in the group that was injected with naloxone after training. In fact, when posttraining administration of naloxone was added to either the EPI or the ACTH posttraining treatment in this experiment, high retention latencies were reinstated (see Table 18.1). At least, manipulations of opioid peptide function do not appear to interact with the intensity of aversive stimuli used during training in a manner comparable to that observed with some other posttraining treatments.

By far the more striking feature of this work now being conducted using opiate treatments, however, is the broad range of testing conditions in which comparable effects on retention are being found. Opiate antagonists, for example, can produce improved retention when rewarding contingencies rather than aversive contingencies occur during training. In an initial set of experiments, we examined the effects of opiate antagonist treatment on retention of a food-rewarded spatial learning task using the eight-arm radial maze (Gallagher, King, & Young, 1983). The training procedure was based on that originally introduced by Olton and Samuelson (1976), in which rats are trained to visit each arm of the maze once during a session in order to obtain a pellet of food placed at the end of each arm. In our experiments we took advantage of the fact that in performing this task rats normally use extramaze cues provided by spatial information in the room surrounding the testing apparatus. Another notable feature of the performance of rats on this task is that animals can exhibit good retention of the initial arm choices when a delay is introduced between the fourth and fifth arm choices. In a number of laboratories, including our own, rats have been found to remember the initial four arm choices and accurately choose the remaining

**TABLE 18.1.** Retention of Passive Avoidance Conditioning following Posttraining Treatments

| | | Training-test step-down latency treatment | |
|---|---|---|---|
| Treatment | *n* | Median (sec) | Mean (sec) |
| Saline | 13 | 180.00 | 108.37 |
| $ACTH_{1-24}$ (2.0 μg/kg) | 10 | 1.53 | 2.64 |
| Epinephrine (50.0 μg/kg) | 11 | 9.53 | 31.54 |
| Naloxone (.4 mg/kg) | 13 | 180.00 | 180.00 |
| $ACTH_{1-24}$ + naloxone | 10 | 180.00 | 144.45 |
| Epinephrine + naloxone | 10 | 180.00 | 134.98 |

*Note.* From Izquierdo and Dias (1983). Reprinted by permission.

four arms at delays up to approximately 6 hours (Beatty & Shavalia, 1980; Gallagher *et al.*, 1983).

In our experiments rats were initially trained on an eight-arm radial maze to a criterion performance consisting of no more than two errors on three consecutive days, using a 6-hour delay imposed between the fourth and fifth arm choices. Experimental testing occurred following this initial training when rats were challenged by placing the maze in new spatial environments. The effects of posttraining opiate antagonist treatment on the development of criterion performance in new spatial environments are presented in Table 18.2. In this experiment two groups of rats were used to assess the effects of two different opiate antagonists, naloxone and diprenorphine. Both groups received initial training and then both groups were tested in two novel environments. For each group, an opiate antagonist—either naloxone (2 mg/kg) or diprenorphine (1 mg/kg)—was administered following the first four arm choices in one of the new rooms, and posttraining injections of the saline–vehicle were administered when rats were tested in the other room. The order of opiate antagonist and saline treatments was counterbalanced for both groups. Compared to the saline–vehicle treatment, posttraining opiate antagonist administration enhanced maze performance. Every animal in the naloxone treatment group took fewer trials to reach criterion and fewer errors when compared to the performance of the same animals in the vehicle condition. These results are part of a growing body of evidence indicating that opiate antagonists can improve performance irrespective of whether the reinforcement contingencies during training are aversive or rewarding. In other research there is evidence that enhanced retention can be produced by these same agents when animals are exposed to nonreinforced events. The results of these experiments may be particularly important in understanding the functional role of opioid peptides in memory processes because in such tasks (i.e., habituation, latent

**TABLE 18.2.** Effects of Posttraining Opiate Antagonist Administration on Maze Performance

| Experiments and treatments | Trials to criterion[a] | Errors to criterion[a] |
|---|---|---|
| Experiment A ($n = 8$) | | |
| Saline treatment | 5.38 ± .71 | 12.0 ± 2.89 |
| Naloxone treatment (2 mg/kg) | 3.25 ± .63[b] | 4.4 ± 2.74[b] |
| Experiment B ($n = 10$) | | |
| Saline treatment | 4.90 ± .70 | 12.2 ± 3.03 |
| Diprenorphine treatment (1 mg/kg) | 3.60 ± .49[b] | 5.8 ± 2.89[b] |

*Note.* From Gallagher, King, and Young (1983). Copyright 1983 by the American Association for the Advancement of Science. Reprinted by permission.

[a] Values given are means ± *SEM*.

[b] $p < .005$ when compared to saline-treatment condition.

inhibition) any increment in the arousal of the animal induced by environmental stimuli or the action of a drug could be expected to interfere with normal retention.

Izquierdo (1979) first examined the effects of posttraining administration of morphine and naloxone on a measure of long-term habituation in rats. The training experience consisted of a single session in which a neutral auditory stimulus was repeatedly presented. As a component of the orienting response, rats were observed to exhibit a rearing response to the initial tone presentations. When normal animals were presented with a second session of tone presentations 24 hours later, less rearing was observed, reflecting long-term habituation to the tone stimulus. Posttraining administration of morphine following tone presentations on the first day was found to decrease retention of habituation as reflected in the amount of rearing on the second test day, in which the behavior of drug-treated animals was roughly equivalent to that observed during the initial session. Posttraining opiate antagonist administration, on the other hand, apparently increased retention of habituation; these animals exhibited significantly less rearing during the second session than the control group.

Another testing procedure used by Rodgers, Richards, and Precious (1984) has recently yielded rather similar results. In their study, mice were tested for a 5-minute session in an open field over which time a modest decline in activity was observed. After removal from the open field, mice in the experimental groups were injected with different doses of naloxone ranging from .1 to 10 mg/kg. All animals were retested in the open field 24 hours later for a 5-minute session. The groups that received naloxone, even at the lowest dose, exhibited lower levels of activity and less rearing than the control group with no differences observed among the groups on a measure of defecation. In this study, additional experiments demonstrated that the effective doses of naloxone in the open field test did not exhibit any aversive properties in tests for place preference or conditioned taste aversion, a result leading these authors to conclude that the opiate antagonist could be acting on a memory process reflected in enhanced familiarity with the testing environment.

Finally, we have begun to examine the effects of posttraining opiate treatments upon another measure that can be used to assess retention of exposure to nonreinforced events. The phenomenon of latent inhibition (LI) is observed when animals are exposed to repeated presentations of a neutral stimulus later to be used as a CS. The preexposure effect is reflected in a subsequent decrement in conditioning referred to as LI (Lubow, 1973). In the LI experiments we are conducting, opiate treatments are administered after the animals are preexposed to repeated presentations of an auditory stimulus. Retention of the preexposure experience is then measured 24 hours later when the auditory stimulus is used as a CS in a standard Pavlovian conditioning task. These experiments are being conducted using rabbits as subjects, and the behavioral measure of LI is a classically conditioned heart rate response produced by pairings of an auditory CS with a shock US.

In the first LI experiment we conducted, we found the conditioned heart rate response (CR) to be quite sensitive to CS preexposure. When rabbits received 45 presentations of the CS prior to the day on which conditioning occurred, a large decrement in the development of CRs was observed in the LI groups. Nonetheless, injection of naloxone following preexposure was found to result in a significantly greater LI effect (Bostock & Gallagher, 1982). This finding was recently replicated in our laboratory using a smaller number of tone presentations. The CR data observed in this experiment are presented in Figure 18.3. Animals in the LI groups received 20 tone presentations 24 hours prior to the conditioning session. One group of rabbits received a subcutaneous injection of vehicle; the other, an injection of naloxone (2 mg/kg). These injections were administered following the preexposure session 24 hours prior to conditioning. The LI–vehicle group exhibited a modest but significant decrement in the emergence of conditioned responding when compared to the normal conditioning group. The LI–naloxone group, however, displayed a pronounced preexposure effect, exhibiting a significant attenuation of conditioned responding compared to

**FIGURE 18.3.** Change in heart rate to the CS from pre-CS baseline during conditioning trials. Latent inhibition groups received a single CS preexposure session 24 hours prior to conditioning. Latent inhibition groups received either saline or naloxone (2.0 mg/kg) injected subcutaneously immediately following the preexposure session. The data points on the graph prior to the first five-trial blocks represent for each group the mean heart rate change to the CS presentation on trial 1 prior to conditioning. The attenuation of conditioning in the LI–naloxone group was significantly greater than that observed in the LI–vehicle group, $p < .001$.

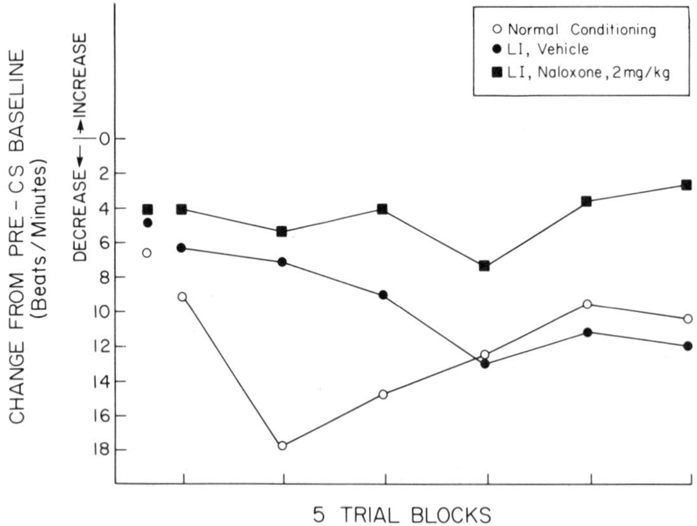

the LI–vehicle group. The increased magnitude of the LI effect in naloxone-injected animals can be interpreted as an increased retention for the pre-exposure to the CS.

An interesting profile of results has emerged from studies examining the effects of posttraining opiate manipulations. As a result of the generality of the effects of opiate treatments across behavioral paradigms, there has been a discernible shift in this work away from interpretations that originally emphasized the results of research using aversive tasks. In the context of more general formulations about the function of memory modulation, opioid peptides do not appear to regulate retention for events by altering any "nonspecific" arousal process. Indeed, retention of habituation and latent inhibition can normally be disrupted by interpolating events that increase the arousal of the animal. That posttraining opiate treatments alter retention for such events in a manner that parallels their effects on a range of other reinforced learning tasks has led to suggestions that the retention of familiarity for stimuli is being influenced by opiate-sensitive mechanisms. This speculation is interesting in light of recent reports by Izquierdo and his colleagues in which exposure of animals to novelty or to unexpected events with a familiar context appears to constitute an adequate stimulus for activation of some components of brain opioid peptide systems (Izquierdo, Souza *et al.*, 1980). Indeed, opioid peptides may serve a role in memory for exposure to complex novel stimuli in primates as suggested by a recent report that reliable, though modest, improvements in recognition memory were obtained in monkeys given naloxone (Martin, Aigner, Brown, & Mishkin, 1984).

## THE ORGANIZATION OF MODULATORY SYSTEMS: A HYPOTHESIS CONCERNING OPIOID PEPTIDES

A major focus of our research program is aimed at identification of the component opioid peptide systems that regulate memory processes. It might be expected that such information will provide a necessary basis for further exploration of the functional role of opioid peptides in memory as well as the sites and mechanisms involved. Already it is quite clear that not all components of opioid peptide systems serve a comparable memory function. For example, administration of morphine into the periaqueductal grey region of the midbrain, a site that is sensitive to the analgesic properties of morphine, does not alter retention of avoidance conditioning in rats (Kesner & Calder, 1980). On the other hand, intracranial administration of opiates, both agonists and antagonists, into the amygdala complex of rats mimics the effects of systemic administration on retention of avoidance conditioning (Gallagher & Kapp, 1978). The bed nucleus of the stria terminalis (BNST) also appears to be sensitive to opiate manipulations. Injection of naloxone into the BNST blocks the amnestic effect of posttraining electrical stimulation within the amygdala complex (Liang, Messing, & McGaugh, 1983). Based on more indirect evidence, other limbic system opioid peptides may be involved in memory processes. Collier and Routtenberg (1984) have proposed that naloxone prevention of retrograde amnesia produced by electrical stimulation in the dentate gyrus may be due to blocking the effects of opioid peptides released within the hippocampus.

A role for limbic opioid peptides in memory processes would certainly be consistent with prevailing views of limbic system function. However, some components of limbic opiate peptide systems may be part of a more widespread neural system that serves to regulate memory. The following discussion of this concept will provide a potentially important interface between opioid peptides and at least two other neurochemical systems that have been of longstanding interest in the pharmacology of memory. These are the ascending norepinephrine (NE) system, arising in large part from the neurons of the locus ceruleus (LC), and the cholinergic (acetylcholine) basal forebrain system. These systems both provide important inputs to limbic structures as well as widespread regions of cortex. In addition, both of these systems are regulated by opioid peptides.

A wide variety of information indicates that opiates and opioid peptides are capable of inhibiting NE activity through opiate receptor mechanisms, probably of the mu receptor subtype, in both the soma/dendritic and the terminal fields of NE neurons. Both systemic administration of morphine (Korf, Bunney, & Aghajanian, 1974) and direct iontophoretic application of opiates and the enkephalins (Bird & Kuhar, 1977; Young, Bird, & Kuhar, 1977) are capable of inhibiting the firing rates of LC neurons. It is likely that endogenous opioid peptides are capable of inhibiting NE neurons because direct synaptic connections have been visualized between immunoreactive terminals labeled with an enkephalin antibody and dendrites labeled with a marker for NE in both the LC and A2 regions (Pickel, Joh, Reis, Leeman, & Miller, 1979). In addition to enkephalin-containing neurons that are present in the LC region, this NE cell group receives a projection from β-endorphin-containing neurons located in the hypothalamus (Bloom *et al.*, 1978). In cats, stimulation of the arcuate region of the hypothalamus produced profound inhibition of LC neurons that was blocked by naloxone administration (Strahlendorf, Strahlendorf, & Barnes, 1980). This observation is consistent with an inhibitory role for β-endorphin input to the LC. Interestingly, in their study Strahlendorf and colleagues (1980) noted that in the absence of arcuate stimulation, naloxone increased the spontaneous firing rate of some LC neurons, perhaps reflecting an interference with endogenous opioid peptide inhibition of these cells. These findings support the general interpretation that in the LC and perhaps the A2 regions, NE neurons are normally regulated in an inhibitory manner by opioid peptides.

Other evidence indicates that opioid peptides are capable of regulating the release of NE at the level of the terminal fields of NE neurons. Numerous studies using *in vitro* brain slices have reported that the evoked release of $[^3H]$NE is inhibited by the presence of opiates in a stereospecific and naloxone-reversible manner (Montel, Starke, & Weber, 1974; Starke, 1979). This effect is shared by several opioid peptides, including met-enkephalin (Taube, Borowski, Endo, & Starke, 1976) and β-endorphin (Arbilla & Langer, 1978). The opiate antagonist naloxone was also found to enhance [$^3$H]NE release evoked by the presence of high $K^+$ concentrations (Taube *et al.*, 1976). There is, as yet, little research exploring the effects of opiates on NE release *in vivo*. However, a reduction in terminal field excitability determined by antidromic frontal cortex activation of LC neurons has been reported following local cortical perfusion with opiates (Nakamura, Tepper, Young, Ling, & Groves, 1982). In addition, these investigators noted that in a minority of the LC neurons tested (35%), naloxone perfusion of cortex enhanced terminal field excitability, an effect that could reflect interference with a tonic action of endogenous opioid peptides on NE terminals. Although no direct connections between opioid peptide-containing neurons and NE terminals have yet been visualized, some indirect evidence suggests that opiate receptors may be located presynaptically on NE neurons. Degeneration of NE terminals in cortex produced by 6-hydroxydopamine (6-OHDA) lesions of the dorsal noradrenergic bundle was found to result in a reduction of opiate binding sites in cortex (Llorens, Martres, Baudry, & Schwartz, 1978).

Information regarding the regulation of acetylcholine (ACh) activity by opiates and opioid peptides is, as yet, relatively sparse but nonetheless interesting. In particular, there is a growing interest in the regulation of the basal forebrain cholinergic system by opioid peptides. These cells are located in several groupings that were well characterized recently in both the rodent and primate brain by Mesulam and colleagues (see Mesulam, Mufson, Levey, & Wainer, 1983; Mcsulam, Mufson, Wainer, & Levey, 1983). These neurons provide a major cholinergic input to the hippocampus (CH1 and CH2 groupings) and to the amygdala complex (CH4). The cholinergic neurons of CH4 located predominantly in the nucleus basalis of Meynert are, in addition, the source of a major cholinergic innervation of neocortex.

Investigations originally describing elevated cholinergic activity in animals during precipitated abstinence from morphine (see Crossland, 1970) led to an interest in the influence of opiates on ACh function. Acute systemic administration of morphine was subsequently found to inhibit ACh release in cortex, an effect that was antagonized by naloxone (Jhamandas, Phillis, & Pinsky, 1971; Jhamandas, Sawynok, & Sutak, 1977; Jhamandas & Sutak, 1980; Wood & Stotland, 1980). Conversely, systemic administration of naloxone or naltrexone was found to enhance the *in vivo* release of cortical ACh (Jhamandas & Sutak, 1976, 1980). These effects of opiates, originally observed on the spontaneous release of ACh, have also been observed on the release of ACh evoked by stimulation of the contralateral sensorimotor cortex (Coutinho-Netto, Abdul-Ghani, & Bradford, 1982).

Because a majority of studies have found little effect of opioid peptides or opiates, either agonists or antagonists, when these agents are perfused onto cortex or applied to *in vitro* cortical slices, it has been suggested that a subcortical interaction between opiate receptors and cholinergic neurons is normally involved (Beani, Bianchi, & Siniscalchi, 1982; Jones & Marchbanks, 1982). The possibility that opiates regulate ACh function at the cell body level has received recent support from research on the septo-hippocampal cholinergic system. Cholinergic neurons residing in the medial septal area (CH1) provide a significant cholinergic input to the hippocampus. Intraseptal administration of β-endorphin or morphine decreases ACh turnover in hippocampus (Moroni, Cheney, & Costa, 1977; Wood, Cheney, & Costa, 1979) and elevates ACh content in hippocampal terminals (Botticelli & Wurtman, 1982). The effects of intraseptal β-endorphin administration on hippocampal ACh are blocked by naloxone and by acute unilateral transection of the fimbria–superior fornix (Botticelli & Wurtman, 1982). There is as yet no information regarding whether this interaction reflects a direct effect of opiates on cholinergic neurons. It is also not clear whether direct administration of opiates or opioid peptides into other basal forebrain sites containing ACh neurons will alter cholinergic activity in cortex (Wenk, 1984; Wood, McQuade, & Vasavan Nair, 1984).

It is intriguing that opioid peptides appear to play upon two systems that have independently been implicated in memory processes. If interference with NE and ACh activity has detrimental effects on memory processes (Squire & Davis, 1981), then it is certainly plausible that the amnestic effects of opiates and opioid peptides could be due an inhibitory influence of these compounds on the function of the NE and ACh systems through the mechanisms described above. Further, the facilitating effects of opiate antagonist administration on memory processes could be due to a release of these same systems from opioid peptide-caused inhibition. At the very least, these hypotheses can lead to specific predictions about the sites and mechanisms through which opiate agents influence memory processes.

Some studies have indeed found that enhancement of memory processes produced by opiate antagonist administration is sensitive to pharmacological treatments that interfere with NE or ACh function (Barrati *et al.*, 1984; Izquierdo & Graudenz, 1980). Recent experiments in our laboratory have been aimed at testing predictions about the specific systems that may be involved in opioid peptide interactions with both NE and ACh function. In a first set of experiments we examined whether memory enhancement produced by naloxone depends upon intact brain NE function by assessing the effects of opiate antagonist treatment in animals with 6-OHDA lesions of the dorsal noradrenergic bundle (DNB) (Gallagher, Rapp, & Fanelli, in press). Three weeks prior to behavioral testing, 6-OHDA lesions of the DNB were performed during stereotaxic surgery. The behavioral testing procedure consisted of a one-trial step through a passive avoidance task previously used in this laboratory. Animals that received control vehicle injections into the DNB during surgery had normal levels of brain catecholamines and exhibited enhanced retention when naloxone (2.0 mg/kg) was administered immediately following the training trial (Figure 18.4). The effect of posttraining

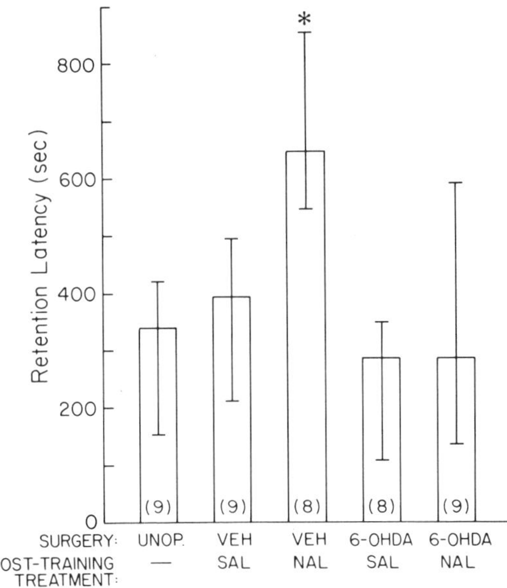


**FIGURE 18.4.** Effect of posttraining systemic naloxone administration on retention latencies for animals with DNB lesions. Median retention latencies and interquartile ranges are indicated for each group. The numbers in parentheses indicate the number of animals in each group. The unoperated and VEH–SAL groups did not differ from one another. $^*p < .01$, Mann–Whitney *U* test (two-tailed) compared to VEH–SAL group. NAL, naloxone; 6-OHDA, 6-hydroxydopamine; SAL, saline; UNOP., unoperated; VEH, vehicle.

naloxone administration was not, however, observed in animals with 6-OHDA-induced lesions of the DNB that produced significantly reduced levels of NE in the forebrain. To assess whether this effect of 6-OHDA treatment was specifically due to its neurotoxic action on NE neurons, additional groups of animals were included that received pretreatment with the NE uptake inhibitor desmethylimipramine (DMI) prior to 6-OHDA injections during surgery. This pretreatment resulted in significant protection of the ascending NE system and, importantly, restored sensitivity to the retention-enhancing effect of posttraining naloxone administration (see Figure 18.5).

Our results have been confirmed by other investigators who found that depletion of brain NE produced by *N*-(2-chloroethyl) *N*-ethyl 2-bromobenzlamine (DSP-4) administration rendered mice insensitive to the retention-enhancing effect of naloxone administration following avoidance training (Introini, 1984). It is perhaps important to note that brain NE depletion does not apparently render animals insensitive to the effects of all pharmacological treatments because posttraining epinephrine administration was found to enhance retention of avoidance conditioning in DSP-4-treated rats (Bennett,

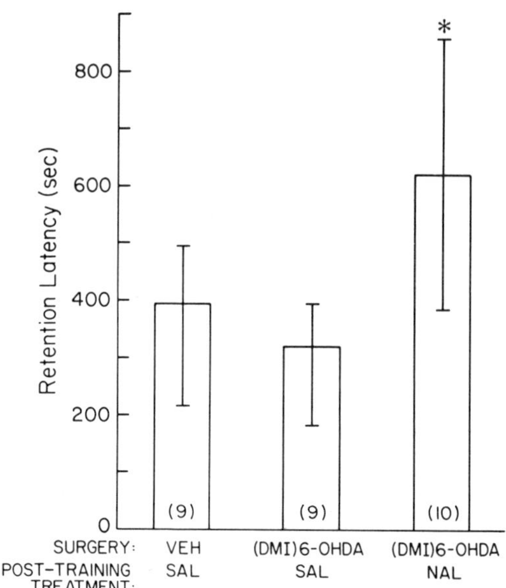


**FIGURE 18.5.** Effect of posttraining systemic naloxone (NAL; 2.0 mg/kg) administration on retention latencies in rats given desmethylimipramine (DMI) prior to 6-hydroxydopamine (6-OHDA) treatment. Bars represent median and interquartile ranges. The numbers in parentheses indicate the number of animals in each group. $^*p < .01$, Mann–Whitney *U* test (two-tailed) compared to VEH–SAL group. SAL, saline: UNOP., unoperated; VEH, vehicle.

Kaleta, Arnold, & McGaugh, 1984). We have subsequently extended our investigation of the effects of NE depletion on the response to opiate antagonist treatment to include a nonaversive task (Fanelli, Rosenberg, & Gallagher, 1985). Lesions of the DNB induced by 6-OHDA were found to prevent the enhancing effect of naloxone administration in rats tested on the radial maze in novel spatial environments (Table 18.3). In this experiment every animal in the control surgery group exhibited improved performance on the maze in the naloxone treatment condition. In animals with 6-OHDA lesions of the DNB, naloxone administration did not significantly alter the acquisition of criterion performance when animals were tested in novel spatial environments.

Because the amygdala complex is a brain site that has been demonstrated to be sensitive to the effect of intracranial naloxone administration on retention (Gallagher & Kapp, 1978) and is also a limbic system site where the NE system and opioid peptides exhibit a high degree of overlapping distribution (Fallon, Koziell, & Moore, 1978; Gros *et al.*, 1978; Simantov, Kuhar, Uhl, & Snyder, 1977), we have examined the behavioral effects of naloxone administration into the amygdala complex in rats with DNB lesions (Gallagher, Rapp, & Fanelli, in press). Behavioral results for groups of animals in this experiment (Figure 18.6) revealed that naloxone increased retention in animals that received control vehicle injections into the DNB. This effect was abolished

**TABLE 18.3.** Effects of Naloxone on Maze Performance in Rats with Dorsal Noradrenergic Bundle (DNB) Lesions

| Treatments and criteria | DNB lesion | Control surgery |
|---|---|---|
| Saline treatment | | |
| Trials to criterion | 6.3 ± 0.73 | 5.9 ± 0.80 |
| Errors to criterion | 13.1 ± 2.05 | 12.0 ± 2.25 |
| Naloxone treatment | | |
| Trials to criterion | 5.4 ± 0.39 | 3.7 ± 0.42[a] |
| Errors to criterion | 11.4 ± 1.37 | 5.0 ± 1.07[a] |

[a] $p < .01$.

by 6-OHDA lesions of the DNB. The results of these experiments demonstrate that within the context of the behavioral testing procedures used, the effect of opiate antagonist administration on memory processes depends upon intact NE function. This requirement may indeed reflect an underlying neural substrate for opiate regulation of memory—that the effects normally obtained with opiate antagonists are due to release of NE function from

**FIGURE 18.6.** Effect of posttraining naloxone (2.5 n*M*) administration into the amygdala complex on retention latencies in animals with DNB lesions. Bars represent medians and interquartile ranges. The numbers in parentheses indicate the number of animals in each group. The vehicle used for intracranial injections was a Krebs–Ringer phosphate solution, designated as K in the figure. *$p < .01$, Mann–Whitney *U* test (two-tailed) compared to VEH–K group. NAL, naloxone; 6-OHDA, 6-hydroxydopamine; UNOP., unoperated; VEH, vehicle.

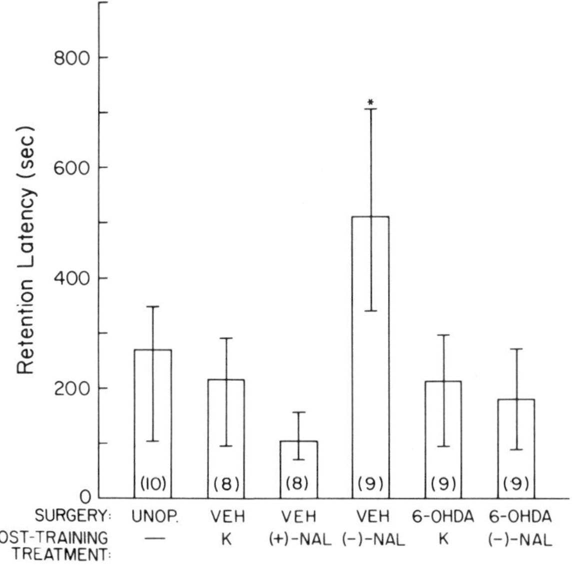

inhibition by endogenous opioid peptides. The fact that the effect of intracranial naloxone administration into the amygdala was absent in NE-denervated animals suggests that presynaptic regulation of NE release by opioid peptides in this region may normally be capable of altering memory. This interpretation is consistent with previous research indicating that intact NE function within the amygdala is necessary for normal retention; post-training injection of β-adrenergic antagonists into the amygdala produces profound retrograde amnesia for passive avoidance conditioning (Gallagher, Kapp, Musty, & Driscoll, 1977).

An interest in the neural mechanisms underlying the effects of opiate treatments on memory should probably not be limited to those opioid peptide and NE systems within the amygdala complex. Indeed, a consideration of other neuroanatomical circuits may prove essential for understanding the wide scope of opiate effects on different measures of retention. This expectation is based in part on observations that animals with amygdala lesions perform normally on some tasks, such as maze learning, that are nonetheless sensitive to opiate treatments (Gallagher *et al.*, 1983). In addition, pharmacological research linking the effects of opiate antagonists on memory to cholinergic function, in combination with the prevailing evidence that interactions between these systems primarily occur at the level of cholinergic cell bodies, would also point to other sites of action for opiates on memory. To assess whether opiate-sensitive mechanisms at sites that are likely to provide an interface between opioid peptides and cholinergic function are involved in memory processes, we have begun to examine the effects of opiate manipulations within the medial septal area (MSA). Our preliminary results indicate that this region, through which opioid peptide mechanisms are known to requlate septo-hippocampal cholinergic function, is sensitive to the memory-altering properties of opiate administration when animals are tested using a latent inhibition task (Gallagher, Fanelli, & Bostock, in press).

## CONCLUSION

There remains much uncharted territory in neurobiological research on learning and memory. The emergence of the concept of modulation has directed attention over the past decade toward neural and hormonal systems that may regulate the adaptive capacities of the brain. This chapter has set forth a core set of systems in the mammalian brain that may serve a modulatory function. Several general points are raised by the research summarized in this presentation.

There is a striking proliferation of neurochemical systems that have been proposed to regulate some aspect of learning and memory processes. Numerous recently investigated peptides have joined a number of more well studied biogenic amines as candidate mechanisms involved in learning and memory. Investigation of interrelationships among the functions of candidate modulators may reveal some degree of integration within the circuitry in the mammalian brain that regulates neural plasticity. Of interest, for example, are proposals that the effects of vasopressin on memory may be due to regulation of NE function (e.g., see Kovács, Bohus, & Versteeg, 1979). It is most probable that regulation of neural plasticity as embodied in the concept of modulation is not dependent upon any single integrating system in the brain. Nonetheless, few efforts up until now have focused upon delineating the specific circuitry used by modulators that would indicate the extent to which they function independently.

A second feature of the research described in this chapter is the relative absence of information regarding the specific sites/circuits upon which modulators presumably act to preserve information in higher species. For example, although there is growing evidence favoring a modulatory role for the ascending NE system upon specific forms of neural plasticity in the mammalian brain such as long-term potentiation (Bliss *et al.*, 1983; Hopkins & Johnston, 1984) and developmentally linked brain changes (Brenner, Mirmiran, Uylings, & Van Der Gugten, 1983; Kasamatsu & Pettigrew, 1976; O'Shea, Saari, Pappas, Ings, & Stange, 1983; Pettigrew & Kasamatsu, 1978), the relevance of these specific processes for learning and memory has not been clearly established. It may be anticipated, however, that the efforts of investigators using neural systems approaches will in the process of identifying circuits where neural changes occur during learning also provide an important guide to those sites where modulatory systems may act to regulate forms of neural plasticity that can be more directly linked to learning and memory in higher species (e.g., see D. H. Cohen, Chapter 2, this volume). Indeed, it may be expected that the various approaches to the neurobiological study of learning and memory in which the concept of modulation has recently emerged will ultimately complement each other in providing a clearer understanding of brain function in this most vital area of research.

## ACKNOWLEDGMENTS

This work was supported by NIMH Grants MH 35554 and MH 39180 and a Research Scientist Development Award (NIMH, K02-MH00406) to M. Gallagher. I thank my collaborators (see references) and Pat Eichman for the preparation of the manuscript.

## REFERENCES

Arbilla, S., & Langer, S. Z. Morphine and β-endorphin inhibit release of noradrenaline from cerebral cortex but not of dopamine from rat striatum. *Nature (London)*, 1978, *271*, 559–561.

Barrati, C. M., Introini, I. B., & Huygens, P. Possible interaction between central cholinergic muscarinic and opioid peptidergic systems during memory consolidation in mice. *Behavioral and Neural Biology*, 1984, *40*, 155–169.

Beani, L., Bianchi, C., & Siniscalchi, A. The effect of naloxone on opioid-induced inhibition and facilitation of acetylcholine release in brain slices. *British Journal of Pharmacology*, 1982, *76*, 393–401.

Beatty, W. W., & Shavalia, D. A. Spatial memory in rats: Time course of working memory and effect of anesthetics. *Behavioral and Neural Biology*, 1980, *28*, 454–462.

Bennett, C., Kaleta, S., Arnold, M., & McGaugh, J. L. Epinephrine facilitates inhibitory avoidance retention of adrenal denervated rats treated with a high dose of DSP4. *Society for Neuroscience Abstracts*, 1984, *10*, 254.

Bird, S. J., & Kuhar, M. J. Iontophoretic application of opiates of the locus coeruleus. *Brain Research*, 1977, *122*, 523–533.

Bliss, T. V. P., Goddard, G. V., & Riives, M. Reduction of long-term potentiation in the dentate gyrus of the rat following selective depletion of monoamines. *Journal of Physiology (London)*, 1983, *334*, 475–491.

Bloom, F. E., Rossier, J., Battenberg, E. L. F., Bayon, A., French, E., Henriksen, S. J., Siggins, G. R., Segal, D., Browne, R., Ling, N., & Guillemin, R. β-endorphin: Cellular localization, electrophysiological and behavioral effects. In E. Costa & M. Trabucchi (Eds.), *Advances in biochemical psychopharmacology* (Vol. 18). New York: Raven Press, 1978.

Bostock, E., & Gallagher, M. Naloxone-induced facilitation of latent inhibition in rabbits. *Society for Neuroscience Abstracts*, 1982, *8*, 148.

Botticelli, L. J., & Wurtman, R. J. Septohippocampal cholinergic neurons are regulated transsynaptically by endorphin and corticotropin neuropeptides. *Journal of Neuroscience*, 1982, *2*, 1316–1321.

Brenner, E., Mirmiran, M., Uylings, H. B. M., & Van Der Gugten, J. Impaired growth of the cerebral cortex of rats treated neonatally with 6-hydroxydopamine under different environmental conditions. *Neuroscience Letters*, 1983, *42*, 13–17.

Carrasco, M. A., Dias, R. D., & Izquierdo, I. Naloxone reverses retrograde amnesia induced by electroconvulsive shock. *Behavioral and Neural Biology*, 1982, *34*, 352–357.

Castellano, C. Effects of morphine and heroin on discrimination learning and consolidation in mice. *Psychopharmacologia*, 1975, *42*, 235–242.

Castellano, C. Strain-dependent effects of naloxone on discrimination learning in mice. *Psychopharmacology*, 1981, *73*, 152–156.

Castellano, C., & Pavone, F. Naloxone-reversible effects of ethanol on passive avoidance behavior in mice. *Physiological Psychology*, 1984, *11*, 291–295.

Castellano, C., Pavone, F., & Puglisi-Allegra, S. Morphine and memory in DVA/2 mice: Effects of stress and of prior experience. *Behavioral Brain Research*, 1984, *11*, 3–10.

Collier, T. J., & Routtenberg, A. Selective impairment of declarative memory following stimulation of dentate gyrus granule cells: A naloxone sensitive effect. *Brain Research*, 1984, *310*, 384–387.

Coutinho-Netto, J., Abdul-Ghani, A.-S., & Bradford, H. F. Morphine suppression of neurotransmitter release evoked by sensory stimulation *in vivo*. *Biochemical Pharmacology*, 1982, *31*, 1019–1023.

Crossland, J. Acetylcholine and the morphine abstinence syndrome. In E. Heilbronn & A. Winter (Eds.), *Drugs and cholinergic mechanisms in the C.N.S.* Stockholm: Försavarets, Forskrugsanstalt, 1970.

Eysenck, M. W. *Attention and arousal*. Berlin: Springer-Verlag, 1982.

Fallon, J. H., Koziell, D. A., & Moore, R. Y. Catecholamine innervation of the basal forebrain. II. Amygdala, suprarhinal cortex and entorhinal cortex. *Journal of Comparative Neurology*, 1978, *180*, 509–532.

Fanelli, R. J., Rosenberg, R. A., & Gallagher, M. Role of noradrenergic function in the opiate antagonist facilitation of spatial memory. *Behavioral Neuroscience*, 1985, *99*, 751–755.

Fulginiti, S., & Cancella, L. M. Effect of naloxone and amphetamine on acquisition and memory consolidation of active avoidance responses in rats. *Psychopharmacology*, 1983, *79*, 45–48.

Gallagher, M. Naloxone enhancement of memory processes: Effects of other opiate antagonists. *Behavioral and Neural Biology*, 1982, *35*, 375–382.

Gallagher, M., Fanelli, R. J., & Bostock, E. Opioid peptides: Their position among other neuroregulators of memory. *International Congress of Psychology*, *23*, in press.

Gallagher, M., & Kapp, B. S. Manipulation of opiate activity in the amygdala alters memory processes. *Life Sciences*, 1978, *23*, 1974–1978.

Gallagher, M., & Kapp, B. S. Influence of amygdala opiate-sensitive mechanisms, fear-motivation responses, and memory processes for aversive experiences. In J. L. Martinez, Jr., R. A. Jensen, R. B. Messing, H. Rigter, & J. L. McGaugh (Eds.), *Endogenous peptides and learning and memory processes*. New York: Academic Press, 1981.

Gallagher, M., Kapp, B. S., Musty, R. E., & Driscoll, P. A. Memory formation: Evidence for a specific neurochemical system in the amygdala. *Science*, 1977, *198*, 423–425.

Gallagher, M., King, R. A., & Young, N. B. Opiate antagonists improve spatial memory. *Science*, 1983, *221*, 975–976.

Gallagher, M., Rapp, P. R., & Fanelli, R. J. Opiate antagonist facilitation of time-dependent memory processes: Dependence upon intact norepinephrine function. *Brain Research*, in press.

Gold, P. E., & McGaugh, J. L. Neurobiology and memory: Modulators, correlates and assumptions. In T. Teyler (Ed.), *Brain and learning*. Stamford, Conn.: Greylock, 1978.

Gros, C., Pradelles, P., Humbert, J., Dray, F., Le Gal La Salle, G., & Ben-Ari, Y. Regional distribution of met-enkephalin within the amygdaloid complex and bed nucleus of the stria terminalis. *Neuroscience Letters*, 1978, *10*, 193–196.

Hopkins, W. F., & Johnston, D. Frequency-dependent noradrenergic modulation of long-term potentiation in the hippocampus. *Science*, 1984, *226*, 4672.

Introini, I. B. *Participación de peptidos opioides endógenos en el proceso de consolidación de la memoria: Su posible interacción con otros sistemas neuronales*. Unpublished doctoral dissertation, Universidad de Buenos Aires, 1984.

Izquierdo, I. Effect of naloxone and morphine on various forms of memory in the rat: Possible role of endogenous opiate mechanisms in memory consolidation. *Psychopharmacology*, 1979, *66*, 199–203.

Izquierdo, I. Effect of beta-endorphin and naloxone on acquisition, memory and retrieval of shuttle avoidance and habituation learning in rats. *Psychopharmacology*, 1980, *69*, 111–115.

Izquierdo, I., & Dias, R. D. Retrograde amnesia caused by met-, leu- and des-tyr-met-enkephalin in the rat and its reversal by naloxone. *Neuroscience Letters*, 1981, *22*, 189–193.

Izquierdo, I., & Dias, R. D. Effect of ACTH, epinephrine, β-endorphin, naloxone and of the combination of naloxone or β-endorphin with ACTH or epinephrine on memory consolidation. *Psychoneuroendocrinology*, 1983, *8*, 81–87.

Izquierdo, I., & Graudenz, M. Memory facilitation by naloxone is due to release of dopaminergic and beta-adrenergic systems from tonic inhibition. *Psychopharmacology*, 1980, *67*, 265–268.

Izquierdo, I., Paiva, A. C. M., & Elisabetsky, E. Posttraining intraperitoneal administration of leu-enkephalin and β-endorphin causes retrograde amnesia for two different tasks in rat. *Behavioral and Neural Biology*, 1980, *28*, 246–250.

Izquierdo, I., Souza, D. O., Carraso, M. A., Dias, R. D., Perry, M. L., Eisinger, S., Elisabetsky, E., & Vendite, D. A. Beta-endorphin causes retrograde amnesia and is released from the rat brain by various forms of training and stimulation. *Psychopharmacology*, 1980, *70*, 173–177.

Jensen, R. A., Martinez, J. L., Jr., Messing, R. B., Spiehler, V., Vasquez, B. J., Soumireu-Mourat, B., Liang, K. C., & McGaugh, J. Morphine and naloxone alter memory in the rat. *Society for Neuroscience Abstracts*, 1978, *4*, 260.

Jhamandas, K., Phillis, J. W., & Pinsky, C. Effect of narcotic analgesics and antagonists on the *in vivo* release of acetylcholine from the cerebral cortex of the cat. *British Journal of Pharmacology*, 1971, *43*, 53–66.

Jhamandas, K., Sawynok, J., & Sutak, M. Enkephalin effects on release of brain acetylcholine.

*Nature (London)*, 1977, *269*, 433–434.

Jhamandas, K., & Sutak, M. Morphine–naloxone interaction in the central cholinergic system: The influence of subcortical lesioning and electrical stimulation. *British Journal of Pharmacology*, 1976, *58*, 101–107.

Jhamandas, K., & Sutak, M. Action of enkephalin analogs and morphine on brain acetylcholine release: Differential reversal by naloxone and an opiate pentapeptide. *British Journal of Pharmacology*, 1980, *71*, 201–210.

Jones, C. A., & Marchbanks, R. M. Effects of (D-alanine$^2$, methionine$^5$) enkephalinamide on the release of acetylcholine and noradrenaline from brain slices and isolated nerve terminals. *Biochemical Pharmacology*, 1982, *31*, 455–458.

Kasamatsu, T., & Pettigrew, J. D. Depletion of brain catecholamines: Failure of ocular dominance shift after monocular occlusion in kittens. *Science*, 1976, *194*, 206–209.

Kesner, R. P., & Calder, L. D. Rewarding periaqueductal gray stimulation disrupts long-term memory for passive avoidance learning. *Behavioral and Neural Biology*, 1980, *30*, 237–249.

Kety, S. The biogenic amines in the central nervous system: Their possible roles in arousal, emotion and learning. In F. O. Schmitt (Ed.), *The neurosciences: Second study program*. Cambridge, Mass.: MIT Press, 1970.

Kety, S. Biological concomitants of affective states and their possible role in memory processes. In M. R. Rosenzweig & E. L. Bennett (Eds.), *Neural mechanisms of learning and memory*. Cambridge, Mass.: MIT Press, 1976.

Korf, J., Bunney, B. S., & Aghajanian, G. K. Noradrenergic neurons: Morphine inhibition of spontaneous activity. *European Journal of Pharmacology*, 1974, *25*, 165–169.

Kovács, G. L., Bohus, B., & Versteeg, D. H. G. The effects of vasopression on memory processes: The role of noradrenergic transmission. *Neuroscience*, 1979, *4*, 1529–1537.

Krasne, F. B. Extrinsic control of intrinsic neuronal plasticity: An hypothesis from work on simple systems. *Brain Research*, 1978, *140*, 197–216.

Liang, K. C., Messing, R. B., & McGaugh, J. L. Naloxone attenuates amnesia caused by amygdaloid stimulation: The involvement of a central opioid system. *Brain Research*, 1983, *271*, 41–49.

Llorens, C., Martres, M. P., Baudry, M., & Schwartz, J. C. Hypersensitivity to noradrenaline in cortex after chronic morphine: Relevance to tolerance and dependence. *Nature (London)*, 1978, *274*, 603–605.

Lubow, R. E. Latent inhibition. *Psychological Bulletin*, 1973, *79*, 398–407.

Lucion, A. B., Rosito, G., Sapper, D. B., Palmini, A. L., & Izquierdo, I. Intracerebroventricular administration of nanogram amounts of β-endorphin and met-enkephalin causes retrograde amnesia in rats. *Behavioral Brain Research*, 1982, 4, 111–115.

Madden, J., IV, Akil, H., Patrick, R. L., & Barchas, J. D. Stress induced parallel changes in central opioid levels and pain responsiveness in the rat. *Nature* (*London*), 1977, *265*, 358–360.

Martin, S., Aigner, T., Brown, M., & Mishkin, M. Effects of naloxone on recognition memory in monkeys. *Society for Neuroscience Abstracts*, 1984, *10*, 253.

Martinez, J. L., Jr., & Rigter, H. Endorphins alter acquisition and consolidation of an inhibitory avoidance response in rats. *Neuroscience Letters*, 1980, *19*, 197–201.

McGaugh, J. L. Time-dependent processes in memory storage. *Science*, 1966, *153*, 1351–1358.

McGaugh, J. L. Hormonal influences on memory storage. *Psychological Review*, 1983, *38*, 161–174.

McGaugh, J. L., & Gold, P. E. Modulation of memory by electrical stimulation of the brain. In M. R. Rosenzweig & E. L. Bennett (Eds.), *Neural mechanisms of learning and memory*. Cambridge, Mass.: MIT Press, 1976.

Messing, R. B., Jensen, R. A., Martinez, J. L., Spiehler, V. R., Vasquez, B. J., Soumireu-Mourat, B., Liang, K. C., & McGaugh, J. L. Naloxone enhancement of memory. *Behavioral and Neural Biology*, 1979, *27*, 266–275.

Messing, R. B., Rigter, H., & Nickolson, V. J. Memory consolidation in senescence: Effects of $CO_2$, amphetamine and morphine. *Neurobiology of Aging*, 1982, *3*, 133–139.

Messing, R. B., Rijk, H., & Rigter, H. Facilitation of hot-plate response learning by pre- and posttraining naltrexone administration. *Psychopharmacology*, 1983, *81*, 33–36.

Mesulam, M.-M., Mufson, E. J., Levey, A. I., & Wainer, B. H. Cholinergic innervation of the cortex by the basal forebrain: Cytochemistry and cortical connections of the septal area, diagonal band nuclei, nucleus basalis (substantia inominata) and hypothalamus of the rhesus monkey. *Journal of Comparative Neurology*, 1983, *214*, 170–197.

Mesulam, M.-M., Mufson, E. J., Wainer, B. H., & Levey, A. J. Central cholinergic pathways in the rat: An overview based on an alternative nomenclature (Ch1–Ch6). *Neuroscience*, 1983, *10*, 1185–1201.

Mondadori, C., & Waser, P. B. Facilitation of memory processing by posttrial morphine: Possible involvement of reinforcement mechanisms? *Psychopharmacology*, 1979, *63*, 297–300.

Montel, H., Starke, K., & Weber, F. Influence of fentanyl, levorphanol and pethidine on the release of noradrenaline from rat brain cortex slices. *Naunyn-Schmiedeberg's Archives of Pharmacology*, 1974, *283*, 371–377.

Moroni, F., Cheney, D. L., & Costa, E. Inhibition of acetylcholine turnover in rat hippocampus by intraseptal injections of β-endorphin and morphine. *Naunyn-Schmiedeberg's Archives of Pharmacology*, 1977, *299*, 149–153.

Nakamura, S., Tepper, J. M., Young, S. J., Ling, N., & Groves, P. M. Noradrenergic terminal excitability: Effects of opioids. *Neuroscience Letters*, 1982, *30*, 57–62.

Olton, D. S., & Samuelson, R. J. Remembrance of places past: Spatial memory in rats. *Journal of Experimental Psychology: Animal Behavior Processes*, 1976, *2*, 97–116.

O'Shea, L., Saari, M., Pappas, B., Ings, R., & Stange, K. Neonatal 6-hydroxydopamine attenuates the neural and behavioral effects of enriched rearing in the rat. *European Journal of Pharmacology*, 1983, *92*, 43–47.

Pettigrew, J. D., & Kasamatsu, T. Local perfusion of noradrenaline maintains visual cortical plasticity. *Nature (London)*, 1978, *271*, 761–763.

Pickel, V. M., Joh, T. H., Reis, D. J., Leeman, S. E., & Miller, R. J. Electron microscopic localization of substance P and enkephalin in axon terminals related to dendrites of catecholaminergic neurons. *Brain Research*, 1979, *160*, 387–400.

Rodgers, R. J., Richards, C., & Precious, J. I. Naloxone administration following brief exposure to novelty reduces activity and rearing in mice upon 24-h retest: A conditioned aversion? *Psychopharmacology*, 1984, *82*, 322–326.

Simantov, R., Kuhar, M. G., Uhl, G. R., & Snyder, S. H. Opioid peptide enkephalin: Immunohistochemical mapping in rat central nervous system. *Science*, 1977, *74*, 2167–2171.

Squire, L. R., & Davis, H. P. The pharmacology of memory: A neurobiological perspective. *Annual Review of Pharmacology and Toxicology*, 1981, *21*, 323–356.

Starke, K. Presynaptic regulation of release in the central nervous system. In D. M. Paton (Ed.), *The release of catecholamines from adrenergic neurons*. New York: Pergamon Press, 1979.

Stein, L., & Belluzzi, J. D. Brain endorphins: Possible mediators of pleasurable states. In E. Usdin, W. E. Bunney, Jr., & N. S. Kline (Eds.), *Endorphins in mental health research*. New York: Oxford University Press, 1979.

Strahlendorf, H. K., Strahlendorf, J. C., & Barnes, C. D. Endorphin-mediated inhibition of locus coeruleus neurons. *Brain Research*, 1980, *191*, 284–288.

Taube, H. D., Borowski, E., Endo, T., & Starke, K. Enkephalin: A potential modulator of noradrenaline release in rat brain. *European Journal of Pharmacology*, 1976, *38*, 377–380.

Tazi, A., Dantzer, R., Mormede, P., & Le Moal, H. Effects of post-trial administration of naloxone and β-endorphin on shock-induced fighting in rats. *Behavioral and Neural Biology*, 1983, *39*, 192–202.

Walters, E. T., & Byrne, J. H. Associative conditioning of single sensory neurons suggests a cellular mechanism for learning. *Science*, 1983, *219*, 405–407.

Wenk, G. L. Pharmacological manipulations of the substantia innominata–cortical cholinergic pathway. *Neuroscience Letters*, 1984, *51*, 99–103.

Wood, P. L., Cheney, D. L., & Costa, E. An investigation of whether septal X-aminobutyrate-containing interneurons are involved in the reduction in the turnover rate of acetylcholine elicited by substance P and β-endorphin in the hippocampus. *Neuroscience*, 1979, *4*, 1479–1484.

Wood, P. L., McQuade, P. S., & Vasavan Nair, N. P. Gabaergic and opioid regulation of the substantia innominata–cortical cholinergic pathway in the rat. *Progress in Neuro-Psychopharmacology and Biological Psychiatry*, 1984, *8*, 789–792.

Wood, P. L., & Stotland, L. M. Actions of enkephalin, μ and partial agonist analgesics on acetylcholine turnover in rat brain. *Neuropharmacology*, 1980, *19*, 975–982.

Young, W. S., Bird, S. J., & Kuhar, M. J. Iontophoresis of methionine-enkephalin in the locus coeruleus area. *Brain Research*, 1977, *129*, 366–370.

Zornetzer, S. F., & Gold, P. E. The mnemon and its juices: Neuromodulation of memory processes. *Behavioral and Neural Biology*, 1983, *38*, 151–189.

CHAPTER 19

# Varieties of Conditioning

**N. J. Mackintosh**
University of Cambridge
Cambridge, England, UK

## INTRODUCTION

The study of animal learning has changed character in the past quarter-century. That much is common knowledge. But it is rather more difficult to characterize the nature of the enterprise as it is now practiced. This is partly, perhaps, because several different streams have branched off from what was once a broad, gently flowing (less charitably, stagnant) river. On the one hand are those who proclaim that they are studying cognitive processes in animals, and although this is a much-abused term, it can be given a meaning that is moderately familiar to practitioners of human experimental psychology and would include the study of varieties of memory (e.g., Grant, 1984; Maki, 1984; Roitblat, 1984); perceptual analysis, including the perception of time (Gibbon & Church, 1984) or space (see Barnes & McNaughton, Chapter 3, this volume; Morris, Chapter 25, this volume); and reasoning and problem solving (Gillan, 1981; Gillan, Premack, & Woodruff, 1981). A second group, exemplified by Shettleworth's contributions to this volume (Chapter 13), has taken seriously the possibility that not only an animal's behavior, but also its perceptual, cognitive, and learning processes may be determined by the ecological niche to which it is adapted. There may, as yet, be relatively little hard evidence to support this suggestion, (as Macphail, Chapter 15, this volume, would argue), but it is both interesting and plausible, and should surely be pursued.

Yet a third area of research within animal learning has, superficially at any rate, changed least. Those who still study classical and instrumental conditioning use techniques, procedures, and vocabulary much of which has hardly changed in the last 25 years. And the fundamental theory of conditioning can, of course, be traced back very much further than that, to the origins of associationist philosophy. The concept of an association is indeed a powerful one, not to be lightly abandoned, and students of conditioning have not done so. But it would be grossly misleading to suggest that their theories have remained the same. In some respects the changes in theory have been more marked than in any other aspect of the study of conditioning. But they have left some fundamental features unchanged. For example, present-day theories of conditioning are often described as more cognitive than their predecessors, and this is true in this sense at any rate, that a theorist will now be at least as interested in inferring what animals know as in predicting what they will do. But this can be achieved simply by abandoning the supposition embedded in stimulus–response (S-R) theory that there is a strict isomorphism between associative knowledge and behavioral output. The relationship is looser (a conditioned response, or CR, is now treated as a convenient index of what an animal knows about the relationship between conditioned and unconditioned stimuli, or CS and US), and very much worse understood than S-R theory ever supposed. And this liberation, as I shall argue below, allows current associative theory of conditioning to include associations between almost any pair of events, not just between stimulus and response. Finally, and in some ways most interesting, it is now widely accepted that the conditions determining whether a CS will be associated with a US are notably more complex than simple temporal contiguity; put informally, they seem to include the requirement that the occurrence of the US not be already predicted by some other event.

The more powerful, but still associative, account of conditioning that has emerged in recent years enjoys, I should judge, a reasonably wide measure of acceptance (Mackintosh, 1983; Rescorla, 1985)—even if there is little argreement on the details of the appropriate theory. And most theorists would also argue that this associative system is one of considerable generality, which can be studied in a variety of animals in a number of different paradigms, including salivary conditioning in dogs, autoshaping in pigeons, nictitating membrane or eyelid conditioning in rabbits, conditioned suppression or conditioned food aversions in rats. All reveal the operation of similar functional laws of associative learning. It seems entirely possible, indeed, that these fundamental laws are common to all vertebrates.

But if there is an important common core to the learning studied in simple conditioning experiments in a wide range of animals and paradigms, it is also possible that certain distinctions can and should be drawn. At one level of analysis, conditioning is a remarkably simple process: The experimenter pairs a CS and a US, or arranges that a reinforcer will be delivered if and only if the animal performs some arbitrarily defined response; as a consequence of exposure to these contingencies, the animal's behavior changes in certain more or less well defined ways; and the theorist infers that these changes occur because the animal has formed certain associations. But the nature of these associations may not always be the same, or at least the nature of the events associated may differ and these differences may have implications for the nature of the behavioral changes to be expected. And it is even possible that some of the changes observed in some experimental paradigms may be nonassociative in origin.

In what follows, I shall consider three distinctions, or sets of contrasts, that have been suggested: those between procedural and declarative learning, those between preparatory and consummatory conditioning, and finally those between associative and nonassociative learning. In each case, I shall suggest some possible implications that the distinction may hold for other issues in the neurobiology of learning and memory.

## PROCEDURAL AND DECLARATIVE LEARNING

The distinction between knowing how and knowing that is one to which philosophers drew attention some years ago (e.g., Ryle, 1949; Wittgenstein, 1953). But animal psychologists had been arguing about the distinction, without knowing it, for many years before that (Dickinson, 1980). If declarative knowledge is knowledge of facts or of propositions about events in the world, knowing that one event regularly predicts the occurrence of another is a form of declarative knowledge, to be contrasted with procedural knowledge, defined as knowing what to do, or what response to perform, in the presence of a particular stimulus. Hull's and Guthrie's stimulus–response theory, in other words, asserts that conditioning produces procedural knowledge; whereas Tolman's expectancy theory asserts that conditioning produces declarative knowledge about what stimulus follows another.

Both theories can, in principle, account for the acquisition of conditioned responding in classical or instrumental conditioning experiments: the procedural theory accounts for it by saying that the animal learns to perform the CR in the presence of a CS or to perform the instrumental response in the presence of a discriminative stimulus; the declarative theory accounts for it by saying that the animal learns that the CS signals the US or that the discriminative stimulus signals that a particular response will be reinforced. The declarative account, of course, then requires some response-production rules, a complication that has for a long time militated against its wide acceptance. But there is now widespread agreement that conditioning procedures do result in the acquisition of declarative knowledge. Even more important, however, is the recognition that this does not necessarily imply that conditioning never involves procedural learning. A general associative theory of conditioning can, as noted earlier, allow that stimuli are associated with responses as well as with other stimuli or reinforcers, or that responses can be associated not only with their consequences but also with antecedent stimuli.

The most direct evidence for declarative knowledge in conditioning comes from experiments in which the value of a reinforcer is changed after conditioning has taken place and the effects of this revaluation on conditioned responding are then studied. Holland and Straub (1979), for example, gave rats conditioning trials on which a CS signaled the delivery of 45-mg food pellets. Once conditioned responding to the CS had been established, the value of the food pellets was reduced for experimental animals. After being allowed to eat the pellets in their home cages, they were given an injection of lithium chloride sufficient to condition an aversion to the pellets. When returned to the conditioning chambers, these experimental animals showed a significant reduction in conditioned responding to the CS. The result does not seem particularly surprising, but it is not predicted by a procedural account of conditioning. If all that an animal knows about a CS paired with food pellets is that the CS makes it salivate, then the fact that the pellets subsequently make it feel ill will not stop its salivating to the CS. If the new association between food pellets and illness is to affect the old tendency of the CS to elicit salivation, the associative path from CS to salivation must be via some central representation of the food, which is itself associated with illness in the devaluation phase of the experiment. The animal must know, in other words, that the CS signals the food pellets and that the pellets make it ill in order to draw the inference that the CS itself is no longer an attractive stimulus.

Similar devaluation effects have been reported in instrumental conditioning. Rats that are trained to press a lever for food pellets and to pull a chain for sucrose, and then are made ill after consuming the pellets, will selectively refrain from performing the response that used to produce the pellets (Colwill & Rescorla, 1985; see also Adams & Dickinson, 1981). Once again, the implication is that the rat knows that lever pressing produces certain consequences and will press the lever only so long as those consequences retain their value.

By the same token, however, the failure of reinforcer revaluation to produce an appropriate change in conditioned responding, although interpretable in a number of different ways, does suggest the possibility that conditioning sometimes produces procedural knowledge, or a stimulus–response habit. Dickinson (1985), for example, has argued that instrumental conditioning will be based on a declarative representation of the relationship between instrumental response and reinforcer only when there is a good correlation between rate of responding and rate of reinforcement, as during the acquisition of responding on ratio schedules. A weaker correlation—for example, that produced by interval schedules of reinforcement or by exposure to only a small part of the range of possible rates of responding and of reinforcement, which will happen once the well-trained animal has settled down to a steady pattern of responding—may result in a procedural representation. Both the nature of the instrumental schedule and the amount of exposure to that schedule can indeed affect the outcome of revaluation experiments. But it is possible that extended practice of a particular response in an unchanging environment may produce a stimulus–response habit by sheer repetition (Neuenschwander, Fabrigoule, Cotton, & Mackintosh, in press).

The distinction between procedural and declarative knowledge, at least as interpreted by conditioning theorists, is thus not so much between conditioning and other more cognitive forms of behavior; rather it is between different representations of knowledge, both of which may result from exposure to the contingencies of a conditioning experiment. We do not yet have any very clear understanding of the circumstances that favor one sort of representation over the other. All we do know is that it requires detailed theoretical and experimental analysis of the circumstances of learning and the factors controlling performance to decide what is happening in any given situation. In particular, because conditioned responding is not necessarily based on procedural knowledge, the fact (if it be a fact) that amnesic patients show normal acquisition and retention of Pavlovian conditioning (Weiskrantz & Warrington, 1979) is not sufficient to establish that amnesia abolishes declarative learning, but spares procedural learning (Squire & Zola-Morgan, 1983). Either the distinction being suggested is rather different from that which I have outlined here—in which case it becomes important to specify just what this new distinction is—or, if we are talking about the same distinction, one would expect Pavlovian conditioning based solely on procedural learning to show quite different characteristics from that seen in normal subjects.

A more recently developed example of a procedural theory of Pavlovian conditioning is that proposed by Hawkins and Kandel (1984) and alluded to by D. H. Cohen (Chapter 2, this volume). The suggestion here is that the function of the US in conditioning is to augment, or prevent habituation of, activity in the pathway between the CS and the unconditioned response (UR) it normally elicits. The CR observed as a consequence of conditioning is in reality an augmented version of the UR elicited by that CS before conditioning began. Just how such a theory could account for the dependence of the CR on the nature of the US used to support conditioning is not clear, but if it provides an adequate model of conditioning in *Aplysia*, then here too one would expect to see important differences in the response of the system to, say, postconditioning changes in the value of the US. Results reported by Cooke, Delaney, and Gelperin for the slug, *Limax* (Chapter 10, this volume), do not provide much support for this implication.

## CONSUMMATORY AND PREPARATORY CONDITIONING

The distinction first drawn by Konorski (1967) between consummatory and preparatory conditioning was based on at least three different criteria: the form of the CR, the nature of the underlying representations that were associated, and the conditions of training that produced such learning. Consummatory conditioning was said to involve discrete, phasic CRs, whereas preparatory conditioning involved diffuse, affective CRs. Paradigm examples of the former included eyelid or leg flexion CRs, and of the latter, changes in heart rate or conditioned suppression. Consummatory conditioning was based on an association between the CS and a precise sensory representation of the US, whereas preparatory conditioning was based on an association between the CS and the emotional or affective tone of the US (e.g., whether it was appetitive or aversive). And whereas consummatory conditioning proceeded relatively slowly and ideally required a relatively short interval between onset of CS and of US, preparatory conditioning could occur in one or two trials even when the interval between CS and US was several minutes.

In practice, Konorski assumed, most forms of conditioning are a mixture of the two; put more precisely, most conditioning experiments involve both processes in varying degrees. But the reality of the distinction is supported by several converging lines of evidence. Whereas conditioning of the rabbit's eyeblink requires a large number of trials and a CS–US interval no longer than a few seconds, pairing of the same CS and same US will produce changes in heart rate to the CS after one or two trials with a CS–US interval two or three times as long (Schneiderman, 1972). That the CS is associated with different representations of the US in different paradigms is suggested by the results of blocking experiments. If a compound CS—consisting, say, of a buzzer and a light—is paired with a US, conditioning to one element of the compound may be prevented or blocked if the other element has already been established as a signal for that US (Kamin, 1969). Blocking is reliably observed in rabbit eyelid conditioning, but only if the previously conditioned element was a signal for exactly the same US as that occurring on compound trials. If the pretrained CS signals shock to one eye and the compound shock to the other, there is no evidence of blocking (Stickney & Donahoe, 1983). In experiments on conditioned suppression, by contrast, blocking is still observed even when the pretrained CS and the compound are paired with quite different aversive events (Bakal, Johnson, & Rescorla, 1974; Dickinson & Dearing, 1979).

Neurobiological analysis also attests to the importance of the distinction between consummatory and preparatory conditioning. The work of Thompson, Moore, Yeo, and their associates (Desmond & Moore, 1982; Thompson, 1983; Yeo, Hardiman, Glickstein, & Russell, 1982) strongly suggests that the integrity of the cerebellum is essential for successful acquisition of two paradigm examples of defensive, consummatory CRs—eyelid and leg flexion responses. Diffuse, preparatory CRs, however (such as changes in heart rate), which can be abolished by the administration of opiates, are entirely spared by the cerebellar lesions that abolish eyelid and flexion CRs. Conversely, a well-established eyelid CR can survive opiate administration, although (confirming the role of preparatory conditioning in the initial acquisition of any CR) after only moderate training opiates can abolish this response also.

One further interesting distinction between consummatory and preparatory CRs is that they appear to be forgotten at different rates, even when they are measured in the same experiment. Conditioned suppression, as an example of largely preparatory conditioning, is retained remarkably

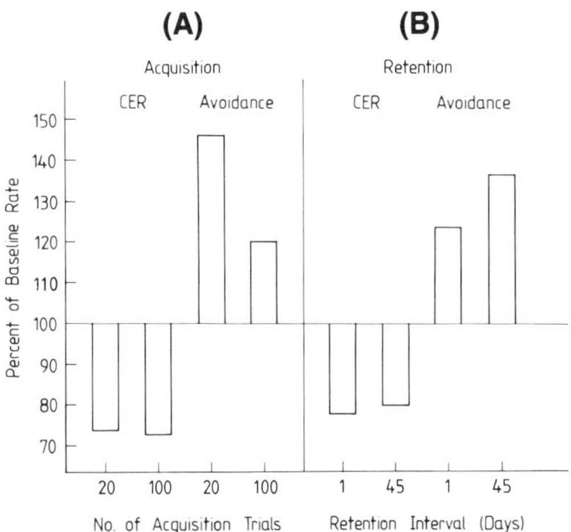


**FIGURE 19.1.** Acquisition and retention of conditioning to a CS paired with an airblast, when conditioning is measured either by the ability of the CS to suppress rewarded lever pressing (CER) or by its ability to enhance the rate at which animals perform an avoidance response (Avoidance). The CER measure reveals suppression of baseline responding, which is acquired within 20 conditioning trials and maintained when animals are given 100 conditioning trials (A), and is retained, essentially without loss, over a 45-day retention interval (B). The Avoidance measure reveals enhancement of baseline responding which is *greater* after 20 than after 100 CS–US pairings (A), but which recovers, after 100 pairings, over a long retention interval (B). (Data from Henderson, Patterson, & Jackson, 1980.)

well over intervals of 2 months or more (Gleitman & Holmes, 1967; Henderson, Patterson, & Jackson, 1980). But Henderson *et al.* found that other measures of conditioning to a CS paired with their aversive US (a blast of air) showed relatively rapid forgetting. Such a CS not only suppresses appetitively reinforced instrumental responding, as in conditioned suppression, it can also increase the rate at which animals perform a well-established avoidance response, even though it signals a US (air blast) different from the footshock used to reinforce avoidance responding (see Figure 19.1). That this enhancement of avoidance responding reflects the preparatory component of conditioning to the CS is suggested by the observation illustrated in Figure 19.1A—that a small number of conditioning trials is sufficient to produce maximum enhancement, which then declines with continued training as the CS is associated with a more precise representation of the US. The critical finding, illustrated in Figure 19.1B, is that enhancement can then be restored by interposing a delay of 45 days between conditioning and test trials, thus indicating that the general affective reactions conditioned to the CS are well retained while information about its precise consequence is forgotten.

Knowledge of the general affective consequences of a CS is thus both acquired more rapidly and forgotten more slowly than knowledge of the precise sensory attributes of the US it signals. Even in simple Pavlovian conditioning, therefore, different measures will produce quite different answers to the question concerning what animals have learned from, or how much they remember of, a conditioning episode. It should come as no surprise, then, if different measures of recall also reveal different outcomes in human experiments. It would certainly not be surprising, for example, if amnesic patients were to show good retention of a conditioned emotional response at the same time that they professed total ignorance of the precise consequences of a stimulus.

## ASSOCIATIVE AND NONASSOCIATIVE LEARNING AND MEMORY

Modern conditioning theory is, as I have argued, fundamentally associationist in outlook. Experimenters arrange certain relationships between events, and their subjects show that they have detected these relationships and associated these events by changing their behavior appropriately. But some instances of learning and memory, even in conditioning experiments, may not involve associating one event with another.

Simple, repetitive presentation of a single stimulus has effects on an animal's behavior toward that stimulus that seem to depend on the retention of information about it. Some of the reactions initially elicited by a novel stimulus habituate or disappear with repeated presentation of the stimulus; and because habituation is retained over intervals of a day or more and can be distinguished from transient receptor adaptation or effector fatigue, it can reasonably be regarded as dependent on learning (Thompson & Spencer, 1966). Repeated presentation of a stimulus also affects the readiness of an animal to associate that stimulus with a US in a Pavlovian conditioning experiment or to use it as a signal for action in an instrumental experiment (Lubow, 1973). This effect, usually termed "latent inhibition," is also retained over intervals of several days and must also, therefore, reflect some long-term learning.

A novel stimulus, therefore, both elicits various unconditioned reactions and enters rapidly into association with other events; a familiar stimulus does neither. The question is why. On the face of it, it does not seem likely that either habituation or latent inhibition should reflect any associative learning. All that the experimenter does to produce these phenomena is to present a stimulus, which is followed by no further consequence, in an unchanging environment. With what could this stimulus be associated that it should cease to elicit responses and be slow to condition? In fact, associationist theorists do not give up that easily, and two quite different associative accounts of habituation and latent inhibition have been proposed. One suggestion has been that the stimulus is associated with the context in which it is repeatedly presented (Wagner, 1976, 1978, 1981). There is good reason to believe that associations are established between a CS and the context in which it occurs (e.g., Marlin, 1982; Rescorla, 1984). According to Wagner, when an animal is replaced in a context in which a stimulus has previously been presented, contextual stimuli retrieve a representation of the stimulus into a short-term store; he assumes that a stimulus will be worse processed if, when it is presented, there is already a representation of it in the short-term store. Long-term habituation and latent inhibition, therefore, depend on context–stimulus associations ensuring that a representation of the stimulus is retrieved before the stimulus is actually presented.

A quite different class of theory assumes that habituation and latent inhibition occur because the repeatedly presented stimulus is followed by no event of consequence and is associated with just this state of affairs. Informally, perhaps, the suggestion is that a novel stimulus elicits startle responses because it might be dangerous; they habituate as the animal learns that it is not. A more formal suggestion is that the stimulus is associated with inhibition of the arousal system (Stein, 1966). Latent inhibition can be interpreted as a case of proactive interface: Learning that a stimulus is followed by nothing interferes with later learning that it is followed by a US (Testa & Ternes, 1977; see also Staddon, Chapter 16, this volume).

There are difficulties, I shall argue, with both of these associative analyses. Wagner predicts that both habituation and latent inhibition should be context-specific: If a stimulus is repeatedly presented in one context, it should habituate and be slow to condition in that context, but its apparent novelty should be restored simply by presenting it in an entirely different context. In the case of habituation there is little or no evidence of any such effect: Marlin and Miller (1981) could detect no effect of a change in context on habituation of startle responses to an auditory stimulus; Hall and Channel (1985), although finding significant dishabituation of the orienting responses to a light when it was presented in a totally novel context, observed no such effect when it was presented in a different, but equally familiar, context from that in which it had been habituated. Dishabituation by novelty *per se* is more consistent with the dual-process account of habituation (Groves & Thompson, 1970) than with Wagner's associative account.

There is good evidence, on the other hand, that latent inhibition is sensitive to a change in context: Repeated exposure to a stimulus in one context will retard subsequent conditioning in that context, but not if the stimulus is presented in a different, but equally familiar context (Channel & Hall, 1983; Hall & Minor, 1984; Lovibond, Preston, & Mackintosh, 1984). Although this seems consistent with Wagner's account, there is reason to believe that it must happen for rather different reasons. According to Wagner, latent inhibition occurs when a stimulus is conditioned in the context in which it was originally exposed because it has been associated with that context. The implication is that latent inhibition would be significantly reduced, if not abolished altogether, if these context–stimulus associations were extinguished. One way to achieve this should be simply to place subjects in that context without presenting the stimulus, but such extinction trials have only rarely been reported to reduce latent inhibition to a previously presented stimulus (Baker & Mercier, 1982; Hall & Minor, 1984). An even more effective way of weakening the association between the preexposed stimulus and the context of this preexposure should be to alternate sessions in that context during which the stimulus is not presented with sessions in another, discriminably different context during which the stimulus is presented. According to Wagner this negative correlation treatment should severely reduce latent inhibition in the first context; but no such effect can be detected (Hall & Minor, 1984).

The other class of associative account fares no better. If latent inhibition and habituation occur because the stimulus is associated with its zero consequence, they should respond in the same way to treatments that affect other forms of associative learning, for example, the association between CS and US in Pavlovian conditioning. Thus, the finding that lesions to the hippocampal system tend to interfere with the course of habituation and of latent inhibition but have no comparable effect on simple Pavlovian conditioning must argue against the attempt to apply a common associative theory to all three phenomena (Gray, 1982; Solomon & Moore, 1975). Purely behavioral experiments have also established clear-cut differences. A second stimulus presented during the interval between a CS and a US can interfere with the course of conditioning to this first CS, but this interference or overshadowing effect depends on the novelty of the interfering stimulus. It it is familiar and, therefore, through latent inhibition, is not itself readily associated with the US, its presence will not interfere with conditioning to the first, target CS (Revusky, 1971; D. R. Shanks & G. C. Preston, unpublished experiments). Shanks and Preston, however, went on to show that habituation of responding to the first stimulus is interfered with by the presentation of the second stimulus, whether the latter is familiar or not.

Behavioral evidence of the difference in mechanism between latent inhibition and conditioning is suggested by the effects of contextual change. It has long been known that if animals are conditioned to a CS in one context, they will often respond less to the CS if tested in another, different context. But it appears that much, if not all of this effect can be attributed to the fact that the second context is usually an unfamiliar place, in which animals have never received any conditioning trials. If animals are conditioned to two CSs, A and B, one always presented in context 1, the other in context 2, the two CSs can be tested in the opposite contexts with no evidence of generalization decrement whatsoever (Lovibond *et al.*, 1984). But even when conditioning transfers perfectly from one context to another, latent inhibition does not: Lovibond *et al.* found marked context specificity of latent inhibition using the same stimuli, contexts, and general procedures that yielded no evidence of context specificity of conditioning. Their results are shown in Figure 19.2.

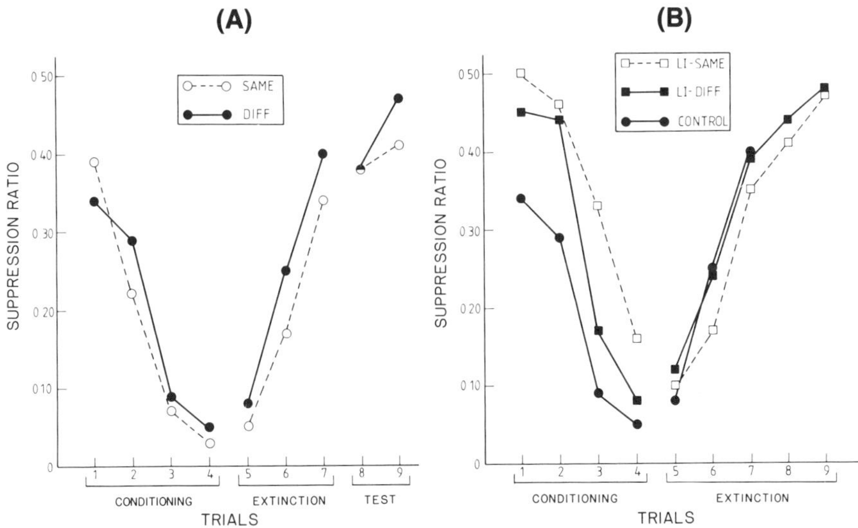


**FIGURE 19.2.** The effect of a change in context on conditioning (A) and on latent inhibition (B). In the conditioning experiment (A), animals received conditioning trials to a tone paired with shock in context 1 and to a light paired with shock in context 2. Both CSs were then extinguished, either in the same contexts as in original conditioning (group SAME) or with the light in context 1 and the tone in context 2 (group DIFF). Finally, the tone and light were tested again, for both groups, in their original conditioning contexts. Contextual specificity of conditioning and extinction would be evidenced if the group DIFF showed more rapid extinction than the group SAME but a recovery of suppression when the two CSs were tested in their original conditioning contexts. No such effect was apparent. In the latent inhibition experiment (B), tone and light were initially presented, without reinforcement, in contexts 1 and 2, respectively, this being followed by a series of conditioning trials in which tone and light were each paired with shock, either in the same (LI-SAME) or different (LI-DIFF) contexts. The control group received no preexposure to the two CSs before the start of conditioning. Both LI groups were slower to condition than the controls, but this retardation was significantly greater in LI-SAME than in LI-DIFF. Indeed, the difference between controls and LI-DIFF is largely due to a difference in initial, unconditioned suppression, on trial 1. This unconditioned suppression had habituated in the two LI groups (note that this habituation seems to have transferred perfectly well from one context to the other). (Data from Lovibond, Preston, & Mackintosh, 1984.)

In spite of their plausibility, therefore, there are some grounds for rejecting both varieties of associative account of habituation and latent inhibition. If a familiar stimulus does not cease to elicit startle responses or become a poorer CS because it is associated with the context in which it is presented or with its zero consequences, we must look for some nonassociative account. It is not really so difficult to do so. One suggestion is that repeated presentation of a stimulus results in the establishment of a stored representation of that stimulus (by a process of learning about which we no doubt know rather little) and that incoming stimuli are compared against this model. If they match, they are recognized as familiar (Konorski, 1967; Sokolov, 1963). Habituation and latent inhibition are tests of recognition memory; it is stimuli recognized as familiar that no longer elicit startle responses and are only slowly associated with new consequences.

This conclusion may seem well-nigh vacuous: To say that a particular phenomenon is a test of recognition memory is hardly to provide a complete explanation of that phenomenon. What it may suggest here, however, is some interesting parallels with the human case, and those may help us to understand some puzzling discrepancies that, to this point, I have rather carefully glided over. Consider the case of the contextual specificity of conditioning, habituation, and latent inhibition. I have claimed that Pavlovian conditioning can transfer without loss from one context to another, but that even when it does, latent inhibition does not. One possibility, of course, is that this discrepancy is an artifact of measurement, or of differences in sensitivity; but there is no good evidence for this suggestion, and the reproducibility of the difference does little to support it. Similarly, Hall and Channell (1985) have argued that latent inhibition may be disrupted by a change in context when habituation is not. This difference too might reflect a problem of measurement, and this is a possibility that will certainly require further research. But if the differences are real, how are they to be explained?

Pavlovian conditioning may be regarded as a test of cued recall: The CS is a retrieval cue (more precisely a list retrieval cue), and the occurrence of the CR indicates that the presentation of the CS has resulted in successful retrieval of a representation of the US associated with it. If latent inhibition is regarded as a test of recognition, then the discrepancy in the effects of a change of context amounts to this: A stimulus can act as an effective retrieval cue even if it is presented in a different context, but it is recognized as the same stimulus only when it is presented in the same context as before. But this difference between the outcome of a test of cued recall and of a test of recognition, however paradoxical it may seem, will be quite familiar to students of amnesia. Amnesic patients, as both Schacter (Chapter 20, this volume) and Weiskrantz (Chapter 21, this volume) make clear, often display precisely this dissociation between recognition and cued recall. It appears that amnesic patients can perform well on tests of cued recall provided they interpret the task as a matter of giving the first answer that comes into their head rather than as one that requires them to recognize why the answer is correct, for example, by saying whether the item had been part of a previously studied paired-associative list (Graf, Squire, & Mandler, 1984).

The animal data also suggest that there may be a difference between latent inhibition, which is sensitive to a change in context, and habituation, which is not. It may seem paradoxical to insist that both are tests of recognition, but amnesic patients also provide a clear example of the distinction between two senses of recognition. They are, in fact, capable of discriminating between items that they have seen before and those that they have not;

indeed they can discriminate between more and less familiar items. But they are extremely bad at saying whether an item is more familiar because it was seen today rather than yesterday, or because it was seen three times rather than once (Huppert & Piercy, 1976, 1978). This sort of finding, indeed, has been used to suggest that there are at least two processes of recognition, one automatic and based on a sense of familiarity and the other reflective and based on search and justification (Baddeley, 1982; Mandler, 1980). It seems possible that latent inhibition is sensitive to the extent to which an animal recognizes why a stimulus seems familiar (because it has been presented before in this context) in a way in which habituation is not.

## CONCLUSIONS

These are, undoubtedly, somewhat speculative comments, but an occasion when people from different backgrounds are brought together to discuss common interests must be one where some speculation is licensed. My aim will have been achieved if I have persuaded anyone studying the neurobiology of conditioning in simple systems or amnesia in humans that animal conditioning experiments are more complicated and therefore potentially more interesting than they had supposed. If conditioning is still conceptualized as a matter of associating temporarily related events, the variety of events that can be associated and the variety of ways in which they can be represented means that conditioning is neither monolithic nor simple. An animal can learn a number of different things in a conditioning experiment, and these differences in knowledge will be reflected in differences in behavior. And even if conditioning itself is associative, other nonassociative forms of learning are implicated in conditioning experiments, which therefore may be able to comment on some of the distinctions between different forms of human memory and to illuminate some little-understood puzzles.

## ACKNOWLEDGMENTS

The preparation of this chapter was supported by a grant from the U.K. Science and Engineering Research Council. I am indebted to G. Hall, G. C. Preston, and D. R. Shanks for permission to cite unpublished work.

## REFERENCES

Adams, C., & Dickinson, A. Actions and habits: Variations in associative representation during instrumental learning. In N. E. Spear & R. R. Miller (Eds.), *Information processing in animals: Memory mechanisms*. Hillsdale, N.J.: Erlbaum, 1981.

Baddeley, A. D. Domains of recollection. *Psychological Review*, 1982, *89*, 708–729.

Bakal, C. W., Johnson, R. D., & Rescorla, R. A. The effect of change in US quality on the blocking effect. *Pavlovian Journal of Biological Sciences*, 1974, *9*, 97–103.

Baker, A. G., & Mercier, P. Extinction of the context and latent inhibition. *Learning and Motivation*, 1982, *13*, 391–416.

Channell, S., & Hall, G. Contextual effects in latent inhibition with an appetitive conditioning procedure. *Animal Learning and Behavior*, 1983, *11*, 67–74.

Colwill, R. M., & Rescorla, R. A. Post-conditioning devaluation of a reinforcer affects instrumental responding. *Journal of Experimental Psychology: Animal Behavior Processes*, 1985, *11*, 120–132.

Desmond, J. E., & Moore, J. W. A brain stem region essential for the classically conditioned but not unconditioned nictitating membrane response. *Physiology and Behavior*, 1982, *28*, 1029–1033.

Dickinson, A. *Contemporary animal learning theory*. Cambridge: Cambridge University Press, 1980.

Dickinson, A. Actions and habits: The development of behavioural autonomy. *Philosophical Transactions of the Royal Society of London, Series B*, 1985, *308*, 67–78.

Dickinson, A., & Dearing, M. F. Appetitive-aversive interactions and inhibitory processes. In A. Dickinson & R. A. Boakes (Eds.), *Mechanisms of learning and motivation*. Hillsdale, N.J.: Erlbaum, 1979.

Gibbon, J., & Church, R. M. Sources of variance in an information processing theory of timing. In H. L. Roitblat, T. G. Bever, & H. S. Terrace (Eds.), *Animal cognition*. Hillsdale, N.J.: Erlbaum, 1984.

Gillan, D. J. Reasoning in the chimpanzee: II. Transitive inference. *Journal of Experimental Psychology: Animal Behavior Processes*, 1981, *7*, 150–164.

Gillan, D. J., Premack, D., & Woodruff, G. Reasoning in the chimpanzee: I. Analogical reasoning. *Journal of Experimental Psychology: Animal Behavior Processes*, 1981, *7*, 1–17.

Gleitman, H., & Holmes, P. A. Retention of incompletely learned CER in rats. *Psychonomic Science*, 1967, *7*, 19–20.

Graf, P., Squire, L. R., & Mandler, G. The information that amnesic patients do not forget. *Journal of Experimental Psychology: Learning, Memory and Cognition*, 1984, *19*, 164–178.

Grant, D. S. Rehearsal in pigeon short-term memory. In H. L. Roitbalt, T. G. Bever, & H. S. Terrace (Eds.), *Animal cognition*. Hillsdale, N.J.: Erlbaum, 1984.

Gray, J. A. *The neuropsychology of anxiety*. London: Oxford University Press, 1982.

Groves, P. M., & Thompson, R. F. Habituation: A dual-process theory. *Psychological Review*, 1970, *77*, 419–450.

Hall, G., & Channell, S. Differential effects of contextual change on latent inhibition and on the habituation of an orienting response. *Journal of Experimental Psychology: Animal Behavior Processes*, 1985, *11*, 470–481.

Hall, G., & Minor, H. A search for context-stimulus associations in latent inhibition. *Quarterly Journal of Experimental Psychology*, 1984, *36B*, 145–169.

Hawkins, R. D., & Kandel, E. R. Is there a cell-biological alphabet for simple forms of learning? *Psychological Review*, 1984, *91*, 375–391.

Henderson, R. W., Patterson, J. M., & Jackson, R. L. Acquisition and retention of control of instrumental behavior by a cue-signaling airblast: How specific are conditioned anticipations? *Learning and Motivation*, 1980, *11*, 407–426.

Holland, P. C., & Straub, J. J. Differential effects of two ways of devaluing the unconditioned stimulus after Pavlovian appetitive conditioning. *Journal of Experimental Psychology: Animal Behavior Processes*, 1979, *5*, 65–78.

Huppert, F. A., & Piercy, M. Recognition memory in amnesic patients: Effects of temporal context and familiarity of material. *Cortex*, 1976, *12*, 3–20.

Huppert, F. A., & Piercy, M. The role of trace strength in recency and frequency judgments by amnesic and control subjects. *Quarterly Journal of Experimental Psychology*, 1978, *30*, 347–354.

Kamin, L. J. Predictability, surprise, attention and conditioning. In B. Campbell & R. Church (Eds.), *Punishment and aversive behavior*. New York: Appleton-Century-Crofts, 1969.

Konorski, J. *Integrative activity of the brain*. Chicago: University of Chicago Press, 1967.

Lovibond, P. F., Preston, G. C., & Mackintosh, N. J. Context specificity of conditioning, extinction and latent inhibition. *Journal of Experimental Psychology: Animal Behavior Processes*, 1984, *10*, 360–375.

Lubow, R. E. Latent inhibition. *Psychological Bulletin*, 1973, *79*, 398–407.

Mackintosh, N. J. *Conditioning and associative learning*. Oxford: Oxford University Press, 1983.

Maki, W. S. Some problems for a theory of working memory. In H. L. Roitblat, T. G. Bever, & H. S. Terrace (Eds.), *Animal cognition*. Hillsdale, N.J.: Erlbaum, 1984.

Mandler, G. Recognizing: The judgment of previous occurrence. *Psychological Review*, 1980, *87*, 252–271.

Marlin, N. A. Within-compound associations between the context and the conditioned stimulus. *Learning and Motivation*, 1982, *13*, 526–541.

Marlin, N. A., & Miller, R. R. Associations to contextual stimuli as a determinant of long-term habituation. *Journal of Experimental Psychology: Animal Behavior Processes*, 1981, *7*, 313–333.

Neuenschwander, N., Fabrigoule, G., Cotton, M. M., & Mackintosh, N. J. Changes in the control of signalled avoidance responding with overtraining. *Quarterly Journal of Experimental Psychology*, *37B*, in press.

Rescorla, R. A. Associations between Pavlovian CSs and context. *Journal of Experimental Psychology: Animal Behavior Processes*, 1984, *10*, 195–204.

Rescorla, R. A. Associations in animal learning. In L.-G. Nilsson & T. Archer (Eds.), *Perspectives on animal learning and human memory*. Hillsdale, N.J.: Erlbaum, 1985.

Revusky, S. The role of interference in association over a delay. In W. K. Honig & P. H. R. James (Eds.), *Animal memory*. New York: Academic Press, 1971.

Roitblat, H. L. Representations in pigeon working memory. In H. L. Roitblat, T. G. Bever, & H. S. Terrace (Eds.), *Animal cognition*. Hillsdale, N.J.: Erlbaum, 1984.

Ryle, G. *The concept of mind*. London: Hutchinson, 1949.

Schneiderman, N. Response system divergencies in aversive classical conditioning. In A. H. Black & W. F. Prokasy (Eds.), *Classical conditioning II*. New York: Appleton-Century-Crofts, 1972.

Sokolov, Y. N. *Perception and the conditioned reflex*. Oxford: Pergamon Press, 1963.

Solomon, P. R., & Moore, J. W. Latent inhibition and stimulus generalization of the classically conditioned nictitating membrane response in rabbits following dorsal hippocampal ablation. *Journal of Comparative and Physiological Psychology*, 1975, *89*, 1192–1203.

Squire, L. R., & Zola-Morgan, S. The neurology of memory: the case for correspondence between the findings for human and nonhuman primate. In J. A. Deutsch (Ed.), *The physiological basis of memory* (2nd ed.). New York: Academic Press, 1983.

Stein, L. Habituation and stimulus novelty: A model based on conditioning. *Psychological Review*, 1966, *73*, 352–356.

Stickney, K. J., & Donahoe, J. W. Attenuation of blocking by a change in US locus. *Animal Learning and Behavior*, 1983, *11*, 60–66.

Testa, T. J., & Ternes, J. W. Specificity of conditioning mechanisms in the modification of food preferences. In L. M. Barker, M. R. Best, & M. Domjan (Eds.), *Learning mechanisms in food selection*. Waco, Tex.: Baylor University Press, 1977.

Thompson, R. F. Neuronal substrates of simple associative learning: Classical conditioning. *Trends in Neuroscience*, 1983, *6*, 270–275.

Thompson, R. F., & Spencer, W. A. Habituation: A model phenomenon for the study of neuronal substrates of behavior. *Psychological Review*, 1966, *173*, 16–43.

Wagner, A. R. Priming in STM: An information-processing mechanism for self-generated or retrieval-generated depression in performance. In T. J. Tighe & R. N. Leaton (Eds.), *Habituation: Perspectives from child development, animal behavior, and neurophysiology*. Hillsdale, N.J.: Erlbaum, 1976.

Wagner, A. R. Expectancies and the priming of STM. In S. H. Hulse, H. Fowler, & W. K. Honig (Eds.), *Cognitive processes in animal behavior*. Hillsdale, N.J.: Erlbaum, 1978.

Wagner, A. R. SOP: A model of automatic memory processing in animal behavior. In N.E. Spear & R.R. Miller (Eds.), *Information processing in animals: Memory mechanisms*. Hillsdale, N.J.: Erlbaum, 1981.

Weiskrantz, L., & Warrington, E. K. Conditioning in amnesic patients. *Neuropsychologia, 17*, 1979, 187–194.

Wittgenstein, L. *Philosophical investigations*. Oxford: Blackwell, 1953.

Yeo, C. H., Hardiman, M. J., Glickstein, M., & Russell, I. S. Lesions of cerebellar nuclei abolish the classically conditioned nictitating membrane response. *Society for Neuroscience Abstracts, 8*, 1982, 22.

CHAPTER 20

# Multiple Forms of Memory in Humans and Animals

**Daniel L. Schacter**
University of Toronto
Toronto, Ontario, Canada

For much of the past quarter-century, the empirical, theoretical, and even metatheoretical concerns of investigators in different sectors of memory research have existed in relative isolation from one another; there has been little consensus about or convergence upon issues of cross-disciplinary concern. In recent years, however, a good deal of research and theory in cognitive psychology, neuropsychology, and neuroscience has begun to converge upon a common theme. A growing number of investigators have argued that memory should not be viewed as a unitary or monolithic entity; instead, they have proposed that memory comprises distinct "forms," "systems," or "types" that may function in qualitatively different ways. Although the specific ideas proposed by different investigators vary widely, the general notion that it may be necessary to postulate multiple forms of memory has been endorsed by researchers in diverse sectors of psychological and neurobiological research (e.g., Cohen, 1984; Deutsch, 1984; Goldberg, 1984; Graf, Squire, & Mandler, 1984; Hirsh, 1974, 1980; Johnson, 1984; Kinsbourne & Wood, 1975, 1982; Mishkin, Malamut, & Bachevalier, 1984; Mishkin & Petri, 1984; Moscovitch, 1982; Oakley, 1981, 1983; O'Keefe & Nadel, 1978; Olton, Becker, & Handelmann, 1979; Rolls, 1984; Schacter & Moscovitch, 1984; Schacter & Tulving, 1982; Squire & Cohen, 1984; Thomas, 1984; Tulving, 1972, 1983; Warrington & Weiskrantz, 1982).

In the present chapter I shall delineate some of the phenomena that have provided a basis for postulating multiple forms of memory, discuss problems that arise when interpreting these phenomena, and consider the prospects for integrating relevant human and nonhuman research. My own research activities focus exclusively on normal and amnesic humans, hence the bulk of the chapter will be concerned with issues that arise from experiments conducted with these populations. However, I believe firmly that the problem of multiple forms of memory requires cross-disciplinary convergence and will not be resolved on the basis of research with human subjects alone (see Schacter, 1984, in press-b). Thus, I shall also discuss some of the relevant data and theory that have been generated by studies of nonhuman organisms.

The chapter is divided into two main sections, corresponding to two major phenomena that have provided a basis for postulating multiple forms of memory in humans. In the first section, I shall consider briefly studies of amnesic patients that have revealed a dissociation between intact skill learning and conscious recollection. In the second section, I shall discuss in greater detail evidence that reveals a similar dissociation between direct priming effects and conscious recollection in both normal and amnesic subjects. I hope to delineate and perhaps clarify several of the problematic interpretive issues surrounding such studies. Within each of the two main sections, I shall also discuss how the phenomena observed in humans may be related to observations reported in the animal literature.

## ASSUMPTIONS AND TERMINOLOGY

Before discussing the relevant data, it may be useful to state briefly what is meant by phrases such as "multiple forms of memory" or "multiple memory systems." These phrases mean different things to different people, and the resulting semantic confusions sometimes constitute a source of needless controversy. In the present chapter, I shall use the phrase "multiple forms of memory" to refer to the notion that there are qualitatively different memorial consequences of an experience that are mediated by processes that can, but may not always, function independently of one another. At the current stage of our deliberations, I view the postulation of multiple forms of memory as a *descriptive*, rather than as an *explanatory* enterprise. To postulate that performance on different types of memory tasks is mediated by "different forms of memory" does not explain the nature of the underlying processes, but it can provide a useful description of the data and hence point the way toward an explanation. Thus, the notion of multiple forms of memory, as used in this chapter, should not be viewed as an attempt to postulate separate "boxes in the head" that account for performance on different tasks, nor is it contrary to or inconsistent with a process-oriented view of memory (cf. Craik & Lockhart, 1972). Rather, it is a hypothesis that distinct classes or clusters of memory processes can be identified. These different classes of memory processes undoubtedly share many features in common and frequently interact with one another during the performance of memory tasks. However, if the hypothesis of multiple forms of memory is correct, the principles that are ultimately needed to explain one type of memory will not be sufficient to explain another.

One further background issue merits brief commentary. The evidence that will be considered in this chapter suggests that skill acquisition and direct priming effects are mediated by a type of memory that can function independently of the process or system that underlies conscious recollection of recently experienced events and information. It is not clear at present whether skill learning and priming effects both depend upon the same form of memory or whether they depend upon different forms of memory. The striking similarity between the two phenomena is that neither require conscious or explicit recollection; this point of resemblance has led several investigators to propose that skill learning and priming depend upon a common system (e.g., Cohen, 1984; Squire & Cohen, 1984). However, as will become clear later in the chapter, there are also important differences between the two phenomena (see also Schacter, in press-a). Unfortunately, there has been virtually no research that has directly explored the relation between skill learning and priming, so it is not possible to provide a firm, empirically based answer to the question of how they are related. My own reading of the literature is that the two may ultimately turn out to be based on distinct and dissociable types of memory. For purposes of exposition, however, I shall refer to skills and priming as manifestations of an implicit form of memory and shall refer to recall and recognition as manifestations of an explicit form of memory. In conformity with the preceding comments, I use the terms "implicit" and "explicit" in a general, descriptive sense (cf. Graf & Schacter, 1985). Although these terms are similar to ones employed by other investigators, I use them to avoid various difficulties with existing characterizations that have been discussed elsewhere (Schacter, in press-a). Implicit memory is revealed on tasks that do not require reference to a specific prior episode; explicit memory is revealed on tasks that do. The theoretical challenge is to characterize the processes and structures underlying these forms of memory and to elucidate the principles that are required to explain them.

## SKILL LEARNING IN AMNESIA

A necessary condition for the postulation of multiple forms of memory is the observation of dissociations between tasks, or classes of tasks, that are hypothesized to be differentially sensitive to different forms of memory. In the absence of dissociation, there would be no basis for questioning the view that memory is a unitary entity that can be understood in terms of a single set of basic principles. It is only when we have evidence of dissociation that the hypothesis of multiple forms of memory can even be entertained.

One of the most compelling dissociations has been provided by studies of patients with organic amnesia. The amnesic syndrome occurs as a consequence of various types of neurological dysfunction, including bilateral lesions of the medial temporal regions, Korsakoff syndrome, closed head injuries, ruptured aneurysms, and anoxia (for review, see Cermak, 1982; Hirst, 1982; Schacter & Crovitz, 1977; Squire, 1982; Whitty & Zangwill,

1977). The hallmark of the amnesic syndrome is a profound deficit in the acquisition and retention of new memories that exists in conjunction with relatively intact intellectual function, normal or near-normal immediate memory, and preservation of much premorbid knowledge and skills. The anterograde memory impairment of amnesic patients can be detected on standard laboratory tests of memory, such as free recall, cued recall, and recognition of recently presented words, sentences, paragraphs, pictures, or faces, and is also evident in everyday situations outside of the laboratory. For example, in a recent case study I played two rounds of golf with a densely amnesic patient who was in the early stages of Alzheimer disease (Schacter, 1983). The patient was unable to remember the location of his tee shots when he searched for his ball after a delay of 30–60 seconds and was also unable to remember how many strokes he had taken when questioned at the conclusion of each hole. But the same patient used his premorbid knowledge of golf vocabulary, rules, and strategies normally and also displayed relatively intact golfing skills.

In view of the generality and severity of amnesic patients' anterograde memory disorder, a unitary view of memory might lead one to expect impairments on all tests that require some type of new learning. The first data to disconfirm this expectation were provided by demonstrations of near-normal motor skill learning in the well-known patient H. M. (Corkin, 1965; Milner, 1962; Milner, Corkin, & Teuber, 1968). The most striking feature of these studies was the dissociation between H. M.'s relatively intact ability to acquire various motor skills and his complete lack of explicit memory for the learning sessions. Although H. M.'s rate of motor skill learning was not entirely normal, an outcome that has been attributed to his generally slowed processing speed (cf. Corkin, 1965), subsequent research has established that a variety of amnesic patients can acquire and retain perceptual–motor skills in a normal manner. Intact skill learning has been observed on tasks involving rotary pursuit (Brooks & Baddeley, 1976; Cermak, Lewis, Butters, & Goodglass, 1973; Cohen, 1981), visual maze learning (Brooks & Baddeley, 1976), reading of mirror-inverted words (Cohen & Squire, 1980; Moscovitch, 1982), and puzzle solutions (Brooks & Baddeley, 1976; Cohen, 1984).

The foregoing observations have led a number of investigators to propose that skill learning and conscious recollection are mediated by different memory systems (cf. Cohen, 1984; Cohen & Squire, 1980; Milner, 1962; Moscovitch, 1982; Schacter & Tulving, 1982; Squire, 1982; Squire & Cohen, 1984; Squire & Zola-Morgan, 1983; Tulving, 1983). The logic underlying this argument seems straightforward: Amnesic patients have sustained brain damage that severely impairs their capacity for explicit recollection and has no effect on their ability to acquire skills; hence, it is permissible to infer that the brain system responsible for explicit recollection can function independently of the system that mediates acquisition of skills. A critical component of this argument is the demonstration of *normal* skill learning in amnesic patients. If amnesic patients demonstrated some skill-learning capacities but did not perform normally on skill-learning tasks, it would be difficult to maintain that skill learning and explicit recollection are mediated by qualitatively different forms of memory because amnesic patients would be impaired on both types of tasks. The finding of some residual skill-learning capacity could then be accounted for by postulating that some memory tasks are "easier" than others for all subjects and that the same damaged system mediates amnesic patients' performance on both skill-learning and explicit-memory tasks. Even if amnesic patients seemed less impaired on skill-learning tasks than on explicit-memory tasks, it would be difficult to make meaningful comparisons between them because of substantial differences in the measurement scales involved in the two types of tasks. For these reasons, theoretical accounts of preserved skill learning in amnesia that postulate different memory systems have placed considerable emphasis upon the observation of normal performance in amnesic patients (cf. Cohen, 1984; Squire & Cohen, 1983).

The emphasis on normal performance, though justified, has tended to obscure a point that may be critical for theoretical interpretation: Amnesic patients can exhibit normal performance on skill-learning tasks only when control subjects' capacity for explicit recollection is not helpful for performing a task. If the capacity for conscious recollection facilitates the acquisition of a new skill and if normal subjects make use of this capacity, the performance of amnesic patients would necessarily appear impaired by comparison. Such a finding would not provide strong support for a claim of dissociable forms of memory and might even be used as evidence against it. However, to reject the multiple forms of memory argument on the basis of this observation could be quite misleading. For example, imagine that the "true" underlying state of affairs is one in which skill memory and explicit recollection can be mediated by functionally independent systems. Further imagine that there are skill-learning tasks on which normal subjects can make use of both systems. In this scenario, amnesic patients would frequently reveal "impaired" performance on skill-learning tasks because they do not have recourse to the intact memory system that supplements the performance of control subjects. However, the rejection of a multiple systems view would be incorrect.

In light of the foregoing considerations, the fact that amnesic patients *do* exhibit normal performance on various skill-learning tasks suggests that conscious recollection is neither useful nor necessary for performance of these tasks. It does not follow, however, that all tasks that tap preserved memory functions in amnesic patients are entirely insensitive to the influence of conscious recollection. Indeed, as we shall see shortly, some tasks that are used to evaluate priming effects can be influenced by conscious recollection. Thus, although the observation of normal performance in amnesic patients does provide evidence that is consistent with a multiple-memories interpretation, the failure to observe normal performance does not necessarily rule out such an interpretation. I will elaborate upon this point in the discussion of direct priming effects.

A second point that must be kept in mind when interpreting the evidence for spared learning in amnesia is that not all amnesic patients may perform normally on skill-acquisition tasks. It is entirely conceivable that in some cases of amnesia, brain damage will infringe upon the structures that mediate "preserved" tasks such as skill learning. In fact, there is now evidence that some groups of amnesic patients do not perform normally on mirror-reading tasks or the Tower of Hanoi puzzle (Martone, Butters, Wolfe, & Cermak, 1984). However, as long as evidence exists that some amnesic patients *can* acquire skills normally, the negative findings are not inconsistent with the view that skills and conscious recollection represent different forms of memory.

The claim that skills are mediated by a type of memory different from the one that underlies explicit recollection is buttressed by converging evidence from animal research. This literature has been reviewed ably elsewhere and need not be presented in detail here (see Mishkin *et al.*, 1984; O'Keefe & Nadel, 1978; Olton *et al.*, 1979; Squire & Zola-Morgan, 1983). The general pattern of results is clear: Monkeys and rats that have suffered medial temporal damage are severely impaired on tasks that require memory for a specific episode, such as delayed matching or nonmatching to sample. However, these same animals learn normally on a variety of tasks that are similar to those used to assess skill learning in humans, in the sense that learning is gradual and does not depend upon memory for any one specific event. These tasks include learning of difficult object and pattern discriminations (e.g., Mishkin, 1954; Orbach, Milner, & Rasmussen, 1960; Zola-Morgan, Squire, & Mishkin, 1982) and acquisition of motor skills (Zola-Morgan & Squire, 1984). Once again, however, it is worth noting that the normal performance of amnesic monkeys suggests that performance on tasks such as visual discrimination does not benefit from the capacity for explicit remembering. If explicit remembering had been useful for performing the task, amnesic monkeys should have been at least partially impaired.

## DIRECT PRIMING EFFECTS IN NORMAL AND AMNESIC HUMANS

The second main source of evidence that has been used to support the claim of multiple forms of memory in human subjects is provided by the phenomenon of direct priming. Whereas skill learning builds gradually across trials, direct priming effects occur after a single exposure to an item (e.g., a familiar word) and are revealed by facilitated processing of the item on a variety of retention tasks that need not involve explicit memory for the item's prior occurrence. For example, on a word-completion task, subjects are given fragmented versions of previously presented words and new words and are required to complete the fragments with the first word that comes to mind. In a series of important experiments, Warrington and Weiskrantz (1968, 1970, 1974) demonstrated that completion performance of amnesic patients was increased by prior presentation of a word as much as was the performance of control subjects. However, in spite of this normal priming effect, the amnesic patients exhibited a severe impairment on a Yes/No recognition test in which they were required to remember explicitly the prior occurrence of a word.

The dissociation between intact word-completion performance and impaired recognition memory that was observed by Warrington and Weiskrantz has been replicated and extended by investigators who have studied various types of amnesic patients (Diamond & Rozin, 1984; Graf & Schacter, 1985; Graf *et al.*, 1984). In addition, amnesic patients have demonstrated normal priming effects, in the absence of conscious recollection, on priming tasks such as lexical decision (Moscovitch, 1982) and homophone spelling (Jacoby & Witherspoon, 1982).

The data from amnesic patients are complemented by two other types of evidence that suggest that priming and remembering may be mediated by qualitatively different forms of memory. First, several studies have revealed that experimental variables that have a large influence on explicit recall and recognition have little or no effect on the magnitude of priming, such as retention interval (Jacoby & Dallas, 1981; Scarborough, Gerard, & Cortese, 1979; Tulving, Schacter, & Stark, 1982), level of processing of study materials (Carroll & Kirsner, 1982; Graf *et al.*, 1984; Jacoby & Dallas, 1981), and modality of study and test presentation (Jacoby & Dallas, 1981; Scarborough *et al.*, 1979; Vanderwart, 1984). Second, it has been shown that the magnitude of priming effects is statistically independent of performance on recognition memory tasks (Eich, 1984; Jacoby & Witherspoon, 1982; Schacter, McLachlan, Moscovitch, & Tulving, 1984; Tulving *et al.*, 1982).

The present discussion of priming effects will be divided into two sections. The first section will examine some methodological points that bear upon the interpretation of data that are derived from priming tests. The second section will focus upon more general theoretical issues concerning the nature of priming effects.

## INTERPRETING THE OUTCOME OF PRIMING TESTS: SUBTLE INFLUENCES OF EXPLICIT REMEMBERING

One of the major differences between tasks that are used to assess priming effects and those that are used to assess skill learning is that tasks of the former class seem to be more easily influenced by explicit remembering than tasks of the latter class. Because this point has substantial implications for understanding the nature of priming effects, I will consider studies that demonstrate that each of the three types of evidence for dissociation between priming and remembering discussed previously—normal priming in amnesic patients, differential effects of experimental variables on recollection and priming, and stochastic independence between recognition and priming—depend critically upon exactly how a priming task is treated by normal subjects.

Consider first the finding of intact priming of word completion in amnesic patients. A recent study by Graf *et al.* (1984) indicates that whether or not normal performance is observed in amnesic patients depends critically upon the instructions given to the subjects at the time of the completion test. When the completion task was presented as a "filler" task that was unrelated to the previously studied items and subjects were simply told to complete test fragments with the first word that came to mind, performance of amnesic and control subjects was equivalent. However, when subjects were instructed to use the word fragments as cues to remember explicitly the previously studied words, performance of the controls improved with respect to completion instructions, whereas amnesic patients' performance did not change as a function of instructions. Similar findings have been observed in other studies that have compared word-completion performance in normal and amnesic subjects (Graf & Schacter, 1985; Schacter, in press-a). Task instructions can also influence the effect that an independent variable has on subjects' performance. For example, Graf *et al.* (1984) observed that experimental manipulations that influence subjects' encoding processes have little or no effect on word-completion performance: The magnitude of priming is similar following semantic and nonsemantic study tasks. However, when subjects are instructed to use the same word-fragment cues to remember the target words, there is a substantial superiority of semantic encoding over nonsemantic encoding. I have observed a virtually identical pattern of results in a study that used different target materials and is described later in the chapter. The third type of evidence for a dissociation between priming and remembering—stochastic independence between explicit and implicit memory tasks—also depends upon the instructions given to subjects on the completion test. In an as yet unpublished study carried out by Gordon Hayman in Toronto, college students studied common words and were then given a Yes/No recognition test followed by a fragment-completion test. Half of the subjects were instructed to complete the fragments with the first words that came to mind; no connection was made between the completion task and the study list. The other half were instructed to use the fragments as cues to help remember the previously studied words. Hayman found stochastic independence between recognition memory and fragment completion in the former condition but observed significant dependence between the two tasks in the latter condition.

The pattern of results from the foregoing studies demonstrates that test instructions have a powerful influence on word-completion performance.

These results suggest that there are two distinct ways to perform word-completion tasks, one of which is independent of the capacity for explicit recollection and one of which makes use of this capacity. Thus, the kinds of inferences that are made about performance on priming tests depend critically on the degree to which subjects make use of conscious retrieval mechanisms. Even when instructions do not direct subjects to use test cues as memory aids, it is possible that they will do so nonetheless if the instructions lack sufficient constraint. For example, when subjects are told to do their best to identify words on a fragment-completion test and are not further constrained to write down the first word that comes to mind, they may make use of a conscious retrieval strategy if they notice the relation between the study and test materials. Such a strategy is likely to occur when short study lists and brief retention intervals are used or when a priming test includes only cues that represent study list materials and does not include nonlist cues. Two studies illustrate this point. Jacoby (1983a) assessed priming effects with a word-identification task (cf. Neisser, 1954) in which subjects are given brief exposures (on the order of 35 msec) to previously studied words and new words and are required to identify them. A number of studies have revealed that priming in the word-identification task can be dissociated from explicit remembering (Jacoby, 1983b; Jacoby & Dallas, 1981). Jacoby found higher levels of identification performance when a large proportion of the studied items were tested than when a small proportion of items were tested; he suggested that subjects may have treated the word-identification task as a memory task when a large proportion of the target words were included on the test. Relevant data are also provided by an ongoing longitudinal study in our laboratory that includes several groups of amnesic patients (Schacter, McLachlan *et al.*, 1984). The pertinent data come from a word fragment-completion task that was administered to patients in the early stages of Alzheimer disease and to a group of matched controls. Three different versions of the task were given to each subject at 6-month intervals. Because all subjects received the task on multiple occasions, we did not attempt to conceal the fact that the test fragments represented items that had appeared on the study list, reasoning that control subjects would probably "catch on" after several exposures to the task. All of the test fragments had appeared previously, performance was tested immediately after list presentation, and subjects were told to try to identify the words represented by the fragments. Under these conditions, priming effects in Alzheimer patients, though substantial, were smaller than those observed in control subjects. We attributed this difference to the use of retrieval strategies by control subjects that enabled them to gain access to explicit memories that were not available to the Alzheimer patients. We hypothesized that patients' performance was mediated by a relatively "pure" (i.e., implicit) priming effect. Consistent with this interpretation, we have found that Alzheimer patients' performance on the three different versions of the fragment-completion task did not change over the year that we have observed them thus far, whereas their recognition performance on the same task deteriorated across sessions, as did their performance on all other tests of explicit recall and recognition that were used in the study.

The fact that conscious recollection can influence performance on priming tasks, even though priming can occur independently of it, raises some tricky interpretive issues that have not yet been resolved satisfactorily. One critical problem concerns the interpretation of amnesic patients' performance on priming tasks. The finding that densely amnesic patients do show normal priming effects under appropriate test conditions constitutes strong evidence that priming can occur independently of conscious recollection. Suppose, however, that amnesic patients do *not* show normal priming on a particular task under conditions in which test instructions attempt to minimize the influence of conscious retrieval. How should we interpret such data? One possibility is that the negative results are specific to the particular patient or patients who participated in the study. As noted earlier, not all amnesic patients reveal intact skill learning and it is reasonable to suppose that not all will reveal normal amounts of priming. It also bears mentioning that it is not an entirely straightforward matter to determine whether an individual amnesic patient does or does not show "normal priming." In the skill-learning literature, demonstrations of normal performance by H. M. and other individual patients have provided impressive evidence of dissociation. However, the tasks that have been used to assess skill learning are typically based on repeated observations and hence yield relatively stable data for individual subjects. This is not always the case with priming tasks. Here, data usually derive from a single test, and counterbalanced designs are required because results on a particular test form may be powerfully influenced by idiosyncratic item variations or item–subject interactions. Thus, performance of individual subjects—even college students—may depend upon which items appear in which conditions on a particular test form. To obtain reliable evidence concerning an individual subject's performance, it is necessary to administer many versions of a priming test. If, however, lack of priming is consistently found in a group of amnesic patients, a second possibility is that the data indicate that some aspect of the process or system that mediates priming is impaired in amnesic patients. A third possibility, of course, is that a failure to observe priming in amnesia suggests that conscious recollection played some role in normal subjects' performance. Although there is clearly an element of circularity in such an interpretation (i.e., certain aspects of priming are normal in amnesics, hence any abnormalities reflect the use of conscious retrieval strategies by controls), it probably should not be dismissed out of hand.

Recent research that has investigated priming of nonwords—letter strings that do not represent an English word (e.g., *numdy*)—provides an illustration of the problem. Several studies of normal subjects have shown that exposure to nonwords enhances performance on tasks that are frequently used to study priming effects, such as lexical decision (Feustel, Shiffrin, & Salasoo, 1983) and word identification (Jacoby & Witherspoon, 1982). However, amnesic patients show no evidence of priming with nonwords on tachistoscopic identification tasks (Cermak, 1984) or on fragment-completion tasks (Diamond & Rozin, 1984; Rozin, 1976). Does this pattern of results indicate that so-called priming of nonwords in normal subjects reflects the influence of conscious recollection? Does it demonstrate that priming of nonwords occurs independently of conscious recollection in normals but not in amnesic patients? Or does it indicate that the appropriate techniques have not yet been devised to elicit priming of nonwords in amnesic patients? We do not yet know the answer to these questions. However, several characteristics of priming effects observed with nonwords favor the first possibility. Scarborough, Cortese, and Scarborough (1977, Exp. 4) observed that the magnitude of priming effects on a lexical decision task did not decline across an intersession delay when familiar words were used as the critical materials. However, priming of nonwords declined substantially across the same temporal interval; in fact, there was no priming effect at the long delay. Scarborough *et al.* also observed a significant effect of delay when subjects were given an explicit-remembering task (Yes/No recognition) for both words and nonwords. This pattern of findings suggests that "priming" of nonwords was mediated by explicit memory. Consistent with this interpretation, Jacoby and Witherspoon (1982) have reported that the magnitude of priming effects with nonwords is correlated with recognition memory performance, whereas priming of real words is independent of recognition memory. Other investigators have observed that the magnitude of repetition effects is generally smaller with nonwords than with real words and have reported additional differences between priming of words and nonwords in lexical-decision tasks and identification tasks (e.g., Feustel *et al.*, 1983; McKoon & Ratcliff, 1979). Whatever the correct answer to the nonword issue, the general problem illustrated here is likely to arise frequently in the future. Because there is no obvious way to distinguish between the alternative hypotheses on the basis of one or two studies, the best we can do at the present time is to emphasize the need for basing theoretical interpretations on overall patterns of data produced by large numbers of studies.

In summary, conscious recollection can influence performance on tests that are sensitive to priming effects, but it is not necessary for priming to occur. Evidence that priming is based upon—or, more accurately, *can* be based upon—a form of memory fundamentally different from the one that underlies explicit recall and recognition is obtained when test conditions and instructions minimize the influence of conscious retrieval strategies. Failure of amnesic patients to show priming on a particular test is difficult to interpret unambiguously and must be viewed in the broader context of relevant research. However, the observation of normal priming effects in amnesic patients does provide clear evidence that performance on a task can be independent of conscious recollection.

## THE NATURE OF IMPLICIT PRIMING EFFECTS: SOME RECENT EVIDENCE

### Activation of Unitized Structures

The experiments discussed thus far that have provided evidence for dissociation between priming and remembering have used familiar words as study materials. Because familiar words have a preexisting representation in memory prior to their appearance in a study list, it has been argued that priming effects may be based upon the activation of preexisting representations (e.g., Graf & Mandler, 1984; Mandler, 1980; Morton, 1969; Rozin, 1976). By this view, the activation process occurs independently of the processes that mediate explicit remembering; hence, priming can occur normally even when explicit remembering is impaired.

In recent work, we have evaluated the role of preexisting representations in priming effects. More specifically, several studies have examined whether the occurrence of priming effects, independent of explicit recollection, is mediated by the activation of preexisting *unitized structures*. Following Hayes-Roth (1977), I define a unitized structure as a discrete memory representation that can be activated in an all-or-none manner and that behaves as a cohesive, integrated whole. Single words are the most common examples of unitized structures. If, however, the foregoing hypothesis has merit, it should be possible to observe priming effects with unitized structures other than words.

The possibility was examined in a recent experiment that used linguistic idioms as the critical materials. Idioms were used because existing evidence indicates that they have the properties of a unitized structure—they can be activated in an all-or-none manner, and they behave as a single representational entity (Horowitz & Manelis, 1972; Horowitz & Prytulak, 1969). In the experiment, amnesic patients, matched controls, and college students studied idiomatic phrases such as *sour grapes* and *small potatoes* and also studied nonunitized phrases that were formed by recombining the components of the idioms (e.g., *sour potatoes* and *small grapes*). Subjects were then given a free-association test in which the first words of the phrases (e.g., *sour, small*) appeared among a long list of distractor cues, and they were instructed to provide the first word that came to mind in response to the cue. The relevant results of the experiment are presented in Table 20.1. They indicate that there was a substantial priming effect for the idiomatic phrases: Baseline probability of providing a target (e.g., *grapes*) to a cue (e.g., *sour*) was only 1%, whereas it ranged from 23% to 29% following a single exposure to the idiom. Moreover, the magnitude of the priming effect was just as large in the amnesic patients as it was in the two control groups, even though the amnesic patients were severely impaired on a subsequent

**TABLE 20.1.** Percentage of Idioms Completed and Recalled in Amnesic Patients, Matched Controls, and Student Controls

| | Unitized phrases[a] | | Nonunitized phrases[a] | |
|---|---|---|---|---|
| Subject group | W.C. | C.R. | W.C. | C.R. |
| Amnesic patients | 27.2 | 27.2 | .00 | .00 |
| Matched controls | 23.6 | 54.4 | 2.0 | 35.0 |
| Student controls | 29.1 | 75.0 | .00 | 75.0 |
| Mean | 26.6 | 52.2 | 1.0 | 37.0 |

[a] W.C., word completion; C.R., cued recall.

cued-recall test—amnesic patients produced no more targets on the recall test than they had on the free-association test, whereas control subjects produced more than twice as many items with cued-recall instructions (Table 20.1). Table 20.1 also indicates, however, that there was no priming of nonunitized phrases in any of the subject groups. This pattern of results supports the hypothesis that the occurrence of implicit priming effects depends critically upon the activation of unitized structures.

A follow-up experiment that used similar materials compared the effects of semantic versus nonsemantic processing activities on priming and remembering of idiomatic phrases. The aforementioned work of Graf *et al.* (1984) and Jacoby and Dallas (1981) has established that priming of individual words is influenced little if at all by semantic versus nonsemantic processing manipulations, whereas explicit remembering is affected substantially by them. Is the same pattern of results observed with unitized structures other than words? In an attempt to answer this question, I conducted an experiment in which college students were shown a list that included eight idiomatic phrases, and engaged in either a semantic study task (reading a phrase that specified the meaning of the idiom) or a nonsemantic study task (comparing vowels and consonants in the two words). Subjects then provided free associations to list and nonlist cues in the manner described above and subsequently attempted to recall the list targets in response to the same cues that had appeared on the free-association test. The results, displayed in Table 20.2, are consistent with the idea that unitized structures play a crucial role in priming effects. There was a small, nonsignificant effect of semantic versus nonsemantic study task on the magnitude of priming effects. In contrast, the study task manipulation had an extremely large effect on cued-recall performance: 72% of the targets were recalled following the semantic study task, and only 22% were recalled following the nonsemantic study task. Subjects in the latter condition, like amnesic patients in the previous experiment, produced no more targets on the recall test than they had on the free-association test.

**TABLE 20.2.** Percentage of Idioms Completed and Recalled as a Function of Study Task

| | Type of test [a] | |
|---|---|---|
| Study task | W.C. | C.R. |
| Semantic | 28.1 | 72.2 |
| Nonsemantic | 19.4 | 22.3 |

[a] W.C., word completion; C.R., cued recall. Baseline completion rate was 2% in both semantic and nonsemantic conditions.

The observation that priming of idioms occurs normally in amnesia and is not significantly affected by study task manipulations lends support to the view that activation of unitized structures is critically involved in the implicit form of memory that is tapped by priming tasks.

### Implicit Memory for New Associations

In a recent series of experiments, Peter Graf and I have further evaluated the idea that implicit priming effects are mediated by the activation of unitized structures by examining whether priming effects on word-completion tasks are influenced by new associations between normatively unrelated words that are established for the first time during a study trial (Graf & Schacter, 1985). Newly established associations between unrelated words have no preexisting, unitized representation. Thus, if implicit priming effects are mediated entirely by the activation of unitized structures, the magnitude of priming effects should be uninfluenced by new associations that are established for the first time on a study trial.

Previous research with college students has provided inconclusive results concerning this question (cf. Carroll & Kirsner, 1982; McKoon & Ratcliff, 1979; see Graf & Schacter, 1985, for discussion), but studies of amnesic patients suggest that new associations may be expressed independently of conscious recollection (Moscovitch, 1984; Schacter, Harbluk, & McLachlan, 1984; Weiskrantz & Warrington, 1979). Our current research extends the findings of these latter studies and also suggests that priming of new associations differs from priming of unitized structures with respect to the influence of semantic processing activities. In one of our experiments, amnesic patients, matched controls, and college students studied pairs of unrelated words (e.g., *window*—REASON), and then completed three-letter fragments of targets as well as nonlist items with the first word that came to mind. Some of the targets were presented in the *same context* on the completion test (e.g., *window*—REA ____ ), and others were presented in a *different context* (e.g., *mold*—REA ____ ). We reasoned that the presence of a new association between the unrelated words would be indicated if subjects completed fragments of list items more frequently in the same-context condition than in the different-context condition. We further suggested that if amnesic patients revealed a normal associative influence on word-completion performance, the effect could be attributed to an implicit form of memory because amnesic patients are almost entirely incapable of explicitly remembering new associations; indeed, that is one of the central characteristics of patients with memory disorders.

The experiment included 12 amnesics of diverse etiologies, 12 matched control subjects, and 24 college students; all subjects were instructed to generate sentences that included the two words from each pair and were then given a word-completion task. The results of this experiment were clear: Amnesic patients completed significantly more test fragments in the same-context condition than in the different-context condition, and their performance was indistinguishable from that of controls (Figure 20.1). However, on a subsequent cued-recall task in which subjects were asked to *remember* the response in the presence of the cue, the amnesic patients were profoundly impaired; they recalled virtually none of the responses, whereas controls recalled over 50% of them.

The observation that newly acquired associations affected priming in amnesic patients is somewhat surprising, because it is well known that such patients perform poorly on tests of associative learning. Our experiment, however, included patients with a range of memory disorders: Some had relatively mild amnesia, whereas others had severe amnesia. It is thus possible

**FIGURE 20.1.** Mean completion performance for unrelated word pairs that were presented in a task that required generating a sentence for each pair. The completion test showed the initial three letters of the response word from each pair, either with the paired stimulus word from the study list (same context) or with another word (different context). A separate control group was used to obtain an estimate of baseline completion performance on the target response words, shown by the dashed lines. Vertical bars show the standard errors of the means.

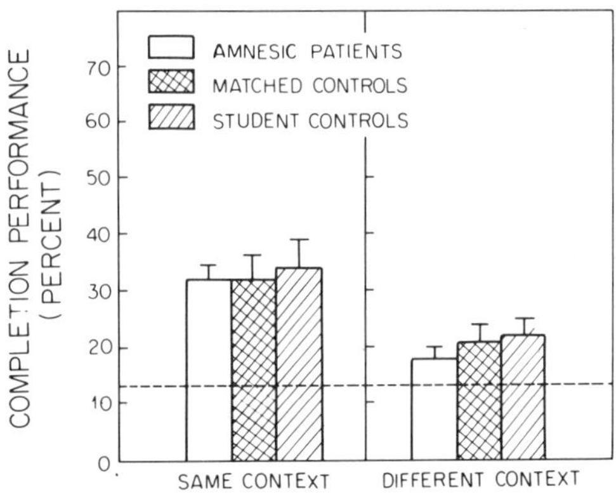

**TABLE 20.3.** Percentage of Words Completed by Mildly and Severely Amnesic Patients as a Function of Test Context

| | Test context | | | |
|---|---|---|---|---|
| | Severely amnesic | | Mildly amnesic | |
| Patient | Same | Different | Same | Different |
| 1 | 37.5 | 45.8 | 37.5 | 16.7 |
| 2 | 29.2 | 16.7 | 29.2 | 16.7 |
| 3 | 29.2 | 33.3 | 41.7 | 29.2 |
| 4 | 20.8 | 20.8 | 29.2 | 25.0 |
| Mean | 29.2 | 29.2 | 34.4 | 21.9 |

that associative influences on completion performance are observed only in those patients with milder forms of memory impairment. To investigate this issue, we recently performed an additional experiment that contrasts the performance of four patients with mild memory problems (three head injuries, one ruptured aneurysm) and four with severe memory problems (two head injuries—one anoxic, one encephalitic). All patients experienced difficulties on standard tests of recall and recognition. However, the patients with mild memory problems had a higher MQ on the Wechsler Memory Scale (84.1) than did the patients with severe amnesia (72.8), even though the two groups' performance on tests of intellectual and cognitive function did not differ. The experiment was similar to our initial study, except that each patient was exposed to and tested on four different lists. This procedure was used in an attempt to generate stable data for each patient.

The results of this study, displayed in Table 20.3, reveal that the mildly amnesic patients showed a consistent trend for more priming in the same- versus the different-context condition. The severely amnesic patients, however, showed no such trend. These data are consistent with the notion that implicit memory for new associations is related to severity of memory disorder. Note, however, that the overall level of priming in the two groups of patients did not differ; the severely amnesic patients showed more priming in the different-context condition than did the mildly amnesic patients. This is a somewhat puzzling result, and it indicates that we must be cautious about the theoretical implications of these data. One speculative possibility, however, seems worth pursuing. To the extent that priming in the different-context condition reflects the activation of preexisting representations (see Graf & Schacter, 1985), whereas priming in the same-context condition is based on a newly established memory representation, it is possible that there are two distinct types of priming effects. One involves the activation of unitized structures, and is preserved in patients with both mild and severe memory disorders; the other involves the establishment of new associations and is preserved only in patients with relatively mild memory impairments.

Further evidence consistent with this view is provided by some recent work that has examined the processing activities that are necessary to support implicit and explicit memory for new associations. In an initial study (Graf & Schacter, 1985, Exp. 1), we found that word-completion performance was affected by new associations only when subjects engaged in elaborative processing (i.e., generating a sentence to relate the words) at the time of study. When subjects engaged in a nonsemantic processing task (i.e., comparing the number of vowels and consonants in the two words), there was no associative influence on word-completion performance; subjects completed about the same number of fragments in the same-context condition and the different-context condition. This pattern of results contrasts with data discussed earlier demonstrating that priming of unitized structures such as words and idioms is unaffected by semantic versus nonsemantic processing activities. Thus, it is possible that priming effects that depend upon elaborative processing occur only in patients with milder forms of amnesia, whereas priming that is independent of elaborative processing occurs in even severely amnesic patients.

In a subsequent experiment, however, we have found that implicit retention of new associations does not depend upon elaborative processing in the same way that explicit recollection does (Schacter & Graf, submitted). Subjects in this experiment were shown a long list of unrelated word pairs. In the *elaborate* condition, subjects were required to generate a sentence for each pair that included the two critical words. In the *rate* condition, subjects were shown a sentence that included the two critical words and were asked to rate how meaningfully the sentence related the words on a scale of 1–7. Word-completion and cued-recall performance were tested in the same manner as described for the previous experiments. One group was tested after a 3-minute delay and a second group was tested after a 24-hour delay.

The results displayed in Figure 20.2 indicate that both the processing manipulation and the retention interval manipulation had large effects on

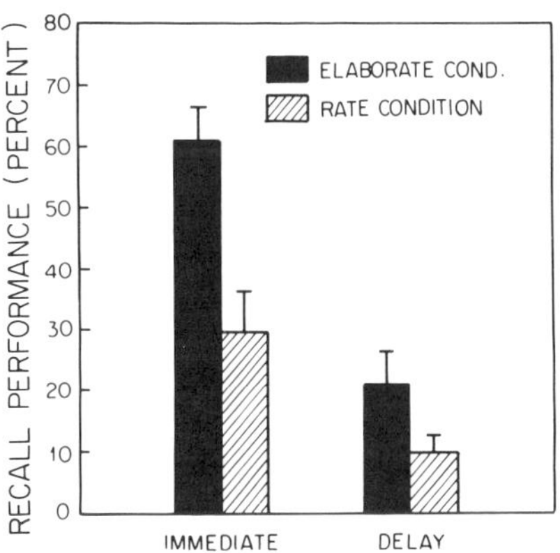


**FIGURE 20.2.** Mean cued-recall performance for unrelated word pairs that were presented in a task that required generating a sentence for each pair (elaborate) or rating the meaningfulness of an experimenter-provided sentence that included the word pair (rate). The cued-recall test presented the stimulus term from the pair and required response recall; it was administered either several minutes after study (immediate) or 24 hours after study (delay). Vertical bars show the standard errors of the means.

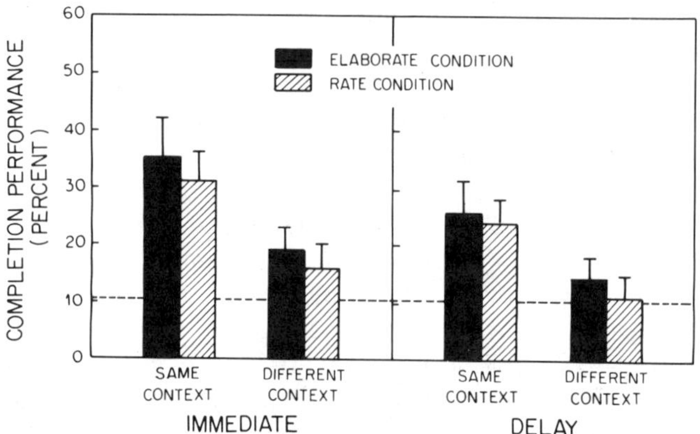


**FIGURE 20.3.** Mean completion performance for unrelated word pairs that were presented in a task that required generating a sentence for each pair (elaborate) or rating the meaningfulness of an experimenter-provided sentence that included the word pair (rate). The word-completion test was administered either 3 minutes after study (immediate) or 24 hours after study (delay). The completion test showed the initial three letters of the response word from each pair, either with the paired stimulus word from the study list (same context) or with another word (different context). The dashed bar represents an estimate of baseline completion performance on the target response words. Vertical bars show the standard errors of the means.

explicit recall. Subjects remembered more than twice as many words in the elaborate condition than they remembered in the rate condition; and they recalled many fewer words after a long delay than after a short delay. By contrast, the data in Figure 20.3 indicate that implicit memory for new associations, as indexed by word-completion performance, was unaffected by type of processing and retention interval. Subjects completed significantly more words in the same-context condition than they did in the different-context condition, and the magnitude of the same/different effect was about the same in each of the experimental conditions.

The foregoing data, in conjunction with the results reported by Graf and Schacter (Exp. 1), suggest that implicit memory for new associations requires some form of meaningful processing at the time of study, but does not require further elaborative activity of the kind that has a large effect on explicit remembering. Although we do not understand precisely what kinds of encoding activities are necessary and sufficient to support implicit memory for new associations, our results indicate that there are similarities as well as differences between the encoding processes underlying implicit and explicit memory for new associations.

## Role of Unitized Structures in Priming of New Associations

The results of the foregoing experiments demonstrate that implicit priming effects cannot be explained entirely in terms of the activation of unitized structures. New associations can also be expressed implicitly, in the absence of conscious recollection. These data, of course, need not imply that unitized structures play no role whatsoever in priming; the results of the idiom experiments discussed earlier suggest that they do. As suggested, it is worth entertaining the idea that there are varieties of implicit priming effects. One type involves the activation of unitized structures and is largely uninfluenced by the nature of encoding activities; a second type entails implicit retention of new associations and depends upon semantic encoding activities.

Several lines of evidence suggest that unitized structures play an important role even in the second type of priming effect. As discussed earlier, when normal subjects study a nonunitized word pair (e.g., *sour potatoes*) and are given the first word (e.g., *sour*) on a free-association test, there is no evidence of priming; subjects almost never provide the target response. Graf and Schacter also observed an absence of priming when amnesic patients studied unrelated word pairs and were asked to provide the first word that came to mind in response to the stimulus term (e.g., *window*— ______ ). To obtain evidence for priming of new associations, it is necessary to include part of the target word—that is, part of a unitized structure—on a completion test (e.g., *window*—REA ____ ). By contrast, explicit remembering occurs even when only one word from a recently studied pair is given as a test cue.

The importance of including part of a preexisting unit as a test target is further illustrated by some of our work with amnesic patients that uses the *method of vanishing cues* (Glisky, Schacter, & Tulving, 1984). We have used this procedure in an attempt to teach patients new vocabulary and to facilitate the acquisition of new associations. In the most pertinent experiment, patients were shown the stimulus terms of unrelated paired-associates and were provided with the successive letters of the target until they guessed it or until the entire word was displayed (e.g., *tobacco*— B __________ ; BO ________ ; BOU ______ ; BOUL _____ ; BOULD ____ ; BOULDE __ ; BOULDER). On successive trials, patients were given one less letter than was required to complete the target on the previous trial, and letters were added until patients provided the correct response. Using this procedure, we found that each of four densely amnesic patients eventually learned to produce the target in the presence of the stimulus without any target letters. The critical finding, however, was revealed by an analysis of the number of trials required to make the initial reduction from $n$ to $n - 1$ letters at each of the pairwise transition points in the task (i.e., the number of trials required to move from needing five letters to needing four, from four to three, three to two, and one to zero). These data revealed that amnesics required 1.7 trials to make each pairwise transition until the final letter was withdrawn. At this point, a striking discontinuity was observed: Amnesics required an average of 24.9 trials to produce the item for the first time in the absence of any target letters. Normal subjects, who treat the task as one of conscious recall, showed no evidence of this discontinuity. We have observed similar results in a vocabulary-learning study that employed the same procedure (Glisky *et al.*, 1984).

The data from the vanishing cues procedure, along with the results of the aforementioned idioms experiments, highlight the critical dependence of priming on the provision of part of a unitized structure as a target response. This dependence in turn suggests that different types of representations are involved in priming effects on the one hand and explicit remembering on the other: The associations acquired by amnesic patients and those expressed by normals on a word-completion test may be quite different from the type of associations that underlie explicit recall and recognition (cf. Wickelgren, 1979). We are just now beginning to investigate these differences. One suggestive possibility, however, is that the new associations that underlie implicit memory in amnesic patients are extremely specific and rigid. An example of this rigidity is provided by a case study in which I attempted to teach some new facts to a densely amnesic patient. The patient was asked questions about little-known facts and was given the answer when he could not produce it himself (e.g., Where was the first game of professional baseball played? *Hoboken*). This patient could sometimes respond correctly when the question was asked again after a brief delay, even though he had no explicit recollection of how he acquired the fact (see Schacter, Harbluk, & McLachlan, 1984). However, the patient could provide the correct response only if the question was repeated in virtually identical form at the time of test. For example, when asked to state what he knew about the history of baseball, the patient provided a number of appropriate answers but never mentioned that the first game had been played in Hoboken. Similarly, when asked to state what he knew about various cities, including Hoboken, he never mentioned anything about baseball. By contrast, control subjects could answer the specific question and could also use their new knowledge to respond to the more general questions. Similar observations have been reported by Cermak (1984).

Further examples of what might be called *hyperspecific associations* are provided by our studies of vocabulary learning in amnesic patients (Glisky *et al.*, 1984). Using the method of vanishing cues, we found that amnesic patients could acquire close to 30 new items of computer vocabulary after many repetitions, and that this new knowledge persisted over delays of weeks and months with little loss. For example, when given the definition "a repeated portion of a program," amnesics eventually learned to respond with "loop" in the absence of any target letters, and they retained this response over a 6-week delay. Although the patients had acquired this new association by visual display of the definition on a computer monitor, they could state the correct answer just as frequently when the definition was simply read to them in a completely different room. Thus, their new knowledge did not depend upon the actual response that they made, was not tied to the environmental context in which they acquired it, and was not modality specific. It did, however, depend critically upon the wording of the question that was put to them. When even relatively small changes in the wording of definitions were made, performance of the amnesic patients was disrupted significantly. In a subsequent phase of this research, we found that amnesic patients could carry out computer commands and even learn to write an extremely simple program. Once again, however, the amnesic patients' ability to use their knowledge depended critically on the precise wording of instructions. For instance, a densely amnesic, head-injured patient had responded consistently to the definition "to store a program" with the correct response "save." However, after the patient had written a brief program and was instructed "Now store your program on the disk," he did not produce the correct response and did so only after being given the initial letter of the word. When asked a rather open-ended question concerning how he would write a program, the patient gave fragmentary and frequently inaccurate answers, even though he could perform the constituent operations and could answer correctly questions concerning these operations when they were similar to the actual commands he had been receiving. Control subjects, by contrast, had no difficulty answering the open-ended questions.

The foregoing examples illustrate that the kind of new associations revealed by amnesic patients may differ qualitatively from the new associations that support explicit remembering. A further relevant finding is that amnesic patients show evidence of classical conditioning, which requires some form of associative learning, in the absence of explicit remembering (Weiskrantz & Warrington, 1979). As has been discussed elsewhere (Schacter & Moscovitch, 1984), these classically conditioned responses seem to be locked into specific stimuli in a rigid manner, without regard to the global context in which the response occurs. Significantly, normal acquisition of classically conditioned responses has been observed consistently in hippocampal animals (see O'Keefe & Nadel, 1978, for review). The observation that amnesic humans and animals may reveal similar effects in classical conditioning raises the question of whether they are based upon the same mechanism. One possibility is that acquisition of conditioned responses in amnesic patients depends in part on the same mechanism that underlies priming of new associations in word completion. Although this is largely a speculative hypothesis, it invites the question of whether direct priming effects might also occur in animals.

## DIRECT PRIMING IN ANIMALS: PROBLEMS AND POSSIBILITIES

It was noted earlier that the animal literature provides converging evidence for the dissociation between skill learning and explicit remembering. However, I am not aware of any animal research that has revealed a phenomenon akin to that of direct priming in the sense that it has been used in this chapter—a facilitation of processing a stimulus after a single exposure to it that can occur independently of explicit recollection (for a somewhat different type of priming, see Wagner, 1978). Moreover, there are several reasons why it may prove difficult to construct an experimental analogue of the priming effects that have been observed in humans. First, as has been discussed in detail, priming effects can be influenced by explicit remembering and hence depend critically upon test instructions. It is not clear how one would prevent an animal from using an "explicit-remembering" strategy on a task, even if one had set up the task in such a way that it could be solved in the absence of explicit remembering (see Olton, 1984b, for a similar point). This difficulty, however, means only that it may be difficult to dissociate priming and remembering in normal animals. It might still be possible to study priming in amnesic animals, which presumably would have little capacity for explicit remembering. Comparison with normal animals could be problematic because controls might rely upon an explicit-remembering strategy, but the question could be investigated empirically. A second, more serious obstacle is presented when one considers the constraints that would have to be observed to construct a priming task for animals. As was discussed earlier, priming effects in normal and amnesic humans seem to depend critically on preexisting unitized representations. Targets typically consist of either well-defined units such as words and idioms or a novel pairing of two preexisting units (e.g., an unrelated word pair). Priming is observed when part of a unit is presented as a cue, and the subjects respond by providing the rest of the unit. In humans, functional units can be defined linguistically. What are the functional units of animal memory, and do they vary across species? It may be crucial to have at least some clues concerning this question before an animal analogue of direct priming effects can be constructed.

The third problem centers upon the notion of explicit remembering itself. To even raise the question of whether it is possible to dissociate priming and explicit recollection in animals presupposes that they can engage in mnemonic activity that is akin to explicit remembering. This issue has long been disputed (e.g., Ruggierio & Flagg, 1976; Schacter, 1982, Chapter 7). Many investigators have assumed that performance on tasks such as delayed matching and nonmatching to sample is based on a form of memory that is similar to what we would call explicit remembering in humans (e.g., Mishkin *et al.*, 1984; Olton, 1984a; Ruggierio & Flagg, 1976; Squire & Zola-Morgan, 1983). My own reading of the literature is consistent with this view: Tasks such as delayed matching and nonmatching to sample appear to make mnemonic demands that are quite similar to those made by the recognition memory tasks used in human research, as is demonstrated by the fact that both amnesic patients and hippocampal monkeys perform poorly on delayed matching and nonmatching tasks (Milner & Taylor, 1972; Olton, 1984a; Sidman, Stoddard, & Mohr, 1968; Squire & Zola-Morgan, 1983). It is conceivable, however, that memory performance on these tasks is mediated by a form of memory that is similar to the one that mediates priming effects in humans. After all, we do not know whether an animal has a conscious "recollective experience" (Tulving, 1983) of an event or whether it simply reveals the effects of recent experiences, independently of conscious recollection, as an amnesic human does. If we accepted the latter alternative, however, it would be difficult to understand why normal monkeys perform at high levels on tasks that reveal substantial impairments in amnesic humans, and why hippocampal lesions impair the animals' performance on the same tasks (see Olton, 1984b, for a similar point). Thus, even though the issue has not been settled decisively, it does seem reasonable to assume that at least some species can engage in mnemonic activity that is analogous to explicit remembering. It should thus be possible, at least in principle, to observe a priming effect in animals that is dissociable from explicit remembering.

The foregoing considerations indicate that experimental study of priming effects in animals will not be easy to achieve. However, ideas proposed by investigators of nonhuman organisms may have potentially interesting implications for understanding the kind of memory that is involved in the priming phenomenon. Based partly on the evidence from classical conditioning mentioned earlier, several investigators have argued that amnesic animals are capable of acquiring new associations that differ fundamentally from the kind of new associations that are acquired by normal animals (e.g., Berger, 1984; Hirsh, 1974, 1980; Mishkin *et al.*, 1984; Oakley, 1981, 1983; Ruggierio & Flagg, 1976). The major difference is that the new associations acquired by amnesic animals are isolated and rigid pairwise bonds in which a particular stimulus can only be associated with one other stimulus or with a single response. By contrast, normal animals also acquire more complex configurations in which a particular stimulus can be related simultaneously to several other stimuli and responses. These organized configurations can function as spatial–temporal maps that provide the animal with a flexible representational structure for interacting with the environment (Hirsh, 1980; Menzel, 1978; Oakley, 1981; O'Keefe & Nadel, 1978).

These ideas apply well to the observations on priming and acquisition of new associations in amnesia discussed earlier. Patients may be limited to the acquisition of rigid pairwise associations that represent linkages between preexisting unitized structures, and they may be unable to acquire flexible new configurations in which multiple relations are formed among constituent units (cf. Mishkin *et al.*, 1984; Schacter, in press-a; Wickelgren, 1979). Further investigation of the hypothesis that fundamentally different types of associations are involved in implicit and explicit forms of memory could provide a focal point for studies of mnemonic dissociations in humans and animals.

## CONCLUDING COMMENTS

It has been noted in this chapter and elsewhere (e.g., Mishkin *et al.*, 1984; Schacter, 1984) that investigators from different sectors of memory research have endorsed the notion that there are multiple forms of memory. The growing support for this hypothesis, particularly in the areas of neurobiology and neuropsychology, represents an exciting development that could yield a rich harvest of new ideas and insights in the coming years. At the same time, however, it is important to keep in mind that research concerning the issue of multiple forms of memory is still in its infancy. We are only beginning to sort out problems pertaining to terminology, assumptions, and theoretical interpretation of experimental data. To provide just one example of the kind of problem that needs to be confronted, consider the evidence on preserved priming effects in amnesic patients. I have argued that this evidence supports a distinction between two different forms of memory. However, an alternative possibility is that amnesic patients suffer from a deficit in retrieving information from a single memory system. That is, amnesics may perform normally on priming tests because partial letter cues provide direct access to stored representations and hence bypass the retrieval processes that are compromised in amnesia. This view does not need to postulate different forms of memory and, thus, would seem to be more parsimonious than a view that does.

Although it cannot be rejected unequivocally, a retrieval-deficit view has problems of its own. First, the aforementioned advantage of parsimony is more apparent than real. A retrieval-deficit interpretation alone cannot account for the fact that when a partial letter cue does elicit a target, the amnesic patient has no explicit memory for a prior episode—he or she does not "acknowledge" that the primed response is a memory (Weiskrantz, 1978). To accommodate this fact, it is necessary to postulate an extra deficit in "awareness" or "monitoring" (cf. Jacoby, 1984). Yet there is no evidence that amnesic patients have an "awareness deficit" that is separate from their memory deficit. In fact, we have recently observed that some amnesic patients are quite good at monitoring certain aspects of memory performance (Schacter, McLachlan *et al.*, 1984). A second problem is that there is evidence that at least some amnesic patients are able to gain access to a great deal of explicit *premorbid* knowledge and can recollect consciously personal experiences from the distant past (cf. Rozin, 1976; Zola-Morgan, Cohen, & Squire, 1983). These observations are difficult to account for by postulating a unitary retrieval deficit because such a deficit should prevent amnesic patients from consciously retrieving information from the distant past as well as from the recent past. Additional difficulties with a retrieval-deficit interpretation have been pointed out elsewhere (Mayes, 1985; Zola-Morgan & Squire, Chapter 26, this volume).

A variety of other problems will also have to be confronted by investigators concerned with the issue of multiple forms of memory: How *many* forms of memory are there, and how can we distinguish among them? How do different forms of memory *interact* during the performance of complex tasks? How can we facilitate the integration of relevant data from different levels of memory research (e.g., cellular, neuropsychological, cognitive) to achieve a broad understanding of the issue? What critical problems in memory research can be clarified by adopting the notion that there are multiple forms of memory? How have the various forms of memory been shaped by natural selection during the course of evolution? Several investigators have addressed these issues (e.g., Hirsh, 1980; Mishkin & Petri, 1984; Nadel & Zola-Morgan, 1984; Schacter, 1984, in press-b; Schacter & Tulving, 1982; Squire & Zola-Morgan, 1983; Tulving, 1983, in press), but it seems clear that a good deal more discussion and debate is required. Although our current ideas concerning the nature of and relations among different forms of memory are rudimentary at best, it seems likely that further pursuit of this issue will shed light on a host of fundamental problems in the psychology and neurobiology of memory.

## ACKNOWLEDGMENTS

This chapter was supported by Grant No. U0361 from the Natural Sciences and Engineering Research Council of Canada and by a Special Research Program Grant from the Connaught Fund, University of Toronto. I am grateful to Peter Graf and Endel Tulving for comments on the chapter, and I thank Carol A. Macdonald for helping to prepare the manuscript.

## REFERENCES

Berger, T. W. Neural representation of associative learning in the hippocampus. In L. R. Squire & N. Butters (Eds.), *Neuropsychology of memory*. New York: Guilford Press, 1984.

Brooks, D. N., & Baddeley, A. D. What can amnesic patients learn? *Neuropsychologia*, 1976, *14*, 111–122.

Carroll, M., & Kirsner, K. Context and repetition effects in lexical decision and recognition memory. *Journal of Verbal Learning and Verbal Behavior*, 1982, *21*, 55–69.

Cermak, L. S. (Ed.). *Human memory and amnesia*. Hillsdale, N.J.: Erlbaum, 1982.

Cermak, L. S. *Some attempts to improve the memory of amnesic patients*. Paper presented to the International Neuropsychological Symposium, Beaune, France, June 1984.

Cermak, L. S., Lewis, R., Butters, N., & Goodglass, H. Role of verbal mediation in performance of motor tasks by Korsakoff patients. *Perceptual & Motor Skills*, 1973, *37*, 259–262.

Cohen, N. J. *Neuropsychological evidence for a distinction between procedural and declarative knowledge in human memory and amnesia*. Unpublished doctoral dissertation, University of California, San Diego, 1981.

Cohen, N. J. Preserved learning capacity in amnesia: Evidence for multiple memory systems. In L. R. Squire & N. Butters (Eds.), *Neuropsychology of memory*. New York: Guilford Press, 1984.

Cohen, N. J., & Squire, L. R. Preserved learning and retention of pattern-analyzing skill in amnesia: Dissociation of "knowing how" and "knowing that." *Science*, 1980, *210*, 207–209.

Corkin, S. Tactually-guided maze learning in man: Effects of unilateral cortical excisions and bilateral hippocampal lesions. *Neuropsychologia*, 1965, *3*, 339–351.

Craik, F. I. M., & Lockhart, R. S. Levels of processing: A framework for memory research. *Journal of Verbal Learning and Verbal Behavior*, *11*, 1972, 671–684.

Deutsch, J. A. Chromomnemonics and amnesia. In L. R. Squire & N. Butters (Eds.), *Neuropsychology of memory*. New York: Guilford Press, 1984.

Diamond, R., & Rozin, P. Activation of existing memories in the amnesic syndrome. *Journal of Abnormal Psychology*, 1984, *93*, 98–105.

Eich, J. E. Memory for unattended events; remembering with and without awareness. *Memory & Cognition*, 1984, *12*, 105–111.

Feustel, T. C., Shiffrin, R. M., & Salasoo, A. Episodic and lexical contributions to the repetition effect in word identification. *Journal of Experimental Psychology: General*, 1983, *112*, 309–346.

Glisky, E., Schacter, D. L., & Tulving, E. *Vocabulary learning in amnesia: Method of vanishing cues*. Paper presented to the American Psychological Association, Toronto, August 1984.

Goldberg, E. Papez circuit revisited: Two systems instead of one? In L. R. Squire & N. Butters (Eds.), *Neuropsychology of memory*. New York: Guilford Press, 1984.

Graf, P., & Mandler, G. (1984). Activation makes words more accessible, but not necessarily more retrievable. *Journal of Verbal Learning and Verbal Behavior*, 1984, *23*, 553–568.

Graf, P., & Schacter, D. L. Implicit and explicit memory for new associations in normal and amnesic subjects. *Journal of Experimental Psychology: Learning, Memory, and Cognition*, 1985, *11*, 501–518.

Graf, P., Squire, L. R., & Mandler, G. The information that amnesic patients do not forget. *Journal of Experimental Psychology: Learning, Memory, and Cognition*, 1984, *10*, 164–178.

Hayes-Roth, B. Evolution of cognitive structures and processes. *Psychological Review*, 1977, *84*, 260–278.

Hirsh, R. The hippocampus and contextual retrieval of information from memory. *Behavioral Biology*, 1974, *12*, 421–444.

Hirsh, R. The hippocampus, conditional operations, and cognition. *Physiological Psychology*, 1980, *8*, 175–182.

Hirst, W. The amnesic syndrome: Descriptions and explanations. *Psychological Bulletin*, 1982, *91*, 435–460.

Horowitz, L. M., & Manelis, L. Toward a theory of redintegrative memory: Adjective–noun phrases. In G. H. Bower (Ed.), *The psychology of learning and motivation* (Vol. 6). New York: Academic Press, 1972.

Horowitz, L. M., & Prytulak, L. S. Redintegrative memory. *Psychological Review*, 1969, *76*, 519–531.

Jacoby, L. L. Perceptual enhancement: Persistent effects of an experience. *Journal of Experimental Psychology: Learning, Memory, and Cognition*, 1983, *9*, 21–38. (a)

Jacoby, L. L. Remembering the data: Analyzing interactive processes in reading. *Journal of Verbal Learning and Verbal Behavior*, 1983, *22*, 485–508. (b)

Jacoby, L. L. Incidental versus intentional retrieval: Remembering and awareness as separate issues. In L. R. Squire & N. Butters (Eds.), *Neuropsychology of memory*. New York: Guilford Press, 1984.

Jacoby, L. L., & Dallas, M. On the relationship between autobiographical memory and perceptual learning. *Journal of Experimental Psychology: General*, 1981, *110*, 306–340.

Jacoby, L. L., & Witherspoon, D. Remembering without awareness. *Canadian Journal of Psychology*, 1982, *36*, 300–324.

Johnson, M. A multiple-entry, modular memory system. In G. H. Bower (Ed.), *The psychology of learning and motivation* (Vol. 17). New York: Academic Press, 1984.

Kinsbourne, M., & Wood, F. Short-term memory processes and the amnesic syndrome. In D. Deutsch & J. A. Deutsch (Eds.), *Short-term memory*. New York: Academic Press, 1975.

Kinsbourne, M., & Wood, F. Theoretical considerations regarding the episodic–semantic memory distinction. In L. S. Cermak (Ed.), *Human memory and amnesia*. Hillsdale, N.J.: Erlbaum, 1982.

Mandler, G. Recognizing: The judgment of previous occurrence. *Psychological Review*, 1980, *87*, 252–271.

Martone, M., Butters, N., Wolfe, J., & Cermak, L. Recognition memory and skill learning in Huntington's disease. *Society for Neuroscience Abstracts*, 1984, *10*, 523.

Mayes, A. *What functional deficits cause amnesia?* Paper presented to the Conference on Cognitive Neuropsychology, Venice, March 1985.

McKoon, G. & Ratcliff, R. Priming in episodic and semantic memory. *Journal of Verbal Learning and Verbal Behavior*, 1979, *18*, 463–480.

Menzel, E. W. Cognitive mapping in chimpanzees. In S. H. Hulse, H. Fowler, & W. K. Honig (Eds.), *Cognitive processes in animal behavior*. Hillsdale, N.J.: Erlbaum, 1978.

Milner, B. Les troubles de la mémoire accompagnant des lésions hippocampiques bilatérales. In P. Passouant (Ed.), *Physiologie de l'hippocampe*. Paris: Centre National de la Recherche Scientifique, 1962.

Milner, B., Corkin, S., & Teuber, H. L. Further analysis of the hippocampal amnesic syndrome: 14 year follow-up study of H. M. *Neuropsychologia*, 1968, *6*, 215–234.

Milner, B., & Taylor, L. Right hemispheric superiority in tactile pattern recognition after cerebral commissurotomy: Evidence for nonverbal memory. *Neuropsychologia*, 1972, *10*, 1–15.

Mishkin, M. Visual discrimination performance following partial ablations of the temporal lobe: II. Ventral surface vs. hippocampus. *Journal of Comparative and Physiological Psychology*, 1954, *47*, 187–193.

Mishkin, M., Malamut, B., & Bachevalier, J. Memories and habits: Two neural systems. In G. Lynch, J. L. McGaugh, & N. M. Weinberger (Eds.), *Neurobiology of learning and memory*. New York: Guilford Press, 1984.

Mishkin, M., & Petri, H. L. Memories and habits: Some implications for the analysis of learning and retention. In L. R. Squire & N. Butters (Eds.), *Neuropsychology of memory*. New York: Guilford Press, 1984.

Morton, J. The interaction of information in word recognition. *Psychological Review*, 1969, *76*, 165–178.

Moscovitch, M. Multiple dissociations of function in amnesia. In L. S. Cermak (Ed.), *Human memory and amnesia*. Hillsdale, N.J.: Erlbaum, 1982.

Moscovitch, M. The sufficient conditions for demonstrating preserved memory in amnesia: A task analysis. In L. R. Squire & N. Butters (Eds.), *Neuropsychology of memory*. New York: Guilford Press, 1984.

Nadel, L., & Zola-Morgan, S. Infantile amnesia: A neurobiological perspective. In M. Moscovitch (Ed.), *Infant memory*. New York: Plenum Press, 1984.

Neisser, U. An experimental distinction between perceptual processes and verbal response. *Journal of Experimental Psychology*, 1954, *47*, 399–402.

Oakley, D. A. Brain mechanisms of mammalian memory. *British Medical Bulletin*, 1981, *37*, 175–180.

Oakley, D. A. The varieties of memory: A phylogenetic approach. In A. Mayes (Ed.), *Memory in animals and humans*. Cambridge: Van Nostrand Reinhold, 1983.

O'Keefe, J., & Nadel, L. *The hippocampus as a cognitive map*. Oxford: Clarendon Press, 1978.

Olton, D. S. Comparative analysis of episodic memory. *Behavioral and Brain Sciences*, 1984, *7*, 250–251. (a)

Olton, D. S. *Learning and memory: Neuropsychological and ethological approaches to its classification*. Paper presented to the Conference on Human and Animal Memory, Umea, Sweden, June 1984. (b)

Olton, D. S., Becker, J. T., & Handelmann, G. E. Hippocampus, space, and memory. *Behavioral and Brain Sciences*, 1979, *2*, 313–365.

Orbach, J., Milner, B., & Rasmussen, T. Learning and retention in monkeys after amygdala–hippocampus resection. *Archives of Neurology*, 1960, *3*, 230–251.

Rolls, E. T. Neurophysiological investigations of different types of memory in the primate. In L. R. Squire & N. Butters (Eds.), *Neuropsychology of memory*. New York: Guilford Press, 1984.

Rozin, P. The psychobiological approach to human memory. In M. R. Rosenzweig & E. L. Bennett (Eds.), *Neural mechanisms of learning and memory*. Cambridge, Mass.: MIT Press, 1976.

Ruggierio, F. T., & Flagg, S. F. Do animals have memory? In D. L. Medin, W. A. Roberts, & R. T. Davis (Eds.), *Processes of animal memory*. Hillsdale, N.J.: Erlbaum, 1976.

Scarborough, D. L., Cortese, C., & Scarborough, H. S. Frequency and repetition effects in lexical memory. *Journal of Experimental Psychology: Human Perception and Performance*, 1977, *3*, 1–17.

Scarborough, D. L., Gerard, L., & Cortese, C. Accessing lexical memory: The transfer of word repetition effects across task and modality. *Memory and Cognition*, 1979, *7*, 3–12.

Schacter, D. L. *Stranger behind the engram: Theories of memory and the psychology of science*. Hillsdale, N.J.: Erlbaum, 1982.

Schacter, D. L. Amnesia observed: Remembering and forgetting in a natural environment. *Journal of Abnormal Psychology*, 1983, *92*, 236–242.

Schacter, D. L. Toward the multidisciplinary study of memory: Ontogeny, phylogeny, and pathology of memory systems. In L. R. Squire & N. Butters (Eds.), *Neuropsychology of memory*. New York: Guilford Press, 1984.

Schacter, D. L. Priming of old and new knowledge in amnesic patients and normal subjects. *Annals of the New York Academy of Sciences*, in press. (a)

Schacter, D. L. Three types of relations between cognitive psychology and neuroscience. In J. Ledoux & W. Hirst (Eds.), *Mind and brain: Dialogues between cognitive psychology and neuroscience*. Cambridge: Cambridge University, in press. (b)

Schacter, D. L., & Crovitz, H. F. Memory function after closed head injury: A review of the quantitative research. *Cortex*, 1977, *13*, 150–176.

Schacter, D. L., & Graf, P. Effects of elaborate processing on implicit and explicit memory for new associations. Submitted for publication.

Schacter, D. L., Harbluk, J. A., & McLachlan, D. R. Retrieval without recollection: An experimental analysis of source amnesia. *Journal of Verbal Learning and Verbal Behavior*, 1984, *23*, 593–611.

Schacter, D. L., McLachlan, D. R., Moscovitch, M., & Tulving, E. *Tracking of memory disorders over time*. Paper presented to the American Psychological Association, Toronto, August 1984.

Schacter, D. L., & Moscovitch, M. Infants, amnesics, and dissociable memory systems. In M. Moscovitch (Ed.), *Infant memory*. New York: Plenum Press, 1984.

Schacter, D. L., & Tulving, E. Memory, amnesia, and the episodic/semantic distinction. In R. L. Isaacson & N. E. Spear (Eds.), *The expression of knowledge*. New York: Plenum Press, 1982.

Sidman, M., Stoddard, L., & Mohr, J. Some additional quantitative observations of immediate memory in a patient with bilateral hippocampal lesions. *Neuropsychologia*, 1968, *6*, 245–254.

Squire, L. R. Comparisons between forms of amnesia: Some deficits are unique to Korsakoff's syndrome. *Journal of Experimental Psychology: Learning, Memory, and Cognition*, 1982, *8*, 560–571.

Squire, L. R., & Cohen, N. J. Remote memory, retrograde amnesia, and the neuropsychology of memory. In L. S. Cermak (Ed.), *Human memory and amnesia*. Hillsdale, N.J.: Erlbaum, 1982.

Squire, L. R., & Cohen, N. J. Human memory and amnesia. In G. Lynch, J. L. McGaugh, & N. M. Weinberger (Eds.), *Neurobiology of learning and memory*. New York: Guilford Press, 1984.

Squire, L. R., & Zola-Morgan, S. The neurology of memory: The case for correspondence between the findings for human and nonhuman primate. In J. A. Deutsch (Ed.), *The physiological basis of memory* (2nd ed.). New York: Academic Press, 1983.

Thomas, G. J. Memory: Time binding in organisms. In L. R. Squire & N. Butters (Eds.), *Neuropsychology of memory*. New York: Guilford Press, 1984.

Tulving, E. Episodic and semantic memory. In E. Tulving & W. Donaldson (Eds.), *Organization of memory*. New York: Academic Press, 1972.

Tulving, E. *Elements of episodic memory*. Oxford: Clarendon Press, 1983.

Tulving, E. On the classification problem in learning and memory. In L.-G. Nilsson & T. Archer (Eds.), *Perspectives in learning and memory*. Hillsdale, N.J.: Erlbaum, in press.

Tulving, E., Schacter, D. L., & Stark, H. A. Priming effects in word-fragment completion are independent of recognition memory. *Journal of Experimental Psychology: Learning, Memory, and Cognition*, 1982, *8*, 336–342.

Vanderwart, M. Priming by pictures in lexical decision. *Journal of Verbal Learning and Verbal Behavior*, 1984, *23*, 67–83.

Wagner, A. R. Expectancies and the priming of STM. In S. H. Hulse, H. Fowler, & W. K. Honig (Eds.), *Cognitive processes in animal behavior*. Hillsdale, N.J.: Erlbaum, 1978.

Warrington, E. K., & Weiskrantz, L. New method of testing long-term retention with special reference to amnesic patients. *Nature (London)*, 1968, *217*, 972–974.

Warrington, E. K., & Weiskrantz, L. Amnesia: Consolidation or retrieval? *Nature (London)*, 1970, *228*, 628–630.

Warrington, E. K., & Weiskrantz, L. The effect of prior learning on subsequent retention in amnesic patients. *Neuropsychologia*, 1974, *12*, 419–428.

Warrington, E. K., & Weiskrantz, L. Amnesia: A disconnection syndrome? *Neuropsychologia*, 1982, *20*, 233–248.

Weiskrantz, L. A comparison of hippocampal pathology in man and other animals. *Ciba Foundation Symposium*, 1978, *58 (new series)*, 373–387.

Weiskrantz, L., & Warrington, E. K. Conditioning in amnesic patients. *Neuropsychologia*, 1979, *17*, 187–194.

Whitty, C. W. M., & Zangwill, O. L. (Eds.). *Amnesia*. London: Butterworth, 1977.

Wickelgren, W. A. Chunking and consolidation: A theoretical synthesis of semantic networks, configuring in conditioning, S–R versus cognitive learning, normal forgetting, the amnesic syndrome, and the hippocampal arousal system. *Psychological Review*, 1979, *86*, 44–60.

Zola-Morgan, S., Cohen, N. J., & Squire, L. R. Recall of remote-episodic memory in amnesia. *Neuropsychologia*, 1983, *21*, 487–500.

Zola-Morgan, S., & Squire, L. R. Preserved learning in monkeys with medial temporal lesions: Sparing of motor and cognitive skills. *Journal of Neuroscience*, 1984, *4*, 1072–1085.

Zola-Morgan, S., Squire, L. R., & Mishkin, M. The neuroanatomy of amnesia: Amygdala–hippocampus versus temporal stem. *Science*, 1982, *218*, 1337–1339.

CHAPTER 21

# On Issues and Theories of the Human Amnesic Syndrome

**L. Weiskrantz**
University of Oxford
Oxford, England, UK

The study of dysfunction is a rich source of inferences about function, and in recent years that has been especially evident in the field of memory disorders. I would like to discuss three issues: (1) the question of different types of amnesia; (2) storage versus retrieval; and (3) the characterization of what is spared in amnesia.

## DIFFERENT TYPES OF AMNESIA?

It has been proposed that there are two different types of patients with anterograde amnesia, a "medial temporal" type and a "diencephalic" type. H. M. is said to be an example of the former, and N. A. and Korsakoff patients of the latter. Other distinctions have also been proposed (e.g., Korsakoff vs. encephalitic), but the issues that arise in considering the first suggested pair can also be extended to other suggested types, as we shall see. It is useful to consider the claim on three fronts: (1) anatomical; (2) memory data; and (3) selection of cases.

### Anatomical

The prototype of the putative diencephalic type of amnesia, it has been argued, is seen in pure form in the case of N. A., whose lesion, as assessed from a CT scan, has repeatedly been described as occurring in the dorsomedial nucleus (MD) of the thalamus (Squire & Moore, 1979). It has also been argued that it is this region that is critical in Korsakoff patients. It is necessary, therefore, to examine the anatomical basis of such claims. It is important to point out, however, that N. A. is atypical in that he is *not* a globally amnesic patient, although this is not often stressed: His memory deficit lies with verbal material and not with nonverbal material, in line with the apparent restriction of the diencephalic lesion to the left hemisphere, sparing the right hemisphere.

The case of N. A. was first reported by Teuber, Milner, and Vaughan in 1968. The injury occurred through an accident with a fencing foil that traveled up the right nostril, penetrated the cribiform plate, and crossed over into the left side of the brain. His verbal memory impairment has persisted since that time. But that is not all that is wrong clinically with N. A.: I can remember Lukas Teuber telling me on very many occasions of one of his main interests in the case, namely that N. A. suffered from Parinaud syndrome—paralysis of upward gaze. Moreover, apparently N. A. still does. Both the clinical (cf. Brain, 1981; Büttner-Ennever, Buttner, Cohen, & Baumgartner, 1982; Pierrot-Deseilligny *et al.*, 1982) and experimental (Pasik, Pasik, & Bender, 1969) evidence place the critical pathological site for Parinaud syndrome in the pretectum. In particular, the work of Pasik *et al.* showed very clearly that a bilateral lesion in the MD of the thalamus is without effect in the monkey on oculomotor performance, whereas a small lesion in the region of the posterior commissure is sufficient to cause disturbances of vertical eye movements. Reasonably enough, in the original report Teuber *et al.* wrote,

> The persistent paralysis of upward gaze, is consistent with the belief that the puncture would have involved the superior quadrigeminal region, entering the brain from below, just to the left of the midline. In addition, the diminished pupillary reaction to light suggests some involvement of the pretectal region. (1968, p. 279)

I have tried to reconstruct the path that the fencing foil is likely to take if it enters the right nostril, avoiding the optic chiasm, and ends up in the anterior tip of left posterior commissure (Figure 21.1) without taking a parabolic route. The foil passes through or very near the mammillary bodies; or if it misses, it is likely to cut the mammillo-thalamic tract. It passes below the MD. I have plotted this conservatively with a foil 2¼ mm in diameter—of course, it may well have been thicker. The CT scan does indicate a lesion in the MD. There is nothing to say that the MD could not be damaged either indirectly (e.g., through bone splinter, infection, vascular lesions). If it is damaged directly by the foil taking a parabolic route (i.e., with indirect damage to the pretectum), the foil would have inflicted even more frontal lobe damage, given that the chiasm was apparently not lesioned; and, of course, tissue between the MD and pretectum would also have been damaged. Whatever the outcome, it is wrong to assume that the MD is the only or even the main "circumscribed" site of damage. Evidence based on negative CT scans from regions outside of the MD (especially taken at only 1-cm slices, and with the available scanners of that period) can readily be false negatives.

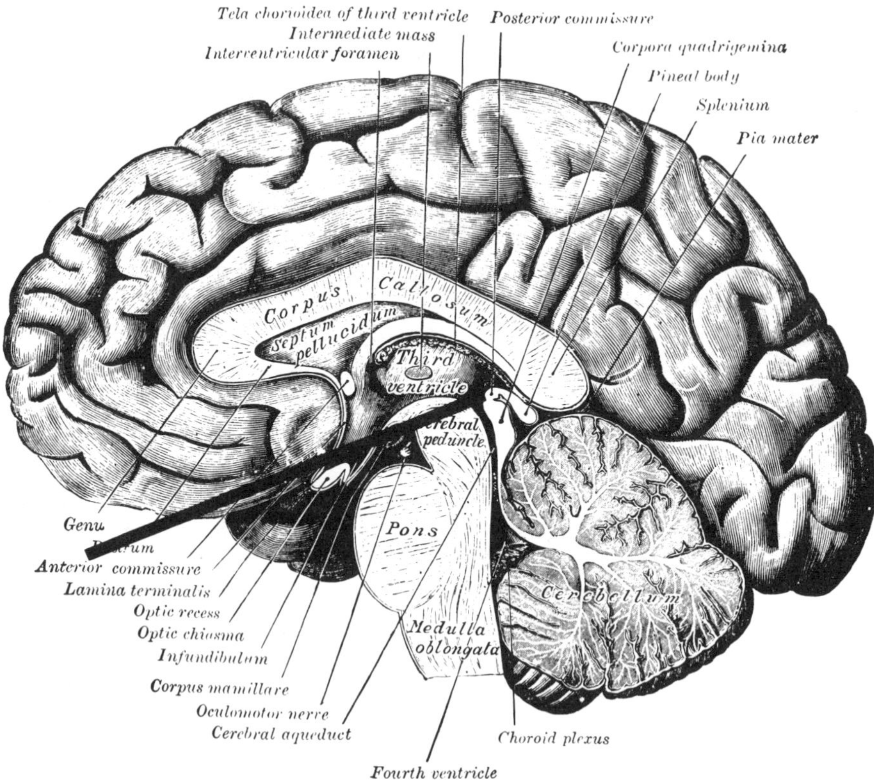


**FIGURE 21.1.** Estimated path of a fencing foil, approximately 2¼-mm diameter, entering nostril and reaching posterior commissure on a direct path avoiding optic chiasm and with minimal damage to frontal lobes. (Drawing of brain from H. Gray, *Anatomy of the Human Body*, 30th ed., C. D. Clemente, Ed. Philadelphia: Lea & Febiger, 1985, p. 989. Reprinted by permission.)

The brains of Korsakoff patients may show damage in the medial thalamus (but not necessarily, as we shall see, in the medial dorsal nucleus) but also consistently in one other region of the diencephalon, the mammillary bodies. There may also be pathology widely but inconsistently scattered throughout other regions, such as the cerebellum. In the two cases described by Mair, Warrington, and Weiskrantz (1979), the fine-grained neuropsychological details of patients who had been studied over several years can be placed beside the neuropathological findings revealed at postmortem. In both patients there was highly conspicuous and circumscribed degeneration in the medial nucleus of the mammillary bodies and a relatively thin band of gliosis in the medial thalamus, in a region lying between the subependymal zone and the main body of the medial dorsal nucleus of the thalamus. In one patient, who had also shown some signs of more general mild intellectual deterioration in the year or two before his death, there was some scattered pathology in other brain regions. The other patient, who remained intellectually quite stable until his sudden death and whose IQ closely approximated his calculated premorbid IQ, had lesions restricted to the two sites mentioned.

The pathological group studies by Victor, Adams, and Collins (1971) of patients with various components of the Wernicke–Korsakoff syndrome are sometimes cited in support of the view that the *true* basis of "diencephalic" amnesia is a lesion in the dorsomedial thalamus. That may turn out to be the case. But Victor *et al.*, however, did not have a single positive case of a lesion restricted to the MD who was amnesic, nor do they claim to have such a case. Their argument, as they made clear, is that they had five *nonamnesic* patients who had mammillary body pathology but *no* medial dorsal thalamic pathology. (Of these five patients, "in 1 the memory defect could be excluded with certainty." The other four died after a brief illness, but there was "no history of memory disorder before admission to hospital and none on admission.") Thus, the inference is based on a double negative: the nonappearance of amnesia and nonpathology of the MD in these cases. Even so, as only a fraction of their patients were amnesic and as only a fraction of the brains were available for examination of the dorsal medial nucleus, it cannot be concluded with certainty that there were no patients who did have dorsal medial pathology but were *not* amnesic.

Nor can it be correct to assert (Squire, 1982c, p. 263) that the MD "was damaged in all 38 of their [Victor *et al.*'s] cases who exhibited amnesia": In fact, there were only at most 24 confirmed Korsakoff patients on whom neuropathological studies of the MD were carried out. [One can only surmise that Squire was mistaken in assuming that the total of 38 patients in whom MD changes were detected were all amnesic (shown in Table 21, p. 88, of Victor *et al.*, 1971). The relevant summaries are instead in Victor *et al.*, 1971, Table 20, p. 83, and Table 28, p. 139.] Victor *et al.* *did* have five patients with memory disorder in which the MD was "virtually the only thalamic nucleus affected" (p. 132). But, again, the thalamus was not available for examination in all cases, and it is worth reminding ourselves that these five patients also had mammillary body pathology. In fact, *all* of the patients of Victor *et al.* with confirmed memory disturbance who came to postmortem had mammillary body pathology. This was the region most conspicuously and severely affected in the patients of Mair *et al.*, together with some gliosis between the subependymal region and the MD of the thalamus.

The most that the evidence reviewed and summarized by Victor *et al.* (1971) and Mair *et al.* (1979) allows one to conclude is that the lesions in mammillary bodies may be necessary but *may* not be sufficient for causing an amnesic syndrome (despite claims of pathology restricted to this site);

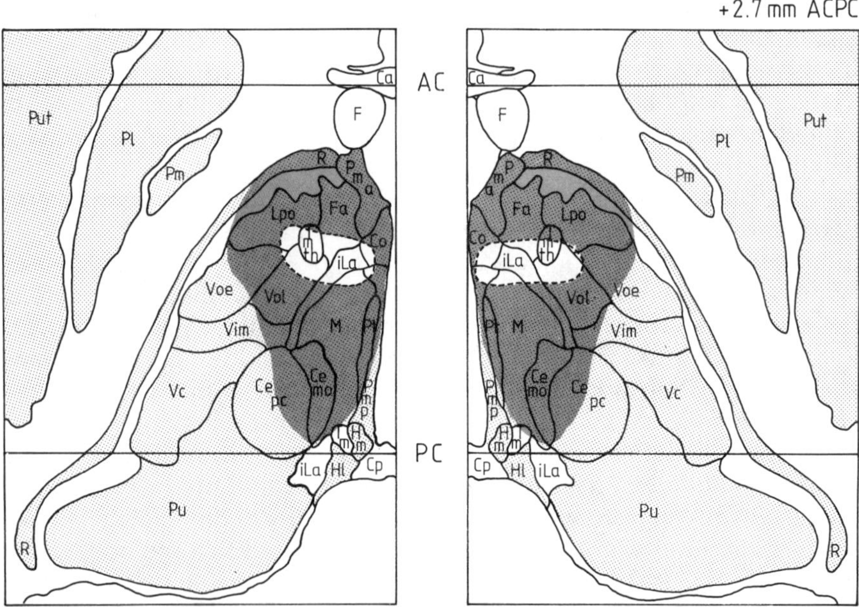


**FIGURE 21.2.** Horizontal section through lower thalamus. The dark gray area corresponds to the territory of the polar and paramedian thalamic arteries. The white area, bounded by dotted lines, is the area of overlap of thalamic infarcts in seven patients, based on CT scans. This area includes the mammillo-thalamic tract and ILA, which carries fiber projections to and from the MD. (From von Cramon, Hebel, & Schuri, in press. Reprinted by permission.)

perhaps lesions in both the mammillary bodies and the thalamus (or the systems in which they are directly involved are necessary for the amnesic syndrome.

Let us consider structures in the medial temporal lobe. Although it is true that Korsakoff patients need have no damage to their medial temporal lobes, including hippocampus, amygdala, subiculum, temporal stem, and neocortex (Mair *et al.*, 1979), it is not the case that it can be assumed that H. M. or other surgical cases (or medial temporal encephalitic cases; cf. Hierons, Janota, & Corsellis, 1978) will not also have consequential degeneration in the mammillary bodies resulting from the primary lesion, which is estimated (H. M. is still alive) to involve the amygdala, hippocampal formation, and surrounding cortex and white matter. As the subiculum and surrounding tissue are thought to have been damaged, the fornix–fimbria will also be affected. He will almost certainly also have thalamic degeneration, although whether this will be where Victor *et al.* (1971) find it (actually, in their population as a whole thalamic degeneration was quite variable) or confined to the restricted zone just lateral to the subependymal region reported by Mair *et al.* (1979), or elsewhere, cannot be predicted with certainty as yet. In any event, there are no grounds for assuming that there is not a large and essential degree of commonality in the diencephalic foci both in Korsakoff cases and in H. M. (and also in the left hemisphere, but not the right, of N. A.; see earlier).

In a recent extensive series of cases of thalamic infarcts associated with neuropsychologically individually very well-documented amnesic conditions, von Cramon [who has kindly given me permission to cite his findings (von Cramon, Hebel, & Schuri, in press)] found the common focus in the thalamus (reconstructed from CT scans) to be anterior and almost entirely outside of the MD but to include the path of entry of the mammillo-thalamic tract, together with a fiber tract (ILA) that he interpreted as "carrying projections from temporal cortex and amygdala to MD" (cf. Figures 21.2 and 21.3). Thus, von Cramon concluded that both the fornix–fimbria system, via the mammillo-thalamic tract, and the thalamically relayed amygdala connections to and from the frontal lobe were involved. The involvement of both systems is thus compatible with the evidence from the estimated lesion in H. M., with confirmed pathology in Korsakoff patients (Mair *et al.*, 1979), with thalamic infarct evidence, and with evidence in monkeys (Mishkin, 1982), although it still remains to be seen whether a *double* disconnection is a

**FIGURE 21.3.** Same subjects illustrated in Figure 21.2, but through the middle thalamic region. "Partial lesions of MD alone were not sufficient to cause an amnesic syndrome as 2 patients *without* memory dysfunction (not depicted here) demonstrate." (Quotation and illustration from von Cramon, Hebel, & Schuri, in press. Reprinted by permission.)

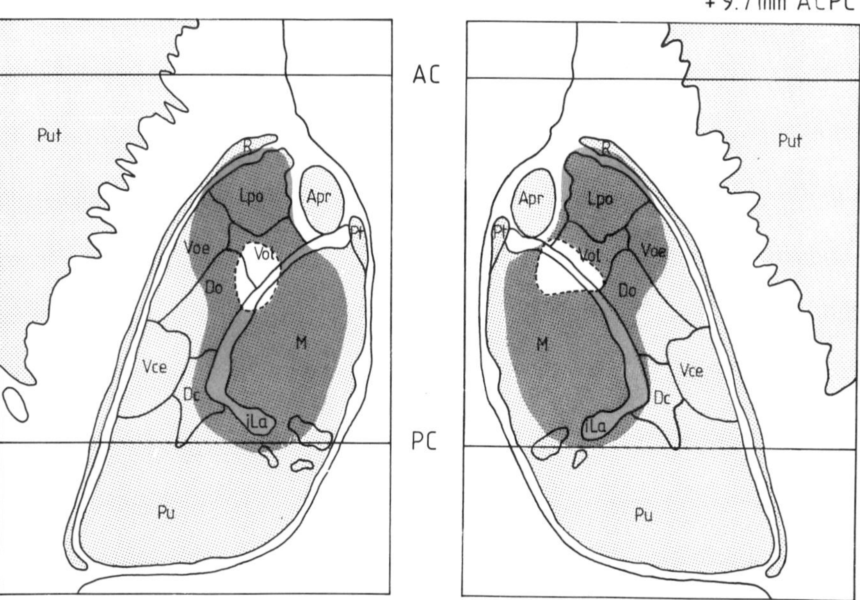

minimal necessity (cf. Mair *et al.*, 1979). However that turns out, the evidence does not serve to support the occurrence of different types of amnesia on anatomical grounds. Moreover, there are good grounds for assuming that certain sites of pathology are shared by all amnesic-syndrome patients.

## Memory Data

One of the grounds for supporting the difference lies in the claim that the two groups show different rates of forgetting. The claim is that H. M., when tested by recognition for pictures, forgets more quickly than do controls or Korsakoff patients. The starting point is a frequently cited study by Huppert and Piercy (1979). When equated at a short retention interval (10 minutes) by adjusting the initial exposure times, forgetting was said to advance more rapidly in the medial temporal group (H. M., $n = 1$) than the normal control group ($n = 2$). But H. M. was then compared with a previously studied Korsakoff group (and a control group now matched for them; Huppert & Piercy, 1978a) and retested with a stimulus exposure that brings him (just) into the range of those groups at the initial retention interval of 10 minutes. His forgetting rate does seem to be faster (Figure 21.4). But if H.M.'s score is plotted to avoid the initial value artifact (Figure 21.5) so that one can compare his forgetting slope directly with the other groups' slopes, the result is hardly impressive, and his scores fall *within* the range of the Korsakoff

**FIGURE 21.4.** Retention as a function of interval between exposure and recognition test of pictures for H. M., Korsakoff patients, and controls, as plotted in Huppert and Piercy (1979). (Reprinted by permission.)

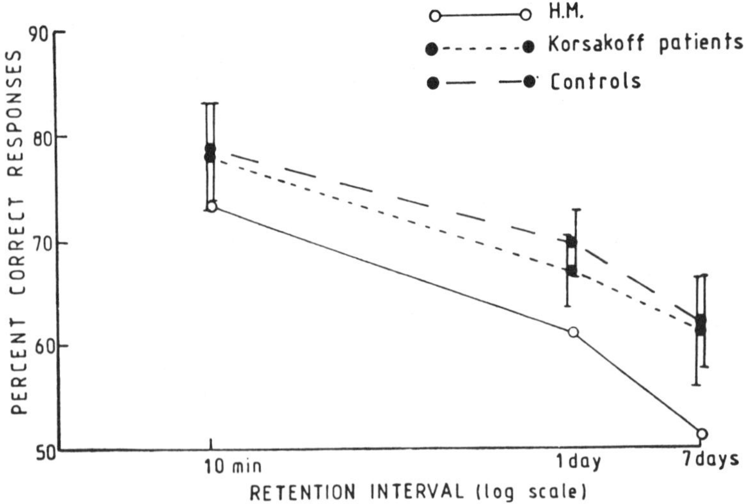

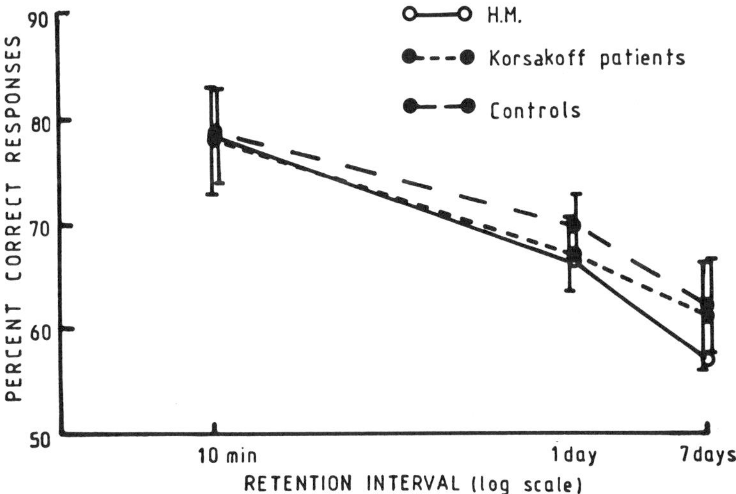


**FIGURE 21.5.** Data of Figure 21.4 replotted so as to match all subjects' means at the earliest retention interval.

group at all intervals. Even if the result were different, basing a quantitative difference between groups on an *n* of 1 shows a notable boldness.

Another basis for the claim lies in estimates of the severity of the retrograde amnesia. These will be considered more fully in the section Storage versus Retrieval. At this point the evidence regarding both rates of forgetting and severity of retrograde amnesia can be briefly summarized as follows: N. A. and Korsakoff patients are reported to be alike in terms of rates of forgetting (Squire, 1981) but different in terms of severity of retrograde amnesia (Squire, 1982c). H. M. and N. A. are said to be rather alike in terms of severity of retrograde amnesia but not in terms of rates of forgetting. Electroconvulsive therapy (ECT) patients are like H. M., but temporarily so. Post hoc explanations are sometimes used to try to iron out such differences, such as appealing to a cognitive overlay and/or damage beyond the putatively prototypical lesions in either type of case. But such differences are more easily explained as differences in *quantitative* severity plus multiple deficits (see later) rather than as qualitative differences. It would generally be considered that evidence of differences between categories of neuropsychological patients should be supported by double dissociation. No such consistent support has appeared for the distinction between diencephalic and medial temporal amnesic categories.

## Selection of Patients

Before proceeding to the data actually available, two preliminary comments are in order: first, a reminder of an earlier injunction:

> two methodological issues bedevil interpretation at this stage of research. . . . Those features of the patients' performance that are "obligatory" must be separated from those that are "optional." This is not a question of reliability, but of dissociation. Independent deficits may be highly correlated in occurrence because of multiple targets of the neuropathology or neurosurgery. Where we know that certain impairments can be produced in other patients who are not amnesic, as with short-term memory deficits, we have special reasons for caution. (Weiskrantz & Warrington, 1975a, p. 425)

In this connection the conclusions that Squire reached (1982a) on the basis of a variety of tests are apposite (see also Moscovitch, 1982):

> [Korsakoff patients'] deficits appear to be related to frontal lobe damage and are superimposed on a more basic memory disorder. Theories of amnesia should be founded on the basic memory disorder and not on deficits such as these, which have no obligatory relationship to amnesia. (p. 560)

On this point it is good to be able to agree. The distinction between encephalitic and Korsakoff patients (Butters & Cermak, 1980; Lhermitte & Signoret, 1972) is subject to the same rider. Clinical groups of Korsakoff patients, even when within normal intelligence limits, are apt to be overlaid with frontal symptomatology which, although it is relevant to theories of amnesia (Warrington & Weiskrantz, 1982), can be empirically dissociated from it. Korsakoff patients have been included in studies in many places because they happen to be available as a clinical group requiring clinical care. In our own experience, such groups are highly mixed in terms of cognitive and neuropsychological status. In other studies, including our own, all patients, have been deliberately selected as being relatively purely and basically amnesic, minimally uncontaminated by a mixture of disorders. We have seen many patients who have been referred by hospital consultants as "Korsakoff" amnesics; after screening these patients clinically we have rejected them prior to inclusion in any experimental investigations as being too mixed and/or mild to be useful for separating out the signal of the amnesic state from neuropsychological background noise. A related point concerns the presence or absence of short-term memory (STM) deficits, which may confound the analysis of the classic long-term memory (LTM) deficit of the amnesic syndrome (cf. Warrington & Weiskrantz, 1972). Although STM deficits may be commonly associated with other features of the Korsakoff syndrome (Butters & Cermak, 1974), it is also clear that they are not obligatory features and that the LTM core of the amnesic syndrome and STM deficits can be doubly dissociated from each other (Baddeley & Warrington, 1970; Warrington, 1982).

We have attempted to select patients on the basis of their clinical purity and severity rather than on etiology, and such groups have yielded homogeneous patterns of results in experimental studies. Curiously, it has sometimes been claimed that we have restricted certain experimental analyses to one type of etiology. Thus, Squire (1982c) refers to the Warrington and Weiskrantz (1978) study of intrusion errors stating that "it should be emphasized that the study of these errors has been limited to the Korsakoff syndrome" (p. 250). In fact, that study included Korsakoff patients, encephalitics, one temporal lobe surgical case, and a postcardiac case, all of whose retroactive and proactive interference patterns were analyzed quantitatively (see Experiment II of that paper). A similar comparison of a group with mixed etiologies was made in the study of Winocur and Weiskrantz (1976), who examined the intrusion errors quantitatively in a rule-constrained, paired-associate learning task and concluded that the patients "could not be differentiated on the basis of diagnostic condition. . . . Relative qualitative or quantitative differences associated with etiology were not apparent" (p. 109). In fact, *every one* of our studies of partial information methods included non-Korsakoff patients, and no *qualitative* differences in patterns were discerned related to etiology.

Second, patients with transient or irregular profiles, even if these may be genuinely if nonglobally amnesic as far as they go, also make interpretation difficult. Thus, as we have already reviewed above, N. A. is not a global amnesic patient: He is a verbal but not a nonverbal amnesic patient. Difficulties arise because patients can be adept at using intact routes as props or as direct cues in tests (as, for example, in recognition of faces), and for this reason less severe as well as incomplete amnesic profiles make for more complex interpretation. Many patients referred clinically as "amnesic" are apt to be verbally amnesic but nonverbally intact—because in everyday life the verbal memory deficit is much more conspicuous and the nonverbal loss may be missed. Clinicians rarely test for nonverbal memory. We rejected any case not *demonstrated* to be impaired *both* verbally and nonverbally.

Electroconvulsive therapy (ECT) patients are also difficult to interpret alongside other states. Not only are the mnemonic (and probably the affective) effects of ECT largely reversible, but they are complicated by the fact that amnesia can be delayed, as has been shown in animals (Geller & Jarvik, 1968) and also known clinically with head injury: The patient may be less impaired soon after the shock than some minutes or hours later, leading, among other complications, to what might appear to be a fast rate of forgetting. The memory impairment in ECT patients is also cumulative and will depend upon the number of shock treatments and their spacing. As regards retrograde amnesia in ECT patients, it is described as being either "brief" (Squire, 1982c), or extending back for "many years (Squire, 1975), or for "a year or two prior to treatment (Squire, Cohen, & Zouzounis, 1984). Given the reversibility of the retrograde amnesia, it is said that the "defect cannot easily be explained as a failure of consolidation" (Squire, 1975), but elsewhere it is said that "the status of retrograde amnesia in . . . patients receiving ECT is consistent" with a formulation in terms of consolidation (Squire, 1981). And although these kinds of patients have been described repeatedly as having amnesia that "is present as a relatively circumscribed disorder, in the absence of general confusion, attentional disorders, or impairment in general intellectual capacity" (Squire, 1981, p. 636), elsewhere it is stated that "cognitive deficits after ECT are most apparent during the 30-minute confusional state that follows *each* treatment. . . . *Nevertheless, cognitive deficits can be detected at other times with appropriately sensitive neuropsychological tests*" (Squire, 1982b, p. 171, italics added).

Despite these complications, it has often been assumed that all of these various categories of amnesia are more or less equivalent in terms of severity of anterograde amnesia, and indeed they have been matched on recognition scores after 10 minutes in order to measure rates of forgeting (see earlier). But severity of the clinical state itself has by no means been controlled for by matching after a short interval. It is worth considering seriously the proposition that *all differences between "types"—once "nonobligatory" features are filtered out (i.e., those features from which amnesia is doubly dissociable)—can be accounted for by differences in severity of the clinical amnesic state.*

Let us look at what methods and data are available regarding severity. The traditional method of estimating this is to measure the difference between IQ and the "Memory Quotient" derived from Wechsler's Memory Scale (WMQ). The latter is widely acknowledged to be less than ideal, to put it conservatively (cf. Mair *et al.*, 1979; cf. also Hirst, 1982), and does not correlate perfectly with clinical assessments of severity (cf. Scoville & Milner, 1957); but as unsatisfactory as it is, it is the best we have in many studies, and in many others we do not even have that.

For example, I have not been able to discover the IQ − WMQ in any of the publications regarding either the ECT patients or N. A.[1] In their recent paper, Graf, Squire, and Mandler (1984) summarize their description of patient groups by saying, "This detailed description of the amnesic patient population is intended to demonstrate the circumscribed and severe nature of the memory deficit" (p. 167). This "detailed" description offers no memory quotients for their alcoholic controls (by no means without interest) or for the ECT patients, although it is provided for the Korsakoff (mean IQ − WMQ of 25.2) and two anoxic patients (difference of 20 points in each case). Evidence of cognitive normality in the amnesic group is presented in full as follows, using a phrase that appears in many papers by one of these authors: "Neuropsychological screening and independent neurological examination indicated that memory impairment was the only remarkable deficit of higher cortical function. All of the patients could draw a cube and a house in perspective and none had aphasia or apraxia." And evidence of

1. Since writing this chapter, my attention has been drawn to this information for N. A. IQ − WMQ for N. A. is stated as being 27 points by Wetzel and Squire (1982). Thus, N.A.'s verbal deficit is less than 2 *SD*'s, and he would fall into the moderate rather than the severe category. (I am grateful to Dr. Stuart Zola-Morgan for sending me the reference.)

putatively severe amnesia is described in full as follows: "None could recall any part of a short paragraph after a 15-min delay," and (for the two anoxic patients only) "their average recall of 10 unrelated noun-noun pairs after each of three successive presentations was 0, 1, 0, and 2.0 words" (p. 167). For the Korsakoff patients we are also referred to two other papers for further details by Squire, which, however, provided no further information about severity. This is scarcely sufficient evidence to demonstrate either a "circumscribed" or "severe" memory deficit, on the one hand, or cognitive normality, on the other, although it is more information than some authors provide; nor does it help to provide any quantitative index of the *degree* of severity of the amnesic state, beyond the IQ − WMQ scores when offered.

The scores of IQ − WMQ in this study (Graf *et al.*, 1984), it will be noted, were in the 20s, and this is quite typical of a very large bulk of studies of Korsakoff patients, and all of the studies by Squire and co-workers, as far as I can determine. In the Boston series of amnesics of Butters and co-workers, the cut-off for inclusion appears to be one standard deviation (SD), that is, a difference of 15 points between IQ and WMQ. The only comment I can find in Butters and Cermak's book (1980, p. 9) is, a "20–30 point scatter between IQ and MQ is the psychometric hallmark of the amnesic symptomatology of alcoholic Korsakoff patients." It is of interest that they were prepared to generalize about this: It is not the hallmark of our own studies, whether of Korsakoff patients (or any other group), as we will see. The Korsakoff studies by Meudell and colleagues appear to fall in the same range (e.g., in Meudell, Northern, Snowden, & Neary, 1980) the mean IQ − WMQ was 22.4. It presumably applies, also, to the patients who were studied by Huppert and Piercy (1978a) and were reported to have normal rates of forgeting; these investigators used patients from the Boston group and Manchester group (although these authors do not provide IQ − WMQ scores, merely describing their patients as "severely amnesic").

All of these patients are of the type who, it is said, show a temporally graded retrograde amnesia (more, however, of this later), although going back some years. Their rates of forgetting for recognition are said to be relatively slow.

In contrast, H. M. had an IQ − WMQ difference of 45 points, that is, 3 *SD*'s. The severe amnesic patient reported by Heilman and Sypert (1977) with Korsakoff syndrome induced by a posterior fornix lesion had a difference of 36 points (this study is useful, also, in reporting normal STM performance). The encephalitic patient studied by Cermak (1976) had normal STM but a very severe retrograde amnesia without a temporal gradient and an IQ − WMQ difference of 49.5.

Finally, let us look at the data from our own patients: Because of the inadequacies of the Wechsler Memory Scale, Warrington has been working on the development of a standardized memory battery at the National Hospital based on 200 normal subjects, with age corrections, and also on a range of neuropsychological patients. It includes both verbal and nonverbal memory recognition components, the scales for which were recently published (Warrington, 1984). No patient who scores less than 2 *SD*'s (30 points) below the age-corrected norm (full-scale memory quotient mean of 100) on *both* verbal *and* nonverbal measures is admitted as amnesic. The two Korsakoff patients who were studied by us for several years and finally came to postmortem both fell well off the bottom of the scale, which itself extends to 2.67 *SD*'s below the normal mean (Mair *et al.*, 1979). Both of these patients had flat retrograde amnesia gradients extending back at least 25 years. Their rate of forgetting for forced-choice recognition both of verbal and of nonverbal material must have been rapid because they were both at chance when tested immediately after presentation of 50 items in each category. These two patients were Korsakoff patients, but similar levels of severity were characteristic of all of our patients regardless of etiology.

Two points emerge from this survey: First, there is not an inevitable or "characteristic" score for Korsakoff patients or any other group. This depends on patient selection or availability. Second, it cannot be claimed that studies reviewed in the literature deal with patients of equal severity, even when these occur within a single study. If we define "severe" as a deviation of at least 2 *SD*'s from the mean, then it covers the single medial temporal group (H. M.) and others of the surgical group reviewed by Scoville and Milner (1957), the Boston encephalitic patients (Cermak, 1976), the Heilman and Sypert fornix-section patient (1977), and all of our patients. If we define as "mild to moderately severe" anything between 1 and 2 *SD*'s (all of which would have been excluded from our studies), then this includes mainly the California, Boston, and Manchester (UK) Korsakoff patients. It does not include our own Korsakoff patients, as we have seen. As regards N. A. and the ECT patients, we are in the dark; but in any event N. A. would have been excluded firmly from our studies because he is not a global amnesic.

Thus, it is parsimonious to assume that there is just one core form of the amnesic syndrome that is revealed if one selects and equates for severity and also eliminates dissociable nonobligatory deficits. Such a hypothesis predicts that rate of forgetting will increase with increasing severity—indeed, the usual *clinical* end point in a case of severe amnesia is complete loss of *recognition* beyond the STM limits. It also predicts that retrograde amnesia will extend further back in time and display flatter gradients with increasing severity (see later). I suspect that the savings on a recognition test that Squire (1981) was still able to find after an interval of 32 hours (clinically well outside our experience) reflects the lack of severity of his Korsakoff group—combined, perhaps, with the administration of the test with a stress on guessing, dependent on priming, rather than recognizing, which may also be how "familiarity" as opposed to "recognition" judgments may be based (Huppert & Piercy, 1978b). Equally, the failure by Warrington (1974) to confirm Piercy and Huppert's (1972) finding of good retention by Korsakoff patients in a recognition test would have a similar explanation (aside from the ceiling effect in the unconfirmed study). This hypothesis is the simplest one that will account for discrepancies in the literature, and it is the most conservative we can adopt until it is proved inadequate.

The moderate degree of severity of the Boston group of patients helps one to understand the "naturalistic" account of one of their patients who was taken to visit North Station (Zola-Morgan & Oberg, 1980). A day or more later (how many days is not clear), the patient recalled a visit and a lunch (accurately), commenting: "Dr. Zola and I sat across from Miss Oberg" (p. 550). We have not taken any of our patients to North Station, but we have talked to them over many years, during which their venue has changed, and about a large number of topics, and we would judge that such a degree of good specific recall of a recent episode is well beyond any of our patients' capacities. This Boston patient had an IQ − WMQ difference of 22 points.

It is noteworthy, in this connection, that the encephalitic patients of Cermak's (1976) and all of our patients had very extended retrograde amnesias without gradients, whereas temporal gradients have been claimed for the less severe Korsakoff patients studied by the Boston group and by Squire. The various measures of retrograde amnesia reported in the literature are by no means equivalent and so direct comparisons are risky (see later). However, both animal and clinical evidence suggest that the greater the degree of anterograde amnesia induced by disease, injury, or treatment, the greater the retrograde amnesia—the end point as severity increases being, one may suggest, a flat gradient with loss extending backward over a very long period (provided one measures this with an adequate test; see later).

Whether, once patient groups are selected to be of equivalent and marked severity and to be uncontaminated by other dissociable deficits, they will turn out to display a common pathology site remains an open question, although the current evidence suggests that this is at least a strong possibility (cf. review by Mair *et al.*, 1979).

We have seen that even when restricting ourselves to one diagnostic category (e.g., Korsakoff) different groups differ in severity and undoubtedly in degree of contamination. If the purpose is to characterize a custodial group, then one can appreciate why profiles of everything from olfactory discrimination to sensory scaling might be interesting to study, but theoretical understanding is advanced by concentrating on dissociations rather than associations. *Dis*sociations reveal what is essential and nonessential about a neuropsychological condition, and they allow both logical analysis and appropriate selection of cases for study. *As*sociations may merely uncover multiple handicaps and, more seriously, generate empirical results that are contaminated because of handicaps (e.g., perceptual or attentional) that intrude into performance but are not essentially linked to amnesia as such.

Having said this, there is no doubt that the detailed empirical criteria for selection are not well established. It is easier to detect a potentially contaminating deficit than it is to establish the null hypothesis. Further empirical work will no doubt sharpen the criteria as further dissociations emerge. But at this stage we are at least able to ask, as minimal requirements, for a quantitative estimate of the severity of the amnesic condition, its globality, and estimates of premorbid intelligence, using methods such as those of Nelson and O'Connell (1978). Good cases are rare and it might not help the analysis for the search to be carried out where there happens to be a lamppost rather than in the shadow where the coin was dropped.

## STORAGE VERSUS RETRIEVAL

It is surprising how provocative it has been to suggest that the amnesic patient's difficulty may be one of retrieval rather than one of storage (Warrington & Weiskrantz, 1970). Consolidation appears to be a flag to which many have felt they must rally at all costs. There is no doubt that consolidation is intuitively compelling from clinical experience and anecdote, which is why it first suggested itself and remained the only hypothesis before it was demonstrated that amnesic patients could both learn and retain information that went well beyond motor skills. But it was those very further instances that failed to be predicted by the same intuition, which was one reason why they were so surprising and led to quite fresh theoretical analyses.

The present discussion will be brief, because modern interpretations of memory processing tend to cut across such monolithic and neat categories. However, leaving aside a variety of intermediate or alternative positions, it is still fair to ask, if a patient cannot remember, is this because he never stored the experience in the first place or because, for a variety of possible reasons, the information is there but inaccessible?

Let us be clear about, in the presence of a memory loss, what *cannot* rule out the possibility of a retrieval impediment. There are more possibilities than that of mutism caused by a "sore throat" in the read-out from store, although even that crude hypothesis is not without some support for certain aspects of amnesia.

First, it is not necessary for premorbid events to be as severely affected as postmorbid events. Premorbid events will have benefited from an increase in strength and recoding in various ways from which new events will be protected if they cannot be further readily accessed.

Second, it is not necessary for retrograde amnesia gradients to be flat—a point I shall be taking up shortly.

Third, it is not necessary that the pattern of strengths and weaknesses of the amnesic patient's performance be denied to normal subjects when subjected to mnemonic degradation. It may, or it may not be, that the pattern of amnesic memory can be approximated in some respects by severely degraded memory in normal subjects, but unless one has a complete theory of normal forgetting in which changes in retrieval play no part, the issue is neutral. To support the consolidation view literally with such a comparison, one presumably would have to consider the argument that normal memory, as it becomes degraded over long intervals, shows "wearing off" of consolidtion—"de-consolidation," if you will—whereas, on other evidence, it is just the opposite assumption that is usually accepted.

Fourth, a cue that helps an amnesic patient to restore him to *complete* normality is not necessary. As we will see, and despite perverse claims to the contrary, it happens in several cases that amnesic patients *do* perform just as well as controls (and even better in some experiments, e.g., with unique cues; Warrington & Weiskrantz, 1978), but it would be absurd to hang a whole hypothesis upon a three-letter cue completely overcoming an accessibility impediment, any more than a pacemaker completely normalizes defective cardiac action.

Fifth, and finally, it is not necessary for normal subjects to be entirely unhelped by retrieval cues; although characteristically, of course, they are helped less, if at all, than are amnesic patients (and need such help less).

The methodological point can be illustrated by an example from another ballpark (to mix metaphors). Suppose, for example, that we know of an athlete who is bored and lacking in motivation—he *walks* at a respectable enough rate, but, when asked to *run*, he just slouches around the racetrack lackadaisically (not that I would like to suggest that amnesic patients are merely lackadaisical mnemonists, but simply to cite an example of type of "retrieval" problem). Right; now we electrify the grid and offer attractive rewards for fast performance, and, lo and behold, he achieves a much better running score. But forget it: all the other athletes also improve their performance somewhat, so there is nothing specific about the motivation of our runner. And if they were not already at ceiling, they would improve still more. Moreover, when we allow our normal athletes to become old and infirm, or maybe just bored with racing, they too show weaker running, although they can walk reasonably normally. But one can be confident that even elderly runners would speed up their running a bit on an electrified track. Using this form of logic, one cannot only dismiss the original motivational argument but can even advance the claim that the slouchy athletes are prematurely senile.

In formal terms, one seeks a significant interaction term; but the advantages conferred by the "rule of differential effects" (Schacter & Tulving, 1982) does not require in principle that normal subjects be entirely impervious to treatments or that amnesic subjects be completely normalized by them, as often seems to be assumed. But the issues involved in identifying a "cure" are more complex than those involved in identifying a deficit: Normal behavior may not be optimal, the scale units on which changes are based may not be equal over the whole range, and all behavioral measures are sensitive to multiple causal factors, some relevant and some irrelevant to the initial disturbance. The problem lies in deciding which are which. The issues have been discussed in more detail elsewhere (Weiskrantz, 1968).

All five of these points have been advanced oversimplistically against a retrieval view, but none is conclusive. Having said that none of these conditions is necessary, it can also be said that it is not easy to specify the conditions that are *sufficient* to force one to accept a retrieval explanation. Sustained impairment of memory by itself will always be inconclusive: A minimal condition for demonstration of a retrieval impairment is the reversibility of the memory loss. But even this is not sufficient because, for example, it could always be the case that it was the stored trace that was initially damaged but only incompletely so, and that it could recover through normal processes of "consolidation," rehearsal, or what have you. But if the reversal is *rapid*, if it is *substantial*, and if it is *extensive*, embracing both premorbid and postmorbid events, one is strongly led, through parsimony if not through absolute logical necessity, to entertain a retrieval explanation very seriously.

All three of the properties can be seen in reversal of memory loss in the amnesic state. Needless to say, cueing works very quickly, and it also works extensively over a wide time span. It is also substantial. H. M. is often taken to be the prototype of the "consolidation" failure case because his postmorbid amnesia is so severe (and, it is argued, because his premorbid retention is less severely affected). The study by Marslen-Wilson and Teuber (1975) is frequently cited in support. But the effects of cueing for both premorbid and postmorbid events were quite remarkable in their study (Figure 21.6): Even postmorbid events that were scarcely detectable by routine methods jumped up to 80–90% correct with prompts. A similar improvement was seen in Korsakoff patients (Figure 21.7). (The fact that their postmorbid performance without prompts is better than H. M.'s performance would support the view that they are less severely amnesic than he is. No IQ – WMQ data are given, but the patients came from the Boston Veteran's Administration Hospital, which would be consisent with this surmise.) It may be that controls are also helped, or would be if their memories were not also so good without prompts, but even Marslen-Wilson and Teuber comment: "The findings of our present study may serve to underscore the extent to which, even in amnesia as severe as H. M.'s such an uncovering of seemingly lost memory traces is possible" (p. 361).

Rapidly reversible retrograde amnesia can also be seen in clinical experiments and routines (cf. Weiskrantz, 1966). For example, the sodium amytal technique is used to determine speech lateralization and also to predict whether surgery would be in danger of producing memory disorders of the type found with bilateral temporal lobe pathology. During the anesthesia, temporally graded retrograde amnesic effects can be present in patients

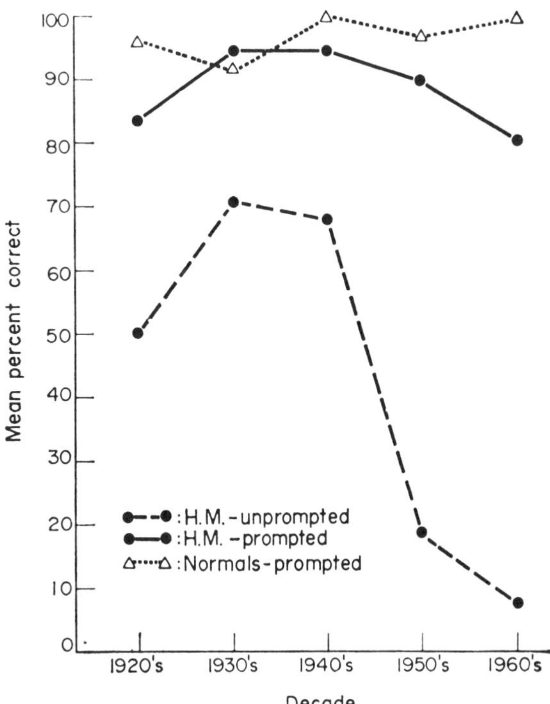


**FIGURE 21.6.** Percentage of correct identifications of faces with and without prompts in each decade by H. M. and (prompted scores only) by normal control subjects. (From Marslen-Wilson & Teuber, 1975. Reprinted by permission.)

already suffering from contralateral temporal lobe dysfunction. These are reversed in the postanesthesia state (Milner, Branch, & Rasmussen, 1962)—memories return. Note that the retrograde amnesia is temporally graded but the recovery is rapid, "all patients being able to recall the pictures and sentence which had been presented before the injection, once the effects of the drug had worn off" (Milner, 1966, p. 123).

An especially instructive study was reported several years ago by Bickford, Mulder, Dodge, Svien, and Rome (1958). These investigators studied the effects in conscious patients of brief trains of electrical stimulation delivered through deep electrodes implanted in the temporal lobes. Such stimulation produced a temporally graded retrograde amnesia. Significantly, the interval over which the resulting retrograde amnesia extended backward in time varied directly with the duration of electrical stimulation. For example, with a stimulus of 1 second, the amnesia was for the preceding few minutes. With a stimulus of 5 seconds, it is extended back a day or so. With a 10-second stimulus, the retrograde amnesia went back as far as several weeks.

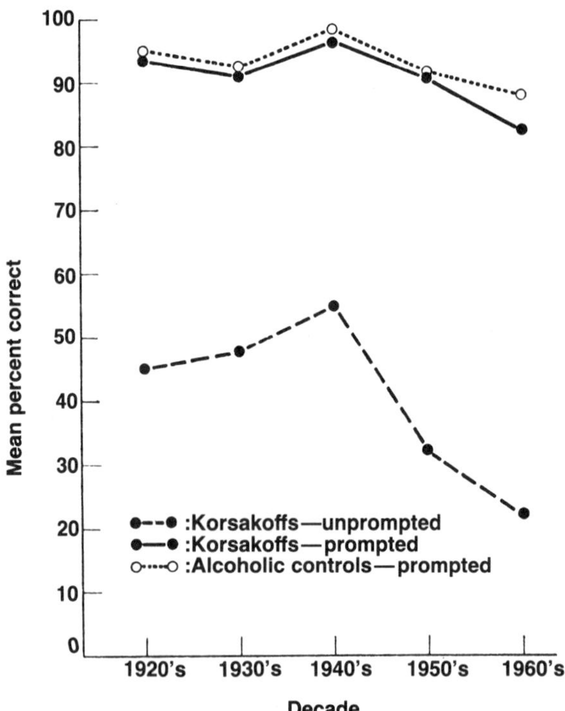


**FIGURE 21.7.** Percentage of correct identifications of faces with and without prompts in each decade by Korsakoff patients and (prompted scores only) by alcoholic controls. (From Marslen-Wilson & Teuber, 1975. Reprinted by permission.)

Moreover, the retrograde amnesia was reversible, recovery occurring within 1 to 2 hours after a 10-second stimulus (less for shorter stimulus durations). When we extrapolate—if the dysfunction were to become increasingly chronic and continuous—as an end point we might expect the retrograde amnesia to stretch back over decades, with a flat gradient, as in patients who are severely amnesic by our definition. This appears to have been the situation in the four encephalitic patients of Butters and Cermak (1980)—but note, even in these severe cases there was reversal:

> Conclusions . . . should be made cautiously as, of the four encephalitic patients, only S. S. and H. C. are still truly amnesic upon clinical examination. . . . Although N. S. was amnesic at the time the STM [short-term memory] tests were administered, *she has made a full recovery and now displays neither anterograde nor retrograde memory problems*. (p. 128, italics added)

These patients had had retrograde amnesia problems stretching back over decades. Obviously their traces were not destroyed when they were in the amnesic state, but they had been rendered inaccessible.

Recovery, in fact, is not uncommon in the amnesic syndrome. Victor *et al.* (1971, pp. 42–43) reported that 21% of their clinical population who could be followed (104 cases) showed "complete" recovery and another 25% showed "significant" recovery from Korsakoff psychosis. Of those that recovered completely, almost all did so within a period of 1 to 10 months (see also Adams, 1969, p. 99). Similar recovery is seen after ECT:

> In the case of the one- to two-year retrograde amnesia associated with ECT [the type of patient included in his studies by Squire], the memory impairment is largely temporary and is recovered substantially during the months following treatment. . . . Thus ECT does not erase these memories but causes them to be temporarily inaccessible in a way that depends on their age at the time of treatment. (Squire, Cohen, & Nadel, 1984, p. 192)

Despite the kinds of evidence just reviewed, loyalty to an unqualified consolidation interpretation seems to be both complacent and stubborn. It is possible to have a cake and eat it, but not without danger of sticky fingers and dyspepsia.

H. M. has often been claimed to be an exception to the generalization that severe amnesia is associated with extensive retrograde amnesia, and this is often used as evidence against a retrieval explanation (inconclusively, as we have argued, even if true). Therefore, it is worth looking at the only quantitative evidence available on the point, namely, the study, already cited, by Marslen-Wilson and Teuber (1975). It is important to stress that in their questionnaire they used publicly highly rehearsable material—past U.S. presidents, scientists, inventors, politicians, film stars. They comment, "We did not attempt to find public figures whose fame might have faded after a particular period; our concern was to identify the approximate date when their fame began." Indeed, some of their material was drawn from the 1920s, and H. M. was born in 1926, but on their criteria it would have been legitimate to have included George Washington. That is, they were concerned with the maximum period that a public figure could have been known, not the minimum. Old and culturally popular material is likely to benefit from reexposure, and it becomes impossible to estimate the mnemonic age of any particular item. Very well established public figures, like George Washington, become part of the cultural pool of repeatable knowledge. On the other hand, less important figures gradually fade. H. M.'s premorbid gradient appears to be an amalgam of these two trends: very "old" material is still retained, but material from the two decades prior to his surgery is retained somewhat better (see Figure 21.7).

In contrast, Sanders and Warrington (1971) (whose methods were used on the Mair *et al.*, 1979, cases that came to postmortem, among others) deliberately tried to avoid such publicly persistent material, and this is frankly acknowledged by Marslen-Wilson and Teuber: "Sanders and Warrington took pains to concentrate their choices of test photographs on those public figures whose fame had come and gone. They were explicitly concerned with what they called the 'fate of old memories' which we could not, strictly speaking, evaluate with our procedures" (p. 362). It is rare for this clear acknowledgment to be contained in reviews. The Sanders and Warrington cases showed, with their method, flat and extensive retrograde amnesias.

Thus, despite the frequent assertion that H. M. has been demonstrated to show good retention of old premorbid material (e.g., "*formal* testing of remote memory in two well-circumscribed cases of memory dysfunction [cases H. M. and N. A.] has *demonstrated* that premorbid memory can be less affected than postmorbid memory" Squire, 1982c, italics added); in fact, the assertion is based on clinical anecdote rather than quantitative demonstration. This may be why the same author has also made just the opposite assertion to the one just quoted: "It has *not* yet been possible to identify retrograde amnesia in this individual [H. M.] with *formal* tests" (Squire, Cohen, & Nadel, 1984).

More recently it has been reported (Corkin, 1984) that with new retrograde amnesia tests (details as yet unpublished), H. M.'s retrograde amnesia is now estimated to extend back to 11 years prior to his surgery (rather than the 2 years in the original report based on anecdotal clinical evidence), or apparently even longer with, for example, "famous tunes." Interestingly, in relation to our review of relative severity of amnesia, it is stated that "a comparison of H. M.'s performance with that of two other amnesic patients suggests that the severity of the remote memory loss may be related to the severity of anterograde amnesia" (p. 257). Details are awaited. As of now, I can discover no published account of H. M.'s having been tested with a proper "episodic" test, with prior rehearsal equalized among items as far as possible; and until that happens, no comparisons or firm conclusions about his retrograde amnesia are possible; the existing evidence on the recovery of H. M.'s pre- and postmorbid experiences with prompts (see above) is certainly consistent with a retrieval explanation.

Clearly, to measure retrograde amnesia with validity it is necessary to try to avoid publicly very rehearsable material, as Sanders and Warrington (1971) did in their original study, and as Squire and Slater (1975) have done with his television material. Albert, Butters, and Levin (1979) have made some partial attempt with their "hard" items, but even these have an expected public life of up to a decade—Rosemary Clooney (one of the "hard" items) is still shown on British television. It was with their material that the encephalitic patients already cited showed an extensive R. A. with a flat gradient. Similarly all of our subjects showed a flat gradient (with the Sanders and Warrington methodology).

The methodological problems in measuring retrograde amnesia are difficult but by no means intractable. The original method invented and developed by Warrington and Sanders (1971), based on some 350 subjects (plus another 200 in a partner study), used as controls young students who were not around when the items first appeared on the scene and hence were not entitled to the memory for such items. The same method was used (without acknowledgment) by Squire (1974), with similar results. The "improved" questionnaire of Squire and Slater (1975) used items based on television shows and race horses, which is a clever and useful advance as it can make use of television viewing records. Of course, similar methodological issues arise in this, as in all questionnaire methods, namely that it must be assumed that television shows did not change in memorability from one time to another, were never repeated or discussed subsequently in the press or elsewhere (a difficult condition to meet, as it happens in passing, on British television). In addition, to be practical, the population has to have at least a minimal obsession with race horses, and not to discuss them or to do so with uniformity. These are problems necessarily inherent in any method that attempts to quantify retrograde amnesia, as discussed in the original paper by Warrington and Sanders; and, in fact, given the great methodological difficulties inherent in such methods, the similarity of findings of normal forgetting (especially if one does not allow Squire and Slater the convenient *ad hoc* exception of 1957–1958 television programs) is close enough for comfort.

Finally, there have been various attempts, in effect, to dismiss flat retrograde amnesia gradients by arguing either that they are caused by cognitive impairments superimposed on the amnesia or that they reflect a slow onset of the initial anterograde amnesic state itself. Neither hypothesis is secure. Regarding "cognitive" impairments in, say, Korsakoff patients, we saw no such evidence in either of the extensively studied cases of Mair *et al.* (1979) at the time when their retrograde amnesia was measured. These results have been curiously, but very misleadingly misquoted by Cohen and Squire:

> It should be noted that Mair, Warrington, and Weiskrantz reported two patients with Korsakoff syndrome who at autopsy were found to have rather restricted lesions but who had nevertheless displayed extensive remote memory impairment. *In this report, too, the patient with the more extensive pathology (in the thalamus* [sic] *and cerebral cortex) had exhibited more extensive remote memory impairment.* (Cohen & Squire, 1981, italics added)

In fact, what was found was:

> The duration of the retrograde amnesia in each case was extensive, *extending over the whole time span sampled in this study (thirty years for E. A. and twenty-five years for H. J.).* Memory for remote events was not spared nor did it appear to be less impaired than that for recent events. (Mair *et al.*, 1979, p. 756, italics added)

In other words, retrograde amnesia was found to have extended back uniformly over at least a 25-year period in both patients, for the full limit of the scale used for each, and there was no evidence of a difference in severity in the two cases. Interestingly, the encephalitic patient studied by Cermak (1976), also with a flat and very extensive retrograde amnesia, was normal on STM tasks (as were all of our patients, regardless of etiology).

As regards the view that a slow and long onset of amnesia might provide an explanation of long and gradientless retrograde amnesia in Korsakoff patients (because of a gradual buildup of alcohol consumption and addiction prior to coming to the clinical attention), as is suggested by Meudell *et al.* (1980) and others, there can be a lack of credibility when the facts are looked at in detail. For example, in the study in question, in which there was a relatively flat gradient for retrograde amnesia in alcoholic Korsakoff patients, it would appear that one of the patients, at least, would have had to become alcoholic 1 year or so before birth for this explanation to have force. But, in any event, there are several, well-attested cases of relatively abrupt onset, either because of temporal lobe or fornix surgery, or especially because of encephalitis (where no such explanation can obtain), who nevertheless have very extended and gradientless retrograde amnesia; and these cases, moreover, can be qualitatively indistinguishable in this regard from Korsakoff cases (cf. Sanders & Warrington, 1971).

## WHAT IS SPARED IN AMNESIA?

But there has long been (e.g., cf. Weiskrantz, 1978, p. 380) an alternative to *either* a generalized consolidation *or* a retrieval position, namely, that some types of memory systems are spared and others are impaired. If this line of approach is taken, the question is left open as to whether those selectively impaired systems are affected at the storage stage (including, as one possibility, a consolidation impediment) or, as we have speculated, a retrieval impairment due to a disconnection between two systems (Warrington & Weiskrantz, 1982), or simply "ablated" *in toto*. But at least there is now considerable agreement, both for animal and human clinical evidence, about the *empirical* support for intact learning and retention that goes well beyond the original finding of spared motor-skill learning (Corkin, 1968; cf. Brooks & Baddeley, 1976). We have summarized the evidence (Weiskrantz & Warington, 1979) from several authors as including at that time visual discrimination learning, recall of pictures and words with a variety of cues, retention of learning of anomalous pictures in the McGill Anomalies Test, rule-governed verbal paired-associate learning and retention, retention of stereoscopic perception of random dot stereograms, retention of the McCulloch color-grating illusion, retention of facilitation for solving specific jigsaw puzzles, retention for arranging specific words into specific sentences, and classical eyelid conditioning. To that list should be added the more recent findings with good learning and retention of the Tower of Hanoi problem (Cohen & Squire, 1980), mathematical problem solving (Wood, Ebert, & Kinsbourne,

1982), and mirror reading (Cohen & Squire, 1980) (although, parenthetically, it seems likely that learning a new oculo*motor* skill is entailed in mirror reading—that, as well as priming of specific words).

Whatever characterization will emerge as the best fit for the supposedly intact system in amnesic patients (and it is probably not yet on the list), it will have to encompass *both* (1) facilitation through priming and (2) the acquisition of new relationships (cf. Warrington & Weiskrantz, 1982).

1. In the first category fall not only, as we have seen, all the examples of cued recall using fragmented or partial information cues, but possibly such phenomena as facilitation of stereoscopic perception, semantic or rhyme paired-associate learning, and specific facilitation of jigsaw puzzle solutions. Even a simple priming interpretation is challenged, it is worth noting (as did Rozin some years ago in 1976), by retention over very long periods (e.g., 4 months by H. M. of fragmented drawings) and the lack of decay over an interval of a week by controls (Tulving, Schacter, & Stark, 1982).

2. But there is also evidence of learning of perceptual-motor skill and problem-solving skill, eyelid conditioning, simple maze learning, the learning of anomalous pictures (which, by definition, involve new relationships), and the anecdotal but compelling evidence by Claparède (1911) and by Korsakoff himself (cf. Delay & Brion, 1969, p. 17) of conditioned emotional responses. This category cannot be handled by a priming explanation alone, although there are no doubt some aspects of priming involved in all the examples cited.

In the first category (facilitation through priming), the most extensive evidence comes from the method of fragmented or partial information cues. [There is a problem of nomenclature. We have called such methods either "partial' or "fragmented" information and, generically, "cued recall," but Graf *et al.* (1984) restrict the last term to one in which the instructions explicitly require the subject to refer to an earlier list—when, in fact, the method does not work—and prefer instead to use terms such as "letter cues" or "fragmented pictures." Butters and Cermak (1980) classify partial information methods under "paired-associate" learning, which is also confusing because amnesic subjects are classically extremely poor at conventional paired-associate learning. Cohen and Squire (1980) have referred to incomplete figures testing as a "recognition memory test," which is clearly misleading, and elsewhere Squire & Slater (1977) label the results of a yes/no recognition procedure as "cued recall"—equally inappropriate.] The method was first used in a formal way with amnesic patients by Warrington and Weiskrantz in 1968, followed up in a series of studies. There are several variations of method and of material, but the general procedure is to expose a list of items, words, or pictures, and after an interval—which can vary from minutes to weeks—to show a fragment of the item and ask the subject to identify the complete item. In our initial study we used literally fragmented pictures and words of varying degrees of completeness (Warrington &

Weiskrantz, 1968), but later we also used the first few letters of a complete word (Warrington & Weiskrantz, 1970; Weiskrantz & Warrington, 1970b), which has the advantage of placing verbal material under close control in terms specifying the number of alternatives the fragment has to the set of possible whole items. We discovered that, to our surprise, the amnesic subject shows an increased probability, in response to the partial cue, of making a correct identification of items that had been previously exposed. There is a clear dissociation between the good performance with partial information cues, on the one hand, and the severely impaired performance, on the other hand, with conventional retention procedures such as free recall or yes/no recognition of the same items (Warrington & Weiskrantz, 1970, 1974).

As much discussion of the method has appeared in the literature, it is worth examining the status of the evidence closely. There is no doubt that the early results were surprising because they appeared to violate clinical impressions and also to extend intact long-term storage of motor-skill learning (which heretofore was the only exception) to the learning and retention of verbal items. But despite early skepticism, the findings were soon confirmed in H. M. (Milner, Corkin, & Teuber, 1968), although it was suggested that the method might have worked because it was so easy for all subjects. [They have also been more recently confirmed (Corkin, 1984) using partial letter cues for words, with apparently precisely the same pattern of results as we originally reported with our patients—a dissociation between the good performance with partial cues and the poor recognition performance. Ironically, there is now no citation of the findings of partial information methods on any other patients by other workers: the only citation in the paper is to J. D. E. Gabrieli, N. J. Cohen, and S. Corkin, unpublished data.] Since that time there have been persistent efforts to discount the findings, and as these are in danger of being accepted through sheer echoic repetition by some reviewers, it is important to examine the data. Thus, the following type of criticism has been advanced:

> Tests based on fragmented drawings have been given to H. M. (Milner *et al.*, 1968), and tests involving either fragmented drawings, fragmented words or the initial letters of words have been given to patients with Korsakoff syndrome (Warrington & Weiskrantz, 1968; Weiskrantz & Warrington, 1970b). These patients exhibited considerable retention over intervals of one hour or more [viz., 4 months in the case of H. M.] *but nevertheless failed to attain the level of performance exhibited by control subjects.* (Squire, 1982c, p. 249, italics added)

Preserved function is therefore dismissed: "Thus, reports of good performance by amnesic patients on incomplete figures (Warrington & Weiskrantz, 1968, 1970) do not necessarily mean that these tasks demonstrate preserved function. Amnesic patients often do rather well in recognition [*sic*] memory tasks compared with free recall tasks, but the advantage of recognition memory over free recall applies to control subjects as well" (Cohen & Squire, 1980, p. 210). The same type of claim is made quite explicit by Squire and Slater (1977):

> Clearly the method by which memory is tested can influence the performance of amnesic patients, but the method of testing also influences the performance of normal subjects. Thus compared to their scores in free recall, the scores of both amnesic and control subjects were higher when they were tested by recognition (Warrington & Weiskrantz, 1970; . . .). (Squire & Slater, 1977, p. 401)

If we turn to the cited study by Warrington and Weiskrantz (1970), we do indeed find that the recognition scores are higher than recall for both groups. Here is Table 2 from that paper:

TABLE 2 (Warrington & Weiskrantz, 1970)

| | Controls | Amnesics |
|---|---|---|
| Recall | 48% | 14% |
| Recognition | 94% | 59% [chance = 50%] |
| Fragmented words | 96% | 94% |

The recognition score *is* higher—it cannot fall below an average of 50%, whereas recall can be zero. But the amnesic subjects were at chance on recognition. Later in the same paper by Warrington and Weiskrantz, we find the following summary of Experiment 2:

> Retrieval by recognition was superior to retrieval by recall in the control group ($p < 0.0001$) *but not in the amnesic group*, while retrieval by partial information was superior to retrieval by recall in the amnesic group ($p < 0.05$) but not in the control group. (p. 629, italics added)

But, aside from this study, there are two further studies—omitted from the citations above—that bear directly on the question (Warrington & Weiskrantz, 1974, 1978); the two graphs in Figures 21.8 and 21.9 are reproduced from these studies.

Thus, there is good evidence that amnesic and control patients can show equivalent performance on partial information methods—with supporting evidence, as we shall see, from other authors—despite repeated assertions to the contrary. But there has been another attack on the positive findings with such methods, namely, that "subsequent work, however, has shown that this result is a consequence of the scoring procedures used to evaluate different retention procedures (ref. to Squire, Wetzel, & Slater, 1978)" (Squire, 1980, p. 370).

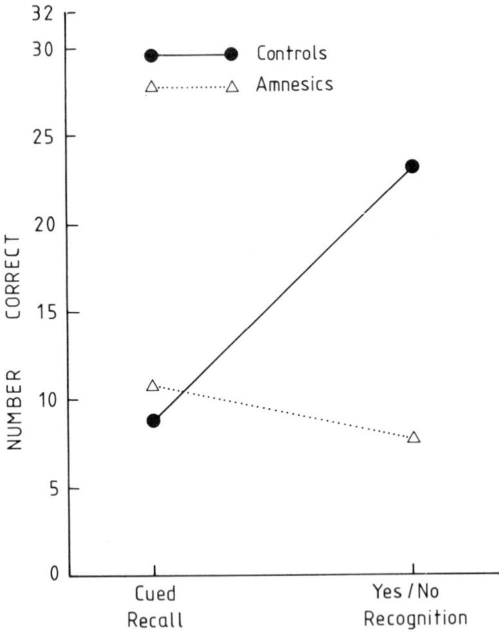


**FIGURE 21.8.** Results of retention tests of amnesic and control subjects using cued recall procedure (cueing words by first three letters) versus yes/no recognition of whole words. It can be seen that amnesic subjects achieved normal (in fact, slightly, but insignificantly superior) retention levels using cued recall. (From Warrington & Weiskrantz, 1974. Reprinted by permission.)

This is a more serious charge, namely, of a failure to replicate with a scoring method implied to be superior. It is necessary to examine the cited Squire, Wetzel, and Slater study to see how far it is justified.

First, some points of detail: The study was done entirely with ECT patients (and controls) and not the kind of organic amnesic patient used in our studies. Moreover, there were different testing schedules for ECT patients and controls, a detail that is not trivial because the essential comparison that emerged in their study is between ECT patients at one retention interval and controls at longer intervals. Our studies used a single testing session and one retention interval.

Second, they changed not only their scoring but their method of selection of items, using target words with a relatively high probability of correct guessing ($p = .28$), thereby entailing a need for guessing correction, whereas we used low probability items ($.1 > p > 0$). Our method of selection did not require the alternative scoring method.

But, in fact, with their guessing correction applied, at their shortest retention interval they obtained exactly the same interaction as we did (cf.

Figure 21.8), with ECT patients displaying a performance qualitatively different (low on yes/no recognition, relatively better on partial information) from that of controls. The only difference was that with one method of scoring, but not the other, the pattern of performance by controls, when their memories were degraded by a 7-day interval, was similar to that of the ECT patients at 20 minutes. In other words, the argument has been switched from our result, which was nicely confirmed by them, to whether amnesic memory might be simulated by the degraded memory of controls. That is an interesting but quite different question, which we had already addressed (Weiskrantz & Warrington, 1975b; cf. also Warrington & Weiskrantz, 1982) saying, briefly, that the matter is neutral and open, but is no cause for embarrassment—unless, that is, one has an entirely complete explanation of how normal long-term forgetting occurs.

There is one other attempted replication with negative results. Citing others' work on prompts with fragments, Squire and Slater (1977) used their own system of prompting and concluded that their "results provide no evidence for the notion that amnesia reflects a retrieval defect easily reversible by prompting procedures. It is suggested that procedures that improve the performance of amnesics may similarly improve the performance of normal subjects" (p. 398). This is what was done in that study:

**FIGURE 21.9.** "Reversal" learning. For each recall cue (the initial three letters), there were only two common English words available as possible responses. Subjects were first taught one set of words (List 1) and then were given four trials with the alternative set (R1–4). the same cues were used on all five trials. It can be seen that amnesic subjects achieved normal levels of retention on List 1 but were impaired when required to switch to the alternative response. (From Warrington & Weiskrantz, 1978. Reprinted by permission.)

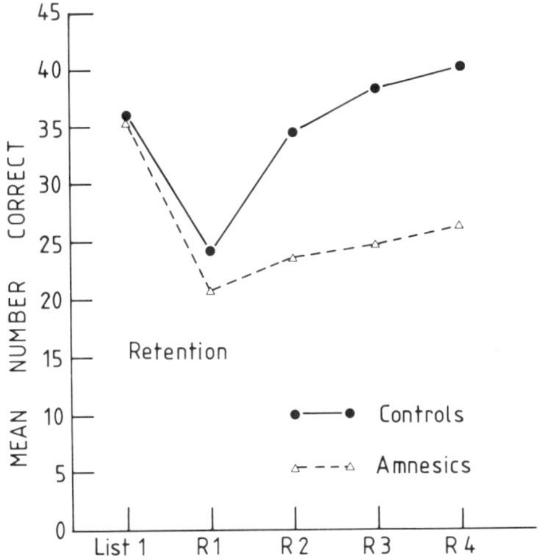

> We next asked whether N. A.'s performance on . . . remote memory tests might be improved by prompting procedures. For prompting we compiled the 154 different facts about news events and the 140 different facts about television programs that had been produced by the control subjects and by N. A. Six months after the free recall session, each subject was read all the facts in this list and asked to "say yes if you specifically remember this detail to be true; say no if you do not." (p. 399)

In other words they administered a yes/no recognition test (which they strangely label as "cued recall" in their figure) after a 6-month interval, and from that argue that there was no specific effect of prompts on this patient relative to controls. But we already know that yes/no recognition behaves differently from prompting (see Figure 21.8 and Warrington & Weiskrantz, 1970, 1974, 1978), and the latter cannot be validly tested, and dismissed, by testing something else.

Much more recently, Graf *et al.* (1984) produced a strong and unambiguous confirmation of the power of the partial information method: Amnesic subjects display normal retention performance using letter cues for words, with "guessing" instructions. Their study also makes it clear that the type of instruction is of crucial importance: Amnesic subjects perform below normal levels if they are instructed to *recall* the target words from the previous list. This is a point of some importance to the understanding of the syndrome. Amnesic subjects do not have an experienced "memory" for items that are facilitated in a priming procedure. Indeed, it was Warrington's idea originally to use the method just because it avoided asking the patient to "remember." The partial information method works because, among other reasons, it avoids asking a subject explicitly about his or her memory for or acknowledged recognition of material that is nevertheless incremented in store. Instead the subject is simply given a cue and asked to provide a compatible response, by guessing if necessary, irrespective of acknowledged recall or recognition. Attention is explicitly drawn to just this feature of the method in Weiskrantz (1978) and Warrington and Weiskrantz (1982) in terms of the sparing of a system in which priming can still operate.

The confirmation by Graf *et al.* (1984) adds to those of other workers (Milner *et al.*, 1968; Corkin, 1984; Schacter, Chapter 20, this volume) and attests to the reality and the power of the method of partial information, which moreover are seen in amnesic patients with a variety of etiologies, including medial temporal surgical cases, Korsakoff patients, and encephalitic patients. There are interesting implications, of course, for the operation of separate systems in normal subjects (Tulving *et al.*, 1982).

The second category (acquisition of new relationships) concerns the learning of new relationships and skills rather than the facilitation of already established items. This category, too, shares a property with the previous category in that the subject need not be asked to "remember" or "recognize" as such: He or she is given a stimulus or placed in a particular situation and asked to respond accordingly. But this property cannot be a sufficient feature for adequate retention: The internal informational characteristics of the material or the task also are critical. The same external situation can sometimes yield either excellent or very poor learning and retention, depending on the structure of the material. Thus, amnesic patients can readily learn rule-determined paired associates (Winocur & Weiskrantz, 1976) or certain other paired-associate tasks (Warrington & Weiskrantz, 1982) but conventional paired-associate learning with random pairs is consistently very poor.

Nor does it seem possible to distinguish between these two categories on the basis of parameters characteristically adopted or time constants that normally apply, despite the analysis that Graf *et al.* (1984) have attempted. Thus, for example, both categories—not only learning of new relationships and skilled procedures, but also priming—may show retention over very long time intervals. We have measured relatively slow rates of forgetting of items cued by partial information over days in amnesic patients (Weiskrantz & Warrington, 1970a), and H. M. showed retention of fragmented pictures over 4 months (Milner, 1970). Equally, both categories can be arranged so that there are relatively few or very many degrees of freedom of responses. We have arranged cues in a priming category task so that they uniquely specified the items being cued (Warrington & Weiskrantz, 1974), with good retention over 24 hours by amnesic patients, as well as using cues that matched several possible response words. Similarly, visual maze learning, which must involve acquiring new relationships, studied with H. M. can be simple, which he can learn, or complex, which he cannot (Milner *et al.*, 1968).

The ability of amnesic subjects to learn new relationships has been characterized in a variety of ways, one of which has been to describe it as "procedural learning" (Cohen, 1981). "Procedural learning" suggests that rules and routines can be learned as well as applied, just as it was found earlier that amnesic subjects can quite effectively acquire and persist in using (without any instruction to do so by the experimenter) a semantic or a rhyming rule in paired-associate learning (Winocur & Weiskrantz, 1976). But, while "procedural learning" is an example of learning by amnesic subjects, it is not the case that all examples of learning of new relationships by them are the learning of a "procedural skill," unless this is made true by definition. Therefore, to characterize the intact system as "procedural" does not by itself account for how new *specific* material and relationships are introduced, such as classical conditioning, discrimination learning, McGill anomalies, or arranging specific random sequences of words into sentences. In classical conditioning, for example, one learns a specific association, that A and B go together, which *may* be the result of a procedure, but not the learning of a procedural skill as such, unless some forms of conditioning are tautologically defined as "procedural." Even so, further quite searching analysis is required to establish a putative difference between stimulus–stimulus and stimulus–response conditioning (Mackintosh, Chapter 19, this volume), and this analysis is, in fact, probably more advanced in animal than in human studies. And some classical conditioning with amnesic patients [if the Claparède (1911) story is valid] can occur in just a single trial, that is, without a repeated procedure. A procedural rule can be held constant but the relationship between items operating under the rule made to vary, as in paired-associate learning with varying degrees of closeness of association between items. The amnesic subject responds differentially to the variable affecting the items (Warrington & Weiskrantz, 1982). It also appears from Schacter (Chapter 20, this volume) that new relationships between words can be acquired using a priming method. Conversely, amnesic subjects can be impaired for some forms of procedural learning. "Reversal learning" using a word completion method is a procedure, yet amnesic subjects are markedly impaired (Warrington & Weiskrantz, 1974, 1978; Winocur & Weiskrantz, 1976).

It is for such reasons that we consider that a characterization based on the demands of the internal cognitive relationships among items to be retrieved is most likely to encompass the broadest range of currently known empirical evidence. Warrington and Weiskrantz (1982) have argued that whenever an event can be predicted reliably from another, there is redundancy and hence the possibility of automatic programming, as in classical conditioning, rule-determined paired-associate learning, discrimination learning ("habits"), and the learning of rules themselves (as in learning to mirror read or to solve puzzles and also in the learning of the rules in rule-determined paired associates). Amnesic patients can acquire and retain such material. They can also benefit from automatic facilitation through repetition, as in priming. What they cannot learn or retain is information that requires ordering, reordering, matching, reflecting about items from store. Nor do they appear to be able to *acknowledge* memory for such material as they are able to acquire, which, we argue, requires an active "cognitive mediational system" and which, we speculate, has become disconnected from the residual system that can cope with redundancy.

Thus, amnesic subjects are impaired in using imagery to aid in connecting random pairs of words in paired-associate learning (Baddeley & Warrington, 1973; Jones, 1974). They are severely impaired on "reversal learning," when they must switch the learned response of one word to a cue to an alternative response to the same cue, although they have no difficulty learning the original word (Warrington & Weiskrantz, 1974, 1978). Such switching in "reversal" presumably depends upon, or is at least helped by, active comparison of the relative order or contexts of the two competing items. This and other examples are reviewed in Warrington and Weiskrantz (1982). On the other hand, amnesic patients, who typically have no impairment of semantic knowledge or vocabulary, can be dissociated from patients who do have semantic knowledge deficits but are not amnesic clinically despite the severe limitations imposed by their semantic impairments (Warrington, 1975, Warrington & Taylor, 1978). This line of argument leads the distinction between two interacting but dissociable memory systems (among others) in man (Warrington, 1979), a "cognitive mediational system," and a stable knowledge system. In the past few years there has been considerable convergence and similarity of the types of characterizations offered for the putative memory system damaged in the amnesic syndrome (cf. Warrington & Weiskrantz, 1982, and Graf *et al.*, 1984, for summaries), such as "active cognitive strategies (Cutting, 1978), "evaluative memory" (Baddeley, 1982; Mandler, 1980), "chunking" and "vertical" associations (Wickelgren, 1979), "declarative knowledge" (Cohen, 1981).

Animal evidence also supports a distinction between those forms of learning of which the animal appears to have knowledge of consequences—and hence can show flexibility when the consequences are altered—and those in which responses are emitted relatively automatically and inflexibly (Dickinson, 1985; Mackintosh, Chapter 19, this volume). One source of the difference appears to be whether the contingencies are arranged so as to give the normal animal closely correlated feedback of his own behavior as the circumstances change (Dickinson, 1985) during training. There is an emerging convergence of views that the animal with lesions intended to model that of the human amnesic state may also be able to acquire those tasks in which reordering is not necessary but not those in which it is (Hirsch, 1974; Mahut & Moss, 1985; Mahut, Zola-Morgan, & Moss, 1982; Mishkin, 1982; Squire & Zola-Morgan, 1983; Weiskrantz, 1982). As in work with amnesic subjects, it is the details of the relatedness of the items to be learned that appear to matter, and how much performance might benefit in efficiency from flexible reordering.

The accumulation of so much varied evidence over the past 20 years for residual acquisition and retention by patients has not only forced a reinterpretation of the nature of amnesia itself but has led to specifications and speculations about different systems within normal memory. The convergence of theoretical views from several authors would appear to mark some agreement about the direction in which further thinking should go. But the next challenge will be to design the quite new theoretical formulations and practical techniques necessary to approach the "evaluative" or "cognitive mediational system" damaged in such patients, and "the operation of some, as yet little understood, memory system" (Tulving *et al.*, 1982, p. 336) that remains.

## REFERENCES

Adams, R. D. The anatomy of memory mechanisms in the human brain. In G. A. Talland & N. C. Waugh (Eds.), *The pathology of memory*. New York: Academic Press, 1969.

Albert, M. S., Butters, N., & Levin, J. Temporal gradients in the retrograde amnesia of patients with alcoholic Korsakoff's disease. *Archives of Neurology (Chicago)*, 1979, *36*, 211–216.

Baddeley, A. D. Amnesia: A minimal model and an interpretation. In L. S. Cermak (Ed.), *Human memory and amnesia*. Hillsdale, N. J.: Erlbaum, 1982.

Baddeley, A. D., & Warrington, E. K. Amnesia and the distinction between long- and short-term memory. *Journal of Verbal Learning and Verbal Behavior*, 1970, *9*, 176–189.

Baddeley, A. D., & Warrington, E. K. Memory coding and amnesia. *Neuropsychologia*, 1973, *11*, 159–165.

Bickford, R., Mulder, D. W., Dodge, H. W., Svien, H. J., & Rome, H. P. Changes in memory function produced by electrical stimulation of the temporal lobe in man. *Research Publications—Association for Research in Nervous and Mental Disease*, 1958, *36*, 227–243.

Brain, W. R. *Diseases of the nervous system* (8th ed.) (revised by J. N. Walton). London: Oxford University Press, 1981.

Brooks, D. N., & Baddeley, A. D. What can amnesia patients learn? *Neuropsychologia*, 1976, *14*, 111–122.

Butters, N., & Cermak, L. S. Some comments on Warrington and Baddeley's report of normal short-term memory in amnesic patients. *Neuropsychologia*, 1974, *12*, 283–285.

Butters, N., & Cermak, L. S. *Alcoholic Korsakoff's syndrome*. New York: Academic Press, 1980.

Büttner-Ennever, J. A., Buttner, U., Cohen, B., & Baumgartner, G. Vertical gaze paralysis and the rostral interstitial nucleus of the medial longitudinal fasciculus. *Brain*, 1982, *105*, 125–150.

Cermak, L. S. The encoding capacity of a patient with amnesia due to encephalitis. *Neuropsychologia*, 1976, *14*, 311–326.

Claparède, E. Récognition et moiïté. *Archives psychologie Geneva*, 1911, *11*, 79–90.

Cohen, N. J. *Neuropsychological evidence for a distinction between procedural and declarative knowledge in human memory and amnesia*. Unpublished doctoral dissertation, University of California, San Diego, 1981.

Cohen, N. J., & Squire, L. R. Preserved learning and retention of pattern analyzing skill in amnesia: Dissociation of knowing how and knowing that. *Science*, 1980, *210*, 207–209.

Cohen, N. J., & Squire, L. R. Retrograde amnesia and remote memory impairment. *Neuropsychologia*, 1981, *19*, 337–356.

Corkin, S. Acquisition of motor skill after bilateral medial temporal-lobe excision. *Neuropsychologia*, 1968, *6*, 225–265.

Corkin, S. Lasting consequences of bilateral medial temporal lobectomy: Clinical course and experimental findings in H. M. *Seminars in Neurology*, 1984, *4*, 249–259.

Cutting, J. A cognitive approach to Korsakoff's syndrome. *Cortex*, 1978, *14*, 485–495.

Delay, J., & Brion, S. *Le syndrome de Korsakoff*. Paris: Masson, 1969.

Dickinson, A. Actions and habits: The development of behavioural autonomy. In L. Weiskrantz (Ed.), *Animal intelligence*. London: Oxford University Press, 1985.

Geller, A., & Jarvik, M. E. The time relations of ECS induced amnesia. *Psychonomic Science*, 1968, *12*, 169–170.

Graf, P., Squire, L. R., & Mandler, G. The information that amnesic patients do not forget. *Journal of Experimental Psychology: Learning, Memory, and Cognition*, 1984, *10*, 164–178.

Heilman, K. M., & Sypert, G. W. Korsakoff's syndrome resulting from bilateral fornix lesions. *Neurology*, 1977, *27*, 490–493.

Hierons, R., Janota, I., & Corsellis, J. A. N. The late effects of necrotizing encephalitis of the temporal lobes and limbic areas: A clinico-pathological study of 10 cases. *Psychological Medicine*, 1978, *8*, 21–42.

Hirsch, R. The hippocampus and contextual retrieval of information from memory: A theory. *Behavioral Biology*, 1974, *12*, 421–444.

Hirst, W. The amnesic syndrome: Descriptions and explanations. *Psychological Bulletin*, 1982, *91*, 435–460.

Huppert, F. A., & Piercy, M. Dissociation between learning and remembering in organic amnesia. *Nature (London)*, 1978, *275*, 317–318. (a)

Huppert, F. A., & Piercy, M. The role of trace strength in recency and frequency judgments by amnesic and control subjects. *Quarterly Journal of Experimental Psychology*, 1978, *30*, 347–354. (b)

Huppert, F. A., & Piercy, M. Normal and abnormal forgetting in organic amnesia: Effect of locus of lesion. *Cortex*, 1979, *15*, 385–390.

Jones, M. K. Imagery as a mnemonic aid after left temporal lobectomy: Contrast between material-specific and generalized memory disorders. *Neuropsychologia*, 1974, *12*, 21–30.

Lhermitte, F., & Signoret, J. -L. Analyse neuropsychologique et différenciation des syndromes amnésiques. *Revue Neurologique*, 1972, *126*, 161–178.

Mahut, H., & Moss, M. The monkey and the sea horse. In R. L. Isaacson & K. H. Pribram (Eds.), *The hippocampus* (Vol. 3). New York: Plenum Press, 1985.

Mahut, H., Zola-Morgan, S., & Moss, M. Hippocampal resections impair associative learning and recognition memory in the monkey. *Journal of Neuroscience*, 1982, *2*, 1214–1229.

Mair, W. G. P., Warrington, E. K., & Weiskrantz, L. Memory disorder in Korsakoff's psychosis: A neuropathological and neuropsychological investigation of two cases. *Brain*, 1979, *102*, 749–783.

Mandler, G. Recognizing: The judgment of previous occurrence. *Psychological Review*, 1980, *87*, 252–271.

Marslen-Wilson, W. D., & Teuber, H. L. Memory for remote events in anterograde amnesia: Recognition of public figures from news photographs. *Neuropsychologia*, 1975, *13*, 353–364.

Meudell, P. R., Northern, B., Snowden, J. S., & Neary, D. Long term memory for famous faces in amnesic and normal subjects. *Neuropsychologia*, 1980, *18*, 133–139.

Milner, B. Amnesia following operation of the temporal lobe. In C. W. M. Whitty & O. L. Zangwill (Eds.), *Amnesia*. London: Butterworth, 1966.

Milner, B. Memory and the medial temporal regions of the brain. In K. H. Pribram & D. E. Broadbent (Eds.), *Biology of memory*. New York: Academic Press, 1970.

Milner, B., Branch, C., & Rasmussen, T. Study of short-term memory after intracarotid injection of sodium amytal. *Transactions of the American Neurological Association*, 1962, *87*, 224–226.

Milner, B., Corkin, S., & Teuber, H. -L. Further analysis of the hippocampal amnesic syndrome: 14-year follow-up study of H. M. *Neuropsychologia*, 1968, *6*, 215–234.

Mishkin, M. A memory system in the monkey. In D. E. Broadbent & L. Weiskrantz (Eds.), *The neuropsychology of cognitive function*. London: Royal Society, 1982.

Moscovitch, M. Multiple dissociations of function in the amnesic syndrome. In L. S. Cermak (Ed.), *Human memory and amnesia*. Hillsdale, N.J.: Erlbaum, 1982.

Nelson, H. E., & O'Connell, A. Dementia: The estimation of premorbid intelligence levels using the new adult reading test. *Cortex*, 1978, *14*, 234–244.

Pasik, P., Pasik, T., & Bender, M. B. The prectectal syndrome in monkeys. I. Disturbances of gaze and body posture. *Brain*, 1969, *92*, 521–534.

Piercy, M., & Huppert, F. A. Efficient recognition in organic amnesia. *Nature (London)*, 1972, *240*, 564.

Pierrot-Deseilligny, C., Chain, F., Gray, F., Serdaru, M., Escourolle, R., & Lhermitte, F. Parinaud's syndrome: Electro-oculographic and anatomical analyses of six vascular cases with deductions about vertical gaze organization in the premotor structures. *Brain*, 1982, *105*, 667–696.

Rozin, P. The psychobiological approach to human memory. In M. R. Rosenzweig & E. L. Bennett (Eds.), *Neural mechanisms of learning and memory*. Cambridge, Mass.: MIT Press, 1976.

Sanders, H. I., & Warrington, E. K. Memory for remote events in amnesic patients. *Brain*, 1971, *94*, 661–668.

Schacter, D. L., & Tulving, E. Amnesia and memory research. In L. S. Cermak (Ed.), *Human memory and amnesia*. Hillsdale, N.J.: Erlbaum, 1982.

Scoville, W. B., & Milner, B. Loss of recent memory after bilateral hippocampal lesions. *Journal of Neurology, Neurosurgery and Psychiatry*, 1957, *20*, 11–21.

Squire, L. R. Remote memory as affected by aging. *Neuropsychologia*, 1974, *12*, 429–435.

Squire, L. R. A stable impairment in remote memory following electroconvulsive therapy.

*Neuropsychologia*, 1975, *13*, 51–58.

Squire, L. R. Specifying the defect in human amnesia: Storage, retrieval and semantics. *Neuropsychologia*, 1980, *18*, 369–372.

Squire, L. R. Two forms of human amnesia: An analysis of forgetting. *Journal of Neuroscience*, 1981, *1*, 635–640.

Squire, L. R. Comparisons between forms of amnesia: Some deficits are unique to Korsakoff's syndrome. *Journal of Experimental Psychology: Learning, Memory, and Cognition*, 1982, *8*, 560–571. (a)

Squire, L. R. Neuropsychological effects of ECT. In R. A. Abrams & W. B. Essman (Eds.), *Electroconvulsive therapy: Biological foundations and clinical applications*. New York: Spectrum Press, 1982. (b)

Squire, L. R. The neuropsychology of human memory. *Annual Review of Neuroscience*, 1982, *5*, 241–273. (c)

Squire, L. R., Cohen, N. J., & Nadel, L. The medial temporal region and memory consolidation: A new hypothesis. In H. Weingartner & E. Parker (Eds.), *Memory consolidation*. Hillsdale, N.J.: Erlbaum, 1984.

Squire, L. R., Cohen, N. J., & Zouzounis, J. A. Preserved memory in retrograde amnesia: Sparing of a recently acquired skill. *Neuropsychologia*, 1984, *22*, 145–152.

Squire, L. R., & Moore, R. Y. Dorsal thalamic lesion in a noted case of chronic memory dysfunction. *Annals of Neurology*, 1979, *6*, 503–506.

Squire, L. R., & Slater, P. C. Forgetting in very long-term memory as assessed by an improved questionnaire technique. *Journal of Experimental Psychology*, 1975, *104*, 50–54.

Squire, L. R., & Slater, P. C. Remote memory in chronic anterograde amnesia. *Behavioral Biology*, 1977, *20*, 398–403.

Squire, L. R., Wetzel, C. D., & Slater, P. C. Anterograde amnesia following ECT: An analysis of the beneficial effects of partial information. *Neuropsychologia*, 1978, *16*, 339–348.

Squire, L. R., & Zola-Morgan, S. The neurology of memory: The case for correspondence between the findings for human and nonhuman primate. In J. A. Deutsch (Ed.), *The physioligal basis of memory* (2nd ed.). London: Academic Press, 1983.

Teuber, H. -L., Milner, B., & Vaughan, H. G. Persistent anterograde amnesia after stab wound of the basal brain. *Neuropsychologia*, 1968, *6*, 267–282.

Tulving, E., Schacter, D. L., & Stark, H. A. Priming effects in word-fragment completion are independent of recognition memory. *Journal of Experimental Psychology: Learning, Memory, and Cognition*, 1982, *8*, 336–342.

Victor, M., Adams, R. D., & Collins, G. H. *The Wernicke–Korsakoff syndrome*. Oxford: Blackwell, 1971.

von Cramon, D., Hebel, N., & Schuri, U. The anatomical basis of thalamic amnesia. *Brain*, in press.

Warrington, E. K. Deficient recognition memory in organic ammesia. *Cortex*, 1974, *10*, 289–291.

Warrington, E. K. The selective impairment of semantic memory. *Quarterly Journal of Experimental Psychology*, 1975, *27*, 635–657.

Warrington, E. K. Neuropsychological evidence for multiple memory systems. *Ciba Foundation Series*, 1979, *69* (new series), 153–166.

Warrington, E. K. The double dissociation of short- and long-term memory deficits. In L. S. Cermak (Ed.), *Human memory and amnesia*. Hillsdale, N.J.: Erlbaum, 1982.

Warrington, E. K. *Recognition memory test*. Windsor, England: NFER-Nelson, 1984.

Warrington, E. K., & Sanders, H. I. The fate of old memories. *Quarterly Journal of Experimental Psychology*, 1971, *23*, 432–443.

Warrington, E. K., & Taylor, A. M. Two categorical stages of object recognition. *Perception*, 1978, *7*, 695–705.

Warrington, E. K., & Weiskrantz, L. New method of testing long-term retention with special reference to amnesia patients. *Nature (London)*, 1968, *217*, 972–974.

Warrington, E. K., & Weiskrantz, L. Amnesic syndrome: Consolidation or retrieval? *Nature (London)*, 1970, *228*, 628–630.
Warrington, E. K., & Weiskrantz, L. An analysis of short-term and long-term memory defects in man. In J. A. Deutsch (Ed.), *The physiological basis of memory*. New York: Academic Press, 1972.
Warrington, E. K., & Weiskrantz, L. The effect of prior learning on subsequent retention in amnesia patients. *Neuropsychologia*, 1974, *12*, 419–428.
Warrington, E. K., & Weiskrantz, L. Further analysis of the prior learning effect in amnesic patients. *Neuropsychologia*, 1978, *16*, 169–176.
Warrington, E. K., & Weiskrantz, L. Amnesia: A disconnection syndrome? *Neuropsychologia*, 1982, *20*, 233–248.
Weiskrantz, L. Experimental studies of amnesia. In C. W. M. Whitty & O. L. Zangwill (Eds.), *Amnesia*. London: Butterworth, 1966.
Weiskrantz, L. Some traps and pontifications. In L. Weiskrantz (Ed.), *Analysis of behavioral change*. New York: Harper & Row, 1968.
Weiskrantz, L. A comparison of hippocampal pathology in man and other animals. *Ciba Foundation Series*, 1978, *58* (new series), 373–387.
Weiskrantz, L. Comparative aspects of studies of amnesia. In D. E. Broadbent & L. Weiskrantz (Eds.), *Neuropsychology of cognitive function*. London: Royal Society, 1982.
Weiskrantz, L., & Warrington, E. K. A study of forgetting in amnesic patients. *Neuropsychologia*, 1970, *8*, 281–288. (a)
Weiskrantz, L., & Warrington, E. K. Verbal learning and retention by amnesic patients using partial information. *Psychonomic Science*, 1970, *20*, 210–211. (b)
Weiskrantz, L., & Warrington, E. K. The problem of the amnesic syndrome in man and animals. In R. L. Isaacson & K. H. Pribram (Eds.), *The hippocampus* (Vol. 2). New York: Plenum Press, 1975.
Weiskrantz, L., & Warrington, E. K. Some comments on Woods' and Piercy's claim of a similarity between amnesic memory and normal forgetting. *Neuropsychologia*, 1975, *13*, 365–368. (b)
Weiskrantz, L., & Warrington, E. K. Conditioning in amnesia patients. *Neuropsychologia*, 1979, *17*, 187–194.
Wetzel, C. D., & Squire, L. R. Cued recall in anterograde amnesia. *Brain and Language*, 1982, *15*, 70–81.
Wickelgren, W. A. Chunking and consolidation: A theoretical synthesis of semantic networks, configuring in condition, S-R versus cognitive learning, normal forgetting, the amnesic syndrome, and the hippocampal arousal system. *Psychological Review*, 1979, *86*, 44–60.
Winocur, G., & Weiskrantz, L. An investigation of paired-associate learning in amnesic patients. *Neuropsychologia*, 1976, *14*, 97–110.
Wood, F., Ebert, V., & Kinsbourne, M. The episodic-semantic memory distinction in memory and amnesia: Clinical and experimental observations. In L. Cermak (Ed.), *Human memory and amnesia*. Hillsdale, N.J.: Erlbaum, 1982.
Zola-Morgan, S., & Oberg, R. G. Recall of life experiences in an alcoholic Korsakoff patient: A naturalistic approach. *Neuropsychologia*, 1980, *18*, 549–557.

# CRITICAL COMMENTARIES

C H A P T E R 22

# Levels of Analysis in Memory Research: The Neuropsychological Approach

**Neal J. Cohen**
The Johns Hopkins University

The chapters in this section have focused largely on neuropsychological data and on the neuropsychological approach to the study of learning and memory. It is important to note that the term "neuropsychology" is often used in both a narrow sense and a broad sense. In the *narrow* sense, it refers to the study of cognitive deficits exhibited by patients with insult to the brain. The pattern of cognitive impairment produced by damage to various critical brain structures can reveal a great deal about the organization of normal cognitive processes and systems. This is the sense of neuropsychology intended by the contributors to the section of this volume of which this chapter is a part. Neuropsychology in the *broad* sense refers to the various research efforts directed at understanding the way in which behavior is mediated by the functioning of the intact brain. This echoes the more general theme of this volume as a whole.

Both senses of neuropsychology will be addressed here in the course of discussing some of the progress made in our understanding of learning and memory. The present treatment begins by considering neuropsychology in the broad sense. I shall first present some examples of the kinds of observations that investigators have taken to be relevant to discussions of brain–behavior relationships in memory research, and then I shall describe one way in which these observations may be incorporated into a more complete understanding of learning and memory. This treatment starts with the following three basic assumptions:

1. The scientific study of learning and memory, as presently conducted, proceeds at several distinct levels of analysis, each characterized by the attempt to describe and formalize a class of empirical generalizations.
2. A *complete* understanding of learning and memory will require moving from empirical generalizations of the phenomena at any given level to explanatory accounts of the way in which the phenomena at each level

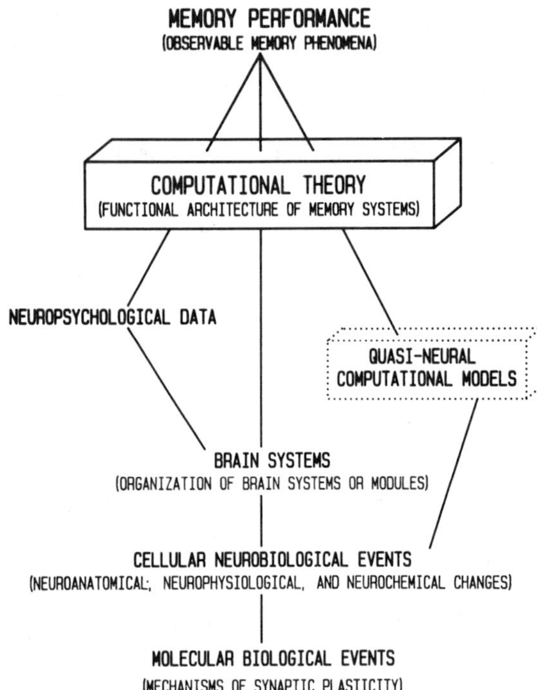


**FIGURE 22.1.** Levels of analysis in the scientific study of learning and memory.

give rise to learning and memory performance, and how the levels interrelate with one another.

3. The different levels bear some likeness to those depicted in Figure 22.1 and discussed individually in the following analysis.

## MEMORY PERFORMANCE

This level of analysis deals with observed memory phenomena, that is, with the ways in which performance reveals the influence of previous experience. Work at this level, then, attempts to discover empirical generalizations that describe the categories of memory performance and the principles or laws that govern its regularities. It is these empirical generalizations that all of the other levels of analysis attempt to explain and for which the models at any level of analysis must provide an account. Let us illustrate this with some examples from work discussed in this volume: The concerns of this level of analysis include describing the relative efficiency of memory for spatial locations or spatial cues in different species of animals (see Gould, Chapter 11, this volume; Shettleworth, Chapter 13, this volume) or with outlining the laws of associative versus nonassociative learning and instrumental versus Pavlovian conditioning (Rescorla, Chapter 12, this volume; Mackintosh, Chapter 19, this volume), both examples in the context of normal memory. It also is concerned with empirical generalizations about impaired memory performance taken from neuropsychological data, such as categorizing the dissociation between spared and impaired memory performance in amnesic patients in terms of spared acquisition of skills and repetition priming, on the one hand, and impaired explicit remembering (e.g., recall or recognition), on the other (Schacter, Chapter 20, this volume; the present chapter).

## COMPUTATIONAL THEORY

This level of analysis and those still to be described (with the exception of the section Neuropsychological Data) are explanatory levels, attempting to provide an explanatory account of the phenomena and generalizations of memory performance. The level of explanation with which computational theory is concerned is the cognitive-level account of memory. It aspires to a formal, computational theory of the particular processes and representations that constitute what might be called the functional architecture of memory. Such a theory would explain how memory is effected at the functional level, characterizing the encoding, storage, and retrieval processes that operate on incoming or stored information and the nature or format of the representations on which these processes operate. Examples from this volume of questions directed at this level of analysis include whether the memory representation of honey bees involves a set of discrete "features" or "parameters" that describe the world, as in a "checklist," or instead involves "pictures" or whole images of experienced scenes (Gould, Chapter 11, this volume); whether animals maintain a spatial or other cognitive map of the environment (Barnes & McNaughton, Chapter 3, this volume; Morris, Chapter 25, this volume); and whether the phenomenological dissociation in amnesia between acquisition of skills and repetition priming, on the one hand, and explicit remembering, on the other, is accounted for by two memory systems that are distinguishable on representational and processing grounds (e.g., procedural vs. declarative systems), by three or more distinct memory systems, or instead by separate retrieval processes with differential access to distinct knowledge domains within a single representational system (Schacter, Chapter 20, this volume; Crowder, Chapter 23, this volume; Kean, Chapter 24, this volume; the present chapter).

Note that this theory level provides the explanatory link between the memory-performance level of analysis and those levels of analysis dealing with the brain systems or basic neural mechanisms that give rise to memory. It is the first step and, I will argue, a particularly crucial one in moving from the empirical generalizations about memory performance to the various explanatory accounts of the systems and mechanisms that support it (see

Figure 22.1; and later discussion). That is, memory performance is mediated by the particular processes and representations that form the functional architecture of memory, as specified by the computational theory. It is these processes and representations, and not memory-task performance itself, that has particular neural instantiation. Accordingly, the *functional significance* for memory performance of particular neural events can be understood only with respect to the processing role they play at the computational level; and an account of memory in terms of neural events must specify in computational terms the precise functional contributions to memory played by each neural event. To explain, note that the attempt to identify those neural events, among the set of all neural events, that are associated with learning and memory requires that our approach include a functional analysis. The neural events associated with learning and memory are grouped together in such an analysis in virtue of their common function, and not in virtue of purely physical or neurobiological characteristics; that is, the subset of interest can be distinguished from the set of all other neural events only by virtue of its participation in memory functioning. It follows from this argument that an account of the way in which the brain supports learning and memory must have both neural and functional terms. The functional terms that must be included in such an account are taken from the computational theory, specifying the processing and representational contributions of the neural events to memory performance. Accordingly, an explanatory account of memory at any neural level of analysis (i.e., brain systems, cellular neurobiological events, or molecular biological mechanisms; see Figure 22.1) would therefore be framed in the context of "mechanism–process pairs," where "mechanism" is here understood to refer to a given neural system, event, or mechanism, and "process" is understood to refer to the particular component processes or representational systems mediated by the neural system, event, or mechanism.

One consequence of the position taken here is that a statement of the functional role of a particular neural system, event, or mechanism, say, the hippocampus, in terms of the *tasks* that individuals with hippocampal damage fail to perform or in terms of the *tasks* with which activity in hippocampal neurons is correlated, is merely a statement of association between performance and some neural level of analysis. Although this is an important step, to be sure, it is not an explanatory account of learning and memory unless it makes contact with the computational-theory level; the functional role of the hippocampus must be stated in terms of the critical component memory processes or storage mechanisms to which it contributes.

## NEUROPSYCHOLOGICAL DATA

This level of analysis deals with neuropsychology in the narrow sense. We have already noted that neuropsychological data provide one set of observations about memory performance to be accounted for in any explanation of learning and memory. What makes this level particularly interesting for our present purposes is that to the extent that memory deficits are specific to particular aspects of memory, inferences can be drawn about the status of particular component memory processes and representational systems; and to the extent that the deficits occur reliably in association with damage to particular critical brain regions or brain systems, the brain systems can be related at least tentatively to the compromised memory processes. Accordingly, this data level contributes to the development of explanatory accounts both at the computational-theory level (of the functional architecture of the memory system) and at the brain-systems level (of the neuroanatomical architecture of the involved brain systems), as well as providing one important source of data useful in constructing a theory of how the various levels of analysis of memory research can be bridged.

Two examples from the present conference that have important implications for both the computational-theory level and the brain-systems level of analysis are the dissociation between preserved and impaired memory capacities in amnesia, and the issue of whether multiple forms of amnesia occur as a consequence of damage to different brain regions (Weiskrantz, Chapter 21, this volume; Schacter, Chapter 20, this volume; Crowder, Chapter 23, this volume; Kean, Chapter 24, this volume). Further discussion of the first of these examples appears in a later section of this chapter.

## BRAIN SYSTEMS

This level of analysis is concerned with identification of the brain systems that contribute to memory and a description of their anatomical organization. Thus, the work of various participants in the present conference has been directed toward establishing the participation in vertebrate learning of the hippocampus, amygdala, locus ceruleus–NE system, pituitary–adrenal hormone system, and various visual pathway structures (D. H. Cohen, Chapter 2, this volume; Barnes & McNaughton, Chapter 3, this volume; Abraham & Goddard, Chapter 4, this volume; Berger & Sclabassi, Chapter 7, this volume; Deadwyler, Chapter 8, this volume; Wenzel & Matthies, Chapter 9, this volume; Gallagher, Chapter 18, this volume). This work constitutes impressive progress in our understanding of which brain systems are active in memory performance. Considerably less progress, however, has been made in our understanding of the precise functional roles played by these various systems. To understand the functional contributions made to memory by the various brain systems requires that a theory of the anatomical organization of the disparate brain systems, that is, a description of their input–output relations, be mapped onto a computational theory of the functional architecture of memory, that is, a description of the processing functions they support, thereby specifying a mechanism–process pair. By thus specifying the relationship between particular brain systems and particular memory processes, we contribute another level of explanation to a complete understanding of learning and memory.

## CELLULAR NEUROBIOLOGICAL EVENTS

At this level of analysis investigators seek to understand the cellular substrate of memory. The goal at this level is to provide a description of the neuronal changes that mediate memory. Recent years have seen enormous progress in our understanding of events at this level of analysis. From the chapters in this volume alone, numerous examples can be found, including long-term potentiation (LTP) or enhancement (LTE) following high-frequency electrical stimulation in hippocampus (Barnes & McNaughton, Chapter 3, this volume; Abraham & Goddard, Chapter 4, this volume; Berger & Sclabassi, Chapter 7, this volume; Wenzel & Matthies, Chapter 9, this volume); increased excitability during behaviorally effective CS–US conditioning in dentate granule cells, hippocampal CA1 cells, or visual pathway cells (Alkon, Chapter 1, this volume; D. H. Cohen, Chapter 2, this volume; Wenzel & Matthies, Chapter 9, this volume); and synaptogenesis (i.e., creation of new synapses) following behavioral training or electrical stimulation in cortex or the CA1 region of hippocampus (Greenough, Chapter 5, this volume).

The neurobiological events listed in the preceding paragraph are all robust examples of cellular plasticity, that is, different examples of changes that occur to neurons or at synapses between neurons as a consequence of experience. The list indicates that plasticity is expressed by a variety of different neurobiological events. But it is unclear at this point whether any functional significance should be attributed to the length of such a list. An important question, then, is whether the different neurobiological events all support the same or different computationally specified memory processes; or, to put it another way, whether it is the type of neurobiological event or just the occurrence of plasticity that is important to understanding the functional role of cellular neurobiological events. Examination of the relationship between particular neurobiological events and the various brain systems in which they are expressed suggests that the localization of plasticity to particular brain systems (e.g., hippocampus vs. visual cortex) may be a more critical determinant of the functional role played by the plasticity than is the nature of the particular neurobiological event that gives rise to it. This is made clearer by considering the following scenarios.

- If, across brain systems, cellular plasticity were expressed by different kinds of neurobiological events such that there were different examples of neuronal or synaptic change for each brain system, then the occurrence of a given neurobiological event would always be a marker of change in the particular brain system that permits its expression. The functional significance of the neurobiological event, then, would be to express change relevant to and determined by the processing role of the host brain system; an account of its functional role would be stated in terms of the computationally specified processing contribution made by that brain system, that is, by the kind of information the system handles and the type of processing it supports. Given that various brain systems differ anatomically with respect to both their input–output relations and the details of their internal organization, it is reasonable to expect that different classes of neurobiological events would have evolved to express plastic changes in the different systems. But when considered in functional terms, all examples of neurobiological events, regardless of the particular system in which they occur, serve the same function of expressing plasticity: They alter the quantity of the particular class of information that the brain system handles, or they change the efficiency with which processing of a particular type is achieved.[1]

• If, in all brain systems, plasticity were expressed by the same common set of neurobiological events, then the occurrence of any particular type of neurobiological event would be distinguishable functionally from another occurrence of that type of event only in respect to the activity of the brain system that permits its expression. Thus, the functional significance of a given example of neuronal or synaptic change occurring as a consequence of experience would be determined by the functional role of that system. On this scenario, the only alternative to the notion that the processing role of a particular neurobiological event is determined by where in the brain it occurs is the notion that memory is coded by the pattern of neurobiological events defined over different, and informationally unrelated, systems, that is, that something like a field theory of memory is an accurate neurobiological description. This is a notion to which few subscribe. Now, this is not to deny that LTP and synaptogenesis are likely to have different memorial consequences. But the difference would be in terms of their *time course* and not their *informational content*. Consider that to understand the processing contribution of either neurobiological event, that is, to complete the mechanism–process pair that ties events at this level to computationally specified processes and representations, we must know about the particular processing system in which either of these events is expressed: Both LTP and synaptogenesis surely have different implications for memory performance when they occur in the hippocampus rather than in the visual cortex.[2]

1. Although it is reasonable to suppose, as we have just done, that the different computational demands placed on different brain systems might be reflected in the specialization of distinct classes of cellular neurobiological events, it must be noted here that current evidence argues firmly against the scenario of different kinds of neurobiological events for each distinct brain system. For example, it is now clear that LTP-like phenomena occur not only in the hippocampal formation but also in neocortex (Lee, 1983) and, conversely, that synaptogenesis occurs not only in neocortex but also in the hippocampal formation (Greenough, Chapter 5, this volume).

2. Only if different types of neurobiological events were distributed among brain systems such that each system had a subset of all possible types of neurobiological events, and if the particular distribution had informational specificity beyond the level of individual brain structures, might functional significance be attributed to the nature of the neurobiological event giving rise to plasticity. In such a case, the nature of the neurobiological event mediating plasticity

## MOLECULAR BIOLOGICAL EVENTS

This level of analysis is concerned with identifying the mechanisms of plasticity, that is, the molecular mechanisms underlying various cellular neurobiological events. Progress at this level is illustrated elegantly in this volume by the analysis of changes in potassium channels and currents as a consequence of experience in *Hermissenda* and in rat hippocampus (Alkon, Chapter 1, this volume).

In attempting to extend the neural analysis of memory to the molecular mechanisms of cellular neurobiological events, we are building a bridge between neuroscience and molecular biology and are gaining a more complete understanding of learning and memory in the sense of coming closer to explicating all of the steps in the causal chain of biological events leading to memory performance. The success of such an enterprise would be a monumental achievement. Yet, as with any of the other levels of analysis, an account of the way in which events at this level support memory performance (in this case, an understanding of how molecular mechanisms give rise to the different categories of normal memory phenomena) requires making contact with the computational theory level to specify the relationship between particular mechanisms and particular cognitive processes.

## BRIDGING THE LEVELS

Having outlined the various levels of analysis of learning and memory with which research in the field has been concerned, a few words need to be said about how the different levels could be bridged to produce the complete explanation that we seek. This is an enormously challenging task, for which few answers are available. I will offer only a few basic observations, considering one way in which the interrelations among levels might be viewed. A theory specifying the *causal* links among events at the different levels, however, remains only a distant goal.

On the present view, the fundamental question would seem to be how to fit together into a coherent framework the different mechanism–process pairs constituting the relationship between particular neural systems, events, and mechanisms, on the one hand, and particular computationally specified processes and representations, on the other. It is instructive in this context to consider the model-systems approach to learning and memory, in which a simple or simplified preparation amenable to a variety of experimental

---

would indeed convey important information about its functional role in memory. But note that rather than demonstrating the functional implications of the neurobiological-events level of analysis considered at the computational-theory level, this case may be demonstrating the need to have a functionally defined neuroanatomy in which structures are distinguished on functional grounds rather than cytoarchitectonic ones. And, in the final analysis, it is the anatomical connections of these functionally defined circuitries that would determine their role in memory processing.

manipulations is used to study some behavioral memory phenomenon at multiple levels of analysis. The model-systems approach assumes (and derives its justification from the notion of) significant conservation of basic mechanisms across species, with the more complex mechanisms and behavioral phenomena of higher species being constructed of the mechanisms and phenomena found in the model systems. The critical question for the present purposes is whether conservation of mechanism at one level, say, the molecular-events level, implies conservation of the functional role of that mechanism considered at the computational-theory level. For example, can we assume that the changes in potassium channels and currents observed both in *Hermissenda* and in rat hippocampus (Alkon, Chapter 1, this volume) play the same functional role in memory for the two species? Perhaps; but not necessarily. We have argued that description at the molecular-mechanisms level of analysis should already include the functional role of mechanisms in mechanism–process pairs, thus specifying the precise relationship between mechanisms and cognitive processes. Only then can the processing contribution of the mechanism under discussion here be compared across the two species. Moreover, a thorough evaluation of the mechanism–process pairs that form part of the explanation of memory at this level of analysis will also need to take into account the mechanism–process relationships framed at other levels of analysis. For example, is there any structure in *Hermissenda* that plays the same role in memory as the hippocampus does for the rat? If not, then in line with our earlier discussion of the relationship between neural events and brain systems, there is little reason to expect the functional role of the plasticity expressed by potassium channels to be the same for the two species.

The real issue here has less to do with making inferences across species than with the degree of abstraction with which we may take explanation at a particular level of analysis to help us in understanding a different level of analysis. An account of memory at the brain-systems level—for example, an explanation of the functional role of the hippocampus in memory—will take little note of the nature of the neurobiological events or molecular mechanisms that mediate plasticity in the hippocampus, that is, whether hippocampal plasticity is mediated by changes in potassium channels, as shown by Alkon (Chapter 1, this volume), or by changes in ion channels in general, or indeed by any membrane changes. Yet analysis of the precise molecular mechanisms of memory is essential for generating an explanatory account of memory framed at the mechanisms level. For this latter level, we would seek to discover whether there are indeed different functional implications for memory of different classes of membrane changes, including changes in the different classes of ion channels.

Similar conclusions obtain about modulation of excitability of neurons within any particular brain system (such as hippocampus or visual cortex) that occurs as a result of intervention by some extrinsic modulatory system. By analogy with the argument presented earlier, the functional significance of modulation in any particular brain system depends little on how exactly it is produced, unless we are interested in specifying the processing role of the modulatory system itself. In that case, we would go on to study the functional consequences of modulation of neuronal excitability in various brain systems produced by the locus ceruleus–NE modulatory system, as in D. H. Cohen's work (Chapter 2, this volume), by aminergic modulation in general, or by any other example of synaptic transmission.

One other observation on this theme is that in studying the molecular mechanisms that mediate plasticity, it is just not feasible to examine the mechanisms of each type of neurobiological event in each brain system during the performance of each type of behavioral task. Hence, a small set of examples must be selected carefully, and their generality is difficult to determine. This is a reasonable strategy from the perspective of explanation at higher levels of analysis to the extent that the nature of the neural mechanisms that permit plasticity to be expressed plays no part in a functional account of the processing role of particular neurobiological events or brain systems, when framed at these other levels of analysis. Yet relationships among levels of analysis become important when moving in the other direction. On the present view, the nature of the neurobiological events and brain systems that particular molecular mechanisms serve bear importantly on (if not actually determine) the functional role of these mechanisms. This seems equally true of each successively higher, neural level of analysis, serving as a useful reminder that memory performance is mediated by the complex of activity at all levels: Molecular mechanisms are undoubtedly well suited to support the specific neurobiological events likely to be needed by each particular brain system playing its specified functional role in memory performance. It seems reasonable to suppose that entire "vertical" systems evolve in concert to support specific processing roles required for particular performances.

These considerations suggest the difficulty in deriving a complete understanding of learning and memory that encompasses all levels of analysis. But they also provide some guidelines. Explanation at each level must be framed as a mechanism–process pair. Consideration of the functional role of each neural system, event, or mechanism helps to inform us about the appropriate degree of abstraction of the phenomenon of interest. Also, looking back up toward memory performance from the more molecular levels of analysis reminds us of the obligatory interrelationship of the events at the different levels in accomplishing memory performance.

Let us close by returning to the neuropsychological approach, as construed narrowly. As already discussed, this level of analysis is concerned with the bridge between the neighboring levels of computational theory and brain systems, and between both of these and memory performance (see Figure 22.1). Accordingly, it is worth considering how well neuropsychological phenomena fit into the larger scheme of developing a complete explanation of learning and memory. One neuropsychological phenomenon discussed at length in this volume concerned the dissociation between preserved and impaired memory capacities in amnesia. This refers to the finding that despite a severe and pervasive disorder of learning and memory, amnesic patients demonstrate preserved memory capacities capable of supporting the acquisition and retention of a variety of perceptual, motor, and cognitive skills (Brooks & Baddeley, 1976; Cermak, Lewis, Butters, & Goodglass, 1973; Cohen & Corkin, 1981; Cohen, Eichenbaum, DeAcedo, & Corkin, in press; Cohen & Squire, 1980; Corkin, 1968; Kinsbourne & Wood, 1975; Martone, Butters, Payne, Becker, & Sax, 1984; Milner, 1962), and the ability to show repetition priming effects involving facilitation or other alteration of performance in naming, spelling, or categorization as a function of prior exposure to the to-be-tested materials (Graf, Squire, & Mandler, 1984; Jacoby & Witherspoon, 1982; Moscovitch, 1982; Schacter, Chapter 20, this volume; Warrington & Weiskrantz, 1968, 1970, 1974). In all cases, previous experience exerts its influence on subsequent performance normally, despite amnesia for the testing occasions, the test materials, and the facts that ordinarily would be acquired during the course of experience (see Cohen, 1984). This phenomenological dissociation, at the level of memory performance, has led several authors to propose that human memory is mediated by a number of distinct systems, that is, that there is a distinction among systems at the level of computational theory (for various ideas about the nature of the dissociation, see Cermak, 1984; Cohen, 1981, 1984, 1985; Kinsbourne & Wood, 1975; Schacter & Moscovitch, 1984; Schacter & Tulving, 1983; Squire & Cohen, 1984; Warrington & Weiskrantz, 1982). Still others have reached similar conclusions on the basis of work with animals (Eichenbaum, Fagan, & Cohen, submitted for publication: Hirsch, 1980; Mishkin, Malamut, & Bachevalier, 1984; O'Keefe & Nadel, 1978; Olton, Becker, & Handelmann, 1979; Squire & Zola-Morgan, 1983; Winocur, 1980). The particular formulation of the dissociation with which I have been associated (cited earlier) distinguishes the development and expression of skilled performance from the accumulation and explicit remembering of specific facts or events, attributing the former to a procedural memory system (preserved in amnesia) and the latter to a declarative memory system. Somewhat different views are presented by Weiskrantz (Chapter 21, this volume) and by Schacter (Chapter 20, this volume).

These phenomena also have relevance for the brain-systems level of analysis. Because amnesia is associated consistently with damage to one or more of a set of critical brain regions, we may conclude that these regions are involved with one (declarative) but not the other (procedural) memory system. It is not yet clear which brain structures contribute to the (procedural) memory system preserved in amnesia. One view is that the basal ganglia play the same role for this memory system as the hippocampus and related medial temporal lobe or diencephalic structures damaged in amnesia play for the other (declarative) system (Mishkin *et al.*, 1984). The interruption of this brain system would be expected to produce a global impairment in the ability to acquire new skills and exhibit repetition priming effects. Another view, derived from the procedural–declarative framework, suggests that the memory phenomena mediated by the procedural system are a collection of plasticities each dedicated to particular processing and action systems; skilled performance in the visual domain would be mediated by changes limited to visual processing structures (e.g., area 17 or area TE), motor performance would be sensitive to plasticity restricted to motor structures (e.g., basal ganglia or cerebellum), and so forth (Cohen, 1984, 1985). On this view, there is no single brain system the damage of which would cause a global procedural memory deficit. Damage to the basal ganglia would cause impairment of only those motor and planning skills the *performance* of which depends upon the integrity of the system.

Although the different memory phenomena and hypothesized processing components under discussion have been related to particular brain regions, work at the molecular-events level may also bear an important relationship. In a series of studies directed at understanding the mechanisms of LTP in hippocampal neurons, Lynch and Baudry (1984) have described a set of membrane changes including protein phosphorylation and the uncovering of glutamate receptors. Important for the present purposes are the findings that this mechanism of synaptic plasticity is located only in some brain regions and not others, and that its abolition through pharmacological intervention interferes with only some memory capacities and not others. A characterization of the difference between the memory capacities preserved and impaired in this preparation has not yet been undertaken; accordingly, the relationship at the memory-performance level between this dissociation and that discussed earlier for amnesic patients cannot be ascertained at this time. Of interest is the potential bridge between particular mechanisms of plasticity, particular components of memory processing, and, consequently, particular categories of memory performance. An important question from the point of view of the effort to bridge various levels, and consistent with our discussion earlier, is whether the critical variable in explaining the observed dissociation in memory performance is the particular kind of mechanism of plasticity or the particular brain system in which it is expressed.

The selective localization of the mechanisms discussed by Lynch and Baudry (1984) to particular brain regions, namely, the forebrain regions (including the hippocampus) that undergo such extensive growth in phylogeny, has already been mentioned. Given the relationship noted several times earlier between brain systems and neural events or mechanisms, the functional significance of these mechanisms of plasticity would appear to be understood only in light of the functional role of the brain systems that permit them to be expressed.[3] These considerations illustrate the necessity

3. Thus, if the hippocampus plays a critical role in accomplishing declarative memory, the fact that a particular molecular mechanism found in the hippocampus may be related obligatorily to this kind of memory should not be surprising. The presence of the particular mechanism in the hippocampus no doubt is essential for accomplishing its role in memory; but, so too is

of considering an explanation at a given level of analysis to be complete only when it has described the functional role of the phenomena of interest in the form of mechanism–process pairs. In attempting to make explicit the explanatory link between neural substrate (i.e., neural systems, events, and mechanisms) and computational theory, we become better informed about the kinds of data and empirical generalizations necessary to construct a complete account of the way in which the brain orchestrates neural events at all levels to mediate learning and memory performance.

## ACKNOWLEDGMENTS

The preparation of this chapter was supported by a Biomedical Research Support Grant (S07 RR07041) from the Division of Research Resources, NIH. I wish to thank Alfonso Caramazza, James L. McClelland, Terrence Sejnowski, David Olton, Howard Eichenbaum, and Matthew Shapiro for critical discussion.

## REFERENCES

Brooks, D. N., & Baddeley, A. What can amnesic patients learn? *Neuropsychologia*, 1976, *14*, 111–122.

Cermak, L. S. The episodic–semantic distinction in amnesia. In L. R. Squire & N. Butters (Eds.). *Neuropsychology of memory*. New York: Guilford Press, 1984.

Cermak, L. S., Lewis, R., Butters, N., & Goodglass, H. Role of verbal mediation in performance of motor tasks by Korsakoff patients. *Perceptual and Motor Skills*, 1973, *37*, 259–262.

Cohen, N. J. *Neuropsychological evidence for a distinction between procedural and declarative knowledge in human memory and amnesia*. Unpublished doctoral dissertation, University of California, San Diego, 1981.

Cohen, N. J. Preserved learning capacity in amnesia: Evidence for multiple memory systems. In L. R. Squire & N. Butters (Eds.), *Neuropsychology of memory*. New York: Guilford Press, 1984.

Cohen, N. J. Neuropsychological analysis of memory: Identifying component memory processes. In J. L. Martinez, Jr. & R. P. Kesner (Eds.), *Learning and memory: A biological view*. New York: Academic Press, 1985.

Cohen, N. J., & Corkin, S. The amnesic patient H. M.: Learning and retention of cognitive skill. *Society for Neuroscience Abstracts*, 1981, *7*, 517–518.

Cohen, N. J., Eichenbaum, H., DeAcedo, B. S., & Corkin, S. Different memory systems underlying acquisition of procedural and declarative knowledge. *Annals of the New York Academy of Sciences*, in press.

Cohen, N. J., & Squire, L. R. Preserved learning and retention of pattern analyzing skill in amnesia: Dissociation of knowing how and knowing that. *Science*, 1980, *210*, 207–210.

Corkin, S. Acquisition of motor skill after bilateral medial temporal lobe excision. *Neuropsychologia*, 1968, *6*, 255–265.

Eichenbaum, H., Fagan, A., & Cohen, N. J. Normal olfactory discrimination learning set and

the presence of connections with the brain systems that provide the hippocampus with sensory information of various modalities and of connections with the systems that provide an appropriate output mechanism to communicate the results of its computations. Only by considering the level of description at which the anatomy, physiology, and molecular biology come together into particular brain systems can the functional roles of a given molecular mechanism or neurobiological event be meaningfully understood.

facilitation of reversal learning after combined or separate lesions of the fornix and amygdala in rats. Submitted for publication.

Graf, P., Squire, L. R., & Mandler, G. The information that amnesic patients do not forget. *Journal of Experimental Psychology: Learning, Memory and Cognition*, 1984, *10*, 164–178.

Hirsh, R. The hippocampus, conditional operations, and cognition. *Physiological Psychology*, 1980, *8*, 175–182.

Jacoby, L. L., & Witherspoon, D. Remembering without awareness. *Canadian Journal of Psychology*, 1982, *36*, 300–324.

Kinsbourne, M., & Wood, F. Short-term memory processes and the amnesic syndrome. In D. Deutsch & J. A. Deutsch (Eds.), *Short-term memory*. New York: Academic Press, 1975.

Lee, K. S. Sustained modification of neuronal activity in the hippocampus and neocortex. In W. Seifert (Ed.), *Neurobiology of the hippocampus*. London: Academic Press, 1983.

Lynch, G., & Baudry, M. The biochemistry of memory: A new and specific hypothesis. *Science*, 1984, *224*, 1057–1063.

Martone, M., Butters, N., Payne, M., Becker, J., & Sax, D. S. Dissociations between skill learning and verbal recognition in amnesia and dementia. *Archives of Neurology (Chicago)*, 1984, *41*, 965–970.

Milner, B. Les troubles de la mémoire accompagnant des lésions hippocampiques bilatérales. In P. Passouant (Ed.). *Physiologie de l'hippocampe*. Paris: Centre de la Recherche Scientifique, 1962.

Mishkin, M., Malamut, B., & Bachevalier, J. Memories and habits: Two neural systems. In G. Lynch, J. L. McGaugh, & N. M. Weinberger (Eds.), *Neurobiology of learning and memory*. New York: Guilford Press, 1984.

Moscovitch, M. A neuropsychological approach to perception and memory in normal and pathological aging. In F. I. M. Craik & S. Trehub (Eds.), *Aging and cognitive processes*. New York: Plenum Press, 1982.

O'Keefe, J., & Nadel, L. *The hippocampus as a cognitive map*. London: Oxford University Press, 1978.

Olton, D. S., Becker, J. T., & Handelmann, G. E. Hippocampus, space, and memory. *Behavioral and Brain Sciences*, 1979, *2*, 313–365.

Schacter, D. L., & Moscovitch, M. Infants, amnesics, and dissociable memory systems. In M. Moscovitch (Ed.), *Infant memory*. New York: Plenum Press, 1984.

Schacter, D. L., & Tulving, E. Memory, amnesia, and the episodic/semantic distinction. In R. L. Isaacson & N. E. Spear (Eds.), *Expression of knowledge*. New York: Plenum Press, 1983.

Squire, L. R., & Cohen, N. J. Human memory and amnesia. In G. Lynch, J. L. McGaugh, & N. M. Weinberger (Eds.), *Neurobiology of learning and memory*. New York: Guilford Press, 1984.

Squire, L. R., & Zola-Morgan, S. The neurology of memory: The case for correspondence between the findings for human and nonhuman primates. In J. A. Deutsch (Ed.), *The physiological basis of memory* (2nd ed.). New York: Academic Press, 1983.

Warrington, E. K., & Weiskrantz, L. A new method of testing long-term retention with special reference to amnesic patients. *Nature (London)*, 1968, *217*, 972–974.

Warrington, E. K., & Weiskrantz, L. The amnesic syndrome: Consolidation or retrieval? *Nature (London)*, 1970, *228*, 628–630.

Warrington, E. K., & Weiskrantz, L. The effect of prior learning on subsequent retention in amnesic patients. *Neuropsychologia*, 1974, *12*, 419–428.

Warrington, E. K., & Weiskrantz, L. Amnesia: A disconnection syndrome? *Neuropsychologia*, 1982, *20*, 233–248.

Winocur, G. The hippocampus and cue-utilization. *Physiological Psychology*, 1980, *8*, 280–288.

CHAPTER 23

# On Access and the Forms of Memory

**Robert G. Crowder**
Yale University

## ON PATHOLOGY LEADING THE MAINSTREAM

The study of amnesic patients led the way to our growing recognition that some distinction, similar to that between procedural and declarative memory, is likely to be indispensable for any general theory of memory. Among the groups represented here, investigators of animal learning and of human memory and clinical neuropsychologists all agree on the importance of what Weiskrantz (Chapter 21, this volume) has referred to as a "convergence" of views about multiple systems of memory. I used to argue, sometimes obnoxiously, that pathological functioning had never really contributed much to mainstream science in the analysis of human memory (Crowder, 1982). I claimed rather that theoretical trends in the study of pathological subject populations had *followed* the mainstream with boring consistency and at a measurable lag of several years. (The same was true, and I think still is, in the study of developmental populations at each end of the age scale.) I held this state of affairs up against what have been crucial, decisive contributions of pathological function in others of the behavioral sciences. For example, color blindness was a basic challenge for early theories of color vision. Also, the linguistic consequences of stroke were crucial for the understanding of hemispheric localization of function. Now at last, we have an instance in which clinical dissociations of process actually *led the way* theoretically, and I want to pause to celebrate this circumstance.

In almost the same breath, I should raise a cautionary note. At least once before, the field of mainstream memory theory has seen an apparently exciting convergence with clinical neuropsychology. This was in the heyday of two-store theories of memory such as those of Waugh and Norman (1965) and Atkinson and Shiffrin (1968). In fact, Scoville and Milner first published their dissociations of "recent memory" from other memory functions in 1957, and so some claim to historical priority could even be documented. Of course, in this case, the archetypal neuropsychologist Hebb (1949) anticipated both the clinical and mainstream disciplines with his original version of dual-trace theory. Certainly, when short-term memory (STM) became the New Look in human memory theory, there were plenty of appeals to the amnesia literature as clinching the case. Some textbook writers even referred to the clinical dissociations of STM and long-term memory (LTM) as the *strongest cases* for two-store theory.

The dual-trace theory of memory may have heuristic merit at some level of discourse, but it no longer animates research the way it used to. At least the distinction between STM and LTM plays no appreciable role in contemporary theory. None of the presentations in this volume has even referred to it. Yet, 20 years ago, you could have seen the same excitement about dissociations of multiple memory systems—STM versus LTM—that we are experiencing here. So, as we celebrate amnesic patients' having led the way, we should recall that the convergence of fields is not unprecedented and reserve our final judgment for some years ahead.A model that has

## ON THE INSIDIOUS INFLUENCE OF OUR TASKS

Behavioral scientists are only human. A research program on a new subject is notorious for false starts, for difficulty finding just the right organism in some cases, for selecting just the right stimuli in others, for mistaken guesses about what response measures to use, and for a gradual fumbling for just the right task. When we finally hit on the right task, most of us will concede, as Larry Jacoby once put it, "we marry it." And naturally we pay a price. Several examples occurred to me in this collection.

### Word Learning

The learning of verbal units has dominated the experimental psychology of human learning and memory from the beginning. So much so that our specialty used to be called Verbal Learning. We threw out that term, with horror, some time ago, but I think we threw it out largely for its surplus meaning. Our experiments still ask participants to learn and then remember words. There are good reasons for this dependence on what Tulving (1983) calls "word events." They abstract in controllable form the real events that mark our daily lives and they engage the all-important linguistic systems, among other reasons. However, reliance on verbal materials probably postponed recognition of what amnesic patients were trying to tell us: It was reported nearly 20 years ago that H. M. and other amnesic patients could learn and retain *motor skills* readily (Corkin, 1968). But such was the alienation and bad reputation of motor-skill learning as a specialty in those days that this sparing of motor skills was regarded more as a curiosity than as a fundamental insight. It was only when reports of normal processing by amnesic patients on *verbal* materials began to come in—largely a series of reports by Weiskrantz and Warrington in the 1970s (Warrington & Weiskrantz,

1974)—that mainstream memory workers paid proper attention. Now, experiments like the recent ones of Graf, Squire, and Mandler (1984) have verified what amnesic patients can and cannot do with our trusty verbal lists, and people are paying attention in a big way.

In the same vein, I want to scold Schacter (Chapter 20, this volume) in the gentlest possible way for his attitude that verbal *priming* is a more or less integral behavior. This attitude results in his quest for a plausible animal counterpart to verbal priming. But the fact of direct priming of words in humans is not by itself the important target. Instead, what this priming tells us about the underlying system is the goal. Trying to get animals to mimic priming is an act of linguistic chauvinism. The reification of priming was also evident when Schacter distinguished "priming" from "remembering." I would rather consider priming as an expression of knowledge of a verbal event, explicit recall and recognition being other expressions of that same knowledge. All imply remembering in some sense. Schacter also classifies priming separately from skill. But I do not understand why. Are perceptal skills any the less complex, tediously learned, or smoothly coordinated than rotary pursuit? Kolers and Roediger (1984) have made the point that much of memory may be little more than the persistence of skilled perceptual operations. Consider the processes of speaking aloud or writing. Are we really prepared to classify these expressive activities as skill but not the corresponding receptive activities of speech perception and reading? Priming is precisely the enhanced perceptual processing accorded information that has occurred recently. But we already knew various verbal and cognitive skills were spared in amnesia. Why consider the perceptual skills engaged by perceptual priming separately from other skills?

## Punishment in Neuroscience

Gallagher (Chapter 18, this volume) documents the evolution of thinking and research on hypermnesic and amnesic modulators over recent years. She shows how reliance on punishment training (which for some reason is called "passive avoidance" in neuroscience circles) postponed our understanding of how these agents work. In particular, opioid peptides were thought to moderate aversive reinforcement, until it was found that they also compromised learning and memory under positive reinforcement. Going back even futher than she does, we see how this overreliance happened: The classic study of Duncan (1949) found apparently amnesic effects of electroconvulsive shock following learning of an escape task. But we all remember the telling criticism (Coons & Miller, 1960) that revealed this to be a flawed procedure. (Because amnesic and aversive properties of the shock could potentially produce the same result.) Using punishment training (inhibitory avoidance) and *directly* testing for the punitive effects of post-training events solved this problem (Madsen & McGaugh, 1961). But Gallagher also shows how modern researchers have employed appetitive procedures coupled with checks against possible unwelcome aversive properties of their posttraining events. Gallagher's review makes clear that the search for task generality in the effects of posttraining treatments on memory is an important priority, just as task generality is an increasingly crucial concern in human memory research.A model that has

## ON SPECIFICITY OF PROCESS

Research strategies on memory follow two complementary tacks, transfer and interference. We try to determine what has been learned by observing how knowledge can be applied to new situations and by observing what other learning will interfere. Numerous examples of each can be found in the contributions in this volume. I shall mention three instructive examples:

1. The first of these is in Gallagher's (Chapter 18, this volume) discussion of the early work on *modulators*. As I just mentioned, opioid peptides were originally thought to modulate learning through a moderating effect on the consequences of negative reinforcement. Now, however, the same substances have been shown to have a similar effect on learning established with positive reinforcement or even with no reinforcement at all. Thus, the operation of this class of modulators must be less specific by far than had been supposed originally, and Gallagher has some properly tentative suggestions about how novelty might be the common factor.

2. At the other extreme of specificity is Schacter's (Chapter 20, this volume) discussion of *hyperspecific associations* by amnesic patients. Thus, one patient could express newly learned knowledge about baseball and the city of Hoboken, but only if the question were asked just the same way every time. This same tendency was observed in Schacter's studies, with Graf, of context-sensitive priming. A previously presented word was primed only if its later occurrence was accompanied by the same context word. This hyperspecificity in amnesic patients' new learning raises a paradoxical point however: Precisely the nature of what is spared in amnesia has been characterized by Kinsbourne and Wood (1982) as *context-free*, rather than *context-bound* memory. Thus, in source amnesia, people show they have picked up new information but have no idea how or where. It is only when the context of learning needs to be reinstated somehow that amnesic patients perform disastrously. What amnesic patients learn is thus apparently context dependent to a high degree but not accessible in relation to that context.[1]

3. Finally, Mackintosh (Chapter 19, this volume) shows us in his chapter how context sensitivity of learning can be used as a *theoretical diagnostic*. In

1. There are important differences between "context" as the experimental setting and "context" as the linguistic environment. As Dan Schacter pointed out in discussion after my presentation, the paradox is less worrisome when this distinction is made.

discussing associative and nonassociative forms of learning, he concludes that habituation transfers across different contexts whereas latent inhibition does not. Therefore, although the experimental operations for these two are very similar, they must have somewhat different explanations.

## ON BLENDS OF PROCESS AND THE LEARNING–PERFORMANCE DISTINCTION

Most of the presentations in this volume have concerned *distinctions* within learning or memory systems. An extraordinarily healthy theme in these presentations has been how real-life performance uses blends of these theoretically dissociable components. For example, Schacter (Chapter 20, this volume) showed that performance of normals in memory experiments includes the same information that is available to amnesic patients but mixed with deliberate goal-directed strategies that capitalize on accessibility of contextual information. Similarly, Mackintosh (Chapter 19, this volume) followed his treatment of the procedural/declarative distinction with cautions that most observed conditioning situations engage both systems.

## ON CONSCIOUSNESS

I see new interest in *consciousness* these days among specialists in human memory. There are three notable signs of this: First, our ideas about *short-term memory* have returned increasingly to William James's (1890) original remarks about Primary Memory as the backward reach of the conscious present. Writers have always done lip service to James's remarks, even while they violated its spirit by proposing a unitary short-term storage system with set capacity and one form of coding, perhaps phonetic. The identification of short-term memory with consciousness implies instead that primary memory can "contain" whatever a person happens to be concentrating on at the time, phonetic, visual, or other forms of information. Short-term or primary memory is thus not a place in any sense. It is a state of activation of a subsystem—potentially any subsystem—of the information-processing apparatus. However, this theme is not one that has been emphasized here, and so I shall turn to other issues.

A second conspicuous appearance of consciousness as a respectable constituent of memory theory is found in Tulving's recent (1983) revision of his views on *episodic and semantic memory*. The previous articulation (Tulving, 1972) of this distinction allowed for what he called the "pragmatic" interpretation—that episodic memory is at stake when it is a question of specified learning from a single learning event, such as a laboratory event, and that semantic memory is at stake when it is a question of general knowledge brought with a person into the laboratory. Now Tulving has restricted the range of episodic memory to require "recollective experience"—consciousness at the time a memory is contacted that one is in some sense reliving an episode from one's past, almost an emotional reaction to being transported into one's own personal history. As he said in the new book (Tulving, 1983), this phenomenon has received almost no attention in research—ever. (Schacter's [1983] recent experiment is an exception.) So defined, episodic memory excludes what amnesic patients can remember and it does so *by fiat*. For surely the one thing amnesic patients lack is this element of recollective experience. What are we to do, then, with evidence reviewed by Schacter that amnesic patients can show memory for a recently presented word in a manner that is absolutely unimpaired so long as they can rely on implicit expressions of that memory? That a certain word occurred in a certain context is evidenced by the fact of priming, even if the context is utterly inaccessible and the retrieval missing the element of recollective experience. Tulving is certainly within his rights to redefine a term he introduced us to in any way he chooses. However, now, we need a new term to refer to memory for specifically dated laboratory episodes.

This leads directly to the third eruption of consciousness into recent ideas on memory, and one that stems from the dissociations shown for amnesic patients and for normal subjects between explicit and implicit memory. It is tempting to appeal to the procedural/declarative distinction here because of its honored history in philosophy as well as its prior use in psychological theory (such as in Anderson's [1976] ACT model). Equating, thus, the procedural/declarative distinction with the unconscious/conscious distinction provides what seems like a neat generalization about amnesic patients—that they are specifically deficient in declarative memory. It is also consistent with such other dissociations of conscious processes as are to be seen in blindsight (Weiskrantz, 1980), visual masking (Marcel, 1983), and decision processes (Nisbett & Wilson, 1978).

But as Kinsbourne and Wood (1982) have observed, the distinction between conscious and unconscious remembering does not take us very far theoretically. It is perhaps suitable as a description of the data—as is the distinction between implicit memory and explicit memory—but we need to look beyond the notion of awareness and find out just what amnesic patients are, and are not, aware of in their memories. There is, as Kinsbourne and Wood (1982) said, no evidence that amnesic patients are any less conscious, as such, than anyone else. Nor, when recalling a bit of premorbid information, are amnesic patients unaware that they are doing so. Rather some almost metacognitive awareness that a piece of information was the result of a particular episode comes closer to the trouble amnesic patients have.

Second, as Mackintosh (Chapter 19, this volume) made clear in his presentation, associative theories of conditioning have been informed and advanced by distinguishing procedural and declarative knowledge by reference to what we used to call stimulus–response and stimulus–stimulus learning, respectively. This seems to me an extraordinarily *healthy* theoretical development, finally releasing associative theory from the grip of stimulus–response dominance, without resorting to sloppy "mentalistic" language. Classical associative theory always dealt with the association of ideas rather than with stimuli and responses. Whether animals possess consciousness is a topic for college bull sessions, but not for professional psychologists. If we are to insist on declarative knowledge being consciously accessible, or potentially so, we are forcing extra and unnecessary stipulations into a perfectly clear and otherwise useful distinction.

## ON METACOGNITION

Metacognitive skills are those that allow us to reflect on our own cognitive functions. To know that to memorize 12 numerals would be harder than to memorize only 9 is such a skill, and one that has been studied in children. To fail to *recall* a bit of information and yet accurately predict whether or not we will be able to *recognize* the correct answer subsequently is another metacognitive skill, one that Schacter (1983) has investigated at some length. Amnesic patients are, in a way, deficient in metacognitive skills; they can possess information in memory and yet have no awareness of that information, or ordinary access to it. The resources we now know they possess for learning and remembering are quite outside their strategic management. Accordingly, in the absence of evidence to my knowledge,[2] it is fair to expect that amnesic patients would be especially impaired at metacognitive skills. Indeed, one can go far with the suggestion that a metacognitive deficit is *their main problem*, as opposed to the range of other terminology that has been used to capture the distinction.

In connection with aging, this suggestion that amnesic patients' main difficulty is with metacognition raises a fascinating paradox: In conditions such anoxia, the Korsakoff syndrome, and Alzheimer disease, classic amnesia symptoms are correlated with increasing age. (This may explain why H. M. was such a popular case.) And as we have seen, there are performance aspects of memory that are spared in amnesia. This might lead to the expectation that *normal aging* would entail, in gradual and less dramatic form, the same pattern of spared performance and reduced metacognition as shows up in amnesia. Indeed, older people are prone to complain of memory loss as the most annoying cognitive circumstance of advancing age.

This expectation that normal aging would mimic the more severe clinical symptoms or organic amnesia in mild form would be wrong. The facts of the matter seem to show the opposite for the normal aging of healthy

2. Dan Schacter informed me, after the meeting, that amnesic patients' control of metacognition concerning premorbid knowledge is intact. Monitoring of new memories in conventional paradigms is necessarily close to zero because overt retrieval is close to zero.

individuals. Lachman and Lachman (1980), for example, reported that performance on tests of factual knowledge declined with age and yet, for the range they studied, metacognitive skills—the so-called Feeling of Knowing—remained unimpaired for even their oldest subjects. The older individuals could remember fewer facts, but in predicting accurately which *unrecalled* facts were likely to be *recognizable* later, they were as good as the younger subjects. Note that it is not just that the older people realistically thought they would have many blocks of memory. When a block in recall occurred, rather, the older subjects could accurately discriminate, somehow, among their failed retrievals and predict accordingly which answers would be correctly recognized and which not. They were indeed aware of the relative strengths of memories they could not even retrieve!

Thus, in summary, organic amnesia, as clinically defined, leads to an opposite pattern of deterioration from normal aging. In organic amnesia, there are spared performance capacities but impaired metacognitive skills, whereas in normal aging, the performance suffers but the metacognition holds up. Of course, there are many gaps in our information about aging. We do not know whether and how word priming, for example, declines with age. But at the very least, this paradox underlines what perhaps we knew all along—that diseases like Korsakoff syndrome and Alzheimer disease are very far from normal conditions. In memory performance, forgetfulness that comes with age seems to be not in any sense a milder version of the organic pathologies. Elderly forgetfulness ought to be examined in parallel with amnesic disorders, using the same array of new tasks that seem to have so clarified the latter recently.

## ACKNOWLEDGMENTS

Preparation of this chapter was supported, in part, by NSF Grant 82-19661.

## REFERENCES

Anderson, J. R. *Language, memory and thought*. Hillsdale, N. J.: Erlbaum, 1976.

Atkinson, R. C., & Shiffrin, R. M. Human memory: A proposed system and its control processes. In K. W. Spence & J. T. Spence (Eds.), *The psychology of learning and motivation* (Vol. 2). New York: Academic Press, 1968.

Coons, E. E., & Miller, N. E. Conflict versus consolidation of memory traces to explain "retrograde amnesia" produced by ECS. *Journal of Comparative and Physiological Psychology*, 1960, *53*, 524–531.

Corkin, S. Acquisition of motor skill after bilateral medial temporal-lobe excision. *Neuropsychologia*, 1968, *6*, 255.

Crowder, R. G. General forgetting theory and the locus of forgetting. In L. Cermak (Ed.), *Human memory and amnesia*. Hillsdale, N. J.: Erlbaum, 1982.

Duncan, C. P. The retroactive effect of electroshock on learning. *Journal of Comparative and Physiological Psychology*, 1949, *42*, 32–44.

Graf, P., Squire, L., & Mandler, G. The information that amnesics do not forget. *Journal of Experimental Psychology: Learning, Memory, & Cognition*, 1984, *10*, 164–178.

Hebb, D. O. *The organization of behavior*. New York: Wiley, 1949.

James, W. *Principles of psychology*. New York: Henry Holt, 1890.

Kinsbourne, M., & Wood, F. Theoretical considerations regarding the episodic-semantic memory distinction. In L. Cermak (Ed.), *Human memory and amnesia*. Hillsdale, N. J.: Erlbaum, 1982.

Kolers, P. A., & Roediger, H. L. Procedures of mind. *Journal of Verbal Learning and Verbal Behavior*, 1984, *23*, 425–449.

Lachman, J. L., & Lachman, R. Age and the actualization of world knowledge. In L. W. Poon, J. L. Fozard, L. S. Cermak, D. Arenberg, & L. W. Thompson (Eds.), *New directions in memory and aging*. Hillsdale, N. J.: Erlbaum, 1980.

Madsen, M. C., & McGaugh, J. L. The effect of ECS on one-trial avoidance learning. *Journal of Comparative and Physiological Psychology*, 1961, *54*, 522–523.

Marcel, A. J. Conscious and unconscious perception: An approach to the relations between phenomenal experience and perceptual processes. *Cognitive Psychology*, 1983, *15*, 238–300.

Nisbett, R. E., & Wilson, T. DeC. Telling more than we know: Verbal reports on mental processes. *Psychological Review*, 1978, *84*, 231–259.

Schacter, D. L. Feeling of knowing in episodic memory. *Journal of Experimental Psychology*, 1983, *9*, 39–54.

Scoville, W. B., & Milner, B. Loss of recent memory after bilateral hippocampal lesions. *Journal of Neurology, Neurosurgery and Psychiatry*, 1957, *20*, 11–21.

Tulving, E. Episodic and semantic memory. In E. Tulving & W. Donaldson (Eds.), *Organization of memory*. New York: Academic Press, 1972.

Tulving, E. *Elements of episodic memory*. London: Oxford University Press, 1983.

Warrington, E. K., & Weiskrantz, L. The effect of prior learning on subsequent retention in amnesic patients. *Neuropsychologia*, 1974, *12*, 419–428.

Waugh, N. C., & Norman, D. A. Primary memory. *Psychological Review*, 1965, *74*, 89–104.

Weiskrantz, L. Varieties of residual experience. *Quarterly Journal of Experimental Psychology*, 1980, *32*, 365–386.

CHAPTER 24

# Disconnected Memories

**Mary-Louise Kean**
University of California, Irvine

The dominant theme in recent work on amnesia has been distinguishing those domains where amnesic subjects, human and infrahuman, show normal or near normal success on learning and memory tasks from those where they are radically impaired. The patterns of sparing and loss observed have led to the development of dichotomous accounts of memory (Squire & Cohen, 1984) as well as more agnostic descriptive accounts that appeal to multiple forms of memory (cf. Schacter, Chapter 20, this volume). Both classes of analyses critically appeal to domain-independent qualities of memory, the central assumption being that the nature of memorial capacity is not contingent in general or in particular on specific cognitive capacities (domains), for example, face recognition or "visual" imaging. Human linguistic capacity is the one domain which is typically excepted from this generalization. If, however, human linguistic capacity is memorially distinctive, it is *a priori* equally plausible that other cognitive domains are as well.

The representational systems that are exploited in behavior are autonomous, of necessity distinctively characterized; that is, I am trusting that no one will dispute that both psychologically and neurally our capacities for voice recognition and face recognition are independent in significant respects as are knowledge of one's native language and the spatial layout of one's house. The extent to which cognitive systems are autonomous constrains the potential descriptive and, ultimately, explanatory scope of domain-independent accounts of memory. Put somewhat differently, any thesis of autonomy entails that cognitive systems are fragmented, hence current approaches to learning and memory arising out of the study of amnesia are only motivated to the extent that the patterns of impairment seen are not a function of the fragmentation of cognitive systems.

It does not follow from the autonomy of systems that their individual functions can be manifested independently. Behavior, whether viewed psychologically or neurobiologically, and no matter how "passive," would seem to involve the interaction of a host of systems. Any consideration of the question of the possible extent of structural memorial autonomy of cognitive systems requires, therefore, consideration of interaction among such systems as well as their internal constitution. It is to the former issue that my comments here are primarily addressed. Specifically, I want to consider how patterns of interaction among independent systems may underlie domain-dependent multiple forms of memory.

If two autonomous systems interact, then there must be a mapping function from one to the other; in the absence of such a mapping function, the two systems would reduce, not be autonomous. So, the issue becomes one of mapping functions. What is of concern is how one gets from some system A to some system B—say, for example, from the system that recognizes faces as familiar faces to a system that allows for the naming of familiar faces. Given that such systems involve complex processes, they must be conceived as multicomponent processes. For the sake of simplicity, my discussion will focus for the moment only on the unidirectional flow of information, as from face recognition to naming. However, it should be clear that the kind of system at issue has bidirectional properties, that we can resurrect the mental image of a person's face from his or her name.

One way in which a mapping can be effected from one system to another is if there are subcomponents of the systems that share some representation feature or features; they can only be shared representational features and not identical representational features because in the latter case the two subcomponents would not be distinct. It is a property of such a mapping function (Figure 24.1) that there will be a loss of information; $B_i$ is an effective filter of representational information from $A_i$, which is not consistent with the representational constitution of $B_i$; thus, there will be a

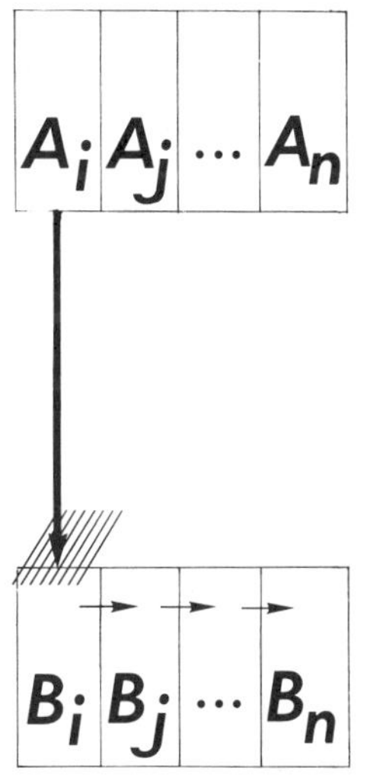


**FIGURE 24.1.** Schematic illustration of mapping system between two functional loci. For example, the A system might be that for face recognition while the B system might be that for naming familiar faces. The /// are to indicate the fact that some representational information from $A_i$ will be filtered out by the representational constitution of $B_i$.

loss of $A_i$ information in $B_i$. Psychologically this kind of mapping function can be illustrated by considering two of the component processes of our capacity to understand sentences, the analysis of individual words and the analysis of the structural relations that hold among words in a sentence. When you hear a sentence that contains the word *profanity*, it is critical to your understanding of that item that you appreciate both that it is a noun and that it is derived from the adjective *profane* (Bradley, 1980). Having identified the word, it is then necessary to assign that word an appropriate structural role in the sentence being heard if you are to understand the sentence. In terms of the structural analysis of the sentence, all that matters is that *profanity* is a noun; the information that it was derived from an adjective is irrelevant and inaccessible (Fodor, Bever, & Garrett, 1974). Disconnection syndromes involving cortico-cortico connections provide neurological evidence of this sort of mapping function (Geschwind, 1965). Such syndromes arise when the pathway(s) between two or more functional loci are disconnected. If, for example, there is a disconnection between left hemisphere language areas and the motor area, there will be a compromise in an individual's ability to perform various acquired motor behaviors to verbal command, for example, be unable to appropriately respond when asked to make a fist or show how you brush your teeth, although the person will be unimpaired in spontaneously carrying out such activities (Geschwind, 1967). Other common disconnection syndromes include conduction aphasia (Wernicke, 1874/1977), pure alexia without agraphia (Dejerine, 1892), and the visual agnosias (Brown, 1972; Geschwind, 1965).

The second obvious way to effect a mapping between two systems A and B is for the outputs of the components of A, or some proper subset of them, to be projected to a third system, an A–B system, which in turn projects to the components of B, or some proper subset (Figure 24.2). In this case there is a convergence of A representations on A–B, which in turn projects to B. In such a process there will be a loss of information as well; if A were replicated in A–B, then A would not be autonomous. Such a mapping function differs from the previous one in that it must be bidirectional, A–B receiving inputs from B as well as from A. Taking A–B to be a functionally combinatorial system, given an A input, the output is distributed across B (or some proper subset of B). At the same time, because the system is bidirectional, the output of A–B will also be distributed back across A. Various subcortical structures, notably the thalamus, are eminently well placed and connected to involve candidate A–B systems. Behaviorally, such a system is arguably required for transcoding between visual images and speech acts.

Combining both these types of mappings, we derive a system with multiple inputs to B from A, one direct and one indirect (Figure 24.3). For the sake of complexity, let us add one more system: some system C, where C and B interact in much the same way as A and B (Figure 24.4). Given

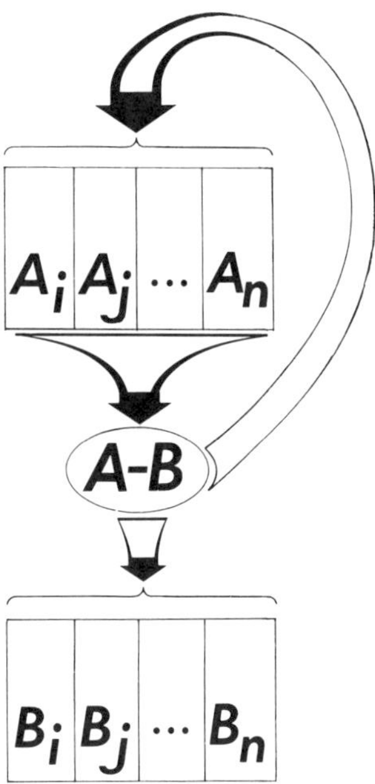


**FIGURE 24.2.** Schematic illustration of a mapping function between two functional loci that is mediated by an intervening combinatorial system. The input to A–B involves a convergence of representational information from the subcomponents of A; the output of A–B is a representation that distributes across (a subset of) the components of both A and B.

such a system, in virtue of A's having activated B, B will activate C, giving the superficial appearance of there being a *direct* relation between A and C, although none in fact actually exists. Thus, for example, it might be thought that all that is needed to read aloud a nonsense word such as *BLICK* is the same system for transcoding letter sequences into sound sequences that is used in reading known words aloud. However, this is not so. The reading of a nonsense word is mediated not only through the letter/sound system(s) but, beyond that, through a third system: an individual's dictionary of the words that he or she knows. Thus, there are people who can read known occurring words but not nonsense words (see Coltheart, Patterson, & Marshall, 1980, for a number of papers dealing with this disorder, "deep dyslexia").

It is not only the case that such a scheme has *prima facie* psychological plausibility as an approach to the problem of fragmentation, it also has, as has already been suggested, considerable neuroanatomical plausibility. It comports with the facts of there being cortico-cortico connections, significantly among functionally distinctive cortical loci, and with there a complex array of ascending and descending pathways between various cortical systems and various subcortical structures. That is, the anatomical design features of the brain seem hardly functionally interpretable unless one assumes something on this order. Unless one makes the certainly false assumption of full redundancy among all subcortical systems, it follows that amnesias

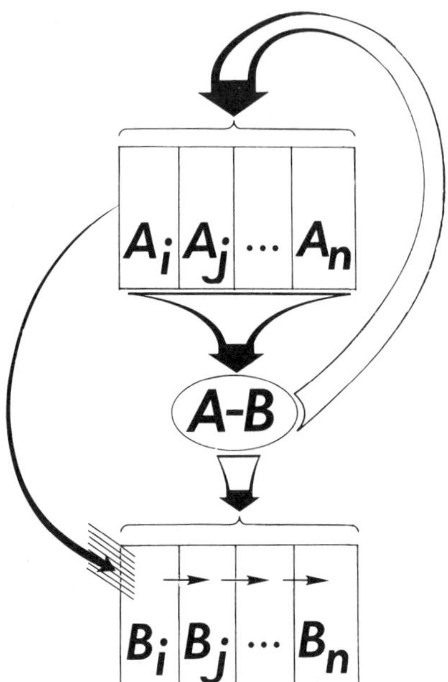


**FIGURE 24.3.** Schematic illustration of a system that combines both a direct mapping between two functional loci (Figure 24.1) and an indirect mapping between the same two loci mediated by an intervening combinatorial system (Figure 24.2).

arising from disruption of different A–B-type systems will be different, as indeed it would seem they are; furthermore, it enables us to consider (at least some) amnesias as disconnection syndromes, a possibility Warrington and Weiskrantz (1982) have put forward.

Perhaps even more striking is the physiological parsimony that arises from this kind of treatment of the problem of fragmentation. It is just this sort of organization that one would expect on the basis of work on long-term potentiation (LTP). First, the efficacy of the system is supported by multiple overlapping inputs. Second, it provides for cumulative activation. Rather than activation proceeding in a linear sequence, because of the feedback properties of the system, even one exposure to a stimulus allows for iterated activation. Third, it is consistent with the selectivity of LTP. These three features—multiple overlapping inputs, iterated activation, and selectivity—are the defining features of LTP (see Seifert, 1984, for several reviews and discussions).

A relatively straightforward developmental interpretation of the treatment is also available. Returning to the simple case of two interacting systems (Figure 24.3), direct activation of both A and B serves to sculpture A–B and its connections in the course of development; at the same time, as A–B is refined through development, it contributes to the sculpturing of A and B. That is, there must in some measure be a reciprocal developmental relationship between A and B, on the one hand, and A–B, on the other; without this the effective combinatorial "interdigitation" of A with B through A–B could not arise with respect to acquired knowledge. The multiple activation of $B_i$ by both $A_i$ and A–B would serve to increase the efficacy of either input alone. Thus, for any instantiated representational relation, impairment to A–B should cause relatively little problem, while for any representational system not instantiated, impairment to A–B should be relatively catastrophic. The neurological evidence would seem to support this. For example, young children become aphasic and are compromised in language acquisition consequent to thalamic lesions (M. Dennis, personal communication); to the extent that one finds adults suffering acquired loss of language (aphasia) consequent to thalamic lesions these are inevitably characterizable, by contrast, as disconnection syndromes (transcortical aphasias). On the other hand, N. A. provides evidence that at least some selective thalamic lesions do lead to significant impairment in learning, although instantiated representational systems are relatively spared (Squire, 1981); studies of the

**FIGURE 24.4.** Schematic illustration of an expansion of a system of the type illustrated in Figure 24.3 to include a third functional system. Such systems can be expanded to involve an arbitrary number of functional systems of the type A, B, or C; possible combinatorial systems can likewise be elaborated. Furthermore, there is no *a priori* limit on the number of systems that might combine in an A-B-type system.

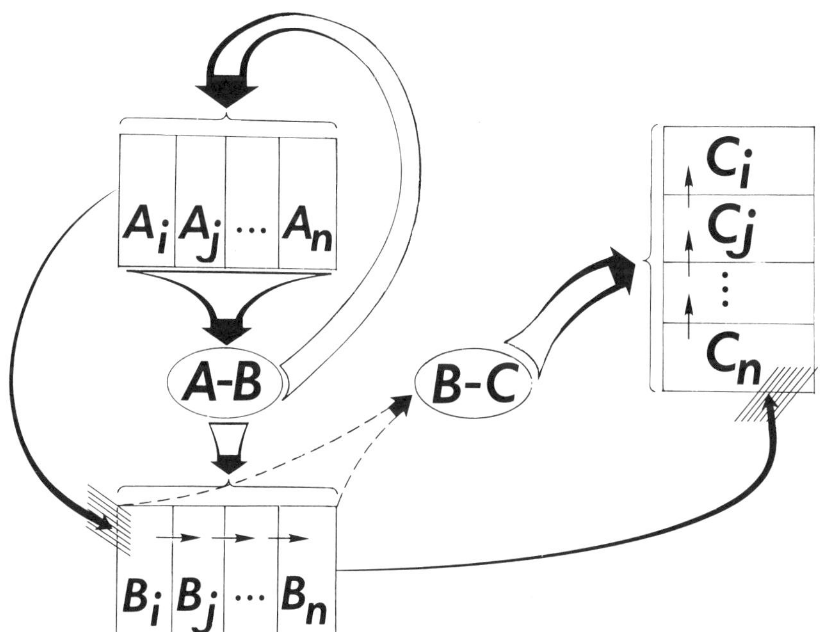

effects of ventrolateral thalamotomy for dyskinesias provides similar evidence (Vilkki, 1978; Vilkki & Laitinen, 1974).

It would also be anticipated from this perspective that cortical lesions, that is, lesions to A- and B-type systems, would have a more profound effect on learning than subcortical lesions. This is simply because the substrate for laying down domain-specific information has been radically eroded. This is also true in the intended sense. An adult who becomes aphasic in consequence to a cortical lesion not only is radically impaired in language use, but also has a profound anterograde linguistic amnesia, more profound apparently than that of H. M. Neal Cohen (personal communication) has found that H. M. has acquired some new vocabulary items in the time since he was operated, though his acquisition is quite significantly below that of control subjects. By contrast, G. R., who became aphasic due to a bullet wound in 1944—the bullet entered in the vicinity of the left Sylvian fissure and emerged in the parietal lobe, a trajectory consistent with predominantly cortical damage and certainly sparing of significant subcortical structures (Newcombe & Marshall, 1980)—has evidently acquired just one new word in the last 40 years—he spends a lot of time in pubs and has learned the name of a brand of beer that is new since the war (J. C. Marshall, personal communication).

This kind of approach makes one prediction about amnesia that runs counter to the common conventional wisdom. Let us assume that A–B is impaired, leaving only the $A_i$ to $B_i$ connection for the activation of B given activation of A by some stimulus. For any premorbidly well-acquired representational relation, I have already suggested that it should be the case that the $A_i/B_i$ connection is sufficient for the activation of $B_i$. Furthermore, as $B_i$ is integrated in the complex of B, its activation should serve to activate the other components of B. From this, however, it does not necessarily follow that the realization of B will function normally if there is no learning demand. In particular, the claim is that the inputs from A–B overlap with other inputs to the components of system B and not that they are coextensive with them. Given this, one would anticipate that while there might generally be an appearance of intact function of B, there would in fact be limitations.

The analysis of faces provides a relevant example. Based on tachistoscopic studies with normal adults, we can distinguish a bilateral face recognition system and a face-selective, right-hemisphere system that plays a critical role in the mature analysis of faces. The bilateral system, although sensitive to the organization of facial features, is relatively orientation insensitive to the rotation of a face on a plane and is keyed to striking features, seemingly recognizing faces as faces on the basis of constituent elements, whereas the right-hemisphere system functions over a highly restricted range of orientations (rotations) and is keyed to the analysis of the planes and angles of faces. This right-hemisphere mature system functionally emerges around the onset of puberty; its emergence does not mark the demise of the striking feature system, although it clearly gains functional ascendency (Carey & Diamond, 1980).

On the basis of lesion studies in humans (Meadows, 1974; Whitely & Warrington, 1977) and of physiological studies in monkeys (Gross, Rocha-Miranda, & Bender, 1972; Perrett, Rolls, & Caan, 1982; Rolls, Judge, & Sanghera, 1977), these two systems are arguably associated with distinct anatomical loci: the fundus of the superior temporal sulcus and inferotemporal cortex. The system of the superior temporal sulcus is orientation tolerant and responsive to constituent elements of faces whereas the inferotemporal system apparently has neither of these properties. In addition to there being cortico-cortico connections between these systems, there are also subcortically mediated systems. Thus, in all respects, these components of the face-recognition system have the required design features.

It is a well-known observation, both anecdotal and experimental, that amnesic patients are significantly impaired in the learning of new faces. In this respect they are much the same as individuals with prosopagnosia; the lesions, of course, are distinct, prosopagnosia being associated with an inferotemporal cortical lesion. What is noteworthy is that at least some amnesic patients seem to show an impairment in face analysis even when there is no memorial demand. In a study of Korsakoff patients, Drinker, Butters, Berman, Samuels, and Carey (1978) found that the patients performed near chance in selecting which of two pictures in a triad were of the same individual when attire was selectively manipulated to "confuse"; neurologically intact subjects almost inevitably selected the correct pair.

A typical analysis of such data—indeed, the one offered—is that the amnesic subjects do not engage in the same depth of processing as normal subjects and alcoholic controls. In some sense that is surely true, but the question is what sense, or, rather what is the mechanism that precludes their carrying out a "deep" analysis. The proposal here is that the analysis of unfamiliar faces requires both cortico-cortico activation of the system that analyzes particular faces and the indirect activation of that system mediated by subcortical structures; that is, multiple overlapping inputs are necessary for the efficacious analysis of particular unfamiliar faces. Under such an analysis, the poor performance of the Korsakoff patients, their lack of "depth of analysis," follows from a compromise of the pathways and or structures that mediate the indirect activation.

Other experiments suggest themselves immediately. For example, how would amnesic patients perform on a task that involves the interaction between linguistic knowledge and visual images? To take just one such case, would we find normal performance on the following task? A subject hears a sentence containing an ambiguous word; the subject's task is to accept or reject as appropriate in the context of the sentence a picture that flashes on just after the occurrence of the ambiguous word and that depicts one of the meanings of that word. Another line of critical research would involve consideration of cross-modal priming.

I am not suggesting that such tasks be used in studies of amnesia merely to test a particular prediction of the view I have been outlining. The view I have been outlining dictates that such tasks are central to the study of amnesia because the claim is that what is critical in learning and memory is the way in which systems interact. It should be clear from both the faces example and the proposed line of experimentation that under this perspective amnesia is not an impairment of learning and memory, writ large, but rather that the learning and memory impairments of amnesia must arise, in some measure at least, in consequence of there being a circumscription of the capability for distinct functional systems to interact. The possibility that there are multiple forms of memory only to the extent that there are interactive autonomous systems cannot be excluded in the absence of evidence delineating domain-dependent constraints on learning and memory.

## REFERENCES

Bradley, D. C. Lexical representation of derivational relation. In M. Aronoff & M.-L. Kean (Eds.), *Juncture*. Saratoga, Calif.: Amni Libri, 1980.

Brown, J. W. *Aphasia, apraxia and agnosia*. Springfield, Ill.: Charles C. Thomas, 1972.

Carey, S., & Diamond, R. Maturational determination of the developmental course of face encoding. In D. Caplan (Ed.), *Biological studies of mental processes*. Cambridge, Mass.: MIT Press, 1980.

Coltheart, M., Patterson, K., & Marshall, J. C. (Eds.). *Deep dyslexia*. London: Routlege & Kegan Paul, 1980.

Dejerine, J. Contribution à l'étude anatomo-pathologique et clinique des differérentes variétés de cécité verbale. *Mémoires Société de la Biologique*, 1892, *4*, 61.

Drinker, J., Butters, N., Berman, G., Samuels, I., & Carey, S. The recognition and encoding of faces by alcoholic Korsakoff and right hemisphere patients. *Neuropsychologia*, 1978, *16*, 683–695.

Fodor, J. A., Bever, T., & Garrett, M. F. *The psychology of language: An introduction to psycholinguistics and generative grammar*. New York: McGraw-Hill, 1974.

Geschwind, N. Disconnexion syndromes in animals and man. *Brain*, 1965, *88*, 237–294, 585–644.

Geschwind, N. The apraxias. In E. W. Strauss & R. M. Griffith (Eds.), *Phenonemology of action and will*. Pittsburgh: Duquesne University Press, 1967.

Gross, C. G., Rocha-Miranda, C. E., & Bender, D. E. Visual properties of neurons in inferotemporal cortex of the macaque. *Journal of Neurophysiology*, 1972, *35*, 96–111.

Meadows, J. C. The anatomical basis of prosopagnosia. *Journal of Neurology, Neurosurgery and Psychiatry, 1974, 37*, 489–501.

Newcombe, F., & Marshall, J. C. The conceptual status of deep dyslexia: An historical perspective. In M. Coltheart, K. Patterson, & J. C. Marshall (Eds.), *Deep dyslexia*. London: Routlege & Kegan Paul, 1980.

Perrett, D. I., Rolls, E. T., & Caan, W. Visual neurones responsive to faces in the monkey temporal cortex. *Experimental Brain Research*, 1982, *47*, 329–342.

Rolls, E. T., Judge, S. J., & Sanghera, M. K. Activity of neurones in the inferotemporal cortex of the alert monkey. *Brain Research*, 1977, *130*, 229–238.

Seifert, W. (Ed.). *Molecular, cellular, and behavioral neurobiology of the hippocampus*. New York: Academic Press, 1984.

Squire, L. R. Two forms of human amnesia: An analysis of forgetting. *Journal of Neuroscience*, 1981, *1*, 635–640.

Squire, L. R., & Cohen, N. J. Human memory and amnesia. In G. Lynch, J. L. McGaugh, & N. M. Weinberger (Eds.), *Neurobiology of learning and memory*. New York: Guilford Press, 1984.

Vilkki, J. Effects of thalamic lesions on complex memory and perception. *Neuropsychologia*, 1978, *16*, 427–437.

Vilkki, J., & Laitinen, L. V. Differential effects of left and right ventrolateral thalamotomy on receptive and expressive verbal performances and face-matching. *Neuropsychologia*, 1974, *12*, 11–19.

Warrington, E. K., & Weiskrantz, L. Amnesia: A disconnection syndrome? *Neuropsychologia*, 1982, *20*, 233–248.

Wernicke, C. *The aphasia symptom complex: A psychological study on an anatomical basis*, 1874. [Reprinted in G. H. Eggert (Ed.), *Wernicke's works on aphasia*. The Hague: Mouton, 1977]

Whitely, A. M., & Warrington, E. K. Prosopagnosia: A clinical, psychological, and anatomical study of three patients. *Journal of Neurology, Neurosurgery and Psychiatry*, 1977, *40*, 395–403.

CHAPTER 25

# Moving On from Modeling Amnesia

**Richard G. M. Morris**
University of St. Andrews
St. Andrews, Fife, Scotland

## THE ARGUMENT

The task of modeling amnesia in animals is an important and useful one. Animal studies provide a comparative perspective to the problem and, in particular, an opportunity for delineating the crucial neuropathology in a precise, histologically identifiable way.

However, I believe it may also be an appropriate time to move on from too focused a preoccupation in animal lesion studies with modeling amnesia. The argument rests largely on three propositions: first, certain characteristics of the amnesic syndrome in humans point to limitations of current animal models, limitations that are unlikely to be overcome in the immediate future; second, that preoccupation with modeling human amnesia ignores the possibility that animal experimentation may reveal other kinds of fractionation of learning and memory distinct from those that have shown up clinically; and third, in a more positive spirit, that we should move on and take advantage of the progress that the amnesia modeling studies have brought about. Although we do not yet have an adequate theory of amnesia, knowledge about tasks that are or are not impaired by lesions of relevant brain circuitry could be exploited to address fundamental issues concerned with the neurobiology of learning and memory.

## THE VALUE OF ANIMAL MODELS

This argument is in no way intended to belittle the importance of animal modeling studies; nor to deny the progress that has been made, particularly in recent years. Research on human amnesia has thrown up a number of issues that have been, and continue to be, addressed in animal experimentation. These include questions to do with the critical neuropathology (e.g., Horel, 1978; Mair, Warrington, & Weiskrantz, 1979), dissociable subtypes of amnesia (Huppert & Piercy, 1978; Lhermitte & Signoret, 1972, cited by

Squire & Cohen, 1984; Squire, 1981), and issues concerning residual learning abilities (Cohen & Squire, 1980), to mention just three examples. Recognition that human amnesia entails residual learning capacity, extending beyond mere motor skills, demands that some care be taken in choosing tasks for animals that are appropriate to these issues. At one extreme are procedures, such as delayed nonmatching to sample in primates (Mishkin & Delacour, 1975) and spatial learning in rats (O'Keefe, Nadel, Keighly, & Kill, 1975), about which there is good agreement as to the deleterious effects of lesions similar to those believed to cause amnesia in humans; at the other extreme, are tasks believed to be unaffected by such lesions, such as simple conditioning and visual discrimination procedures (Mishkin, Malamut, & Bachevalier, 1984). There is, of course, substantial disagreement at a deeper theoretical level as to how these and other tasks should be characterized. Novel interpretations of the psychological aspects of animal models of amnesia continue to be proposed (e.g., Gaffan, 1985; Rawlins, in press); but, whatever the merits of these proposals, it is possible to make progress with tasks the differences of which are recognized at only a descriptive level. Thus, in addressing Horel's (1978) proposal that damage to temporal stem white matter could be the cause of amnesia in humans, Zola-Morgan, Squire, and Mishkin (1982) have used primates and delayed nonmatching to sample: Temporal stem lesions alone did not cause impairments of performance, although hippocampus and amygdala lesions caused rapid forgetting as previously reported by Mishkin (1978). Likewise, Aggleton and Mishkin (1983a, 1983b) have considered the effects of diencephalic lesions upon object recognition. They have also shown that these lesions produce impairments on single-trial, but not multitrial, object-reward associations (see Mishkin *et al.*, 1984). Animal studies will continue to be useful to address questions for which progress will be slow in work using amnesic patients. For example, the issue of possible differences in forgetting rate after either diencephalic or bitemporal lesion (see Squire & Cohen, 1984, pp. 10–12; Weiskrantz, Chapter 21, this volume) could be studied using monkeys; similarly, animal studies might provide useful information about whether an extensive or a more restricted retrograde amnesia is found after lesions that cause rapid anterograde forgetting.

## LIMITATIONS OF ANIMAL MODELS

However, the thrust of the argument raised earlier is to point to various limitations of the animal modeling exercise. By "limitations," I do not mean outstanding controversies (e.g., whether the spatial deficit in rats after hippocampal lesions is a special case of a more general memory impairment); rather, I mean difficulties that are inherent in any comparative perspective of amnesia. A first example will serve to illustrate the type of problem that has not yet, in my view, been adequately addressed in animal studies.

As both Schacter (Chapter 20, this volume) and Weiskrantz (Chapter 21, this volume) pointed out, global amnesia is distinguished from dementia (and other disorders of cerebral function) as a general impairment in memory combined with a retention of normal intellectual function. The latter is usually as measured in IQ tests. The amnesic patient H. M. has a full-scale IQ of 108 (tested 1983; see Corkin, 1984), barely changed over the 30 years beginning before the medial temporal lobe resection that caused his global amnesia. Thus, in constructing an animal model of amnesia, showing that hippocampus and amygdala monkeys demonstrate rapid forgetting on visual, tactile, and spatial recognition tasks is, strictly speaking, only half of the exercise complete. For, in addition to showing that these animals' amnesia is multimodal, one would also like to have some indication that the monkeys are, like H. M., unimpaired intellectually. In part, this is shown by the mere fact that the monkeys continue to "understand" the rules of the task: In some important sense, that they continue to select between the discriminanda, reach for the rewards when available, and wait out short delay intervals without becoming severely distracted, implies that the lesions have not caused gross dementia. Likewise, as pointed out by Zola-Morgan in discussion, the spared capacity for quite complex motor skills (e.g., the "lifesaver" task; Zola-Morgan & Squire, 1984) and the lack of *any* deficit on discrimination tasks learned by normal monkeys relatively slowly (e.g., 400 trials) also argues for a lesion-induced dementia. However, given that IQ is measured in humans using tasks that entail reasoning but not memory, it would seem worthwhile to establish that hippocampus- and amygdala-lesioned monkeys can (still) reason. Perhaps some of the tasks developed by Premack (1983) would be suitable vehicles to explore residual intellectual capacity in (putatively) amnesic monkeys. An important spin-off of the effort so expended would be a range of procedures for distinguishing animal models of global amnesia from models of Alzheimer disease.

A second limitation of animal studies concerns the question, raised by Schacter, whether monkeys do actually "engage in a mnemonic activity that is akin to explicit remembering" (Schacter, Chapter 20, this volume). In his recent monograph, Tulving (1984a) stated categorically that "members of no other species possess quite the same ability to experience again now, in a different situation and perhaps in a different form, happenings from the past, and know that the experience refers to an event that occurred in another time and in another place." In assessing such an assertion, we all share the inescapable problem that animals cannot speak. Nevertheless, it would surely be a mistake of a classic behaviorist kind to assume that because an animal cannot talk, he cannot have a recollective experience. The chimpanzee may not be able to tell us about the day when the BBC filmed him wrestling with David Attenborough, an unforgettable piece of film, but he may, perhaps, reflect from time to time on this unusual event. More seriously, Schacter (Chapter 20, this volume) claims that delayed nonmatching to sample probably makes the same demands as those made by recognition memory tasks used in human memory research (i.e., it requires explicit memory), but he points out that effective performance could be mediated "by the form of memory that is similar to the one that mediates priming effects by humans." This is an excellent point, but his rejection of the possibility has an air of circularity to it. The argument runs as follows: (1) Humans use explicit remembering in recognition tasks. (2) When asked to explicitly remember, amnesic patients do worse than normals. (3) Hippocampus- and amygdala-lesioned monkeys do badly on recognition tasks. (4) Therefore, normal monkeys explicitly remember. The claims may be correct, but the argument is circular. The balance of probability surely favors Schacter's conclusion, but the problem that deserves scrutiny is the thorny issue of how to give "instructions" to animals. It is only in recent years that we have advanced from thinking of rewards as reinforcement for particular responses to viewing them as agents that, to be sure, change behavior (see Mackintosh, 1983, pp. 20ff.) but that also serve as baits to guide animals toward an understanding of what is required of them. Thus, what has to be done in animal studies to address the problems arising from the new work on priming in relation to amnesia requires an altogether new level of sophistication in instructing animals. It is now known that humans behave quite differently in various tests of memory, such as when requested to write "the first word that comes to mind" (Graf, Squire, & Mandler, 1984, p. 168) or to "pick out the word that I showed you on a card" (p. 170). It is not at all obvious how to differentially instruct a monkey to "choose the first object that comes to mind" on one occasion, while on another to instruct him to "remember the one I showed you before." Selective reward might be the basis for the latter type of instruction, but how might an animal experimenter realize the former? The implication of the discussion so far is that animal studies, for all the remarkable progress made in the last 10 years, do not address at least two major issues of concern in work on human amnesia.

## OTHER KINDS OF FRACTIONATION OF LEARNING AND MEMORY

The second proposition of the argument is that animal experimentation may reveal other kinds of fractionation of learning and memory processes distinct from those that have shown up clinically.

The fact that the sorts of phenomena that have been observed and studied in animals have been very different from those studied in humans and have involved widely differing tasks may seem too obvious to be worth pursuing at length. To be sure, some tasks given to animals for studying memory are closely modeled on their human counterparts. Kesner and Novak's (1982) recent work on serial position effects in list-learning by rats, conducted using a radial maze, is one example. Other learning tasks have their origins in thinking about clinical problems, although not necessarily problems concerned with memory pathology (e.g., active-avoidance learning; see Mowrer & Miller, 1942). However, many procedures are so different (e.g., DRL schedules, partial reinforcement) that a measure of discontinuity between animal and human neuropsychological work is inevitable. The history of this discontinuity is discussed by Weiskrantz (1982). In addition, numerous lesion-induced impairments that have been observed in animals have no obvious counterpart in the clinical literature. But what are we to make of such observations? Do they imply that different learning processes exist in animals? The parsimonious view must be that differences at the task level, and the phenomena they give rise to, may be quite superficial with respect to underlying mechanisms. It is essential to remember, always, that experimental procedures are the inventions of experimenters. Although it is not always appreciated, the tasks used in behavioral experimentation should not be viewed as the substance of investigation. Procedures are, in a sense, like biochemical assays. They are mere techniques for getting at the underlying psychological processes or neurobiological mechanisms of memory. Thus, although animal neuropsychologists use tasks very different both from each other and from their human neuropsychological colleagues, they share a general belief in the biological continuity of learning and memory processes between animals and man (cf. Macphail, 1982). One example of this is the similarity between Olton, Becker, and Handelmann's (1979) distinction between working memory and reference memory, drawn exclusively on the basis of animal work, and Tulving's concepts of episodic memory and semantic memory (see Tulving, 1984b). Another example is O'Keefe and Nadel's (1978) assertion of a continuity between spatial mapping in animals and cognitive mapping in man.

The implication of a biological continuity argument is that, for all the superficial differences between animal and human studies of cerebral function, the second proposition of the present argument is false. It should *not* be possible to observe fractionations of memory processes in animals that cannot also be observed in humans, and vice versa. Moreover, it may be that higher mammals have just two broad categories of learning/memory processes (namely, a category of those that are spared in amnesia, and a category of impaired processes) and that lesions to any part of the midbrain cause impairments (of varying severity) restricted to the latter category only. However, matters are not quite as simple as this. For there is no *a priori* reason to believe that the kinds of pathology of memory shown by humans exhausts the possible types of pathology that could, in principle, be experimentally demonstrated. Certain cognitive or behavioral deficits may occur in isolation only in animals because they are caused by circumscribed lesions which, in turn, can only be made experimentally. Disruption of taste aversions after discrete lesions of the amygdala (Ashe & Nachman,

1980) is one such example. Another is the selective loss of conditioned responses after lesions of the dentate interpositus nuclei (Thompson *et al.*, 1984). Novel dissociations between subsystems of memory may emerge after lesions that are, at best, exceedingly unlikely in humans (e.g., neurotoxin-induced depletions of particular subfields of cells in the hippocampus; e.g., Jarrard, 1985; Sutherland, Whishaw, & Kolb, 1983). And certain learning impairments in animals (e.g., of olfactory learning) may offer avenues to understanding general neurobiological principles (Lynch, Submitted for publication) even though they may seem of tangential interest to students of human memory pathology.

Thus, preoccupation with modeling amnesia may lead to a fruitless search for a unifying theory of the neuropsychology of memory. However desirable on grounds of parsimony such a general theory might be, the alternative scenario of a constellation of dedicated memory subsystems (albeit ones that share some common principles of operation) should be borne in mind. It is also worth pointing out, by way of conclusion, that differences in the perceived domains of explanation of any given theory can sometimes cause confusion. In his review of comparative aspects of amnesia, Weiskrantz (1982) discusses and dismisses both the working-memory (Olton *et al.*, 1979) and the spatial-memory (O'Keefe & Nadel, 1978) theories. But in his own work (Mair *et al.*, 1979), Weiskrantz has stressed that some particularly well studied amnesic patients have no detectable neuropathology in the hippocampus. It is puzzling that two theories, which are expressly concerned with hippocampal function, should be dismissed for failing to be adequate theories of phenomena that need not be caused by hippocampal pathology.

## MOVING ON FROM MODELING AMNESIA

As pointed out earlier, there is presently considerable theoretical disagreement about the subsystems of memory that are impaired after diencephalic and hippocampal lesions. Elsewhere (Morris, 1983) I have suggested that testing the rival theories will prove difficult, as they often make superficially similar predictions about numerous tasks (see also Rawlins, in press). But the job of building better theoretical models of animal and human amnesia must and will continue.

But, in standing back from the theoretical disagreements, it is possible to see the progress that has been made; and the opportunities for taking advantage of it. In particular, the fact that amnesia is associated with spared cognitive function suggests the possibility of using a range of sensitive and insensitive tasks to investigate neurobiological issues. As examples, consider various topical issues that are not ordinarily considered in relation to work on amnesia: What role, if any, does reactive synaptogenesis play in mediating recovery of function after brain damage (Ramirez & Stein, 1984)? What types of disorders of memory function, if any, can embryonic transplants into adult brain improve (Cotman & Nieto-Sampedro, 1984; Gage, Bjorklund, Steneri, Dunnett, & Kelly, 1984)? And what role, if any, does synaptic plasticity play in learning or memory (Morris & Baker, 1984; Teyler & Discenna, 1984)? Study of these and other issues could be significantly advanced by taking advantage of our knowledge of spared and impaired function after midbrain lesions.

Recently, together with Michel Baudry and Elizabeth Anderson (Anderson, Baudry, Lynch, & Morris, in press) I have investigated the effects of one of the new range of amino acid antagonists upon memory. Aminophosphonovaleric acid (APV) is one of a group of antagonists with particular affinity for hippocampal NMDA (*N*-methyl-D-aspartate) receptors (Evans, Francis, Jones, Smith, & Watkins, 1982). It is also known, from work with hippocampal slices, that APV blocks long-term potentiation (LTP) (Collingridge, Kehl, & McLennan, 1983) and that this blockade is specific to the D stereoisomer of APV (Harris, Ganong, & Cotman, 1984). Thus, it is of interest to the general question of the functions of synaptic plasticity whether APV has any effect upon learning. Accordingly, we have conducted two parallel experiments: In the first, rats were implanted with osmotic minipumps containing either DL-APV, L + APV, or saline. Together with a group of unoperated control rats, they were then trained on a spatial water-maze task that was chosen precisely because of its sensitivity to hippocampal lesions (Morris, 1984). After training for 5 days, during which the DL-APV rats showed a mild acquisition impairment, all rats were given a single transfer test lasting 60 seconds. The escape platform was removed from the pool for this test. The results showed that DL-APV-treated rats were severely impaired in searching in a spatially selective way for the now-absent platform (Figure 25.1). In parallel with this study, we implanted other groups of rats with minipumps as before, but then conducted an acute electrophysiological investigation of LTP in each rat under urethane anesthesia. For some (but not all) rats, the experimenter was blind with respect to which rats had received DL-APV, L + APV, or saline. The results of this second study confirmed the earlier hippocampal-slice work in showing that DL-APV caused a selective impairment in the induction of LTP. Thus, a stereospecific blockade of LTP.

In designing this study, we took advantage of knowledge derived from modeling amnesia in animals to choose a learning task that we know to be sensitive to hippocampal lesions. Clearly it will be valuable to follow up these preliminary observations, using a range of tasks known to be sensitive or insensitive to lesions that cause amnesia. In choosing such tasks, we can remain neutral with respect to the theoretical reasons for sensitivity/insensitivity. But the work on modeling amnesia will prove valuable in drawing links between dissociations drawn at a strictly psychological level and underlying neurobiological mechanisms of information storage. Moving on

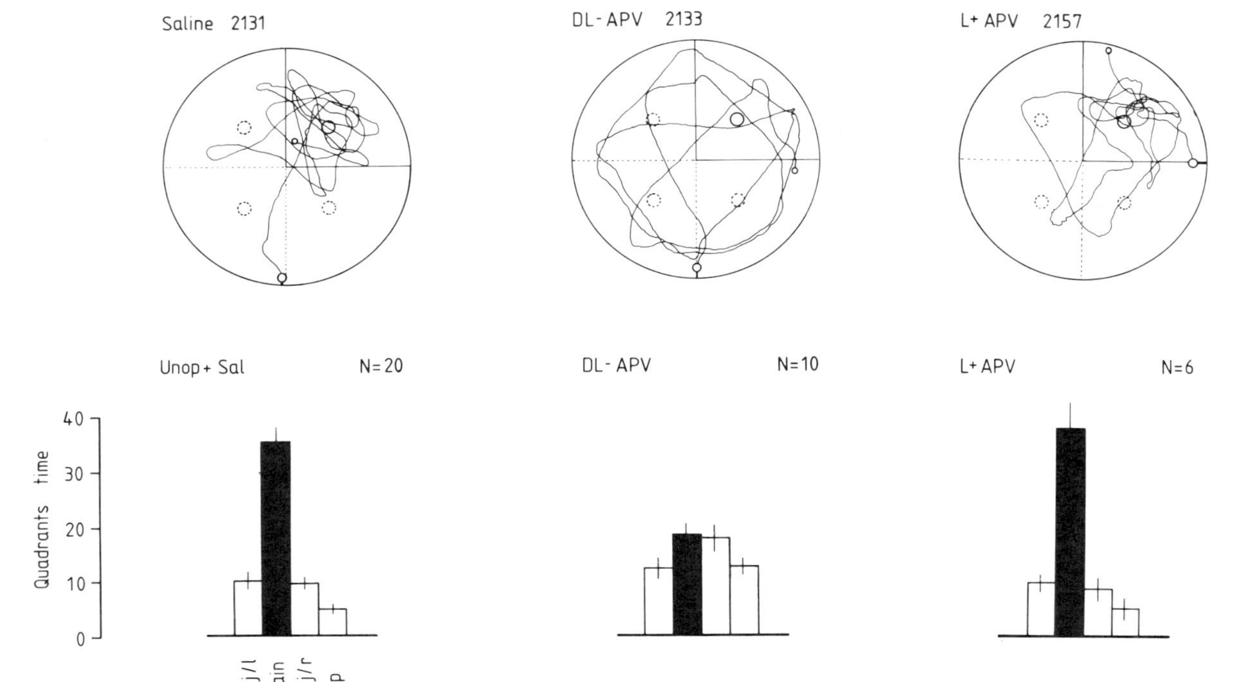


**FIGURE 25.1.** Paths taken (top row) during the transfer test by the three median rats in each group; and (bottom row) mean time spent in each of the four quadrants of the pool by all rats. For each rat shown, the original training quadrant was Northeast. The impairment in distribution of searching by the DL-APV group was highly significant ( $p < .0001$). Adj/l, adjacent quadrant to the left; Adj/r, adjacent quadrant to the right; APV, aminophosphonovaleric acid; Opp, opposite to training quadrant; Unop, unoperated animal (control); Sal, saline; Train, training quadrant.

from modeling amnesia entails taking advantage of the progress made so far. Or as Sir Henry Head put it, "It is not the injury that should capture our attention . . . [but] how through injury or disease, normal function is laid bare."

## ACKNOWLEDGMENTS

I am grateful to Michel Baudry and Eric Harris for drawing my attention to APV; to Elizabeth Anderson for her assistance in running the experiment referred to above; and to Marjorie Anderson for assistance in the preparation of the manuscript. This work was supported by a grant from the Medical Research Council (G83/14974N).

## REFERENCES

Aggleton, J. P., & Mishkin, M. Memory impairments following restricted medial thalamic lesions in monkeys. *Experimental Brain Research*, 1983, *52*, 199–209. (a)

Aggleton, J. P., & Mishkin, M. Visual recognition impairment following medial thalamic lesions in monkeys. *Neuropsychologia*, 1983, *21*, 189–197. (b)

Anderson, E., Baudry, M., Lynch, G., & Morris, R. G. M. Selective impairment of learning and blockade of long-term potentiation by an *N*-methyl-D-aspartate receptor antagonist, APV-5. *Nature (London)*, in press.

Ashe, J. H., & Nachman, M. Neural mechanisms in taste aversion learning. In J. M. Sprague & A. E. Epstein (Eds.), *Progress in psychobiology and physiological psychology* (Vol. 9). London: Academic Press, 1980.

Cohen, N. J., & Squire, L. R. Preserved learning and retention of pattern-analysing skill in amnesia: Dissociation of knowing how and knowing what. *Science*, 1980, *210*, 207–210.

Collingridge, G. L., Kehl, S. J., & McLennan, H. Excitatory amino acids in synaptic transmission in the Schaffer collateral commissural pathway of the rat hippocampus. *Journal of Physiology (London)*, 1983, *334*, 19–31.

Corkin, S. Lasting consequences of bilateral medial temporal lobectomy: Clinical course and experimental findings in H. M. *Seminars in Neurology*, 1984, *4*, 249–259.

Cotman, C. W., & Nieto-Sampedro, M. Cell biology of synaptic plasticity. *Science*, 1984, *225*, 1287–1293.

Evans, R. H., Francis, A. A., Jones, A. W., Smith, D. A. S., & Watkins, J. C. The effects of a series of ω-phosphonic-carboxylic amino acids on electrically evoked and excitant amino acid induced responses in isolated spinal cord preparations. *British Journal of Pharmacology*, 1982, *75*, 65–75.

Gaffan, D. Hippocampus: Memory, habit and voluntary movement. *Philosophical Transactions of the Royal Society of London, Series B*, 1985, *308*, 87–99.

Gage, F. H., Bjorklund, A., Steneri, U., Dunnett, S. B., & Kelly, P. A. T. Intrahippocampal septal grafts ameliorate learning impairment in aged rats. *Science*, 1984, *225*, 533–536.

Graf, P. R., Squire, L. R., & Mandler, G. The information that amnesic patients do not forget. *Journal of Experimental Psychology*, 1984, *10*, 164–178.

Harris, E. W., Ganong, A. H., & Cotman, C. W. Long-term potentiation in the hippocampus involves activation of *N*-methyl-D-aspartate receptors. *Brain Research*, 1984, *323*, 132–137.

Horel, J. A. The neuroanatomy of amnesia: A critique of the hippocampal memory hypothesis. *Brain*, 1978, *101*, 403–445.

Huppert, F. A., & Piercy, M. Dissociation between learning and remembering in organic amnesia. *Nature (London)*, 1978, *275*, 317–318.

Jarrard, L. E. Selective hippocampal lesions and behaviour: Implications for current research and theorizing. In R. L. Isaacson & K. Pribram (Eds.), *The hippocampus*. New York: Plenum Press, 1985.

Kesner, R. P., & Novak, K. J. Serial postion curve in rats: Role of the dorsal hippocampus. *Science*, 1982, *218*, 173–174.

Lynch, G. S. Synapses, circuits and the beginnings of memory. Manuscript submitted for publication.

Mackintosh, N. J. *Conditioning and associative learning*. London: Oxford University Press, 1983.

Macphail, E. *Brain and intelligence in vertebrates*. London: Oxford University Press, 1982.

Mair, W. G. P., Warrington, E. K., & Weiskrantz, L. Memory disorder in Korsakoff's psychosis. *Brain*, 1979, *102*, 749–783.

Mishkin, M. Memory in monkeys severely impaired by combined but not by separate removal of amygdala and hippocampus. *Nature (London)*, 1978, *273*, 297–298.

Mishkin, M., & Delacour, J. An analysis of short-term visual memory in the monkey. *Journal of Experimental Psychology: Animal Behaviour Processes*, 1975, *1*, 326–334.

Mishkin, M., Malamut, B., & Bachevalier, J. Memories and habits: Two neural systems. In G. Lynch, J. L. McGaugh, & N. M. Weinberger (Eds.), *Neurobiology of learning and memory*. New York: Guilford Press, 1984.

Morris, R. G. M. Modelling amnesia and the study of memory in animals. *Trends in Neurosciences*, 1983, *6*, 479–483.

Morris, R. G. M. Developments of a water-maze procedure for studying spatial learning in the rat. *Journal of Neuroscience Methods*, 1984, *11*, 47–60.

Morris, R. G. M., & Baker, M. Does long-term potentiation/synaptic enhancement have anything to do with learning or memory? In L. R. Squire & N. Butters (Eds.), *Neuropsychology of memory*. New York: Guilford Press, 1984.

Mowrer, O. H., & Miller, N. J. A multi-purpose learning-demonstration apparatus. *Journal of Experimental Psychology*, 1942, *31*, 163–171.

O'Keefe, J., & Nadel, L. *The hippocampus as a cognitive map*. London: Oxford University Press, 1978.

O'Keefe, J., Nadel, L., Keighly, S., & Kill, D. Fornix lesions selectively abolish place-learning in the rat. *Experimental Neurology*, 1975, *48*, 152–166.

Olton, D. S., Becker, J. T., & Handelmann, G. E. Hippocampus, space and memory. *Behavioral and Brain Sciences*, 1979, *2*, 313–315.

Premack, D. The codes of man and beasts. *Behavioral and Brain Sciences*, 1983, *6*, 125–167.

Ramirez, J. J., & Stein, D. G. Sparing and recovery of spatial alternation performance after entorhinal cortex lesions in rats. *Behavioral Brain Research*, 1984, *13*, 53–61.

Rawlins, J. N. P. Associations across time: The hippocampus as a temporary memory store. *Behavioral and Brain Sciences*, in press.

Squire, L. R. Two forms of human amnesia: An analysis of forgetting. *Journal of Neuroscience*, 1981, *1*, 635–640.

Squire, L. R., & Cohen, N. J. Human memory and amnesia. In G. Lynch, J. L. McGaugh, & N. M. Weinberger (Eds.), *Neurobiology of learning and memory*. New York: Guilford Press, 1984.

Sutherland, R. J., Whishaw, I. Q., & Kolb, B. A behavioural analysis of spatial localisation following electrolytic, kainate-, or colchicine-induced damage to the hippocampal formation in the rat. *Behavioral Brain Research*, 1983, *7*, 133–153.

Teyler, T. J., & Discenna, P. Long term potentiation as a candidate mnemonic device. *Brain Research Reviews*, 1984, *7*, 15–28.

Thompson, R. F., Clark, G. A., Donegan, N. H., Lavond, D. G., Lincoln, J. S., Madden, J., IV, Mamounas, L. A., Mauk, M. D., McCormick, D. A., & Thompson, J. K. Neuronal substrates of learning and memory: A "multiple-trace" view. In G. Lynch, J. L. McGaugh, & N. M. Weinberger (Eds.), *Neurobiology of learning and memory*. New York: Guilford Press, 1984.

Tulving, E. *Elements of episodic memory*. London: Oxford University Press, 1984. (a)

Tulving, E. Precis of episodic memory. *Behavioral and Brain Sciences*, 1984, *7*, 223–268. (b)

Weiskrantz, L. Comparative aspects of studies of amnesia. *Philosophical Transactions of the Royal Society of London*, 1982, *298*, 97–109.

Zola-Morgan, S., & Squire, L. R. Preserved learning in monkeys with medial temporal lesions: Sparing of motor and cognitive skills. *Journal of Neuroscience*, 1984, *4*, 1072–1085.

Zola-Morgan, S., Squire, L. R., & Mishkin, M. The neuroanatomy of amnesia: Amygdalar hippocampus vs. temporal stem. *Science*, 1982, *218*, 1337–1339.

CHAPTER 26

# Complementary Approaches to the Study of Memory: Human Amnesia and Animal Models

**Stuart Zola-Morgan**
**Larry R. Squire**
Veterans Administration Medical Center, San Diego
and University of California, San Diego

One of the hopes for behavioral neuroscience is that information about neural systems and function obtained from experimental animals will eventually illuminate the biological foundations of cognition in humans. The problem of memory holds particular promise in this regard because memory can be studied in experimental animals at both the cellular and neural systems levels and because the work with animals has begun to make contact with neurological and neuropsychological studies of human memory and amnesia. Human amnesia itself has been illuminating because the disorder can be strikingly selective and severe and because analysis of the deficit can suggest how the damaged neural systems contribute to normal memory function. This kind of information could, in principle, guide animal work in a number of ways as well as lead to more detailed neurobiological studies.

For several reasons, neuropsychological approaches to human amnesia have begun only recently to live up to this promise. Historically, descriptions of memory problems were often based on anecdotes or clinical impressions, particularly in the domain of retrograde amnesia. Neuropathological information was seldom available in patients who had been carefully tested. Even now, the amnesic patients available for study often are an etiologically mixed group, have lesions of uncertain location, and sometimes have additional lesions that do not themselves cause amnesia but do alter the presentation of the memory disorder.

In recent years, neuropsychological work has become more rigorous and uniform. Standing populations of patients with similar etiologies have become available for continuous study, and the work has begun to yield cumulative information. These developments promise to resolve a number of issues that have been long debated. (1) Does amnesia consist of a single disorder or of multiple disorders? (2) Where are the effective lesions? (3) How severe is the impairment in individual patient populations and how can one compare across studies that involve different patients? This chapter outlines briefly the present status of these issues.

## AMNESIA: UNITARY OR MULTIPLE DISORDER?

Whether the brain is highly differentiated and specialized or whether large brain regions operate as equipotential, nondissociable entities has been a focus for discussion throughout the history of neuroscience. Although functional information is still very primitive, dissociable brain systems that relate to particular aspects of behavior can be identified. Moreover, certain syndromes that were originally described very broadly, such as the Klüver–Bucy syndrome, have been fractionated into functional components with distinct loci. In the case of amnesia, the syndrome has long been linked to medial temporal or diencephalic damage. Damage to these brain regions causes difficulty establishing new memories as well as difficulty retrieving information learned before the onset of amnesia.

A central question is whether careful analysis of amnesia will reveal multiple systems contributing to memory functions. There are three possibilities. First, the brain areas damaged in amnesia might operate together as a unitary functional system that cannot be divided into smaller functional units in any meaningful fashion. Second, the areas damaged in amnesia might contribute to memory processing in different ways. For example, differences might exist in the contributions made by the medial temporal and diencephalic regions even if the two regions belonged to a neural system that functions together in some sense. A third possibility, independent of the first two, is that certain features of impaired performance, ordinarily considered an integral part of the amnesic disorder, might turn out to be unrelated to amnesia and to depend on damage outside the medial temporal and diencephalic areas.

Weiskrantz (Chapter 21, this volume) adopts the view that the memory impairment in amnesic patients reflects a unitary disorder affecting both the establishment of new memories and the retrieval of old memories. According to this view, the deficit is qualitatively the same regardless of which part of the system is damaged. However, there are several aspects of amnesia that suggest a different view. In the first place, during the past decade the core disorder in amnesia has been repeatedly redefined as particular deficits have been dissociated from amnesia. For example, frontal lobe dysfunction leads to certain phenomena, such as failure to release from proactive interference (Moscovitch, 1982) and special difficulty in making temporal order judgments (Milner, 1971), that might have been taken as obligatory to amnesia because they typically occur in patients with Korsakoff syndrome. However, because these features are absent in amnesic patients whose memory impairment is as severe as that seen in Korsakoff patients (Cermak, 1976; Squire, 1982b), they are no longer considered essential components of anterograde or retrograde amnesia. Indeed, the importance of identifying deficits that are dissociable from amnesia is widely recognized (see Moscovitch, 1982; Squire, 1982a; Weiskrantz, Chapter 21, this volume; Weiskrantz & Warrington, 1975).

Amnesia has also been defined more narrowly as the result of demonstrations that some memory functions are preserved in amnesia (motor skills, cognitive skills, and priming; Schacter, Chapter 20, this volume; Squire & Cohen, 1984; Weiskrantz, Chapter 21, this volume). These developments mean that it is difficult to know *a priori* what features of amnesia must appear together, and it is reasonable to suppose that more dissociations will be found. As each dissociation is demonstrated and confirmed, the concept of unitary disorder can be retained only by revising its meaning and applying it to a smaller set of deficits.

One recent focus of interest concerns the forgetting rates exhibited by different amnesic patients. A technique was used in which patients were given more exposure to stimulus material than were normal subjects—to equate performance at short learning-retention intervals. Forgetting rates were then assessed across longer intervals. It was suggested originally that H. M. had a rapid forgetting rate and that Korsakoff patients had a normal rate (Huppert & Piercy, 1979). These findings were ambiguous because H. M. was more amnesic than were the patients with Korsakoff syndrome and because the data for H. M. were difficult to interpret (Squire & Cohen, 1984). More recent results for H. M., using the same technique, suggested that he forgets at a normal rate (Freed, Corkin, & Cohen, 1984), but the data were variable and sometimes nonmonotonic.

The possibility that forgetting rate might be a neuropsychological signature of different forms of amnesia was placed on firmer ground by the finding that patients prescribed electroconvulsive therapy (ECT) and patients with Korsakoff syndrome differed in forgetting rates, despite an equivalent severity of amnesia (Squire, 1981). Whether forgetting rates will consistently dissociate forms of amnesia depends on a matching of amnesic patients with respect to initial learning ability and on the use of sensitive measures of forgetting. Ideally, one should compare two groups of patients with known lesions and an equivalent severity of amnesia. The importance of forgetting rates has not yet been resolved, and studies of monkeys with identified surgical lesions will probably be needed to settle this issue.

The status of remote (premorbid) memory is also relevant to the problem of how to characterize amnesia. Remote memory can be nearly intact in amnesia or severely affected across all the decades of adult life. The question is what determines its extent and severity. In some instances, it is clear that the extent of retrograde amnesia is correlated with the severity of anterograde amnesia (e.g., in traumatic amnesia; Russell & Nathan, 1946), and it has been presumed to be correlated with anterograde amnesia in the case of medial temporal amnesia (Squire, Cohen, & Nadel, 1984; Weiskrantz, Chapter 21, this volume; Wickelgren, 1979).

In other instances, and particularly in patients with diencephalic lesions, the relationship between anterograde and retrograde amnesia is less clear. Consider first the best-studied example of diencephalic amnesia, Korsakoff syndrome. Patients with Korsakoff syndrome exhibit a severe and extensive impairment of remote memory that affects the majority of their adult lives (Albert, Butters, & Levin, 1979; Cohen & Squire, 1981; Meudell, Northern, Snowden, & Neary, 1980; Sanders & Warrington, 1971; Seltzer & Benson, 1974). The remote memory impairment in these patients appears to be distinct from and not related to their anterograde amnesia. In one recent study eight patients with Korsakoff syndrome (Shimamura & Squire, in press) were given nine tests of anterograde amnesia and two tests of remote memory covering the past four decades (1940s–1970s). The severity of anterograde amnesia correlated only with the ability to remember events that had occurred in the 1970s. Test questions about the 1970s probably measured the anterograde amnesia that was already present or developing during that time period. There was no correlation between the severity of anterograde amnesia and the overall severity of remote memory. Thus, the ability to recall very remote events seems to depend on mechanisms distinct from those required for new learning and for recall of more recent events.

Two cases reported by Mair, Warrington, and Weiskrantz (1979) support this point. On tests of anterograde amnesia (p. 757), the two patients performed similarly. Patient H. J. actually performed slightly more poorly than did patient E. A. on three tests and the same as E. A. on a fourth. Yet, on a multiple-choice test of remote memory (p. 756), patient E. A. was distinctly more impaired. The same point has been made previously, based on comparisons between patients with Korsakoff syndrome, a severely amnesic postencephalitic patient (S. S.), and other patients (Butters, Milliotis, Albert, & Sax, 1984; Cohen & Squire, 1981). The remote memory impairment associated with Korsakoff syndrome and patient S. S. is both more severe and more extensive than that in most other groups of amnesic patients, even though the severity of anterograde amnesia compared across groups can be similar.

Perhaps the best example of this point comes from a study of memory for famous faces involving diencephalic amnesic patients with Korsakoff syndrome and patient H. M. with bilateral medial temporal lesions (Marslen-Wilson & Teuber, 1975). H. M. performed worse than the average Korsakoff patient at recognizing faces from the 1950s and 1960s (H. M. became amnesic in 1953). Indeed, H. M.'s anterograde amnesia is widely recognized to be more severe than that of most other amnesic patients that are available for study. Yet, H. M. was normal at recognizing faces from the 1940s and 1930s, whereas the Korsakoff patients were markedly impaired. More recent studies of H. M. have found on some tests evidence for remote memory impairment covering a period up to 11 years prior to his surgery (Corkin, 1984). Yet H. M. was still able to recall well-formed episodes of particular events from before that time and to score normally on tests that asked about events from before that time. In this respect he clearly excels over other amnesic patients who have been carefully studied (e.g., Butters *et al.*, 1984; Cermak, 1976; Cohen & Squire, 1981; Damasio, Eslinger, Damasio, Van Hoesen, & Cornell, 1985).

Apparently, a severe and extensive remote memory impairment does not inevitably follow from severe anterograde amnesia, and an extensive remote memory impairment is a dissociable deficit from anterograde amnesia. This same idea has been discussed by others (Butters *et al.*, 1984; Goldberg, Antin, Bilder, Hughes, & Mattis, 1981; Parkin, 1984). To confirm this idea, and to determine what is responsible for extensive remote memory impairment, it will be necessary to apply the best possible neuropsychological techniques. Unfortunately, many case reports still evaluate retrograde amnesia only by informal interview. Formal tests must be used, and even they are sometimes not sensitive enough to detect remote memory impairment when it is present, unless they go beyond multiple-choice methods (Cohen & Squire, 1981). Moreover, patient groups must always be rigorously compared with respect to anterograde amnesia, if anything meaningful is to be concluded about the relationship between anterograde amnesia and remote memory.

## WHERE ARE THE LESIONS? ANIMAL MODELS OF AMNESIA

Whereas careful neuropsychological descriptions of amnesic patients have contributed enormously to the understanding of how memory is organized in the brain, it has also become clear that the final resolution of many of the issues depends significantly on knowing the specific brain structures that, when damaged, cause amnesia. Identification of the sites of damage would provide independent criteria for neuropsychological analysis. Which lesions lead to which neuropsychological findings? Are there lesions within the medial temporal and diencephalic structures linked to amnesia that produce different deficits? Which features of amnesia depend on lesions within these structures, and which depend on other lesions?

Clinicopathological material from amnesic patients with diencephalic and medial temporal lesions has been accumulating since the last decade of the 19th century (Bechterev, 1900; Gudden, 1896). In trying to piece together from this literature whether damage to a particular structure causes amnesia, one encounters two problems. First, information about the extent of damage is based on lesions that do not neatly honor neuroanatomical boundaries and often on an incomplete analysis of areas of the brain that appear normal on gross examination. Second, quantitative data describing the memory impairment often are not available. In the case of patients with Korsakoff syndrome, for example, the mammillary bodies and the mediodorsal thalamic nucleus frequently have been correlated with the amnesia. However, it is not yet clear which of these structures deserves the most emphasis, and it is not known whether they must be damaged in combination (Mair *et al.*, 1979; Squire, 1982a; Victor, Adams, & Collins, 1971).

Patients with amnesia and diencephalic lesions other than those with Korsakoff syndrome are also pertinent to this issue. Bilateral infarctions resulting from occlusion of the thalamo-subthalamic paramedian artery can produce severe memory loss (Mills & Swanson, 1978; Winocur, Oxbury, Roberts, Agnetti, & Davis 1984), and damage to the mediodorsal nucleus is common to all the reported cases (Guberman & Stuss, 1983). In addition, for N. A., who has material-specific amnesia for verbal material (Kaushall, Zetin, & Squire, 1981; Teuber, Milner, & Vaughan, 1968), radiographic evidence has identified a lesion in the region of the left mediodorsal thalamic nucleus (Squire & Moore, 1979). These data suggest that damage to the mediodorsal nucleus, without damage to the mammillary bodies, are sufficient to cause amnesia.

N. A.'s amnesia is the result of an accident in 1960, when a miniature fencing foil entered his brain through the right nostril. There must be some additional damage beyond the dorsal thalamus as a result of the path taken by the foil. Moreover, N. A. has mild paralysis of upward gaze, a condition implying damage in the pretectal region, which is located just caudal to the mediodorsal nucleus. However, the presumed pretectal lesion need not have been caused by the foil directly because vertical gaze paralysis and memory loss can occur together following a single circumscribed neurological event—infarction of the territory supplied by the paramedian artery (Mills & Swanson, 1978). In any case, N. A.'s memory impairment does raise the important question of whether the mammillary bodies could have been damaged by the foil. Considering the position of the mammillary bodies in the ventral surface of the brain and the fact that the foil passed through the base of the skull, this is a reasonable possibility.

We have tried to resolve this question using an intact male human cadaver to determine what structures could be damaged when the brain is penetrated through the nasal passage. A hand-held, sharp trocar (approximately 2.0 mm in diameter) was introduced into the right nostril through the base of the skull and into the brain. The trocar was filled with blue latex solution before removing it, so that the path taken by the trocar could later be reconstructed. A number of passes were attempted, but despite repeated attempts by a full-grown adult male to push the trocar through, the thickness of the skull prevented entry into the brain except in the area of the cribriform plate. We made three separate passes through the cribriform plate, each at a different angle relative to the base of the skull. Two passes went through frontal cortex and ended in the genu of the corpus callosum. In a third pass, we attempted the most oblique angle in a posterior direction that would still allow penetration of the skull. In this case, the trocar passed through the sphenoid bone at the border of the cribriform plate, just anterior to the sphenoid sinus, and it entered the brain anterior to both the optic chiasm and the pituitary stalk. The path was approximately 1 cm in front of the border of the mammillary bodies, and it ended in the anterior nucleus of the thalamus, approximately 3 mm from the border of the mediodorsal nucleus.

In none of the attempts were we able to pass the trocar near the mammillary bodies. We were also unable to replicate the angle of approach illustrated in Figure 21.1 of Weiskrantz (Chapter 21, this volume), being limited by the structure of the nasal passage and the bones of the skull [but see a recently reported case of suicide by brain injury (Yamamoto, Yamada, & Sato, 1985), which shows a more ventral pathway]. Although direct injury to the mammillary bodies is unlikely to have occurred in N. A., precisely which structures are damaged in his case remains uncertain. The radiographic evidence, which shows a lucency in the region of the mediodorsal nucleus, can reveal only the minimal extent of the damage. For example, if the anterior nucleus were damaged in conjunction with the mediodorsal thalamic nucleus, then some retrograde degeneration could be expected in the mammillary bodies. This case, like the others in the human neuropathological literature, have not yet settled definitively the question of which specific diencephalic structures are important for memory functions (Squire, 1980, p. 53).

Recent successes in developing an animal model of amnesia in the monkey (Mishkin, Spiegler, Saunders, & Malamut, 1982; Squire & Zola-Morgan, 1983; Zola-Morgan & Squire, 1985a) will enable investigators to identify empirically the specific structures in the diencephalon and medial temporal region that must be damaged to cause amnesia. Two recent studies showed that thalamic lesions including the mediodorsal nucleus caused amnesia in monkeys (Aggleton & Mishkin, 1983a, 1983b); a third showed that even a small lesion limited to the posterior portion of the mediodorsal nucleus produced a marked memory deficit (Zola-Morgan & Squire, 1985b).

It has been difficult to produce circumscribed and selective lesions of the mammillary bodies because of their proximity to life-sustaining brain stem areas and to the blood supply of the circle of Willis. Four laboratories (Aggleton & Mishkin, 1985; Holmes, Jacobson, Stein, & Butters, 1983; Saunders, 1983, 1984; Zola-Morgan & Squire, in preparation) have successfully produced mammillary body lesions in monkeys; and studies are currently underway to determine whether these lesions cause amnesia. One study reported only a mild memory impairment following mammillary body lesions (Aggleton & Mishkin, 1985). The deficit was less severe in the monkeys with mammillary body lesions than in monkeys tested in the same task following lesions of the anterior (Aggleton & Mishkin, 1983b) or posterior

(Zola-Morgan & Squire, 1985b) portion of the mediodorsal nucleus. Further studies with animals should be able to determine whether combined damage to the mammillary bodies and mediodorsal nucleus produces a greater memory impairment than damage to either structure alone and whether other diencephalic lesions produce amnesia. The animal models move the problem of the neuroanatomy of amnesia beyond the uncertain human neuropathological literature and provide a way to develop quantitative, cumulative information.

## SELECTION AND QUANTITATIVE TESTING OF PATIENTS

Although at this stage neuroanatomical questions about memory will probably be answered more satisfactorily by work with monkeys than by studies of patient material, there can be no substitute for careful neuropsychological analysis of patients. Yet here, too, the work in monkeys makes an important point. Study of monkeys has benefited from the ability to compare across laboratories quantitative scores obtained from the same tasks. Although it is relatively straightforward to quantify memory impairment in patients, it has not been so easy to compare results across studies. Two commonly used instruments—delayed prose recall and paired-associate learning—are helpful; but often study patients score close to zero on these tests, so that only coarse comparisons between studies can be made (Squire, 1985). Multiple-choice recognition tests of the kind used by Warrington (1984) in her battery might be helpful, although here, too, amnesic patients can score at only 61% correct for verbal material and 55% correct for nonverbal material (chance = 50%; Warrington, 1974).

The best approach at this time probably is to follow the standing populations of patients that have been tested repeatedly over a number of years. Published test results for such patients provide a cumulative record of quantitative information that can be used for comparison in other investigations. A more satisfactory method would be to develp a set of standard tests that are free of floor and ceiling effects and that could come into such regular use that their results would be reported in the "Subjects" section of all experimental reports involving amnesic patients.

The Wechsler Memory Scale (WMS) is commonly used, and it provides a rough estimate of the severity of the deficit. However, the WMS has long been regarded as inadequate for this purpose because much of the test measures functions that are not affected in amnesia. Accordingly, amnesic patients can score less than two standard deviations below normal on the WMS (IQ − MQ differences of 20–30 points), even though the same patients deviate from normal subjects by three standard deviations or more on conventional memory tests such as list learning, paired-associate learning, and delayed recall. For example, consider the results for paired-associate learning obtained by control subjects and by amnesic patients studied in our laboratory. Subjects are given three successive trials to learn ten unrelated word pairs (Jones, 1974). The total number of pairs recalled correctly after three trials (maximum score = 30) was 24.8 ± 2.71 (mean ± standard deviation) for 6 healthy control subjects, 19.2 ± 7.21 for 35 alcoholic control subjects, and 22.1 ± 4.2 for 19 medical inpatients. Eight patients with Korsakoff syndrome averaged 2.4 ± 1.6, three other amnesic patients (hypoxic ischemia) averaged 2.8 ± 1.7, and N. A. scored 2.0. The IQ − MQ differences were 24.6, 23.7, and 27 for the Korsakoff patients, the three amnesic patients, and N. A., respectively.

Despite the problems associated with the available tests, they have been widely used, and something is known about the relative severity of memory impairment in different patient populations. Patients with Korsakoff syndrome constitute the largest class of amnesic study subjects, and these have been studied especially in Boston, London (England), Manchester (England), and San Diego. The IQ − MQ difference for these populations averages 20–30 points (Butters & Cermak, 1980; Meudell *et al.*, 1980; Squire, 1982b). IQ − MQ differences have not been reported for the patients studied in London (England). Nevertheless, it seems reasonable to suppose that these amnesic groups are all roughly similar in severity. Winocur gave the same multipart memory test to British amnesic patients (three Korsakoff patients, one post encephalitic patient, and one patient of unknown etiology) and to Korsakoff patients in the London (Ontario, Canada) and Boston areas (Winocur & Kinsbourne, 1978; Winocur & Weiskrantz, 1976). They performed nearly identically (Table 1, p. 673, Winocur & Kinsbourne, 1978). Moreover, San Diego patients obtained nearly the same score as the British patients after two presentations of related paired associates (Shimamura & Squire, 1984; Winocur & Weiskrantz, 1976). What adjective one selects to label the severity of these patients (mild, moderate, severe) can be debated. But patients with MQ − IQ differences of 20–30 who fail at paired-associate learning and delayed recall are so impaired that they live abnormal lives in supervised environments. It seems inappropriate to term such patients mildly amnesic, although recognizing this point does not deny that amnesia can be even more severe (e.g., patient H. M.).

In addition to comparing the severity of amnesia across patient groups, it is also important to screen patients (especially the heterogeneous Korsakoff group) for signs of cognitive impairment beyond memory. Tests of parietal lobe function (which emphasize constructional abilities and spatial orientation) and tests of frontal lobe function are especially useful in this regard. The point is that findings from amnesic patients are most valuable when the deficit is very circumscribed.

## PROGRESS

One point on which there has been striking agreement in recent years is that amnesia spares some memory functions. The learning of specific skills and the phenomenon of priming are intact. Preserved skill learning has also been demonstrated in monkeys with medial temporal lesions (Zola-Morgan & Squire, 1984). These findings provide evidence for the existence of multiple memory systems. One distinction derived from the neuropsychological work contrasts declarative memory, which is impaired in amnesia, and procedural memory, which is spared (Cohen, 1981; Squire & Cohen, 1984). Similar distinctions have been suggested by others (see Squire & Zola-Morgan, 1985).

Historically, it took some time for the idea of multiple memory systems to come to the foreground. It was shown more than 20 years ago that a perceptuo-motor skill could be learned by an amnesic patient (Milner, 1962), but discussions of memory and amnesia tended to set aside these motor-skill data and to adhere to a unitary view for the rest of memory. It was also recognized that short-term and long-term memory were distinct and that amnesia spared certain old, well-established memories, such as vocabulary (Warrington, 1979), but amnesia was still considered to affect all new learning except motor skills.

Demonstrations of unexpectedly good learning and retention by amnesic patients on other than motor-skill tasks date back to 1968 (Milner, Corkin, & Teuber, 1968; Warrington & Weiskrantz, 1968). However, there were two reasons why these findings, and those that followed in the next several years, did not lead to proposals of multiple memory systems. First, even when the performance of amnesic patients was good, it often fell short of normal levels. Second, in those cases where amnesic patients appeared to perform normally, some favored the explanation that amnesia was therefore a retrieval deficit (Warrington & Weiskrantz, 1970, 1974, 1978). Even as recently as the late 1970s, it was possible to dismiss the idea of multiple memory systems (Weiskrantz, 1978, p. 380 ff.) and to propose that the deficit lay in accessing memory (Weiskrantz, 1978, pp. 378, 385; Weiskrantz & Warrington, 1979).

At the same time, quite apart from issues of interpretation, there was uncertainty about the claim that amnesic patients could sometimes perform normally. For example, amnesic patients had been reported to perform normally on tests that used three-letter word stems as cues for previously presented words (Warrington & Weiskrantz, 1974, 1978), that is, a demonstration of what would later be termed priming. Because the critical importance of the instructions given to the subjects at retention testing was not widely appreciated, several laboratories failed to confirm the original findings (Mayes, Meudell, & Neary, 1978; Mortensen, 1980; Squire, Wetzel, & Slater, 1978; Wetzel & Squire, 1980); and the theoretical importance of these early findings was therefore overlooked.

Later it was shown that only one kind of instruction resulted in normal performance by amnesic patients (e.g., "use this stem to form the first word that comes to mind"); whereas with conventional memory instructions (e.g., "use this cue to find the previously presented word"), normal subjects always performed better than amnesic patients (Graf, Squire, & Mandler, 1984). The fact that amnesic patients can perform normally when the three-letter cue test is structured appropriately, that is, that amnesic patients exhibit normal priming effects, is now generally taken as evidence for the operation of a separate memory process or system, one that is spared in amnesia (Warrington & Weiskrantz, 1982; Schacter, Chapter 20, this volume; Squire & Cohen, 1984). This formulation is, of course, independent of the interpretation given to the impaired functions of (declarative) memory that do occur in amnesia, for example, whether there is an impairment in encoding, consolidation, or retrieval. This question has been considered at length elsewhere (Squire, 1982a; Squire & Cohen, 1984).

The other important insight that led to the idea of multiple memory systems was that motor skills are not separate and special after all, but rather they are a subset of a larger domain of learning and memory that includes cognitive skills. Both motor and cognitive skills are spared in amnesia. A number of reports of long-term retention by amnesic patients had already accumulated by the late 1970s (see Cohen, 1981; Squire & Cohen, 1984; Weiskrantz, 1978), although many were either anecdotal or based on studies that did not include a control group to determine whether amnesic patients actually performed normally. More formal studies (e.g., Brooks & Baddeley, 1976; Cohen, 1981; Cohen & Squire, 1980) confirmed that amnesic patients can be entirely intact at several kinds of skill learning. Because the kind of information acquired successfully by amnesic patients seemed to differ in a principled way from the kind of information that they could not acquire, a distinction was suggested between kinds of memory or memory systems (Baddeley, 1982; Cohen, 1981; Cohen & Squire, 1980; Moscovitch, 1982; Warrington & Weiskrantz, 1982; Wickelgren, 1979). A similar point of view had developed even earlier in the animal literature, based on the behavioral effects of damage to the limbic system (Gaffan, 1974; Hirsch, 1974; O'Keefe & Nadel, 1978), and the most recent treatments of this issue seem to bring the animal work and the human work into close correspondence (Mishkin, Malamut, & Bachevalier, 1984; Mishkin *et al.*, 1982; Squire & Zola-Morgan, 1983; Weiskrantz, 1982).

## PERSPECTIVE

This is a promising time for neuropsychological work on these problems. Through parallel study of human amnesic patients and animal models, it should be possible to identify the structures that, when damaged, produce amnesia, relate these to neural systems, and these to function in experimental animals and humans. One difficulty here is the simple fact that amnesic patients differ in terms of their pattern of lesions and in terms of what damage is present in addition to the damage that causes anterograde amnesia. It will be necessary to match groups of patients in terms of particular memory deficits and then to determine their pattern of performance on other aspects of memory function. The work will require thorough and repeated neuropsychological studies of standing populations and cooperation among laboratories.

## ACKNOWLEDGMENTS

This work was supported by the Medical Research Service of the Veterans Administration, by NIH Grant NS19063, and by NIMH Grant MH24600. We thank Dr. Arthur Shimamura for his critical discussions of the issues considered here and Drs. David Amaral and Mark Kritchevsky for their invaluable assistance in carrying out the trocar pathway experiment. We also thank Mr. John Sykes, curator of the prosectorium, University of California, San Diego, School of Medicine.

## REFERENCES

Aggleton, J. P., & Mishkin, M. Visual recognition impairment following medial thalamic lesions in monkeys. *Neuropsychologia*, 1983, *21*, 189–197. (a)

Aggleton, J. P., & Mishkin, M. Memory impairments following restricted medial thalamic lesions in monkeys. *Experimental Brain Research*, 1983, *52*, 199–209. (b)

Aggleton, J. P., & Mishkin, M. Mammillary-body lesions and visual recognition in the monkey. *Experimental Brain Research*, 1985, *58*, 190–197.

Albert, M. S., Butters, N., & Levin, J. Temporal gradients in retrograde amnesia of patients with alcoholic Korsakoff's disease. *Archives of Neurology*, 1979, *36*, 211–216.

Baddeley, A. Amnesia: A minimal model and an interpretation. In L. Cermak (Ed.), *Human memory and amnesia*. Hillsdale, N.J.: Erlbaum, 1982.

Bechterev, W. V. von. Demonstration eines Gehirns mit Zerstorung der vorderen und inneren Theile der Hirnrinde beider Schlaffenlappen. *Neurologisches Centralblatt*, 1900, *19*, 990–991.

Brooks, D. N., & Baddeley, A. What can amnesic patients learn? *Neuropsychologia*, 1976, *14*, 111–122.

Butters, N., & Cermak, L. S. *Alcoholic Korsakoff syndrome: An information processing approach to amnesia*. New York: Academic Press, 1980.

Butters, N., Milliotis, P., Albert, M. S., & Sax, D. S. Memory assessment: Evidence of the heterogeneity of amnesic symptoms. In G. Goldstein (Ed.), *Advances in clinical neuropsychology* (Vol. 1). New York: Plenum, 1984.

Cermak, L. S. The encoding capacity of a patient with amnesia due to encephalitis. *Neuropsychologia*, 1976, *14*, 311–326.

Cohen, N. J. *Neuropsychological evidence for a distinction between procedural and declarative knowledge in human memory and amnesia*. Unpublished doctoral thesis, University of California, San Diego, 1981.

Cohen, N. J., & Squire, L. R. Preserved learning and retention of pattern analyzing skill in amnesia: Dissociation of knowing how and knowing that. *Science*, 1980, *210*, 207–209.

Cohen, N. J., & Squire, L. R. Retrograde amnesia and remote memory impairment. *Neuropsychologia*, 1981, *19*, 337–356.

Corkin, S. Lasting consequences of bilateral medial temporal lobectomy: Clinical course and experimental findings in H. M. *Seminars in Neurology*, 1984, *4*, 249–259.

Damasio, A. R., Eslinger, P. J., Damasio, H., Van Hoesen, G. W., & Cornell, S. Multimodal amnesic syndrome following bilateral temporal and basal forebrain damage. *Archives of Neurology*, 1985, *42*, 252–259.

Freed, D. M., Cohen, N. J., & Corkin, S. Rate of forgetting in H. M.: A reanalysis. *Society for Neuroscience Abstracts*, 1984, *10*, 383.

Gaffan, D. Recognition impaired and association intact in the memory of monkeys after transection of the fornix. *Journal of Comparative and Physiological Psychology*, 1974, *86*, 1100–1109.

Goldberg, E., Antin, S. P., Bilder, R. M., Jr., Hughes, J. E. O., & Mattis, S. Retrograde amnesia: Possible role of mesencephalic reticular activation in long-term memory. *Science*, 1981, *213*, 1392–1394.

Graf, P., Squire, L. R., & Mandler, G. The information that amnesic patients do not forget. *Journal of Experimental Psychology: Learning, Memory and Cognition*, 1984, *10*, 164–178.

Guberman, A., & Stuss, D. The syndrome of bilateral paramedian thalamic infarction. *Neurology (Cleveland)*, 1983, *33*, 540–546.

Gudden, H. Klinische und anatomische Beitrage zur Kenntnis der miltiplen Alkoholneuritis nebst Bemerkungen uber die Regenerationsvorgang im peripheren Nervensystem. *Archiv für Psychiatrie und Nervenkrank-heiten*, 1896, *28*, 643–741.

Hirsch, R. The hippocampus and contextual retrieval of information from memory: A theory. *Behavioral Biology*, 1974, *12*, 421–444.

Holmes, E. J., Jacobson, S., Stein, B. M., & Butters, N. Ablations of the mammillary nuclei in monkeys: Effects on postoperative memory. *Experimental Neurology*, 1983, *81*, 97–113.

Huppert, F. A., & Piercy, M. Normal and abnormal forgetting in organic amnesia: Effects of locus of lesion. *Cortex*, 1979, *15*, 385–390.

Jones, M. K. Imagery as a mnemonic aid after left temporal lobectomy: Contrast between material-specific and generalized memory disorders. *Neuropsychologia*, 1974, *12*, 21–30.

Kaushall, P. I., Zetin, M., & Squire, L. R. A psychosocial study of chronic, circumscribed amnesia. *Journal of Nervous and Mental Disease*, 1981, *169*, 383–389.

Mair, W. G. P., Warrington, E. K., & Weiskrantz, L. Memory disorder in Korsakoff psychosis. A neuropathological and neuropsychological investigation of two cases. *Brain*, 1979, *102*, 749–783.

Marslen-Wilson, W. D., & Teuber, H. -L. Memory for remote events in anterograde amnesia: Recognition of public figures from newsphotographs. *Neuropsychologia*, 1975, *13*, 353–364.

Mayes, A. R., Meudell, P. R., & Neary, D. Must amnesia be caused by either encoding or retrieval disorders? In M. M. Bruneberg, P. E. Morris, & R. N. Sykes (Eds.), *Practical aspects of memory*. London: Academic Press, 1978.

Meudell, P. R., Northern, B., Snowden, J. S., & Neary, D. Long-term memory for famous voices in amnesic and normal subjects. *Neuropsychologia*, 1980, *18*, 133–139.

Mills, R. P., & Swanson, P. D. Vertical oculomotor apraxia and memory loss. *Annals of Neurology*, 1978, *4*, 149–153.

Milner, B. Les troubles de la mémoire accompagnant des lésions hippocampiques bilatérales. In P. Passouant (Ed.), *Physiologie de l'hippocampe*. Paris: Centre National de la Recherche Scientifique, 1962.

Milner, B. Interhemispheric differences in the localization of psychological processes in man. *British Medical Bulletin*, 1971, *27*, 272–277.

Milner, B., Corkin, S., & Teuber, H. -L. Further analysis of the hippocampal amnesic syndrome: 14-year follow-up study of H. M. *Neuropsychologia*, 1968, *6*, 215–234.

Mishkin, M., Malamut, B., & Bachevalier, J. Memories and habits: Two neural systems. In G. Lynch, J. L. McGaugh, & N. Weinberger (Eds.), *Neurobiology of learning and memory*. New York: Guilford Press, 1984.

Mishkin, M., Spiegler, B. J., Saunders, R. C., & Malamut, B. J. An animal model of global amnesia. In S. Corkin, K. L. Davis, J. H. Growdon, E. Usdin, & R. J. Wurtman (Eds.), *Toward a treatment of Alzheimer's disease*. New York: Raven Press, 1982.

Moretensen, E. L. The effects of partial infromation in amnesic and normal subjects. *Scandanavian Journal of Psychology*, 1980, *21*, 75–82.

Moscovitch, M. Multiple dissociations of function in amnesia. In L. Cermak (Ed.), *Human memory and amnesia*. Hillsdale, N.J.: Erlbaum, 1982.

O'Keefe, J., & Nadel, L. *The hippocampus as a cognitive map*. London: Oxford University Press, 1978.

Parkin, A. J. Amnesic syndrome: A lesion-specific disorder? *Cortex*, 1984, *20*, 479–508.

Russell, W. R., & Nathan, P. W. Traumatic amnesia. *Brain*, 1946, *69*, 290–300.

Sanders, H. I., & Warrington, E. K. Memory for remote events in amnesic patients. *Brain*, 1971, *94*, 661–668.

Saunders, R. C. Impairment in recognition memory after mammillary body lesions in monkeys. *Society for Neuroscience Abstracts*, 1983, *9*, 28.

Saunders, R. C. The effects of hippocampal-mammillary body system lesions on association memory in monkeys. *Society for Neuroscience Abstracts*, 1984, *10*, 385.

Seltzer, B., & Benson, D. F. The temporal pattern of retrograde amnesia in Korsakoff's disease. *Neurology*, 1974, *24*, 527–530.

Shimamura, A. P., & Squire, L. R. Paired-associate learning and priming effects in amnesia: A neuropsychological study. *Journal of Experimental Psychology: General*, 1984, *113*, 556–570.

Shimamura, A. P., & Squire, L. R. Korsakoff's syndrome: The relationship between anterograde amnesia and remote memory impairment. *Behavioral Neuroscience*, in press.

Squire, L. R. The anatomy of amnesia. *Trends in Neuroscience*, 1980, *3*, 52–54.

Squire, L. R. Two forms of human amnesia: An analysis of forgetting. *Journal of Neuroscience*, 1981, *1*, 635–640.

Squire, L. R. The neuropsychology of human memory. *Annual Review of Neuroscience*, 1982, *5*, 241–273. (a)

Squire, L. R. Comparisons between forms of amnesia: Some deficits are unique to Korsakoff syndrome. *Journal of Experimental Psychology: Learning, Memory and Cognition*, 1982, *8*, 560–571. (b)

Squire, L. R. The neuropsychology of memory dysfunction and its assessment. In I. Grant & K. Adams (Eds.), *Neuropsychological assessment of neuropsychiatric disorders*. New York: Oxford University Press, 1985.

Squire, L. R., & Cohen, N. J. Human memory and amnesia. In G. Lynch, J. L. McGaugh, & N. M. Weinberger (Eds.), *Neurobiology of learning and memory*. New York: Guilford Press, 1984.

Squire, L. R., Cohen, N. J., & Nadel, L. The medial temporal region and memory consolidation: A new hypothesis. In H. Weingartner & E. Parker (Eds.), *Memory consolidation*. Hillsdale, N.J.: Erlbaum, 1984.

Squire, L. R., & Moore, R. Y. Dorsal thalamic lesion in a noted case of chronic memory dysfunction. *Annals of Neurology*, 1979, *6*, 503–506.

Squire, L. R., Wetzel, C. D., & Slater, P. C. Anterograde amnesia following ECT: An analysis of the beneficial effect of partial information. *Neuropsychologia*, 1978, *16*, 339–347.

Squire, L. R., & Zola-Morgan, S. The neurology of memory: The case for correspondence between the findings for human and nonhuman primate. In J. A. Deutsch (Ed.), *The physiological basis of memory* (2nd ed.). New York: Academic Press, 1983.

Squire, L. R., & Zola-Morgan, S. Neuropsychology of memory: New links between humans and experimental animals. In D. Olton, S. Corkin, & E. Gamzu (Eds.), *Conference on Memory Dysfunctions*. New York: New York Academy of Sciences, 1985.

Teuber, H. -L., Milner, B., & Vaughan, H. G. Persistent anterograde amnesia after stab wound of the basal brain. *Neuropsychologia*, 1968, *6*, 267–282.

Victor, M., Adams, R. D., & Collins, G. H. *The Wernicke–Korsakoff syndrome*. Philadelphia: F. A. Davis, 1971.

Warrington, E. K. Deficient recognition memory in organic amnesia. *Cortex*, 1974, *10*, 289–291.

Warrington, E. K. Neuropsychological evidence for multiple memory systems. In *Brain and mind* (CIBA Foundation Symposium). Amsterdam: Elsevier, 1979.

Warrington, E. K. *Recognition memory test*. Windsor: NFER-Nelson, 1984.

Warrington, E. K., & Weiskrantz, L. A new method of testing long-term retention with special reference to amnesic patients. *Nature*, 1968, *217*, 972–974.

Warrington, E. K., & Weiskrantz, L. The amnesic syndrome: Consolidation or retrieval? *Nature*, 1970, *228*, 628–630.

Warrington, E. K., & Weiskrantz, L. The effects of prior learning on subsequent retention in amnesic patients. *Neuropsychologia*, 1974, *12*, 419–428.

Warrington, E. K., & Weiskrantz, L. Further analysis of the prior learning effect in amnesic patients. *Neuropsychologia*, 1978, *16*, 169–177.

Warrington, E. K., & Weiskrantz, L. Amnesia: A disconnection syndrome? *Neuropsychologia*, 1982, *20*, 233–248.

Weiskrantz, L. A comparison of hippocampal pathology in man and other animals. In K. Elliot & J. Whelan (Eds.), *Functions of the septo-hippocampal system* (CIBA Foundation Symposium No. 58). Amsterdam: Elsevier, 1978.

Weiskrantz, L. Comparative aspects of studies of amnesia. In D. E. Broadbent & L. Weiskrantz (Eds.), *Philosophical transactions of the Royal Society of London* (Vol. 298). London: The Royal Society, 1982.

Weiskrantz, L., & Warrington, E. K. The problem of the amnesic syndrome in man and animals. In R. L. Isaacson & K. H. Pribram (Eds.), *The hippocampus* (Vol. 2). New York: Plenum Press, 1975.

Weiskrantz, L., & Warrington, E. K. Conditioning in amnesic patients. *Neuropsychologia*, 1979, *17*, 187–194.

Wetzel, C. D., & Squire, L. R. Encoding in anterograde amnesia. *Neuropsychologia*, 1980, *18*, 177–184.

Wickelgren, W. A. Chunking consolidation: A theoretical synthesis of semantic networks, configuring in conditioning, S-R v. cognitive learning, normal forgetting, the amnesic syndrome and the hippocampal arousal system. *Psychological Review*, 1979, *86*, 44–60.

Winocur, G., & Kinsbourne, M. Contextual cueing as an aid to Korsakoff amnesics. *Neuropsychologia*, 1978, *16*, 671–682.

Winocur, G., Oxbury, S., Roberts, R., Agnetti, V., & Davis, C. Amnesia in a patient with bilateral lesions of the thalamus. *Neuropsychologia*, 1984, *22*, 123–144.

Winocur, G., & Weiskrantz, L. An investigation of paired-associate learning in amnesic patients. *Neuropsychologia*, 1976, *14*, 97–110.

Yamamoto, I., Yamada, S., & Sato, O. Unusual craniocerebral penetrating injury by a chopstick. *Surgical Neurology*, 1985, *23*, 396–398.

Zola-Morgan, S., & Squire, L. R. Preserved learning in monkeys with medial temporal lesions: Sparing of motor and cognitive skills. *Journal of Neuroscience*, 1984, *4*, 1072–1085.

Zola-Morgan, S., & Squire, L. R. Medial temporal lesions in monkeys impair memory in a variety of tasks sensitive to amnesia. *Behavioral Neuroscience*, 1985, *99*, 22–34. (a)

Zola-Morgan, S., & Squire, L. R. Amnesia in monkeys after lesions of the mediodorsal nucleus of the thalamus. *Annals of Neurology*, 1985, *17*, 558–564.(b)

Zola-Morgan, S., & Squire, L. R. In preparation.

# AUTHOR INDEX


Abdul-Ghani, A.-S., 323, 330*n*.
Abraham, W. C., 64–68, 70, 72, 73, 75*n*., 107, 108, 116, 120, 136, 138, 139, 146*n*., 151, 157, 423, 424
Abrams, T. W., 254, 275*n*.
Abzug, C., 55, 61*n*., 137, 145, 149*n*.
Acosta-Urquidi, J., 15, *15*, *16*, 17, 24*n*.
Acuña, K., 196, 209*n*.
Adams, C., 338, 347*n*.
Adams, R. D., 383, 399, 411*n*., 414*n*., 468, 476*n*.
Adinolfi, A. M., 94, 99*n*.
Aggleton, J. P., 453, 460*n*., 469, 474*n*.
Aghajanian, G. K., 108, 119*n*., 322, 332*n*.
Agrid, Y., 110, 119*n*.
Agnati, L. F., 118*n*.
Agnetti, V., 468, 477*n*.
Aigner, T., 321, 332*n*.
Akasu, T., 108, 118*n*.
Akil, H., 315, 332*n*.
Albert, M. S., 400, 411*n*., 466, 474*n*.
Alexander, G., 79, 102*n*.
Alger, B. E., 64, 73, 75*n*., 76*n*., 151, 168*n*.
Alkon, D. L., 10, *11*, *13*, 14, *14*, 15, *15*, *16*, 17, *18*, 19, *21*, 22, *22*, 23, 24*n*., 25*n*., 26*n*., 27, 42, 46*n*., 79, 80, 107, 108, 116, 119*n*., 120, 134, 135, 137, 146*n*., 173, 190*n*., 254, 282, 296, 424, 426, 427
Andersen, P., 63, 64, 66, 73, 75*n*., 121–123, 126, 132*n*., 138, 146*n*., 151, 168*n*.
Anderson, A. M., 201, 202, 208*n*.
Anderson, C. L., 97, 100*n*., 134, 147*n*., 169*n*.
Anderson, E., 458, 460*n*.
Anderson, J. R., 438, 440*n*.
Antin, S. P., 467, 475*n*.
Arbilla, S., 323, 329*n*.
Armstrong, D. L., 266, 278*n*.
Armstrong-James, M., 94, 99*n*.
Arnold, M., 326, 330*n*.
Ashe, J. H., 42, 48*n*., 108–111, *111*, 116, 117*n*., 118*n*., 456, 460*n*.
Asratyan, E. A., 224, 229*n*.
Atkinson, R. C., 433, 440*n*.
Avery, M., 232, 250*n*.

Bachevalier, J., *302*, 306*n*., 351, 377*n*., 429, 432*n*., 453, 461*n*., 473, 475*n*.
Baddeley, A. D., 347, 347*n*., 354, 375*n*., 388, 402, 410, 411, 411*n*., 412*n*., 429, 431*n*., 473, 474*n*.
Bahr, E., 245, 249*n*.
Bailey, C. H., 255, 270, 274*n*.
Bajjalieh, S. M., *85*, 86, 101*n*.
Bakal, C. W., 340, 348*n*.
Baker, A. G., 344, 348*n*.
Baker, M., 458, 461*n*.
Balda, R. C., 232, 235, 245, 248, 249*n*., 303, 306*n*.
Balda, R. P., 232, 235, 236, 249*n*., 250*n*.
Balzer, J. R., 121, 132*n*.
Baptista, L. F., 257, 274*n*.
Baranyi, A., 62, 75*n*.
Barchas, J. D., 315, 332*n*.,
Barker, J. L., 14, 26*n*.
Barnes, C. A., 49, 51, 53–55, 57–59, 59*n*., 60*n*., 61*n*., 66, 73, 76*n*., 93, 103*n*., 107, 108, 120, 131, 137, 151, 157, 161, 335, 421, 423, 424
Barnes, C. D., 322. 333*n*.
Barnes, E. S., 26*n*.
Barrati, C. M., 315, 324, 330*n*.
Barrionuevo, G., 134, 138, 147*n*.
Barry, S. R., 175, 191*n*.
Bateson, G., 256, 274*n*.

Battenberg, E. L. F., 330*n*.
Baudry, M., 79, 80, 102*n*., 134, 135, 148*n*., 151, 166, 168*n*., 169*n*., 272, 276*n*., 323, 332*n*., 430, 432*n*., 458, 460*n*.
Baumgartner, G., 381, 412*n*.
Bayon, A., 330*n*.
Beatty, W. W., 318, 330*n*.
Bechterev, W. V., von, 467, 474*n*.
Bechterev, W. V., von., 467, 474*n*.
Becker, J. T., 57, 61*n*., 351, 377*n*., 429, 432*n*., 456, 461*n*.
Becker, L. E., 266, 278*n*.
Beckstead, R. M., 122, 132*n*.
Behrends, P., 300, 306*n*.
Belford, G. R., 42, 48*n*.
Belluzzi, J. D., 315, 333*n*.
Beltz, B., 185, 190*n*.
Benardo, L. S., 110, 117*n*.
Ben-Ari, Y., 331*n*.
Bender, D. E., 449, 450*n*.
Bender, M. B., 381, 413*n*.
Benfenati, F., 118*n*.
Benjamin, P. R., 181, 190*n*.
Bennett, C., 326, 330*n*.
Bennett, E. I., 151, 170*n*.
Bennett, E. L., 80, 82, 97, 99*n*., 100*n*., 102*n*.
Bennett, W., 116, 117*n*.
Benson, D. F., 466, 476*n*.
Berard, D. R., 272, 274*n*.
Berger, T. W., 48*n*., 57, 58, 59*n*., 121, 131, 132*n*., 134, 137, 147*n*., 148*n*., 151, 170*n*., 373, 375*n*., 424
Berkowitz, R., 82, 102*n*.
Berman, G., 449, 450*n*.
Bernardi, G., 110, 118*n*.
Berry, M., 272, 274*n*.
Berry, S. D., 48*n*.
Berthier, N. E., 45, 46*n*.
Best, P. J., 49, 61*n*.
Bever, T., 444, 450*n*.
Bianchi, C., 324, 330*n*.
Bickford, R., 397, 412*n*.
Bilder, R. M., Jr., 467, 475*n*.
Bird, S. J., 322, 330*n*., 334*n*.
Birt, D., 42, 46*n*.
Bischoff, S., 110, 111, 117*n*., 119*n*.
Bitterman, M. E., 283, 284, 285*n*., 300, 306*n*.
Bittiger, H., 110, 117*n*.
Bjorklund, A., 458, 460*n*.
Black, J., 90, 100*n*.
Bliss, T. V. P., 50, 59*n*., 62–65, 68, 70, 71, 75*n*., 109, 116, 117*n*., 121, 132*n*., 151, 169*n*., 311, 329, 330*n*.
Bloch, V., 55, 59*n*., 60*n*.
Bloom, R. E., 322, 330*n*.
Bockaert, J., 111, 117*n*.
Bogdany, F. J., 207, 208*n*., 291, 294*n*.
Bohus, B., 329, 332*n*.
Bolles, R. C., 216, 229*n*., 301, 306, 307*n*.
Boothe, R. G., 272, 276*n*.
Borowski, E., 323, 333*n*.
Bostock, E., 320, 328, 330*n*., 331*n*.
Botticelli, L. J., 324, 330*n*.
Bourne, R., 97, 103*n*.
Bouton, M. E., 216, 229*n*.
Boyle, M. B., 173, 190*n*.
Bradford, H. F., 323, 330*n*.
Bradley, D. C., 444, 450*n*.
Bradley, P., 272, 274*n*.
Bragin, A. G., 151, 169*n*.
Brain, W. R., 381, 412*n*.
Branch, C., 397, 413*n*.
Branch, M., 49, 61*n*.
Brandon, J. G., 267, 270, 272, 274*n*., 275*n*.
Brassel, S., 71, 75*n*., 139, 148*n*.
Bremner, B., 245, 249*n*.
Brenner, E., 329, 330*n*.
Brett, L., 255, 230*n*., 291, 294*n*.
Brion, S., 403, 412*n*.
Brons, J. F., 62, 75*n*.
Brooks, C. McC., 108, 117*n*.
Brooks, D. N., 354, 375*n*., 402, 412*n*., 429, 431*n*., 473, 474*n*.
Brown, J. W., 444, 450*n*.
Brown, M., 321, 332*n*.
Brown, T. H., 62, 75*n*., 134, 136, 138, 147*n*.
Browne, R., 330*n*.
Browning, M., 116, 117*n*.
Broyles, J. L., 29, 30, 37, 39, 47*n*., 48*n*.
Brunelli, M., 109, 117*n*.
Budtz-Olsen, O. E., 82, 100*n*.
Bullock, T. H., 79, 100*n*., 182, 190*n*., 231, 249*n*.
Bunney, B. S., 322, 332*n*., 333*n*.
Burgess, J. W., 267, 270, 271, 274*n*.
Burghagen, H., 257, 275*n*.

Bursick, D. M., 121, 132*n*.
Butters, N., 354, 356, 375*n*., 377*n*., 388, 398, 400, 403, 411*n*., 412*n*., 429, 432*n*., 449, 450*n*., 466, 467, 469, 471, 474*n*., 475*n*.
Buttner, U., 381, 412*n*.
Büttner-Ennever, J. A., 381, 412*n*.
Buzsaki, G., 71, 75*n*.
Byers, D., 266, 274*n*.
Byrne, J. H., 254, 278*n*., 311, *312*, 333*n*.
Byus, C. V., *115*, 118*n*.

Caan, W., 449, 450*n*.
Calabresi, P., 110, 118*n*.
Calas, A., 110, 119*n*.
Calder, L. D., 321, 332*n*.
Camardo, J. S., 135, 148*n*.
Camel, J. E., 82
Campbell, D. T., 287, 294*n*.
Cancella, L. M., 315, 331*n*.
Cardozo, J. N., 97, 103*n*.
Carew, T. J., 254, 275*n*.
Carey, S., 449, 450*n*.
Carrasco, M. A., 315, 330*n*., 331*n*.
Carroll, M., 357, 364, 375*n*.
Cartwright, B. A., 202, 208*n*.
Castellano, C., 315, 330*n*.
Castellucci, V. F., 109, 116, 117*n*.
Castro, A. J., 84, 100*n*.
Cegavske, T. W., 48*n*.
Celeni, M., 118*n*.
Cermak, L. S., 353, 354, 356, 361, 370, 375*n*., 377*n*., 388, 391–393, 398, 402, 403, 412*n*., 429, 431*n*., 465, 467, 471, 474*n*.
Chain, F., 413*n*.
Chan, F., 266, 278*n*.
Chang, F.-L., 82, *83*, 91, *92*, 94, 97, 98, 100*n*., 151, 153, 157, 166, 169*n*.
Chang, J. J., 179, 190*n*.
Changeaux, J.-P., 89, 100*n*., 197, 208*n*.
Channel, S., 343, 346, 348*n*.
Chen, M., 255, 274*n*.
Chen, S., 272, 274*n*.
Cheney, D. L., 324, 334*n*.
Chetail, M., 182, 190*n*.
Christian, E. P., 139, 140, 144, 147*n*., 148*n*.
Church, R. M., 335, 348*n*.
Ciarolla, D. A., 121, 132*n*.
Claparède, E., 403, 409, 412*n*.
Clark, G. A., 48*n*., 91, 103*n*., 461*n*.
Clark, R. B., 14, 25*n*.
Clark, R. D., 267, 274*n*.
Cohen, B., 381, 412*n*.
Cohen, D. H., 27–30, *29*, *31*, 33, *34*, *35*, 36–39, *36*, *38*, *40*, 42, 43, *43*, 46*n*., 47*n*., 48*n*., 107, 108, 120, 135, 147*n*., 150, 181, 288, 329, 339, 423, 424, 428
Cohen, J. L., 181, 191*n*.
Cohen, L. B., 173, 183, 190*n*., 191*n*.
Cohen, N. J., 57, 59*n*., 78, 103*n*., 136, 146, 147*n*., 148*n*., 197, *302*, 307*n*., 351, 353–355, 374, 375*n*., 378*n*., 379*n*., 389, 399, 400–405, 409, 411, 412*n*., 414*n*., 429, 430, 431*n*., 432*n*., 442, 448, 451*n*., 453, 460*n*., 461*n*., 465–467, 472, 473, 474*n*., 475*n*., 476*n*.
Cole, S., 280, 285*n*.
Collett, T. S., 202, 208*n*.
Collier, T. J., 322, 330*n*.
Collingridge, G. L., 458, 460*n*.
Collins, G. H., 383, 414*n*., 468, 476*n*.
Coltheart, M., 445, 450*n*.
Colwill, R. M., 218, *218*, 227, 229*n*., 338, 348*n*.
Conner, J. A., 189, 191*n*.
Connor, J., 10, 25*n*.
Connor, J. R., 267, 274*n*.
Cooke, I., 253, 254, 282, 290, 339
Coons, E. E., 435, 440*n*.
Copeland, J., 183, 190*n*.
Corkin, S., 354, 376*n*., 377*n*., 400, 402, 404, 408, 412*n*., 413*n*., 429, 431*n*., 434, 440*n*., 460*n*., 465, 467, 472, 474*n*., 475*n*.
Cornell, S., 467, 475*n*.
Corsellis, J. A. N., 384, 412*n*.
Cortese, C., 357, 361, 378*n*.
Coss, R. G., 255–258, 260–263, 265–267, 270–272, 274*n*., 275*n*., 276*n*., 277*n*., 278*n*., 296
Costa, E., 324, 334*n*.
Cotman, C. W., 72, 75*n*., 89, 100*n*., 458, 460*n*.
Cotton, M. M., 338, 349*n*.
Coulter, D. A., 15, 25*n*.

Coulter, J. D., 86, 103*n*.
Coupland, R. E., *81*, 100*n*.
Coutinho-Netto, J., 323, 330*n*.
Couvillon, P. A., 284, 285*n*.
Cowan, W. M., 110, 119*n*., 122, 132*n*., 133*n*.
Cowie, R. J., 232–234, 236, 238, 249*n*., 250*n*.
Cragg, B. G., 97, 100*n*.
Craik, F. I. M., 352, 376*n*.
Crawford, M. R., 109, 117*n*.
Croll, R. P., 181, 190*n*.
Crossland, J., 323, 330*n*.
Crovitz, H. F., 353, 378*n*.
Crow, T., 10, 17, 22, 25*n*., 26*n*.
Crowder, R. G., 421, 423, 433, 440*n*.
Cruse, H., 201, 208*n*.
Culligan, N., 179, 190*n*.
Cummins, R. A., 82, 100*n*.
Cunningham, C. L., 214, *215*, 229*n*.
Curcio, C. A., 272, 275*n*.
Cutting, J. A., 411, 412*n*.
Cynader, M. S., 48*n*.

Dale, R. H. I., 242
Dallas, M., 357, 359, 363, 376*n*.
Daly, J. W., 109, 117*n*.
Daly, M., 300, 306*n*.
Damasio, A. R, 467, 475*n*.
Damasio, H., 467, 475*n*.
Dantzer, R., 315, 333*n*.
Dauchin, A., 89, 100*n*., 197, 208*n*.
David, H., 151, 170*n*.
Davies, C. A., 82, 102*n*., 173
Davis, C., 468, 477*n*.
Davis, D. L., 266, 274*n*.
Davis, H. P., 324, 333*n*.
Davis, W. J., 181, 190*n*.
DeAcedo, B. S., 429, 431*n*.
Deadwyler, S. A., 72, 75*n*., 139, 140, 143, 144, 147*n*., 148*n*., 423
Dearing, M. F., 340, 348*n*.
DeGraan, P. N. E., 118*n*.
DeGroot, D., 94, 100*n*.
Dejerine, J., 444, 450*n*.
Delacour, J., 237, 249*n*., 453, 461*n*.
Delaney, K., 175, 179–181, 190*n*., 253, 254, 282, 290, 339
Delanoy, R. L., 109, 118*n*.
Delay, J., 403, 412*n*.
DeLorenzo, R., 26*n*.
Dembitzer, H. M., 272, 276*n*.
Denti, A., 55, 59*n*.
Descarries, L., 108, 119*n*.
Desmond, J. E., 348*n*.
Desmond, N. L., 97, 100*n*., 134, 147*n*., 151, 157, 166, 169*n*., 270, 275*n*.
Deutsch, J. A., 351, 376*n*.
Devine, J. V., 84, 102*n*.
DeVoogd, T. J., 94, 101*n*.
Deweer, B., 55, 59*n*.
Diamond, D. M., 108, 119*n*.
Diamond, J., 256, 275*n*.
Diamond, M. C., 80–82, 97, 99*n*., 100*n*., 101*n*., 267, 274*n*.
Diamond, R., 357, 361, 376*n*., 450*n*.
Dias, R. D., 315, 316, *317*, 330*n*., 331*n*.
Dickinson, A., 285, 285*n*., 337, 338, 340, 347*n*., 348*n*., 411, 412*n*.
Di Giamberardino, L., 80, 100*n*.
Discenna, P., 91, 103*n*., 157, 162, 166, 170*n*., 458, 461*n*.
Dismukes, R. K., 109, 117*n*.
Doble, K. E., 191*n*.
Dodge, H. W., 397, 412*n*.
Dollinger, J., 196, 208*n*.
Dolphin, A. C., 64, 71, 75*n*., 111, 117*n*., 151, 169*n*.
Domjan, M., 300, 306*n*.
Donahoe, J. W., 340, 349*n*.
Donegan, N. H., 461*n*.
Donoghue, J. P., 86, 100*n*.
Douglas, R. M., 50, 54, 59*n*., 60*n*., 151, 169*n*.
Dray, F., 331*n*.
Drinker, J., 449, 450*n*.
Driscoll, P. A., 328, 331*n*.
Droz, B., 80, 100*n*.
Dubois, M. P., 185, 191*n*.
Duff, T. A., 36, 47*n*.
Duffy, C., 151, 161, 166, 169*n*.
Duncan, C. P., 435, 441*n*.

Dunnett, S. B., 458, 460*n*.
Dunwiddie, T., 116, 117*n*., 138, 148*n*.
Durkis, D. A., 196, 208*n*.
Durlach, P. J., 215, 216, 220, 225, 226, 229*n*.
Dyson, S. E., 89, 94, 100*n*.

Eaton, R. C., 256, 275*n*.
Ebert, V., 402, 415*n*.
Eccles, J. C., 122, 132*n*., 150, 169*n*.
Egan, M., 183, 190*n*.
Egyhazi, E., 87, 101*n*.
Eich, J. E., 357, 376*n*.
Eichenbaum, H., 429, 431*n*.
Eidelberg, E., 71, 75*n*.
Eisinger, S., 331*n*.
Elisabetsky, E., 315, 331*n*.
Ellen, P., 245, 249*n*.
Elliott, C., 82, 102*n*.
Ellisman, M. H., 97, 101*n*.
Endo, T., 323, 333*n*.
Erber, J., 199, 200, *200*, 209*n*.
Errington, M. L., 151, 169*n*.
Escourolle, R., 413*n*.
Eslinger, P. J., 467, 475*n*.
Evans, R. H., 458, 460*n*.
Ewert, J.-P., 257, 275*n*.
Eysenck, M. W., 314, 330*n*.

Fabrigoule, G., 338, 349*n*.
Fagan, A., 429, 431*n*.
Fallon, J. H., 326, 330*n*.
Fanelli, R., 324, 326, 328, 330*n*., 331*n*.
Farley, J., 10, 14, 17, 19, 22, 23, 25*n*., 26*n*.
Fass, B., 89, 100*n*.
Feher, O., 62, 75*n*.,
Ferron, A., 108, 119*n*.
Feustel, T. C., 361, 376*n*.
Feustel, W. A., 146, 148*n*.
Fietz, A., 283, 285*n*.
Fifkova, E., 94, 97, 100*n*., 102*n*., 134, 147*n*., 151, 158, 166, 169*n*., 170*n*., 270, 278*n*.
Fischer, W., 284, 285*n*.
Fitch, H. S., 258, 275*n*.
Flagg, S. F., 372, 373, 378*n*.
Fletcher, W. H., *115*, 116, 118*n*.
Floeter, M. K., 98, 101*n*.
Flood, J. F., 151, 170*n*.
Fodor, J. A., 444, 450*n*.
Forgays, D. G., 82, 101*n*.
Forman, R., 10, 23, 25*n*.
Foster, K., 79, 101*n*.
Foster, T. C., 143, 144, 147*n*.
Fraisse, P., 284, 285*n*.
Francis, A. A., 458, 460*n*.
Freed, D. M., 465, 475*n*.
Freedman, R., 108, 118*n*.
Freire, M., 94, 101*n*.
French, E., 330*n*.
Fricke, R., 122, 132*n*.
Friesen, W. O., 121, 132*n*.
Frotscher, M., 150, 170*n*.
Fuchs, J. L., *85*, 86, 87, 101*n*.
Fulginiti, S., 315, 331*n*.
Fulton, J. F., 262, 275*n*.
Fuxe, K., 109, 118*n*.

Gabbott, P. L., 97, 103*n*.
Gabriel, M., 42, 47*n*., 79, 101*n*.
Gabrieli, J. D. E., 404
Gaffan, D., 453, 460*n*., 473, 475*n*.
Gaffan, E. A., 245, 249*n*.
Gage, F. H., 49, 61*n*., 458, 460*n*.
Gage, P. W., 270, 275*n*.
Galef, B. G., 300, 306*n*.
Gallagher, M., 58, 315, *316*, 317, 318, *318*, 320, 321, 324, 326, 328, 330*n*., 331*n*., 333*n*., 423, 435, 436
Gallistel, C. R., 79, 101*n*.
Gamlin, P. D. R., 30, 39, 47*n*.
Ganong, A. H., 458, 460*n*.
Garcia, E., 225, 229*n*.
Garcia, J., 225, 230*n*., 253, 275*n*., 291, 294*n*.
Gardner, B. T., 300, 306*n*.
Gardner, R. A., 300, 306*n*.
Gardner-Medwin, A. R., 50, 59*n*., 64, 75*n*.

Garrett, M. F., 444, 450*n*.
Garrud, P., 49, 60*n*.
Gart, S., 10, 25*n*.
Geller, A., 389, 412*n*.
Gelperin, A., 49, 61*n*., 173, 175, 179–181, 183, 185, 188, 189, 190*n*., 191*n*., 192*n*., 253–255, 275*n*., 282, 290, 296, 339
Gerard, L., 357, 378*n*.
Gerren, R. A., 136, 147*n*.
Geschwind, N., 444, 450*n*.
Gibbon, J., 335, 348*n*.
Gibbs, C. M., 37, 39, 42, 47*n*., 48*n*., 225, 229*n*.
Gibbs, M. E., 88, 102*n*.
Gibson, J. J., 254, 275*n*.
Gillan, D. J., 335, 348*n*.
Gispen, W. H., 116, 117*n*., 118*n*.
Glaser, E. M., 284, 285*n*.
Gleitman, H., 340, 348*n*.
Glickstein, M., 340, 350*n*.
Glisky, E., 369, 370, 376*n*.
Globus, A., 256, 267, 272, 275*n*.
Goddard, G. V., 50, 60*n*., 64, 65, 67, 68, 73, 75*n*., 107–109, 116, 117*n*., 120, 136, 138, 139, 311, 330*n*., 423, 424
Gold, P. E., 109, 118*n*., 311, 313, 314, 331*n*., 332*n*., 334*n*.
Goldberg, E., 351, 376*n*., 467, 475*n*.
Goh, Y., 14, 25*n*.
Goodglass, H., 354, 375*n*., 429, 431*n*.
Goodwin, B. G., 265, 278*n*.
Gordon, J., 196, 208*n*.
Goren, C. C., 256, 275*n*.
Gorman, C., 94, *96*, 101*n*.
Gormezano, I., 225, 229*n*.
Gould, J. L., 193, 194, *195*, 196–199, *199*, 202, 204, 205, 208, 208*n*., 209*n*., 210*n*. 248, 253, 255, 257, 266, 270, 283, 288, 296, 306*n*., 420, 421
Gould, R., 26*n*.
Graf, P., 346, 348*n*., 351, 353, 357, 358, 362–364, 366–368, 369, 376*n*., 378*n*., 390, 391, 404, 408, 409, 411, 412*n*., 429, 432*n*., 435, 441*n*., 455, 460*n*., 473, 475*n*.
Grant, D. S., 335, 348*n*.
Grau, J. W., 216, 229*n*.
Graudenz, M., 324, 330*n*.
Gray, E. G., 94, 101*n*., 272, 278*n*., 348*n*.
Gray, F., 413*n*.
Gray, H., *382*
Gray, J. A., 344, 348*n*.
Green, B. F., 305, 306*n*.
Green, E. J., 82, 93, *93*, 101*n*.
Green, K. F., 253, 275*n*.
Greenberg, J., 79, 102*n*.
Greenberg, M. J, 183, 191*n*.
Greene, S. L., 247, 250*n*., 281, 286*n*., 293, 293*n*., 295*n*.
Greengard, P., 116, 117*n*., 119*n*.
Greenough, W. T., 80–84, *81*, *83*, *85*, 86, *87*, *88*, 89–91, *92*, 93, *93*, 94, *95*, *96*, 97, 98, 99, 100*n*., 101*n*., 102*n*., 103*n*., 107, 120, 134, 135, 146, 147*n*., 151, 153, 157, 166, 169*n*., 267, 270, 424
Greenspan, R. J., 266, 277*n*., 304, 307*n*.
Gribkoff, V. K., 72, 75*n*., 109–111, *111*, 116, 118*n*., 138, 148*n*.
Grieshaber, J. A., 267, 278*n*.
Gros, C., 326, 330*n*.
Gross, C. G., 449, 450*n*.
Groves, P. M., 323, 333*n*., 343, 348*n*.
Guberman, A., 468, 475*n*.
Gudden, H., 467, 475*n*.
Guillemin, R., 330*n*.
Guillery, R. W., 94, 101*n*.
Guttman, N., 290, 294*n*.

Hafner, S., 50, 61*n*., 62, 76*n*., 79, 102*n*., 161, 170*n*.
Haftorn, S., 232, 246, 249*n*.
Haig, K. A., 245, 249*n*.
Hailman, J. P., 196, 209*n*.
Hainsworth, F. R., 280, 285*n*.
Hall, G., 343, 344, 346, 348*n*.
Hall, R. D., 86, 101*n*.
Halpain, S., 151, 169*n*.
Hamaguchi, T., 270, 276*n*.
Hambley, J., 88, 102*n*.
Hamont, M., 111, 117*n*.
Hampson, R. E., 143, 144, 147*n*.
Handlemann, G. E., 57, 61*n*., 351, 377*n*., 429, 432*n*., 456, 461*n*.
Hankins, W., 225, 230*n*., 291, 294*n*.
Hansel, H. C., 245, 249*n*.

Harbluk, J. A., 364, 370, 378*n*.
Hardiman, M. J., 340, 350*n*.
Harley, C. W., 70, 76*n*.
Harlow, H. F., 298, 306*n*.
Harrigan, J., 25*n*.
Harris, E. W., 458, 460*n*.
Harter, S., 298, 306*n*.
Hashiguchi, T., 109, 118*n*.
Hatton, J. D., 97, 101*n*.
Hawkins, R. D., 49, 59*n*., 173, 189, 191*n*., 197, 209*n*., 254, 275*n*., 282, 283, 285*n*., 287, 294*n*., 339, 348*n*.
Hay, B., 14, 17, 25*n*., 26*n*.
Hayes-Roth, B., 362, 376*n*.
Hebb, D. O., 74, 76*n*., 150, 169*n*., 433, 441*n*.
Hebel, N., *384*, 385, *385*, 414*n*.
Hebert, M., 82, 99*n*.
Heilman, K. M., 391, 392, 412*n*.
Heinrich, B., 206, 209*n*.
Heldman, E., 10, 23, 25*n*., 26*n*., 108, 119*n*.
Henderson, R. W., 340, 341, *341*, 348*n*.
Hennessy, D. F., 258, 260, 275*n*.
Henriksen, S. J., 330*n*.
Henrikson, C. K., 267, 278*n*.
Herrmann, T., 245, 249*n*.
Hertz, M., 201, 209*n*.
Hess, E., 196, 209*n*.
Hierons, R., 384, 412*n*.
Hill, A. J., 49, 60*n*.
Hillman, D. E., 272, 274*n*., 276*n*.
Hinds, J. W., 272, 275*n*.
Hinman, C. L., 121, 126, 132*n*.
Hirai, K., 108, 109, 118*n*.
Hirano, A., 272, 276*n*.
Hirsch, H. V. B., 267, 278*n*., 411, 412*n*.
Hirsh, R., 58, 60*n*., 145, 146, 147*n*., 351, 373, 375, 376*n*., 429, 432*n*., 473, 475*n*.
Hirst, M., 188, 191*n*.
Hirst, W., 353, 376*n*., 390, 412*n*.
Hockberger, P., 189, 191*n*.
Hodos, W., 298, 306*n*.
Hoefer, I., 206, 209*n*.
Hoffman, C. A., *85*, 86, 101*n*.
Holland, P. C., 211, 213, 225, 230*n*., 337, 348*n*.
Holloway, R. L., 80, 101*n*.
Holmes, E. J., 469, 475*n*.
Holmes, P. A., 340, 348*n*.
Holmqvist, B., 122, 132*n*.
Hopfield, J. J., 173, 188, 190*n*., 191*n*., 254, 275*n*.
Hopkins, W. F., 109, 116, 118*n*., 329, 331*n*.
Horel, J. A., 452, 453, 60*n*.
Horn, G., 88, 97, 101*n*.
Horner, J., 196, 197, 206, 209*n*., 292, 294*n*.
Horowitz, L. M., 362, 376*n*.
Horridge, G. A., 182, 190*n*.
Horsfall, C. R., 82, 100*n*.
Hotson, J. R., 113, *115*, 118*n*.
Hubel, D. H., 89, 102*n*.
Hughes, J. E. O., 467, 475*n*.
Humbert, J., 331*n*.
Hunter, B. E., 64, 75*n*.
Hunter, W. S., 297, 306*n*.
Huppert, F. A., 347, 348*n*., 386, *386*, 391–393, 412*n*., 413*n*., 452, 461*n*., 465, 475*n*.
Huygens, P., 315, 330*n*.
Hwang, H.-M., 94, *95*, *96*, 101*n*.
Hyden, H., 87, 101*n*.
Hymovitch, B., 98, 101*n*.

Ings, R., 329, 333*n*.
Introini, I. B., 315, 325, 330*n*., 331*n*.
Ishikawa, K., 110, 118*n*.
Ito, M., 62, 76*n*.
Izquierdo, I., 315, 316, *317*, 319, 321, 324, 330*n*., 331*n*., 332*n*.

Jackson, R. I., 341, *341*, 348*n*.
Jacobson, S., 469, 475*n*.
Jacoby, L. L., 357, 359, 361, 363, 374, 376*n*., 429, 432*n*.
Jahn, E. G., 188, 192*n*.
James, P. C., 233, 249*n*.
Janota, I., 384, 412*n*.
Jarrard, L. E., 49, 57, 60*n*., 457, 461*n*.
Jarvik, M. E., 389, 412*n*.
Jasper, H. H., 108, 119*n*.
Javay-Agrid, F., 110, 119*n*.

Jenkins, H. M., 220, 229*n.*, 306*n.*
Jennings, H. S., 287, 294*n.*
Jensen, R. A., 315, 331*n.*, 332*n.*
Jhamandas, K., 323, 331*n.*, 332*n.*
Joh, T. H., 322, 333*n.*
Johnson, M., 351, 376*n.*
Johnson, R., 94, 97, 99*n.*, 100*n.*, 116
Johnson, R. D., 340, 348*n.*
Johnson, R. E., 267, 274*n.*
Johnston, D., 109, 118*n.*, 138, 147*n.*, 329, 331*n.*
Johnston, T. D., 253, 276*n.*, 300, 303, 306*n.*
Jones, A. W., 458, 460*n.*
Jones, C. A., 324, 332*n.*
Jones, D. G., 89, 94, 100*n.*
Jones, E. G., 94, 101*n.*
Jones, M. K., 410, 412*n.*, 471, 475*n.*
Jones Leonard, B., 55, 60*n.*
Jork, R., 118*n.*
Joschko, M., 170*n.*
Joschko, R., 170*n.*
Judge, S. J., 449, 451*n.*
Juraska, J. M., 82, *83*, 94, 101*n.*, 102*n.*

Kalat, J. W., 248, 250*n.*
Kaleta, S., 326, 330*n.*
Kamil, A. C., 232, 235, 245, 248, 249*n.*, 280, 285*n.*, 303, 306*n.*
Kamin, L. J., 213, 229*n.*, 340, 348*n.*
Kammerer, E., 110, 119*n.*, 150, 170*n.*
Kandel, E. R., 27, 29, 39, 42, 47*n.*, 48*n.*, 49, 59*n.*, 78–80, 102*n.*, 109, 117*n.*, 134, 135, 147*n.*, 148*n.*, 173, 189, 191*n.*, 197, 209*n.*, 254, 255, 275*n.*, 276*n.*, 282, 283, 285*n.*, 287, 294*n.*, 339, 348*n.*
Kapp, B. S., 315, 321, 326, 328, 331*n.*
Kappers, C. U. A., 90, 102*n.*
Karreman, G. A., 79, 101*n.*
Karten, H. J., 30, 47*n.*
Kasamatsu, T., 108, 118*n.*, 311, 329, 332*n.*, 333*n.*
Kato, E., 109, 118*n.*
Katz, H. B., 82, 102*n.*
Kauer, J. S., 183, 191*n.*
Kaufmann, W., 170*n.*
Kaushall, P. I., 468, 475*n.*
Kavaliers, M., 188, 191*n.*
Kawato, M., 270, 271, 276*n.*
Kean, M.-L. 421, 423
Keenan, C. L., 270, 276*n.*
Kehl, S. J., 458, 460*n.*
Kehoe, E. J., 225, 229*n.*
Keighly, S., 453, 461*n.*
Keightly, S., 49, 61*n.*
Keith-Lucas, T., 290, 294*n.*
Kelly, P. A., 458, 460*n.*
Kesner, R. P., 58, 60*n.*, 146, 148*n.*, 321, 332*n.*, 455, 461*n.*
Kessler, M., 151, 160, 169*n.*
Ketter, R. N., 48*n.*
Kety, S. S., 108, 118*n.*, 311, 313, 314, 332*n.*
Kiger, J. A., 266, 274*n.*
Kill, D., 49, 61*n.*, 453, 461*n.*
Killackey, H. P., 42, 48*n.*
King, R. A., 317, *318*, 331*n.*
Kinsbourne, M., 146, 148*n.*, 351, 376*n.*, 377*n.*, 402, 415*n.*, 429, 432*n.*, 436, 438, 441*n.*, 471, 477*n.*
Kirsche, W., 150, 170*n.*
Kirsner, K., 357, 364, 375*n.*
Klein, M., 135, 148*n.*
Klose, K. J., 79, 102*n.*
Klosterhafen, S., 284, 285*n.*
Kobayashi, H., 108, 109, 118*n.*
Koch, C., 270–272, 276*n.*, 277*n.*
Koenig, H. L., 80, 100*n.*
Koketsu, K., 108, 109, 118*n.*
Kolb, B., 49, 58, 60*n.*, 61*n.*, 457, 461*n.*
Kolers, P. A., 435, 441*n.*
Koltermann, R., 206, 209*n.*
Konorski, J., 339, 346, 349*n.*
Konstantinos, T., 82, 100*n.*
Koopowitz, H., 270, 276*n.*
Korf, J., 110, 117*n.*, 322, 332*n.*
Korr, H., 80, 102*n.*
Kovac, M. P., 181, 190*n.*
Kovács, G. L., 329, 332*n.*
Koziell, D. A., 326, 330*n.*
Krasne, F. B., 311, 312, 332*n.*
Krauss, J., 110, 117*n.*
Krausz, H. I., 121, 124, 132*n.*
Kravitz, E., 185, 190*n.*, 191*n.*
Krebs, J. R., 232, 234, *234*, 235, 238–240, *239*, 244, 246, 249*n.*, 250*n.*, 254, 278*n.*

Krech, D., 80, 99*n*.
Kroin, J. S., 121, 126, 132*n*.
Krug, M., 151, *156*, 162, 169*n*.
Krushinskaya, N. L., 248, 249*n*.
Kuba, K., 109, 118*n*.
Kubie, J. L., 49, 60*n*.
Kuhar, M. J., 322, 326, 330*n*., 333*n*., 334*n*.
Kumamoto, E., 109, 118*n*.
Kuno, M., 270, 276*n*.
Kupfermann, I., 181, 191*n*.
Kuypers, K., 82, 103*n*.

Lachman, J. L., 440, 441*n*.
Lachman, R., 440, 441*n*.
Ladak, F., 258, 277*n*.
Laitinen, L. V., 448, 451*n*.
Landauer, T. K., 289, 294*n*.
Langer, S. Z., 323, 329*n*.
Laroche, S., 55, 60*n*.
Larson, J. R., 84, *87*, *88*, 98, 99, 102*n*.
Lashley, K. S., 41, 48*n*., 202, 209*n*.
Lauer, J., 206, 209*n*.
Lavond, D. G., 48*n*., 461*n*.
Lederhendler, I., 10, 17, *18*, 22, 23, 25*n*., 26*n*., 108, 119*n*., 135, 146*n*.
Lee, K. S., 50, 60*n*., 91, 97, 102*n*., 134, 136, 148*n*., 151, 158, 166, 169*n*., 270, 276*n*.
Lee, Y. W., 121, 124, 132*n*.
Leeman, S. E., 322, 333*n*.
Le Gal La Salle, G., 331*n*.
Leger, D. W., 257, 258, 265, 275*n*., 276*n*.
Lehman, H. K., 191*n*.
Lekawa, M. L., 116, 118*n*.
LeMoal, H., 315, 333*n*.
LeMoal, M., 110, 119*n*.
LeVay, S., 89, 91, 102*n*.
Levey, A. J., 323, 333*n*.
Levin, J., 400, 411*n*., 466, 474*n*.
Levins, R., 265, 276*n*.
Levy, W. B., 64, 66, 67, 71, 75*n*., 76*n*., 97, 100*n*., 109, 118*n*., 134, 138, 139, 147*n*., 148*n*., 151, 157, 166, 169*n*., 270, 275*n*.
Lewis, D., 136, 148*n*.
Lewis, R., 354, 375*n*., 429, 431*n*.
Lewontin, R. C., 265, 276*n*.
Lhermitte, F., 388, 413*n*., 452
Liang, K. C., 321, 331*n*., 332*n*.
Libet, B., 108, 109, 111, 117*n*., 118*n*.
Lichtman, J. W., 89, 102*n*., 267, 277*n*.
Liley, A. W., 50, 60*n*.
Liman, E., 19, 25*n*.
Lincoln, J. S., 57, 60*n*., 461*n*.
Lindauer, M., 199, 206, 209*n*.
Lindholm, E. P., 86, 101*n*.
Lindner, B., 97, 100*n*.
Ling, L. J., 19, 25*n*.
Ling, N., 323, 330*n*., 333*n*.
Livingstone, M. S., 185, 191*n*.
Llínas, R., 255, 272, 276*n*., 277*n*.
Llorens, C., 323, 332*n*.
Lockhart, R. S., 352, 376*n*.
LoLordo, 216, 229*n*.
Lømo, T., 50, 59*n*., 62–64, 68, 75*n*., 76*n*., 121–123, 126, 132*n*.
Lorenz, K. Z., 255, 256, 276*n*.
Lossner, B., 151, 169*n*.
Lovibond, P. F., 343, 344, *345*, 349*n*.
Loyning, Y., 122, 132*n*.
Lubow, R. E., 227, 229*n*., 319, 332*n*., 342, 349*n*.
Lucion, A. B., 315, 332*n*.
Ludescher, F. B., 232, 249*n*.
Lund, J. S., 267, 272, 276*n*.
Lund, R. D., 272, 276*n*.
Lynch, G., 72, 75*n*., 79, 80, 91, 102*n*., 116, 117*n*., 134, 135, 138, 148*n*., 151, 156, 160, 166, 168*n*., 169*n*., 270, 272, 276*n*., 301, 302, 306*n*., 430, 432*n*., 457, 458, 460*n*., 461*n*.

Macagno, E. R., 173, 190*n*.
Mack, K., 82, 102*n*.
Mackintosh, N. J., 146, 212, 213, 229*n*., 282, 286*n*., 336, 338, 343, *345*, 349*n*., 409, 411, 421, 436–438, 455, 461*n*.
MacLennan, A. J., 258, 277*n*.
Macphail, E. M., 195, 281–283, 285*n*., 296, 299–301, 303, 304, 306*n*., 335, 456, 461*n*.
Madden, J., IV, 134, 148*n*., 151, 170*n*., 315, 332*n*., 461*n*.

Madsen, M. C., 435, 441*n*.
Magleby, K. L., 50, 60*n*.
Mahut, H., 411, 413*n*.
Maier, N. R. F., 297, 306*n*.
Mair, W. G. P., 383–386, 390, 392, 393, 399, 401, 413*n*., 452, 457, 461*n*., 466, 468, 475*n*.
Maki, W. S., 242, 250*n*., 281, 285*n*., 335, 349*n*.
Malamut, B., *302*, 306*n*., 351, 377*n*., 429, 432*n*., 453, 461*n*., 469, 473, 475*n*.
Malthe-Sorenssen, D., 79, 103*n*., 134, 148*n*.
Mamounas, L. A., 461*n*.
Mandler, G., 346, 347, 348*n*., 349*n*., 351*n*., 362, 376*n*., 377*n*., 390, 411, 412*n*., 413*n*. 429, 432*n*., 435, 441*n*., 455, 460*n*., 473, 475*n*.
Manelis, L., 362, 376*n*.
Marcel, A. J., 438, 441*n*.
Marchand, C.-R., 185, 191*n*.
Marchbanks, R. M., 324, 332*n*.
Marciani, M. G., 110, 118*n*.
Margolis, R., 196, 209*n*.
Mariscal, S., 196, 209*n*.
Marin-Padilla, M., 266, 272, 276*n*.
Marler, P., 193, 194, 196–198, 209*n*., 256, 276*n*., 306*n*.
Marler, P. R., 257, 276*n*.
Marlin, N. A., 343, 349*n*.
Marmarelis, P. Z., 121, 132*n*.
Marr, D., 57, 60*n*., 146, 148*n*., 255, 276*n*.
Marshall, J. C., 445, 448, 450*n*.
Marslen-Wilson, W. D., 396, *397*, *398*, 399, 413*n*., 466, 475*n*.
Martin, S., 321, 332*n*.
Martinez, J. L., Jr., 315, 331*n*., 332*n*.
Martone, M., 356, 377*n*., 429, 432*n*.
Martres, M. P., 323, 332*n*.
Marx, I., 151, 170*n*.
Masuhr, J., 200, 209*n*.
Matera, C. M., 181, 190*n*.
Mates, S. L., 267, 276*n*.
Matthews-Bellinger, J., 270, 276*n*.
Matthies, H., 110, 118*n*., 119*n*., 150–153, 157, 170*n*., 423, 424
Mattis, S., 467, 475*n*.
Mauk, M. D., 48*n*., 461*n*.
Mayes, A., 374, 377*n*.
Mayes, A. R., 472, 475*n*.
Mayr, E., 266, 277*n*., 382
McAfee, D. A., 62, 75*n*., 136, 147*n*.
McBurney, R. N., 270, 275*n*.
McCann, G. D., 121, 132*n*.
McCormick, D. A., 48*n*., 57, 60*n*., 461*n*.
McDonald, J. F., 266, 277*n*.
McGaugh, J. L., 110, 118*n*., 301, 306*n*., 311, 313, 321, 326, 330*n*., 331*n*., 332*n*., 435, 441*n*.
McGowan, B. K., 253, 275*n*.
McKenna, T. M., 108, 119*n*.
McKoon, G., 361, 364, 377*n*.
McLachlan, D. R., 357, 359, 364, 370, 374, 378*n*.
McLennan, H., 458, 460*n*.
McNaughton, B. L., 49, 50, 53–55, 57–59, 59*n*., 60*n*., 61*n*., 64, 66, 68, 73, 76*n*., 93, 103*n*., 107, 108, 120, 131, 137, 138, 148*n*., 151, 157, 161, 169*n*., 335, 421, 423, 424
McQuade, P. S., 324, 334*n*.
Mead, A., 245, 249*n*.
Meadows, J. C., 449, 450*n*.
Megela, A. L., 73, 75*n*.
Melone, J. H., 267, 274*n*.
Menzel, E. W., 254, 257, 277*n*., 373, 377*n*.
Menzel, R., 199, 200, *200*, 209*n*., 283, 284, 285*n*.
Mercier, P., 280, 285*n*., 344, 348*n*.
Merrin, J., 109, 118*n*.
Merzenich, M. M., 42, 48*n*.
Messing, R. B., 315, 321, 331*n*., 332*n*., 333*n*.
Mesulam, M.-M., 323, 333*n*.
Meudell, P. R., 391, 402, 413*n*., 466, 471, 472, 475*n*.
Meyer, R. L., 267, 277*n*.
Milgram, N. W., 50, 61*n*., 62, 76*n*., 79, 102*n*., 161, 170*n*.
Miller, J. D., 42, 47*n*., 102*n*.
Miller, J. P., 271, 277*n*.
Miller, M., 94, 102*n*.
Miller, N. E., 435, 440*n*.
Miller, N. J., 456, 461*n*.
Miller, R. J., 322, 333*n*.
Miller, R. R., 343, 349*n*.

Milliotis, P., 466, 476*n*.
Mills, R. P., 468, 475*n*.
Milner, B., 354, 356, 373, 377*n*., 378*n*., 381, 390, 392, 397, 404, 408, 409, 413*n*., 414*n*., 429, 432*n*., 433, 441*n*., 464, 468, 472, 475*n*., 476*n*.
Minor, H., 343, 344, 348*n*.
Mirmiran, M., 329, 330*n*.
Mishkin, M., 237, 249*n*., *302*, 306*n*., 321, 332*n*., 351, 356, 372–375, 377*n*., 379*n*., 385, 411, 413*n*., 429, 432*n*., 453, 460*n*., 461*n*., 462*n*., 469, 473, 474*n*., 475*n*.
Miyagawa, M., 108, 118*n*.
Mohr, J., 373, 378*n*.
Mondadori, C., 315, 333*n*.
Montel, H., 323, 333*n*.
Moore, J. W., 45, 46*n*., 344, 348*n*., 349*n*.
Moore, R. Y., 326, 330*n*., 380, 414*n*., 468, 476*n*.
Moretensen, E. L., 472, 476*n*.
Morimoto, H., 82, 99*n*.
Mormede, P., 315, 333*n*.
Moroni, F., 324, 333*n*.
Morris, R. G. M., 49, 57, 60*n*., 61*n*., 335, 421, 460*n*., 457, 458, 461*n*.
Morton, J., 362, 377*n*.
Moscovitch, M., 351, 354, 357, 364, 371, 377*n*., 378*n*., 388, 413*n*., 429, 432*n*., 464, 465, 473, 476*n*.
Moshkov, D. A., 97, 102*n*., 151, 169*n*.
Moss, M., 411, 413*n*.
Mountcastle, V., 197, 209*n*.
Mowrer, O. H., 456, 461*n*.
Mufson, E. J., 323, 333*n*.
Mulder, D. W., 397, 412*n*.
Murakami, F., 270, 276*n*.
Murray, E. A., 86, 103*n*.
Musty, R. E., 328, 331*n*.
Mutt, V., 118*n*.

Nachman, M., 456, 460*n*.
Nadel, L., 49, 57, 61*n*., 136, 146, 148*n*., 351, 356, 371, 373, 375, 377*n*., 399, 400, 414*n*., 429, 432*n*., 453, 456, 457, 460*n*., 466, 473, 476*n*.
Nagle, G. T., 191*n*.
Naka, K.-I., 121, 132*n*.
Nakamura, S., 323, 333*n*.
Nairn, A. C., 117*n*.
Naito, S., 26*n*.
Nathan, P. W., 465, 476*n*.
Neary, D., 391, 413*n*., 466, 472, 475*n*.
Neary, J. T., 15, *15*, *16*, 17, 24*n*., 26*n*.
Nei, M., 261, 277*n*.
Neisser, U., 359, 377*n*.
Nelson, H. E., 394, 413*n*.
Nelson, R. J., 48*n*.
Nestler, E. J., 116, 119*n*.
Neuenschwander, N., 338, 349*n*.
Neuman, R. S., 70, 76*n*.
Newcombe, F., 448, 450*n*.
Nickerson, R. S., 282, 285*n*.
Nickolson, V. J., 315, 333*n*.
Nieto-Sampedro, M., 89, 100*n*., 458, 460*n*.
Nisbett, R. E., 438, 441*n*.
Noreen, G. K., 121, 132*n*.
Norman, D. A., 433, 441*n*.
North, K. A. K., 50, 60*n*.
Northern, B., 391, 413*n*., 466, 475*n*.
Nottebohm, F., 231, 248, 250*n*.
Novak, K. J., 455, 461*n*.

Oakley, D. A., 351, 373, 377*n*.
Oberg, R. G., 393, 415*n*.
O'Connell, A., 394, 413*n*.
Oestereicher, B., 189, 191*n*.
Ogura, H., 124, 132*n*.
O'Keefe, J., 49, 57, 60*n*., 61*n*., 136, 146, 148*n*., 351, 356, 371, 373, 377*n*., 429, 432*n*., 453, 456, 457, 461*n*., 473, 476*n*.
Olds, M. E., 42, 46*n*.
Oleson, T. D., 42, 48*n*.
Oliver, M., 91, 102*n*., 134, 148*n*., 151, 169*n*., 270, 276*n*.
Olson, D. J., 242, 249*n*., 250*n*., 281, 285*n*.
Olton, D. S., 49, 57, 61*n*., 146, 148*n*., 240, *241*, 245, 250*n*., 280, 285*n*., 286*n*., 317, 351, 356, 372–373, 377*n*., 429, 432*n*., 456, 457, 461*n*.
Opfinger, E., 200, 209*n*.

Orbach, H., 173, 190*n.*, 356, 378*n.*
Orona, E., 79, 101*n.*
Orr, W. B., 57, 58, 59*n.*, 137, 147*n.*
O'Shea, L., 329, 333*n.*
Ott, T., 110, 118*n.*, 151, 169*n.*
Overton, W. F., 255, 277*n.*
Owings, D. H., 255, 257, 258, 260–263, 265, 266, 275*n.*, 276*n.*, 277*n.*
Owings, S. C., 265, 277*n.*
Oxbury, S., 468, 477*n.*

Painter, S. D., 191*n.*
Paiva, A. C. M., 315, 331*n.*
Palay, S. L., 89, 103*n.*
Pallaud, B., 99, 103*n.*
Palmini, A. L., 315, 332*n.*
Pappas, B., 329, 333*n.*
Parkin, A. J., 467, 476*n.*
Pasik, P., 381, 413*n.*
Pasik, T., 381, 413*n.*
Passingham, R. E., 298, 299, 304, 307*n.*
Patrick, R. L., 315, 332*n.*
Patterson, J. M., 341, *341*, 348*n.*
Patterson, K., 445, 450*n.*
Patterson, M. M., 48*n.*
Paula-Barbosa, M. N., 272, 278*n.*
Pavone, F., 315, 330*n.*
Payne, M., 429, 432*n.*
Pearson, O. P., 301, 307*n.*
Pellionisz, A., 255, 277*n.*
Pepper, S. C., 256, 277*n.*
Perkel, D. H., 255, 270–272, 275*n.*, 277*n.*
Perkel, D. J., 270, 271, 277*n.*
Perrett, D. I., 449, 450*n.*
Perry, M. L., 331*n.*
Peters, A., 94, 102*n.*
Peterson, G. M., 84, 102*n.*
Petri, H. L., 351, 375, 377*n.*
Petrinovich, L., 257, 274*n.*, 301, 307*n.*
Petrovskaya, L. L., 97, 102*n.*, 151, 169*n.*
Pettigrew, J. D., 311, 329, 332*n.*, 333*n.*
Phifer, C. B., 179, 191*n.*
Phillis, J. W., 323, 331*n.*
Pickel, V. M., 322, 333*n.*
Piercy, M., 347, 348*n.*, 386, *386*, 391–393, 412*n.*, 413*n.*, 452, 461*n.*, 465, 475*n.*
Pierrot-Deseilligny, C., 381, 413*n.*
Pinel, J. P., 258, 263, 277*n.*
Pinsky, C., 323, 331*n.*
Pitts, L. H., 30, 47*n.*
Poggio, T., 270, 271, 276*n.*
Pohle, W., 151, 152, 169*n.*, 170*n.*
Popov, N., 152, 170*n.*
Poran, N., 261, 263, 275*n.*
Powell, T. P. S., 94, 101*n.*
Pradelles, P., 331*n.*
Precht, W., 272, 276*n.*
Precious, J. I., 319, 333*n.*
Premack, D., 302, 303, 306, 307*n.*, 335, 348*n.*, 454, 461*n.*
Preston, G. C., 343, 344, *345*, 349*n.*
Price, D., 191*n.*
Prince, D. A., 110, 113, *115*, 117*n.*, 118*n.*
Prior, D. J., 179, 183, 191*n.*
Pritchard, D., 70
Prytulak, L. S., 362, 376*n.*
Puglisi-Allegra, S., 315, 330*n.*
Puro, D., 108, 118*n.*
Purpura, D. P., 266, 277*n.*
Purves, D., 89, 102*n.*, 267, 277*n.*
Quinn, W. G., 266, 277*n.*, 304, 307*n.*

Racine, R. J., 50, 54, 59, 61*n.*, 62, 70, 76*n.*, 79, 91, 102*n.*, 161, 170*n.*
Rall, W., 271, 277*n.*
Ramirez, J. J., 457, 461*n.*
Ranck, J. B., Jr., 49, 60*n.*
Randich, A., 216, 229*n.*
Rapp, P. R., 324, 326, 331*n.*
Rasmussen, T., 58, 356, 378*n.*, 397, 413*n.*
Ratcliff, R., 361, 364, 377*n.*
Rausch, G., 267, 277*n.*
Rauschenberger, J., 300, 306*n.*
Rawlins, J. N. P., 49, 61*n.*, 245, 249*n.*, 453, 457, 461*n.*
Read, J. M., 82, 101*n.*
Reader, T. A., 108, 119*n.*
Redman, S., 270, 277*n.*
Reingold, S. C., 179, 190*n.*
Reis, D. J., 322, 333*n.*
Reivich, M., 79, 101*n.*, 102*n.*
Rescorla, R. A., 146, 179, 191*n.*, 211, 213–

216, *215*, 218–221, *218*, *222*, *223*, 224–227, *225*, 229*n*., 230*n*., 240, 253, 254, 257, 284, 291, 336, 338, 340, 343, 348*n*., 349*n*., 421
Revusky, S. H., 289, 294*n*., 344, 349*n*.
Richards, C., 319, 333*n*.
Richards, W., 17, 19, 25*n*., 26*n*.
Richer, J. M., 256, 277*n*.
Riddell, W. I., 299, 304, 307*n*.
Riedl, R., 255, 277*n*.
Rifkin, B., 227, 229*n*.
Rigter, H., 315, 332*n*., 333*n*.
Riives, M., 64, 75*n*., 109, 117*n*., 311, 330*n*.
Rijk, H., 315, 333*n*.
Rinzel, J., 271, 277*n*.
Riopelle, A. J., 298, 307*n*.
Risch, H., 121, 126, 132*n*.
Roberts, R., 468, 477*n*.
Roberts, W. A., 237, 241, 242, 250*n*.
Robinson, G. B., 70, 76*n*.
Robinson, H., 272, 277*n*.
Robinson, J. H., 139, 147*n*., 148*n*.
Rocha-Miranda, C. E., 449, 450*n*.
Rodgers, R. J., 319, 333*n*.
Roediger, H. L., 435, 441*n*.
Roemer, R. A., 48*n*.
Rogers, C. J., 64, 75*n*.
Roitblat, H. L., 290, 294*n*., 335, 349*n*.
Rolls, E. T., 351, 378*n*., 449, 450*n*., 451*n*.
Romanes, G. J., 297, *297*, 307*n*.
Rome, H. P., 397, 412*n*.
Ronacher, B., 201, 209*n*., 210*n*.
Ropartz, P., 99, 103*n*.
Rose, S. P. R., 88, 97, 102*n*., 103*n*., 255, 277*n*.
Rosen, S. C., 181, 191*n*.
Rosenberg, R. A., 326, 330*n*.
Rosenzweig, M. R., 80, 82, 97, 99*n*., 100*n*., 102*n*., 151, 170*n*.
Rosito, G., 315, 332*n*.
Rossier, J., 330*n*.
Routtenberg, A., 322, 330*n*.
Rowe, M. P., 258, 275*n*., 278*n*.
Rowgaski, M. A., 108, 119*n*.
Rozin, P., 248, 250*n*., 300, 307*n*., 357, 361, 362, 374, 376*n*., 378*n*., 403, 413*n*.
Rudy, J. W., 49, 61*n*., 175, 179, 189, 191*n*., 192*n*.
Ruggierio, F. T., 372, 373, 378*n*.
Rusiniak, K., 225, 230*n*., 291, 294*n*.
Russell, I. S., 340, 350*n*.
Russell, W. R., 465, 476*n*.
Ruthrich, H.-L., 152, 170*n*.
Ryle, G., 337, 349*n*.
Ryugo, D. K., 42, 48*n*.

Saari, M., 329, 333*n*.
Saavedra, M. A., 220, 230*n*.
Sæther, O. A., 256, 278*n*.
Sahley, C. L., 49, 61*n*., 175, 179, 185, 189, 191*n*., 192*n*.
Sakakibara, M., 10, 14, 17, 25*n*., 26*n*., 108, 119*n*.
Sakharov, D. A., 182, 192*n*.
Sakurai, M., 62, 76*n*.
Salasoo, A., 361, 376*n*.
Salpeter, M. M., 270, 276*n*.
Saltwick, S. E., 42, 47*n*., 79, 101*n*.
Samuels, I., 449, 450*n*.
Samuelson, R. J., 240, *241*, 250*n*., 280, 285*n*., 317, 333*n*.
Sanders, H. I., 399–402, 413*n*., 414*n*., 466, 476*n*.
Sanderson, K. J., 86, 102*n*.
Sanghera, M. K., 449, 451*n*.
Sapper, D. B., 315, 332*n*.
Sarty, M., 256, 275*n*.
Sato, O., 469, 477*n*.
Saunders, R. C., 469, 475*n*., 476*n*.
Sawynok, J., 323, 332*n*.
Sax, D. S., 429, 432*n*., 466, 474*n*.
Scarborough, D. L., 357, 361, 378*n*.
Scarborough, H. S., 361, 378*n*.
Scatton, B., 110, 117*n*., 119*n*.
Schacter, D. L., 346, 351–354, 357–359, 364, 366–375, 376*n*., 378*n*., 379*n*., 395, 403, 408, 410, 413*n*., 414*n*., 421, 423, 429, 432*n*., 435–439, 436*n*., 439*n*., 441*n*., 442, 454, 465, 473
Schaeffer, S. F., 185, 191*n*.
Schafer, S., 283, 285*n*.
Scheich, H., 267, 277*n*.
Schetzen, M., 121, 124, 132*n*.
Schleidt, W. M., 257, 278*n*.
Schlossberg, P., 280, 286*n*.

Schmaltz, G., 55, 59*n*.
Schneiderman, N., 340, 349*n*.
Schnetter, B., 201, 210*n*.
Schnierla, T. C., 297, 306*n*.
Schnur, P., 227, 229*n*.
Schoppmann, A., 48*n*.
Schottler, F., 91, 102*n*., 134, 148*n*., 151, 160, 169*n*., 270, 276*n*.
Schröder, H., 110, 119*n*.
Schulzeck, S., 152, 170*n*.
Schürg-Pfeiffer, E., 257, 275*n*.
Schuri, U., *384*, 385, *385*, 414*n*.
Schwab, M. E., 110, 119*n*.
Schwartz, B., 196, 198, 210*n*.
Schwartz, J. C., 323, 332*n*.
Schwartz, J. H., 27, 42, 47*n*., 78–80, 102*n*., 117*n*., 255, 276*n*.
Schwartzkroin, P. A., 113, *115*, 118*n*.
Schwartzman, R. J., 79, 102*n*.
Sclabassi, R. J., 121, 126, 132*n*., 423, 424
Scoville, W. B., 390, 392, 413*n*., 433, 441*n*.
Seeman, P., 111, 119*n*.
Segal, D., 330*n*.
Segal, M., 14, 26*n*.
Seifert, W., 446, 451*n*.
Seligman, M. E. P., 253, 278*n*.
Seltzer, B., 466, 476*n*.
Senseman, D. S., 183, 191*n*.
Serdaru, M., 413*n*.
Shalter, M. D., 257, 278*n*.
Shambes, G. M., 86, 102*n*.
Shanks, D. R., 344
Shapiro, E., 135, 148*n*.
Sharp, P. E., 55, 61*n*., 93, 103*n*.
Shashoua, V., 136, 148*n*., 151, 161, 166, 169*n*., 170*n*.
Shavalia, D. A., 318, 330*n*.
Shell, W. F., 298, 307*n*.
Shepard, R. N., 290, 294*n*.
Sherman, S. M., 42, 48*n*.
Sherry, D. F., 232, 234, 235, 238–240, 243, *243*, 246, 248, 249, 249*n*., 250*n*.
Shettleworth, S. J., 196, 210*n*., 234, *234*, 235, *239*, 238–240, 244, 246, 250*n*., 253, 254, 266, 278*n*., 280, 289, *294*, 294*n*., 296, 303, 335, 420
Shiffrin, R. M., 361, 376*n*., 433, 440*n*.
Shimamura, A. P., 466, 471, 476*n*.
Shipley, M. T., 122, 133*n*.
Shoukimas, J. J., 10, 22, 23, 25*n*., 135, 146*n*.
Sidman, M., 373, 378*n*.
Siegelbaum, S. A., 135, 148*n*.
Siegelman, J., 39, 47*n*.
Siggins, G. R., 330*n*.
Signoret, J.-L. 388, 413*n*., 452
Sigurdson, J. E., 284, 286*n*.
Simantov, R., 326, 333*n*.
Simmelhag, V., 287, 295*n*.
Simon, H., 110, 119*n*.
Simonsen, L., *88*
Siniscalchi, A., 324, 330*n*.
Sirevaag, A. M., 97, 103*n*.
Skrede, K. K., 63, 75*n*., 79, 103*n*., 121, 132*n*., 134, 148*n*.
Slater, P. C., 400, 401, 403, 405, 407, 414*n*., 472, 476*n*.
Smith, D. A. S., 458, 460*n*.
Smith, D. G., 261, 275*n*., 278*n*.
Smith, M. C., 245, 249*n*.
Smith, W. J., 257, 278*n*.
Snowden, J. S., 391, 413*n*., 466, 475*n*.
Snyder, S. H., 326, 333*n*.
Sokolov, Y. N., 346, 349*n*.
Sokolove, P. G., 182, 185, 191*n*., 192*n*.
Solina, A., 39, 47*n*.
Solomon, P. R., 48*n*., 91, 103*n*., 146, 148*n*., 344, 349*n*.
Sørensen, K. E., 122, 133*n*.
Sotelo, C., 89, 103*n*., 266, 272, 278*n*.
Soumireu-Mourat, B., 331*n*., 332*n*.
Souza, D. O., 321, 331*n*.
Spalding, D. A., 255, 278*n*.
Spear, P. D., 42, 48*n*.
Spence, K. W., 220, 230*n*.
Spencer, W. A., 29, 39, 48*n*., 134, 147*n*., 342, 349*n*.
Spiegler, B. J., 469, 475*n*.
Spiehler, V. R., 331*n*., 332*n*.
Squire, L. R., 41, 48*n*., 57, 58, 59*n*., 61*n*., 78, 103*n*., 136, 146, 147*n*., 148*n*., *302*, 307*n*., 324, 333*n*., 339, 346, 348*n*., 349*n*., 351, 353–356, 372–375, 375*n*., 376*n*., 378*n*., 379*n*., 380, 383, 387–391, *390*,

392, 399–405, 407, 411, 412*n.*, 413*n.*, 414*n.*, 415*n.*, 429, 431*n.*, 432*n.*, 435, 441*n.*, 442, 451*n.*, 453–455, 460*n.*, 461*n.*, 462*n.*, 465–473, 474*n.*, 475*n.*, 476*n.*, 477*n.*
Staddon, J. E. R., 199, 210*n.*, 242, 250*n.*, 287–289, 291–293, 294*n.*, 295*n.*, 296, 343
Standing, L. 282, 286*n.*
Stange, K., 329, 333*n.*
Stanton, M., 79, 101*n.*
Stanzione, P., 110, 118*n.*
Stark, H. A., 357, 379*n.*, 403, 414*n.*
Starke, K., 323, 333*n.*
Stefano, G. B., 188, 192*n.*
Stein, B. M., 469, 475*n.*
Stein, D. G., 457, 461*n.*
Stein, L., 315, 333*n.*, 343, 349*n.*
Steneri, U., 458, 460*n.*
Stephens, D. W., 239, 250*n.*
Stevens, A., 232, 250*n.*
Stevens, C. F., 270, 278*n.*
Stevens, T. A. D., 238, 240, 244, 250*n.*
Steward, O., 64, 66, 67, 71, 75*n.*, 76*n.*, 89, 94, 100*n.*, 103*n.*, 109, 118*n.*, 138, 139, 148*n.*
Stewart, M. G., 97, 103*n.*
Stickney, K. J., 340, 349*n.*
Stoddard, L., 373, 378*n.*
Stotland, L. M., 323, 334*n.*
Strahlendorf, H. K., 322, 333*n.*
Strahlendorf, J. C., 322, 333*n.*
Straub, J. J., 337, 348*n.*
Stryker, M. P., 48*n.*
Stuss, D., 468, 475*n.*
Summers, R. J., 242, 250*n.*, 281, 286*n.*
Sundberg, S. H., 64, 75*n.*, 138, 146*n.*, 151, 168*n.*
Sutak, M., 323, 332*n.*
Sutherland, N. S., 282, 286*n.*
Sutherland, R. J., 49, 58, 60*n.*, 61*n.*, 457, 461*n.*
Sveen, O., 64, 75*n.*, 138, 146*n.*, 151, 168*n.*
Svien, H. J., 397, 412*n.*
Swanberg, P. O., 240, 250*n.*
Swann, J. W., 64, 75*n.*, 138, 146*n.*, 151, 168*n.*
Swanson, L. W., 71, 76*n.*, 109, 110, 119*n.*, 122, 133*n.*
Swanson, P. D., 468, 475*n.*
Sypert, G. W., 391, 392, 412*n.*

Tabata, M., *14*, 22, 26*n.*
Takashima, S., 266, 272, 278*n.*
Tanaka, T., 108, 118*n.*
Tank, D. W., 173, 190*n.*, 254, 275*n.*
Taube, H. D., 323, 333*n.*
Tavares, M. R., 272, 278*n.*
Taylor, A. M., 410, 414*n.*
Taylor, B., 245, 249*n.*
Taylor, L., 373, 377*n.*
Tazi, A., 315, 333*n.*
Tepper, J. M., 323, 333*n.*
Ternes, J. W., 343, 349*n.*
Teskey, G. C., 188, 191*n.*
Testa, T. J., 343, 349*n.*
Teuber, H.-L., 354, 377*n.*, 381, 396, *397*, *398*, 399, 404, 413*n.*, 414*n.*, 466, 468, 472, 475*n.*, 476*n.*
Teyler, T. J., 48*n.*, 64, 71, 73, 75*n.*, 76*n.*, 91, 103*n.*, 109, 119*n.*, 136, 148*n.*, 151, 157, 161, 166, 168*n.*, 169*n.*, 170*n.*, 458, 461*n.*
Thomas, G. J., 351, 379*n.*
Thompson, E. B., 270, 274*n.*
Thompson, J. K., 461*n.*
Thompson, R. F., 27, 39, 41, 42, 48*n.*, 57, 60*n.*, 71, 76*n.*, 78, 91, 103*n.*, 109, 119*n.*, 134, 136, 137, 148*n.*, 151, 170*n.*, 340, 342, 343, 348*n.*, 349*n.*, 457, 461*n.*
Thorndike, E. L., 297, 307*n.*
Tieman, S. B., 267, 278*n.*
Tinbergen, N., 256, 278*n.*
Tomback, D. F., 232, 233, 238, 250*n.*
Tomie, A., 216, 230*n.*
Tongroach, P., 62, 76*n.*
Treit, D., 258, 277*n.*
Tulving, E., 301, 302, 307*n.*, 351, 354, 357, 369, 373, 375, 376*n.*, 378*n.*, 379*n.*, 395, 403, 408, 411, 413*n.*, 414*n.*, 429, 432*n.*, 434, 437, 438, 441*n.*, 454, 456, 462*n.*
Turek, R. J., 235, 236, 249*n.*
Turner, A. M., 81, *81*, 89, 103*n.*
Turvey, M. T., 253, 276*n.*

Uhl, G. R., 326, 333*n*.
Ungerer, B., 99, 103*n*.
Ushiyama, N. S., 109, 118*n*.
Uttley, A., 74, 76*n*.
Uylings, H. B. M., 82, 103*n*., 329, 330*n*.

Van Bergeijk, W. A., 284, 286*n*.
Van Der Gugten, J., 329, 330*n*.
Vander Wall, S. B., 232, 235, 236, 238, 240, 250*n*.
Vanderwart, M., 357, 379*n*.
Van Dongen, C. J., 118*n*.
Van Harreveld, A., 97, 100*n*., 135, 147*n*., 151, 166, 169*n*., 170*n*., 270, 278*n*.
Van Hoesen, G. W., 467, 475*n*.
Van Minnen, J., 182, 192*n*.
Van Mol, J., 182, 192*n*.
Van Veldhuizen, N., 242, 250*n*.
Vasavan Nair, N. P., 324, 334*n*.
Vasquez, B. J., 330*n*., 332*n*.
Vaughan, H. G., 381, 414*n*., 468, 476*n*.
Vaughan, W., 247, 250*n*., 281, 286*n*., 293, 293*n*., 295*n*.
Vaughn, J. E., 267, 278*n*.
Veltman, W. A. M., 82, 103*n*.
Vendite, D. A., 331*n*.
Veratti, E., 182, 192*n*.
Verbeek, N. A. M., 233, 239*n*.
Versteeg, D. H. G., 329, 332*n*.
Victor, M., 383, 384, 414*n*., 468, 476*n*.
Vilkki, J., 448, 451*n*.
Virginia, R. A., 258, 277*n*.
Volkmar, F. R., 80, 82, *83*, 101*n*.
Volterra, V., 121, 133*n*.
von Cramon, D., *384*, 385, *385*, 414*n*.
von Frisch, K., 199, 200, 204, 206, 210*n*.
Voorhoeve, P. E., 122, 132*n*.
Voronin, L. G., 298, 303, 307*n*.
Vrensen, G., 94, 97, 100*n*., 103*n*.
Vries, J. K., 121, 132*n*.

Waddington, C. H., 256, 278*n*.
Wagner, A. R., 214, 216, 220, 226, 227, 230*n*., 342, 349*n*., 372, 379*n*.
Wainer, B. H., 323, 333*n*.
Walker, J. A., 49, 57, 61*n*.
Wall, J. T., 37, 48*n*.
Walmsley, B., 270, 277*n*.
Walsh, R. N., 82, 100*n*.
Walters, E. T., 254, 278*n*., 311, *312*, 333*n*.
Warrington, E. K., 339, 350*n*., 351, 357, 364, 371, 379*n*., 382, 388, 389, 392, 394, 395, 399–411, *400*, *405*, *406*, *407*, 411*n*., 413*n*., 414*n*., 415*n*., 429, 432*n*., 434, 441*n*., 446, 449, 451*n*., 452, 461*n*., 465, 466, 470, 472, 473, 475*n*., 476*n*., 477*n*.
Waser, P. B., 315, 333*n*.
Watkins, J. C., 458, 460*n*.
Waugh, N. C., 433, 441*n*.
Weber, F., 323, 333*n*.
Webster, G., 265, 278*n*.
Wehner, R., 201, 202, 204, 210*n*.
Weibel, E. R., *81*, 103*n*.
Weinberger, N. M., 42, 48*n*., 50, 61*n*., 108, 119*n*., 136, 147*n*., 301
Weiskrantz, L., 136, 339, 346, 350*n*., 351, 357, 364, 371, 374, 379*n*., 382, 388, 389, 394–396,402–411, *405*, *406*, *407*, 413*n*., 414*n*., 415*n*., 423, 429, 432*n*., 433, 434, 438, 441*n*., 446, 451*n*., 452–454, 456, 457, 461*n*., 462*n*., 464–466, 469, 471–473, 475*n*., 477*n*.
Weiss, K. R., 181, 191*n*.
Weisz, D. J., 48*n*., 91, 103*n*.
Welker, W., 86, 102*n*.
Wenk, G. L., 324, 334*n*.
Wenzel, J., 150, 151, 153, *154*, 170*n*., 423, 424
Wenzel, M., 170*n*.
Wernicke, C., 444, 451*n*.
West, A., 10, 22, 23, 26*n*.
West, M. O., 139–141, 143, 144, 147*n*., 148*n*.
West, R. W., 94, 97, 101*n*., 103*n*.
Wetzel, C. D., *390*, 405, 414*n*., 415*n*., 472, 476*n*., 477*n*.
Whishaw, I. Q., 49, 58, 60*n*., 61*n*., 457, 461*n*.
Whitehead, M. C., 267, 278*n*.

Whitely, A. M., 449, 451*n*.
Whitty, C. W. M., 353, 379*n*.
Wickelgren, W. A., 370, 373, 379*n*., 411, 415*n*., 466, 473, 477*n*.
Wieland, S. J., 183, 185, 188, 192*n*.
Wiener, N., 121, 124, 133*n*.
Wiesel, T. N., 89, 102*n*.
Wigström, H., 54, 61*n*., 64, 73, 75*n*., 76*n*., 138, 146*n*., 151, 168*n*.
Wild, J. M., 36, 37, 43, 48*n*.
Wilkie, D. M., 242, 250*n*., 281, 286*n*.
Will, B., 99, 103*n*.
Williams, D. R., 290, 295*n*.
Williams, H., 290, 295*n*.
Wilson, C. J., 270, 278*n*.
Wilson, F. D., 117*n*.
Wilson, R. C., 64, 76*n*.
Wilson, T. DeC., 438, 441*n*.
Winocur, G., 389, 408–410, 415*n*., 429, 432*n*., 468, 471, 477*n*.
Winson, J., 55, 61*n*., 131, 133*n*., 137, 145, 149*n*.
Wise, S. P., 86, 100*n*., 103*n*.
Withers, G. S., *87*
Witherspoon, D., 357, 361, 376*n*., 429, 432*n*.
Wittgenstein, L., 337, 350*n*.
Wolf, L. L., 280, 285*n*.
Wolfe, J., 356, 377*n*.
Wong, R. K. S., 14, 25*n*.
Wood, F., 146, 148*n*., 324, 334*n*., 351, 376*n*., 377*n*., 402, 415*n*., 429, 432*n*., 436, 438, 441*n*.
Wood, P. L., 323, 324, 333*n*.
Woodbury, C. B., 220, 230*n*.
Woodruff, G., 335, 348*n*.
Woodward, D. J., 108, 118*n*.
Woody, C. D., 17, 26*n*., 62, 75*n*., 116, 119*n*., 149*n*.
Wu, P. Y. K., 257, 275*n*.
Wurtman, R., 324, 330*n*.
Wyss, J. M., 110, 119*n*.

Yamada, S., 469, 477*n*.
Yamamoto, I., 469, 477*n*.
Yamane, T., 189, 191*n*., 192*n*.
Yang, B., 91, 103*n*.
Yarosh, C. A., 109, 117*n*.
Yeo, C. H., 340, 350*n*.
Young, J. Z., 270, 278*n*.
Young, N. B., 317, 331*n*.
Young, R. A., 48*n*., 151, 169*n*.
Young, S. J., 323, 333*n*.
Young, W. S., 317, *318*, 322, 334*n*.
Yuen, A. R., 267, 274*n*.

Zangwill, O. L., 353, 379*n*.
Zengel, J. E., 50, 60*n*.
Zetin, M., 468, 475*n*.
Zini, I., 118*n*.
Zola Morgan, S., 339, 349*n*., 354, 356, 372–375, 377*n*., 379*n*., 393, 411, 413*n*., 414*n*., 415*n*., 429, 432*n*., 453, 454, 462*n*., 469, 470, 472, 473, 476*n*., 477*n*.
Zoli, M., 118*n*.
Zook, J. M., 48*n*.
Zornetzer, S. F., 314, 334*n*.
Zouzounis, J. A., 389, 414*n*.
Zs-Nagy, I., 182, 192*n*.
Zwiers, H., 118*n*.

# SUBJECT INDEX

A2 region, 322
Abstract representation, 303
AB-US arrangement, 212–220
Acetylcholine
  opiate effects, 323, 324
    latent inhibition tasks, 328
  slow postsynaptic potentials, 109
Acetylcholine receptor changes, 88
Acquisition
  brain slice technique, 23
  *Hermissenda*, and mammals, 17, 23
Across-fiber pattern, 290
ACT model, 438
ACTH, and opiate antagonists, 317
Active cognitive strategies, 411
Adenylate cyclase, 111
Affective aspects, conditioning, 339, 341
African jewel fish, 256, 267, 268*n.*, 270
Age factors
  memory loss, and amnesia, 439, 440
  spatial learning, rats, hippocampus, 51, 53
  synaptogenesis, and environment, 82
Aged rats, 51, 53
Aging process, and metacognition, 439, 440
Alanine-deficient diet, *Limax*, 175–178
Alcohol, and perforant path, 70
Alexia, 444
Alpha conditioning
  and associative learning, 197, 200, 202, 288
  existence of, evaluation, bees, 283
Alphabet ot learning, 287
Alzheimer disease, 359, 360
Amakihi, 280
Aminophosphonovaleric acid, 458, 459*n.*
4-Aminopyridine, 15*n.*, 16*n.*
Amnesia (*see also* Anterograde amnesia; Retrograde amnesia)
  and aging, 439, 440
  animal models, 372–375, 452–457, 463–474
  and awareness, 374, 438
  and disconnection, 445–450, 464, 467
  hyperspecific associations, 370, 371
  issues and theories, 380–411
  medial temporal versus diencephalic, 380–386, 464–467
  and memory forms, 351–375
  modeling, 452–460, 463–474
  and new associations, 365, 366
  partial information method importance, 402–408
  priming effects, 356–375
  and recognition, types of, 346, 347
  reversal of, 396–403
  severity measurement, 390–392
  skill learning, dissociation, 353–356
  spared memory types, 402–411, 453
  storage versus retrieval, 394–403
  unitized structures in, 362–371
  vocabulary learning, 370, 371
Amnesia severity, 390–392
Amygdala
  animal models, amnesia, 454
  conditioning mediation, pigeon, 32*n.*, 33
  damage to, amnesia, 384, 385, 454
  naloxone administration, 326–328
  opiate effects, conditioning, 321, 326–328
  taste aversion effect, generality, 456, 457
Analogue conditioning model, 39
Animal models, amnesia, 372–375, 452–457, 463–474

Anterograde amnesia
  Korsakoff syndrome, 466, 467
  measurement, 390–393
  retrograde amnesia correlation, 465–467
  reversibility, 398
Antidromic spike, 72, 73
*Aplysia*
  ecological factors, learning, 282, 283
  and levels of analysis, 254, 255
  procedural theory, 339
Appetitive conditioning, *Limax*, 174
Archistriatum mediale, pars dorsalis, 32*n.*, 33*n.*
Arctic ground squirrels, 263
Arousal, and memory modulation, 314
Associative learning
  amnesics, 371
  and catalytic effects, 227
  cause detection, 285
  cellular analysis, *Hermissenda*, 12*n.*, 13*n.*
  conditions for, neuronal changes, 44, 45
  context effects, 216, 217
  contiguity in, consequences, 211–228
  and habituation, 342–347
  *Hermissenda* potential for, 10
  hippocampus, 136
  innate aspects, ethology, 196, 197, 201, 203
  and latent inhibition, 342–347
  in *Limax*, 174
  and memory system dichotomy, 302, 303
  multiplicity in, and neurobiology, 219, 220
  neuronal modification, pigeon, 36–39, 40*n.*, 44, 45
  versus nonassociative learning, 342–347
  species comparison, 302
Associative recall, and priming, 366–371
Attentional tuning, 146
Auditory conditioning, 42
Auditory discrimination, and synapse, 139–144
Auditory evoked potentials, 139–144
Autistic children, 256
Autoconditioning, 198
Autonomic system, and plasticity, 108
Autoshaping
  catalytic effects, conditioning, 225, 225*n.*, 226
  conditional discrimination, 220–224
Aversive conditioning, *Limax*, 175–181
Aversive stimulus, and modulation, 314
Avian amygdala homologue, 33*n.*
Avoidance conditioning
  epinephrine response variability, 314
  opioid peptide modulation, 315
  sensory pathway modification, 42
Awareness, amnesics, priming, 374, 438
Axo-dendritic contacts, 156–160
Axo-spine synapses, 158

B-US association, 213
Backward conditioning, *Limax*, 179
Bait-shyness learning, 300
Basal ganglia, 429
Bed nucleus, 321
Bees (*see* Honey bees)
Beta-adrenergic antagonists, 328
Beta-endorphin
  cholinergic effects, hippocampus, 324
  locus ceruleus inhibition, 322
  norepinephrine inhibition, 323
Birds (*see also* Food-storing birds)
  food storing 231–249, 280, 281
  song learning, 194, 195
  spatial memory models, 240–245
Black-capped chickadees, 233, 243*n.*
Blindsight, 438
Block of conditioning
  catalytic effects, 225, 226
  consummatory versus preparatory conditioning, 340
  in *Limax*, 174, 175
  LIMAX model, 189
Blue tits, food storing, 232
Brain damage, skill learning, 356
Brain lesions, and memory site, 19, 22
Brain slice technique, 23
Brain thickness, 82
Brain weight, 82
8-Bromoadenosine 3′,5′-cyclic monophosphate, 116

Buffer process, 144
Bungarotoxin binding, 88
Butaclamol, 111

CA1 neurons
  conditioning, E-S curve, 64
  dopamine effect, excitability, 110–116
  *Hermissenda* membrane similarity, 10, 14, 15
  and hippocampal slices, ribosomes, 160–168
  long-term potentiation, 92*n.*, 94
  ribosomal systems, learning, 152–168
  synaptogenesis, 94
  trace independence, 73
CA3 neurons, 152–160
Calcium, *Hermissenda*, membranes, 10–24
California ground squirrel, 257–260, 266
Cardiac motoneurons, 30, 33–38
Catalytic functions, contiguity, 224–228, 284, 291
Catecholamines (*see also* Dopamine)
  long-term potentiation influence, 109
  and neuronal plasticity, 107–117
Caudate-putamen, 85*n.*
Causality
  conditioned stimulus identification, 288, 289
  and intelligence, ecology, 285
Cebus monkeys, 298, 299
Cellular excitability, 108–116
Cellular models
  *Hermissenda* conditioning, 23
  vertebrates, pigeon, 27–46
Cellular plasticity (*see* Neuronal plasticity)
Cerebellum, 340
Cerebral cortex
  disconnection syndromes, lesions, 448
  maze training effects, 82
Cerebral ganglion, *Limax*, 186, 187*n.*
Chickadees, food storing, 232–249
Chimpanzees, language learning, 300
Cholinergic system, 323, 324, 328
Chunking, 411
Circadian rhythms, 290
Circuits, memory systems, 79
Circular platform task, 51*n.*
Clark's nutcracker, 232, 233, 235, 236, 240, 300
Classical conditioning
  amnesics, 371, 373, 409, 410
    animals, 373
  conditional control in, 222–224
  contiguity in, 211–228
  heart rate, pigeon, 28–39
  *Hermissenda*, and mammals, 17
  innate aspects, ethology, 196, 197, 255, 256
  and neural system properties, 131
  neuromodulation in, 311, 312, 312*n.*
  operant conditioning comparison, 198
  and procedural learning, 409, 410
  procedural versus declarative learning, 337–339
  temporal contiguity, 288, 289
Coal tits, food storing, 232
Cochlear nucleus, plasticity, 42
Cognition
  in amnesia, 410
  and levels of analysis, 421, 422
  memory system dichotomy, 302, 303
  species comparison, 302, 303
Cognitive maps, 57–59, 257
Cognitive mediational system, 410
Color learning, bees, 200, 201
Command neurons, LIMAX, 188, 189
Comparative psychology, 280, 281, 452–457
Complex learning, 301–303
Compound conditioning, *Limax*, 174
Compound stimulus presentation
  contiguity consequences, 215
  new elements, 220, 221, 222*n.*
Computational theory, 421, 422
Computer models
  and levels of analysis, 255
  LIMAX, 188, 189
Conditioned discrimination, 220–224
Conditioned inhibition (*see also* Latent inhibition)
  honey bees, 202, 283
  as paradigm, interpretation, 223, 224
Conditioned response
  conditioned stimulus dependence, 222–224

consummatory versus preparatory, 339–342
innate aspects, ethology, 196, 197
sensory pathway modification, 42, 44, 45
versus spatial learning, physiology, 57
temporal properties, pigeon, 33–36
Conditioned stimulus
catalytic function, 224–228
cellular models, *Hermissenda*, 23
conditioned response dependence, 222–224
and declarative learning, 337, 338
heart rate, pigeon, 28
*Hermissenda* learning, and mammals, 17–22
identification rules, animals, 288, 289
innate aspects, ethology, 196, 197
nerve pathways, pigeon, 36, 37, 42–45
temporal aspects, 33–36
and neuromodulation, 311, 312
neuronal modification, 44, 45
pairwise associations, contiguity, 212–220
temporal factors, *Limax*, 178, 179
Conditioned suppression, 340, 341
Conditioning (*see also* Associative learning; Classical conditioning; First-order conditioning; Operant learning; Second-order conditioning
associative and nonassociative, 342–347
cellular models, *Hermissenda*, 23
consummatory versus preparatory, 339–342
contiguity in, consequences, 211–228
*Hermissenda* channel changes, 9–24
in *Limax*, 174–189
LIMAX model, 188, 189
and long-term potentiation, 137, 138
procedural and declarative learning in, 337–339
versus spatial learning, physiology, 57
varieties of, 335–347
vertebrates, 27–46
Conduction aphasia, 444
Conscious recollection, 353–375
Consciousness, 437–439
Consolidation
in amnesia, versus retrieval, 394–402
ECT effects, 389, 399
Constancy
honey bees, 292
and long-term memory, birds, 293, 294*n*.
Consummatory conditioning
forgetting rates, 340, 341
neurobiology, 340
preparatory conditioning distinction, 339–342
Contact zone curvature, 94
Context effects
associative learning, 216, 217, 342, 343
conditional role, 224
definition, alternative view, 257, 258
latent inhibition explanation, 342–345
priming, amnesics, 364–366, 436
Contextual presentation, 145, 146
Contiguity
and associative learning, 211–228
catalytic functions, 224–228
and causality, learning, 288
Contingency requirement
conditioning principles, 289
*Hermissenda*, and mammals, 17
Cortico-cortico connections, 444, 446
Corvids, food storing, 231–249
Covert alpha conditioning, 197, 200
Crested tits, 232
Cross-correlation technique, 124
*Crotalus viridis oreganus*, 258–266
Cues
amnesics, recall, 346, 347, 395, 396, 400, 402–411
bird food-storing, 240
hierarchies of, learning, 206, 207
honey bee learning, 201, 206, 207, 283, 284
time-specific interactions, 206–208
and innate learning, ethology, 196, 197
and intact memories, amnesics, 402–408, 472, 473
Cyclic-AMP-dependent protein kinase, 113–116

Cyclic-AMP-dependent protein kinase inhibitor protein, 114–116

Decay kinetics
long-term potentiation, 70
spatial memory, kinetics, 53, 54
Decision processes, 438
Declarative memory
amnesia syndrome, 411, 472
in conditioning, 337, 338
and consciousness, 438
memory system dichotomy, 302, 429
procedural learning distinction, 337–339
and sensory discrimination, hippocampus, 145, 146
and spatial memory, hippocampus, 59
Default rule, 293
Delayed-alternation, 292, 293
Delayed matching to sample
mnemonic demands, animals, 372, 373
recency principle, 292, 293
tests of, and memory models, 242, 243
Delayed nonmatching to sample
animal models, amnesia, 453–455
mnemonic demands, animals, 372, 373
Delayed prose recall, 470
Delayed spatial alternation, 242, 243, 281
Dendritic fields, 80–84
Dendritic shaft synapse, 156–160, 166
Dendritic spines
adjustability of, 267, 269*n.*, 270–273
genetic-epigenetic restraints, 272
ion flux, and regulation, 270, 271
length of, 271–273
and synaptogenesis, 92*n.*, 93, 94, 95*n.*, 96
Dentate fascia (*see* Fascia dentata)
Dentate gyrus
auditory discrimination, EPs, 139–144
environmental complexity, synapse, 91, 93, 93*n.*,
long-lasting traces, 62–74
mechanisms, 71, 72
long-term potentiation effect, 128–130, 139, 140
and nonlinear systems, 120–131
norepinephrine, trace independence, 70
ribosomal system, learning, 154–160
sensory evoked potentials, 139–144
2-Deoxyglucose uptake, 85*n.*, 86–89
Depolarization
cAMP role, dopamine, 113–116
dopamine effect, CA1 neurons, 111–116
granule cells, conditioning, EPSPs, 72, 73
*Hermissenda* neuronal membranes, 10–19
Deprivation-rearing, 255, 256
Descending pathways, 30, 32*n.*, 33
Desmethylimipramine, 325, 326
Developmental overproduction, synapses, 89–96
Dextrallorphan, 316*n.*
Diencephalon
amnesia theories, 380–394, 464–467
lesions of, animals, amnesia, 453, 467–470
Differential two-tone discrimination, 139–144
Diprenorphine, 316*n.*, 318*n.*
Disconnected memories, 442–450
Discrimination learning
honey bees, 284
new elements formation, 220, 221, 222*n.*
synaptic changes, hippocampus, LTP, 139–144
Dissociation
in amnesia, skill learning, 353–356
in amnesia, versus unitary, 464–467
animal models, amnesia, 452, 453, 457
and brain systems, 429
measurement of, amnesia, 393, 394, 452, 453
pathological studies, 433
priming effects, amnesia, 356–375
Distributed network, learning, 42–44
Diurnal cycle, 290
Dopamine
cellular excitability modulation, 108–116
hippocampal CA1 cells, excitability, 110–116
*Limax* feeding behavior, 183, 184, 186, 187

storage pool effects, 188
microtopical application, 110–112
opiate agonist modulation, mollusks, 188
synaptic modulation, 108–116
Dopamine-sensitive adenylate cyclase, 111
Dorsal noradrenergic bundle, 324–327
Dorsomedial thalamic nucleus
animal models, lesions, 468–470
Korsakoff amnesia, 380–394
versus mammillary bodies, amnesia, 383, 384
Double-hoarding design, 239
Douglas ground squirrels, 260–265
Drive, 194
*Drosophila melanogaster*, 266, 303, 304
DSP-4, 325
Dual-trace theory, 434
Dyadic form, learning, 291
Dyslexia, deep, 445

E. A., patient, 466
Ecology, 279–285, 300, 301, 355
Ectostriatal neurons, 37
Eidetic images, 201
Electrical changes
conditioning, brain slices, 28
hippocampal synapses, 50
Electrical stimulation
and amnesia, reversibility, 397, 398
hippocampus, synaptic change, 49–59
and learning, 23, 24
multiple trace production, 62–74
synaptogenesis, hippocampus, 91, 92*n*.
Electroconvulsive shock
and amnesia types, 387
forgetting rates, 465
learning effects, 226
memory consolidation effects, 399
mnemonic effects, 389, 390
spared memory, 405–407
Embryonic transplants, 458
Encephalitic amnesia
versus Korsakoff patients, 388
reversibility, 398
Encephalization, 299
Endorphins (*see* Beta-endorphin)
Engram
*Limax* food memory, 181, 182
vertebrate models, 41, 42
Enkephalins
locus ceruleus effect, 322
norepinephrine inhibition, 323
Entorhinal cortex neurons (*see also* Perforant path)
auditory discrimination, 139, 140
Environment (*see also* Field studies)
and memory capacity, 281, 282
Environmental complexity
long-term potentiation, hippocampus, 91, 93, 93*n*.
polyribosomal aggregate, 94, 96, 96*n*.
synaptic changes, rats, 80, 81, 81*n*., 82, 94, 96
Epinephrine
dose-response function, 314
level variability, conditioning, 314–317
Episodic memory
and consciousness, 437, 438
and sensory discrimination, 146
Ergonovine, *Limax*, 187, 188
E-S left shift, 65–74
E-S potentiation, 64–70
E-S slope depression, 65–74
Ethanol, perforant path, 70
Ethology
and laboratory studies, bridges, 280, 281
of learning, 193–199
Eurasian nutcracker, 235, 236
Evaluative memory, 411
Evolution
and memory capacity, species, 282
restraints on learning, 253–273
Excitatory postsynaptic potentials, 63–74
Expectancy theory, 337
Experience expectant information storage, 146
Explicit memory
in animals, 372, 373, 455
and consciousness, 438
definition, 353
and priming, amnesics, 356–375
skill learning, amnesics, 353–356
Extinction
in *Limax*, 174

Extinction (*continued*)
LIMAX model, 189
on phylogenetic time scale, 260–265
Eye occluders, 82–84

Facial features, gestalt, 256
Facial recognition, disconnection, 442–450, 466, 467
Facilitation
catalytic effects, 226
and conditional control, 222–224
Familiarity, 347
Famous faces, 466, 467
Fascia dentata
electrical stimulation, 51, 52*n*.
long-term potentiation effect, 154–160
spatial memory, synapses, 50–59
Feed neurons, 188
Feedback, bird song learning, 194
Feedback pathways, 122, 123, 123*n*.
Feedforward inhibition, 71
Feedforward pathways, 122, 123, 123*n*.
Feeding behavior
isolated brain preparation, *Limax*, 179–181
localization of, 181–188
Feeding motor program, *Limax*, 179–188
Field studies
and laboratory studies, 279–281
and level of analysis, 253–255
Fimbria-superior fornix, 324
First order conditioning, *Limax*, 174, 182
Fisher ground squirrels, 260–265
Flat retrograde amnesia, 402, 403
Flatworms, dendritic spines, 270
Flee neurons, 188
Flower handling, bees, 206
FMRFamide
*Limax* feeding, immunoreactivity, 183–186, 186*n*.
somatostatin colocalization, 185
Food aversion learning, *Limax*, 175–181
Food-storing birds, 231–249
ecological restraints, 300, 301
evolutionary constraints, 266
laboratory and field studies, 280
memory capacity, recency, 292, 293, 294*n*.
versus pigeons, memory, 281
and radial mazes, model, 240–245
Forager honey bees, 267, 269*n*., 270, 271*n*., 272
Forelimb reaching studies, 84–89
Forgetting rates, 386, 387, 465
Fornix-fimbria system, 384, 385
Fragment-completion test (*see also* Word-completion tests)
nonword effects, priming, 361
priming effects, 359, 360, 402–408
Fragmentation, problem of, 446
Fragmented drawings, 402–408
Free recall tasks, 404–408
Frontal lobe dysfunction, 464
Functional architecture of memory, 420*n*., 421, 422

GABA, *Limax* feeding, 183–187
Gene mutations, and learning, 266
General process theories, 283, 284
Genetics, and learning, 253–273
Geniculo-striate visual pathway, 30
Geraniol odor, 201
Gestalt principles, 256, 257
Gopher snakes, 258–266
G. R., patient, 448
Granule cells, dentate gyrus
feedback pathways, 123*n*.
long-term potentiation, ribosomes, 158–160
multiple traces, perforant path, 62–74
and nonlinear systems analysis, 120–131
ribosomes, learning, 154–160
spike-EPSP curve, 65, 66
Great tits, food-storing, 2, 232
Ground squirrels, 258–266
Gyrus dentatus (*see* Dentate gyrus)

Habit
memory system dichotomy, 302
species comparison, 302
Habituation
associative and nonassociative theories, 342–347
and catalytic effects, 227
context effects, 342, 343
*Hermissenda*, and mammals, 17

innate aspects, ethology, 196
opiate effects, 319
as recognition memory, 346, 347
Hawks, conditioning, 291
Heart rate
latent inhibition, opiates, 320, 320*n.*
visual conditioning, pigeon, 28–39
*Hemichromis bimaculatus*, 256
*Hermissenda*, 9–24
cellular analysis, learning, 12*n.*, 13*n.*
conditioning-induced channel changes, 9–24
ecological factors, learning, 282, 283
intersensory integration, 14*n.*
mammalian brain relevance, 9–24, 426
synaptic interactions, schematic, 11*n.*
Herring gull chicks, 196
Heterogeneous summation, 196, 197, 201
Heterosynaptic EPSP depression, 66–69
Hierarchies, learning, 206, 207
Hindlimb motor cortex, 86, 87
Hippocampal monkeys, 372, 373, 454
Hippocampal slice preparation
long-term potentiation study, 109
ribosomal systems, LTP, 160–168
Hippocampus (*see also* CA1 neurons; Dentate gyrus; Perforant path)
bird food storers, 248
cholinergic system, opiates, 324
cognitive map versus working memory, 57–59
in learning and memory, systems, 134–146
long-term enhancement site, 50–59, 458
monkey models, amnesia, 372, 373, 454
morphological change, memory, LTP, 150–168
multiple traces, neural activity, 62–74
nonlinear systems analysis, 120–131
spatial learning, synapse, 49–59
storage model, 57
synaptogenesis, electrical stimulation, 91, 92*n.*
H. J., patient, 466
H. M., patient
amnesia measurement, 391, 392
consolidation failure, 396, 399, 400
dissociation, 354
facial recognition, 466, 467
forgetting rates, 386, 387, 465
as medial temporal amnesia type, 380–394
Holography, 79
Homophone spelling, 357
Homosynaptic long-term potentiation, 67–74
Honey bees, 193–208
evolutionary restraints, 266–272
learning and memory in, 193–208, 291, 292
ecological factors, 283, 284
picture mode, 292
spine density, foragers, 267, 269*n.*, 270, 271*n.*, 272
time learning, 206–208, 283, 284
catalytic aspect, 291
Hormones, time-dependent memory, 313
Hull's and Guthrie's theory, 337
Humans, versus nonhuman vertebrates, 299, 300
6-Hydroxydopamine
dorsal noradrenergic bundle, 324–327
and opiate binding sites, 323
Hyperpolarization
cAMP role, dopamine, 113–116
dopamine effect, CA1 neurons, 111–116
Hyperspecific associations, 370, 371, 436
Hyperstriatum ventrale, 32*n.*, 33*n.*

$I_A$ current, *Hermissenda*, 10, 13*n.*, 14, 14*n.*
Idiomatic phrases, priming, 362–364, 363*n.*, 364*n.*
Imagery, amnesia, 410
Imaginal representation, 303
Immunocytochemistry, *Limax*, 183–185
Implicit memory
and consciousness, 438
definition, 353
and priming, amnesics, 356–375
skill learning, amnesics, 353–356
Imprinting
and bird song learning, 194, 195
synapse structure changes, 97
*In vitro* expression, memory, 179–181
*In vivo* expression, memory, 179–181

Incomplete figures, amnesics, 402–408
Inference, 287–294
Inferior colliculus, 85*n.*
Inferotemporal cortex, 449
Innate behavior
  bird song learning, 194, 195
  color learning, bees, 201
  mechanisms, 193–196, 201, 255–257
    criticism, 255–257
Innate learning triggers, 196
Instinct
  and learning, 255–265
  and spine-stem shortening, bees, 271, 271*n.*
Instructions, and performance, 358, 359, 408
Instrumental learning (*see* Operant learning)
Intelligence
  and causality, 285
  definition, 279
  and ecology, 279–285, 299–306
Intelligence quotient, 390–392, 470, 471
Interference, 225, 226, 436
Internal states, 55, 56
Interneurons
  *Limax* food memory, engram, 181–183
  LIMAX model, 189
  trace mechanisms, dentate gyrus, 72, 73
Interstimulus interval, 126, 130, 131
Invariability principle, 288, 289
Invertebrates, 283–285
Ionic channels, 13–24
  *Hermissenda* learning, and mammals, 13–24
  *Hermissenda* photoreceptor similarity, 10
  versus synaptogenesis, memory, 80, 135
Isolated brain preparation, *Limax*, 179–181
Iterated activation, 446

Jewel fish, 256, 267, 268*n.*, 270
Jigsaw puzzle solutions, 402, 403

Kamin blocking effect
  catalytic aspects, 225
  in *Limax*, 174, 175
Kenyon cells, 267, 269*n.*, 271*n.*, 272
Korsakoff amnesia
  anterograde and retrograde amnesia, 466
  and consolidation, 396–398, 401, 402
  diencephalic amnesia, 380–394
  facial recognition, disconnection, 449
  forgetting rates, 386, 387, 465
  quantitative testing, 470, 471
  severity measurement, 390–394

Laboratory studies
  bird food-storing, weaknesses, 236, 253, 254
  level of analysis, 253–255
  and neurobiology, 254, 255
Landmark learning, bees, 202, 204*n.*, 205*n.*
Language, chimpanzees, 300
Latent inhibition
  associative and nonassociative explanations, 342–347
  catalytic effects, 227
  context effects, 342–345
  versus habituation, 346, 347
  opiate effects, 319, 320, 320*n.*, 321
    acetylcholine, 328
  as recognition memory, 346, 347
Lateral geniculate equivalent, 37–39, 40*n.*, 46
Lateral perforant path, 63*n.*, 66–68
Laughing gulls, 196
Learning (*see also* Associative learning; Discrimination learning; Operant learning; Passive-avoidance learning)
  distributed network, 42, 43
  evolutionary restraints, 253–273
  hippocampal systems, 134–146
  in honey bees, 193–208
  instinct adjustment, 255, 271
  isolated brains, *Limax*, 179–181
  in *Limax*, 174, 175, 179–181
  long-term potentiation, 136, 137
  performance distinction, 437
  selectionist view, 287–290
  species comparison, 296–305
Learning sets, 298, 299
Lemniscal ventral medial geniculate, 42
Lesions, brain, 19, 22

Leucine uptake, reversal training, 88
Levallorphan, 316*n.*
Lexical decision tasks
  nonword effects, priming, 361
  priming effects, amnesics, 357
LI experiments, 319, 320, 320*n.*
*Limax maximus,* 173–189
  anatomical localization, 182, 183
  associative learning function, 173
  complex computation in, 173–189
  ecological factors, learning, 282, 283
  and levels of analysis, 254
  immunocytochemical localization, 183–185
  isolated brains, learning, 179–181
  modeling studies, 188, 189, 287, 288
  neurochemical manipulations, 185–188
  postingestive conditioning, 175–178
  stimulus timing, 178, 179
LIMAX model, 188, 189, 290
Lip–brain preparation, *Limax,* 179–181, 183–188
Lips, *Limax* learning, 179–183
Location learning, bees, 204, 205
Locus ceruleus
  conditioning role, 39
  opioid/norepinephrine interaction, 322, 323
Long-lasting traces, 64–74
Long-term enhancement (*see also* Long-term potentiation)
  age differences, rats, hippocampus, 51, 53
  definition, 50
  and long-term memory, 59
  sleep–waking cycle effect, 55, 56
  and spatial memory, 50–59, 137
Long-term habituation, 319
Long-term memory
  and constancy principle, birds, 293*n.*, 294*n.*
  in Korsakoff amnesia, diagnosis, 388, 389
  and long-term enhancement, 59, 109
  synaptic modification, hippocampus, 50–59
  synaptogenesis, versus receptors, 80
Long-term potentiation (*see also* Long-term enhancement)
  amnesia models, 458
  catecholamines, 108–116
  and conditioned cellular changes, 137, 138
  decay time course, 70, 73
  and disconnection, 446
  hippocampal morphology, 150–168
  hippocampal neurons, slices, 109
  hippocampal slices, ribosomes, 160–168
  as level of analysis, 424, 425, 430
  long-term memory model, 109
  and nonlinear systems analysis, 120–131
  perforant path, electrical stimulation, 64–74
  perforant path–dentate system response, 128–131
  protein synthesis, 161–166
  structural changes, hippocampus, 150–168
  synaptogenesis, hippocampus, 91, 92*n.*
  trace independence, 68–74
*Loxop virens,* 280

Maier three-table task, 245
Mammals, mollusk relevance, 78
Mammillary bodies
  animal models, lesions, 468–470
  Korsakoff patients, amnesia, 381–384
Mapping functions, 443
Marine flatworms, 270
Marsh tits, food-storing, 232–249
Matrix data structure, 291
Maze training (*see also* Radial maze)
  occipital cortex dendritic fields, 82
  operant learning, 131
McCulloch color-grating illusion, 402
McGill Anomalies Test, 402
Medial dorsal nucleus (*see* Dorsomedial thalamic nucleus)
Medial forebrain bundle, 32*n.*, 33*n.*
Medial perforant path, 63*n.*, 66–70
Medial septal area, 324, 328
Medial septal nucleus, 139, 140
Medial temporal amnesia
  amnesia theories, 380–394, 464–467
  forgetting rates, 386, 387

Medial temporal amnesia (*continued*)
lesion studies, models, 467–470
preserved skill learning, 471, 472
Mediodorsal thalamic nucleus (*see* Dorsomedial thalamic nucleus)
Medullary raphe, 32*n*.
Membrane-bound ribosomes, 152, 153, 158, 161–168
Membrane channels, 9–24
Membrane input resistance
cAMP role, dopamine, 113–116
dopamine effect, CA1 neurons, 111–116
Membrane potentials, dopamine, 111–116
Memory capacity
comparative studies, 281, 282, 303, 304
gene mutation, *Drosophila*, 303, 304
and recency, animals, 293, 294
Memory consolidation (*see* Consolidation)
Memory performance, 420, 421
Memory systems, plurality, 301–303
Mental representation, 290–294
Mesencephalic reticular formation, 55
Met-enkephalin, 188
Metacerebral giant cell, 186
Metacognition, 439, 440
Methionine-deficient diet, *Limax*, 175–178
Method of vanishing cues, 369, 370
*N*-Methyl-D-aspartate, 458
α-methyl-*p*-tyrosine, 188
Metoclopramide, 111
Mirror-reading tasks, 354, 356, 403
Model-systems approach, 426–431 (*see also* Animal models)
Modulation
evolution of concept, 313–315
functional significance, 315–321, 427, 428
opioid peptides, 315–329, 436
review of, 311–329
Molecular approach, 425, 426, 430, 431
Mollusks
complex computation in, 173–189
dendritic spines, 270
ecological factors, learning, 282, 283
and levels of analysis, 254, 255
and localized memory, adequacy, 78
Monitoring, amnesics, priming, 374
Monkeys
explicit memory, amnesia, 372, 373, 455
learning set differences, 298, 299
mediodorsal thalamic nucleus lesions, 469
as model, amnesia, 454, 455, 469
recognition memory, naloxone, 321
skill learning, amnesia, 356
Morphine
cholinergic effects, 323, 324
long-term habituation effect, 319
molluscan dopaminergic synapses, 188
retention impairment, 315
Motor neurons
heart rate conditioning, 30, 33–38
*Hermissenda*, learning, 22
Motor programs, 194–198
Motor-sensory forelimb cortex, 85*n*., 86–89
Motor skill learning, 354, 402, 403, 471–473
Multiple-choice recognition tests, 470
Multiple overlapping inputs, 446
Muscarinic receptors, 109

$N_1$ component, 139–144
$N_2$ component, 139–144
N. A., patient
amnesia measurement, 390, 392
as diencephalic amnesia type, 380–394, 468, 469
paired-associate testing, 471
Naloxone
amygdala complex effect, 321, 322, 326–328
cholinergic effects, 323, 324
and increased retention, 315, 316*n*., 317
latent inhibition effect, 319, 320, 320*n*.
long-term habituation effect, 319
nonaversive tasks, 317, 318, 318*n*., 326, 327
norepinephrine enhancement, 323
and memory, 324–327
recognition memory, monkeys, 321
in reward contingencies, 317, 318, 318*n*., 326, 327
Naltrexone, 316*n*., 323

Natural environment (*see* Field studies)
Natural selection
  and innate behavior, 257
  instinct as product of, 255, 256
  and memory capacity, 282, 303
Nectar-feeding birds, 280
Negative components, EPs
  discrimination learning, hippocampus, 139–144
  trial sequence effect, 141–144
Nei's model, 261
Neocortex, reach training, 84–89
Neostriatum intermedium, pars mediale, 32*n*., 33*n*.
Neural networks, LIMAX model, 188, 189
Neural representation, 290–294
Neural systems, nonlinear analysis, 120–131
Neurobiological approach, 424, 425
Neurobiotaxis, 90
Neuronal density, 80, 81, 81*n*.
Neuronal membrane channels (*see* Ionic channels)
Neuronal plasticity
  and amnesia models, 458
  catecholamines, 107–117
  in conditioning, models, 41, 42, 79
  evolutionary aspects, and experience, 265–273
  hippocampus, 135, 136
  as level of analysis, 424, 425
  modulation implications, 312, 329
  nonlinear systems analysis, 121–131
Neuronal substrate, and evolution, 266–270
Neuropsychological approach, 419–430
New associations
  implicit memory for, 364–368
  and priming, amnesics, 366, 371, 373
  and spared memories, amnesics, 408–411
  unitized structures in, 368–371
Nictitating membrane conditioning
  as model, 39
  sensory pathway modification, 42
  versus spatial learning, physiology, 57
Nonassociative learning
  versus associative learning, 342–347
  catalytic effects, 227
Nonlinear systems analysis. 120–131
Nonsemantic encoding, 358, 363
Nonverbal amnesia, 389, 392
Nonverbal memory scale, 392
Nonwords, priming effect, 360, 361
Norepinephrine
  amygdala complex role, 326–328
  in locus ceruleus, and opioids, 322
  and long-term potentiation, traces, 70
  opioid peptide inhibition, 322, 328
    and memory, 324–328
Northwestern crow, 233
Nose–brain preparation, *Limax*, 183
Nucleus dorsolateralis posterior, 32*n*., 33*n*.
Nucleus rotundus, 31*n*., 32*n*., 33*n*., 37
Null hypothesis question, 282–285, 304, 305
Nutcrackers, food storing, 232–249, 300

Obligatory performance, 388
Occipital cortex
  and environmental complexity, rats, 80–82, 81*n*., 94
  polyribosomal aggregates, synaptogenesis, 94, 96
Octopus, 282
Oculomotor skills, 403
Odor stimuli
  honey bees, 199, 200
    conditioned inhibition, 283
  *Limax* memory, localization, 181–183
Olfactory nerves, *Limax*, 182
"On demand" synapses, 89–96
Ontogenetic considerations, 255–273
Operant learning
  associative learning in, 217–219
  catalytic effects, 226–228
  classical conditioning comparison, 198
  discriminative stimulus in, 225
  general rules, 289, 290
  honey bees, 206
  innate aspects, ethology, 198, 199
  laboratory studies, weaknesses, 254
  and neural system properties, 131
  procedural versus declarative learning, 337, 338

Operant Learning (*continued*)
  and response-outcome associations, 217–219
Opiate agonists, mollusks, 188
Opiate antagonists (*see also* Naloxone)
  and increased retention, 315–317
  and rewarding contingencies, 317, 318, 326, 327
Opioid peptides/opiates (*see also* Morphine)
  locus ceruleus effect, 322, 323
  memory modulation, 315–329
  norepinephrine regulation, 322, 323
Optic tectum, 268*n*.
Optic tract, 31*n*.
Optional performance, 388
Overt alpha conditioning, 197

Paired-associate tasks
  amnesics spared memory, 408–410
  amnesics testing, 470, 471
  rule-determined type, 408
Paired-impulse paradigm, 123, 126
Pairing specificity, *Hermissenda*, 17
Pairwise associations, 212–220
Parameter hypothesis, 202
*Paridae*, 232–240, 293, 294*n*.
Parinaud syndrome, 381
Partial information cues
  amnesics, intact memories, 402–408
  instructions, importance of, 408
Passive-avoidance learning
  epinephrine levels, 314
  opioid peptide levels, 315–317
  synapse structure changes, 97
  task factors, 435, 436
Pattern learning, bees, 201, 202, 203*n*.
Pavlovian conditioning (*see* Associative learning; Classical conditioning)
Pavlov's work, 297, 298
Perceptual-motor skills (*see also* Motor skills)
  dissociation, amnesia, 354
Perforant path
  auditory evoked potentials, 139–144
    trial sequence effect, 143, 144
  environmental complexity, synapses, 93, 93*n*.
  EPSP-spike curves, 64–70
  granule cell excitability, feedback, 123*n*.
  long-term potentiation effect, 128–130, 154–160
    ribosomes, 154–160
  and mnemonic functions, systems, 131
  multiple trace activity, synapses, 62–74
  and nonlinear systems analysis, 120–131
Perforant path–dentate system, 123–131
Perforations, synaptic densities, 97
Performance, 437
Persistence of memory, 238, 247
Phenylalanine-deficient diet, 176
Phosphorylase kinase, 15, 15*n*.
Phosphorylation (*see* Protein phosphorylation)
Photoreceptors, *Hermissenda*, 10–24
Phylogenetic considerations, 45, 46, 253–273
Picture hypothesis, 202, 292
Picture mode, bees, 292
Pigeon
  conditioned heart rate, 28–39
  versus food-storing birds, memory, 281
  memory capacity, 293, 294
Pinyon jay, food-storing, 232
*Pituophis melanoleucus catenifer*, 258–266
Place learning
  long-term potentiation effect, 49–59, 137
  synaptic strength, hippocampus, 49–59
Plasticity (*see* Neuronal plasticity)
Polyribosomal aggregates, 94, 95*n*., 96, 96*n*.
Polysomes
  hippocampal slices, 160–168
  and learning, hippocampus, 152–154
  long-term potentiation effect, 158–168
Pons, 32*n*.
Population spike, 63–74
  dopamine effect, CA1 cells, 110, 111
  in nonlinear systems, 122–131
  perforant path stimulation, 63–74, 122, 124, 126
Posteromedial hypothalamus, 30, 32*n*., 33

Postingestive conditioning paradigm, 175–178
Postmorbid amnesia, 396, 397, 400
Postnatal synaptogenesis, 93
Postsynaptic changes, LTP, 156–160
Postsynaptic density
  long-term potentiation, hippocampus, 156–160
  synaptogenesis, electrical stimulation, 94
Postsynaptic spine, 156–160
Postassium channels, *Hermissenda*, 10, 13–19
Potentiation
  catalytic effects, conditioning, 225, 226
  versus enhancement, 50
Preexisting representations, 362
Preexposure effect, 216
Premorbid amnesia
  and consolidation, 396, 397, 400, 401
  extent and severity, 465–467
  and metacognition, 439*n*.
  and retrieval-deficit explanation, 374
Premorbid knowledge, 374, 439*n*.
Preparatory conditioning
  consummatory conditioning distinction, 339–342
  forgetting rates, 340, 341
  neurobiology, 340
Preparedness, 253
Presynaptic terminal size, 156–160
Pretectum, amnesia, 381, 468
Primacy effect, 238, 244
Primary memory, 437
Primates (*see also* Monkeys)
  abstract representation, 303
  amnesia model, 453–454
Priming
  in amnesics, dissociation, 356–375
  in animals, 371–375, 455
  and conscious retrieval mechanisms, 359
  context effects, 366
  and intact memories, amnesics, 403–409, 471–473
  reification of, criticism, 435
  unitized structures in, 362–371
Principal optic nucleus, 31*n*.
Proactive interference, 464
Procedural memory
  amnesics new learning, 409, 410, 472
  and consciousness, 438
  declarative learning distinction, 337–339
  memory system dichotomy, 302, 429
  Pavlovian conditioning, *Aplysia*, 339
Procerebral lobes, *Limax*, 182, 183
Programs, 194–198, 287
Prompts, and amnesia, 407, 408
Prosopagnosia, 256
Protein kinase inhibitor protein, 114–116
Protein phosphorylation
  CA1 neurons, dopamine, 116
  evolutionary conservation, 15
  *Hermissenda* learning, 13*n*., 15, 15*n*.
Protein synthesis
  hippocampus, memory and LTP, 150–168
  synaptogenesis, learning, 88, 89
Punishment, 435, 436 (*see also* Passive-avoidance learning)
Pupillary conditioning, 42
Puzzle solutions, 354

Quinidine sulfate, 179–181
Quinuclidinyl benzilate binding, 88

Radial maze
  and food storing, birds, 240–245
  natural environment generalization, 280
  opiate antagonist effects, 317, 318, 326
  recency principle, 292–294
  Skinner box comparison, 242
Random stimulus train input, 123–131
Rank order, cues, bees, 206, 207
Rate of decay, 53, 54
Rats
  animal model, amnesia, 453
  skill learning, amnesia, 356
  spatial memory, radial mazes, 241, 242
Rattlesnakes, 258–266
Reach-training apparatus, 85*n*.
Recall
  and aging, 440

Recall (*continued*)
amnesics intact memory, 404–408
as explicit memory, 353, 370
Recency effect
auditory evoked potentials, 144
bird food storing, 238, 239, 244
hippocampal memory, 145
and memory capacity, birds, 293*n*., 294*n*.
radial maze learning, 292–294
Receptors, versus synaptogenesis, 80
Reciprocal coding, 202
Recognition memory
amnesics intact memory, 404–408, 454, 455
animal models, amnesia, 454, 455
comparative studies, capacity, 281, 282
as explicit memory, 353, 370
naloxone, monkeys, 321
nonword priming, 361
types of, 346, 347
word-completion tests, priming, 357
Recollection, dissociation, amnesia, 353–356
Recollective experience, 437, 438
Recovery functions, 126–128
Red nucleus, 39
Reference memory
as model, 456
in radial mazes, 242
Reflection, and recognition, 347
Rehydration, *Limax*, reinforcement, 179
Reinforcement, and modulation, 313, 314
Reinforcer revaluation, 337, 338
Releasers, definition, 193, 194
Remote memory, 465–467 (*see also* Premorbid amnesia)
Representation, 287–294, 303
declarative versus procedural learning, 339
role in learning, 287–294
and unitized structures, priming, 362
Rescorla–Cunningham procedure, 218
Response learning, contiguity, 217–219
Response–outcome associations, 217–219
Retention
brain slice technique, 23
*Hermissenda*, and mammals, 17
modulation, opioid peptides, 315–321
Retention intervals
bird food storing, 238
preparatory conditioning, 340, 341
and priming, amnesics, 366–368
radial maze model, pigeons, 242
Retinal ganglion cells, 35, 36, 43
Retrieval-deficit view
priming, amnesics, 374
versus storage, amnesics, 394–403
Retrograde amnesia
and amnesia types, 387
anterograde amnesia correlation, 465–467
beta-adrenergic antagonists, 328
ECT effects, 389, 390
Korsakoff' syndrome, 466, 467
methodological problems, 400, 401
modulation concept, 313
reversibility, and consolidation, 396–403
severity measurement, 390–393
Revaluation experiments, 337, 338
Reversal learning
amnesics, 407, 410
and neural systems, 131
Reward, opioid antagonists, 317, 326, 327
Rhyming, paired-associates, 409
Ribosomes
hippocampal slices study, 160–168
learning behavior, hippocampus, 152–154
long-term potentiation effect, 154–168
Right-hemisphere systems, 448, 449
RNA/DNA ratio, maze training, 82
Romanes system, 296, 297
Rotary pursuit, amnesics, 354
Rule-determined paired-associates, 408, 410
Rule of differential effects, 395

Sacramento Delta squirrels, 261–263, 266
Safflower seeds, birds, 239, 240
Salivary burster neuron, 183–185
Salivary nerve, *Limax*, 183–185
Saturation, place responding, 137
Savings, *Hermissenda*, and mammals, 17

Schaffer collaterals, 160–168
Scrub jay, food-storing, 232, 233
Search and capture hypothesis, 272
Second-order conditioning
  *Limax*, 174
  modeling, LIMAX, 188, 189
  new elements formation, 220, 221, 222*n.*
  temporal aspects, *Limax*, 179
Selection, and learning, 287–290
Selectivity, and potentiation, 446
Semantic encoding
  and consciousness, 437, 438
  priming effects, 358, 363, 364
  unitized structures in, 369
Semantic paired-associates, 409
Sensitive period, 194
Sensitization
  and catalytic effects, 227
  *Hermissenda*, and mammals, 17
Sensory discrimination learning
  spatial memory comparison, hippocampus, 146
  synaptic changes, hippocampus, LTP, 139–144
Sentence understanding, 444
Septo-hippocampal cholinergic system, 324
Serial array, 42
Serial learning, 146
Serotonin, *Limax*, 183
Sessile spine synapses, 92*n.*, 94, 95*n.*, 96, 153
Shaft synapses, 92*n.*
Shape learning, bees, 201, 202
Short-lasting representation, 146
Short-term memory
  and consciousness, 437
  in Korsakoff amnesia, 388
Sierra ground squirrels, 261, 266
Sign stimuli
  definition, 193, 194
  innate aspects, ethology, 196, 197, 256
Signal-consequent learning, 212–214
Simple representations, 57
Size perception, bees, 292
Skill learning
  brain damage effects, 356
  dissociation, amnesia, 353-356, 471-473
Skinner box, 242
Sleep–waking cycle, 55, 56
Slow postsynaptic potentials, 108–116
Slow-wave sleep, 55, 56
Social cages, rats, 80, 81, 81*n.*
Social deprivation, 256
Sodium amytal technique, 396, 397
Sodium pentobarbital, 56
Somatosensory cortex, 84–89
Somatostatin, 185
Spatial data structure, 291
Spatial delayed matching, 242, 243
Spatial frequency, bees, 201, 202
Spatial information storage, 49–59
Spatial memory/learning
  age differences, rats, 51, 53
  animal models, amnesia, 453, 457
  birds, food-storing, 231–249
    comparative studies, 245–248
  versus conditioned learning, physiology, 57
  hippocampus, 136
  laboratory tests, and models, 242, 243
  and long-term enhancement, 50–59
  neurobiology of, birds, 248, 249
  nonspatial memory comparison, 146
  radial mazes, rats, 241–243
*Spermophilus beecheyi*, 257–266
Spider monkeys, 298
Spike-EPSP relationship, 64–70
Spine synapses, 92*n.*, 93, 94, 95*n.*, 96, 158, 267, 269*n.*, 270
Spiroperidol, 110, 111
Split-brain procedure, 82–84
Spontaneous alternation, 293
Squirrel monkeys, 299
S. S., patient, 466
Stellar's jay, 232
*Stentor*, 287
Stereoscopic perceptions, amnesia, 402
Stimulus intensity, 126, 130, 131
Stimulus interval, 130, 131
Stimulus-response conditioning
  procedural versus declarative knowledge, 337–339, 438, 439
  temporal aspects, *Limax*, 179
Stimulus specificity, *Hermissenda*, 18, 19

Stimulus–stimulus conditioning
and association theory, 438, 439
catalytic factors, 291
temporal factors, *Limax*, 179
Stimulus timing (*see also* Temporal factors)
*Limax*, conditioning, 179
Storage model
in amnesia, versus retrieval, 394–402
and hippocampus, 57
Stratum radiatum, CA1 cells, 153, 160–168
Stria terminalis, 321
Sulpiride, 111
Sunflower seeds, birds, 239, 240
Superior cervical ganglion, 108, 109
Superior colliculus, 85*n.*
Superior temporal sulcus, 449
Sympathetic cardiac neurons, 33–36
Sympathetic ganglion, 108, 109
Synapse formation (*see also* Synaptic modification)
adjustability of, 267–273
and amnesia models, 457
behavioral acquisition, hippocampus, 150–160
genetic and environmental factors, 267–273
versus ion channel permeability, 80, 135
as level of analysis, 425
memory process, 77–99
morphology, 93, 94, 95*n.*
postnatal period, 93
Synapse turnover, 89–96
Synapses on demand, 89–96, 267
Synaptic cleft width, 94
Synaptic density
and learning, rats, 80, 81, 81*n.*
perforations in, learning, 97
short-term learning, hippocampus, 153
Synaptic depression, 69, 70
Synaptic excitability, dopamine, 108–116
Synaptic interactions, *Hermissenda*, 11*n.*, 17–19
Synaptic modification (*see also* Synapse formation)
evolutionary restraints, 265–273
versus ion channel permeability, 80, 135
and levels of analysis, 255
spatial learning, hippocampus, 49–59
spontaneous changes, spatial learning, 54, 55
Synaptic plasticity (*see* Neuronal plasticity)
Synaptic vesicles, 156, 157
Synaptogenesis (*see* Synapse formation)

Tachistoscopic tasks, 361
Task instructions, importance, 358, 359, 408
Tasks, influence of, 434–436
Taste aversion
amygdala lesions, generality, 456, 457
and evolution, 253
*Limax* memory, localization, 179–188
Taste–taste aversion experiments, 180, 181, 188
Tectofugal pathway, 30, 31*n.*, 32*n.*, 37
Tectothalamo-extrastriate pathway, 30
Telencephalon, visual conditioning, 30, 32*n.*, 33*n.*
Temporal factors
and conditioning, principles, 288, 289
hippocampus, learning, 136
honey bees, 206–208, 283, 284
catalytic aspects, 291
*Limax*, conditioning, 178, 179
Temporal order judgments, 464
Temporal specificity, *Hermissenda*, 17, 19
Temporal stem lesions, 453
Temporally graded amnesia, 391–393
Thalamofugal pathway, 30, 31*n.*, 32*n.*, 37
Thalamus (*see also* Dorsomedial thalamic nucleus)
damage to, amnesia, 384, 385
and disconnection syndromes, 447, 448
visual conditioning mediation, 32*n.*, 33*n.*
Three-letter word stems, 364, 365, 472, 473
Three-table task, 245

Time course, dopamine modulation, 108, 109
Time learning (*see also* Temporal factors)
  honey bees, 206–208, 283, 284, 291
Tits, food-storing, 231–249
Tolman's expectancy theory, 337
Tone discrimination, 139–144
Tower of Hanoi puzzle, 356, 402
Traces, neural activity, 62–74, 139
Transcortical aphasias, 447
Transfer, 436, 437
Transplants, embryonic, 458
Trial-and-error learning, 198, 199
Tryptophan-deficient diet, 176
Twin-impulse paradigm, 123
Two-choice tests, bees, 199–201
Two facing eyes, 256, 267
Two-store theory, 433, 434
Two-tone discrimination, 139–144
Type B photoreceptors, 10
Tyrosine-deficient diet, 176

Ultraviolet sensitivities, bees, 201
Unconditioned stimulus
  catalytic function, 224–228
  cellular models, *Hermissenda*, 23
  consummatory versus preparative response, 339–342
  context effects, 216, 217, 224
  heart rate, pigeon, 28, 33–36, 42–45
  *Hermissenda* learning, and mammals, 17–22
  innate aspects, ethology, 196, 197
  locus ceruleus role, 39
  temporal aspects, *Limax*, 178, 179
  temporal aspects, nerve pathways, 33–36
  time-specific associations, bees, 207, 208
Unitized structures, 362–371
Upward gaze paralysis, 381
Urethane, 56

Vagal cardiac neurons, 35
Vanishing cues procedure, 369, 370
Vasopressin, 329
Venom resistance, 261–265
Ventral Area of Tsai, 32*n*.
Ventral pons, 32*n*.
Ventrolateral medulla, 32*n*., 33*n*.
Ventromedial brain stem, 30, 32*n*.
Verbal amnesia, 389
Verbal learning, 434, 435
Verbal memory scale, 392
Vertebrates
  engram localization, 41–44
  humans versus nonhumans, learning, 299, 300
  memory properties, 27–46
  as model system, prognosis, 39–41
  Pavlovian associative learning, 211–228
Vertical associations, 411
Vertical eye movements, 381
Vesicles, synaptic, 156, 157
Violet, honey bee learning, 200, 201
Visual agnosias, 444
Visual conditioning, 27–46
Visual cortex, 80, 81, 81*n*.
Visual discrimination training, 97
Visual masking, 438
Visual maze learning, 354, 409
Visual pathways, 29, 30
Vocabulary learning, amnesics, 370, 371
Voltage-sensitive dyes, 183

Weaver mice, 266
Wechsler's Memory Scale, 390–392, 470, 471
White-crowned sparrows, 194, 195
Win-shift strategy
  and environmental resources, 281, 300, 301
  laboratory and field studies, 280
Within-stimulus learning, 214, 215, 220, 221, 222*n*.
Word-completion tests
  in amnesics, priming, 356–358, 365, 367
  instructions effect, priming, 358, 359
  new associations effect, 367
Word identification
  nonword effects, priming, 361
  structural analysis, 444

Word learning, 434, 435
Word stems, 472, 473
Working memory
  long-term enhancement comparison, 57–59
  as model, 456, 457
  in radial mazes, 241, 242
  and sensory discrimination, hippocampus, 146

*x*-intercept
  cAMP effect, dopamine, 113–115
  long-term potentiation, CA1, 64–66

Yes/No recognition test, 357, 406, 408, 409

GSC
GLASSBORO STATE COLLEGE

Milliotis, P., 466, 476*n*.
Mills, R. P., 468, 475*n*.
Milner, B., 354, 356, 373, 377*n*., 378*n*., 381, 390, 392, 397, 404, 408, 409, 413*n*., 414*n*., 429, 432*n*., 433, 441*n*., 464, 468, 472, 475*n*., 476*n*.
Minor, H., 343, 344, 348*n*.
Mirmiran, M., 329, 330*n*.
Mishkin, M., 237, 249*n*., *302*, 306*n*., 321, 332*n*., 351, 356, 372–375, 377*n*., 379*n*., 385, 411, 413*n*., 429, 432*n*., 453, 460*n*., 461*n*., 462*n*., 469, 473, 474*n*., 475*n*.
Miyagawa, M., 108, 118*n*.
Mohr, J., 373, 378*n*.
Mondadori, C., 315, 333*n*.
Montel, H., 323, 333*n*.
Moore, J. W., 45, 46*n*., 344, 348*n*., 349*n*.
Moore, R. Y., 326, 330*n*., 380, 414*n*., 468, 476*n*.
Moretensen, E. L., 472, 476*n*.
Morimoto, H., 82, 99*n*.
Mormede, P., 315, 333*n*.
Moroni, F., 324, 333*n*.
Morris, R. G. M., 49, 57, 60*n*., 61*n*., 335, 421, 460*n*., 457, 458, 461*n*.
Morton, J., 362, 377*n*.
Moscovitch, M., 351, 354, 357, 364, 371, 377*n*., 378*n*., 388, 413*n*., 429, 432*n*., 464, 465, 473, 476*n*.
Moshkov, D. A., 97, 102*n*., 151, 169*n*.
Moss, M., 411, 413*n*.
Mountcastle, V., 197, 209*n*.
Mowrer, O. H., 456, 461*n*.
Mufson, E. J., 323, 333*n*.
Mulder, D. W., 397, 412*n*.
Murakami, F., 270, 276*n*.
Murray, E. A., 86, 103*n*.
Musty, R. E., 328, 331*n*.
Mutt, V., 118*n*.

Nachman, M., 456, 460*n*.
Nadel, L., 49, 57, 61*n*., 136, 146, 148*n*., 351, 356, 371, 373, 375, 377*n*., 399, 400, 414*n*., 429, 432*n*., 453, 456, 457, 460*n*., 466, 473, 476*n*.
Nagle, G. T., 191*n*.
Naka, K.-I., 121, 132*n*.
Nakamura, S., 323, 333*n*.
Nairn, A. C., 117*n*.
Naito, S., 26*n*.
Nathan, P. W., 465, 476*n*.
Neary, D., 391, 413*n*., 466, 472, 475*n*.
Neary, J. T., 15, *15*, *16*, 17, 24*n*., 26*n*.
Nei, M., 261, 277*n*.
Neisser, U., 359, 377*n*.
Nelson, H. E., 394, 413*n*.
Nelson, R. J., 48*n*.
Nestler, E. J., 116, 119*n*.
Neuenschwander, N., 338, 349*n*.
Neuman, R. S., 70, 76*n*.
Newcombe, F., 448, 450*n*.
Nickerson, R. S., 282, 285*n*.
Nickolson, V. J., 315, 333*n*.
Nieto-Sampedro, M., 89, 100*n*., 458, 460*n*.
Nisbett, R. E., 438, 441*n*.
Noreen, G. K., 121, 132*n*.
Norman, D. A., 433, 441*n*.
North, K. A. K., 50, 60*n*.
Northern, B., 391, 413*n*., 466, 475*n*.
Nottebohm, F., 231, 248, 250*n*.
Novak, K. J., 455, 461*n*.

Oakley, D. A., 351, 373, 377*n*.
Oberg, R. G., 393, 415*n*.
O'Connell, A., 394, 413*n*.
Oestereicher, B., 189, 191*n*.
Ogura, H., 124, 132*n*.
O'Keefe, J., 49, 57, 60*n*., 61*n*., 136, 146, 148*n*., 351, 356, 371, 373, 377*n*., 429, 432*n*., 453, 456, 457, 461*n*., 473, 476*n*.
Olds, M. E., 42, 46*n*.
Oleson, T. D., 42, 48*n*.
Oliver, M., 91, 102*n*., 134, 148*n*., 151, 169*n*., 270, 276*n*.
Olson, D. J., 242, 249*n*., 250*n*., 281, 285*n*.
Olton, D. S., 49, 57, 61*n*., 146, 148*n*., 240, *241*, 245, 250*n*., 280, 285*n*., 286*n*., 317, 351, 356, 372–373, 377*n*., 429, 432*n*., 456, 457, 461*n*.
Opfinger, E., 200, 209*n*.

Orbach, H., 173, 190*n.*, 356, 378*n.*
Orona, E., 79, 101*n.*
Orr, W. B., 57, 58, 59*n.*, 137, 147*n.*
O'Shea, L., 329, 333*n.*
Ott, T., 110, 118*n.*, 151, 169*n.*
Overton, W. F., 255, 277*n.*
Owings, D. H., 255, 257, 258, 260–263, 265, 266, 275*n.*, 276*n.*, 277*n.*
Owings, S. C., 265, 277*n.*
Oxbury, S., 468, 477*n.*

Painter, S. D., 191*n.*
Paiva, A. C. M., 315, 331*n.*
Palay, S. L., 89, 103*n.*
Pallaud, B., 99, 103*n.*
Palmini, A. L., 315, 332*n.*
Pappas, B., 329, 333*n.*
Parkin, A. J., 467, 476*n.*
Pasik, P., 381, 413*n.*
Pasik, T., 381, 413*n.*
Passingham, R. E., 298, 299, 304, 307*n.*
Patrick, R. L., 315, 332*n.*
Patterson, J. M., 341, *341*, 348*n.*
Patterson, K., 445, 450*n.*
Patterson, M. M., 48*n.*
Paula-Barbosa, M. N., 272, 278*n.*
Pavone, F., 315, 330*n.*
Payne, M., 429, 432*n.*
Pearson, O. P., 301, 307*n.*
Pellionisz, A., 255, 277*n.*
Pepper, S. C., 256, 277*n.*
Perkel, D. H., 255, 270–272, 275*n.*, 277*n.*
Perkel, D. J., 270, 271, 277*n.*
Perrett, D. I., 449, 450*n.*
Perry, M. L., 331*n.*
Peters, A., 94, 102*n.*
Peterson, G. M., 84, 102*n.*
Petri, H. L., 351, 375, 377*n.*
Petrinovich, L., 257, 274*n.*, 301, 307*n.*
Petrovskaya, L. L., 97, 102*n.*, 151, 169*n.*
Pettigrew, J. D., 311, 329, 332*n.*, 333*n.*
Phifer, C. B., 179, 191*n.*
Phillis, J. W., 323, 331*n.*
Pickel, V. M., 322, 333*n.*
Piercy, M., 347, 348*n.*, 386, *386*, 391–393, 412*n.*, 413*n.*, 452, 461*n.*, 465, 475*n.*
Pierrot-Deseilligny, C., 381, 413*n.*
Pinel, J. P., 258, 263, 277*n.*
Pinsky, C., 323, 331*n.*
Pitts, L. H., 30, 47*n.*
Poggio, T., 270, 271, 276*n.*
Pohle, W., 151, 152, 169*n.*, 170*n.*
Popov, N., 152, 170*n.*
Poran, N., 261, 263, 275*n.*
Powell, T. P. S., 94, 101*n.*
Pradelles, P., 331*n.*
Precht, W., 272, 276*n.*
Precious, J. I., 319, 333*n.*
Premack, D., 302, 303, 306, 307*n.*, 335, 348*n.*, 454, 461*n.*
Preston, G. C., 343, 344, *345*, 349*n.*
Price, D., 191*n.*
Prince, D. A., 110, 113, *115*, 117*n.*, 118*n.*
Prior, D. J., 179, 183, 191*n.*
Pritchard, D., 70
Prytulak, L. S., 362, 376*n.*
Puglisi-Allegra, S., 315, 330*n.*
Puro, D., 108, 118*n.*
Purpura, D. P., 266, 277*n.*
Purves, D., 89, 102*n.*, 267, 277*n.*
Quinn, W. G., 266, 277*n.*, 304, 307*n.*

Racine, R. J., 50, 54, 59, 61*n.*, 62, 70, 76*n.*, 79, 91, 102*n.*, 161, 170*n.*
Rall, W., 271, 277*n.*
Ramirez, J. J., 457, 461*n.*
Ranck, J. B., Jr., 49, 60*n.*
Randich, A., 216, 229*n.*
Rapp, P. R., 324, 326, 331*n.*
Rasmussen, T., 58, 356, 378*n.*, 397, 413*n.*
Ratcliff, R., 361, 364, 377*n.*
Rausch, G., 267, 277*n.*
Rauschenberger, J., 300, 306*n.*
Rawlins, J. N. P., 49, 61*n.*, 245, 249*n.*, 453, 457, 461*n.*
Read, J. M., 82, 101*n.*
Reader, T. A., 108, 119*n.*
Redman, S., 270, 277*n.*
Reingold, S. C., 179, 190*n.*
Reis, D. J., 322, 333*n.*
Reivich, M., 79, 101*n.*, 102*n.*
Rescorla, R. A., 146, 179, 191*n.*, 211, 213–